Wow! A rich treasure trove of practical coaching skills, guiding framewor[...] that spans the depth and breadth of supporting the human journey into more of our [...] for Transformation includes working with change at the social-cultural level, as well as inner shadow work.
—John Kinyon, Co-Founder of Mediate Your Life Training and co-author of *From Conflict to Connection* and *Choosing Peace*

*Coaching for Transformation* is a guide to a holistic coaching practice that integrates the mind, body, heart and spirit. By openly addressing the usually taboo issues of power and privilege, it prepares coaches to enable their clients to live their best lives and to coach for social change.
—Deborah Howard, Esq., author of *Repairing the Quilt of Humanity*

*Coaching for Transformation* is profound, insightful, informative and expansive. It is a great resource for new and experienced coaches.
—Andrea Sigetich, President, SageCoach and author of *An Entrepreneur's Trail Guide*

With the addition of in-depth examples of real-life coaching, *Coaching for Transformation: Pathways to Ignite Personal and Social Change* lays out an integrated, compassionate, holistic, and culturally accessible approach to coaching. This book is an excellent resource for both new and experienced coaches for years to come.
—Sarah Reiff-Hekking, Ph.D. True Focus Coaching Inc.

Genuine transformation is a Soulful process of deep emotional trust. *Coaching for Transformation* offers an empathic and intuitive coaching model that is rooted in self-awareness and emotion. It is a potent guide book for any coach who is passionate about the inner journey.
—Leza Danly, Founder, Lucid Living

*Coaching for Transformation: Pathways to Ignite Personal and Social Change* is a significant contribution to the field. The work of personal and social change coaching honors our interconnection and interdependence. The more we recognize this fundamental tenet the better off we will all be.
—Michele Bertran

*Coaching for Transformation* is brimming with practical wisdom for coaches. Enlightening it is, page after page.
—Ike Lasater, co-author of *From Conflict to Connection*

A wonderful resource…just reading it ignited personal change. The emphasis on the spirit and the soul I found thought provoking. The chapters I appreciated most addressed cross cultural coaching, power and privilege in coaching and coaching for social change.
—Dr. Ansley LaMar, Psychology Professor, New Jersey City University

I found *Coaching for Transformation* to be an enlightening and important tool. Several topics that I found particularly powerful and useful to my journey as a coach, mediator, and collaborative lawyer are: the integration of the mind, body, and Spirit of both the client and coach; the need to be culturally competent; building one's coaching business; and particularly, coaching for social change.
—Stephanie R. Bush-Baskette, Esq., Ph.D.

*Coaching for Transformation* offers a highly readable and inspiring guide on a holistic practice of coaching that integrates a spiritual, empathic, somatic and social/intra-personal way of empowering others and ourselves. This method repeatedly reminds us of our interdependence as a species and our innate capacity for possibility and change.
—Dian Killian, Ph.D., author of *Connecting across Differences*

# COACHING for Transformation

## SECOND EDITION

### Pathways to Ignite
### Personal & Social Change

Martha Lasley | Virginia Kellogg
Richard Michaels | Sharon Brown

**Coaching for Transformation: Pathways to Ignite Personal & Social Change**

**Second Edition**

Discover Press. Printed in the United States of America.

For information: Coaching for Transformation, PO Box 224, Troy, PA 16947

ISBN 978-0-9742000-4-0

# Table of Contents

# Acknowledgements

Coaching for Transformation has been a collaborative process from day one and we are so thankful for the many, many people who have supported us. This revised edition bears the collective imprint of hundreds of Coaching for Transformation certified coaches whose feedback and experience have molded and shaped the pages that follow. We thank our clients and students for the many hours we've spent together deepening our collective learning.

All four of us want to express our endless love for Charlotte Morse for her strategic thinking, savvy editing, clear-cut graphics and for driving the process with astonishing ease.

We are grateful to all the people who explored the edges with us, generated ideas and contributed content, especially Belma González, Guthrie Sayen, Steven Filante, Anne Yardley, Kena Acuña and Michael Wright.

For all those who shared stories, coaching examples and learning tips, we appreciate your contribution that demonstrates the transformative impact of coaching on individuals and organizations: Altaf Shaikh, Anuradha Prasad, Bill Plotkin, Damon Azali-Rojas, Ivy Woolf Turk, J.R. Reynolds, Jagruti Gala, Johnny Manzon-Santos, Jonelle Naude, Karen Romine, Kathleen Moore, Kim Fowler, Leanne Whiting, Leslie Brown, Lupita González, Manish Srivastava, Maria Rogers Pascual, Marilyn O'Hearne, Michael Wise, Mike Scott, Nirupama Subramian, Pailin Chirachaisakul, Pernille Plantener, Rebecca Aced-Molina, Rob McGowan, Sangita Kumar, Shruti Sonthalia, Sonali Kelkar and Sushma Sharma.

Many colleagues have generously contributed their wisdom and time. We are deeply grateful for the feedback and support from Suzie Bichovsky, Madhu Maron, Stacey Strongarone, Anna Matthisen and Cindy Nicole.

Last, we thank each other—what a joy it's been to clarify our thinking and discover the depth of our alignment. We raise a glass to Sharon for her precious clarity, Richard for his wholehearted vision, Virginia for her commitment to expanding the coaching profession and Martha for her passion for learning.

# Section I:
# Getting Started

*I will not die an unlived life.*
*I will not live in fear*
*of falling or catching fire.*
*I choose to inhabit my days,*
*to allow my living to open me,*
*to make me less afraid,*
*more accessible;*
*to loosen my heart*
*until it becomes a wing,*
*a torch, a promise.*
*I choose to risk my significance,*
*to live so that which came to me as seed*
*goes to the next as blossom,*
*and that which came to me as blossom,*
*goes on as fruit. —Dawna Markova*

Welcome to the world of coaching! Even if you've been coaching for years, the journey of becoming a professional coach holds both promise and uncertainty about the unknown. We invite you into the mystery of this new path knowing that both your life and the lives of others will change as a result.

Section I orients you to the foundation of Coaching for Transformation—the approach, core principles and process, building relationships with clients, and developing the core skills for truly effective coaching. May your journey be richly rewarding—for you and for those whose lives you touch.

# 1
# Welcome to Coaching

*Tell me, what is it you plan to do with your one wild and precious life? —Mary Oliver*

## Welcome

Whether you choose to establish a coaching practice, integrate coaching into your current profession, or use coaching skills to enhance your interpersonal relationships or for social justice, welcome to this transformational journey. As you step into coaching, you create sacred relationships with people that take them to the core of their being. These relationships are the foundation for their discovery of who they are, what they want and how they contribute to their family, workplace, community and the world. Coaching invites people to take action that reflects their power, creativity and authenticity.

The journey of coaching takes you deep into your heart and far out into the world. As you support transformation in others, you awaken your own inner transformational process.

In Chapter 1, we explore the foundation of coaching and the Coaching for Transformation process. In this orientation we look at definitions, guidelines, core principles and coaching competencies, and introduce how coaching can make our world a better place.

## What is Coaching?

Coaching emerged as a way to provide support and guidance for individuals moving through a change process toward greater effectiveness and fulfillment. Coaching is part of the cultural shift from a pathology worldview to a resourceful worldview. In the pathology worldview, problems are identified, evaluated, and solutions are implemented, usually by outside experts. In contrast, coaches work with people from a resourceful point of view—collaborating to explore opportunities and identify resources to create an exciting future based on awareness, choice and action. Coaching is world-changing, as well as life-changing work.

Although coaching is a fast-growing profession, many people confuse coaching with giving people advice. In practice, coaching is an empowering process where the coach asks rigorous questions and provides sacred space so people can discover their own creative solutions.

Coaching is a partnership that maximizes human potential. We define coaching as a skillset and a mindset that taps into the resourcefulness of people to initiate creative solutions. We can create coaching partnerships with individuals, groups, organizations or communities.

As coaches, we are trained to listen, observe and ask empowering questions. We reflect what we see and hear to help people clarify their feelings and values, leading to insight and action. We customize our approach based on the individual's, organization's or community's challenges, experiences, cultural norms, values and knowledge. We trust that our partners are resourceful and that they have the inner wisdom to overcome obstacles and generate compelling strategies and action plans. Our job is to provide support to enhance the skills, resources and creativity they already have. In addition, Coaching for Transformation is a holistic coaching process that combines awareness of body, mind, soul and spirit. We delve into the impact of cultural identity, power and privilege, and institutionalized inequities to support deep, lasting and real transformation.

Coaching helps people articulate their vision, identify their needs and core values, bring their inner and outer worlds into alignment, set goals they feel passionate about and create a plan for their own development. Coaching provides a structure to continuously reflect and capture learning, and take that new learning directly into action. Through the coaching partnership, people can build capacity, expand possibilities and achieve greater fulfillment and success while staying on track with their objectives.

How does coaching differ from other helping professions?

Coaching is not mentoring, consulting, training, psychotherapy or counseling. While coaching shares the end goals of learning and growth with these professions, the focus and process of coaching differ in significant ways.

**Therapy** (psychotherapy or counseling) frequently focuses on the past and healing—assisting clients in healing psychological problems such as depression, anxiety, phobia, trauma, destructive behaviors and addiction. Coaches are not trained to heal psychological problems and make referrals to therapists when warranted. Instead of analyzing the past, coaching looks forward to create a deeper engagement with the present and a more desirable future. Coaching is primarily for expanding awareness and designing actions that move people toward the fulfillment of their life purpose, dreams and goals. Although coaching is not therapy, coaching can be a very healing process.

**Consulting** typically focuses on developing the whole organization systemically. Consultants work with senior leaders providing expertise and interventions to develop leadership skills, strategies, structures, policies and procedures to improve the effectiveness of the organization. Consultants are usually hired to address specific problems, design interventions and offer solutions. In contrast, coaches support staff in discovering and creating their own solutions. Many consultants offer coaching as part of their services or integrate a 'coach approach' into their consulting.

**Training** and **teaching** are professions in which knowledge is imparted to support learning. Rather than teaching how to do something, coaches support and challenge people to access their own inner and outer learning resources.

## What is Transformation?

*You can think of the kind of transformation described here as drawing new water out of your old well—by going deeper than you ever dipped before. The way to get your bucket deeper into your well is by taking on powerful questions, instead of jumping at attractive-looking answers. —John Scherer*

Humans have the potential and deep desire to learn, grow and evolve. Transformation is a process of profound and radical change that arises from deep awareness and leads to fresh orientation and new direction. Transformation honors what is, while reaching deep within us to find what is emerging—the birthing of something brand new. Instead of denying the past or the present, the transformational process cradles or embraces our life force. Coaches act as midwives to the birthing process—the creation of something new and exciting.

Transformation happens when people are deeply seen, heard, understood and recognized for their gifts. Ironically, when we try to change people, they resist. In contrast, coaching helps people become more of who they already are. Simply witnessing the process and being fully present has a transformational impact.

In holistic coaching we create an essence-to-essence relationship of reciprocity. We look for and bring out the client's essence and, at the same time, bring our own essence to the relationship. In this essence-to-essence relationship, both coach and client experience transformation. The coach is transformed just by witnessing the powerful shifts in the client. Naming what is happening in the moment on a physical, emotional and energetic level amplifies the transformation. Naming the impact the client has on the coach can serve as a source of inspiration.

Transformation is the change that happens within to bring people into greater alignment. For example, a young father wants to honor his values of family and responsibility, and at the same time he wants freedom. The exploration leads to transformation and a new way of being in the world. Transformation nearly always involves a change in pattern, be it a pattern of thinking or a pattern of behavior. Instead of looking for the big "aha" moment, we notice that transformation can happen in any moment.

# Leadership that Works

Leadership that Works began offering coaching and training programs to visionary leaders in 1997. The Coaching for Transformation process, developed by the partners at Leadership that Works, stands on the shoulders of the human development field, psychology, soul work from indigenous cultures and philosophies of the East. We are committed to building awareness of cultural norms, power, privilege and social inequities. On the cutting edge of the expanding profession of coaching, we integrate the heart and mystery of transformation with the practical world of tools, skills and results. As part of our mission, we help people awaken their gifts and access inner wisdom in service of individual and global transformation.

## Deep awareness of emotions and needs

Lasting, sustainable change is rooted in deep awareness. Traditionally, most coaching models focus on helping people achieve their goals by taking action. Often the change is temporary. The Coaching for Transformation process helps people break through limiting beliefs, become aware of the wisdom of their bodies, identify their emotions and understand their needs and values. From that grounded, centered place of deep awareness, people can develop strategies and take actions that honor their values. The coach's deep empathic presence does more to facilitate transformation than pushing people toward end-goals. By developing a fierce heart connection, we prioritize depth of awareness before moving into action.

## Holistic—body, mind, soul and spirit

Our holistic approach combines awareness of body, mind, soul and spirit with solid coaching skills. As we exercise the right and left brain, we integrate the heart, mind and body with logic and the mystery of transformation.

## Cultural awareness and commitment

We are committed to changing the demographics of the coaching profession by making coaching available to diverse communities. We actively seek faculty with deep roots in multicultural competencies and participants that represent many different communities and backgrounds. We look for creative ways to bring coaching to people who traditionally don't have access to coaching—the social sector, communities of color, LGBTQQ and more.

## The coach's stand

We take a stand for deep, transformative coaching. As we replace rote, predictable coaching with coaching that comes from listening for what is beneath the surface, we respond with clarity, energy and boldness.

By developing our own personalized coach's stand, we can step into a powerful way of being that mobilizes transformation. The coach's stand is a set of physical, visual and spiritual practices and commitments that a coach embodies in order to make each coaching moment, session and relationship more powerful. Together, the practices create an orientation that allows us to effectively call out our clients' power. By taking risks and following our intuition about what we sense is possible, we hold a vision for clients that is larger than what they have been able to see on their own. This calls clients into being whole, humane, loving and powerful.

### Focus on transformation for the client as well as the coach

Although we hold the focus on the transformation of people we coach, the coach's life is also transformed by the process and there is no going back to a mediocre life.

### Values

At Leadership that Works, we build relationships and make decisions based on our core values. We draw inspiration from these guiding principles that are reflected through daily interactions within the organization and with students, clients, partners and communities.

**Heart Connection**—We believe our human capacity for empathy and compassion builds trust, cultivates authentic and meaningful relationships, and empowers collaboration. We are committed to creating space for every part of every one of us. We believe in the power of love and generosity to support, challenge, respect and inspire each other.

**Social Change**—We take a stand for social, economic and environmental justice. We believe that each of us represents a complex mix of lived experiences, social identities, spiritual traditions and cultural backgrounds. We are committed to practicing cultural humility, and to authentically exploring issues of power, privilege and rank within ourselves and our communities, within our institutions and societal systems.

**Integrity**—We strive for excellence in everything we do, from innovative leadership programs to inclusive organizational practices grounded in accountability. We are committed to earning and sustaining trust with all our stakeholders and communities. We create and deliver rigorous learning experiences that impact human evolution.

**Collaboration**—We believe that working together unlocks greater potential than we can achieve on our own. Creating conscious relationships and teams encourages each of us to make a uniquely powerful contribution. We enthusiastically partner with other entities in order to expand our collective knowledge and ignite synergy.

**Innovation**—We embrace our existing wisdom, curiosity and entrepreneurial spirit to explore realms of possibility and to identify natural openings and real-time opportunities. We are committed to cultivating wildly creative and supportive spaces that invite us to play at, and go beyond, our edges. We celebrate our successes as well as our failures in service of our collective learning.

## Core Principles

The foundation of holistic coaching is built on our beliefs about human beings and the coaching process. These beliefs form the core of effective communication, impacting the relationships we build, the level of trust that develops and the client's willingness to share vulnerably. Our beliefs permeate our body language, energy and the signals we send while coaching. When we internally integrate these beliefs, or core principles, we can create even more powerful relationships based on all that is possible.

1. People are whole, and simultaneously moving toward a fuller experience of their wholeness.
2. People are inherently resourceful and wise.
3. Honoring the full diversity of experience expands awareness.
4. People have the freedom to choose how they respond.
5. Much more is possible than any of us can imagine.

The core principles help us create the container for powerful and transformational coaching relationships. We can share the core principles with clients because these powerful foundational beliefs about life can build authentic connection.

## WHOLENESS: People are whole, and simultaneously moving toward a fuller experience of their wholeness.

Consider the power of being in relationship from a place of wholeness, honoring all that is present, while holding the space for all that is yet to be born. The pathology worldview focuses on what's wrong or needs improvement, creating comparisons and images of brokenness. Seeing people as whole shifts the paradigm to one of reverence and respect, setting the foundation for a powerful, resourceful partnership.

*Example:*
Mai was told she was too shy and soft-spoken to be a strong leader. Her coach worked with her to understand what positive intent drives her behavior. Mai realized she didn't have to be loud and out-going to lead well; she just needed more confidence. She developed her unique ability to develop people and foster effective leadership in the organization.

## DIVERSITY: Honoring the full diversity of experience deepens awareness.

When we support people to embrace the fullness of their life, including their cultural experience, we help them honor and integrate all parts of themselves. This leads to deeper awareness as they notice what's important across the spectrum of their inner and outer world. The more aspects of ourselves that we acknowledge and accept, the more accepting we are of diversity in the external world.

*Example:*
Ashanti wanted to change her profession. She dreamt of healing the trauma of internalized oppression. She was torn between her passion for making a difference and her fear of losing the security of her stable job. Her coach helped her savor both parts of herself fully. In that space she created an action plan, based on embracing two important values—contribution and security.

## RESOURCEFULNESS: People are inherently resourceful and wise.

Trusting that our clients are wise and resourceful allows us to remain curious and hold space for what is emerging. We support them in tapping into a deep well of resourcefulness that connects them with new insights, creativity and action.

*Example:*
Johan has a long-term belief that he is "not good with people." His coach gets curious about this belief and Johan realizes he tells himself this often to prevent criticism. But deep down he has a strong desire to have great relationships. He decides to journal all the times he is "good with people," and begins to discover that he listens fully, supports his friends and helps colleagues grow.

## FREEDOM: People have the freedom to choose how they respond.

When we remember that clients have the freedom to choose their response to circumstances in their lives, we free ourselves from judgment and from taking responsibility for them. We acknowledge their life experiences, honor their choices and create a space where powerful, respectful connection and cultural humility exist between us.

*Example:*
Liv frequently used words like, "I must, I should, I have to…" so her coach asked her to rephrase her sentences starting with, "I choose to…"

## POSSIBILITY: Much more is possible than any of us can imagine.

The beauty and mystery of the transformative process is that neither the coach nor the client can imagine all that's possible. The journey has no fixed destination, but holds great promise and rich rewards. As coaches, when we remain open and curious, we have greater access to our right brain, our intuition and extraordinary solutions. Far more is possible than any of us realize.

*Example:*
Rose said, "With the glass ceiling here, I have no options," so her coach asked her to brainstorm all the options that seemed impossible. Quickly she realized that items on her "impossible" list actually were possible and she began to see new options for action.

# Coaching for Transformation Process

We create sacred coaching relationships that take people to the core of their being. These relationships form the foundation for their discovery of who they are, what they want and how they want to contribute to the world.

Coaching for Transformation is a dynamic process, where we bring our full curiosity, compassion and courage to the coaching relationship. Yet our primary focus is on the person being coached. Whatever clients bring, whether a question, a dream or a desire, we support them to move into awareness, alignment and action.

## Coach

The coach cultivates uncompromising presence by bringing these three qualities to every coaching session:

**Curiosity**—the opposite of judgment, curiosity invites us to accept all that is and explore the unknown. Every judgment, whether directed at ourselves or our client, has a built-in antidote—curiosity. With the curiosity of a child, we can awaken playfulness, joyfulness and creativity.

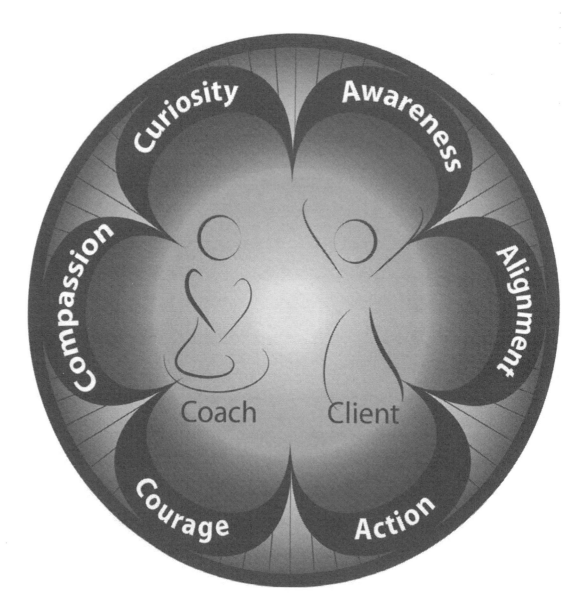

*Coaching for Transformation Process*

**Compassion**—empathic connection unlocks the heart because people are seen, heard and deeply understood. If we notice resistance, we can consciously choose to put our attention on our compassion. When we open our hearts, our clients open theirs.

**Courage**—bold, authentic communication helps us build trusting relationships. Courage supports clarity and can include trusting our intuition, being transparent, accessing spiritual guidance and supporting cultural consciousness. We sense what is missing and bring in our voice to explore what is emerging. Courage means coming from the heart even when feeling fear.

To engage in a mutually empowering relationship, coaches need a strong inner foundation. We enter our inner relationship to own, heal and transform our inner world. To create intimacy with people we coach, we first need to create space for self-intimacy. When we put attention on our inner landscape, we can access an empowering inner freedom which we carry into the coaching relationship. As we cultivate mindfulness, we connect deeply to the life force in ourselves and in our clients.

## Client

The word "client" refers to the person receiving coaching and can be someone who hires us as a coach, or someone in our organization or community. We can coach our boss, our peers and our direct reports. The coaching relationship is infused with equality and possibility. We support the client to develop presence by focusing on:

**Awareness**—tuning into whatever is present. Mindfulness leads to sparks of insight and awakens clients to their own inherent wisdom and inner clarity. We support the client to become more grounded, reflective and conscious.

**Alignment**—finding congruence between the inner and outer experience. Putting attention on aliveness and radiance supports convergence of different aspects of the self, including body, mind and spirit. The sense of "coming home" to oneself awakens vitality and full engagement.

**Action**—purposefully moving forward. Creative action that arises from awareness and alignment has beauty and power. By connecting with the heart we enliven the process of exploring options, planning action steps and building in accountability.

The client determines the desired outcomes for each coaching session. The possibilities are endless. As we hold their agenda, we also hold the intention for the client to deepen their awareness, move toward alignment and step into action. Creating space for reflection gives clients access to their inner-knowing. As they move toward new insights and deeper learning, we support integration, which allows them to consciously receive, savor and build upon their wisdom. When actions arise from that place of self-connection, their goals manifest more easily.[1]

## The coaching relationship

Connection comes first. Nothing happens without connection. Fierce love and unconditional support build trust and a flourishing relationship. The coach and client share power equally. This relationship is a space for experimentation, alchemy and human evolution. In the deeply connecting space of the coaching relationship, intuition blossoms for both the client and the coach.

## Transformation for both the client and the coach

The coach never stops listening for transformation. One of the ways to accentuate what's emerging in the client is for the coach to simultaneously track the transformational processes in the coach's inner world. Honoring the transformational process of the client awakens transformational possibilities in the coach. In every moment, transformation is possible for both the client and the coach. Even more broadly, the ripple effect of transformation impacts all the systems the client and coach touch. Both parties expand their capacity to hold space for transformation that goes way beyond the coaching relationship.

---

1    The client side of the CFT model, "awareness, alignment, action" was coined by Vikram Bhatt, which inspired a group of CFT faculty to collaborate to develop the coach side of the model, "curiosity, compassion, courage". Graphic design by Charlotte Morse.

## The Three Levels of Coaching

At Leadership that Works, we support three levels of coaching:

**Level One** coaching supports transformation at the *personal level.*

Creating a healthy relationship with self

Honoring internal wisdom and trusting intuition

Moving from awareness to alignment to action

**Level Two** coaching supports transformation at both the personal and the *interpersonal level.*

Deepening conversations

Supporting connection and collaboration

Creating conscious relationships that serve

**Level Three** coaching supports transformation at the personal, interpersonal and the *collective level.*

Honoring the spiritual dimension

Creating transformation in communities and organizations

Supporting systemic change that leads to social justice

## Core Competencies

The International Coach Federation (ICF) is the leading credentialing agency for coaches around the globe. The Coaching for Transformation program is an ICF Accredited Coach Training Program (ACTP). The ICF core competencies are outlined below and detailed in Appendix II. These competencies form the heart of the ICF credentialing process.

### A. Setting the foundation

Meeting ethical guidelines and professional standards

Establishing the coaching agreement

### B. Co-creating the relationship

Establishing trust and intimacy with the client

Coaching presence

### C. Communicating effectively

Active listening

Powerful questioning

Direct communication

## D. Facilitating learning and results

Creating awareness

Designing actions

Planning and goal setting

Managing progress and accountability[2]

---

**COACHING *in Action* | The Power of Coaching** *by Rob McGowan*

I am super shy, so I was nervous about Damon coaching me with 30 people watching, but my relationship with Damon spans some years. We're both social justice organizers and we really connect as fathers of sons who had some health challenges. My middle son passed away from brain cancer. We've had some profound conversations about our sons. As black men, we know our children are in danger. They are here today and can be gone tomorrow.

Already connected, we started the coaching session by jumping into a deep intimate issue around being a father, being a black man and what that means. I'm 6'1" tall, dark skinned, and grew up in Alabama. My mom drilled into me how to act, because anything perceived as a threat could cost me my life. She wanted to protect me and I felt the same about my sons.

Damon got me to talk about what was most important to me—the spiritual and mental health of my black sons who at any moment could be taken away. When my oldest son graduated from high school, I felt I hadn't had the conversations I'd wanted to have before he went off to college. I had missed a lot because I'd spent 10 years mismanaging the balance of my personal and professional life in the social justice movement. Little things, little conversations that were not had. I wanted my relationship with my youngest son to be different.

Damon said to me, "You say these things are important to you, I believe they are important to you, but what have you done to make time with your family, time with your son, time with yourself?" I was blown away because in social justice work we don't do that enough. I couldn't continue to lie to myself about my good intentions, because there was no action. I had to take a hard look in the mirror.

That coaching session was deep and transformative for me. He helped me re-focus on things that are important. Ever since my son transitioned, I've wanted to start a foundation, but hadn't. I started the foundation for my son, because Damon said, "When are you going to get the paperwork done? Give me some dates. When will you have the conversations?" We set some deadlines and he asked me to check in with him, and when I did, a lot had changed.

I started looking at my health, losing weight and spending more time with my son. Because of coaching, my whole life changed. When my youngest son wants to talk to me, he gets my attention. I'm more involved in his life. I've made changes with my oldest son also. Our conversations are more focused... more present in the moment. The same is true with my wife and my friendships.

Amazing things were put in motion. Once I earnestly committed to the people and things that really mattered in my life, the universe got out of my way. Many things fell in place, because I let go of the grind and focused on my real desires. It's a tough journey for black men in the United States. I care about my son's safety. I can't prepare him for this world if I'm not around. There is no part of my life that hasn't improved. Later, I encouraged my wife to participate in an introductory coaching course and the afternoon that she finished, we had the most transformative conversation in 17½ years of marriage.

---

2    International Coach Federation. Retrieved from http://www.coachfederation.org

## Beginning the Journey

The Coaching for Transformation core values, principles, process and levels of coaching form the foundation for the coaching skills, pathways to alignment and opportunities we explore throughout this book. Whether you are new to coaching or a seasoned coach deepening your skill set, you are part of a community of people doing life-changing and world-changing work. We are honored to be on the journey with you!

# 2

# Cultivating Presence

*Presence is a rare quality in a world of 20-second sound bites, nonstop stimulation, and gnawing anxiety. What underlies presence? …People with presence have an ineffable quality about them; they are "present," surprisingly attentive, and undistracted. A fullness, a centeredness, a wholeness radiates from them. We enjoy being "in their presence." You can build presence. It is the natural radiance of heart security. —Doc Childre and Bruce Cryer*

Imagine you are an artist preparing yourself to create a masterpiece. How do you engage with your environment? What is your mental and emotional state? Where do you go within yourself to prepare? What is your attitude toward the paints, brushes and canvas in front of you?

How do you shift your focus from your daily responsibilities and tune into your inner resources? How do you fully use your senses to awaken a spontaneous outpouring of your heart?

The focus of this chapter is similar—preparing you to create effective coaching relationships, to tap all of your inner resources, and to care for yourself as a coach so that you are fully responsive to the challenges and possibilities of the moment. So… relax, take a few deep breaths and get ready to explore the ways you can cultivate presence.

## Awareness

*We've come to believe that the core capacity needed for accessing the field of the future is presence. We first thought of presence as being fully conscious and aware in the present moment. Then we began to appreciate presence as deep listening, of being open beyond one's preconceptions and historical ways of making sense. We came to see the importance of letting go of old identities and the need to control and, as Salk said, making voices to serve the evolution of life. Ultimately, we came to see all these aspects of presence as leading to a state of "letting come," of consciously participating in a larger field for change. When this happens, the field shifts, and the forces shaping a situation can shift from re-creating the past to manifesting or realizing an emerging future. —Peter Senge*

Awareness involves the flow of our whole organism: emotions, thoughts, energy and physical sensations. Many of us rely on *thinking* most of the time, but as coaches we continuously attune to the whole symphony of awareness. Fritz Perls, the father of Gestalt therapy said, "It's the awareness, the full experience of how you are stuck, that makes you recover." Perls said that learning equals discovery and what you are discovering is yourself. Awareness is a means to discovery. As a coach, you'll use awareness to help people tap their inner knowing, including the wisdom of the body, mind, emotion, soul and spirit.

Coming into awareness; coming into the moment, creates a clear mind. People become freer emotionally, giving them access to creativity and inner resourcefulness. When we create the space for awareness, clients do the work themselves, and they create solutions that neither of us would have imagined.

## Four simple steps for developing awareness

We have access to our awareness in every moment and we can develop deeper awareness through practice. We would not expect our muscles to be strong without practice. These techniques deepen our ability to be aware of our self, our clients and the environment. We can deepen our contact with the here and now by simply noticing, *without judging*. Allow whatever is occurring to happen without forcing change. Notice thoughts that arise without engaging with them.

### 1. Notice the breath

Sit, close your eyes and focus your attention on your breath without trying to change it. Notice how your body expands and contracts as you breathe. Pay attention to the subtle sensations of the air flowing in and out of your nose.

*What effect does focusing on the breath have on your body, emotions and energy?*

### 2. Notice physical sensations

Now turn your focus to whatever sensations you are aware of in your body. You may notice tingling, tension, coolness or relaxation. Do not try to change the sensations, judge them or create a story about what the sensations mean. Simply notice.

*What effect does focusing your attention on physical sensations have on your breath, emotions and energy?*

### 3. Notice your emotions

Now shift your attention to whatever emotions are present. Accept whatever emotions are present without judging, changing or engaging in inner dialogue about them. You may notice contentment or restlessness, joy or sadness, fear or love, or numbness.

*What effect does focusing your attention on your emotions have on your breath, body and energy in this moment?*

### 4.  Notice your energy

Now shift your attention to whatever energy lives in you. Accept whatever energy flows through you without trying to change it or engage in inner dialogue about your energy. You may notice desire or blockages, intensity or flow.

*What effect does focusing your attention on your energy have on your breath, body and emotions in this moment?*

We can use focused attention to notice what is happening in nature, the environment or in communication with other people. The practice of simply *noticing*, engages our awareness and brings us into the moment. When we notice our clients are entangled in thought, we can guide them into awareness. This provides access to a clear mind and intuition and opens our creativity, resourcefulness and wisdom.

## Listening

The human spirit and the human condition improve when people hear each other deeply.

Listening is foundational to the coaching process. The three levels of listening are self-focused listening, client-focused listening and transformation-focused listening.

### Self-focused listening

Self-focused listening includes paying attention to our thoughts, body, emotions and intuition. When we bring awareness to what is happening within, in the moment, we recognize the choice to shift from reaction and judgment to the wisdom of the entire body-mind system. This heightened awareness makes intuition more accessible.

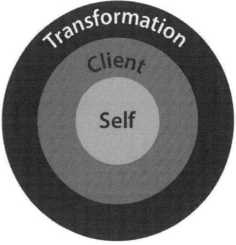

**Listening Focus**

For instance, in the middle of a session, if we notice tension or we start thinking about a conflict from yesterday, we can bring our attention into the tension and the body lets go. Our physical sensations and emotions can be a distraction or they can inform the coaching. If we sense that we are distracted by our inner experience, we can choose to come back to be more fully present with the client.

If we sense our thoughts are stimulated by our client's experience, we can ask, "What does my inner conflict want?"

When we cultivate inner awareness and follow our intuition, the coaching is more in tune with what is happening in the moment. We become more effective and model the practices we want our clients to develop. Self-awareness nourishes our ability to listen deeply to another.

Self-focused listening ranges from paying attention to transient thoughts to deep awareness of what is happening in the moment. When our attention is focused in the *now*, we shift from thinking to awareness. Awareness has the brilliant function of allowing choice and is more in tune with the needs in the moment. When we notice what is happening within ourselves, without judging, we are more successful in being present and available.

*Examples:*

Noticing our limiting beliefs about what the client is saying

Staying present with or exploring the meaning of the butterflies in our stomach

Listening to our intuition telling us to explore our feeling of alarm

Trusting our desire to share a metaphor

Noticing that we are triggered, we choose in the moment to journal after coaching so that we can be present with our client now

## Client-focused listening

In client-focused listening we narrow our focus so all our attention is on the other person. Listening to content and word choice gives us clarity about what is most important to the speaker. But we also listen for what the client is *not* saying. We pay attention to the nuances of their mannerisms, pace, volume and tone. Conscious, clear, empathic listening fosters self-awareness and affirms their experience.

*Examples:*

Hearing the words of the story and listening for the underlying desires

Listening for the values at stake when the client appears to be stuck

Noticing the excitement as the voice gets louder or more energized

Hearing the change in emotions when the client shifts to new revelations

Sensing the underlying desire for relief as our client repeatedly says he doesn't want to talk about sadness

## Transformation-focused listening

Transformation-focused listening is being attentive to all that's happening within ourselves, our clients and the environment. Hearing the whole symphony, we have a heightened sense of the flow of the coaching conversation and the clients' inner process. We can sense the openings, new possibilities, emerging opportunities and forces that generate change.

Awareness is inherent in transformation-focused listening, which creates an environment that fosters opportunities for profound personal transformation. As a coach, we intuit moments of opening—opportunities for our clients to explore feelings and insights and to become aware of what is waiting to be born.

At the heart of transformation-focused listening we attune to who people are becoming and what possibilities are emerging. Holding people as resourceful and whole supports transformational listening.

*Examples:*

Noticing the shift when the client is talking about something ordinary and then sees a bigger picture

Sharing intuition that takes the client to an intriguing realization

Focusing on the same thing at the same time in an effortless flow with the client that moves into new territory

Following the client's lead with a mutual sense of unfolding creativity as you go

Noticing the client's words are particularly charged with energy and sensing her attunement with her inner truth

## Shifting the focus of listening

We can hold our attention on all three areas of listening simultaneously, or we can hold our focus on one area, staying continuously aware of what will serve the client. For instance, we may shift through all three areas of focus rapidly when we connect with our intuition. Intuition is informed by self-focused awareness, and when we share it, we pick up the reaction as we shift to a client focus, and then shift to the focus on transformation.

## Enhancing our listening

We can enhance our listening by practicing the following:

Creating trust—reduces resistance

Being curious—cultivates receptivity

Staying in the moment—increases engagement

Reflecting core values—enhances ownership

Allowing for silence—creates space for intuition and feeling

Capturing opportunities—generates proactive behavior

## Clarifying, reflecting and distilling

When we consciously direct our listening to all three levels, we sense the essence of what is expressed. Listening for the essence includes three aspects: clarifying, reflecting and distilling. Clarifying ensures understanding, reflecting reinforces awareness and distilling captures the essence of what's emerging. When we focus on the words, tone and body language, and then reflect back what we hear, see and sense, we build trust. Trust leads to understanding and growth. Listening for the essence means hearing and supporting true self-expression.

As a coach, we listen for what is most important to our clients. Reflection leads to deeper understanding of values, beliefs, aspirations, fears and dreams that are the heart of our client's experience. Reflection can help people gain clarity, feel heard and deepen self-understanding.

"I follow you," "I'm with you," or "I understand," don't contribute to connection as much as distilling or summarizing the emotional and energetic content. Instead of saying you understand, show that you understand. Show that you understand deeply, accurately and without judgment.

Even if your reflection isn't quite accurate, when clients see that you are trying to understand, they experience an energy shift and willingly explore more deeply.

Reflecting is more than just parroting what was said. Reflecting might take the form of rephrasing so that your client can take it in on a deeper level. Pay attention to the particular words which seem to catch the essence of what is expressed. You might articulate what you see happening in your client, in the space or in the coaching relationship.

> *Examples of listening for the essence:*
>
> Phil: I am not creating this chapter for the book the way I had hoped.
>
> Coach (clarifying): You are hoping for something more?
>
> Coach (reflecting): So you are not creating what you'd hoped?
>
> Coach (distilling): You want access to your creativity?

## Disempowering reflections

Many habitual responses or reflections do not contribute to awareness and learning. By avoiding disempowering responses, we help people gain their own insight and power. The following examples can disempower the people we coach:

**Agreeing with judgments:** Yes, that guy is obnoxious.

**Asking for more information:** So she insulted you. Who else was there and what did they say?

**Consoling:** It wasn't your fault; anyone else would have done the same thing.

**Denying feelings:** You shouldn't feel angry that your boss is exerting power over you. He's only trying to help.

**Disagreeing:** How can you say that? She's so smart!

**Educating:** I hope you will learn that you have got to be more assertive if you want people to listen to you.

**Giving advice:** If I were you, I'd go to the beach.

**Judging:** You have no people skills.

**Moralizing:** That was a really insensitive thing to do. I think you need to apologize.

**Reassuring:** You'll be fine. By tomorrow this will all blow over.

**One-upping:** That's nothing; something much worse happened to me…

**Shifting away from concerns:** You sound pretty riled up. Let's focus on next week's meeting.

**Solving the problem:** All you have to do is cancel the contract and move on.

**Sympathizing:** Oh, you poor thing…

**Telling someone what to feel:** I don't see why you feel marginalized. Even if you are the only Korean in the division, you should be happy about how much money you're making!

**Telling your own story:** Something very similar happened to me…

## Turn unproductive behaviors into productive interventions

**Approval and disapproval:** Instead of sharing your evaluation, reflect what matters.

**Comparing yourself:** Instead of thinking about who is smarter or how your experience is different, or what you would have done, stay focused on the uniqueness of your client's experience.

**Evaluating or analyzing:** Instead of interpreting or psychoanalyzing, reflect the content or the emotions and needs.

**Ignoring nonverbal cues:** Listen to the essence of the content, but also name the body language, tone of voice, rate of speech and energetic cues.

**Jargon:** If you notice you're using words and phrases that your client wouldn't use in a casual conversation, that's a sign you're using jargon. Use conversational street language as much as possible.

**Leading:** Instead of reflecting where you think they are going next, reflect where they are right now.

**Long-windedness:** Simple, short interruptions help people self connect.

**Multi-tasking:** Instead of cleaning off your desk and trying to listen at the same time, give 100% attention. Show that you care by suspending all other activities.

**Pointing out contradictions:** When clients contradict something they've said earlier, instead of pointing out the discrepancy, reflect the most recent comment and acknowledge their change, progress, new clarity or the appearance of a new voice or part.

**Pretending you understand:** If you get confused, say so. "I'm not following you. Could you say that another way?"

**Suggesting a particular response:** "I think you ought to go in there and tell him off," doesn't lead to understanding. Nor is the suggested strategy likely to benefit anyone. Ask, "What do you want to happen?" or "If you were to put consequences aside for a moment, what might you do?"

**Understating or overstating:** If your client expresses mild annoyance, instead of saying, "You sound really angry," reflect back the same level of intensity and energy. Likewise, if the speaker is loudly expressing outrage, she won't feel understood if you quietly reflect, "You sound a little annoyed." Meet her where she is.

# Intuition

Intuition is a broad cognitive term that refers to information, ideas, knowledge and understanding that come to us outside the rational and logical channels of thinking. It may come to us as an image, spontaneous thought, feeling or a strong sense. Intuition is a response to all that is present, right now. When we share our intuition in the moment, new possibilities can emerge. If we rely solely on our thinking, we miss out on vast sources of knowledge.

When we over-analyze or second-guess the messages that come through our body-emotional intelligence, we miss out. Worst case scenario, our hunch is not fruitful and we learn from that. Best case, we gain from the experience of synchronicity with our client and deepen our relationship with this wider field of communication that comes from beyond the conscious mind.

The appreciation of intuition in modern society is growing and has room to grow still, for it contributes to nearly all of our decisions every day. Coaching relationships give both of us the opportunity to grow intuition, test it and learn how to trust it.

### Seven steps to intuitive development

In her book, *Practical Intuition,* Laura Day offers the following stages on the path to developing one's intuition:

Opening

Noticing

Pretending

Trusting

Reporting

Interpreting

Integrating

As we cultivate openness to our intuition, we can expand the ways we use our coaching skills. When following our intuition, coaching is more in tune with what is happening in the moment. We share our sense, or intuitive hits with the people we coach and assess how they receive it.

*Examples:*

I'm getting a sense of a little girl in a corner of a dark room. Does that resonate with you?

I have a hunch that you'll go into this meeting with all your boldness, as though you're Queen Latifah... What comes up for you?

I can hear the complexity of all you're facing. What does your intuition say about it?

My instincts tell me you're in the calm before the storm. Is there anything worth exploring here?

I'm getting an image of a bear eating honey and ignoring the bee stings. Does that have any meaning for you?

Whether our intuition resonates with our client or not, stating our intuitive messages may open up new avenues of exploration and awareness.

## Curiosity

Curiosity dwells at the center of learning. When we choose to see the world with brand new eyes, we adopt a curious mindset. No matter how negative or perplexing the topic, we can stay open and curious. To do that, we approach our coaching sessions without thinking we know exactly what to do. What might be possible? We can acknowledge whatever is present or alive without being in a hurry to get somewhere else. As we keep company with emotions and get curious, the deeper needs emerge. Without applying pressure, we simply open to what is emerging.

There is no such thing as judgmental curiosity. To be curious is to be in a state of openness. If we embody the enthusiasm of a child exploring a creek, we approach our coaching sessions with wonder and awe.

The wisdom of *not* knowing allows us to be present to something new unfolding. But what if we *do* know? Suppose something similar has happened to us and we know exactly what the client should do? Since their experience is unique, we stay curious about what we *don't* know.

We can embody curiosity by stepping into the unknown with childlike openness for the sake of exploring what is possible. Instead of responding to the situation as a problem, we explore with a beginner's mind and resist the temptation to problem solve. For example, we can say, "So you are stuck. What is that like for you?"

Typically, giving the *right* answer may serve in the short run, but in the long run, we've done nothing to help the person we're coaching to grow. People feel far more empowered when given the opportunity to access their own answers. Even when we can anticipate the solution, instead of becoming attached to our ideas and strategies, we expect people to build on what's possible and to come up with an even more fitting solution than anything we could possibly imagine.

So we take great pleasure in *not knowing*, and cherish the opportunities to uncover buried treasure. It takes persistent practice to avoid looking for a fast answer, and to shift into exploring the client's deeper wisdom.

Karen:  I can't seem to get to all of the things I want to do. I need help prioritizing them.

Coach:  What are the pieces that are important to you?

Karen:  Well, I'm really excited about the work I'm doing now. I'm independent and I really help people, but I want more time for leisure, family, spiritual connection and taking care of things in my home.

Coach:  If you had all of that, what would it give you?

Karen:  Deep joy—joy beyond belief—and a sense of a life well-lived!

Coach:  I'm hearing peace, satisfaction and gratitude. What would a day well-lived look like?

Karen:  (tunes in and notices) I would start the day with yoga, prayer and meditation. I would work until I noticed my energy sagging and then go for a walk. Connecting with nature would energize me for my afternoon work and I want to use my evenings for working to protect the environment.

Coach:  So you see how your business, service and spiritual pieces come together. My intuition tells me to ask about family and leisure time.

Karen:  Yes! That's very important. I see Saturday as a day for leisure, and want Sundays to be real family days.

Coach:  What leisure activities connect you with your deepest joy?

> Karen: Reading inspirational books, walking at the lake, spending time with my dog, family dinners.
>
> Coach: What are you noticing as you share these joyful aspects of your life?
>
> Karen: I'm noticing how energized and excited I feel.
>
> Coach: How can you keep that energy and excitement alive?
>
> Karen: I'm going to take a picture of me smiling and looking radiant and put it on my desk. It will remind me to make space each day for something that makes me smile.
>
> Coach: I'm going to leave you with an inquiry. How can you make each day well-lived?

Although Karen was seeking a quick fix, the coach in this example remained curious and resisted the urge to move into action. As a result, she experienced for herself the impact of what really mattered to her.

## Creating Trust

We can open our sessions as though we are opening a gift box with a rare gem inside. We hold our own agenda lightly as we tune into the client's agenda. As coaches, we are not the expert, the problem solver or the one responsible for the results of the session. We don't have to offer a life-changing piece of wisdom. We don't have to make them change. All we need to do is witness their exploration. Witnessing becomes a building block for authentic change and empowerment.

We create safe space by including the five elements of trust: reliability, acceptance, openness, straightforwardness and caring. When we consistently do what we say we'll do, accept others without judgment, openly give and receive feedback, speak our truth and show we care, we build trust.

> *Example:*
> Julio, I am moved by your courage and the loving way you explained to your parents about being gay. I honor your commitment to your authenticity, and I'm touched by the depth of love you feel toward your parents while wanting them to see all of you.

The author Mary Rose O'Reilley talks about how listening like a cow helps people establish radical presence. She says, "Cows cock their big brown eyes at you and twitch their ears when you talk. This is a great antidote to the critical listening that goes on in academia, where we listen for the mistake, the flaw in the argument." Critical listening crushes the spirit and weakens trust. Empathic listening builds awareness and trust and encourages hidden talents.

### Holding the container

There are tangible and subtle ways that we create a "container" or an environment of trust and support. The tangible ways include clarity about the process, regularity, reliability, keeping agreements, tracking progress, clear boundaries, follow-up on requests, challenges and homework. The subtle ways of holding the container include all the core principles, such as seeing our client as resourceful with unlimited potential. In service of the client's agenda, the container of coaching holds both safety as well as fierce courage, and this in turn opens the door to authentic exploration.

When a coach walks the talk and engages in soulful and spiritual development, there is more room for clients to do their own exploration in these areas. The dual exploration that happens in coaching is invigorating—as our clients do their inner work, they call us into working more deeply on ourselves.

## Natural Flow

Leaps of insight, awareness or creativity are spontaneous. When a natural opening presents itself, we can mine the vein of gold. To be in the natural flow, we recognize openings, let go of our agenda, follow our intuition and respond in the moment.

For example, a client says she is sick and tired of the same old same old. Rather than trying to find a solution the same old way, the coach hears that new felt sense, interrupts and acknowledges, "What's the easy way out of being 'sick and tired'?"

If we get an image of the client flying, instead of deliberating the pros and cons, we can respond to that moment by saying, "I see you flying," which may open the client to a whole new way of seeing life.

Natural openings are not thought out. We simply respond. After we learn coaching skills and processes, we can eventually let go of logical practices and flow with our clients, meeting them with what is called for in the moment.

Being in the flow means we pay attention to opportunities, which are often verbal—a slip of the tongue, saying the same thing twice, or talking about other people as a means to explore the self. When the client says, "A bird just came to my window," we can see this as a distraction, or as a natural opening. "Talk to the bird..." can be far more empowering than asking, "What are you avoiding?"

Awareness of body language often supports the natural flow. When a client picks a piece of lint off her clothing, the coach can explore the natural opening by connecting the action to what she is saying. The coach might ask, "What would you like to get rid of?" or "What's annoying you?" With a client who is highly aware and attuned to self discovery, the coach might simply say, "You just removed a piece of lint," and leave space for her to explore or make her own meaning.

As coaches, we have hundreds of options when it comes to ways to go with the natural flow. Connecting the natural opening to the client's agenda for the session, tying the micro-movement to values or vision, or making the connection to the client's goals supports the natural flow of coaching.

## Transformational Relationship

Not all coaching methods emphasize the *transformational relationship*. Coaching for Transformation is a pioneering model that embraces the value of focusing on the client, while embracing the transformational relationship between coach and client. We can simultaneously step wholeheartedly into both sides of the coaching equation by sharing our own transformation. As coaches, we share the impact of the clients' transformation for the purpose of adding value to their experience, not to upstage or take away from their personal transformation.

# Self-Care for the Coach

*Allow your work and your recreation to be one and the same…*
*Serve others and cultivate yourself simultaneously…*
*Understand that true growth comes from meeting and*
*Solving the problems of life in a way that is*
*Harmonizing to yourself and to others. —Lao Tzu*

What are the ways we care for our mind, body and soul? How much meaning, inspiration and purpose do we want in our lives? How regularly do we exercise and take time for spiritual practices? How does diet support our optimal functioning?

Using a journal to reflect on our own self-care, we can ask:

How is our energy level?

How are our spirits?

What inspires us?

How is our health?

Do we want a change of viewpoint?

Life balance and living in ways that are deeply nourishing is part of walking our talk as coaches. Through the process of self-reflection, we can also access greater wisdom, creativity and happiness.

Instead of looking for a textbook definition of balance, we find our own pathway to satisfaction. What is the cost when we do not provide the self-care we need? Since we are always making choices, what is the choice we want to make regarding self-care? The most valuable resources we have as coaches are our health, energy, empathy and clarity of mind. Connecting with these resources allows us to use our coaching toolbox more creatively.

Self-care supports us professionally as well. People hire us mostly because of who we *are*, so the success of our business and our effectiveness as a coach depends upon self-care. We share universal needs, but each person has different priorities. While one person needs eight hours of sleep a night, another only needs six. If our inspiration and self-care are intact, we can work the right amount and fall more deeply in love with our work.

To look at the whole spectrum of values and how they manifest in our lives, use the life balance wheel, such as the one in Chapter 10, *Strategy and Action*.

## COACHING in Action | The Coaching Relationship by Pernille Plantener, CFT Faculty

*"In my early professional years I was asking the question: How can I treat, or cure, or change this person? Now I would phrase the question in this way: How can I provide a relationship which this person may use for his own personal growth?" —Carl Rogers*

Extensive studies in psychotherapy have shown that the most important predictor of client outcome is the therapist-client relationship, as experienced by the client. Studies from the last couple of decades confirm that the importance of the relationship applies to coaching as well.

Even though we put effort into learning the Coaching for Transformation skills and pathways, they merely serve as a scaffold for building and deepening the relationship. As Carl Rogers points to—the relationship is the field in which transformation becomes possible.

### THE QUALITIES OF A HELPFUL COACH-CLIENT RELATIONSHIP

**Unconditional positive regard.** Through unconditional positive regard, we provide optimum conditions for growth where clients accept and take responsibility for themselves. By definition any helping relationship anticipates change. In the coaching relationship, that anticipation presents as Hope—an optimism that something positive will develop to bring about constructive change. Thus, unconditional positive regard means that the coach shows overall acceptance of the client—as distinct from the client's behaviors. The coach sets aside personal opinions and biases to focus on the client's intrinsic worth. No matter what the client says or does, we interpret it as an expression of an intention of something positive—and we nurture that intention.

**Trustworthiness.** When the client trusts the coach, deep explorations can happen. Trust is about honoring agreements, and if agreements need to be broken, we do it with awareness and gentleness. When the client has a sense that the coach is with her, the coaching relationship comes into alignment. We create intimacy so that whatever the client shares, we receive it as a precious gift.

**Authenticity.** We model radical self-acceptance by being authentic moment by moment. If we drift away for a few seconds, or if we don't understand what the client says, or if we are touched or triggered, we let the client know. Holding the coach as a role model, the client is encouraged to self-reveal, which builds trust.

**Vulnerability.** An especially important aspect of authenticity is to let the client experience our vulnerability. Whether we feel insecurity, shame or fear of rejection, we self-manage and bring it in only if we believe sharing our emotions will serve the client. Rather than share long stories, we are more likely to connect if we share our feelings and our longing in the moment.

### FIVE LEVELS OF CONTRACTS

1. **Contract with the world and God—personal ethics**
   The first level of contract is the personal commitment each coach holds—areas where we will not compromise. It might be about holding all human beings as equals, or about not harming the planet, or about working within the law. We can ask ourselves, "What work would I refuse, given my personal ethics? Or what would make me resign from a coaching contract?"

2. **Contract with the client or organization— logistics and expectations**
   The second level of contracting includes administrative aspects—time, place, duration, context, fees, evaluation methods and confidentiality—as well as the learning and development contract. When we coach the employees of an organization, the sponsor may have one agenda for the work, while the people being coached might have others. For example, the sponsor wants a newly promoted employee to enhance her people skills. She might not see any reason to work on that, and would prefer coaching on work-life balance. We hold the confidentiality of the coaching relationship, and encourage transparency and dialogue.

---

**COACHING *in Action* | The Coaching Relationship** *by Pernille Plantener, CFT Faculty*

*(Continued)*

**TRANSFERENCE AND COUNTER-TRANSFERENCE**

3. **Contract for the course of coaching—desired outcomes**

   The arc of the coaching relationship often starts with clarification of values, vision and goals. We contract about using other processes or tools: 360° feedback, assessments and other forms of support. We determine the desired outcomes of the coaching process, and check in regularly on progress, and often recalibrate or change course.

4. **Contract for the session—presenting agenda**

   We also create a contract for each session, starting by finding the presenting and deeper agenda. We check to see if clients are getting what they want from the session. We complete processes thoroughly, such as checking back in with the constricted body parts, making agreements about embodying a new viewpoint, or summarizing action steps. To keep the client on track and on time, we can ask for the bottom line, recap, interrupt or refer to the time.

5. **Contract from moment to moment—what's important now**

   Using our intuition, we track the client's aliveness in every moment. We name it when their energy shifts. If the client steps over something, we can bring them back to what matters most. One of the ways to help clients stay focused is to invite them to "park that for a moment" and come back to it later.

   The art of coaching is to hold all five levels of contracts simultaneously, which builds trust.

Sometimes clients unconsciously relate to the coach as a significant figure in their life, appealing for love, reliving an old drama or testing an abusive pattern. And sometimes coaches relate to the client as someone with whom we have unfinished businesses, such as someone dependent, needing protection, or providing approval. This way of using each other as representatives from our past is common and known as transference and counter-transference.

From the Internal Family Systems work of Richard Schwartz[1], we learn that all of us consist of a multitude of sub-personalities. One part of the internal community might be frozen in the past and relating to the coach as if he was her father, while another part wants to explore this dynamic. By getting curious about the part that is engaging in transference, we can support awareness of the nature and purpose of this part. Working with transference opens the client to embrace the part with loving acceptance, which gradually allows the part to be a constructive partner rather than a powerful terrorist. This way, the coaching relationship becomes a space for transformation.

Likewise, when we are not able to see our clients' resourcefulness, we may be engaging in counter-transference. The ongoing practice of supervision helps us deal with our own unfinished business and limiting beliefs without using our clients for this purpose.

---

1    Schwartz, Richard C. *Internal Family Systems Therapy,* The Guilford Press 1995

## The Coach's Stand

One of the ways to access our commitment and energy is to develop what we call the *coach's stand*. By that, we mean a solid foundation from which we coach and a courageous, empowered attitude that inspires clients.

The coach's stand is a set of physical, mental and spiritual qualities that we embody when we coach. As we stand in our power, we call your clients to step into their own power.

We divide the coach's stand into three parts:

> Physical stand or movement
>
> Metaphor for the coaching relationship
>
> Commitment to what we care about

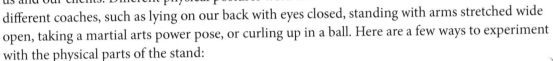

## Physical

Our energy and impact in the world are affected by our physical being. We feel confident and powerful when standing, ready to move. Conversely, we may have trouble being expansive in our thinking if we are seated with our arms and legs crossed. As coaches, we need to explore and discover the postures and movements that most empower us and our clients. Different physical postures work for different coaches, such as lying on our back with eyes closed, standing with arms stretched wide open, taking a martial arts power pose, or curling up in a ball. Here are a few ways to experiment with the physical parts of the stand:

> Dancing
>
> Pushing on a wall
>
> Moving arms energetically
>
> Doodling
>
> Jumping up and down
>
> Walking or pacing
>
> Scanning the body for sensations
>
> Opening your eyes widely
>
> Pretending you are swimming in the air

We can develop a range of physical components of our stand to use at different times. The easiest way to discover these is to try out different postures and movements while coaching and notice the impact on the coach, the client and the energy of the coaching relationship. If we get stuck or the client gets stuck, we move! We can notice the subtle impact our physicality has on our inner experience and outer posture. When we are more present, we may find our breath deepens, we relax, or our back straightens. As we experiment with these points of self-awareness we can be surprised at how much our physical being affects the quality and quantity of energy available to the coaching relationship.

## Metaphor

Metaphors are powerful symbols. Some images invite reflection, some create energy and others evoke action. Our unique metaphor for the coaching relationship brings power to both coach and client.

*Examples of metaphors for the coaching relationship:*

Walking along the beach together as co-explorers

Hovering like a hummingbird, taking in the beauty

Fellow ants in an ant hill, comparing notes on the community

Holding the rope, creating safety for the mountain climber

Offering a mirror that actively reveals what's hidden

Standing shoulder-to-shoulder

Looking out from the crow's nest

Standing behind the boxer in the ring

Persisting like a curious child

Sword cutting through illusion and self-deception

By creating a metaphor that energizes us, we can bring forward the qualities we want to bring to our coaching. Metaphors come from the right brain. They often appear before we *think* of them. Without judging, we can open to whatever images come. As we sit with the image, notice what it calls forth. Metaphors can help you embody the CFT core principles as well as your own principles.

## Commitment

When we commit to something happening in each coaching interaction, we go beyond having a curious conversation. Without commitment, the coaching can drift. We may not know the coaching has run off-track, so we train ourselves to notice when our energy is fading or we have missed opportunities to fully engage. When we make a commitment, it helps us overcome our inner critic.

Sourcing unconditional love for ourselves and our client is a natural state of being that invites intimacy and depth. But sometimes we forget our stand. We get triggered, overwhelmed, or find ourselves on auto-pilot. Instead of judging ourselves, we can welcome the tension and take a moment to review our commitment. Then we can ask, what can I do in this moment to recommit to or change my stand? By sourcing power, we create an environment where passion is stirred and vision evolves into reality. Stretching our imagination and pushing our boundaries unleashes the flow.

Coaching in general focuses on desired behavior, rather than problematic or bad behavior; but sometimes a few bad examples can illuminate the way forward. Here are some examples of commitments that undermine the effectiveness of the coaching.

*Examples of undermining commitments:*

Looking good

Doing it right

Keeping the client from quitting

Helping the client stay comfortable

Avoiding rocking the boat

Being polite

Showing how much I know

Wanting to be liked

*Now ask yourself:*

What stories or commitments do you hold that keep you from stepping into your power as a coach?

How do you develop commitments that enliven and empower you, your client and the relationship?

You may already know what commitments you want to develop. If so, experiment with them and discover how they affect your coaching. If not, the first place to look is the core principles. Holding these principles will ensure your commitment supports your client's agenda rather than replacing or nullifying it.

*Examples of empowering, enlivening commitments:*

My clients connect to their soul and create from their essence

My clients choose powerful actions from full alignment

My clients' freedom is more important than either of us being comfortable

My clients can count on me to bring the best of my coaching to our sessions

I speak to my clients' magnificence and challenge anything less than that

I stretch myself for the sake of my clients' transformational agenda

## Perspective

*To enhance your focus on your client, ask yourself:*

What are the untapped resources in my client's life?

How am I holding back and forgetting my client's resourcefulness?

How is this client already whole and moving toward a greater expression of her wholeness?

How can I stop problem solving and start trusting my client's inherent creativity?

To be a masterful coach, we step past the borders of our knowing. The greatest value to clients comes from our willingness to go to the places where we don't already have the answers. We can be more interested in *their* ideas and what is possible than in *our* ideas. Our personal experience or clever solutions might generate excitement momentarily, but do not empower people in the long run.

Imagine that our job as a coach is to explore the places that neither of us know—the possibilities that have not yet surfaced. New directions and new perspectives live in the land of mystery—that place where neither of us have the answer.

## COACHING *in Action* | **My Coach's Stand** *by Michael Wise, CFT Certified Coach*

I struggled with my coach's stand at first. I thought I had developed several great stands and metaphors, but none of them helped. Lost and confused. I switched my stand a few times but never really connected with one. Eventually I thought, "I can just coach without a stand and I'll be fine." So I tried that for a while and found many sessions didn't go as far as I would like. I let my clients linger in stories for too long or just chat.

My mentor asked what my coach's stand was, and when I shared it, she said she didn't feel any of that intention or energy during the session. In a moment of intuition she said, "As I listen to your coaching I keep getting an image of a flying trapeze." In that moment something clicked and I saw clearly how my coach's stand could support me. Since that day the flying trapeze has been my coach's stand.

Before every coaching session I imagine my client letting go of the bar they have been holding, and reaching for a new bar. My physical stance is with my feet slightly apart and my hands stretched up and out as if reaching for the trapeze bar. My metaphor is the trapeze artist ready to fly to the next bar. My commitment is that I create a safe place where clients connect to their passions and strengths, let go and leap toward what brings them most alive, knowing that if they miss the bar, they will survive and learn something new.

Connecting with this stand has brought my coaching to a new level. When I'm stuck or my client is stuck, I think of the trapeze artist and empowering questions come to me. When I embody my physical stance and envision clients letting go of the bar, I connect them with what is calling them forward. Not only do clients let go and leap, but so do I.

When we are called to be someone we've never been before, or do something we've never done before, we inspire clients to do the same. We can replace rote, predictable coaching with boldness. By taking risks, we hold a vision that is larger than what they can see themselves, which calls them into a deeper space or a bigger game.

We don't develop the ability to stand with boldness and call out the power by ignoring our feelings, but by deepening your awareness. Many experienced coaches say that some of their most powerful and inspired sessions happen when they enter the coaching without much emotional or physical energy, but are able to tap into unexpected energy and resourcefulness. Self-focused listening brings us into an awareness of what is happening in the moment and the inner resourcefulness to reconnect to our power.

What do *you* stand for?

Compassionate action?

Authenticity?

Social Justice?

Transformation?

Deep awareness?

Abundance?

Balance?

Aliveness?

When we speak, listen or take action from your stand, we hold the space for bringing new ways of being into existence. When we boldly and publicly claim our stand, we commit to creating a new future for ourselves and our clients.

**Using the coach's stand**

Once we have developed the three parts of our stand (physical, metaphor, commitment), we use them to call out our clients' power. Before each coaching session, we focus on our commitment, step into the metaphor and embody the physical component.

*Questions to Consider*

Experiment with your coach's stand. What stand feels most powerful for you?

What do you notice as you focus on the three levels of listening in your coaching sessions?

What do you notice about your sense of presence when you trust your intuition?

What do you notice about your sense of being present when you get curious?

How can you give the gift of full presence?

# 3
# Core Skills—The Coach's Palette

*Technique becomes a tool, not an objective…You must know your tools, have the best, and put them in perfect arrangement for service. Painting requires great judgment and skill. —Robert Henri*

Just as an artist gathers brushes, pigments and techniques, coaches have a palette of skills to use with their clients. In Chapter 3 we cover transformational coaching skills, starting with examples of each of the core skills. Then we discuss several aspects of coaching in detail—empowering questions, acknowledging, listening, wisdom of the body, emotions and uncovering the client's agenda.

Coaching skills help us bring out the best in our clients and give them access to their full power. We can choose from a variety of techniques to help them increase awareness and move toward more satisfaction and fulfillment. Mastering the skills of coaching helps us take clients to the fullest expression of their potential.

Coaching for Transformation is a client-centered process. We follow our clients' agendas, attune to their essence as they discover themselves and their highest dreams. As we focus on our client, we can ask ourselves questions like:

What matters most to this client?

How can I focus my coaching on all of what my client brings?

What is the deepest expression of my client's greatness?

How do I empower my client to see a full range of choices?

We ask the questions that our client doesn't dare ask. Using the entire internal and external environment as a resource, we attune to our own sensations, to the words and to what our client is not saying. We feel the energy and use our intuition. Then we let go of any attachment to the outcome and let our client take whatever resonates.

# Transformational Coaching Skills

The following list of core transformational coaching skills gives a range of colors to use. We explore several of them in more detail later in this chapter.

**Acknowledging the Essence**—sharing qualities that we see, hear and sense to support clients in feeling seen at their authentic core. Naming their aliveness or passion.

*Examples: "I hear your compassion for children and commitment to social justice. I sense taking a stand for children is core for you." "As I listen to you talk about speaking your truth I am struck by the depth of your courage."*

**Asking Empowering Questions**—asking open-ended questions to evoke self-reflection, clarity, insight and action.

*Example: "What is important about this?" "What stands out to you?" "What is next?" "What would you do if you knew you couldn't fail?"*

**Brainstorming**—generating ideas, expanding new possibilities or developing strategies.

*Example: "Let's explore some options. What do you see when you step out of the box?"*

**Challenging**—requesting the person stretch beyond perceived limitations. A challenge is more than a simple request. It pushes people beyond what they think is possible so they stretch themselves and end up doing more than they originally thought possible.

*Example: "I challenge you to stop working alone and find three other changemakers to support you this month." Your client can accept, decline or negotiate the challenge.*

**Championing**—believing in and encouraging resourcefulness, and highlighting their desire or ability to take the next step.

*Example: "I have seen you make life-serving decisions before and believe in your ability to be a powerful executive director. What do you need to say yes to this promotion?"*

**Clarifying**—articulating needs and values in order to verify understanding. More than repeating the words, clarifying speaks to the deeper message or implication. Clarifying includes articulating, reframing and asking empowering questions.

*Example: "I sense you are looking for respect and autonomy in this new move. What else is important?"*

**Embracing Polarities**—naming experiences, ideas, feelings or needs that appear to be in conflict, and holding them with respect, without making one side more important than the other.

*Example: "So you want freedom and security. How can you have both?" You may ask your client to step into the experience of freedom, and then into the experience of security and notice the difference in each place.*

**Establishing Accountability**—creating structures to verify the action plan is on track, supporting clients to actively live their values and move toward their vision or goals.

*Example: "What will you do? When will you do it? How will I know?" or "How will you celebrate when you realize your vision by the end of the year?"*

**Facilitating Cultural Awareness**—creating awareness of power and privilege, supporting cultural humility, embracing identities and cultural differences and addressing systemic oppression.

*Example: "How do the power dynamics impact you as a young Asian man?" or "How can you bridge the cultural differences?"*

**Holding Client's Agenda**—identifying what the client wants. Listening for what matters most, both in the big picture of their life, in the coaching session and in the moment.

*Example: "Javier, I know you want to look at how to manage your time. What is most important about that? How will managing your time affect your life?"*

**Holding Silence**—discerning when to create space for the client to look internally. Pausing allows space for self-intimacy, for both the coach's and the client's intuition to emerge.

*Example: "..................................................................................."*

**Interrupting**—cutting through storytelling or reporting to capture the essence of what's expressed. Interrupting is done in service of getting back to exploring what matters most, or moving from discussion to felt experience.

*Example: "Katia, stop. What is the essence of what you are saying? What is important here? What is the feeling that may be difficult to be with?"*

**Intuiting**—trusting inner knowing and expressing gut reactions.

*Example: "I have a sense (hunch, intuition) that there is a black veil over this whole situation. How does that resonate with you?"*

**Making Metaphors**—using images, stories and pictures that engage the right brain and deepen the learning by reflecting the essence of the situation.

*Example: "Jasmine, this difficult conversation you need to have with your sister feels like a stone over your heart." Or "What is an image or metaphor which captures the essence of your experience?"*

**Moving into Action**—co-creating or requesting movement toward goals that are aligned with values, vision and desires. This could include brainstorming ways to create forward movement.

*Example: "What can you do this week to realize your goal?" "What's something you can do to keep the momentum going this month?"*

**Naming What's Present**—succinctly describing what is happening in the moment or what is underneath the surface. Includes naming what we see and sense, distilling what is happening now or what is emerging. We can observe patterns, or name what is not being said, or identify what is happening in the coaching relationship.

*Example: Andy talks about something he is afraid of. You hear growing excitement as well, and say, "You've had enough of living in fear and you're ready to embrace the excitement of this opportunity."*

**Offering an Inquiry**—asking questions that help people explore new learning and insights more deeply over time. Something to ponder between sessions, an inquiry focuses on learning and awareness, not action.

*Example: "Simone, what is love to you?" "What's the relationship between your spiritual connection and the way forward?"*

**Reflecting**—mirroring words, energy, feelings, needs, values or vision. Hearing the deepest motivation by focusing on what your client wants at the core.

*Example: "Zoë, are you excited because you've been longing for mutuality and partnership?" "Chitra, you mentioned sadness. I also hear a desire for connection."*

**Re-Framing**—sharing a new perspective that opens up broader possibilities.

*Example: "This may seem like a dead end to you. How might this serve you or your dream?"*

**Requesting**—asking for a specific action without being attached to the outcome. Client responds with yes, no, or a counter-offer.

*Example: "Ebony, will you spend 20 minutes a day being with the most vocal, powerful part of yourself?"*

**Self-Managing**—noticing that our internal experience or our agenda is affecting our ability to be fully present, and then recovering. Recovering can involve transparency, or letting the client know what has happened. Following our intuition without judging, giving advice or holding back.

*Example: Rich describes a crisis in his relationship, similar to the crisis you face in your own relationship. As coach, you notice you are triggered and set an intention to take time for yourself after the session. Then you return to client-focused listening and ask curious questions.*

**Setting Goals**—setting intentions for desired outcomes and making plans that are specific, measurable, alive, relevant, time-bound and shared.

*Example: "What will you create? What energizes you about the goal? When will you take action? How will that look when it is complete? Who will you talk to about your goals?"*

**Visioning**—exploring the big picture and creating a visual reminder of the desired future. We go into the experience of the vision before asking what they see.

*Example: "Gil, take away all the limits and imagine you are successful beyond your wildest dreams. What do you see?"*

As in any other discipline, coaching mastery comes from practicing the basics until the form becomes second nature. At that point we can step beyond the form into new levels of spontaneous creation.

*Questions to Consider*

Which three coaching skills are you most comfortable using?

Which three coaching skills do you want more practice using?

How can you get more practice with these skills?

# Asking Empowering Questions

Despite conventional perceptions, coaches don't give advice. The whole idea is to get people to consider their situation and come to solutions on their own. The path to this understanding starts with curious, empowering questions. Empowering questions are open-ended questions that invite people to ponder, consider, open, notice, discover and awaken. They create insights, "ah-ha" moments and opportunities. Open questions invite engagement and body-mind connection.

Empowering questions typically begin with "What" or "How" and are often simple, intuitive or spontaneous. Questions that begin with "When" can also be empowering when they are not used to satisfy the coach's desire for information that is extraneous to the client's agenda. "Why" questions tend to create defensiveness and cut off connection. Questions that can be answered with simply "Yes" or "No" are considered closed questions that limit exploration, possibility and dialogue.

## Other criteria for empowering questions

Lead to clarification

Call for introspection

Address a paradox

Connect to the person's needs and desires

Consider a new perspective

Help the person see the issue in a different light

Move into depth or new territory

Bring light to inner conflict

Get to the root of a belief or pattern

Help people face fear and learn from it

Ask something new

Create specific engagement

Invite deep reflection

Elicit feedback

Generate movement

## Examples of empowering questions

### Probing Questions

What do you want?

What's important about that?

What are you excited about?

What is your intention?

What are you overlooking?

### Clarifying Values

What do you care about in this situation?

What value does this experience have for you?

What do you want? If you get that, then what do you want?

How does this plan honor your values?

What are you committed to?

### Setting Stretch Goals

If you knew you'd succeed, what else would you do?

If you were to raise the bar, what would it look like?

How can you play a bigger game?

What's the big picture?

What action would really excite you?

### Expanding Options

What is possible?

If you had a magic wand, what would you do?

What impact would you like to have?

What are your choices?

What would be possible if you did not censor yourself?

### Getting Support

Who can help you navigate the cultural differences?

What do you need help with?

Who can help you with that?

What can you delegate?

What request can you make?

If you knew they'd say yes, who would you ask for help?

### Action Questions

How do you plan to achieve that?

How can you break that down into smaller steps?

What are you going to do? By when? Who will you tell?

Is there anything else you need to do?

On a scale of 1 to 10, how committed are you to this plan?

### Breaking through Barriers

What's stopping you?

In an ideal world, how would you face this problem?

What would motivate you to change?

What would it cost you if things remain the way they are?

Pretend you know the answer…

### Reducing Sense of Overwhelm

What can you say "no" to?

What can you stop doing so that you can make room for what's important?

What can you stop tolerating?

What are you doing now that's working?

If you only focused on one thing, what would it be?

### Eliciting Wisdom

What might you do differently next time?

What does your heart tell you about this?

When you're at your best, what's different?

What do you know in your gut?

What do you really want?

The questions below can be useful as you move into deeper coaching:

### Connecting with Soul

Aliveness—where are you most alive?

Depth—what is the deepest or wildest possibility?

Let go into—what is it to sink into yourself?

Alignment—with what are you most aligned in your life?

Being with—what is it to be with yourself?

### Connecting with Spirit

Wholeness—what does it mean to be whole?

Passion—where does your passion live inside you?

Surrender—what is it to surrender to a greater good?

Trust—what do you trust with every cell in your body?

Stretch—where does the Universe want you to stretch next?

Love—how can you create a loving culture at work?

### Connecting with the Body

Laughter—what brings out your laughter?

Lightness—where do your worries disappear?

Energy—when have you found yourself uplifted?

Movement—what moves you?

Sensuality—in what ways does your body flow?

Beauty—what is it to love and appreciate every part of your body?

### Engaging the Mind

Best thinking—how do you tap the full capacity of your mind?

Ideas—what is possible?

Vision—if you could have anything, what would you want?

Possibility—what else?

Judgment—what values are at stake for you?

Choice—where do you choose to put your attention?

### Connection with Emotions

Acceptance—how can you embrace your emotions?

Happy—what are you celebrating?

Fear—what is your fear calling you to do?

Grief—what opportunities have you missed?

Sadness—what is sweet about sadness?

Shame—what healing are you longing for?

Anger—what about your anger calls you forth?

## Examples of limiting questions

### Close-ended Questions

Are you going to be able to fix it?

Can you get more resources?

Do you have any influence?

These questions ask for a yes/no response. An open-ended question generates new ways of thinking. Examples: How can you fix it? What can you do to get more resources? What influence would you like to have?

### Informational Questions

How many employees do you have?

What did you study in college?

Who else was in the meeting?

All of these questions give us information that we don't really need. Even if we don't have the entire context, we can still coach effectively.

## Why Questions

Why didn't you take action?

Why did you do that?

Why are you going to get help?

"Why" questions ask for the story, the logic, the thinking behind the choices, and they often imply judgment or criticism. "Why" questions can become mental rehashing of old beliefs. Avoid judgmental questions including "why" questions in coaching, so that you honor the needs of past choices and can stay open to celebrating new choices in the future. Of course there are exceptions, such as, "Why is this important to you?"

## Leading Questions

Don't you think you ought to…?

Have you tried…?

Wouldn't it be better if you…?

All of these questions are thinly disguised forms of advice, which is not as empowering as helping people discover their own solutions. Likewise, don't bother asking questions if you already know the answer.

## Judgmental Questions

Do you consider that normal behavior?

Who does she think she is?

Did you expect to get away with that?

Curiosity is the opposite of judgment. To be curious is to be in a state of openness.

## Shrinking Questions

Aren't you taking on a little too much?

Are you sure you can handle all of this?

Do you really think you're ready?

Out of a desire to protect people from possible failure, beginning coaches sometimes encourage people to shrink. Masterful coaches help people expand their vision, but still address potential barriers creatively; e.g., "How can you get past the barriers?"

# Acknowledging, Championing, Celebrating and Appreciating

*Caminante, no hay puentes, se hace puentes al andar. (Voyager, there are no bridges, one builds them as one walks.) —Gloria E. Anzaldúa*

Acknowledging the essence of our client, serving as a champion for their aspirations, celebrating their successes and appreciating the value they add are life-serving coaching skills.

## Acknowledging the essence

Acknowledging the essence is a heart-to-heart way of seeing our clients. We acknowledge clients by sharing qualities that we see, hear and sense as the essence of the person. We do this to support them in feeling seen authentically at their core.

> *Examples*
>
> As I listen to you talk about speaking your truth at work I am struck by your courage. What do you notice?
>
> You're cherishing your self-awareness and the balance you've created at work and at home.
>
> You care deeply about understanding the impact of tokenism.
>
> I want to acknowledge the way you are taking responsibility by acting on what matters most to you.
>
> You sound very connected to your values and you're honoring them fully.
>
> Kudos for stepping out of your comfort zone.
>
> Your commitment to growth is unwavering.

Acknowledgement is different from complimenting, which implies evaluation and judgment.

> *Examples: Vague Compliments*
>
> Good job!
>
> You're amazing!
>
> Way to go!
>
> Outstanding!

Instead, we acknowledge the essence of our client's being at the core. A true acknowledgement is unique to the client in the moment, yet points to their enduring qualities. An acknowledgment can include what we notice about their stand, their growth, their learning or what we see. We name the qualities of the client that seem core or essential in relationship to what's happening in the moment. When we acknowledge our client's unique qualities, they can often step into those qualities more fully.

We can become aware of the client's essence through intuition, felt sense, reading the energy or observation and can share the source to help the client understand the basis of our acknowledgment.

Acknowledging the essence has two and sometimes three steps:

1. Deliver the acknowledgement.

2. Listen for the impact.

3. Follow up if the client did not receive the acknowledgement or received it partially.

Acknowledgment can be more powerful if delivered in few words—go right to the heart of the matter. We don't go on and on. We deliver and pause. At first, some clients want to move on, brush off or negate the acknowledgment. Following up can include slowing down the process, repeating or rephrasing the acknowledgment, asking what stops them from receiving it or inviting them to hold silence and take it in. That doesn't mean we force our acknowledgement on our clients; we stay unattached and check in about the impact. People receive acknowledgments differently so we are sensitive to that. Even if the acknowledgment doesn't resonate with the client, something new may emerge, such as an acknowledgment the client does want to hear.

## Championing

When you champion your clients, you help them see things that might not be obvious to them. You can point to their strengths and core values, underscore their abilities and resourcefulness and help them raise the bar on their personal expectations. Benjamin Disraeli said, "The greatest good you can do for another is not just share your riches, but to reveal to him, his own."

> *Example*
> "Dominique, you took on that big global project last year and although it was a challenge, you delivered it on time and on budget. I believe in your ability to handle this new project equally well!"

Championing means we take a stand for our clients. We call them into their power by reminding them of their values, their vision, their strengths and their past successes. We know they can meet a challenge—personal or professional, internal or external—because they have met challenges before, and we can cite specific examples. Not only can we cite their actions, but also their talents, evolution or expanded consciousness.

When it comes from the heart, championing catapults clients out of the status quo and into fresh possibilities. We have the deepest impact when championing comes up spontaneously. In contrast, if we're doing it to get them to shift, they get the sense that where they are is not okay. When our celebration of our client rises up in us and we can't stop it from pouring out, then we know it's the real deal. "You're more committed to stopping trafficking than anyone I know. One thing I'm sure about you is that giving up is not an option. I challenge you to ask ten people to help you."

Although this skill of taking a stand for our clients is typically used when they are swimming in self-doubt or questioning their capabilities, we can also champion clients when they are coming down the home stretch of a project or even when they are upbeat and confident. "Remember when you launched that change initiative and how you used your peacemaking skills to help those two rival groups to collaborate… Tap into that part of you now."

The two main components to the skill of championing are 1) celebrating, followed by 2) challenging. The synergy comes from the combination of deeper awareness and forward movement. Offering specific examples of what the client has done seeds the challenge.

In contrast, "I believe in you" has a vague emptiness to it until we add what we believe the client can actually do. "You have the connections to fundraise enough money to pilot this initiative by the end of the month."

Championing is not empty cheerleading (You can do it!) because it's based on data. If we are trying to rev them up when they have low energy, we are working way too hard. It's far more genuine and impactful to offer a grounded celebration followed by a challenge that invites them to step toward their yearning. "You have a daily practice of going deep into self awareness. I request you take that self-intimacy into your relationship with your boss and open your heart."

When our clients are in the pit of despair, negating their experience in the moment can leave them feeling disconnected. "You're a strong person—you can snap out of it…" doesn't cut it. Forget about pulling them out of the pit, and notice when they start to climb out themselves, rinse off their hopelessness, or see a glimmer of light, as this is the time to match their energy, and stay present to the momentum that is building. "You're in the darkness, but a light from far away is calling you. Answering the call is both scary and exciting. You have the freedom to move toward the light."

If we're trying too hard, championing can sound saccharine, manipulative or over the top. "You're so courageous…" is a bit flat unless we give examples, "You told a vulnerable story to that group of investors and asked for what you need." Voicing our own experience can add to the quality of connection. "I'm feeling goose bumps as I envision you in the driver seat—owning your leadership, yet sharing authentically your own struggles with power and privilege."

We support clients to believe in themselves and simultaneously move forward. We call them into self-affirmation, and from that place where they are steeped in their own confidence and unique beauty, we call them into action. "As you savor your connection to a higher power, use that energy to create your action plan."

## Celebrating

To experience the joy fully, we celebrate the people we coach. What milestones do our clients want to celebrate? How will they celebrate? We don't wait until goals are complete and visions are realized. We don't wait until the change initiative is complete or the book is finally finished.

Look for opportunities to celebrate the small successes along the way. Changing our behavior is no small feat, so we create milestones and rituals to support these transitions.

Celebrations don't have to be flamboyant or costly. You can say, "I celebrate your courage. You took a big risk and presented a controversial alternative." Or you can ask, "How would you like to celebrate this important step?"

Ultimately, we want to support clients to celebrate themselves by asking empowering questions. We might co-create an image or a metaphor—something memorable—as a way to draw out their internal celebration. "I see you at the hub of many circles of healers. What do you celebrate when you step into the center of all those healers?"

This practice of celebrating can be intense and bold or soft and sensitive. We can create space for clients to receive our energy in a way that works for them. In some cultures, people like to soak in the energy of celebrating slowly and respond best to a subtle dance.

## Appreciating

The way people live their values, develop new insights or take action on what matters often impacts us as coaches. Their inner and outer work can serve as an inspiration to us. While acknowledgement focuses exclusively on your client, expression of appreciation focuses on the coach, which can enhance the interaction and quality of connection. Acknowledgment is often used to help clients see themselves more fully or support the changes they are making in their lives, whereas appreciation is a genuine expression of what's alive in the coach.

A full appreciation has three parts:

1.  The observable behavior of your client
2.  The emotional impact
3.  What is satisfying for the coach

"Keisha, when you shared with me the anger you felt about the healthcare inequities for poor people, I felt grateful that you shared your real feelings. You awaken in me a desire to express myself more authentically."

The relationship deepens when we share what inspires us, how our thinking has changed or how our own growth or transformation is impacted by the work of our clients. Instead of vague compliments like, "I appreciate you," we can deepen intimacy and empower the coaching partnership by sharing the specifics of what we appreciate:

I appreciate the way you explored from the heart because…

Would you like to hear how you've contributed to my well-being?

I feel tenderness and I'm connected to my own desire for…

The most moving part of your work for me was…

I'm touched by your vulnerability—are you interested in what opened up in me?

The specific components of appreciation foster transparency and give people a sense of their power and impact. The two-way street creates a more robust relationship, fostering intimacy and authenticity. When our clients understand their impact on us, the relationship is further enhanced by a sense of equality, mutuality and shared power.

## Requests and Challenges

The main difference between a request and a challenge is that clients generally say yes to our requests, but take a moment to catch their breath before responding to a challenge. In both cases, we listen deeply to what's important to the client, and base our requests on helping them move toward a more desirable future. Free of demand, we ask clients to take action, but we're open to hearing yes, no, or a counteroffer.

Both requests and challenges are for the benefit of the client, not for the benefit of the coach. In the wider world, we make requests that benefit ourselves all the time.

Will you send me the name of the book you're reading?

Will you recommend an orthopedist?

Will you give me feedback on my website?

But in coaching, we focus on requests and challenges that are exclusively for the benefit of the client.

To start creating the relationship you want, will you call your daughter today?

Will you give yourself a break and take the night off?

Will you create an action plan to get the funding you need?

If we're listening deeply, clients generally say yes to our requests, but they are often startled by our challenges, because we take them out of their comfort zone.

When we propose a challenge, a real one, the reaction we get is one of wide-eyed curiosity, with a slight undertone of panic when the full ramifications of that challenge sink in. For example, "You say you've been procrastinating for years, so I challenge you to finish writing your book in one month." At first the client says, "No way," to this bold challenge. But as the coach holds silence, the client's jaw drops and she says, "Do you think that's possible? That would be amazing!"

Ideally, the answer to a challenge is "no," and that's often how we know it's a challenge and not an easy request. Not in the sense that the challenge defies all logic and realism, but in the sense that it defies our client's perceived limitations. If the client can say "yes" without blinking, that's the telltale sign of a request. In contrast, a challenge is often met with a "no" or a counteroffer.

Though a challenge is meant to push a client beyond their perceived limitations, it must be specific and explicit to have impact. "I challenge you to be a better ally," has all the makings of an energizing challenge, but anybody can say yes to it. It's incomplete. A challenge must include something doable!

"I challenge you to ask more people for support," is not specific enough. How much is more? Specifically, what kind of support are you challenging the client to seek?

For a challenge to be explicit, we need to add an action, such as, "Ask ten people to help you with your HIV orphans project," or "Find three partners to help you launch your project," or "Ask five potential donors to contribute to your initiative to ban female genital mutilation." Once we get a reaction, even if it's hesitation, we can add, "by the end of the week." If the client is taken by surprise, don't back off. Ramp it up!

If people say yes to our challenges right away, then we're probably not challenging them—we're making simple requests. If they gasp, sit up taller, or fall out of their chair, we're probably zeroing in on their deepest desires.

A challenge is an expansion of making a clear, positive doable request, but there's another element—the real power of a challenge is that the client feels deeply seen by the challenger. A challenge isn't just about getting someone to take action on something important to them; it's a fierce form of empathy that supports people in connecting with their life force. When people experience deep empathy they usually enter a blissful state. But how do we help people take that blissful state forward and really integrate it into their lives? One example, "So you want more self love? I challenge you to embrace your inner antagonist and meditate for 30 minutes a day for a week—to connect with what your antagonist really wants for you."

The real essence of offering a challenge is about so much more. The first step of offering a challenge is to identify the lost parts of soul that a person is ready to reclaim. That's what makes a challenge so much fun! From the place of supporting clients to move toward being more of who they already are, we can take great delight in challenging old beliefs or assumptions, jolting them out of playing small or unleashing their passion. We can hold their highest dreams and what's possible even if they might not yet see it for themselves.

A challenge is for the benefit of the receiver, not the giver. So it's not about challenging your kids to pick up their socks, or your direct report to complete the project by Friday, because that's about you and your agenda. To make the challenge about the client, we let them know we see their dreams and their full potential. We also express our belief in them. That's how we take their breath away, because they start to see themselves anew.

A few more examples of challenges, which must be tied to the client's agenda, not the coach's agenda:

> You want support, so I challenge you to ask three role models who share your values to mentor you—within the next month.

> You're tired of not having enough money at the end of the month, so I challenge you to reduce your expenses by 10% this month.

> So you want to be a stronger activist? I challenge you to bring together 10 Israelis and 10 Palestinians to develop a change initiative.

If we tie the challenge to the now—the words just spoken—and also to the client's vision and goals, we deepen the way we see our clients. For instance, "You just mentioned how much you want to adopt a special needs child. So I challenge you to commit an hour a day to make that happen. Right now, make the space on your calendar to give a high quality life to a child who needs you."

*Questions to Consider*

What are three requests you'd like to make of yourself?

What are three outrageous challenges you'd like to explore?

## Where to Put Our Attention

With so many options, what do coaches look for and where do we focus?

Key Words—The first words spoken can be very revealing, so pay attention to the very first things said. When phrases are repeated, pick them up and get curious. Notice which words have energy behind them.

Yearning—In every moment, we listen for what the client wants. Even if they continuously talk about what they don't want, or what's not working, we can listen for what they do want.

What's Not Said—Focus on what the client is protecting. Sometimes they'll come right out and say, "I don't want to talk about my loss," an indication they are protecting something of value. Other times what they are avoiding is more subtle. We use our intuition to look under the surface and listen for what's emerging.

What is Showing Up—Notice what is present, or alive or arising. Responding to what is happening opens doorways that might otherwise be missed. These signals show up as emotion, tone of voice, words, energetic shifts, pacing, breath and more. Putting our attention on the here and now leads to awareness, depth and aliveness.

Emotions—The dashboard of the human experience, emotions let us know what's going on under the hood. Pay special attention to tears and laughter—both are indications that something is moving within.

Body—The body reveals all—changes in posture, facial expression and the shrinking or expansion of the space the body occupies. Pay special attention to extremities—the hands and feet give us lots of information.

What's Easy—proactively point clients toward what is working right now or to the easy next step. If the client lacks resourcefulness or possibilities, point the client toward what is already working. Focusing on what is working connects them to their past successes, creativity and resourcefulness whereas focusing on the problem often results in more problems and less creativity. Assume the client knows the way forward and can find where movement is already happening.

## Presenting, Deeper and Transformational Agendas

Our role is to support our client's agenda. How do we do that? What is the client's agenda?

Asking what our clients want coaching on puts the ball in their court and allows them to reflect on and speak about what they want. Their answer is often the tip of the iceberg.

For example, a client wanted to know how to proceed with an important meeting. She wanted more clarity about what she wanted to say, how she wanted to prepare and what she wanted to have happen in the meeting. That's her "presenting agenda" and a goal for the coaching session.

Looking deeper, it becomes clear that she wants to be more authentic and relaxed, rather than put on a show during the meeting. This is her "deeper agenda."

Both the *presenting agenda* and the *deeper agenda* are valid. As coaches, we pay attention to both what the client wants to do and who she wants to be. This allows her flexibility if the meeting moves in an unexpected direction. She will have thought about her viewpoint, what she wants to do about the situation and how she wants to show up.

Clients often come with something to work on and discover there is something underneath that is more important. In this case, she wants to be herself and let go of the expectations that she has to be an expert in all matters. Addressing this, she sees that her expectations of herself are in her way and when she becomes more comfortable with being in her own skin, then the meeting no longer looks ominous. This new light changes how she feels about the meeting and what she needs to do to prepare. By changing her viewpoint, she is more in touch with herself and can respond more fluidly with whatever happens in the meeting.

---

## COACHING *in Action* | Seeking the Deeper Agenda *by Manish Srivastava, CFT Certified Coach*

Coach: So Anya, what would you like to be coached on today?

Anya: Vision. I need some clarity around my vision. To really know what my vision is (*presenting agenda: clarity on vision*).

Coach: Let's see… If you have clarity on your vision, what would it bring to you? (*Looking for deeper agenda*)

Anya: More confidence and concrete action. Knowing where to get business and work for myself (*deeper agenda: getting business*).

Coach: Let's unpack your vision a little bit more. What clarity do you already have about your vision?

Anya: I want to work in the area of women empowerment. Especially those who take a career break and want to go back to work. And…

Coach: (*At this moment, I asked myself, "what is her soul yearning for?" As she spoke about women's empowerment, I started noticing her tentativeness around the word. She spoke the word "empowerment" three times. The stories of women empowerment she told had similarity to her own story. I got an intuitive flash around the word empowerment.*)

As you talk about women's empowerment, I have a question: What would unleash your power?

Anya: (*pauses and sighs*)… Someone else getting that power out of me. It's a struggle for me to unleash my own power. Today I was thinking, if I want to work on women empowerment, how am I empowering myself? When I do it myself, it's a slow process (*transformational agenda—unleashing my power*).

Coach: And where does 'power' reside in your body? (*I pursue further to explore the transformational agenda and follow the natural opening around 'power'.*)

She pointed to her lower stomach/womb and described that her power lies there like a chakra (*wheel of energy*). We used the Embracing the Shadow pathway to engage in a fierce conversation with her chakra. Chakra said that it has not been valued for the last five years and wants to come back in its power. On return to the seat of awareness, Chakra came back to her throat instead of her belly, seeking to express its true power.

Later, while reflecting on the experience, Anya shared that she is feeling as if an old friend is returning. She also shared that five years back (*when Chakra went dormant*), her mother had died. She was longing to reconnect with this inner power (*transformational agenda*) which is now manifesting in her business and practice (*presenting and deeper agenda*).

By clarifying the *deeper agenda*, the coaching includes both the doing and being aspects of the preparation. The client is more self-aware and can draw from her intuition, imagination and excitement.

Another dimension of the client's agenda is listening for who the client is becoming and what else is possible. Transformational listening leads to the *transformational agenda*—the core need or the soul need of the client.

The *transformational agenda* may show up as something that not only connects with the issue, but is imperative for growth, a calling or a life lesson that cuts across many issues in the moment. Sometimes we point it out or we may choose to track it silently. We continuously look for the transformational agenda, holding the space for opportunities to emerge.

In Manish's story above, the client's *transformational agenda* is to fully contribute to the greater good—to learn how to use organizations and technology to serve humanity.

In any coaching session, we hold all three agendas. We know the client wants to have a successful meeting (presenting agenda), and when we explore deeper, we help her to increase her skillfulness and her ability to access her inner power (deeper agenda). What emerges is the transformational agenda (to serve humanity). Simultaneously, we hold our client's transformational agenda, which supports awareness of the body, mind, soul and spirit. Tuning into the client's transformational agenda is like tapping into a bountiful underground spring that feeds life, even if we are not always aware of its existence.

Questions for finding the *presenting agenda*:

What do you want coaching on today?

What is most alive right now?

What would you like to focus on today?

How would you like to see this session unfold?

What would you like to explore?

What do you want from today?

What are you curious about?

How would you like to begin?

What are you feeling in this moment?

What's your agenda for today?

What would you like to get out of this session?

Some questions that help unearth the *deeper and transformational agenda* are:

What's most important to you now?

What is underneath that?

What is deeper than this?

What do you have to access in yourself in order to be successful here?

What matters most about this?

What are your feelings about this?

What do you really want?

As coaches, we can also ask questions of ourselves to help us get in touch with our clients' *transformational agendas*:

What matters most here?

What are the untapped resources?

What is the deepest expression of wonder and greatness?

How is this client already whole and moving toward a greater expression of wholeness?

How am I holding back or forgetting the client's resourcefulness?

What is the difference this client wants to make?

In paying attention to the transformational agenda and asking ourselves these questions, we open to what wants to be born. What is emerging? Who are they becoming? This comes more from our combined intuition, than from logic. As in painting or any act of creation, we go with our intuition and see where it leads. At this level, heart talks to heart. Identifying the transformational agenda

## COACHING *in Action* | Problem Solving or Possibility Seeing *by Michael Wright, CFT Certified Coach*

In coaching parlance, we have a phrase, "coach the client and not the problem." This means that the client's problem shouldn't be the center of gravity in coaching, the client should be. Problems are finite, often relatively limited in scope and duration. Clients, however, are infinite sources of wisdom, depth and knowing. Life itself is at the center of the client.

As a new coach and trained attorney, I wanted very much to help clients resolve their issues. Who doesn't at heart want to help people, to give them a sense of relief? This desire, unbeknownst to me, had me coaching problems, not clients.

To shift away from my problem-solving mentality, I needed to gain trust that, in stepping back from the problem, my work would still have value. So I tested out getting a presenting agenda from the client (the problem as they know it) and then diving for the deeper agenda (the client's heart-based yearning, and the answer to the question: What's important about this to you?). I then started to embrace the deeper agenda as the "North Star." For example,

instead of coaching the problem, "I don't want to be so overcommitted and stressed," we began exploring the client's deeper agenda underneath for "a greater sense of calm, relaxation and space" or even for "greater connection with friends and loved ones."

In the dance with the deeper yearning, the focus of coaching shifted. It became about the inner core, the heart, of the client. It was somewhat frightening to let go at first. But in making the shift, I could sense we were moving out of the old problem-centered paradigm and into a place we are not often as intimate with—our own deepest Self. It's not often we sit with questions about our heart's desires.

This intimacy makes us more conscious of our heart. By breathing life into their heart's desires, I often noticed that client's problems would simply fade out of view. The heart took center stage. Going deep in the heart rooted them in the Self. From there, the vision was no longer one of problems but of new realities and possibilities.

is not about being right; it is about connecting with the aliveness and picking up on the energetic cues of growth in motion.

The *presenting agenda* and the *deeper agenda* are in service to the *transformational agenda*. By being in the moment and opening to our intuition as our clients explore the deeper agendas, we get a sense for the greater opportunity that their presenting agendas and deeper agendas are in service to. We also get clues to the transformational agenda in the discovery session, or the very first session. Much of the purpose of the discovery session is to get a deeper sense of the client. So we celebrate the aliveness, without holding back, and become the midwife for what wants to be birthed.

*Questions to Consider*

What three coaching skills would you like to develop?

Make a list of 100 empowering questions you could ask.

How do your body and your feelings inform your awareness right now?

# 4
# Calling Out the Power

*There is in every organism, at whatever level, an underlying flow of movement toward constructive fulfillment of its inherent possibilities. —Carl Rogers*

Remember a time when you felt powerful—planted firmly in your inner strength and aligned with your core. What was possible from this place? What opened for you? What metaphor describes that sense of power and connection? The metaphor might be a tiger or a volcano or the wind in the trees.

When we connect with the fullness of our personal power, we grow more confident and take actions aligned with our vision and core values. Calling out the power is a process that calls out the depth and breadth of personal power—beyond what is immediately visible. It calls out the fullness of what is emerging. In this chapter, we explore how to call out power in ourselves and in the people we coach.

## The Essence of Calling Out the Power

Calling out the power refers to the ways we engage with clients to move them toward stepping into their creativity, wholeness and sense of possibility. We support transformation when we help clients explore their deepest desires before solving immediate problems. Their natural power awakens and grows when they connect with the wisdom of their bodies, their emotions and their intuitive knowing. They naturally evolve from connecting to their own needs and desires, to discovering what's needed in the world.

Once clients are connected to their power, they perceive, choose and act in ways that are productive for themselves and for all. As they connect to their essence, they become aware of what really matters, develop a sense of purpose and act with clarity.

We call out the power when we sense our clients are ready to step into something much larger than they may be aware of. By voicing what we

**COACHING *in Action* | Calling Out the Power** *by Manish Srivastava, CFT Certified Coach*

When I "call out the power" with my clients, it brings me into my full power and unconditional love. I discover fearless love within me. I stand strong looking deep into my client's soul-yearning. I believe in it and call it forth.

We both step into the unknown and discover the magic. It only happens when I operate from a place of deep love and faith in my client's potential. When I am not in that space (as sometimes happens), I become judgmental, critical or demanding and that's when I fail. My client struggles and retaliates. I become defensive, until I return to my centre, own up to my failure and restart the relationship.

My client had recently moved to become general manager of a coal power plant (a private company) after a long career in the government sector. He found himself losing the race to young, smart, MBAs in the corporate sector and kept judging himself as "not good enough" for this sector. He spoke throughout in a monotonous, flat tone. Given his illustrious career and senior leadership role, I was surprised by his low energy and apparent hopelessness.

I touched my frustration and asked him, "What frustrates you most in this work and life?" For the first time he spoke passionately about the company's lack of responsibility for community and environment. He was angry about how they were polluting water and destroying the water table of nearby villages. When asked what he would like to do about it, he said "Nothing, I do not have much power in this system."

I looked at him... "GM of a power plant, 15 years of public sector career and family legacy of social service. His father led a cooperative and his grandfather was a freedom fighter. What is it that he is not ready to step into?" But instead of asking that, I did something that surprised me. I asked him, "If your father and grandfather could come in the room right now, what would they say?"

I had no idea where this would lead our coaching. The question went like a jolt. He stared at me for a long time. No answer. I held the silence while looking deeply in his eyes. I almost had tears in my eyes. Something connected us beyond the contract. In retrospect, this was one moment I didn't care about the contract or continuity. I was fearlessly in service of his deeper soul-yearning.

After a long silence, I gave him a challenge, "Before we meet next, I request you write a letter to your father (not alive) and ask him to guide you in your journey as a leader. See what he says."

Next month when I met him again, he had very different energy. The passion in his voice and appearance was vivid. He shared that he met villagers personally, involved them in influencing his boss and company owner to get nine water treatment plants sanctioned. Out of which three were already built. All this happened within one month. He not only stepped into his full power, but went beyond the set norms to truly follow his passion. He found a new path in his company as a sustainability leader. After working with him, I realized that our deep source of power often lies in our life journey and seeks expression through the challenges we face in life.

see emerging in our clients, they often shift into a new experience of themselves. Paradoxically, the new, fresh experience can seem like coming home or reclaiming a lost part of themselves.

What do you see in your clients that may be obscure to them?

*Example from a nonprofit founder:*
Near the beginning of my coaching session, I said, "He's antagonistic, even incendiary, but he's politically connected, so I'm thinking about asking him to join the board." My coach said, "Really?" I was silent for a moment, but what really woke me up was when my coach said,

"Incendiary. I hear the five-alarm fire in your voice. I can smell the smoke. What happens if the organization burns to the ground?"

*Example from a political activist:*
I told my coach, "This topic will bore you." She picked up on it and forced me to wake up to my limited thinking. Several times, she said, "This is boring." Instead of treating me like, "Oh, you poor baby…" she said, "Look. This is your life. What do you want to do about it?" She stepped out of her comfort zone, in service of my life. No one had ever done that for me before. She is a very caring, empathic person, and I couldn't imagine her ever saying anything like that, so it came as a surprise. I was shocked out of complacency and my usual way of doing things. She turned into a warrior for the sake of my life.

*And a story from a new executive director:*
I made some mistakes when I first joined the organization. I was just beginning to regain the trust of my staff, when my board insisted that I get executive coaching. I thought this was a slam, and was completely resistant to working with a coach—I've run several highly successful organizations. I entered coaching very reluctantly. You know what won me over? When I explained the situation, my coach listened, but knew right away that I was covering up the seriousness. He said, "So if you don't get this cleaned up, it's game over." I swallowed hard. He stayed silent. Finally I said, "I need help." This was a big moment for me. I don't think I'd ever said those words before and I was surprised at how relieved I felt to say, "I need help."

Coaching is not "rent a friend." Instead of just going with the flow, we consciously create a rigorous, supportive relationship. We advocate for shared power and co-create an empowering relationship by determining how we'll work together. Both parties take risks and seek feedback on how the relationship is working or not working. Together we take a stand for the client's desired outcomes. Based on mutual respect, trust, openness and honesty, we create agreements and structures that awaken clients to their full power.

## Fierce Coaching

Coaching as a profession attracts deeply compassionate, nurturing people who don't always know when to bring out the hard edge. Fierce coaching can be a challenge for those naturally drawn to empathy and encouragement. Coaching requires courage, and fierce coaching is a test of that courage.

Instead of avoiding behaviors that feel uncomfortable, we take risks for the sake of our clients. If we step into fierceness and push ourselves, we bring aliveness and deeper trust into the coaching relationship.

Fierce coaching builds on the work of Frank Farrelly, a therapist dissatisfied with his effectiveness, who developed provocative coaching by exploring new procedures for promoting change in chronic and recalcitrant clients. Rather than using the same old techniques, fierce coaching moves us out on our growing edge as a coach. Instead of relying on what consistently works for us, we stretch ourselves and increase our range by trying new ways of interacting with clients. We can wake up their power by taking risks. If we usually make them toe the line, experiment with creating soft, loving, intimate space. If we habitually offer warmth and support, we can try a crisp, "let's get moving" approach. If you routinely empathize, try radical honesty.

*Examples of Fierce Coaching*

Carmelita: I'm wondering if I should take a leap and confront my boss about his bias against younger employees?

Coach: You already know the answer to that question.

Newt: If I had the guts, I'd leave this job.

Coach: So let me see if I have this right. You're staying in this job so you can be miserable? For the rest of your life?

Nadia: It seems like I am spinning my wheels. I'm sick of it.

Coach: So am I.

Trevor: I've never been good with people.

Coach: Until now.

Suze: I have no idea how to be a good ally.

Coach: My b.s. detector just went off. You know exactly what to do.

Niko: My mother has all the power.

Coach: So when are you going to start driving your own boat?

Joe: So I slammed my fist on the table, told them I wouldn't take no for an answer and threw my phone across the room.

Coach: Sending them an unequivocal message… that you just want to be loved?

Gretchen: I lost so many years when I was sick. All of my friends have achieved big things, and I'm so far behind. Nothing has gone right since my Dad died eight years ago.

Coach: This comes up in many of our coaching sessions. Haven't you had enough of feeling powerless? What are you going to do about it right now?

These short coaching dialogues are some of the countless ways to use fierceness to call out the power of the client. Connecting with our client's power happens in the moment. Responding from a real, empowered place inside, we stay alert to possibilities.

Particularly when clients are stuck coaching on the same issue week after week, consider playing the devil's advocate, spearing old belief systems, making mischief, finding humor, offering outrageous suggestions or holding silence for a very, very long time.

*Some examples of fierce language:*

You've told yourself this for how long?

What's wrong with that?

If that happens, you'll probably die.

So why do you bother?

Either it's your karma or you're in a bad soap opera.

Each of these phrases sounds antithetical to coaching, but delivered with care, they can move people out of a rut quickly. Whether they're shocked, shaken, confused or angry, clients have breakthroughs simply because you love them enough to jolt them into discovering their own insights. Behaviors that seem absolutely impossible to change, suddenly become so repulsive that people can't change fast enough.

## Be prepared

Fierce language might have an undesirable impact. What if clients tighten up, shut down or retreat toward safety? If you've backed them into a corner, stop. We can change the focus of our energy, create more space, back away physically and share our own vulnerability. We can name what is happening in the moment, "It looks like what I'm doing is actually making it harder for you. I'm going to shift and wonder what you need to re-establish trust." Transparent with our feelings, we support connection. As we enroll them in exploring what's alive for them now, we can reconnect by identifying the values they want to honor.

If we have set up an agreement that we're both going to take risks at the beginning of the coaching relationship, we can celebrate how small failures contribute to the long-term trust and ultimate transformation.

Coaching has its challenges. As we fully support clients by being present to their feelings, dreams and goals, we simultaneously challenge their limiting beliefs. How can we be supportive, empathetic champions and fearless truth tellers at the same time? We look to clients for the focus, agenda and goals, and simultaneously hold our agenda in order to serve them fully.

Calling out our client's power often requires us to act in ways that are uncomfortable. We may bring more intense intimacy and connection. We may be fierce, forceful or challenging. We may slow down and create spaciousness. Or speak louder, softer, faster, or slower than usual. We may do things that stimulate discomfort in our clients. It's all part of coaching.

Notice that clients who are fully in their power won't always feel upbeat, cheerful or happy. They can be grieving, hurting or angry and at the same time powerful.

*Questions to Consider*

What is your growing edge for fierce coaching?

How can you take yourself to the edge and beyond?

What was the impact of experimenting with this technique?

## Expanding the Power

Calling out the client's power is not a one-size-fits-all approach. What is powerful in one culture can be offensive in another. We begin calling out the power when we consciously create the relationship. We continue to design the coaching partnership as we discover what empowers or undermines the relationship. Bringing curiosity and humility, we create a strong relationship that honors both the client and the coach, and gives the relationship a solid foundation. We bring our full energy, passion and commitment and as a result, the client experiences being fully understood, honored and empowered.

*What will you consider when calling out the power in a cross-cultural coaching relationship?*

### Opening to our own power

When we open to our own power, we open to calling out the power of the client. One of the beauties of coaching is that even when we are not fully in our power, our intention to move toward full empowerment provides a boost to both coach and client.

Our coach's stand is one resource to reconnect us with our personal power. Our vulnerability also calls out the power by shifting clients from complacency to fierce courage, heart connection, aliveness and authenticity. Instead of being careful and comfortable, we can set an intention to step out of our comfort zone in each coaching session. As we take risks, we gain access to a whole spectrum of playful, irreverent, outrageous interventions that serve life.

*What are some ways you can step more fully into your own power?*

*What will help you remember your personal power?*

### Support vs. empowerment

Whether we're coaching individuals or groups, we support people to move along the continuum toward full empowerment. As people evolve and build their self-connection, instead of "doing the work for people," we can contribute even more by continually moving them toward "doing their own work." In addition to creating spaciousness for inner work, another way to empower people is by shifting the coaching skill to the client. The following table shows the difference between supportive and empowering coaching.

| SUPPORTIVE<br>Coach does more of the work | EMPOWERING<br>Client does more of the work |
|---|---|
| I sense that you feel discouraged because you need progress. Does that resonate with you? | What do you need? |
| Do you want to focus on x or y… | Where would you like to focus? |
| Let's brainstorm. | Would you like to brainstorm some options? |
| What will you do? When will you do it? How will I know? | How would you like to take responsibility? |
| Instead of saying "I should…" will you reframe that as, "I choose to…" | You said, "I should… How does that feel?" |
| You smiled when you said you were scared. Are you afraid because you need acceptance? | You smiled when you said you were scared. Where does that smile come from? |
| Would you like to explore your disappointment or your hunger? | I don't know where to go with this—what does your gut say? |
| Here's a challenge for you… | What's the challenge you'd like to give yourself? |
| My intuition tells me… | What does your intuition tell you? |
| I have an inquiry for you… | What inquiry would you like to think about? |
| I appreciate you because you contribute to my… | What do you appreciate about yourself? |
| I'm hearing a shift in your energy… | What's your energy like right now? |

Although the right side of the chart offers more empowering interventions, the left side can be equally fruitful. The more the coach models each skill, the easier it is for people to do it themselves. Early in the work with new clients, we spend more time in the left column, but as people evolve and take responsibility for their inner and outer work, we acknowledge their increased capacity by shifting to the right column.

We draw this distinction between supportive and empowering coaching because in our desire to contribute, we often stay in the supportive zone far longer than is productive. The other possibility is that coaches move too quickly to empowerment before the client has the self-connection, comfort or skill level. Ultimately we want people to make their own meaning when we offer observations.

Instead of asking suggestive questions, or questions we think we know the answer to, sharing observations can help people explore their inner world and determine where to look next. But how do we determine which observations to offer? At any moment we have access to multiple observations (I notice your voice just got softer; you closed your eyes; when you spoke about Mira, you sat up taller). We can tap our intuition, ask clients for permission to experiment wildly, and get feedback about what's working or not working.

When we model self-connection and empathy, it helps others develop these skills themselves. Because we live in a culture that operates under a huge empathy deficit, most of us need to fill the well, especially when we're triggered or in a charged situation. For instance, if the client says she wants to make a living playing poker and the coach is triggered because a dear friend is addicted to gambling, there are several choices. If the coach is not self-connected and can't stop thinking, "You idiot. How will you ever be able to support your family?" that's a signal the coach needs to get empathy from someone else. But if the coach is more aware, he can self-empathize right then and there—notice he is alarmed because he wants to contribute to his client's well being and support her in creating a meaningful life. From this nonjudgmental, self-connected place, he can get curious about her values, what needs she's hoping to meet by becoming a professional poker player, and support her in developing her own self-awareness.

When clients are in a curious state rather than a judgmental state, or if they are highly aware of their needs, or at least have access to them, that's a great time to ask them to identify their feelings, needs and requests for themselves. Frequently, people need a lot of help with self-empathy because they habitually think about strategy before getting clear about what they really need. When people are disconnected or unaware of their needs, we can help them reconnect before asking them to explore their creativity.

## Edgy Coaching

*When I dare to be powerful, to use my strength in the service of my vision, then it becomes less and less important whether I am afraid. —Audre Lorde*

Too often coaching is predictable, polite and comfortable. When asked what they want more of, most clients say, "I want you to challenge me…"

How do we ramp up our coaching, find our bold voice and take a stand for our clients? First, stop commiserating. Second, wake them up to the opportunity to live life more fully. And third, we call out our own power to move into edgy coaching. Let's start by looking at why we call out our client's power.

Isn't it better to just accept people exactly the way they are? After all, that's when we are most likely to witness transformation—when people are seen, heard and deeply understood, they shift. But there's another piece that supports transformation… when we create the space for them to embody their full power and express their authentic voice.

We all have moments of giving our power away—to family, teachers, colleagues, church, government, doctors, or even entire systems. Most of us were encouraged, taught or expected to give our power away. We were told what to think, how to dress, who to hang out with and what to believe. When truth comes from an external source, it robs us of a deep connection with our intuitive guidance.

So how do we help clients shatter this type of traditional thinking? When they accept disempowering beliefs and negative self-talk as the truth, how do we help them rise above their limitations? What are some ways to help them reconnect to their inner power and authentic voice?

If only it was as easy as giving them reminders: You are the author of your life. Only you have the power to transcend anything that keeps you from accessing your brilliance. But they already know this and if they could stop their self-limiting beliefs, internalized oppression or addiction to email, they would have done so already.

Our role as coaches is to help clients transcend their current level of vibration or state of consciousness, raising the collective energy field. Discordant energy can only be transformed when they come into alignment with their powerful God self. Pure authenticity.

To call out the power, the coach has two primary ways to raise the vibrational energy—support and challenge.

## Calling out the power

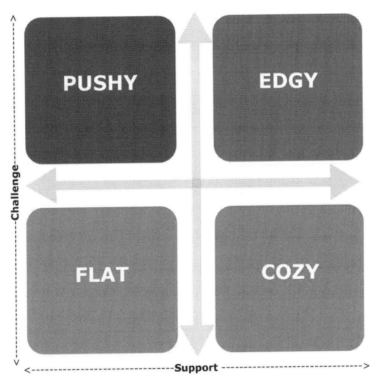

*Adapted from Challenging Coaching by John Blakely and Ian Day*

The most powerful supportive moments come from deep empathy and holding silence. Honoring clients, just the way they are. Why? Because internal shifts happen when we slow down, connect deeply and hold space for awareness to emerge.

However, the most challenging moments come from requesting that clients do something to shift their behavior or limiting beliefs. Why? Because awareness without action leads to "feel good" coaching or wallowing; whereas real learning takes place when people combine fresh awareness with new actions.

In the lower left quadrant of the model, flat coaching is completely disengaging because we offer neither support nor challenge.

We move into the cozy quadrant when we support our clients, but don't challenge them. We're likely to stay in that quadrant if as coaches we are attached to comfort or we value harmony and peace above all. Many clients find the cozy quadrant healing and revitalizing; others find it mushy or indulgent.

In contrast, pushy coaching comes from offering all challenge, but no support. We don't spend much time in this quadrant unless we strongly value awareness, authenticity and courage. Many clients enjoy the excitement and rigor of this quadrant; others find it brutal.

However, there is another way… edgy coaching blends both support and challenge so that clients play at the top of their game. We invite clients to remove their masks and become more real and more powerful than ever before. In this quadrant, rigorous, passionate coaching prevails and clients move into the zone—where their inner and outer world align.

How come it is so difficult to develop edgy coaching? Without wavering, Thomas Leonard, often referred to as the father of coaching, said, "If you cannot afford financially to lose your clients, you WILL be a mouse. Guaranteed. Again, the simple solution is money. Don't put yourself in a position where paying your mortgage is more important than being an honest coach to your clients."

Let's take Leonard's concept a step further. If you care more about being liked than being edgy, you serve no one. Everybody loses. Helping clients reclaim their power requires a whole lot of courage. We have to be willing to risk the loss of the coaching relationship, for the sake of growth and development.

As coaches, we need to step into our own power to help clients step into theirs.

## Ways of being

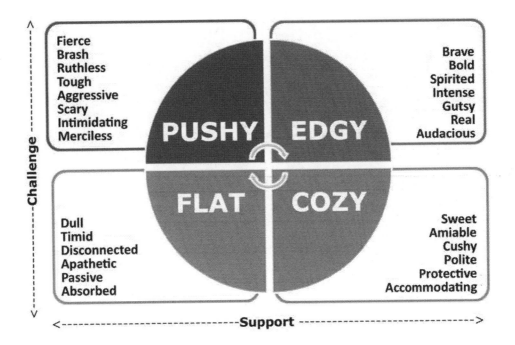

*Both the client and the coach experience these ways of being. So why spend any time at all in the pushy quadrant when it's so antithetical to the principles of the coaching profession? I assert that you can't get to edgy coaching without experimenting with pushy coaching. I know about this because I used to spend 99% of my time in the cozy quadrant, unwilling to rock the boat. If I am not in the edgy quadrant, I ask myself, "how can I love this client enough to move her toward her growing edge?" I coach as if the client's life depends on what I say next. Because it does. —Martha Lasley*

Edgy coaching is not always about demanding clients step into confidence; it could be about helping them step into any unexpressed authentic parts of themselves. For instance, calling out the power can be a wakeup call to embrace the grieving process, explore deep-seated fear or express regret. We can help clients reclaim their self-love, express the depth of their longing, or become the leader they've always wanted to be.

As coaches, we've been called to serve, but how do we answer the call? How do we take responsibility for calling out the power of our clients? It may sound counter-intuitive, but our own honest vulnerability invites clients into their power, which lives right alongside of their powerlessness.

*The key to other people's hearts is finding the key to yours. Got to give to receive, got to open up yourself to get inside somebody else. —Jesse Jackson*

## Calling out the power examples

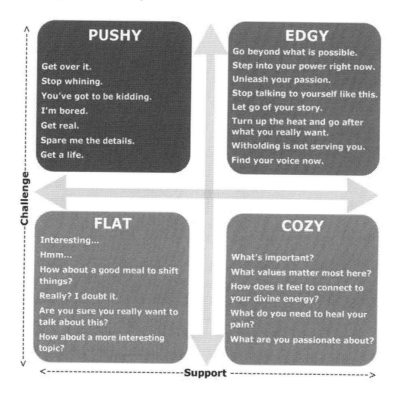

Here are some examples of edgy coaching in response to the client's energy:

Client: I know I'm procrastinating, but I think I'll wait for my son to get a little older.

Coach: Good idea. Your son will be a little older in five minutes.

Client: I'm ready to take action. I went to college with a great film maker—I might get in touch with her. And I also know a producer—not sure if he'd return my call. Maybe I could get a meeting with an agent.

Coach: Too much information. What actions will you actually take?

Client: I can't just play and have fun all the time. That would be irresponsible.

Coach: Responsibility and play are both important to you. Right now, take full responsibility for having more fun and play in your life.

*More examples of edgy coaching:*

What do you really, truly want that you are not allowing yourself?

I've seen you take a lot of risks, but you seem to be shrinking right now. What happens when you expand your breath and your body?

You have told me you want to be challenged. Give yourself the ultimate challenge right now.

You say "I'll try," or "I might," or "Probably." What happens when you shift your language to "I will?" Make a list of what you are saying yes to.

You don't seem invested in this plan. Connect with your heart, expand the plan and make it rock solid.

Enough. What will you stop doing and start doing to accomplish this goal?

What would make your grandchildren proud?

If you owned this company, what would you do?

If you were on the front page of the paper or on TV, how would you like to be portrayed?

## What if your clients don't follow through on their bold commitments?

We can get discouraged when a client doesn't commit, resists the change they know they need to make, or doesn't follow through.

*Ever notice how often your clients make significant strides forward when you're rapidly growing? I hate to break it to you, but our clients serve as human mirrors for ourselves. Their issues are likely to be similar to our issues. If my clients consistently fail to live up to their full potential, I look in the mirror. If I can see where I'm letting myself down, avoiding doing my own work, or copping out, then I can make some changes, and no surprise, my clients usually shift too. Clients respond much more to my energy and authenticity than to my words. —Martha Lasley*

If we're impatient with the pace of change, we may have forgotten to trust the inherent magic of the coaching process. If we're frustrated because a client seems resistant to change, we can consider the possibility that their journey is happening at the perfect pace, and that our frustration is about our own slow pace of change.

We call out the power not just by asking empowering questions, but by offering challenges. As heretical as it sounds, bold coaching sounds an awful lot like directives. Except that our directives are connected to the clients' yearning and we've created a relationship where clients can push back and choose their own direction. Here are some examples of directives that connect to the client's yearning:

Give more than voice to your vision.

Now is the time to honor the playful side of your leadership.

Amplify your desire for social change.

Clients are in charge of their lives. Always. If they hold onto a behavior, belief or action, it must be serving them in some way, even if it's not obvious. We all get stuck occasionally. Profound wisdom and growth arise from our darkest nights. So part of calling out the power is about creating space for the darkness.

Fear is not the enemy, but a signpost of what's important. Recognizing that at the core of fear is pure energy, we can help clients reframe their fear as excitement about what matters most. Our role is to open clients to their own courage which leads to bold action and taking risks.

### How to push our own boundaries: get feedback about our edginess

To expand our own boundaries, we ask clients for feedback. After a coaching session, we can ask, what percent of the time did we spend in each quadrant? Then compare to our own perceptions.

Another way to move toward edginess is to practice coaching with peers. We can ask an observer to put an X in one of the four quadrants every time the coach speaks. As the coaching relationship builds, we can stretch toward edgier coaching.

We also ask clients for specific feedback on which moments were most supportive, most challenging and which moments had BOTH—taking them into their growing edge.

The way we coach changes over time… more support happens early in the coaching relationship, more challenge comes once trust has deepened. But don't wait. Most clients won't even hire a coach who doesn't offer them edgy coaching from the get go. But we can continuously recalibrate the blend of support and challenge based on feedback and what is working for each unique client.

As we move into the zone, any ridiculous pressure to "fix" or "save" our clients melts away. By listening to the subtle changes in the wind, we intuitively know when to catch a wave and when to float during a coaching session. The coach's role is to keep the channels open to aliveness, awakening the client to both their beauty and their blessed unrest.

## Coaching without Questions

Coaching is not a game of Jeopardy where we try to figure out the questions when we already know the answers. Question after question can become tiresome, so instead of relying exclusively on questions, we can expand our level of support by offering observations, statements or directives. While we want people to have choice in every moment, we imply choice more with tone and receptivity, than whether or not we frame it as a question or a statement. Sometimes people need a break from empowering questions and welcome direct statements. The challenge is to offer statements that invoke the power of the client.

Behind most questions is a statement, so we can speak more transparently and directly by offering observations, statements or directives uncolored by judgment.

*A few examples of observations:*

You're sitting on your hands and biting your lip.

Your volume just increased, and you are speaking faster than usual.

*Some examples of statements:*

You changed the agreement.

Dating is not included in your action plan.

*Example of directives:*

Amplify that last word.

Make that into a request.

We take observations for granted because they are so obvious, but when people are deeply immersed in thought, they can miss the observations completely. By stepping out of the mind stream which disconnects us from the flow of life, we can become an observer by simply noticing what we see or hear. When we just observe, without labeling our experience, we learn to see with new eyes. If we simply look without thinking, without attaching words to what we see, we have an entirely different experience. When we perceive directly, without thought, we become one with the objects in our environment. When we give more spaciousness to our observations, we experience life more fully and become more present and aligned with our power. Sharing our observations becomes an art form as we determine which observation to share, and when. Additional examples are provided below.

### Supporting Body Awareness

Your shoulders just slumped.

Notice your body.

Pay attention to your breath.

Exaggerate that gesture.

Scan your body and notice any sensations.

Express that in movement.

Breathe louder.

Loosen any restrictions, relax your throat.

Stand up and dance—whatever comes to you.

Notice what your flexed left foot wants to say to you.

You are holding something in your hand. Open your hand.

You just removed lint from your shirt.

Try a pensive posture to see what thoughts you generate.

Your body is collapsed in on itself.

Your body has a message for you.

Assume everything you communicate verbally or non-verbally has meaning.

Try saying that again while looking skyward with a smile on your face.

Repeat that, "I have so much weight on my shoulders," while I press on your shoulders.

Breathe out what you wish to give; breathe in what you wish to receive.

Describe your posture right now.

Make a sound to go along with the movement in your arms.

When you speak to her, you look at me.

### Supporting Voice Awareness

Your voice trailed off.

Make the sound that expresses your internal feelings.

You swallowed hard. Say the words you've been trying to swallow.

Relax the back of your throat and say that again.

You have something to say.

Give voice to your pelvis.

Amplify one word.

Make the sound that expresses your deepest desires.

Repeat that phrase louder.

Sing a phrase from a song—whatever comes to you.

Say that again, pausing after every noun.

## Supporting Language Awareness

You are talking about yourself in the second person.

Try saying the first thing that comes to you.

If you weren't being polite, you would say...

Change "I should" to "I choose to."

Say that again without qualifiers.

Contradict what you just said.

Say it directly to her. "Cheri, you ..."

Change that question into a statement.

Say the headline only.

Change that to an "I" statement.

Change "I can't" to "I won't."

Shift from the hypothetical to what is real for you.

Refer to him as "Dale" instead of "him."

## Expanding with Imagery

You have a gift.

Notice the first image that comes to you.

Breathe deeply into the part of you that needs more oxygen.

Let yourself fantasize.

Imagine you are killing something.

Ask your future self for advice.

Chew on your experience. Describe the texture and flavor of the food.

Give yourself full permission.

You are giving birth.

I see you in a boat.

### Clarifying Observations

Notice what captures your attention.

Try saying the exact words that trigger you.

Pay attention to what stands out for you.

Become aware of what grabs you.

Remember the moment when you were first irritated.

Put your attention on what matters most.

Notice what's coming up.

Name the observation that stimulates your judgment.

Something is ringing in your ears.

### Clarifying Feelings

Change "He makes me feel," to "I feel."

Something is happening to you.

Your feelings are a gift.

Stay with your feelings.

Act out your feelings.

Unleash the pain.

Affirm the hurt.

Vent.

Get the rage out.

Speak to your feelings.

Connect to the internal experience of your emotions.

Experience the fullness of your relief.

Notice where the joy lives in your body.

### Clarifying Needs

Notice what energizes you.

Connect with your heart's longing.

Slow down. Check in with yourself.

Open your heart first to yourself. Now to the other person.

Make a list of all the things you appreciate about yourself.

Hold onto your needs and rock them like a baby.

Unfreeze the need and imagine that need completely fulfilled.

Take a minute to sit with the beauty of your needs.

Connect with what enlivens you.

### Clarifying Requests

Imagine asking for what you really want.

Make that into a request.

You want to connect, so ask for what you want.

Propose a doable request.

Start your request with, "Will you…"

Try reconnecting with the need before asking for what you want.

Make "I want you to respect me," into a doable request.

Imagine what you want. Ask for that.

Make a request of yourself.

*What do you notice in your coaching when you experiment with coaching without questions?*

# Reframing Disempowering Language

One aspect of calling out our clients' power is bringing awareness to their disempowering language. This language is often habitual and unconscious. Bringing it to the light offers opportunities for clients to see it clearly and choose to change it—moving them to a place of greater personal power.

How do we support our clients to find some comfortable ground and own their language? The beauty of coaching is that we can ask empowering questions that support awareness without making our clients wrong. Over time, they catch themselves and shift their language on their own without prompting from the coach.

| REFRAMING DISEMPOWERING LANGUAGE | | |
|---|---|---|
| **Disempowering Language** | **Examples from the Client** | **Empowering Questions from the Coach** |
| No Choice | I have to, must, can't… | What if you knew you had a choice? |
| Non-Commitment | I'll try, could, might… | What will you actually do? |
| Dualism | It has to be either this or that… | How can you have both? |
| Labels | I'm lazy; he's so smart… | What happens when you let go of that label? |
| Blame | It's my fault, she screwed up… | If no one were to blame, then what? |
| Ambiguity | that, it, those, these, this… | What do you mean when you say, "I'll do it?" |

| REFRAMING DISEMPOWERING LANGUAGE | | |
|---|---|---|
| **Disempowering Language** | **Examples from the Client** | **Empowering Questions from the Coach** |
| No Specificity | few, less, little, many, much, more, several, most, some, enough… | How many is a few? |
| Blanket Statements | All, every, never, always, absolutely… | How does it feel to say, "always"? |
| Uncertainty | Sort of, kind of, almost, maybe, perhaps… | What are you hesitant about? |
| No Time Frame | Soon, sometimes, occasionally, often, eventually… | When is soon? |
| Comparison | He's much more successful than I am… | Would you like to talk about your success without comparing? |
| Moralistic Judgment | Should, ought to, good, bad, right, wrong… | When you unpack that judgment, what are you longing for? |

## Finding Power in the Shadow

For each of our light or sunny emotions, there is a darker counterpart, often referred to as the shadow side. On the other side of joy, there is grief.

As a coach, not only can you acknowledge, validate and embrace the full spectrum of your client's shadow side, you have opportunities to work with those emotions in ways that bring your client into alignment and support transformation.

There is tremendous power in all of these emotions that many coaches and clients are afraid to approach. Only in facing the shadow can we harness its energy. Ignoring it will not make it go away, and may well give it license to manifest in destructive ways. This work is addressed in more detail in Chapter 9, *Embracing the Shadow*.

*Questions to Consider*

What risks can you take in support of your clients' full connection with their power?

What can you do with each of your clients to enhance your ability to call out their power?

What support can you request to step into your power more fully?

How will exploring the shadow equip you in calling out the power?

# Section II:
# Pathways to Alignment

*People say that what we are all seeking is a meaning for life…I think that what we are really seeking is an experience of being alive, so that our life experiences on a purely physical plane will have resonance within our innermost being and reality, so that we can actually feel the rapture of being alive. —Joseph Campbell*

As coaches, we take clients deeper than "figuring out" what they want to do. We take them into the experience of their core aliveness. Grounded in what resonates at the soul level, their life choices become more purposeful, rich and satisfying.

We offer five pathways to alignment, which remind people to connect with their core essence. Each process engages clients with their core aliveness and deepens self-connection. For instance, values clarification is one of the powerful ways to invite clients to "come home" to themselves. This "coming home" speaks to the core principle of valuing diversity, where all parts of self are welcomed home. Each pathway helps clients clarify what matters most, and reconnect with their creative, resourceful core. Regardless of which pathway to alignment you choose, each process supports self-awareness, which leads clients to deeper confidence about their direction, choices and action.

## Self-Alignment

Our clients' true selves are deeply connected, ready and eager to embrace life and create. They also have many parts that compete for attention—parts that tend to shut down creativity and action. Our job as a coach is to help clients become more aware of their highest self and the possibilities that brings, while integrating all parts, including those they've disliked or ignored. As they work with limiting beliefs, old patterns and inner critics, we can help them move toward radical self acceptance. At Leadership that Works, we call this process "bringing the client into alignment."

Supporting self-alignment can be as simple and profound as finding images and metaphors that connect them to their deeper self, offering an embodiment practice that helps them connect with times when they were most alive, or developing declarations or vows that serve as touchstones for how their essence lives in the world. Whatever process we choose, the value of self-alignment is that clients step out of feeling stuck and step into a new relationship with themselves that reconnects them with their inner resources.

Without making any part of our clients wrong, we help them become more self connected by working effectively with all parts of themselves. Each part exists for a reason. Each part, even a destructive part, has a noble purpose. The inner critic, for example, wants the same things that we all want—mastery, love, harmony, safety or connection. It often uses a strategy that we don't enjoy, like screaming at us, but we can help them tap into their yearning and change their strategy. In that way, we learn to recognize the parts of psyche that do most of the heavy lifting in maintaining identity, and keeping us safe physically and psychologically.

When clients are "lined up" with themselves, integrating body, mind and spirit, we sense a palpable energetic shift. New possibilities for action arise easily, along with a sense of movement, aliveness and creativity. When in alignment, our clients are present and engage with life more fully.

Much of the coaching training prepares coaches to both recognize alignment and enhance its expression. The pathways to alignment are processes that help bring out powerful, creative and authentic self-expression. They also get the limiting beliefs to loosen their grip and reduce their power to run out clients' lives.

When clients shed the victim mentality and create from that place of alignment, they connect with their aliveness, empowering beliefs and gratitude. Alignment leads to awareness of new possibilities, new choices and new action. As alignment becomes more sustainable over time, clients engage with the world in a different way. We recognize a radical shift in awareness that continually deepens. The ongoing transformation allows people to celebrate themselves just the way they are, and releases yearning and creative power. They step into actions they were unwilling to take on in the past, or go where they were too frightened to go. As we bring clients into alignment of body, mind and spirit, we don't know what's going to happen. Both the questions and the ground shift. Instead of clients asking, "How do I get more out of my life?" you may notice them asking, "How can I contribute more to life?"

## Transformation

Transformation is the process of moving from limitations to full creativity and full expression. Our clients have opportunities for transformation while on the pathway toward alignment, and new doors open as a result of alignment. We recognize alignment because clients have greater access to inner and outer resources. They let go of old attachments, viewpoints and limiting beliefs.

The evolution occurs both in the movement toward alignment, and in the radical life changes that occur when clients create their lives from the place of full alignment. They become ready and eager to create in the world and more able to see their personal, authentic path and unique contribution.

Wildly different possibilities exist when clients become more aligned. As they become more understanding of their inner critics, creativity and possibility are ignited. Action becomes easy and natural. Transformation includes both an internal shift and a shift in their relationship with the world.

Transformation is not a static, idealized state in which clients never experience limiting beliefs, because actual human development is cyclical and progressive. Transformation is available in every moment. We shift internally and then move to another level with new challenges. So coaching becomes a process of continuous movement toward alignment and breakthrough to transformation, and then we find fresh opportunities that lead to deeper alignment.

*Questions to Consider*

What is your experience with self-alignment?

What has transformed in your life as a result?

## Transformational agenda

Clients need help holding the focus on transforming their lives. Once the transformational agenda emerges, coaches commit to holding onto the possibilities for life transformation and support the discovery of what clients really want. This strong commitment to the transformational agenda keeps the coaching moving toward expansive possibilities and away from quick solutions or business as usual.

Part of holding the transformational agenda is engaging with the mystery. We bring clients to the edge of what they already know and have the courage for, and then move to the edge of what they have the courage to create, and then jump off the cliff into the mystery together. If we stop at "The client has the answer" or "I know what this client is capable of," we miss the real power of coaching—engaging in the places that neither the client nor coach can imagine.

Transformational agenda questions that become part of our stand as a coach can include:

What is possible for this client that they have not considered?

Who is this person becoming?

What is the authentic expression of this individual in the world?

What is beyond what we know is possible?

## Pathways to alignment

The Coaching for Transformation process starts with the key components covered in Section I: Core Principles and the Coach's Stand (Chapter 1), the elements of coaching presence, such as listening, curiosity, awareness and intuition (Chapter 2), all of the resources of the Coach's Palette (Chapter 3) and Calling Out the Power (Chapter 4). To support awareness, additional Coaching for Transformation processes, collectively called pathways to alignment, support clarification and bring clients into alignment with their core self, which leads to transformation. The pathways to alignment help clients develop the capacity to engage with life fully. The pathways, listed below, are covered in the chapters that follow. Experiment with multiple options as you help your clients discover what is emerging.

# Pathways to Alignment

Exploring Needs and Values (Chapter 5)

Experiencing the Moment (Chapter 6)

Envisioning the Future (Chapter 7)

Expanding the View (Chapter 8)

Embracing the Shadow (Chapter 9)

Brought up as a woman in India, the concept of my own needs seemed alien. I had learned to be a pleaser; the role and identity of being a caregiver came with ease. At one point I felt completely drained. Parts of myself suddenly needed care and called out for my attention.

The pathway of **Exploring Needs and Values** came to life as I reached inward for empathy and uncovered my hidden needs. Slowing down, spending time listening to the core needs of conflicting parts, my energy shifted. I felt more spacious within. Different parts weren't at war, and the possibility of them co-existing emerged. I became more present to myself and better equipped for self-care.

Strengthening and empowering my heart, the practice of pausing and **Experiencing the Moment** helped me take in my complete experience. My emotions, body sensations and energetic experiences became a place of anchoring.

Working on aligning these in-the-moment experiences led me to disentangle from many limiting beliefs. As I reflected on the beliefs I held about myself and others, I saw them as stories I was holding, refraining from seeing them as absolute truths. Sometimes I saw the world from the perspective of a 5-year-old, where love was overwhelmed by the complexity of power relationships.

I re-discovered the pathway of **Expanding the View** by embodying new perspectives that felt more joyful and in alignment with my core values. I came to experience the wisdom of Martin Luther King Jr.'s words, "Power without love is reckless and abusive, and love without power is sentimental and anemic." Walking through this path, the possibility of embodying love and power together emerged.

Oscillating between thinking of myself as brilliant and capable, or useless and unworthy, led me to explore the nuances of **Embracing the Shadow**, integrating and healing hidden parts of myself. Discovering the Inner Patriarch that looked down on me for being a woman was extremely overwhelming. Having spent significant time with this part, I began to notice an energy working with this part, that of the Wounded Woman. They seemed to work in tandem. The Inner Patriarch would initially define the rules and the Wounded Woman would obey. After a time, the Wounded Woman would get overwhelmed and move into a tantrum or invite in the Rebellious Woman.

Seeing and understanding these parts and power dynamics gave me a new lens to see my external reality, society and world I lived in. Healing these parts within helped me experience a new inner and outer reality—the security and strength of my inner masculine and vibrant powerful creative energy of my inner feminine. I began to claim my sensuality, power and beauty.

With this also came re-parenting—discovering many young parts of me that needed love, care and attention. Previously I believed that only our inner children need re-parenting so it was a significant learning to realize the amount of care the Inner Mother and Inner Father required. Healing and teaching them a new language, relevant to my reality today became crucial.

During this unfolding, my interests shifted. I was a new person, truly transformed. Aspects of what called me at the beginning of this journey no longer made sense. From feeling restless and unclear about my path, I began to notice that each No (or loss of interest) had a Yes behind it. When I could truly tune in to the Yes behind the No it became a powerful tool that provided clarity and helped me **Envision the Future** of the life I desired.

As the pathways of transformation became a lived experience, I discovered a new me. Lost for years, the twinkle in my eye was back.

Exploring Needs and Values
Experiencing the Moment
Envisioning the Future
Expanding the View
Embracing the Shadow

# Coaching for Transformation

## Pathways to Alignment

### Core Principles

Wholeness   Diversity   Resourcefulness   Freedom   Possibility

## Coach's Palette

| | | |
|---|---|---|
| Empowering Questions | Acknowledging | Client's Agenda |
| Clarifying | Reflecting | Action |
| Brainstorming | Accountability | Naming What's Present |
| Requesting | Self-Managing | Challenging |
| Goals | Interrupting | Cultural Awareness |
| Embracing Polarities | Silence | Reframing |

## Coach's Stand

## Presence

Curiosity

Intuition

Awareness

Listening

Trust

www.LeadershipthatWorks.com

# 5

# Exploring Needs and Values

*Personal leadership is the process of keeping your vision and values before you and aligning your life to be congruent with them. —Stephen Covey*

Exploring Needs and Values is a powerful way to support clients in "coming home" to themselves. It takes them into their core aliveness, so they can effortlessly connect to what matters most. This in turn enables them to take more aligned action, which brings about greater fulfillment, energy and passion. When you explore their unique expression of needs and values, expect to find more than what is on the surface.

## Universal Needs and Values

Everyone is driven by universal needs and values. Even though the language used to describe them varies, and some resonate more strongly than others in different parts of the world, they are still commonly shared across cultures and history. According to psychologist Marshall Rosenberg, everything we do or say is an attempt to meet our needs. We hold values long-term, but our needs are the immediate driving force in our lives.

## Deepening Awareness of Needs

### Exploring the relationship between feelings and needs

Emotions are intimately related to needs. Our feelings serve as indicators of needs met or unmet. Too frequently people ignore how they feel or want to change how they feel, without recognizing the needs that are not being met. Others try to push emotions away to avoid being perceived as "needy."

Instead of colluding with clients and treating emotions as something to get over, we can acknowledge the gift of their emotions. By encouraging emotional awareness, they can open to the life force of their current needs. This simultaneously supports increased awareness and acceptance of the inner world, yielding a greater sense of wholeness.

To support a client in making the connection between their feelings and needs, we can acknowledge emotions and then ask curious questions that uncover the need underneath. Sometimes clients acknowledge an emotion themselves and other times we may name the emotion and follow it with a clarifying question. We can pay particular attention to anything we hear twice, which is usually a sign that the client wants to be heard.

Below are examples of how you might acknowledge emotions and follow up with a curious question that links feelings to needs. For example, your client says, "I can't wait to get out of here!"

> It sounds like you are deeply disappointed—what are you longing for?

> I'm getting a sense that you're really thrilled! What needs are alive in you?

> You sound absolutely furious! What is going on in your heart?

If the client's response includes a focus on what another person is doing or not doing, use it as an invitation to dive deeper. For example, if they respond, "I hate that she left me and caused me so much pain." You can say, "And what's the longing behind that?" Or "What is missing for you?"

By engaging with needs, we help clients develop a close relationship with their inner world. This can include looking at their self-criticism, which we can help them understand in a new light as unmet needs. For example, if a client says, "I'm not smart enough or dedicated enough to realize my vision," we can ask, "So what need is connected to your frustration?" Another empowering question might be, "What need is your inner critic trying to meet by telling you you're not smart enough?"

| UNIVERSAL NEEDS AND VALUES | |
|---|---|
| Expression | celebration, vitality, humor, passion, creativity, imagine, dream, inspiration |
| Harmony | peace, security, safety, order, consistency, calm, stability, relaxation, comfort, ease, reassurance, beauty |
| Autonomy | independence, dreams, freedom, choice, individuality, space, spontaneity |
| Integrity | authenticity, meaning, purpose, justice, fairness, honesty, presence, openness, trust, respect, equality |
| Community | interdependence, trust, bonding, inclusion, belonging, cooperation, unity, synergy, integration, loyalty, participation, partnership, acceptance |
| Contribution | mastery, growth, service, gifts, enrichment, empowerment, support, acknowledgment, help, nourishment |
| Connection | understanding, closeness, appreciation, empathy, support, consideration, love, affection, companionship, mutuality, nurturing, intimacy |
| Play | adventure, challenge, daring, risk-taking, thrill, fun, humor, amusement, laughter, pleasure, sensuality |
| Meaning | awareness, celebration, clarity, competence, consciousness, creativity, understanding, hope, learning, purpose, effectiveness, growth, discovery |
| Well-being | health, sustenance, safety, shelter, rest, sex, food, clothing |

We can repeatedly connect feelings to needs until the client shifts to a new awareness and experience of needs. Sometimes clients are stunned and need a moment to take in their needs. As coaches, we listen for the silence that precedes the shift. Sometimes we hear the transformation as a sigh of relief, an energetic thunk, a burst of emotion, an "ah" or slowing down.

As clients come into greater awareness and alignment, we can support them by anchoring their new insights about feelings and needs with supportive action. Actions can be anything from wearing a piece of jewelry as a reminder of a deep need or making a career change that honors needs more fully.

## Identifying needs

Another way to deepen awareness is to ask open-ended questions that help clients more fully experience, understand and articulate their needs. This approach directly asks about the need, because the client is already connected to their emotions. Let's look at an example, "My partner is driving me crazy!"

You might ask these simple, empowering questions that look beneath the surface of what is happening:

What do you need?

What do you really want in this partnership?

What motivates you?

What is even more important that stops you from creating what you want?

You want something else… What?

Both this approach and exploring the relationship between feelings and needs are intended to help clients experientially discover more about what matters to them and what brings them alive.

## Differentiating between needs and strategies

It can be a seduction, especially for a new coach, to prematurely go for the satisfaction of finding strategies to solve the issues presented rather than first exploring underlying needs. That however may lead a client to action that is not grounded in what matters most to them. By first exploring needs, you can get to what's underneath a presenting issue for a client, so they can then eventually take action that is informed by a deeper sense of what's important to them.

For example, when a client says, "I need a new job," a novice coach, eager to contribute, might ask questions to elicit strategies for finding work, and soon the client has a plan to search the job market, network with colleagues, go back to school and interview for jobs. An experienced coach will slow down the process and dig for what's underneath the desire for a new job, which can surface a deeper agenda with needs that may be served by a very different set of actions.

Here's how it plays out in practice: Jori wanted a new job. By exploring her needs, it became clear she was outraged that her proposal was rejected by her boss and she wanted respect for her ideas. Digging a little deeper, the need for understanding, freedom of expression and the desire to make a contribution became evident and even more important than an action plan to find a new job.

Once she became aware how much she wanted to contribute, many strategies surfaced to meet that need. She decided to discuss her ideas with her boss, take a course to learn to write more influentially and join the board of directors for a social justice organization. She may still decide to get a new job, but she's doing so with an awareness that her primary need is to make a meaningful contribution.

Finding a new job is a strategy to fulfill a particular need. Our clients' success in getting their needs met is directly related to how clearly they recognize what they are. Differentiating between strategies and needs helps clients make life-serving choices.

| STRATEGIES | POSSIBLE UNDERLYING NEEDS |
| --- | --- |
| I need a new career. | To contribute, inspiration, sustainability |
| I need him to listen to me. | Respect, to matter, connection |
| I need her to get out of my life. | Protection from pain, independence, safety |
| I need him to finish the report. | Support, shared understanding, responsibility |
| I need to go on vacation. | Rest, relaxation, fun, adventure, protection |

Even when clients have a lot of clarity about their strategies, when they understand what motivates them (their needs), we can support them to detach from the specific strategy and move more toward a conscious and balanced fulfillment of their needs. By continuously helping them connect to needs, they become aware of what's alive in the moment and what would make life more fulfilling. Often this begins with needs that are not met, because they come to their attention through powerful feelings. Choosing effective strategies also requires awareness of needs that are already met, so we don't sacrifice those when we address unmet needs.

Another way to dive deeper into needs, as opposed to staying at the level of strategies, is through metaphors, dreams or poetry. For people who have little or no access to the felt emotions in their bodies, nor a sense of their needs, imagery can serve as an entryway.

## Our needs connect us to our deepest yearning

Needs are part of our core energy. When we feel low and disconnected, this is a sign that needs are awaiting fulfillment. Recognizing needs supports us in reconnecting and moving into alignment, thereby restoring our experience of wholeness.

Our human needs, for things like safety, shelter and rest, provide the foundation for a well-lived life. Our heart-based needs for service, love, creativity and community point us to some of our deepest and most enlivening yearnings. These yearnings are in the DNA of life, which moves powerfully through each of us. As coaches, we see that these needs, human and heart, are not in conflict. Only our strategies for meeting them are in conflict. Knowing this enables us to look for a new horizon of strategies that can hold the space for all our needs.

Living a full, authentic, compassionate life requires that we allow all parts of life, including our feelings and needs, to live in and move through us. This spiritual practice connects us to our deepest essential self and is vital to our well-being.

**COACHING *in Action* |** **Working with Needs and Values** *by Pernille Plantener, CFT Faculty*

A father wanted support to connect with his teenage daughter who repeatedly accused him of being rude to her. He was in pain, having a hard time remembering his love for her—all he saw was her hostile face and her demanding attitude.

He didn't have easy access to his feelings so I asked what his heart looked like, if viewed from the outside. "It's all tied in barbed wire," he said. I stayed silent while something worked in him. "Well actually it is there to protect, but it hurts me as well."

I asked, "What makes protection so important?"

"This heart is very, very fragile," he said and at that moment, tears came to his eyes.

"What is your heart longing for?" I asked quietly.

"Oh it wants company," he said. "Gentle company."

Again we sat in silence. He obviously connected strongly with the need for gentleness and company and I felt no need to push anything.

After a while, he shifted his attention toward his daughter. "I guess she is trying to find identity," he said. "And perhaps…. Perhaps she wants to push the borders in order to know that she is loved, no matter how she behaves. Perhaps she could do with some gentleness as well."

He walked away with a strong commitment to connect with her and let her know of his vulnerability—as well as willingness to receive hers in whatever form it might take.

This conversation took about 15 minutes and I didn't propose a single feeling, need or strategy. Yet, we swam in the ocean of feelings and needs from beginning to end and completed with a powerful strategy, all in alignment with his values of responsibility and love as a father. The client became self-aware using his own words and found a strategy that was simple and intuitive.

Self-compassion means we approach our feelings and needs in a new way, including those we want to get over and those we seek to avoid. As we recognize that what is inside of us is not the enemy, we enter the space of unconditional acceptance, which then permits integration of all our parts into the whole. This softens us and generates an authentic vulnerability that connects us deeper inside ourselves as well as in the outside world.

## The coach's feelings and needs

Our feelings serve as a barometer to our inner world. When we embrace the full range of our emotions as a coach, we can expand our capacity for self-awareness, self-acceptance and self-management. This allows us to be more fully available to clients. In turn, that personal work furthers our skill at holding space for our client's intense emotions, which creates safety in the relationship.

Self-responsibility (which is very different from self-blame) means we own our full experience. As we explore our inner reality, we notice our thoughts, feelings, body sensations, aliveness and longing. Without resisting all that, we can simply accept what's happening within and breathe into our experience.

In our work, we draw on the wisdom of our body, just as we encourage clients to. The practice of noticing our bodily sensations helps us become fully present and aware of emotions. This practice also helps us notice when our heart is shrinking or expanding, and gives us insight into our deepest needs in the moment.

Our thoughts can include judgments and interpretations, but we recognize that they are actually stories we tell ourselves, not the truth. We then notice we have a choice, to label our experience or to watch how our thoughts change when we slow down and pay attention. In this way we can transform negative self-talk into self-compassion and awareness.

As we honor our needs and values, we come to full clarity about what motivates us at the core. As a result, this practice of self-awareness supports us in communicating with authenticity and passion. With practice, we have easy access to our inner vulnerability, which allows us to be fully present with our heart open. When our hearts are undefended, we can step into powerful coaching.

Inner work is vital, but we don't have to complete our inner work before working with clients. In fact, the client and the coach impact each other's inner work and capacity for transformation. During a session, our attention is on the client, but if we allow ourselves to be moved by the client's transformation, we too can benefit. Just witnessing the client's process can have a profound impact on us.

# Transforming Judgment

The core work of transforming judgment is to help clients recognize and connect with their needs. As we look at how to transform judgments, keep in mind the work we began on understanding needs and values earlier in this chapter.

## Separate opinions from observations

Opinions and observations can easily become entangled, resulting in thoughts based on interpretation and understanding instead of pure facts. When we separate observations from opinions, we distinguish between what actually happened and our opinion of what happened.

Example of an observation: We did not get the grant.

Example of an opinion: I really screwed up the grant proposal.

To help clients separate their opinions from what actually happened, we can ask them for the observations. What did you see or hear that led you to this viewpoint? Sometimes they hold a belief based on something that happened in early childhood and sometimes the belief emerges from whatever occurred just before the session. To support them in identifying clean observations we can ask them what a videotape would capture. [1]

Observations are very different from judgments, assumptions, evaluations, interpretations and diagnosis, but we may have to peel several layers of the artichoke before we get to the heart of the matter. For instance, if you ask for an observation and your client says, "I've never been a strong leader," as far as she's concerned it's a fact, especially since several people would agree with her. When you ask what happened that led her to think this, she'll begin to move toward a clean observation. It may sound more like, "My board president thinks I need leadership training."

---

1    Rosenberg, Marshall B. (2003). *Nonviolent Communication: A Language of Life*. Encinitas, CA: PuddleDancer.

Since no one can know what another thinks, we can ask, "And what did your board president actually say that leads you to imagine you need leadership training?" After a few rounds, your client is likely to identify the actual words. "Right after the meeting he asked me, 'What leadership development programs have you attended?'"

We still don't know what the board president thinks and our focus is on the client, and not the board president anyway! Maybe he admires your client's leadership skills and wants to know where she got them. But at least your client has identified what was actually said. When we help clients state what they observed or heard, rather than how they interpret what happened, they begin to see how much they make up based on a comment or a raised eyebrow.

The importance of this step is in training clients to separate facts from inferences. Once they see how quickly they add embellishments to what actually happened, they can more easily choose an empowering viewpoint.

## Self judgment

Our inner critic is the part of us that generates self judgment. Marshall Rosenberg developed a process of transforming that judgment into awareness of feelings and needs, as behind judgment are unmet needs and pure energy that is waiting to be understood and tapped. We can help clients release that source of energy.

When we support full connection to their needs, we help clients move toward self acceptance, understanding and awareness. Through deep awareness of needs, they come into alignment. Only after that, do we support them in creating strategies to meet their needs. Some common self judgments and underlying needs follow.

| JUDGMENT | UNDERLYING NEED |
|---|---|
| I'm not loveable. | Love |
| I have nothing to offer. | To contribute |
| I am unworthy. | To matter |
| I am not enough. | Belonging |
| I don't deserve it. | Acceptance |

Adapted from the work of Marshall Rosenberg, the steps for transforming self judgment are:

**Identify the Judgment:** A judgment could be a story clients tells themselves, a label, something they think, or anything they believe is absolutely true about themself. As coach, we can ask, *What judgment do you have of yourself?*

**Clarify the Observation:** We can ask for the observation or the exact words. *What happened? What did you actually do or say that led to this judgment?*

**Identify the Needs:**

> **Needs they were attempting to meet by the action**: We help clients identify what needs they were trying to meet when they did whatever they did. Since everything they do is an attempt

to meet a need, we point them toward the need they were trying to meet. We identify the need and not a strategy (which is a way to meet needs). *What needs were you trying to meet when you said that? Savor those needs and notice how you feel.*

**Needs they were attempting to meet by judging themselves**: Since self judgment is an attempt to meet a need, support them in understanding their positive intent in judging themselves. *What needs of yours were you trying to meet by judging yourself? Savor those needs and notice how you feel.*

**Needs they are trying to meet by holding on to the judgment**: If the self judgment is still alive, find out what needs they are trying to meet by holding onto the judgment. *What needs are you meeting by continuing to hold that judgment? Savor those needs and notice how you feel.*

**Action:** We can give clients complete choice in honoring all the needs at stake. *Now that you are steeped in awareness of your needs, what actions can you take that would meet multiple needs at once?*

*Example: Transforming Judgment*

Shanti: I can't believe I told my sister off. She deserved it of course, but I'm tired of being so mean. I was really mean this time.

Coach: What did you actually do or say that leads you to call yourself mean?

Shanti: She isn't doing her share taking care of mom so I told her she was lazy.

Coach: Those were your actual words?

Shanti: Actually I said, "Can't you get off your lazy butt and take her to the doctor instead of always assuming I'm going to do it?" That's not how I want to relate to her. Or anyone else.

Coach: So what needs were you trying to meet when you said that?

Shanti: I wanted help. Support. Some understanding of how hard it is for me to do almost everything for her myself.

Coach: Ah... so just notice how important those needs are for you. Support and understanding. Enjoy those needs for a moment... How does that feel?

Shanti: Yeah. I know that's where I was coming from—wanting support—but it sure didn't sound that way.

Coach: So now let's look at what needs came up when you called yourself mean. What needs were you trying to meet with that self judgment?

Shanti: Argh... When I say I'm mean, underneath it, I want to express myself with love, even when I'm frustrated. I want to care for my sister and for myself. I'd like to be gentler.

Coach: What core needs really matter here?

Shanti: Respect. I want to have an open heart.

Coach: So take a moment and just notice how much you cherish respect and having an open heart. (pause).

Shanti: I'm noticing an internal shift, some relief from tension. But I still worry that I have a mean streak.

Coach: What needs are you trying to meet by holding onto that judgment of yourself?

Shanti: You know what it is? I just want to protect myself and my sister from that kind of suffering. I'd like to trust that I can be loving. Ahhh. I feel a lot of energy flowing through me as I imagine that.

Coach: I've been tracking all the needs you mentioned. Support. Understanding. Expressing yourself with love. Care. Gentleness. Respect. Open-heartedness. Relief from suffering. Love. Take a moment to savor them all. From this place of self-alignment, what actions can you take that would meet multiple needs at once?

Shanti: I think I'll call my sister and just listen to her. Find out what her life is really like. And then we can create a way to take care of mom that works for both of us. Tonight maybe. No, tomorrow would be better.

Coach: Anything I can do to help support your intention?

Shanti: Ask me about our conversation next time we talk, okay?

## Judgment of others

The same process can be used to transform judgment of others, except we ask clients to look at what was actually done or said that didn't meet their needs. Instead of projecting judgments on others, our clients can learn to own their judgment and their needs.

The steps for transforming judgment of others include:

**Identify the judgment:** The judgment could be a story, a label, a thought or a belief. It could be something your client thinks is absolutely true about that person. *What judgment do you have of the other person?*

**Clarify the observation:** What did the person actually do that led to this judgment? Ask for the observation or the exact words. *What did the person actually do or say?*

**Identify needs:**

> **Needs unmet by the other's action**: Help your client identify their needs, savor those needs and notice how they feel. Since the judgment points your client toward an unmet need, make sure they identify a need and not a strategy. Strategies are ways to meet needs. *What needs were unmet for you when the person did or said that?*

> **Needs you were trying to meet by judging**: Since the judgment is an attempt to meet a need, support your client in understanding their positive intent in judging others. *What needs of yours were you trying to meet when you judged the person? Savor those needs and notice how you feel.*

> **Needs you are trying to meet by holding on to the judgment**: You may notice some shift, but if the judgment is still alive in the client, ask what needs the client is trying to meet by holding on to the judgment. *Consider what needs you are trying to meet now by holding on to the judgment you have of the person. Savor those needs and notice how you feel.*

**Action:** Give your client complete choice in honoring all the needs at stake before moving into action. *Now that you are steeped in awareness of your needs, what actions can you take that would meet multiple needs at once?*

Once our clients are fully connected to their deeper needs, their attention may move toward strategies for meeting needs, so encourage them to brainstorm ways to meet the needs of both the chooser (the part of them that chose to act the way they did) and the educator (the part of them that wants them to act differently).

## Transforming Distress into Light

Another practice that deepens awareness is transforming distress into light, a way to harness the energy of distress in life-serving ways. This process is adapted from the work of many practitioners, including: Marshall Rosenberg, Susan Skye, Robert Gonzales and Meganwind Eoyang.

| | |
|---|---|
| Observation: | Describe the stimulus of your distress. |
| | What triggers you? |
| | Describe the moment you first felt pain. |
| | What are you seeing, hearing, smelling, etc? |
| Judgment: | Express your reaction. |
| | What are you telling yourself? |
| | What is your judgment of others or yourself? |
| | Voice all the judgments until you have clarity about your core belief or deepest judgment. |
| Body: | Scan your body. |
| | Sense your body from the inside and experience the wisdom of the body. |
| | What physical sensations do you notice? |
| | Notice any desires in the body—for attention, expression or movement. |
| Emotions: | Experience your feelings. |
| | What are you feeling? |
| | Give voice to your internal emotions. |
| | Honor your deepest feelings without pushing them away. |
| Needs: | Experience your needs fully. |
| | What do you want? |
| | Underneath that, what are you longing for? |
| | Mine all the needs, digging deeper until you identify the bedrock need. |

Mourning:     Grieve the unmet need.

Feel the pain of the unmet need.

What if this need were never met?

Grieve the loss.

Alignment:     Sense the radiance of the need.

Stay with the distress and add the image of a bright light, sustaining this attention until clarity emerges.

Feel the alive energy associated with the exquisite need.

Reaching for life, imagine the deep satisfaction of this need fully met.

Action:     Getting needs met.

What requests can you make of yourself that will help you remember the radiant need?

What requests can you make of yourself to help you honor or meet these needs?

What requests can you make of others that would be most likely to get your needs met?

The transformation of internal distress into light is the psychological alchemy of turning base metal into gold. Holding the light of awareness intently on an internal emotional state alters the frequency of the energy and completely transforms the initial emotion. As we mourn, we touch the sadness of the unmet need, but if we stay with it, we touch the beauty of the need as it lives in us. This connection activates healing and transformation.

This inner practice can also be brought into dialogue. It can support us in coming from our aliveness and fullness, where we're connected to our core authenticity and can share from our passionate, wholehearted desire without expectation or blame of others. Even when our needs remain unmet, the practice of putting our attention on our needs is nurturing and energizing.

*Example: Transforming Distress into Light*

Erika:    My best friend is acting cold and distant lately. She won't say exactly what's wrong. It's been this way ever since I said I didn't want to give her a copy of my report because I didn't want her to use the content inappropriately. I asked her if we could talk about it and she just says there's nothing to talk about.

Coach:    What are you telling yourself about this?

Erika:    I'm so stupid. How could I have said that to her? Why was I mistrustful of her? I will never be able to fix things between us. I've lost her friendship for good. I also think she's being inflexible. She is so stubborn sometimes. How can she end such a long friendship over a misunderstanding?

Coach:    What physical sensations do you notice?

Erika:    I have this deep aching around my heart chakra. The pain is emotional but I feel it physically too. There are tears always near the surface. Sometimes I just let them out. I feel so weighed down.

Coach:   What are you feeling right now?

Erika:   I feel this overwhelming sadness. We've shared so many good times together. I really value her friendship. I feel anguished and heartbroken and regretful. I wish I could take those words back. I don't know how to fix this if she won't talk about it. I'm also feeling hurt and angry by her refusal to have a conversation.

Coach:   What needs are you aware of?

Erika:   I have a deep need for connection and harmony. Also for relief from this intense pain.

Coach:   What if this need were never met?

Erika:   My life would feel so empty and sad and lonely. It would be like sitting alone in a dark room.

Coach:   Stay with the distress and then imagine a bright light entering your body through your head, filling you with bright golden energy...What are you noticing?

Erika:   My heart is wrapped in the yellow light and the light is also encasing my tears. I see the light flowing out of me and toward my friend. I notice some of the tension easing and I'm breathing more deeply and evenly. I'm smiling as the light connects the two of us.

Coach:   What requests can you make to honor or meet your radiant needs?

Erika:   I want to give my friend space to heal, so my requests for myself are that I connect with her possible feelings and needs and that I spend time each day this week journaling about my needs and hers, and envisioning all of them wrapped in the golden light. That will give me some relief and allow me to open to what might be possible for us.

## Personal Values

*At the heart of each of us, whatever our imperfections, there exists a silent pulse of rhythm, a complex of wave forms and resonances, which is absolutely individual and unique, and yet which connects us to everything in the universe. —George Leonard*

Our values are our deeply-held desires that guide us in creating a fulfilling life. When we honor our values, our hearts sing. When values are confused with judgment, including ethical or moral judgment, thoughts of right/wrong or good/bad—we lose our ability to connect with our common humanity. That also reduces our capacity to contribute to making the world a better place.

Energetically, needs and values are the same. Needs and values are nearly identical, except that needs are what we care about right now and values are what we care about long-term. Knowing and articulating our values gives us the opportunity to know what we stand for. Finding compelling language that describes the key driving forces in our lives gives us clarity about our deepest longing.

## COACHING *in Action* | **Values and Needs** *by Nirupama Subramanian, CFT Certified Coach*

Sharmila was a senior marketing manager in a multinational company. Smart, with excellent analytical skills, she was on a fast track for a promotion but something was holding her back. When she received feedback that she needed to be more assertive and speak up during meetings, Sharmila wanted to be coached on her communication skills.

Over the course of coaching, Sharmila connected to her values of respect and need for acceptance. Growing up as a girl in a large family in India, she was taught not to express herself or voice her opinions in front of elders, especially males. She had an older brother who she looked up to, who was given more attention and respect by the family. To Sharmila, disagreeing with authority was disrespectful. Senior male members were supposed to take all key decisions. Girls did not have a voice in her family. Being silent and accepting others met her own need for belonging and acceptance from her family.

As a woman in the corporate world, she felt stifled and small during meetings when she could not contribute fully. She felt hesitant and unsure in large groups with men senior to her. She was not in her full power during these situations. Sharmila realized that her need for freedom and growth were being compromised by staying small and silent. She was also not getting a feeling of belonging and acceptance from the group. She was seen as a good worker but not respected as a potential leader. She realized the childhood strategy for acceptance would no longer work in her current scenario.

During coaching, she understood that she was not being disrespectful by voicing her opinions. Instead she was respecting her own needs for growth and her value of greater contribution to the organization. This realization gave her more confidence in herself and she was able to express herself more freely and without fear.

Most of us have four or five core values that we've held since childhood. To clarify values, we can explore peak experiences when life was exceptionally sweet, when we recognized our highest selves or when we were at the top of our game. If we look for values that feel like second nature, we can identify the qualities of life that support those values and make life worth living. Our values don't change much over time, but our awareness of our values often shifts.

We can help clients become aware of what really matters to them by helping them clarify the unique set of values they treasure over time. Values awareness helps people become true to themselves. When they are aligned with their values; their vision, mission and purpose become clear and easy to define. Over time, when a goal isn't met, it's often because the goal is not linked to a core value.

Values are deeply personal. To support clients in determining the most important values, we listen between the lines. Clarity about values is quite often a revelation and helps them make decisions and take action. When people are uncomfortable, it's often because their needs in the here and now or their long-term values are not honored. When values are fully honored, people come into alignment and feel energized.

## Values Clarification

Clarifying values is one of the primary ways of awakening inherent resourcefulness and wisdom that activates deep levels of creativity. We are fully capable of much more than we can imagine at any moment. When we pay attention to the still small voice within, to the experiences that have shaped us, and to what we love, our values become clearer.

## Asking clarifying questions

Look at snapshots of when your life was really sweet—times when you were fully honoring what was most important to you. What made it sweet?

Recall the challenging times in your life. What were the lessons learned?

Tell me a song that you love, or a movie. What about that makes it special for you?

Look at times when you were particularly upset or angry. What was missing for you?

More coaching questions you can ask to elicit values:

When was a time you felt passionate about your life or work?

When was your life or work particularly meaningful or fulfilling?

What were the greatest lessons you learned from adversity?

What was a time when you felt fully energized about your life?

What insights do these times reveal about your life purpose?

What do you stand for?

What legacy do you want to leave?

What are three intentions you have for your future?

What is a purpose you feel called to fulfill?

Where the importance of a value isn't clear, the client can envision a situation where it is not possible to honor the value. We can ask, what does it feel like without that value present? The degree of discomfort will reveal how important the value is.

## Listening for values in peak experiences

We ask clients to share a "peak" experience, one in which life was wonderful, full, rich and "just right." A peak experience may be a major life experience or a small incident. We ask what stands out about each experience. Look for the qualities of the experience, the interactions and the source of fulfillment. Questions we can ask are:

What was it about this experience that made it special?

What values were being honored?

What's the one value you'd most like to pass on to others (a mentee, your children or someone you care about) as the key to a fulfilling life?

If there were no chance of being laughed at or left out, what would be the most important value you'd like to express through your life?

## Defining moments and metaphors for values

To further ground values, we can explore a client's defining moments or high points and use metaphors to create a reference point for the impact of the values. This helps them reconnect with the specific experience and energetic qualities that embodied particular values.

Where a client's values are clear, we ask them to remember a defining moment when they honored the value fully. Alternatively, where it would help to discover values, we ask them to remember and describe a defining moment, and listen for the values they were honoring at that time.

As a revealing exercise, we can ask clients to prioritize their top seven values and remember a time when they honored each to the fullest. For each value we ask:

What defining moment epitomizes each value?

What is a metaphor that helps you visualize the defining moment?

What is a metaphor that catches the essence of the experience?

When exploring these defining moments with clients, we have them talk about the moment or the metaphor and watch them step out of their head and into an experience and feeling of the value. If they are talking about the experience and value as if telling a story, invite them to step back into the actual experience or ask them how the experience lives in their body.

| Examples of Values, Defining Moments and Metaphors ||
|---:|:---|
| Value: | Adventure |
| Defining Moment / Metaphor: | A woman climbed alone above the snowline on Mount Baker in the winter. She saw herself as a snow goddess. |
| Value: | Connection |
| Defining Moment / Metaphor: | A grandmother planned a huge family reunion, attended by relatives from far and wide. It brought the family closer together. She saw the interconnected web of life. |
| Value: | Recognition |
| Defining Moment / Metaphor: | A coach was asked to head up a ground-breaking project, cutting edge work that had never been tried. She connected to being a freedom fighter. |
| Value: | Catalyzing |
| Defining Moment / Metaphor: | A mentor watches changes in the troubled teens he guides, and envisions himself as a rudder attuned to the roaring river. |
| Value: | Contribution |
| Defining Moment / Metaphor: | An operations manager and her team went to a homeless shelter to clean up the damage from a flood. Their work helped the shelter get back in service to clients in 24 hours. She thought of the experience as a deep pulsing heart. |

## Ways to Use Values

The following are some additional ways to explore values:

**Create a blueprint for making decisions.** Ask, "If you say yes to this project, which of your values will you honor? Which will you ignore?" "How does saying yes honor more values?" "How might honoring your values by engaging in this project impact your life?"

**Remind them what is important.** Their values list can serve as a powerful reminder to pull them back to their center. Connecting with the value as a felt sense or associating a value with a metaphor activates the right or creative side of the brain. Remembering the value impacts their body, emotions and soul, as well as their thoughts.

**Plan life direction and vision.** Include major values in any vision or action plan. Check to make sure values don't counteract each other.

**Make values more conscious.** Clarification of values can be a true eye-opener for the client because they develop a compassionate self-witness, a crucial element of self-acceptance. As they experience and embody their values, they reawaken subconscious forces and deeper energies that move them toward the realization of their visions.

### Difference between espoused values and lived values

Often people have a gap between espoused values and lived values. That doesn't mean they're hypocrites—it can just mean there's a gap between how they live now and how they want to live. Making that gap conscious is an important step in crossing the gap. When their values are aligned and alive, it reinforces the client's trust in the limitless potential of what is possible.

While holding our clients' limitless potential, we can inquire into the specifics of the here and now. For instance, a client may value adventure, but hasn't been honoring that value lately. How she is living adventure now and how she wants to live it may be miles apart. The coaching process helps her take on the challenge of narrowing the gap if adventure is something she truly wants in her life. By looking at the values she is honoring by holding back (such as predictability), the exploration can lead to opportunities to honor multiple values.

A common set of values may translate into different behaviors for different people. How would you know if someone valued creativity? What range of behaviors would you expect? As coaches, we honor our clients' wisdom about what behaviors fulfill a particular value for them. You can help them clarify the values and behaviors and then hold themselves accountable for making the changes they say are important to them.

To have client's explore their values, and the degree to which they are living them, we offer the activity below.

*Activity*
Write a tribute to your own life, or a hypothetical obituary, if you dare. It could be either for your life as it stands now, or for a moment in the future, when you have achieved some of your current goals.

**COACHING *in Action* | Values Coaching** *by Kim Fowler, CFT Faculty*

Jamie: I can't seem to focus. It feels like everything I do, I'm missing something. I'm not at my best at work. I'm not even feeling like I'm at my best with my friends.

Akasha: I can hear the frustration in your voice. I'm also getting a sense of sadness.

Jamie: One of my closest and oldest friends died of liver cancer a couple of months ago. I still break down at times that surprise me. I'll see or hear something that reminds me of him.

Akasha: I'm so sorry. It sounds like you loved him very much.

Jamie: He was like a brother. He meant a great deal to me.

Akasha: So what need is showing up in you right now around his death?

Jamie: I think I need the time to connect to my grief, with no other distractions. I did that when my mom died a few years ago and it was really helpful.

Akasha: So, you need to connect with your grief. We talked a while back about how needs are important in the present and they point to values, which are important over the long term. What value does connecting with your grief point to?

Jamie: Well, I guess at the base of it is that I really want to connect with me, with the soul and heart of me. That comes and goes. I want it all the time. I want to be with the me I really love. It's a long time since I've felt that consistently.

Akasha: If you're aware and living from the value of connecting with the soul of you, what would be different for you?

Jamie: Life would feel easier! I would still feel my grief, and would also start learning what it is to integrate it into me. My thoughts would be clearer. I think I would be sharper at my job. I also think I would be more compassionate with myself and my friends. I'd be more connected.

Akasha: So, what will help you stay in that value of connecting with your soul?

Jamie: I think it has something to do with making sure I connect with myself intentionally every day. Maybe if I do it every day, even if it's only for half an hour, I will gradually grow it to where I want it to be.

Akasha: So you'll connect with yourself for at least 30 minutes a day beginning today?

Jamie: Yes.

Akasha: How does that feel?

Jamie: Like I can breathe a bit easier. Like a start.

Akasha: You have such love for yourself to make this start.

Jamie: Yes, I think I do.

## Prioritizing Values

As an exercise, we ask clients to prioritize their top seven values and how much they are honoring them on a scale of 1 to 10. Then we ask some of the following questions:

What is a time when you honored the value fully?

What is the barrier or obstacle that keeps you from honoring the value now? On a scale of 1 to 10, how strong is the barrier?

What are you learning from identifying the barrier, and how might those lessons help you fulfill the values you want to honor?

What needs to happen for each value to become a "10"? What action can you take to raise your score? Long term? Today?

Values work needs spaciousness, so give clients a chance to feel deeply into each question.

## Values-Based Action

Action is an important follow-up to values and needs work because action changes the situation, so that clients can live a value-centered life. We can coach about needs and values continuously, but their behavior does not change until clients actually do something. When alignment happens organically, they begin to make changes in themselves and their world. That leads to further consideration of needs and values, and further action. Action is covered in more depth in Chapter 10, *Strategy and Action.*

*Questions to Consider*

What are creative ways to help clients gain awareness of their values and needs?

To what extent are your life choices aligned with your values?

How can you close the gap between your espoused values and your lived values?

What is the first step toward living your values more fully?

# 6

# Experiencing the Moment

*All the things that truly matter—beauty, love, creativity, joy, inner peace—arise from beyond the mind.*
*—Eckhart Tolle*

Experiencing the Moment differs from every other coaching pathway, because we do not take the client anywhere, except into their present moment experience. We help the client embrace, embody and include every part of what is happening in the moment. We focus on the present with no desire to fix or move the client toward any outcome or attitude.

The process allows people to claim, experience and integrate parts of themselves that they may have pushed away, denied or avoided. When we do this, we experience a transformation. Experiencing the Moment puts people in touch with their authenticity, power, aliveness and wholeness.

To make themselves more acceptable, some clients avoid shame, discomfort or fear. Reclaiming these lost parts allows for integration and fulfillment.

Experiencing the Moment is a powerful tool for alignment and transformation. We can use it to help clients notice when they have lost connection with a part of their experience, step in to where they are in the moment, and arrive at a place of inclusion and integration where they have a new relationship with the issue they brought to coaching.

## Here and Now—Four Step Process

The Experiencing the Moment process includes four key steps.

### 1. Notice the client's experience

What is happening right now? What is their experience in this moment? What are they having difficulty accepting? We may notice a disconnect between what the client is saying and their tone of voice or emotion. The client may be avoiding a topic, an emotion or an experience. We pay attention when words or phrases stand out as charged with feeling. For example, we may sense a happy voice, sad voice, childlike voice or a parental voice. Our role is not to analyze the voice, but simply to notice when different aspects of the client show up.

## 2. Bring that experience into awareness

We can heighten our client's awareness by asking simple questions, naming what we notice, exploring nuances or asking for clarification. Instead of connecting with how clients felt in the past, we connect with how they feel in this moment. For example:

> What is this experience like for you?

> When you spoke about your friend congratulating you, you started speaking really fast—almost running past the congratulations.

> When you said you were surprised that your friends remembered your birthday, you sounded like a happy child.

> You say you are sad you didn't get the promotion last month. How is that impacting you now?

## 3. Explore here and now

First we invite our clients to step into their experience and explore further. We might say, "It looks like you are having trouble enjoying and celebrating the project completion. What happens if you step into and stay with your experience? A simple question might be: "How do you feel when you give yourself permission to feel your conflicting emotions?

As we take the client into their experience of the moment and keep them there, we allow the process to unfold. Clients experience transformation when they move from avoiding and pushing away the discomfort to including and integrating their experience. As clients notice and reflect on their emotions, sensations, images and thoughts long enough, they create space for transformation. Often clients experience a shift. They move into a different relationship with an experience and/or part of themselves. From this place of alignment they can make new choices and take action.

## 4. Integrate the learning

The client sets the direction, taking the lead and moving toward awareness, learning or action. Often the session ends in action, doing something with the new awareness or learning. Or the action may focus on further reflection and integration. We don't assume that all sessions need to end in action. We might end with a powerful inquiry to take the wisdom deeper, with no action items at all. For example:

> How can you keep that insight alive over the next week?

> How will you stay connected with that powerful metaphor?

> What would it look like to live from the wisdom of your body each day?

## When to Choose Experiencing the Moment

When clients experience intense emotions, resistance or have trouble finding their voice, Experiencing the Moment can help them slow down and get to know themselves. When they are going full speed ahead, ignoring their body, or living in a state of confusion, Experiencing the Moment brings them into full awareness.

Experiencing the Moment is valuable when a client is having trouble fully experiencing or accepting some part of their life. This can show up as a lack of emotion or words not matching their tone or energy.

We use Experiencing the Moment skills in every other alignment pathway and, for many coaches, it's their first choice as a pathway because authenticity becomes paramount. Exploring Needs and Values are more compelling when our clients have a strong, visceral experience of their relationship with their needs in the present moment. Envisioning the Future has more impact when embodied rather than just imagined. Likewise, when we ask our clients to Expand the View, or Embrace the Shadow, their visceral and physical experience is a powerful resource.

When we are present with shifting emotions and needs, we help people connect with their aliveness in times of difficulty as well as joy.

When a client has a psychological condition that we are not trained to work with, we make a referral to a therapist. But this does not mean we stop coaching or avoid looking at what matters most. Some clients work with both a coach and a therapist at the same time, and others find it more effective to take a break from coaching while doing deeper healing work with a therapist. Experiencing the Moment helps us work skillfully with our clients' processes, creating a space of safety and courage that facilitates self-acceptance, understanding and integration.

The essence of Experiencing the Moment coaching is integration. It allows people to include all parts of themselves as they move forward. This place of full acceptance puts people in touch with themselves and enables them to move into action in an aware, integrated and creative way.

## Primary Skills Used in Experiencing the Moment

We use all of our coaching skills in this pathway, in particular:

### Self-management

Inviting clients into the present moment, we welcome all parts of their experience. To become comfortable with a full range of emotions and expression, we shift from judgment to curiosity, and welcome them all. Otherwise, clients take our cue and avoid stepping in, experiencing and expressing what is going on. To develop self-management, we get coached ourselves so we integrate those parts of ourselves we have neglected or pushed away. Once we fully embrace ourselves, we can offer the same to our clients.

### Interrupting

Bring people into the moment, by interrupting with simple empowering questions such as:

How do you feel about what you just said?

How is it for you to notice the joy (sadness, confusion, elation, etc.) of this moment?

What is the impact on you now?

What just happened?

## Naming what's present

State what we see, for example:

I hear you telling the story, but you are not really here.

I sense there is a whole lot you are not saying.

I notice you step into the moment then jump back out. What is happening?

## Intuiting

We share our sense or hunch about what is happening now, without censoring or filtering. We stay unattached to intuition being "right," and check to see if our intuition is useful. Instead of analyzing or interpreting our intuition, we blurt it out and create space for the client to make their own meaning. For instance, if we sense a fog rolling over a client, we name it, "I sense a fog rolling over you," but we avoid interpreting it, "That must be about the loss and confusion you are feeling right now." Instead, we ask the person we are coaching to make their own meaning, "I sense a fog rolling over you. Is there any meaning for you in that?"

I have a hunch...

My sense is...

My gut says...

I have a sixth sense...

My intuition is…

I have an instinct...

My guess is...

These phrases help us voice our intuition and help clients recognize that we act as their partner, not as a guru with the answer. However, we don't overuse intuition because too much sharing of our intuition can rob people of their own insights.

## Cultural humility

We recognize that the client's culture—race, ethnicity, class, gender, age, sexual orientation, geographic connection, etc.—is always present and has an impact. We make room for and avoid judgment about a client's willingness or ability to step into their experience. Also we get curious about how their self-identifications affect what they feel and experience right now while still keeping them in the present moment experience.

What comes up for you specifically, in this moment, as a Latina?

Where does your sense of identity live within you? What does your identity say about your experience right now?

Step into your cultural identity. What is it saying right now?

## Holding silence

Silence allows the power of this pathway to emerge. Being fully present in the moment takes space and time. Experiencing the Moment coaching can mean setting a pace for spaciousness. Creating space for reflection allows people to get to know themselves as they step into their experience. It can be seductive to want to provide the solution that will change people's lives. If we notice the desire to have the answer or be smart, we can slow down, listen and give space for our client's own answers to emerge.

When clients are silent in response to our questions, this doesn't mean they don't have the answer or are stuck. We may have hit on something they want to ponder. If we resist the impulse to jump in, we let them swim in the questions.

We also follow our intuition that points us to ask another question and explore what is going on. We continuously walk the line between giving space and holding the energy of the coaching session. We want to tap their aliveness, but that does not mean we have to be upbeat or moving fast. As we expand our range as coaches, we include a balance of keeping things moving and holding space with silence.

## Metaphors

One way to move from "talking about it" to experiencing the moment is to invite the client to express their experience in a metaphor. They can express the now with an image, a physical posture or movement, or a sound. Then they can step into the metaphor and explore it. Metaphors make it easier to step into, stay with and explore the sensations.

> What image comes as you stay with these sensations?
>
> Step into the cave. What do you see?
>
> What is the temperature?
>
> Reach out, what do you feel with your fingers?
>
> What sounds are here?

## Acknowledging and championing

Experiencing the Moment can lead our clients into difficult or uncomfortable places. When our clients struggle or lose confidence, we can let them know we see their essence which helps them continue the exploration.

> I've seen your courage and willingness to face dark places. You can go even further.

## Reflecting

This lets our client know that we are with them, taking in their experience.

> I hear that this is frightening for you.

## Stay in the here and now

Experiencing the moment means being with the person right now (and then right now, and right now). By truly holding the focus on this moment, the person being coached can experience the depth of whatever is present. If the client starts talking about the past, the future or people who are not present, we bring them back from their flight to the here and now.

How do we bring attention to the here and now? When clients take a trip into the past or future, we can bring them back to their experience right now with simple questions.

What's happening now that reminds you of this story from your childhood?

When you talk about your ideal future, what parts of that do you have access to right now?

Who is in your life now that reminds you of the old experience you are describing?

When you talk about the historical suffering of your people, how does this help you connect with what you are experiencing now?

---

**COACHING in Action | Experiencing the Moment** by Altaf Shaikh, CFT Faculty

A lot of coaching students restrict themselves to working with emotions and the body when using the Experiencing the Moment pathway. For me, it's much bigger than that. Whether the client is happy or sad, an alert coach works with the desire, the yearning, that comes from deep down right in that moment.

Most of my coaching is by phone, and in the beginning I didn't do much with the body, because I've seen so many coaches ask rote questions about the body with no real concern for what the body is wanting. But now I am aware when my clients are seated or walking, because I ask about it. What's shifted? What's released when you move? How are you sitting? What are you looking at?

The client's opening sentences are crucial—both the words and the energy inform the session. If we push for the presenting agenda too early, we may miss the real agenda. Getting very curious and asking simple one word questions, like "So?" or "And?" can add a lot of value at the start of the session. We are not just floating down the river together; I am picking up patterns. So for instance, if the client comes late to the session or says something repeatedly, I look at what is happening. If I bring in my own agenda by asking, "What do you want out of this session," I can actually take the client out of the moment and into the future. Instead, if I stay with the initial sentence, a lot can come forth. Especially if I don't convey urgency, my patience can create spaciousness for what wants to emerge. Even if the client starts with, "I'm blank," that's

an opportunity to just go with it, without trying to take the client somewhere else.

Staying in the here and now is experiential in nature and it takes a lot on the part of the coach to trust the process. If the client steps out of the "here and now" and begins to talk about "there and then" I don't correct them; I gently guide them back to the present moment, by asking about what is going on now.

Here is an example of one session.

My client started with "I'm not able to manage time."

I held silence. Silence is the inquiry. It takes a lot of self-management to slow down, avoid urgency and simply be curious about the client's experience.

After a period of silence, she listed a whole lot of things she does. If I had come in with my own insights or shared something "smart" before I had a felt sense of her experience, she would have lost the opportunity to arrive at her own insights.

She spoke with a lot of emotion about the way she does things and why she is not able to finish any of them.

I could have stated, "I see you're frustrated," but instead asked, "What is happening to you internally as you talk?" An inquiry usually helps the client stay with what is happening now.

*(Continued)*

But in this case, she said, "I think I will have to manage time better." She wanted to problem solve, but I said, "That's what you think. What are you feeling?"

"Frustration!"

It can take longer to get to the presenting agenda (to reduce her frustration) but if we allow the client to find it just by staying present, she takes more ownership.

Getting to the deeper agenda came easily—she wanted to feel light, to release the pain in her shoulder. Staying with what was opening up moment by moment, she checked in with the pain in the shoulder. When she was deviating from the present by talking about her story, she went into blame— her husband and in-laws were not doing much. So I asked, "What is it that you want?" In that moment she wanted clarity and assertiveness.

The key to experiencing the moment is to trust the client. I even asked her if talking about her husband and in-laws would get her what she wanted. As it turned out, she was adamant that she wanted to be heard, because she'd never spoken to anybody about her frustration with her husband or in-laws.

As she talked about "there and then," I listened with curiosity and patience, looking for the opportunity to re-enter the here and now. She came to realize that her heaviness in her body was about blame and anger and she owned her part in creating the situation. She came to awareness that she had made up a story that if she had more freedom to meet people that her husband would not like it. She took personal responsibility that she had placed restrictions on herself. This realization gave her the choice to remove those restrictions and create space to do more things on her own.

Without pressuring my client to state her agenda, the patience allowed something beautiful to come out of it. She recognized her anxiety, came to a new level of consciousness and committed to more assertiveness.

## Wisdom of the Body

*The body is an opening, a way to union even though we may perceive it to be an enclosure, a little fortress with some awareness inside. The body is a passageway, an entry into a cathedral. It is the door to spaciousness. When we become aware of the body in this way, we begin to experience life differently and might even feel the presence of invisible forces, wisdom bearers that can give strength, compassion and understanding to us in our everyday affairs. —Stephen Schwartz*

We can use our body as a fortress or as a cathedral—protecting ourselves from the possibility of pain or danger, or opening ourselves to the beauty and wisdom in every cell. We're taught to trivialize our bodily sensations because we're afraid of suffering, eros or narcissism. So we close ourselves to our deepest yearnings, our desire for love and freedom, our hunger for expressing from the deepest parts of ourselves.

As coaches, we can support people in honoring the intuitive wisdom emanating from their bodies. In every moment, our subconscious speaks to us through our bodies, using a language that is as rich and informative as the language of our native tongue. Our bodies communicate continuously, informing our intuition, which is also known as sixth sense or somatic intelligence.

When we respect the body's intelligence, we raise our consciousness and can make meaning from our immediate experience, without the filters that accompany verbal expression. Language is more abstract—one-step removed from our actual experience—because we edit, label and summarize our somatic-emotional experience.

Instead of relying so heavily on conversation, we can facilitate growth by using the body as a rich resource to process emotions, instincts and intuition. Listening to the full wisdom of the body reveals emotional patterns, energy shifts and opportunities for transformation. Including the body helps people understand their needs at the cellular level and fully embody their conscious choices. Since learning happens in the body, a daily embodiment practice helps people change an old habit into a new one.

Our desire for change starts in our body. When we accept the sacred nature of our bodily experience and attune to our body's vibrations, we receive a felt sense of our internal wisdom that nourishes us. If we don't know how we're feeling, we can scan our bodies for sensations and experience the waves of energy, which invariably have a message that helps us discover our emotions. We may notice trembling, tensing, aching or tingling in different parts of our body.

The world of thought and evaluation is a tiny fraction of the knowledge that is available to us. Paying attention to the body gives us a deeper sense of our innate wisdom. Without evaluating or manipulating our experience, or pressuring ourselves to change, we can come to new discoveries just by witnessing and opening to what is. If we attend to the subtlest cues and stay very quiet, we come into contact with our energy. Whether we're experiencing pure bliss, mild restlessness or utter outrage, riding the waves of energy and honoring the emerging forces within is an act of self-respect.

## Honoring the body and energy

We keep our clients connected to the here and now by having them explore their body sensations and shifts in energy. Tuning into the body and energies automatically brings us to the present moment and disconnects us from planning, worrying and trying to understand. We notice what is present in the moment.

When we bring clients' attention to sensations in the body, we give them permission to stay with their body as we acknowledge, inquire and reflect what is happening.

> What physical sensations do you notice?
>
> Where do you notice that in your body?
>
> Bring your awareness to the sensation and stay with it.
>
> Allow your judgments to flow through you without forcing them to change.
>
> What do you notice now?
>
> Move yourself physically and notice the energy shifts of embodying the feelings.
>
> What is your body trying to tell you?
>
> What part of your body holds your fear?
>
> Where is the joy coming from in your body?
>
> How does your anger live in your body? What shape and color is it?

## Observations

Instead of asking questions, we can further empower people by offering observations and giving them space to make their own meaning.

> You are speaking louder and faster now.
>
> Your energy shifted when you said "I want a partner."
>
> When you described your plan, your voice gained confidence.
>
> One side of your mouth smiled when you said you value risk taking.
>
> You stuttered when you said "sincerity."
>
> You leaned back after the silence.
>
> Your right leg is in constant motion.
>
> You just looked rapidly from left to right.

We don't have to follow every observation with a question. Clients empower themselves when we allow them to ask their own questions about our observations.

## Awareness of the client's body

Authenticity stems from congruent emotions, language, body, thoughts and actions. We're perceived as authentic when our inner world matches our outer expression. This inner and outer alignment helps us choose actions that bring momentum into our lives. When clients are not aware that they are saying one thing and doing another, it's our role to enhance their awareness through observation and curiosity. Body awareness is intimately connected to awareness of feelings and needs.

We not only have brains in our heads, but neuroscience reveals that we have complex and functional neural networks—or brains—in our heart and gut. The brain in our head is responsible for cognitive perception, thinking and making meaning. The brain in our heart processes emotions, values and relational affect. The brain in our gut helps us establish our core identity, protects and keeps us safe and mobilizes us to take action. The brains in our heart and guts communicate with the brain in our head through our neural pathways.

The heart gives us access to far more intelligence than the brain alone,[1] and other body parts also contribute to our understanding. An internal, felt sense of love, care, compassion and appreciation produce measurable, qualitative change in the heart's electrical field. We can support people in honoring the intuitive wisdom emanating from their bodies. We can also learn to read the nuances of body language which serve as a portal to understanding emotions and needs.

## Sources of information about the body

The face is a primary source of information about the body. Eyes watering, muscles quivering, eyes blinking or darting, teeth or jaw clenching, lips tightening, nostrils flaring, brow furrowing, throat constricting, and skin around the eyes moving are all indications that changes are happening within.

---

1    Childre, Doc Lew & Martin, Howard (2000). *The HeartMath Solution: The Institute of HeartMath's Revolutionary Program for Engaging the Power of the Heart's Intelligence.* HarperOne.

Secondary sources of information come from the extremities—movement of the hands and feet, fingers and toes are further away from consciousness, but strong indicators nonetheless.

Information about the body comes many other sources:

Breath—the pace, rhythm, volume and location

Posture—position and balance

Energy—flow of Chi or vital energy

---

**COACHING** *in Action* | **Using the Body's Wisdom** *by Sonali Kelkar, CFT Faculty*

Coach: What's happening?

Anushka: I am feeling very restless.

Coach: What is this restlessness telling you?

Anushka: I don't know… I wish I knew.

Coach: Where in your body do you feel this restlessness?

Anushka: In my hands…in my feet…

Coach: You shook your hands like you were shaking off something.

Anushka: Yes, it's this frustration that I am trying to shake off.

Coach: Where do you feel the frustration the most?

Anushka: Around my chest…it's caging me…it's like a tight ball

Coach: What's its texture… its colour?

Anushka: …It's black … a ball made up of endless string. It's tying itself up… (silence)

Coach: You spoke much slower than you did a minute ago… What's happening?

Anushka: I realize how I am actually tying myself up… I haven't been speaking up …My boss didn't give me a raise and I haven't spoken to her about it.

Coach: What needs get met when you do not speak up about it?

Anushka: None of my needs get met when I don't speak up.

Coach: Really? You must have a need you're trying to meet by not speaking up…

Anushka: Actually, I keep quiet because of my need for harmony and respect.

Coach: Ah… Your voice was so clear when you said that…Looks like harmony and respect are really important for you… And what needs of yours are left unmet?

Anushka: …My need for recognition… growth…

Coach: I noticed your shoulders go backwards and you sat back.

Anushka: Yes, growth is really important for me at this stage of my career. I respect my boss and I'd also like to be recognized for the way I have grown to handle so much more. I am not the same person I was a year ago. And yet I am doing nothing about it.

Coach: Your eyes lit up when you talked about your growth. Growth seems to be very important for you today.

Anushka: Yes! It is…I look to learn and grow every single day… it brings me to work every day.

Coach: What's happening in your body right now?

Anushka: I can feel blood gushing through my legs and my chest. My shoulders feel lighter. I realize I have been pushing aside my need for recognition and growth. Like it's something I shouldn't want… I want to change things. My reality is that I want both—recognition and growth. If I don't stand up for myself, how can I expect others to stand up for me?

Witnessing her body's reaction to her awareness of her needs facilitated Anushka to choose actions that helped her fulfill her needs for recognition and growth, as well as her needs for respect and harmony.

---

Flexibility—spinal flexibility and movement

Blood—the pace of the heartbeat, changing color of the skin

Crying, sighing, fidgeting, yawning and laughing often occur when the client comes in contact with the unknown. This is a good time to create space for what wants to emerge.

The pace and rhythm in the industrialized world exacts a toll on well-being and creativity. Our clients may feel overwhelmed, physically or emotionally, by the speed of movement, thought, speaking and breathing. To enter a rejuvenating flow state, they need a balanced physical structure, heart connection and a calm compassionate awareness of themselves and others.

Although the rational mind, emotions, body and soul, function together as one integral unit, each component can contribute to awareness. When a person lives and breathes as one harmonious unit, alignment is experienced. Living from the inside out ensures authenticity.

## Awareness of your body

As a coach, fluency in the subtleties of your own body language helps you connect more intimately with others. Understanding body language heightens our intuition, compassion and insights into people. When we explore our body, emotions and mind, as we interact with clients, we can increase our awareness of how our energy shifts. Our body serves as a barometer of what is happening in us and in our clients. Inner awareness allows us to become more present, which helps us create the space for them to explore their bodies' energy and their authentic selves.

## Inviting shift

To live authentically we need congruence with emotions, thoughts and actions. Inner and outer alignment helps people choose actions that bring momentum into their lives. Exploring new kinesthetic experiences helps develop sensory awareness, which contributes to greater choice. When the body is alert and free of muscular tension, the whole person is more open to listening, learning and taking action. Freeing the body from old habits unlocks intuition and creativity. Imagine what possibilities open up when people feel energized and connected to their intuition, creativity and choice!

In *Emotional Intelligence*, Daniel Goleman gives us a look inside the workings of our body-mind connection. He says, "Neuroscientists use the term 'working memory' for the capacity of attention that holds in mind the facts essential for completing a given task or problem…signals of strong emotion—anxiety, anger and the like—can create neural static, sabotaging the ability of the working memory…crippling the capacity to learn."[2] The circuits from the senses connect directly to the primitive brain, by-passing the reasoning mind. Thus we cannot simply try to reason away anxiety, fear and anger. When we slow down the breathing and notice our emotional responses, we can notice the gap between our emotions and our responses. This gives us a greater capacity to bring our emotions and thoughts into harmony. Our feelings can serve our thinking, and conversely, our thinking can be enriched by the wisdom of our feelings.

Effective performance is the result of taking in the relevant data and responding intuitively, based on a synthesis of feeling and data. We engage the wisdom and inherent intelligence of all levels

---

2    Goleman, Daniel (2006). *Emotional Intelligence*. New York: Bantam.

**COACHING *in Action* | Coaching with the Energetic Bodies** *by Leanne Whiting, CFT Certified Coach*

Chakra is a Sanskrit word that can be translated to "wheel." There are seven primary chakras, and several minor chakras that correspond to various areas in the body that provide a sophisticated understanding of wholeness and integration of the body, mind and spirit. The study of these energetic wheels date back to over 5000 years ago and are inevitably linked with the ancient art and science of yoga, a philosophy and a practice designed to unite the body, mind and spirit as one.

Our body is our vehicle that takes us through our experiences of life. As we move through our joys, trials, tribulations and transformations our chakras are wheel-like energies that are continuously spinning. Chakras that appear to be moving too slowly or too quickly can be used as gateways of transformation.

Each Chakra holds energy and layers of consciousness that provide a formula to help us connect our physical feelings and sensations with emotions and feelings throughout our various experiences in life.

In Coaching for Transformation, chakras can be used to move the client's awareness into the body to support awareness of what may be holding them back through the shadows of the energy, which tend to move the chakra slower, to the opening of a chakra and awareness of the deeper and transformational energy of what is longing to surface and come alive.

**EXAMPLE OF COACHING WITH CHAKRAS**

James: I'm completely stressed, overwhelmed and don't have enough time.

Leanne: What do you want time for?

James: [pause] I want to take time to write music… but I know that time is not the issue.

Leanne: [Silence}

James: Fear. I'm actually scared.

Leanne: Where do you feel the fear in your body?

James: [pointed to his stomach].

Leanne: That's your third chakra. The shadow of the third chakra is shame.

James: That's it… My shame doesn't allow me to find my drive, motivation or confidence. I need all that to write music. What's holding me back is the shame.

Leanne: You are doing a lot. Always. But you have been quite passive about what is important to you.

James: I didn't think I had so much shame. But that's it. I don't feel good enough to write music.

Leanne: What do you feel in your body now?

James: Pain in my right shoulder.

Leanne: Take a couple of breaths into your shoulder, which is a wing of your heart, your fourth chakra. What does that pain cover?

James: Acceptance, self-love and balance.

Leanne: The shadow of the fourth chakra is grief. The third and fourth chakra work together. Self-love will override shame. [pause] Now what?

James: Meditation practice—I want to sit with that every day.

Allow the shadow of shame to surface—not to override it, but to let the heart open to it.

Leanne: Anything else?

James: I want to create an affirmation so that when I feel pain in my stomach, I bring my awareness to I am whole, I am worthy, I am loved.

Leanne: Will you let me know how that goes for you?

**ADDITIONAL RESOURCE**

See Appendix I: *Coaching with the Energetic Body: Spinning the Chakras for Awakening* or download at www.LTWorks.com/chakras

of our being. Our action is in tune with inner and environmental factors unavailable through the intellect by itself.

We are wired to respond to emotional crisis by short-cutting the logical thinking functions of the brain. Our survival depends on this. Our ancestors didn't have to think about what to do when a tiger was approaching.

In *Looking for Spinoza*, Antonio Damasio says that we create maps in our brains from the recordings that come in through our senses.[3] We learn to rely on those maps. If we were chased by a tiger, the map would get us out alive. However, many of the maps we have stored are outdated.

When we ask empowering questions and slow down, the actual circuitry of our mind maps can be interrupted for reconsideration. Beliefs can shift when seen in a new light as clients respond to their current emotions, thoughts, needs and intuition. By guiding them to pay attention to their bodies, they can interrupt the autopilot of habit. New ways of responding to information become possible.

This circuitry can rewire itself more effectively when people are in touch with their bodies and the natural world. Bringing awareness to the body can restore new energy flows. In this place we can use the core principles of responding to what is showing up and looking for what is easy by recognizing the next natural place that is opening.

## Connecting with Emotions

To be skillful with Experiencing the Moment we become increasingly comfortable with feelings and emotions. In many cultures, people deny their feelings. At home and at work, people are taught to consider feelings a sign of weakness or neurosis. As a result, many people keep their emotions under control and even claim, "I'm not feeling anything," but the only time people aren't feeling something is when they are dead. Even if all they can feel is numb, frozen or still, they always feel something. Helping people connect to their feelings, just sitting with how they feel, without trying to change it, leads them to a radically different awareness of their internal state. As we give them the space to understand their feelings, they shift, which leads to deeper understanding and awareness.

In culturally inexpressive cultures, taboos place many feelings off limits and consequently, many people have no idea what they are feeling. Early in the coaching relationship, some people appreciate having a list of feelings handy to reconnect with what is really going on internally.

In culturally expressive cultures, people who don't express their emotions are considered flat or inauthentic.

When people judge their emotions as good, bad or terrible, they color their experience, which changes it. If we remove the ball and chain and sit patiently, allowing them to have their internal reactions, we find at the core of every emotion a pure wave of energy that is free of moralistic judgment. By trusting that emotions know what they need to heal, we honor their inner wisdom.

---

3    Damasio, Antonio R. (2003). *Looking for Spinoza: Joy, Sorrow, and the Feeling Brain*. Orlando, FL: Harcourt.

Opening to the delicate mystery of emotions generates a sweet acceptance both within and outside the self.

Even when we have a thorough understanding of the beauty of each emotion, we can find ourselves struggling to accept a particular emotion. For instance, a low threshold for anger or boredom could prevent us from recognizing a gift—a profound message for the soul. Instead of steering away from anger or admonishing boredom we can support people to embrace the fullest expression of themselves. When they shun a part of themselves, those emotions continue to torment them. Reclaiming lost parts is the crux of self-healing and emotions are the entry point. Instead of seeing emotions as an Achilles heel, we can open to their life force and honor their profound importance.

When we help people face and embrace their emotions, the vice-like grip loosens and they can experience life more fully and freely.

Sometimes people avoid emotions by telling stories. Or they may talk about the feelings without experiencing the feelings in the now. We can bring them back to the moment by asking, "What happens when you embrace the energy of that feeling?" When we support people to fully trust their life force energy, just as it is, their emotions are no longer stuck because the energy of self-love frees them up to move.

The six core emotions that are evident across cultures are happiness, sadness, surprise, disgust, anger and fear, according to researchers Ekman and Friesen.[4] A more extensive list allows clients to identify the nuances of their feelings.

| FEELINGS | | | | |
|---|---|---|---|---|
| **PEACEFUL** | **LOVE** | **GLAD** | **PLAYFUL** | **ENGAGED** |
| blissful | affectionate | confident | adventurous | absorbed |
| carefree | amorous | delighted | alive | alert |
| centered | empathic | ecstatic | buoyant | aroused |
| composed | friendly | encouraged | energetic | astonished |
| expansive | grateful | excited | exuberant | curious |
| fulfilled | loving | exhilarated | giddy | eager |
| quiet | nurtured | grateful | goofy | engrossed |
| relaxed | open | happy | impish | enriched |
| relieved | radiant | hopeful | inquisitive | enthusiastic |
| satisfied | sensitive | inspired | invigorated | fascinated |
| serene | tender | joyful | lively | intrigued |
| tranquil | trusting | proud | mischievous | surprised |
| trusting | warm | satisfied | refreshed | touched |

4    Ekman, P. & Friesen, W. V. (1975). *Unmasking the Face: A Guide to Recognizing Emotions From Facial Clues*. Englewood Cliffs, New Jersey: Prentice-Hall.

| FEELINGS | | | | |
|---|---|---|---|---|
| **MAD** | **SAD** | **SCARED** | **TIRED** | **UNEASY** |
| agitated | blue | afraid | blah | anguished |
| angry | dejected | anxious | bored | apathetic |
| annoyed | depressed | apprehensive | dull | boggled |
| bitter | despairing | desperate | embarrassed | chagrined |
| concerned | despondent | dread | exhausted | confused |
| disgusted | discouraged | fearful | fatigued | detached |
| edgy | dismayed | frightened | hurt | frustrated |
| enraged | distant | horrified | indifferent | helpless |
| exasperated | distressed | jealous | inert | hesitant |
| frustrated | gloomy | jittery | lethargic | perplexed |
| furious | heavy | lonely | listless | puzzled |
| grouchy | helpless | nervous | mopey | skeptical |
| hostile | lonely | sensitive | overwhelmed | torn |
| impatient | miserable | shocked | passive | troubled |
| irate | overwhelmed | startled | reluctant | uncomfortable |
| irritable | sorrowful | suspicious | restless | unglued |
| livid | troubled | terrified | sleepy | unsteady |
| outraged | unhappy | worried | weary | withdrawn |

How do we help clients build awareness of feelings in the moment? Many people are alienated or cut off from their emotional state and struggle to identify their internal reactions. If asked what they're feeling, they identify their thoughts. Marshall Rosenberg distinguishes feelings from thoughts and asserts that starting a sentence with these words invariably means the speaker is sharing his thinking, not what he is feeling:

> I feel that…
>
> I feel you…
>
> I feel as if…
>
> I feel like…
>
> I feel she…
>
> I feel I…[5]

Following the word "feel" immediately with an emotion (internal state) helps people connect. To relieve alienation, you can awaken capacity for experiencing feelings and support emotional awareness by asking:

> What's your internal reaction?
>
> How do you feel when you think she's betrayed you?
>
> What do your bodily sensations tell you?

---

5    Rosenberg, Marshall B. (2003). *Nonviolent Communication: A Language of Life*. Encinitas, CA: PuddleDancer.

Do you feel sad, angry or hurt?

Which feelings resonate with you?

## Feelings mixed with judgment

Sometimes people use pseudo feelings to describe what they think other people are doing to them. For instance, when Jorge says, "I feel abandoned," that's actually what he thinks someone else is doing, whereas his actual internal feeling is hurt, sad or angry. We can help people identify their emotional response by asking, "How do you feel internally when you think someone has abandoned you?"

| | | | |
|---|---|---|---|
| Abandoned | Degraded | Intruded Upon | Rejected |
| Abused | Despised | Let Down | Ripped off |
| Attacked | Detested | Loved | Shamed |
| Belittled | Diminished | Manipulated | Taken for Granted |
| Betrayed | Discounted | Marginalized | Unappreciated |
| Bullied | Disrespected | Misunderstood | Unpopular |
| Cheated | Distrusted | Patronized | Unwanted |
| Cherished | Hated | Picked on | Used |
| Coerced | Interrupted | Provoked | Valued |
| Cornered | Intimidated | Put-Down | Worthless |

Coaching questions help people shift from thinking to the felt sense of their experience, which gives the feelings a place to call home. Rather than seeing a feeling as something dangerous happening outside of themselves, they develop self-intimacy by honoring their internal emotions.

## Stay present to emotions

How do we work with feelings, creating a space of safety and courage that facilitates self-acceptance, understanding and integration? How can we be fully present with shifting emotions and help people connect with all their inner wisdom in times of difficulty, as well as joy?

### Listen to the body

The body serves as a resource for staying present and deepening awareness of emotions. Just as a lightning rod channels the currents of electricity to prevent destruction, our bodies have the capacity to digest emotions that release turmoil. The first key is to breathe and remind ourselves that we do not have to save our clients, give them the answer or change their experience.

### Transform judgment

Our job is to notice and release judgments, both of our clients and ourselves. To hold a deep caring acceptance of the people we coach, we start with transforming self-judgment into curiosity.

## Hold true

We could say many soothing things that aren't necessarily false, but if they don't come from the heart, we disconnect from our clients. Mollifying or placating our clients serves no one.

## Resist the urge to lead

How do we just be present with our clients? We don't need to lead them through their emotions. With patience, we trust that the process is beneficial, even though it may seem to be "going nowhere."

## Offer presence

Presence means inhabiting our bodies and hearts in ways that tap our personal power, aliveness, creativity and flow. An awakened presence is fully connected to self and others. Being present is to be aware and available in the moment: centered, attuned, focused and attentive. We have the opportunity to be present with whatever emotions arise, while offering compassion, integrity and courage. Our clients know we are with them, because we respect their feelings, and hold space for more feelings to emerge.

## Engage with the intensity

We hold the full range of emotional experience. Sometimes people have a more difficult time being with joy, fulfillment and their own magnificence than sadness or anger. We help them step into all of it. We do this by simply asking them to pay attention to their experience. We breathe with them. We don't need to create an elaborate plan of what to do with what they are noticing. We notice their energy and ask questions that further their self-awareness of their life force.

## Create space for courage

By trusting that our clients have the answers, we help them gain access to their inner well of strength. Especially when they might not immediately see their strengths themselves, we recognize their wholeness and invite them to access their courage for exploration and change.

A pathway to a fulfilling life is to discover the lost parts of ourselves and embrace them. That means loving every aspect of ourselves in every moment. As a coach, we can show people the path to fulfillment by fully accepting every part of them, and all that they experience, no matter what. When we offer unconditional love to the parts of them that are angry, hurt or scared, they realize how to do this for themselves. As those lost parts get welcomed back into the fold, they come back home to themselves. When they love the fragmented parts back into sync, their healing becomes our healing, and transformation is shared.

The work of the coach is to undo the powerful conditioning and unconscious programming that tell people their emotions are bad or their desires are selfish. We empower people to heal themselves as they journey toward unconditional self-love. As we invite them to open their hearts, they fully experience each and every moment as opportunities to love themselves. The healing pathway to wholeness embraces the discarded parts of self which leads to a peace that surpasses all understanding.

Experiencing the Moment refers to witnessing the here and now, honoring what's going on emotionally, understanding deeper needs and processing the inner experience.

Powerful feelings may arise during coaching that open the door to deeper awareness. Our clients' emotional life has great impact on their choices, creativity and action. Becoming adept at being in the present moment helps people feel safe, look deeply and come to greater clarity before moving forward.

When we only work with their thoughts about what they want or what's getting in the way, it's like watering the leaves of a plant without getting water to the roots. Working with emotions brings surprises, deep insight and new energy.

We can help people explore what is below the surface so they can learn to feel into their joy and their wounds with love and compassion. When they stay in that timeless world of their emotional

## COACHING *in Action* | **It All Started with "What's Okay?"** *by Leslie Brown, CFT Faculty*

One of the things that scared me the most when starting my coaching journey was bringing up too much emotion in my youth clients (it wasn't the same with my adult clients). I found this to be a very interesting twist because prior to coaching, a large part of my work had been with foster youth who frequently had huge emotional outbursts that I was responsible for supporting. My initial response was to act as a protector and keep it nice and light by staying in the play space. I felt that I was more in control as a coach and could ensure that the youth would be safe and avoid emotional rollercoasters. However, I noticed that many of my youth clients were unable to maintain momentum because I was avoiding their deeper emotions and transformational agendas.

My safe and careful approach to youth coaching was acting as a barrier. Once I realized my impact as coach, my biggest challenge became increasing my risk and vulnerability to assist my clients to go deeper and gain access to their fullest expression of themselves. I vowed from that point forward to incorporate more vulnerability and take more risk.

When I met Makai, I knew that she would be my opportunity to live my coaching stance and I began coaching from an edgy and vulnerable space. I can clearly remember swallowing my fear and fully digging into my stance that would not allow me to keep it light. My first question to her was "How is life going for you right now?" Her quick response, with a huge smile and giggle was, "It's okay" and then she listed all of the amazing things happening. My intuition quickly told me that buried under all of

the fluff and giggles, Makai wanted more in life. My next question was "What does okay mean to you?" I suddenly noticed a huge shift in her energy as the smile and giggles faded. She took a deep breath and quietly responded "I have no idea what okay means." She went on to say that it was just something she learned to keep conversations going, during her time in foster care.

As we continued to explore the "It's Okay" concept she suddenly became very emotional and started crying hard. Initially I wanted to change the subject, but I remained quiet, holding the space for her. While she continued to weep I went a little deeper in my vulnerability and acknowledged that I could feel her pain and longing to move away from the automatic responses. This acknowledgment supported Makai to move into a more authentic space and she suddenly stopped crying and got really angry. She began sharing many of the things in life that she described as okay, but were not okay.

In the new awareness of her own truth, Makai's energy shifted once more and she was suddenly standing fully in her power. From the place of power she vowed that she would begin questioning everything in life that was "okay" with a critical eye. She planned to address some of the areas of life that were not okay that she had been avoiding. I was completely blown away with what I witnessed unfold through Makai's emotional journey. I learned that my openness to welcome emotions, truth and vulnerability, supported my youth clients in doing the same.

reactions, they experience the freedom to express the fullness of their feelings. They can more readily access their creativity and integrate their experience and take action in a more meaningful way.

Regardless of the language clients use to describe their experience, our role as coaches is to read their feelings and energy so that they experience being received. Meeting people right where they are goes a step beyond seeing, hearing or understanding them.

If a client struggles to identify emotions, we can shift the focus toward bodily sensations. If a client says, "I'm being manipulated and can't seem to touch on how I feel about that," we can ask, "Where does that live in your body?" or "Where is the disappointment?" or "Does your whole body experience it or does it live in your chest or belly?" These questions help the person being coached shift from thinking to the felt sense of the experience, which gives the feelings a place to call home.

Rather than seeing a feeling as something dangerous happening outside the self, we support self-intimacy by honoring the internal emotions.

If a person has a low threshold for a certain emotion, say fury, it may be because of an innate value of tenderness that they'll do anything to protect, even if it means numbing parts of their own bodies. When unconditional love permeates our coaching, experiencing the moment becomes a hotbed for transformation.

## Going into Resistance

As emotional issues come up, our clients may experience resistance. As coaches, rather than resisting the client's resistance, we flow with what is happening in a given moment. That doesn't mean we just let the client wander around aimlessly or that we passively accept oppression or harm. It means when blocks or obstacles arise, we embrace them with curiosity. As a spiritual attitude, we choose to face challenges and explore resistance without trying to change it. Facing whatever troubles arise frees up all the physical and emotional energy that would otherwise be spent in resistance.

If we hear, "I don't want to talk about that," or "This is a waste of time," we use our intuition as we explore. Especially when people are very raw or sensitive around emotional issues, we don't drag them into the process. We let them come to it in their own time. We respect when people don't want to work on certain issues or emotions. However, deep exploration is a means of getting through to powerful places; so we don't avoid what we sense is rich territory. We honor the healer within by exploring resistance to emotions.

### Move toward the resistance

If the client is "grinding away" trying to push through the resistance, we can ask to simply stop and go into the experience of the resistance.

*What is it like being right where you are now?*

### Get curious

We can get really curious about the resistance, rather than trying to get people out of or through the resistance.

*What do you notice about this part of you that does not want you to have awareness of your body. Where are you noticing it? What color is it? Touch it—what do you sense there?*

### Identify the needs behind the resistance

Assuming that people act in their own best interest, we can uncover the motivating forces by peeling the onion and identifying the needs they are trying to meet.

*What needs are you meeting by protecting yourself?*

### No need to "rescue"

There is no need to do anything about resistance, no need to direct them out of it, and no need to rescue them. Humor, caring, love and empathy all help the resistance shift organically.

*What if we took a step into it together?*

### Recognize bracing

Resistance shows up as "bracing against" something. The key is learning how to recognize bracing and also see what they are embracing when they brace against something. What is the yes behind the no? We attune our listening for that energetic stance of "arms out in front, holding something at bay." There is no need to do anything about this; just bring our clients' awareness to it by articulating what we notice.

*I sense you are braced, like you are holding back your desire. What is in that?*

People have a choice about whether to explore emotions. When we hold that choice for our clients, we help them break the automatic reflex to resist. When we hold that people always have choice, there is a sense of control and investment—a partnership dedicated to their growth and understanding.

We can also invite people to exaggerate their bracing or amplify their voice. If we ask them to take a posture or a movement that embodies what they are bracing against and have them hold it, they can be fully present and experience it on a direct level. By going into it directly, often change will happen, and certainly more awareness will result. If the person being coached reports out while in this experience, they can move through it, gain the insights that come up and have the freedom to make the choice to shift.

### Explore negations

When clients say that something is not happening they imply that it is at least in their mind, but disowned or rejected. Instead of negating their negations, we can accept them and get curious. For instance, here are some possible responses that honor the client's negation, yet keep the door open.

Client: I don't want to talk about my boss today.

Coach: Because you are protecting yourself from…?

Client: I went out on a date with him, but nothing happened.

Coach: Nothing?

Client: I'm not stressed out.

Coach: So if you're not stressed, what are you feeling?

Client: My mother doesn't think I should become a lawyer.

Coach: And your viewpoint?

Client: I am not scared.

Coach: Of what?

Client: I wasn't sad.

Coach: About what?

## Asking wicked questions

Wicked questions are designed to help clients explore biases, assumptions and contradictions. The answers aren't obvious, because the questions are often paradoxical or worthy of deep reflection.

*Examples*

What's wrong with being a workaholic?

How can you get your children to be more connected to the family yet more independent?

What's wonderful about stress?

How can you be completely dedicated to your writing and yet fully present for your partner?

How is anger your friend?

What are the benefits of being a marginalized queer woman?

What's so bad about ignoring your loved ones?

What's positive about not having enough money?

What if your behavior is sexist?

What is a good reason why your stepmother is acting so unreasonably?

What is dying to be born?

What are the questions you cannot ask yourself?

What if you do flunk out?

The purpose of "wicked" questions is to support breakthroughs, question biases and liberate us from old ways of thinking.

### Conflicting signals

Conflicting signals can lead us into the unknown. If the mouth is smiling, but not the eyes, we can encourage the client to observe their body which often amplifies the signals and increases awareness. If we name a conflicting signal with a hint of judgment such as, "You say you're open, but your arms are crossed," the client may move into denial, "I'm just cold. Or this is a comfortable position for me." Our curiosity, openness and eagerness to explore are paramount if we want clients to delve into the great mystery of their physical expression. A loving attitude supports the natural flow and includes trusting that a way forward will emerge. Instead of trying to heal clients or solve their problems, trusting their process shows the way forward and puts less pressure on the client to change or do things differently.

## Process Work

Process work is very closely aligned with Experiencing the Moment. This branch of psychology originated in the 1970's with the work of Arthur Mindell, a Jungian analyst. "Mindell discovered that the dreaming process went far beyond our nighttime dreams and could be seen in physical symptoms, relationship difficulties, addictions, extreme states of consciousness and social tensions. All of these dreamlike processes—when approached with curiosity and respect, can lead to new insight and an energetic shift that is vital for our personal development and the evolution of our collective bodies."[6]

Process work involves holding immense curiosity about everything the client is saying.

"If a client speaks about being hurt by an aloof partner, the coach listens as if s/he has no idea what hurt, aloof or partner actually mean. Approached with an empty mind, with no prior experience. Or we might miss the twinkle, we might miss the doorway into something special. If we interpret the client's feelings as hurt or abandoned, we might miss the opportunity to help the client explore her own aloofness."[7]

Process work emphasizes holding curiosity, paying attention to the body, staying in the moment with the client and approaching the client with compassion. Because we want the best for our clients, we sometimes join them in pushing them toward their desired changes. The danger of colluding with clients in this way is that we can take them out of their experience, where awareness and growth are most available. Following the client's process is an invitation to journey to somewhere neither of you have ever been, open to possibilities and experience transformation.

---

6    http://www.processconsulting.org/process_work
7    Diamond, Julie and Jones, Lee Spark (2005). *A Path Made by Walking: Process Work in Practice*, Lao Tse Press, p. 34

# Working with a Sense of Failure

*Success is moving from one failure to another without a loss of enthusiasm. —Winston Churchill*

Failure is a part of life. As coaches, we don't shy away from failure or rush to cushion the blow. To stay in the moment with failure can lead to rich insights. So instead of pushing through the discomfort to get to the learning, we can instead be curious about how it is to experience failure right now in this moment. It can make a big difference to be heard. As we listen for their longing, we help them to deepen the experience. For example:

*I hear deep sadness when you share the mistakes you think you made in the relationship. What is underneath the sadness?*

Using the body can help integrate the feelings associated with failure. As with all the Experiencing the Moment work, including the body helps people integrate the experience and move forward.

*Questions to Consider*

Take a moment to notice the feelings that are present for you right now.

Where are your feelings living in your body?

What is their color, shape or density?

What is a metaphor for any resistance you are feeling now?

As you continue noticing your feelings and your body, what shifts?

How can you support your clients to experience the moment?

# 7

# Envisioning the Future

*The future belongs to those who believe in the beauty of their dreams. —Eleanor Roosevelt*

Imagine your ideal life. Close your eyes and let your imagination soar. What does the future hold that's exciting and fulfilling for you? What difference do you long to make in your life, for your family or in the world? Visioning helps get to the heart of these questions and more. In moving toward your vision, mysteries begin to unfold and dreams come to life. As the first step in the process of creation and world-changing work, visioning unleashes passion and offers new possibilities. Visioning sets the stage for creative action for individuals, corporate teams and communities alike—establishing the blueprint for creating compelling personal, organizational and social change.

Envisioning the Future includes many processes that serve as pathways to alignment, and in this chapter we'll explore: courageous visions, right brain visioning, guided visualization and ritual. One of the things that sets coaching apart from therapy is a focus on the future.

Visioning helps clients open to the expanse of possibilities and alignment with their core values. The process helps them connect with what's waiting to be born and begin shaping their future. As the transformational self comes more clearly into view, both the coach and client sense the possibilities are truly limitless.

Vision work supports the mysterious coming together of desire: seen, felt or sensed. Born in the heart, vision comes alive through action. When vision grows out of an alignment with body, mind and spirit, it sustains us.

Deeply rooted in individuals and communities, visions reflect what people long to bring into the world. Working toward the vision satisfies an inner urge for personal growth and contribution. For some, creating and working toward a vision is a way to honor justice and equity—leaving the world a better place for future generations.

Vision can be cultivated. It is deep and profound. Simple and accessible. This chapter covers processes that lead us to our visions, and our visions to us.

## Setting the Stage

Setting the stage involves seeing from a new perspective. We can prime the pump and fuel our creative juices using some of these suggestions:

**Slow down.** Meditation, yoga, deep breathing or long walks can calm the mind and support presence, openness and receptivity to intuition and creative insights.

**Explore edges.** Dramatic events and powerful emotions can generate dynamic visions. What brings out anger? Tears? Joy? We can explore what we find on the edges of those emotions as a source for vision.

**Stir.** Look outside the comfort zone. Ideas often arise out of necessity, not just desire. Many of us avoid taking risks. We can stir things up and see what arises when we take a departure from daily habits, our long-time friends, our social status or our habits. Step outside our psychological comfort zone, and we can find new vistas.

**Change.** Consider making profound changes in our way of being, or how we live as inspiration for powerful visions. Change can feel difficult—especially if it can lead to instability or crisis. However, choosing change can be an opportunity for learning and seeing things in a new way—and can pave the way for creating a vision of what more may be possible.

**Break the rules.** We all have habitual ways that we get our ideas and make our plans. When those are not working, we can change it. For example, if we usually make a list of possibilities, try thinking without pen and paper. If we like to do things by the book, we can break the rules and see what opens up. We're not suggesting breaking rules that could result in danger, bullying, violence, expulsion, getting fired or incarcerated. We break the rules with a purpose: to try new ways of doing things or seeing the world differently.

**Play.** Sometimes we're trying so hard to create a vision that our ideas are afraid to come out into the light. The conscious mind, especially when it's working full bore, can be an intimidating force. Play can give the delicate, ephemeral wisps of imagination a chance to make their acquaintance. Many of us have lost the habit of play, but we can set aside time for play and humor, and let go of expectations. We can allow play to be random, or unstructured, and can connect with our inner child who still knows how. We don't have to worry about whether we're "doing it right." The playful part of us will guide us if we are willing to follow.

**Retreat.** Consider a change in venue—a place free of distractions. Magical things can happen in the heart and mind when the body leaves its customary domain. When planning a retreat or helping a client plan one, it's helpful to set a clear intention and be open to what might be revealed.

As we look at the lives of visionaries, we see qualities that we all have in some measure. We can use the visionaries as role models. How can we use these qualities in developing our own vision for our coaching?

Visionaries:

Are inherently curious

Convey a clear sense of passion

Explore their own nature unceasingly

Have the courage to dream

Open to the mystery

Expand the sense of possibility

Engage others in their vision

## Courageous Visions

The exercise that follows is a way to engage people in the process of Envisioning the Future. There are no formulas. Visions are the mysteries within waiting to be born. As coaches, we are the catalysts for awakening, and we do that by paying attention to individual ways of accessing and giving expression to the vision.

Helping clients expand their personal vision becomes a springboard for them to make a more meaningful contribution. Storytelling helps people get in touch with the deeper expression of their visions. As we walk them through the seven simple steps of the *Courageous Visions* process they become more engaged with their visions. This process builds upon the values work from Chapter 5. Visions come alive when they emerge from deeply held values.

1. **History: sharing milestones & possibilities**

   Share a story about a peak experience. Choose a time when you felt empowered, in the zone and joyful.

   What life milestones are important to you?

   What about your past will help you embrace the future?

2. **Values: clarifying what matters most**

   Examine your peak experiences and milestones for your personal values.

   Prioritize your top seven personal values.

   Which value is most important to you right now?

3. **Environment: choosing what you want**

   In your ideal future, describe the environment.

   What surrounds you? Who is with you?

   What is your inner experience?

   What's significant about this ideal environment?

   If you had a magic wand, how would you change your physical environment and the ambience?

4. **Action: shaping behaviors and capabilities**

   In your ideal future, determine what capabilities you have mastered. Build your awareness about what you especially enjoy doing.

   What personal capabilities do you already have that you will use even more in the future? Who else is involved?

   What new competencies do you need to master to meet future challenges?

5. **Identity: honing your image**

   Brainstorm the identity or nicknames you would like to earn from people you respect who meet you in the future.

   Imagine that you overhear these people talking about you. What do you want them to say?

   Ten years from now, when people are still talking about you, what do they say?

   What do you want children in your life to learn from you?

6. **Contribution: serving your purpose**

   Think about how you wish to serve. Imagine your ideal contribution. Envision how you take care of yourself so you can contribute fully.

   What do you contribute that's unique? In the short term? In the long term?

   What do you consider the most important contribution you can make?

7. **Vision: picturing your future**

Imagine an online article or blog post honoring you:

What headline introduces the cover story?

You are quoted in the article. What do you have to say about your success? What difference have you made?

What is the visionary story of your life?[1]

Here's a shortened example of the *Courageous Visions* process, from a real coaching session, with the steps noted:

Coach: In our first session, you shared some of the highlights from your life (Step 1) and you clarified your values. (Step 2)

Hope: Yes, and I was really amazed how the peak experiences of my life are a direct window to my core values: contribution, equality, empowerment and fun.

Coach: You light up when you say those words. When we ended our last session, you said you wanted to envision your future, so I'm checking to see if that's still alive for you.

Hope: Absolutely. And I did some of the homework, to envision my ideal future.

Coach: Great. So paint a picture of that ideal future right now. (Step 3)

Hope: I see myself as part of a loving family in a nurturing work environment, with a dynamic career and inner peace. But today, something new is coming into view. I want healing and safety for girls.

Coach: [silence] I can feel the intensity of your longing.

Hope: Yes. I want to live in a world where girls have freedom and respect…where they don't have to live in fear.

Coach: The opposite of fear would be what?

Hope: Courage. Freedom to play, enjoy their innocence, have fun.

Coach: I hear all your top values deeply embedded in your vision. So step into your own courage and let's see if there is anything else coming into view.

Hope: Yeah, but I'm scared that I won't be able to have much of an impact, that girls will go on being abused, trafficked, sold into lives of misery.

Coach: So no wonder this is important to you. Would you like to take a moment to grieve all that misery and just notice what you want instead.

Hope: What I really want is to create sanctuaries for girls to be completely safe.

Coach: What do you need to be or do to create the kind of world where girls are completely safe? (Step 4)

Hope: First I need to be a more influential leader. I would have to get in front of the right people to raise funds. And I need to develop a team that cares deeply.

Coach: How would that team describe you? (Step 5)

Hope: Inspirational. One who shares leadership and power. Fun-loving. Bold.

---

1    Lasley, Martha (2004). *Courageous Visions: How to Unleash Passionate Energy in Your Life and Your Organization.* Burlington, PA: Discover Press.

Coach: Many people share your vision. What's unique about your contribution? (Step 6)

Hope: My team and I empower girls to create their own destiny. With my fundraising background, I can start building these sanctuaries this year. I'm ready to create an action plan today.

Coach: I hear your enthusiasm! Before you create the action plan, let's look at one more aspect of the vision. Imagine an article about this project has gone viral. What's the headline? (Step 7)

Hope: Teenage Girls Ending Human Trafficking in 63 Countries.

Coach: Wow! And you're quoted in the article. What do you say?

Hope: I'm really proud of these girls. They are standing up to the $150 billion dollar human trafficking industry where half the girls are sold for less than $100. They have mobilized girls world-wide to end the sex slave trade, created sanctuaries and programs for girls to maintain their freedom and innocence.

Coach: Take a moment to celebrate your vision. How inspiring for you and for me!

Hope: I can't wait until next week—I'm going to start my action plan today.

Coach: I don't think I could stop you if I wanted to, but as you plan, allow the vision to expand naturally.

Hope: Yes, I can already see some of the donors involved.

Coach: And will you tell 5 people about your vision?

Hope: Not quite ready for that. I need to get a little clearer first.

Coach: So do you want to take that on as homework? Create spaciousness for clarifying your vision?

Hope: Yes, clarifying the vision now, sharing later.

Coach: I hear you! You really want some time to embody your vision. I want to acknowledge the way you honor your values. This vision is full of courage and it's all about living life fully—for girls and for you!

Hope: It's very healing for me. I get to reclaim my childhood—I get to be a very different girl who has tremendous power.

## Creating Vision Using the Right Brain

*The visionary starts with a clean sheet of paper, and re-imagines the world.*
—*Malcolm Gladwell*

So often when we start creating, we only build on the information that our mind offers. We can expand the possibilities and increase the engagement of our clients by engaging the right brain in the visioning process.

One of the keys to right brain vision work is to ask clients to set aside all the rules they live by. Allow space to explore without constraints of money, time, relationships, societal norms, internalized beliefs and physical ability. Reassure them they can get practical later in the process.

Instead of creating their life from circumstances or assumptions, we can support tapping into vitality, energy and choice by using the right brain to create from possibility.

Vision is most compelling when we create from the place inside where we are most alive, by tapping into the seat of creativity. Imagine next year as a piece of music, a poem, a painting, a collection of favorite things, a photo or some other metaphorical representation of what is possible. We can create from these representations by exploring the images and building a plan based on the images that arise.

We explore several other right brain tools to use with clients to expand their visions.

## Right brain vision questions

These questions help people look in places they would not ordinarily look to expand the vision. We can encourage them to look for the "flash" answer without pondering so that we engage the right brain.

What is the theme for your vision?

If your vision were a piece of music, what would it be?

What if your vision were 1,000 times bigger?

What if your vision were 1,000 times deeper?

What metaphor describes the vision?

What does nature have to say to you right now about your vision?

What does the uniqueness of your neighborhood say about your vision?

What does your vision taste like?

What feelings do you associate with your vision?

What are the colors?

If you added one outrageous element to your vision, it would be…?

When you picture your life ten years from now, what are you most excited about?

In what imaginary place would you be at your best?

Who would you like to be for a week?

If someone from the future visited you, what one question about your future would you ask?

What would you do with 100 million dollars?

If all your dreams came true, what would the future look like?

What deeper resource is available to you in creating your vision?

What are you forcing about this vision?

What can you take less seriously about your vision?

What rules need to be bent or broken?

How would a 5-year-old describe where you are headed next?

What if you had no limits?

What outrageous elements could you add to your vision?

What talents and gifts do you have to support your vision?

If you asked God (the Creator, the Divine, Allah, your Higher Power, etc.) about your next steps, what would you hear?

What is the magnet that draws people toward your vision?

What will you feel when you get what you want?

What is the secret to your deep success?

When you sit still and ask yourself what stirs your soul, what comes to you?

Who are you and what might it look like to embody that in your life?

What's the reason you've been put on the planet?

## Right brain vision exercises

Right brain exercises can be an energizing starting point for a coaching session. We can help the client deepen the themes that arise. The key is to avoid literal interpretations and keep the exploration in the land of images as long as possible before making the vision concrete.

When working with clients over the phone, we can ask them to create a right brain representation of their vision, similar to ways we'd work if we were together in the same room. They can send a photo of their collage or painting or simply describe it over the phone. The coaching centers on deepening the image of the representation of their vision, helping them stay very engaged and in the experience of the vision.

We can take our clients out of their heads by offering these visioning techniques:

### 1. Gather your Vision

For a week, several times a day wander around your home and pick up objects that catch your eye. They can be meaningful, silly or inexplicable. Put them in a box. At the end of the week, spread them all out around you and ask yourself what the objects tell you about your vision. Pay attention to the "flash" images and answers.

### 2. Capture the Images

Put a large piece of flip chart paper on the back of a door or anywhere accessible. Label it "My Life." Next to it have a basket of colored markers. Every time you walk by the paper for two weeks, write down something. Don't second guess what you write. You might write a phrase, an idea, a symbol, a drawing or just a word. Don't worry if what you write or draw seems disconnected or makes no sense. At the end of two weeks, look for themes.

### 3. Create a Vision Board

Vision boards can be done from a place of receptivity or intentionality. When approaching them from receptivity, we open to messages that come when we ask ourselves what is ours to create. The vision may come as images, colors, feelings, physical sensations or words. We may get a glimpse of our desire, or a new sense of things. Creating a space for our inner being to express what is emerging is a powerful way to experience the vision that lies deep within.

In this way of visioning we wait for spirit or a spontaneous arising of vision to come to us—trusting all that we receive.

Coming at a vision board from the other pole of creativity, intentionality, we look into the heart of what we want and actively engage in articulating, thinking about and exploring what we want our vision to be. We also pay attention to our feelings and passions. We actively design what we want and manifest our intentions.

Start with a stack of old magazines, greeting cards, post cards or online images. Be on the alert for what is calling you (receptivity) or what represents your vision (intentionality). Choose the images without second guessing yourself. Gather the images over an hour, a week or a month. Arrange your images on a poster board or art board. When they feel right, glue them down. Alternately, you can use various web-based vision board sites.

Hang the board where you can view it daily to reinforce your exciting vision. The magic and mystery of the process comes from watching the images on the board become reality. It is as if the right brain makes requests through the images, and a guiding presence makes them real.

## Guided Visualization

*Dreams are extremely important. You can't do it unless you can imagine it. —George Lucas*

Guided visualization can be a powerful means of bringing clients into a new vision for themselves or an aspect of their lives. The process invites them into a calm and receptive state, perhaps even a meditative or transitional state and then leads them on a path of open imagination, almost as though choreographing a dream. We invite the conscious mind to step aside and observe, while the subconscious provides the imagery. Visualizations brought about this way are often rich and surprising. As an example, we detail a future self visualization below.

### Future self visualization

The future self is simply a way to help clients move toward who they are becoming. In truth, they are already their future self and they sometimes can't own it. We use visualization in discovery sessions or whenever someone wants a clearer sense of themselves or their possible options.

Close your eyes and take slow deep breaths, allowing your body to completely relax. Keep your attention on your breathing, and notice how your breathing welcomes relaxation.

Notice and release any remaining tension in your neck, back, arms and legs.

Imagine yourself walking on a beautiful day and you feel totally at peace. Notice your surroundings—notice the colors and sounds and smells. Make note of what this place looks like and feels like to you. You may feel a guiding presence.

Continue on your walk until you realize you have magically, come to the place where your future self lives, ten years into the future. [pause] Notice what your future home looks like and get the feel of the place.

Your future self, ten years older than you are now, welcomes you. Notice your future self—the appearance, energy, clothing...

As you enter the home of your future self, your home ten years from now, look around. Notice the feel of the space, colors and smells.

Your future self encourages you to sit down to have a conversation. As you gaze into your future self's eyes, get a sense of the wisdom and experience. Notice how you feel.

Now you can ask some questions of your future self.

What has made your life fulfilling? [pause]

What are your greatest gifts? [pause]

What do I need right now? [pause]

What is the greatest contribution you have made over the last ten years? [pause]

What special name do you like to be called? [pause]

Now ask a few questions of your own and notice the answers coming into your being. Receive each response with gratitude.

What's new here that you are in touch with? What is being created anew in this space?

Sit still and gaze into your future self's eyes, taking in any additional insights you receive. As you do, your future self hands you a gift. Explore the gift—and ask your future self the significance of this gift.

Then thank your future self and leave the house and prepare to make the journey home.

As you head back, notice everything around you and take the time to cherishing any new insights.

As you return to your starting point, express your gratitude for this magical inner journey.

Take a deep breath and slowly come back from the visualization to where you are now—opening your eyes and stretching, remaining silent.

Write down the key insights you learned from your journey and time with your future self. Stay fully present and open to even more insights as you write.

*Debrief:*

What stood out for you in that experience?

What did you ask your future self and what answers did you receive?

What was the special name of your future self?

What was the gift and its significance?

What was co-created in that space?

In what ways is your vision now clearer?

## Ways to Work with the Future Self

Below are some methods for working with the future self to help clients stand in a more powerful place, outside the influence of their inner critic.

Go through the visualization at the discovery session or anytime in the coaching relationship. Debrief the experience. See what vision presents itself as a result.

Record the visualization process. Ask clients to listen to it as homework and then journal about the experience. Offer an inquiry such as, "Who are you becoming?"

Help them fully embody the experiences of their future self so they know this resource from the inside out. Have them find the place their future self lives in their body and access that energy through the body.

Ask them to create a concrete image of their future self. This can be a picture, a collage, a poem or a series of words that evokes the feeling. Suggest they keep this image present where they will see it daily.

Suggest spending five minutes each day with their future self, having a conversation over coffee or tea. What brings joy… excitement… goose bumps… tears…?

Ask clients to dress as their future self. Ask "What is the impact of doing this?"

When clients say "I don't know," ask "What does your future self say?" or "If you asked your future self, what would he or she do?"

When they are stuck, have them get up and move around as their future self. Combine this with questions for their future self. Movement itself can open them up to more information.

To help them see that they are already their future self ask, "What parts of you now are part of your future self?"

Ask the future self to comment on all areas of the wheel of fulfillment (in Chapter 10, *Strategy and Action*)—rating their level of satisfaction with each area, or how does their future self find satisfaction in each of the areas?

To spice up fun and recreation, ask clients to plan a vacation as their future self.

Ask your clients to make post card messages from their future self. They can give the cards to you and, sporadically, you send the cards to them.

Who are the friends of your client's future self? How are they different from current friends and family? What are the surprising qualities of these friends?

The client's future self can tell a story or fable based on an issue the client is facing now. The client can voice or journal the story.

On the coaching call prep form, ask "How have I moved toward my future self this week?" "What evidence have I gathered this week that I am already my future self?" "To be my future self today, what needs my attention?"

Use the name or the gift as inspiration for calling out the power of your client.

## Ritual in Visioning

Personal ceremony and ritual help clients align with all parts of their internal and external worlds. Vision fasts, divination cards, writing, drawing, mandalas, collages, mask making and poetry reading, are some of the ways clients can deepen their exploration of vision. Some folks take great pleasure in prayer, meditation, creating an altar, spending time with elders or youth, lighting a candle, looking into a fire, gazing at stars or city lights.

On occasion we work with someone who has difficulty dreaming or creating a vision. When we ask empowering questions or attempt to lead them in a visioning exercise, it falls flat.

What can inhibit people from knowing how to dream? When they have no idea what they want for their future, what can we as coaches do to create an environment where dreams and visions can flourish?

First we can raise our awareness and get curious about what prevents people from dreaming or creating a vision. Usually, it's not because they lack imagination or drive. A few other real examples that have kept people from dreaming:

- After the death of my husband, I couldn't envision loving anyone new who could die.

- After I was sexually assaulted, I wouldn't let anyone get close to me, even though that's what I wanted most.

- During the war, my best friend died in my arms and I felt rage for years, before I could admit what I really wanted: peace.

- I was living the dream when a hurricane took away everything I owned. It shook me to the core and it was a long time before I could dream again.

- When I had leukemia, I was very close to death. I could only see myself as sickly, even when I recovered.

Perhaps they want their vision so badly, they don't dare raise their hopes. To avoid disappointment, they play small.

Personal trauma may leave them feeling too vulnerable to truly explore what they want. The vision process may raise issues of loyalty or feeling different from family members or friends—especially if their dreams threaten to set them apart or change their relationships.

Curiosity is key to creating a space for exploring resistance and creating an opportunity for shifting into new ways to look at possibilities. We can also create space to explore fear, suffering, isolation and whatever else may surface.

For example, the American dream focuses on the success of the individual, not the well-being of all, but it disregards discrimination based on race, religion, gender or national origin. All of these might inhibit people's ability to dream or achieve their goals. Groups or communities who have experienced systemic oppression may resist visioning to protect themselves from further pain. The historical trauma of slavery, genocide, hate crimes or trafficking can motivate people to play safe.

By getting curious about institutionalized racism, sexism, classism, etc. we can impact our clients' ability to create a compelling vision for their future.

As an example, some US federal, state and local governments set explicit intentions to create racially segregated metropolises, or ghettos. The word "ghetto" sometimes implies racist connotations, but a ghetto is actually a part of a city in which members of a minority group live, especially because of social, legal or economic pressure.

How do those pressures impact people's ability to dream? What can happen to the ability to envision a future when events in our lifetime (or in our parents', or ancestors') have limited our access to a just and equitable existence? What happens when policies keep us from improving our lot in life or detrimentally affect our health or life expectancy simply because of the color of our skin, ethnicity, religion, gender or other factors? What happens when dreaming is dangerous or goes against the power structure?

Even if people are of a generation or in a situation where opportunities are available—what happens when they feel the injustice of being the 'lucky one' among family and friends, the one who can have more privilege, when others deserve it just as much? For example, what happens when their vision includes a higher education or a change in economic status that separates them from their community and their culture?

Without making assumptions about what is keeping someone from dreaming or visioning we ask curious questions. We can check our assumptions by remembering this poem of Langston Hughes:

---

**COACHING in Action | Barriers to Visioning** *by Belma González, , CFT Faculty*

*(Continued)*

**A Dream Deferred**

*What happens to a dream deferred?*

*Does it dry up*

*like a raisin in the sun?*

*Or fester like a sore--*

*And then run?*

*Does it stink like rotten meat?*

*Or crust and sugar over--*

*like a syrupy sweet?*

*Maybe it just sags*

*like a heavy load.*

*Or does it explode?*

We support clients by listening for their deferred dreams and honoring the anger or hurt that forced their dreams into hiding. By getting curious, we give them plenty of space to experience heartache and suffering. They may have very good reasons for feeling numb, frozen or immobilized. They may feel completely stuck, unable to access their creativity or imagination. Even when they can't remember their childhood dreams, underneath, their dreams are longing for expression. Listening without judgment, we create space for dreams to re-emerge and evolve.

---

As coaches we can encourage clients to deepen their vision by offering them rituals as fieldwork and planning ways to use the entire universe as a resource for their visions.

Connecting with the body through dancing, walking, swimming or heavy exercise, while focusing on vision, can be a powerful addition to vision work. Drumming, singing, chanting or toning can open people to new ideas. Posing a question and dancing the answer or drumming the answer can offer new insights.

## Discovery Walk

A discovery walk is a walking meditation designed to open to the resources outside ourselves. We can give this process to clients as homework which they can use anywhere. The key to a successful discovery walk is to assume there are resources and answers for us everywhere and simply open to them.

Go to a place where you wish to begin your walk.

Take a deep breath.

Ask a question out loud. Possible questions include: "What is waiting for me?" or "What is the universe ready to offer me?" or "What is the best use of me at this time?" The question can be general or specific.

Let the question go. You don't need to focus on it.

Notice where your attention is drawn and head toward that point.

As you move toward it, notice where else you are drawn and head there.

Continue this process, staying receptive to what draws you.

Do this until you find the place to stop—what place speaks to you?

Stop and pay attention to what is offered in answer to your question.

Offer thanks and gratitude.

We can do a discovery walk anywhere. Try a natural and wild place, in the city, at night, sitting in one place, in your house, following the sounds and smells (getting a buddy to guide us while blindfolded), with our music collection, in a library or in a museum.

## Vision Retreat

As coaches, we may want to do a personal vision retreat or give it as fieldwork to a client.

To access vision it is helpful to:

Set an intention.

Decide on a specific amount of time to set aside.

Choose an environment that will support the vision retreat.

Commit to the time and place in our calendar.

Consider what we need to do, complete, not complete or delegate so we do not clutter our mind when we set out on retreat.

Prepare what we need to have with us.

Prepare the space so it is pleasing to our mind and body.

Begin the process of visioning in a way of our choosing.

Some questions that we can ask are:

Who am I?

What, by my very nature, am I here to fulfill?

What am I passionate about?

What do I love?

What is my life purpose?

What do I long to share?

What is the contribution or difference I want to make?

If life were a project, what would be mine to create?

What does my soul call me to?

What is my place in the circle of life?

What is my place in community?

Each of the visioning processes support clients in getting fully in touch with compelling visions from their place of greatest aliveness. From this place, they fully see and begin to own their power to make their visions a reality. A wealth of creativity and focused action can spring forth when they create visions while connected to this energy or life force.

As we explore these processes with our clients, we can ask ourselves the following questions:

What surprised me most about my client's vision?

What did my client get in touch with that I did not foresee?

What are some of the possibilities I want to hold for this client now?

What blocks my client?

How can I support my client in stepping fully into a grand vision that exceeds what I can see now?

## Purpose

*I hunger for the comfort that can come from devotion to herd wisdom. Yet, at the same time, I remain desperate to flee the soul-wilting thatch of society's rules and standards and fly to the more uncertain but broader possibilities of living originally. —Gordon MacKenzie*

As clients fully engage with their visions, they come into alignment with a greater purpose for their lives. What may start out as personal dreams and desires can take on greater shape as they find themselves wanting to make a difference in themselves and in the world. This is when they awaken to their life purpose—to their calling that is greater than themselves that is beginning to emerge and take hold of them. Many people struggle to find their life purpose. The pathways to alignment, and visioning specifically, connect people to their life purpose without effort or struggle. A new life force, energy and passion compel them forward and fuel the vision crystallizing the legacy they want to leave. Some questions to help people connect with their life purpose consciously include:

What matters most to you about this vision?

What impact can it have on others?

How will your life change once it's real?

What is the difference you see yourself making in your life, community, organization or in the world once you realize your vision?

What legacy do you long to leave as a result of the seeds planted by your vision?

What is the greatest change you hope for as a result of your vision?

*Questions to Consider*

What are the most compelling elements of your vision?

What areas of your life do you envision changing?

What is the impact you hope to have through your coaching?

How will you further explore your vision and keep it alive?

# 8

# Expanding the View

*An old man walked to a neighboring town and came upon a group of workers carrying heavy stones. He sat down to watch, first seeing a man struggling under the weight of a heavy stone, grunting and having a very hard time with the job. The old man asked him, "What are you doing?" The man replied, "Carrying stones," and went on with his work.*

*Then the old man noticed a second worker, carrying a stone much like the stone the first worker carried, but he made the work look easy. This second man was smiling enthusiastically about his work. He asked the second man, "What are you doing?" The man replied, "I am building the greatest cathedral ever."*

## TOPICS

When to Use
Expanding the View

Expanding the View in
Four Steps

Identify a Neutral Topic

Discover Multiple
Viewpoints

Choose a Fresh
Viewpoint

Brainstorm Possible
Actions

In this parable the two stone carriers saw their work differently. Their viewpoint made all the difference in their attitude.

We all have viewpoints about our lives and the situations we face. Our viewpoints are as close as our breath. We hold them as facts, yet they are not. These beliefs affect how we see and interact with the world and how the world interacts with us.

Helping clients recognize that their current viewpoint is just one way of looking at a situation liberates them from their self-imposed thoughts. Once they take the first step of recognizing that their views are not the "truth," they can reframe their way of thinking, make a plan and take action based on a deeper awareness.

Our viewpoints are shaped by everything we experience, including family and culture. In this chapter, we learn how to help clients identify their viewpoints, attitudes and beliefs. We make viewpoints and their impact more conscious, so clients can choose to create from their aliveness, creativity and power. Expanding the View is a simple process that can transform people's viewpoints and people's lives.

Expanding the View rests on three assumptions:

1.  Our attitudes, assumptions, opinions and beliefs impact our experience and affect how the world responds to us.

2.   We can develop the freedom to choose our viewpoint.

3.   When we are free from undermining beliefs, we move toward life-sustaining choices.

## When to Use Expanding the View

We start by recognizing when clients are out of alignment. They may feel stuck, confused or discouraged. We listen for viewpoints (assumptions, beliefs, attitudes, opinions, judgments) that limit or diminish aliveness or possibilities. They may believe their viewpoint is "the truth" or "the way it is."

We recognize opportunities to use Expanding the View when clients seem to believe the "stories" they tell themselves, without question. Their language may convey rigid beliefs, such as:

I never have enough money.

It's impossible for me to have a close relationship with my daughter.

I must get more training before I change my career.

I can never have an intimate partner again.

Because I am good at math, I can't consider jobs in another field.

I have to either do work I hate or have no money.

One way to recognize viewpoints is to look for them everywhere. Listen to ourselves, friends, politicians, teachers, newscasters. What is the attitude or belief behind what we say and how we say it?

The Expanding the View process pushes the boundaries of our well-constructed attitudes about life. The process is an aid for exploring many possible viewpoints about any situation and embracing a fresh viewpoint that offers more possibilities. By noticing our own viewpoints, we begin to attune to viewpoints that our clients carry.

## Expanding the View in Four Steps

We use Expanding the View when we and/or our client notice a limiting viewpoint.

1.   **Identify a neutral topic**

     Separate the topic from viewpoints, opinions or beliefs.

     Examples of opinions: All I do is fundraise. There is no end to it. We can never be sustainable.

     Example of a neutral topic: Sustainability of the organization.

2.   **Discover multiple viewpoints**

     Explore other possible viewpoints about the topic.

     Example of viewpoints: I freak out when asking for money. I'm wildly bold and creative in crafting my pitch. I know what doesn't get funded. I am good at networking. There is an insurmountable class and cultural gap between me, my organization and wealthy people with resources. I am not cut out for this.

3. **Choose a fresh viewpoint**

   Select an empowering viewpoint or attitude to experiment with creatively.

   Examples of viewpoints to create from: I am wildly bold and creative. Fundraising is fun. I can make a difference in my community.

4. **Brainstorm possible actions**

   Explore new possibilities and action steps that open up from the chosen viewpoint. Then commit to at least one action step.

   Examples of possible actions: Oh, now that I know that I want to unleash my creativity, I can identify grantors that are more closely aligned with our mission and write a wildly creative grant proposal. I could ask Rich to mentor me.

   Example of committing to an action step: I'm going to ask Rich to help me write a wildly creative grant proposal this week.

## Identify a Neutral Topic

When a client voices a disempowering viewpoint, the first step is to separate the viewpoint from the topic. Expanding the View works best when we are crystal clear about the topic the client is exploring. This is a crucial part of the process, so we do not skip this step. Our clients are about to shatter long-held beliefs, so meaningful, clearly-defined topics help them focus.

Starting with the simple examples below, let's separate the topic from the viewpoint, just like diagramming a sentence. The goal is to separate the topic from the opinion about the topic.

| STATEMENT | TOPIC | CURRENT |
|---|---|---|
| I never have enough money. | My finances | I manage my money badly. |
| It's impossible for me to have a close relationship with my daughter. | Relationship with my daughter | It's impossible for us to be close. |
| I must get more training before I start my career. | My career | I'm not ready to start my career. |
| I can never have an intimate partner again. | My primary relationship | I'm not loveable. |
| Because I am good at math, I can't consider a career in another field. | Career choices | I have to do what I'm good at. |
| I have to either do work I hate or have no money. | Fulfilling work | I have to choose between money and fulfillment. |

Looking at the topics in the chart, we notice that clients could have any number of possible viewpoints about that topic besides the one they are currently holding. Once we help them pull topics apart from their viewpoints, they may see other possibilities emerge.

Often the statements are as clear as the examples above and it is easy to separate the topic from the disempowering viewpoint. And sometimes people feel so anxious about their situation that coming to a clear topic may take some unearthing. We can ask, "What are you wanting to explore?" or "What is important here?" or "What is at the center of this?" We can guess the topic and listen for how it resonates with the client. When there is more than one potential topic, we help the client choose the one that is most important now. We may start out focused in one area but as we move through the session, it may become clear that another topic is more relevant. By staying open, the topic can shift.

For example, Shana started out thinking her issues were all about her job, but then it started to look more like the topic was about freedom or commitment. All the topics may be important, so we help clients choose the one that has the most energy.

The following chart shows possible topics and viewpoints that might emerge from the presenting statement. In some cases, it takes more exploration to uncover the topic and viewpoint.

| STATEMENT | POSSIBLE TOPICS | CURRENT VIEWPOINT |
| --- | --- | --- |
| He will never break my heart again. | Love/ Connection/ My Relationship with my Ex | I have to protect myself. It is not safe for me to love again. |
| I am a loser. I have been at this job too long. | Choice / Fulfilling Work / My Career | I am not good enough. I'm stuck. I'm not creative. |
| People with power and resources don't take people who look like me seriously. | My Relationship with Power/ Resources/ Respect | It's not easy for me because of my race, class, gender, sexuality. |
| Sometimes I wonder if this is all there is for me? | My Life / Self Expression | My life is not working. I have no prospects for anything better. |
| If I had more money I could do what I want. | Freedom/ Vision/ My Finances | I am limited by money. I can't have what I want. |

In each case, we can tell the speaker feels disempowered, but we may not see the topic immediately. Topics do not include:

Opinions

Solutions

Judgments

Labels

Positions

Neutral topics contribute to the power of Expanding the View process. If the client begins with a topic called "my bad relationship with my father," there is nowhere empowering to go with it. The viewpoint is embedded in the topic. Imagine coming up with empowering viewpoints around the topic of "my bad relationship with my father," and compare it with the topic of "my relationship with my father."

Choosing the exact name for the topic isn't vital because the topic may change, but we name it clearly, so we can refer to it later.

With new clients, we can ask if they want to shift their current viewpoint and if they are willing to try on and embody other ways of looking at the issue. This lets them know what we are doing and gets them to take responsibility for the direction of the coaching.

## Discover Multiple Viewpoints

In this step the client comes up with at least three different viewpoints, embodying each one. Sometimes we brainstorm many viewpoints and then embody each one. Or we get the client to embody each viewpoint before stepping into a new one.

Sometimes people are attached to their current viewpoint and find it difficult to think of new viewpoints. Ways to come up with alternate viewpoints:

A. Directly ask for a different viewpoint

What is a different way to look at this?

What viewpoint is unique to your personal identity?

What is a fresh viewpoint you could try?

What's the wackiest or wildest viewpoint you can imagine?

What seems like an impossible way to look at this?

B. Look through different eyes

Let's look through different eyes.

Whose eyes could you look through and get a different view of this?

What is a viewpoint your ancestors might want for you?

How would a 5-year-old view this?

What would your future self notice?

C. Use a metaphor, an image or sound. After stepping into the experience of the metaphor, notice what viewpoint emerges.

Think of a metaphor. What comes up?

What image comes up? It doesn't have to be related to the topic. Step into it. From this experience what viewpoint emerges?

What song is emerging?

> Take a look out the window. What do you see that calls you?
>
> Like putting on different clothes, what viewpoint you could try on?

D. Use movement. Ask the client to move, change body posture or position and look in a new direction.

> Move to a different part of the room and look in a new direction.
>
> Slowly spin around. What new perspective catches your eye?
>
> Change your body posture and allow your body to inform you. What is the viewpoint that emerges from that?
>
> If you were to dance with this topic, what dance would you choose?
>
> Shift your body and notice what viewpoint your body is wanting to try.

E. Look at the big picture. This gives the client enough distance in space or time to get a different perspective and find out what the new belief is from there.

> Looking down from outer space, what new viewpoint does this gives you?
>
> Imagine you are looking at this from the perspective of your entire life. What is different looking from here?
>
> A hundred years from now, how would you see this?
>
> Imagine you are on a mountaintop. What do you notice from up here?
>
> If your entire community were supporting you, what viewpoint would come up?

The coach can suggest additional viewpoints to bring in a wider variety of ways to look at the situation.

### Embodying shifting viewpoints

Transformation becomes more likely when our clients fully step into a series of viewpoints, living each one as the present moment truth about the situation they are exploring. Until they do this, they are merely *considering* a shift, and Expanding the View feels like an exercise or assignment. We can train our clients to *step into* and *embody* each viewpoint. We start by asking them to embody their current viewpoint, Since they already strongly believe it, they usually find it easy to physically embody.

### Ways to support embodiment of a new viewpoint:

A. Leave the viewpoint by physically moving to a new place. Viewpoints can be sticky. Moving or shaking the body helps the client leave old beliefs behind.

> Shake your arms and legs to get rid of the old viewpoint. Let it go and move to a new place looking in a new direction.
>
> Throw that viewpoint out the window and let a new one come in.
>
> Something shifted in you physically. What are you noticing?

B. Physically step into the new viewpoint. We invite the client to step into the new viewpoint and remind them to find their truth.

Leave the old viewpoint behind. As you move, step into the truth of the new viewpoint.

Imagine the viewpoint is a pool and you are jumping or diving into it.

Keep stepping deeper into this way of looking.

C. Use Experiencing the Moment skills to embody each viewpoint. As we invite the client deeper into the experience of the viewpoint, we create spaciousness. We use our awareness to notice if the client is shifting or staying in the old truth.

What do you notice as you try this on?

What is happening in your body?

It sounds like the old viewpoint is still present. Let's revisit that one for a moment.

What do you yearn for in this point of view?

Step outside of the viewpoint and look at it. What is your relationship with it?

When the client fully steps into and embodies the viewpoint, we notice a shift. It is a little like stepping into a different world where new ways of thinking and acting are possible. Often we see a shift in energy and emotion.

D. Look at what is different about the topic now. Once the viewpoint is embodied we invite the client to look at the topic and notice what is different from here.

Take a look from here.

What is true now about the issue you are exploring?

What is different?

What is possible from here?

Each viewpoint provides new possibilities as they loosen the grip of the original viewpoint. Exploring three viewpoints including the original is usually the minimum, but people often get value from five or more. One way to know if the client has embodied enough viewpoints is noticing how easy and alive the next steps are. If the client has shifted into alignment, then energy, possibilities, choices and actions flow easily. If not, we may choose to return to this step and embody more viewpoints.

## Choose a Fresh Viewpoint

In this step the client chooses a fresh viewpoint to create from. We support clients to choose a viewpoint that enlivens them or opens up new possibilities.

Questions we can ask to support choice:

Which viewpoint would you like to try for the next month?

What view do you choose to inhabit going forward?

What viewpoint will you choose to help you plan from and live from?

> If you choose one viewpoint to embody for the rest of the day, which one energizes you the most?
>
> You don't have to choose this viewpoint forever, but which one would you like to experiment with now?

After trying out several viewpoints in Step 2, we often see a shift in the client's body, voice, energy or attitude toward themselves. This movement to alignment opens a natural transition to Step 3 when the client embraces a new perspective.

The client can combine viewpoints, come up with a new one, or use one already explored. At this stage, occasionally people choose the original viewpoint, but they have a fresh relationship, a new energy, or a different attitude toward that viewpoint. For example, Dory's original viewpoint was, "I don't know." After trying out, "I want to know," "I'll never know," and "I don't have to know," she became very energized when she returned to her original viewpoint. She experienced a sense of awe and wonder as she released the pressure she had put on herself, and began to enjoy the mystery of not knowing. She chose "I don't know," as her fresh viewpoint and moved into Step 4 feeling invigorated and in alignment.

As coaches, we may have an opinion about which viewpoint the client should choose. However, it is extremely unlikely that we are a better judge of this than the client. Without forcing a choice, we can help the client choose a viewpoint that resonates and is full of possibility. Choosing a fresh viewpoint gives the client a foundation and platform to live in and create from.

## Brainstorm Possible Actions

In this last step, the client generates possible actions from a place of alignment, then chooses to commit to at least one action. For most clients, once they are well anchored in the new viewpoint, creativity flows easily.

We start by inviting the client to fully embody the chosen viewpoint and notice possible actions arising. Instead of creating a dull to-do list, we use the energy of alignment to generate new possibilities and new ways of being.

> From this viewpoint, let's explore what is possible.
>
> What could you do?
>
> Who could you be?
>
> What is something wildly different you might try?

As part of brainstorming, we can add our own ideas based on what we have heard. Our suggestions serve to open up and stretch our client's thinking. Without being attached to our ideas, we give clients the power to choose.

At this point the client readily chooses their commitments. These actions usually flow easily with energy and aliveness. If not, we reground the client in the chosen viewpoint and try again. We may need to go back to Step 2 and ask the client to try on more viewpoints.

*Expanding the View Example*

To get a feel for the flow of a session, notice what the coach says to expand the view in this scenario:

Coach:  What's going on?

Tasha:  I'm a failure. I can't do anything on my own. (current viewpoint)

Coach:  What actually happened that led you to think you're a failure and you can't do anything on your own? (seeking clarity about the topic)

Tasha:  For over three years I've been trying to find a partner and I haven't been successful. I don't follow through even with people who are interested. I think there's something wrong with me. (another viewpoint)

Coach:  Anything happen recently that led you to think you're a failure? (seeking more details to determine the actual topic)

Tasha:  I was thinking about trying a new online dating service. (pause) Oh yeah, and my ex just told me he's seeing someone else.

Coach:  Ah, so you're seeing the connection between what happened and what you're thinking. And what do you want coaching on? (seeking the topic)

Tasha:  Dating. No… Partnership. (topic)

Coach:  So as you connect with your desire for partnership, what's your viewpoint right now? (seeking the starting viewpoint)

Tasha:  Ack! I feel overwhelmed. Dating is hopeless. I'll never have a partner.

Coach:  What happens when you fully embody that viewpoint?

Tasha:  I sink even lower. (after a moment, she sits up taller)

Coach:  I'm sensing a shift as you sit with your hopelessness. What's another viewpoint that you would never consider? (noticing the energetic shift, asks for another viewpoint)

Tasha:  I am the most loving partner in the world. But I would never say that! I get the chills just thinking that. (new viewpoint)

Coach:  Take that viewpoint outside your body and notice your relationship with it. (exploring relationship with the viewpoint)

Tasha:  I am so suspicious. This is a viewpoint I cannot trust. But I notice a golden light. (new metaphor)

Coach:  Sit with your suspicion, the mistrust and the golden light. What comes up? (Slows down the process, and gives client freedom to expand)

Tasha:  It's as if I'm going to visit a strange place. (metaphor)

Coach:  Go into that strange place now. Notice how you feel as you dive into the golden pool of light saying, "I am the most loving partner in the world." (experience the metaphor)

Tasha:  I'm in a tropical place. It's warm. There's a waterfall. I feel very alive. But I don't want to dive into the pool. I'm filled with doubt. (metaphor and feelings)

Coach:  How about welcoming that doubt into your body? (inviting attention on the body)

Tasha:  Wow—I notice a big change right away. My heart is open. Nobody gives all of herself the way I do. (shift)

Coach: Stay with it and notice what you're yearning for… (deepen the experience of the yearning)

Tasha: Real partnership. Uh oh. Right away I tell myself I've already had my shot at love. It's all downhill from here. I'm being sucked down by a vortex in a whirlpool. (new viewpoint and metaphor)

Coach: I saw a glimmer in your eyes. What's that about? (points to the body)

Tasha: Who cares? So what? Another person does not define me. A bell just went off. (new viewpoint)

Coach: What does the bell want for you? (giving voice to the metaphor)

Tasha: I am the vibration and the sound of that bell. Power is ringing through my body. It resonates in the center of my being… The bell has a voice that says, "You don't have to work so hard." All you have to do is listen to the bell within. (big shift in viewpoint—deep resonance)

Coach: You're standing taller, your chest is open and you're breathing deeper. (body awareness)

Tasha: Yeah, my lung capacity just doubled.

Coach: Which viewpoint do you want to experiment with this week? (choosing a fresh viewpoint into life)

Tasha: Of course I can find a partner! I don't have to be different. I walk in a way that feels buoyant. Regal. I'm in a very different place. (embodiment)

Coach: Hold that energy. And see if any actions are emerging. (moving into brainstorming actions)

Tasha: The easiest one is to let go of the failure. What's happened in the past does not define the future. I can give myself the freedom to fail in another relationship. Or succeed!

Coach: Sounds freeing. (creating space for insight and action)

Tasha: Absolutely. I'm going to a political rally tonight and I'm going to bring this new way of being with me. The world is my playground.

Coach: How do you keep the playground close to your heart? (keeping the actions connected to the yearning)

Tasha: Every day I'm going to visualize partners and people who want to play with me. Put on a wizard's costume. No, forget that. I'm going to go to a quiet place in nature and listen for guidance. Ask my friends to invite me over. No blind dates. I'll ask friends out instead. (actions that further embody the new viewpoint)

In this scenario, Tasha was familiar with Expanding the View, so the coach gave her a lot of freedom to go through the process in her own way. Instead of forcing her through a linear process, the coach encouraged her to deepen her awareness of whatever emerged. The coach pointed her toward her body, slowed things down to be with her yearning and helped her expand her metaphors. Her new viewpoints popped up spontaneously based on the spaciousness given by the coach. Another example follows of an Expanding the View session that organically emerged. After several coach-guided Expanding the View sessions, it's common for clients to do their own work without much prompting.

## COACHING *in Action* | **Road Map for Expanding the View** *by Steven Filante, CFT Faculty*

Joe is a vibrant, energetic, 45-year-old man who revels in meeting life head on. He came to the session sounding sad, discouraged and weak. He had survived a severe heart attack and said, "My life as I knew it is over." Clearly, Joe was out of alignment.

Joe carried a burden of emotional weight with the experience, and the coach sensed a new viewpoint would shift the load. The coach asked Joe if he was willing to try on and embody other ways of looking at the issue. Joe didn't believe that change was possible, but he really wanted to feel more alive and hopeful about his life. Joe was familiar with the Expanding the View process and stepped in fully.

As his topic, Joe chose: "My Life Going Forward." His starting viewpoint was, "My body betrayed me and my life as I knew it is over." The topic and viewpoint came by checking in about what was important to shift and also some guessing from the coach.

Using a possibility board, the coach mapped out Joe's topic and current viewpoint.

### POSSIBILITY BOARD: VIEWPOINTS

| **Beginning Viewpoint** <br><br> **"My body betrayed me and my life as I knew it is over."** | * | * |
| --- | --- | --- |
| * | **Topic of Coaching** <br><br> **"My Life Going Forward"** | * |
| * | * | * |

*\* Other possible viewpoints*

The coach helped Joe get a visceral feel for his beginning viewpoint and the impact of living in it.

Next, Joe generated other viewpoints to try on. Joe was lucky. Because he got treatment quickly, he had no permanent heart damage. Even so, at the beginning of the coaching the first viewpoint was dominant. With questions from his coach, he easily found several more viewpoints.

**COACHING *in Action* | Road Map for Expanding the View** *by Steven Filante, CFT Faculty*

## POSSIBILITY BOARD: VIEWPOINTS

| Beginning Viewpoint<br><br>**"My body betrayed me and my life as I knew it is over."** | *My body is healing itself. | *I'll probably have another heart attack. |
|---|---|---|
| *This is temporary. I will get better. | **Topic of Coaching**<br><br>**"My Life Going Forward"** | *Like breaking a leg, I may limp, but it won't limit me. |
| *It is time for me to grieve and feel the loss. | *This is a wake up call for something great that is coming. | *My team is cheering me on. I can have the life I dream of. |

*\* Other possible viewpoints*

Joe stepped in to the truth of each viewpoint, deeply embodying and discovering what was available in each one. The possibility board reflects what showed up in each viewpoint, which included imagery, the body, emotions, energy, metaphors or yearning.

## POSSIBILITY BOARD: EMBODYING VIEWPOINTS

| Beginning Viewpoint<br><br>**"My body betrayed me and my life as I knew it is over."**<br><br>**Metaphor of a door slamming in my face.**<br><br>**Yearning to hide and feel safe.** | *My body is healing itself.<br><br>Lighter energy.<br><br>I am partnering with my body. | *I'll probably have another heart attack.<br><br>My fear is real.<br><br>Body is heavy and tight. Very sad and discouraged.<br><br>Wishing for more strength and resilience. |
|---|---|---|
| *This is temporary. I will get better.<br><br>Feeling of hope.<br><br>Image of starting out on a backpacking trip. | **Topic of Coaching**<br><br>**"My Life Going Forward"** | *Like breaking a leg, I may limp, but it won't limit me.<br><br>I can live with this.<br><br>Yearning for healing and quiet. |
| *It is time for me to grieve and feel the loss.<br><br>Body feels heavy and slow.<br><br>Image of someone dying and me grieving the loss.<br><br>Feeling tender and protective of myself. | *This is a wake up call for something great that is coming.<br><br>Feeling a sense of purpose.<br><br>Image of a huge me walking through the world.<br><br>My body feels strong and open. | *My team is cheering me on. I can have the life I dream of.<br><br>Image of all my support people standing with me.<br><br>Body feels open and alive.<br><br>Sense of hope and possibility. |

*\* Other possible viewpoints*

**COACHING in Action | Road Map for Expanding the View** by Steven Filante, CFT Faculty

In Step 3 Joe chose to embody "My team is cheering me on. I don't have to be careful; I am being taken care of." He adapted one of the viewpoints he tried on during the exploration and chose to step into it fully.

At this point the coach moved to Step 4 where Joe stayed with the energy of his chosen viewpoint, brainstormed and committed to specific actions. Joe and his coach used the possibility board to explore actions, putting the topic and chosen viewpoint in the center.

| POSSIBILITY BOARD: ACTIONS | | |
|---|---|---|
| Option:<br><br>Focus on getting better. Enjoy the process. | Option:<br><br>Get a picture showing someone being held in the air by a group of people. | Option:<br><br>Smile at my rehab team and appreciate them. Be friendly and enthusiastic. |
| Option:<br><br>Tell friends I don't want to talk about the heart attack anymore. Let's talk about other things. | **Topic of Coaching**<br><br>**"My Life Going Forward"**<br><br>**Chosen Viewpoint:**<br><br>**"My team is cheering me on. I don't have to be careful. I am being taken care of."** | Option:<br><br>Plan a vacation with Jennifer. |
| Option:<br><br>Spend five minutes a day dreaming about the life I want. | Option:<br><br>Be a partner at rehab. Give them information so they can do their job. | Option:<br><br>Relax and let go of vigilance. Remember my viewpoint. |

Joe felt very differently by the end of the session. He committed to all the options except the vacation plan. He felt excited to go to rehab the next day bringing his new enthusiasm. Very aware that his coach was part of his support team, he continued to use his coaching sessions to create the life he wanted.

## COACHING *in Action* | **Expanding the View** *by J.R. Reynolds, CFT Certified Coach*

Many times our viewpoints of the world are centered more on ourselves and our projections than actual reality. As a result, we form opinions that can often derail even the best intentions.

This can be the case especially if we happen to be part of what social science refers to as a "dominant group." In the United States, examples of dominant groups include: white, male, Christian, heterosexual, non-disabled, upper middle class.

Renee is a middle-aged and upwardly mobile banking executive. One of her core values is giving back to the community. After a negative experience volunteering at a small grassroots nonprofit agency focused on women helping women help themselves, she asked for some coaching.

"Volunteering with them was a disaster," Renee complained.

"What was hard about it?" I asked.

"They just didn't have their sh*t together over there," said Renee.

"How do you mean, Renee?"

"So I get there and the executive director didn't want to see me. Then, I get assigned to do accounting paperwork that any secretary could do."

"How was that for you?"

"I felt insulted," replied Renee.

After deeper exploration of Renee's emotions, I helped her take another look at the agency she had volunteered with.

"What's the annual budget of the nonprofit?"

"Budget? From what I could tell, they were living from pillar to post," said Renee. "They're barely hanging on. It was so sad. How can they help their clients when they can hardly help themselves?"

I nodded, then asked, "You said the agency didn't have their, uh, stuff together and the executive director didn't want to see you. How might those two things be related?"

"Well, actually she did stop over later, while I was reorganizing their financials."

"Hmm, I'm curious; how did that feel?"

"Annoyed at first," admitted Renee. "Then she apologized about not coming out to meet me and explained about the all the 'fires' she was fighting."

"What did her explanation do for you?"

"It made me wonder why she was doing things her assistant should have been doing."

"Where was her assistant?" I asked.

Renee leaned toward me and opened her mouth as if to speak, but stopped. She furrowed her brow. I followed suit and we sat in silence for almost a minute. Finally, Renee spoke.

"It didn't occur to me until just now that she might not have had an assistant," Renee said almost at a whisper.

More silence.

"What's going on with you?" I asked.

"Feeling uneasy."

"Where's that showing up in your body?

"My stomach; it's knotting," Renee said.

The coaching continued with Renee sharing an expanded view of her experience. In the process she admitted her initial interpretation of what transpired might be wrong, including a shift around why she had been assigned what she considered a menial accounting task.

"They just didn't have the capacity to get that work done," Renee concluded. "I also might have been the only one in there who understood what needed to be done."

"Where does that lead you?" I asked.

"I'm starting to see how I might really have been valued over there," Renee smiled. "Here I thought they didn't want me so they gave me that tedious work. Now I see they probably wanted and may have even needed me."

"And how do you feel?"

"Valued. Like I need to pick up the phone to reconnect."

The value of the Expanding the View process is that clients realize they can choose any viewpoint about any situation. As we train clients in the coaching process, over time they can use Expanding the View without the coach. Chapter 10, *Strategy and Action*, goes into more detail about action plans and accountability.

*Questions to Consider*

What are some creative ways you might use the Expanding the View process with your clients?

What viewpoints are you holding about yourself as a coach?

What is your commitment to exploring and standing in an empowering viewpoint?

# 9
# Embracing the Shadow

*Last night, as I was sleeping*
*I dreamt-marvelous error!*
*That I had a beehive*
*Here in my heart.*
*And the golden bees*
*Were making white combs*
*And sweet honey*
*From my old failures. —Antonio Machado*

## TOPICS

The shadow is the unconscious, or hidden parts of the personality. Jung believed, "in spite of its function as a reservoir for human darkness—or perhaps because of this—the shadow is the seat of creativity."[1] The shadow personifies everything we refuse to acknowledge about ourselves, yet project on others. Robert Bly talks about the shadow as "the long bag we drag behind us." He refers to all the parts of ourselves that we have hidden away all our lives because they are unacceptable. We put those parts into that bag that we pull behind us, and rarely engage with these parts of ourselves. We also disown parts of ourselves that we want, such as personal power.

Working with the shadow helps unleash power by embracing all of who we are, not just the happy, positive parts that make us look good on the surface. Instead of operating from the storm of external factors that constantly influence us, our goal in this work is to find the stillness and clarity that comes from integrating shadow members of the internal community.

Embracing the Shadow is built on the work of multiple modalities. We are grateful for Roberto Assagioli's development of psychosynthesis, Carl Jung's work with Active Imagination, Fritz Perl's Gestalt open-chair technique, Hal & Sidra Stone's work with Voice Dialogue, Richard Schwartz's process of Internal Family Systems and Tim Kelley's Inner Harmony work. What all these processes share in common is the

---

1    Kaufman, C. Three-Dimensional Villains: Finding Your Character's Shadow

**RESOURCES**

*Psychosynthesis* by John Firman and Ann Gila

*The Dark Side of the Light Chasers* by Deborah Ford

*Jung on Active Imagination* by C. G. Jung

*Internal Family Systems Therapy* by Richard C. Schwartz

*Gestalt As A Way of Life: Awareness Practices: as taught by Gestalt Therapy founders and their followers* by Cynthia Sheldon and Angela Anderson

*Embracing Our Selves* by Hal and Sidra Stone

*Embracing Your Inner Critic: Turning Self-Criticism into a Creative Asset* by Hal Stone

premise that healthy personalities include many sub-personalities, or parts. Every one of us has many parts—some we identify with strongly, others we reject.

We also appreciate the way the social justice movement informs this work. The beauty of honoring all parts is that it heightens our awareness and sensitivity to power and oppression as we witness how these dynamics operate in ourselves, in our clients and in society. We cannot have a truly healthy psyche if we marginalize some parts, nor can we have a healthy society when we marginalize some groups of people, whether because of their gender, race, sexual orientation, class or other social constructs. And we're grateful to our colleagues and students who continue to explore new ways to embrace the shadow.

## The Internal Community

Similar to the way we interact with our community or family, friends and the world, we also interact with an internal community. The internal community is that group of internal parts of the psyche that direct our lives. Each part has an important purpose, without exception. Our role as coaches is to help clients learn to embrace their parts, exactly as they are. Even when a part behaves harshly, we look beneath the words or vicious behavior to understand its positive intent. If we appreciate each part's attempt to contribute, honor the important role the part is playing and thank it for its years of service, the part feels seen, heard and understood.

The inner critic is one of the most vocal parts of the internal committee. Everyone has one. That's why we require all our coaches to become very familiar with the inner critic and how it operates. For instance, the inner critic has a reputation for spewing out nasty comments, but underneath has the positive intent to keep us from making mistakes or protect us from embarrassment. We especially need to be aware of our own inner critic and how it impacts us while we are coaching.

As coaches, we don't try to change the parts, get them to see things differently or modify their behavior. We don't scold them, give them advice or try to get them to disappear. We don't try to fix them or get rid of them. Members of the internal committee are just like people—if we devalue one member of the committee by shaming it or kicking it out, it is likely to rebel or sabotage what has already been accomplished. As coaches, we don't act as revolutionaries who replace one despot with another, because the change does not last. Sure, ignoring a part might work for a short time, but true change cannot be accomplished by bullying or ostracizing a particular part. Instead, we actively support the evolution of the whole by embracing each part of the internal community.

In our internal conversations, some parts of ourselves dominate others, which can leave us feeling fragmented. This rejection of parts of ourselves leads to internal polarity, blind spots and imbalance. But when we go beneath the surface and really listen to our many parts, we connect vulnerably to our full humanity and begin to have compassion for all of our sub-personalities.

## Parts dialogue

The simplest way to embrace the shadow is to compassionately witness different parts, by creating the space for clients to see and hear each part fully.

As clients explore inner conflict or polarities, we help them honor each voice when it shows up. What does each part have to say? What is it worried about? How does it communicate? We can simply listen to each voice or ask questions. We don't name the parts for the client; we ask each part what it would like to be called.

Our role is to keep our client in the experience and in the conversation instead of talking about it. The beauty of the process is to step fully into the experience of the voice, and become that voice. By embodying each voice, there is more possibility for developing deep self-compassion.

*Parts Dialogue Example*

Carlos: I'm overwhelmed at the thought of adopting a child. I really want to become a father, but I don't want to lose my freedom. We could get a child as early as next month and Juanita would be really upset if I back out now. Why did I say yes to this? What was I thinking?

Coach: I'm hearing two parts of you—one that really wants your freedom and another that wants to be a father.

Carlos: Exactly. The part of me that wants to be a great father is excited and the part that wants to keep my freedom is scared.

Coach: Which part would like to speak first?

Carlos: The part that is scared.

Coach: Will you move to a new place in the room and step into this part that is scared? Allow this part of you to speak without censoring it. The other part will have a chance later. You are not committed to act on what this part is saying—you are simply giving yourself permission to let this part speak.

Coach: And what would you like to be called?

Carlos: You can call me, "Really Scared."

Coach: Okay, Really Scared, what's it like to be you?

Carlos (Really Scared): I notice I'm feeling small. I'm completely overwhelmed and need freedom. I don't want to be tied down.

Coach: What else do you want to say, Really Scared?

Carlos (Really Scared): Carlos is afraid to tell Juanita that he might not be the greatest father—she would be disappointed and hurt. But he should talk to her.

Coach: I hear how much you want Carlos to talk with Juanita. Take a moment to notice what you're feeling…

Carlos (Really Scared): Relieved. I'm glad I'm speaking up.

Coach: Thanks for taking a stand for Carlos to speak up and keep his freedom. Are there any other conditions that would make it okay to adopt a child?

Carlos (Really Scared): A flexible schedule at work.

Coach: Okay, before Carlos can adopt a child, you want him to have his freedom and a flexible schedule. Thanks. Carlos, come back to your original seat... What was it like to listen to the Really Scared part?

Carlos: Interesting. I had no idea how tired this part is. I'm thankful that this part wants me to talk to Juanita.

Coach: Now let's also create space for the part of you that wants to be a great father. What shall I call this part of you?

Carlos: You can call me "Fun Dad," because I love having fun with kids. Even though my father was never around, I think I will be very different. We'd have so much fun every day.

Coach: Let's hear from Fun Dad. Go to a new position in the room where you would like to be.

Carlos (Fun Dad): I'm squatting down, smiling, ready to play.

Coach: And what do you notice?

Carlos (Fun Dad): I am excited and inspired about this opportunity. I have a glimpse of what I want. To help a child have a great life. I have been waiting for this. I think it is a chance for me to trust myself more. To jump in.

Coach: What else is here?

Carlos (Fun Dad): I have wanted to be a fun dad for a long, long time. That's all for now.

Coach: Thanks for saying what you really want. Take a moment to notice your experience in this moment... Then go back to your original seat and be Carlos. Respond to what you just heard.

Carlos: I hear Fun Dad's excitement. I need help. The parenting classes we've been taking are a long way from the real thing. I'm not at all prepared for this. I want to talk to some fathers I admire and ask some questions.

Coach: Okay, so this part has inspired you to ask for support from other fathers. I want to thank both parts for taking care of Carlos. What do you appreciate most about each part: Fun Dad and Really Scared?

Carlos: I'm surprised and grateful. Both parts care about me a lot.

Coach: What do you notice about the energy you are experiencing in this moment?

Carlos: I feel calm and excited at the same time. A tension has left my belly. When I think about sharing all this with Juanita, I can relax. I can't wait to get moving on this.

Coach: I want to acknowledge the honesty of both voices. What was that like for you?

Carlos: I liked hearing from both parts. When they are in my head, they roll around and nothing gets resolved. When I was responding to Really Scared at one point, I wanted to take care of him and not just win him to my viewpoint. I feel more real, more whole.

Coach: What's next?

Carlos: Talk to Juanita and then invite our friends over for some fun. Create a plan to make sure I get some flexibility and still have some freedom.

Notice the coach asked the client to get out of the chair and stand in different places to represent different parts. When each voice has its own discrete and protected territory, clear boundaries support full expression. This creates the possibility to engage on a level of bodily sensation and emotion. In parts dialogue, the aliveness and direct experience of what was hidden awakens the shift. The paradox is that separation of the parts leads to integration.

As a coach, we do not need to interpret the experience at all; we just let them see what awareness is created out of the experience. Curiosity is the gateway to compassion. If we truly trust the process of Embracing the Shadow, we simply listen deeply to whatever emerges.

Getting to know their parts helps clients relate to themselves with far more curiosity, confidence and compassion. Spontaneously, their inner dialogues change. They stop berating themselves and get to know their sub-personalities, which helps them achieve balance and harmony internally.

When we use the Embracing the Shadow process, we help clients explore polarized aspects of their personalities. Since each part wants something positive, we help them respect the concerns of each part. As we empathically connect with each part, integration of the polarities takes place. To fully integrate the shift, we encourage clients to voice or physically express what they truly appreciate and respect in each part.

## Using the body

Each member of the community has likely taken up residence in some particular place in the body, and we can use the body to access each part of the internal community. The body stores our experience on all levels—physical, emotional, mental and spiritual. It serves as a filing cabinet for the soul. We may have forgotten what we ate three weeks ago or an argument six months ago, but our bodies remember everything.

When clients can be present to their bodies, they have an entry point into the more subtle emotional field. Staying in the head and talking about our experience is not as effective as exploring the body's wisdom. We often see the body shift when a new part emerges. Body awareness initiates the ability to come into the moment and go to the heart of the matter.

## Honoring all parts

The beauty of Embracing the Shadow is that we create opportunities for inclusion. As a result, people develop a loving relationship with themselves and others. This radical approach to coaching includes deep listening and gratitude for the role each part plays.

The human psyche has many parts, which is natural and healthy. All parts of the psyche have a positive intent, even parts that are stuck in contentious roles. As coaches, we listen for the noble purpose of all parts, regardless of their role. We listen to parts the same way we listen to people, picking up on their longing for transformation.

By creating opportunities for each part to be heard, the parts come to know and appreciate each other's role. In the example that follows, the leader and resistor become valued members of the inner team instead of viciously opposing each other. When we hold the belief that there are no bad

## COACHING *in Action* | **Discomfort with Leadership** *by Rebecca Aced-Molina, CFT Faculty*

Here is an example of how Embracing the Shadow supported an emerging leader to find her unique leadership style. Lucia is in her early 30's, a Latina woman from an immigrant family, the first in her family to go to college. She is a new Program Director in a large non-profit organization, grappling with creating sound organizational systems without losing the organic grassroots feel of the work.

Lucia: I'm not comfortable being in a leadership position. I've always been so critical of leaders. I don't have any good role models really. Many of the leaders I've observed have been very divorced from the work on the ground.

Coach: How would you describe a positive leader, practicing leadership in ways you could feel good about?

Lucia: It is really important to me to set goals and make sure our actions are moving us toward accomplishing those goals. But I don't want to be a dictator.

Coach: It sounds like there is a part of you that has some clear ideas about how to lead an organization and another part that is resisting.

Lucia: YES!

Coach: Let's hear from both of them. Would you be willing to allow each voice, the organizational leader and the resistor, to speak from their own perspective?

Lucia: Absolutely!

Coach: Let's both agree that when we hear from each voice, no matter what they say, we won't try to make one right and the other wrong. Is that okay with you to put our judgments aside?

Lucia: Yes.

Coach: Okay. So which part would like to speak first?

Lucia: Let's start with the organizational leader.

Coach: I invite you to get up out of your chair and find a place in the room where you can sit or stand as the organizational leader. How are you standing or sitting?

Lucia (Leader): Standing really straight. I kind of brushed off my pants and lifted up my chin.

Coach: Great. And what's important to the organizational leader part of you?

Lucia (Leader): Wow! I just realized, I've worked really hard to get to where I am. I've studied and worked hard. It is really important to make Lucia's parents proud.

Coach: Okay. So you are realizing you want some recognition about how hard you have worked and that being in this position is a source of pride.

Lucia (Leader): Yes, and I have great ideas.

Coach: Okay. Come back to being Lucia. Why don't you take a minute and honor the organizational leader part. Tell her how much you appreciate her. Do it silently and let me know when you are done.

Lucia: Okay.

Coach: How was that for you?

Lucia: Pretty amazing. I feel more open to her. She isn't doing anything wrong and I realized how much I have been judging her. I definitely want to let go of some of that.

Coach: Great! So let's hear from the resistor part. Why don't you move to another place in the room and sit or stand like the resistor. (pause) You there?

Lucia: Yes.

Coach: So what do you notice about the resistor part?

Lucia: Well. I've got one hand on my hip and my other hand is waving a finger saying, "Don't forget where you came from!"

Coach: I am going to speak to you as if you are this resistor part fully right now; okay? You can answer in the first person, fully embodying this part of you. Resistor part, "What do you care deeply about?"

Lucia (Resistor): Just that I have been through hard times, my parents have been through hard times, and that those struggles are a part of me too.

**COACHING *in Action* | Discomfort with Leadership** *by Rebecca Aced-Molina, CFT Faculty*

*(Continued)*

Coach: What are you resisting?

Lucia (Resistor): Well. I believe in honoring my elders and being humble. It is part of my culture. It just feels weird to assume I am at the center of anything. It is just not how I was raised.

Coach: What do you need to feel okay about Lucia taking on leadership?

Lucia (Resistor): I just need her to know that her purpose as a leader is to build up the community as a whole and that she's not going to lose sight of that.

Coach: Okay. Thank you, resistor. I can see you have a lot of insights to offer Lucia. Let's come back to Lucia. After hearing from both parts, what are you more aware of now?

Lucia: Just that it makes sense now! I see why I've been having such a hard time. And I also realize that I don't need to get rid of either of these parts. In fact, the opposite is true. I need to embrace both of them.

Coach: Wonderful. I would encourage you to take some time to journal and express to both these parts what you appreciate about them. How does that sound?

Lucia: It sounds great. I can't wait!

parts, we create an environment of inclusion, which makes it safe for other parts to come forth. We honor every part because each has a desire to serve.

When we invite opposites to be heard, they often feel relieved to be understood. Wherever there's a rule-maker, there is a rebel. If the sage needs to be heard, so does the jester. Just like most working committees, these inner committee members have never been trained to hear each other's needs or understand the valuable role each fulfills. Often they have been using strategies since childhood and they've never been taught to collaborate. When we support a client's internal parts being heard, we activate a powerful internal wisdom council where each member brings insights and support for fulfilling the client's life's calling.

People are often relieved to find out that they are not their parts. They have parts, but they are not their parts. Only a part of them is ruthless, another part is kind and compassionate. Only a part of them is a workaholic, another part just wants to have fun. One part is not better than another part. All parts add value to the system.

## Types of parts

Although we all have countless parts, we focus on two main categories: protectors and those they protect. Typically, the protector's role is to make the protected parts safe, by ensuring they do not experience pain or suffering, by any means necessary.

### The Protector Parts

The protectors are the parts of us that come to our aid when the child parts have been hurt. Not only do they rescue the wounded child, they take extraordinary precautions to keep the child from ever being wounded again. These protectors work hard, using strategies developed when we were very young. They help us to survive—they plan ahead and ensure that we are socially acceptable.

Many of these protector parts showed up in the system when we were too young to protect ourselves.

Years later, the strategies of the protectors no longer serve us, but the intent to serve is still active. Protectors either prevent some parts from being heard or they distract us from the pain when those parts become active. We all have many protectors, and each one has a different strategy for shielding us from pain.

Some of the most common names for protectors are:

- critic
- pusher
- pleaser
- procrastinator
- controller
- skeptic
- rescuer
- perfectionist

There are many more parts that protect us and we can give key players of our internal committee personalized names. They may distract us by replacing the emotional pain with various addictions, physical maladies, or keeping us so busy we don't have time to feel anything. They come in swiftly whenever they get the scent of danger, and are committed to keeping us out of trouble.

Despite some of their seemingly dysfunctional behaviors, protectors really need to be appreciated for their vigilance. They became activated during a time of stress or danger and their stance is, "NEVER AGAIN!" Even if it means armoring against all emotions or getting stoned every day, they are serious about avoiding pain. They push some parts out of the system to protect the internal family from their pain.

**The Protected Parts**

The hurt parts that are being protected have been marginalized to the outer edges of the internal community. These parts are usually vulnerable or child parts, frozen in time, but still carrying the burden of fear and shame from long ago. These child parts are often rejected, punished or ridiculed for being different in some way. If they hold family secrets, they could be considered a threat to the family of origin, so they get sent away. Sometimes the only way hurt parts have been able to survive is by becoming invisible.

Some of the common names for protected parts are:

- wounded child
- whiner
- bad boy
- gifted child
- unloveable
- too smart

- overly emotional
- too needy

These protected parts have been locked away so long that they are completely unaware that things have changed since the original incident or trauma. They remain childish and overwhelmed. For the most part, they live undetected in the far realms of the psyche and many people have no awareness that they even have a wounded child.

These child parts come alive when they are triggered by something similar to the original pain. When the protected parts bring in strong emotions such as fear, anger or grief, the protectors act swiftly to keep danger at bay. They try to induce guilt or shame by criticizing us, punishing us or giving directives that must be obeyed. Not surprisingly, their voices often sound similar to our teachers or parents. "Quit acting like a girl." "Go back to where you came from." "Shut up or I'll give you something to cry about." They protect the system from being overwhelmed by the hurt parts.

Despite these ruthless techniques and harsh words, the protectors' goal is to protect the hurt part from experiencing powerful emotions that could lead to self-destruction. Their vigilance has kept us alive and they intend to keep doing whatever it takes to keep us safe. They are deeply committed to making sure we do not experience fear or helplessness. Ironically, the reason they criticize us is to protect us from humiliation from others. Both protector parts and protected parts can be male or female, regardless of the client's gender. And some parts do not have a discernable gender.

**Dominant Parts**

A few powerful parts usually dominate our psyche, strong-arming weaker parts into submission. The dominant parts of the internal committee are those who think they are running the show and they usually take up the most air-time. We may have 4-5 dominant parts that speak to us often, but we have hundreds of other parts on the sidelines waiting to be heard. While a few parts dominate our consciousness, we remain unconscious of many other parts.

Each dominant part has an opposite that it tries to curtail, or protect, also known as a "shadow" part, or unconscious part. For instance, the Pleaser, who tries to make everyone else happy, prevents the Selfish part from speaking. The Pusher blocks the efforts of the Procrastinator. The Rule Follower forces the Freedom Fighter into submission. These polarized parts come in pairs, one dominating the other, one conscious, the other unconscious.

All these parts function like a large family, each with a vital role that contributes to the larger system. Each part is valuable to the system, the same way a healthy ecosystem needs all its parts. When we accept each part as a valued member of the family, they become more appreciative of each other's roles and more collaborative.

Sometimes, clients identify with a particular part so strongly that they become confused or think they are the part. A one-time protective measure becomes a pattern that is difficult to change, even when the part itself recognizes that its behavior is self-destructive. The part moves into survival mode and has no intention of relinquishing its role. When a person experiences trauma or neglect, strong parts take over the personality and can overtake the leadership position of the

Self. Sometimes dominant parts come to believe they are the "whole personality." An example of this is when we describe ourselves as "selfish" or "bitter" or "proud" or "stupid" because we have identified so strongly with a part and we start to believe that is who we are. Meanwhile, other parts notice that the domineering parts have taken over, and they lose trust in the Self's capacity to lead.

Once that compassionate internal leadership is lost, we can restore a healthy internal system by separating parts from the Self and listening to each. The heart of the work is to distinguish parts from the Self and re-create conscious, respectful relationships with each part. Once the Self resumes the role of compassionate leader, and welcomes each part, the Self can make decisions that benefit the whole. The entire system breathes more deeply when the Self takes the lead.

## COACHING *in Action* | **Identifying Parts** *by Guthrie Sayen, CFT Faculty*

Once you realize that a part is calling for attention or blocking your progress, you need to find the right one so that you can talk to it. It is crowded in your psyche; just calling for any part is like shouting "Hey, you!" at a party. You'll probably get a response, but not necessarily from the one you want. So, how do you identify and call the part you're looking for?

### NAME

The simplest way to invite a part into a dialogue is to ask for it by name:

"I want to talk to my Protector (or Critic, Perfectionist, Pleaser, Skeptic, etc.)"

This often works with the major players in your psyche, the parts that run your life on a daily basis. It also works for parts that you have engaged in the past, when you and the part have agreed on a name for it.

### FUNCTION

You can ask for a part that does something specific:

"I want to talk to the part that distracts me."

"I want to speak to the part that objects to me finding a life partner."

"I want to speak to the part that likes to socialize in large groups."

"I want to speak to the part that knows how to organize projects."

### EMOTION OR BODY SENSATION

You can also call a part forth by emotion or body sensation:

"I want to talk to the sadness."

"I want to talk to the part that is feeling angry."

"I want to talk to the pain in my low back."

"I want to talk to the part that is creating the headache."

### BELIEF

And, finally, you can invite a part forward by what it believes:

"I want to talk to the part that believes expressing power is dangerous."

"I want to talk to the part that believes I am unworthy of love."

"I want to talk to the part that believes living my purpose is bad for me."

You don't have to have a name for a part to talk to it; you just need a simple way to differentiate it from other parts. You can use these same categories to identify your client's parts.

# Self Integration

At the center of the psyche is the Self, which is compassionate and wise. The Self integrates the work of the parts as they help us to cope, deal with difficulties or protect us from pain. The Self is not a part; it acts as a witness or a conductor who becomes increasingly aware of parts and can bring all parts into alignment. The Self sits in the seat of benevolent sovereignty. When the coach helps the client separate parts from the Self, and listens to each, it creates opportunities for choice that benefit the whole system.

According to Schwartz, the Self is the natural leader of the psyche, and different from all the parts. The energy of the Self is calm, balanced, vibrant, connected, confident, joyful, peaceful and more. The Self has the capacity to take leadership of the parts, resolve inner conflicts and return balance to the system.

Embracing the Shadow becomes a spiritual practice of continuously opening our hearts to all parts. Not by forcing the Self to be more loving, but by allowing compassion to naturally arise just by listening to and accepting all parts. The awareness that we all have similar parts supports the sense that we are all connected. From a reservoir of deep wisdom, the Self serves the whole as a compassionate witness. The Self is not attached to a particular agenda, but is a resource for centered action.

When a part finishes speaking and we thank the part, we can give the Self time to reflect on what's been said. Given a chance to speak, parts often have profound insights, so giving the Self a chance to reflect creates the opportunity to cherish all parts and integrate their collective wisdom.

Richard Schwartz says, "the goal is not to fuse all these smaller personalities into a single big one. It is instead to restore leadership, balance and harmony, so that each part can take its preferred, valuable role."[2]

Helping clients interact with their protectors—to understand, appreciate and honor them, no matter how destructive their behavior has been—is a way of helping all parts to trust the Self to take the lead.

# Structuring a Session

### Prepare for the session

1. Take a moment to self-connect, remember your coach's stand and set your intention to serve your client.

2. Connect with your client.

3. Get clear about your client's intention for the session.

4. Explain the purpose of Embracing the Shadow—to create space for parts to be acknowledged.

5. Ensure that your client is ready to begin.

---

2    Schwartz, Richard, Ph.D.. (1995) Internal Family Systems. The Guilford Press, New York, N.Y.

### Begin the session

1. Identify a part that would like to be understood more fully.

2. Get permission from the protectors to talk to the part.

3. Ask the client to move to a new place in the room to embody that part.

4. Get to know the part by asking curious questions.

5. Ask the part what it would like to be called.

6. When that part has finished speaking, thank the part for its service.

7. Ask your client to move back to the original position of the Self.

### Debrief the session

1. Check in with the Self to learn how it is reacting to what the part just shared.

2. Give the Self some reflection time to make meaning from the experience.

3. Ask the Self to summarize what the part said and describe the impact on the Self.

4. Share your impression or your sense of how the part serves.

5. Ask if there is anything else the Self needs for closure.

6. If a new or opposite part wants to be heard, ask the new part to choose another location and repeat the process.

### Getting permission to work with parts

The first step in working with parts is to get permission. Embracing the shadow only succeeds if we respect all parts. If we ignore them, don't believe them or make their fears seem inconsequential, we ostracize them and reduce the chances of bringing parts into alignment. If we judge them, banish them or argue with them, the whole system loses trust.

It's only natural for parts of the psyche to have reservations about change. If we insist on change, without getting all parts on board, the change won't be sustainable. The resistor comes back with a vengeance. Furthermore, resistors always have our best interest in mind. If a part doesn't want us to revisit a childhood trauma, it has a good reason. If it doesn't want us on the stage, it has a good reason for that too. Every part is invested in our well-being. Maybe it's blocking our progress because we truly aren't ready for the change or our life is in danger. Maybe we will get fired or get hurt or lose our friends if we change. Whatever the reason, if a part is unwilling to give us permission to do shadow work, we need to honor their fears and discover their underlying positive intent.

With that in mind, we ask all parts for permission to do the work. If we don't get permission, we don't move forward. The easiest way to gain permission is simply to ask for it and then listen. If a part comes forth with some reservations, and we listen to their fears with reverence, permission is often granted. If that's not enough, we can get curious about the part and learn about their worst fears. Only then do we negotiate; not by arguing or convincing, but by listening respectfully to objections and asking for the part's conditions or requests. We can ask:

What topics are off limits?

What would make it possible to have a discussion?

What conditions would you like to set?

If you sense any danger, will you let me know?

If you start to feel unsafe, will you stop the process?

Whatever agreements we make, we keep our end of the bargain. If the part wants to stop the process, we don't say, "Can I ask you just one more question?" We stop immediately, thank the part for taking a stand, for insisting on safety and for its honorable service. That way we can build trust over time and can keep the door open for future conversations.

### Getting Permission Example

When Lara came to coaching, she'd already done a lot of work on herself. She was widely known as a leader in her field. As an Asian woman, she was angry that women and Asians weren't promoted in her organization. Part of her wanted to speak out and change policies and another part didn't want to rock the boat. Lara had already been doing some parts work so she wanted to explore these two parts more deeply.

Coach: I would like to talk to the part that wants to speak out and change policies. Will you check in to see if any parts object or want to set some conditions?

Lara: [silence] My protector is saying that it's okay to talk to the part that wants to change as long as you also talk to the part that doesn't want to rock the boat.

Coach: Okay. Agreed. Can I talk to your protector for a moment?

Lara: Sure.

Coach: Okay, so step out of your Self and become the protector. Go to a place in the room where you feel most comfortable.

Lara: [moves to the window] Okay, he is ready to talk to you.

Coach: Good. So protector, can you say that again, "I am ready to talk to you." (requesting Lara to be the protector, speak in the first person, instead of talking about the protector).

Lara (Protector): I am ready to talk to you. It's okay to talk to this part that wants change, but you must also listen to the part that doesn't want to rock the boat.

Coach: Sounds important.

Lara (Protector): Very important. She could lose her job.

Coach: So your role is crucial. You keep Lara from losing her job.

Lara (Protector): Yes. I'm fiercely protective of her.

Coach: Thank you for protecting her. For keeping her safe.

Lara (Protector): I'm astounded that you're thanking me, because Lara doesn't like me very much. She wishes I'd just go away.

Coach: What touches me is that you're still willing to serve Lara, even though you think she doesn't like you. Such dedication.

Lara (Protector): Thank you. I work hard.

Coach:  Is there anything else you want Lara to know?

Lara (Protector): It wouldn't hurt for her to appreciate me once in a while.

Coach:  And what would you most like to be appreciated for?

Lara (Protector): For making sure she's respected. Keeping her employed. Making sure people like her. Also I want to make sure she knows how much I care about her. Without me, she'd be miserable.

Coach:  I will tell her you care about her and how hard you've worked to make sure she's respected.

Lara (Protector): Thanks.

Coach:  So you've set the condition that we also talk to the Don't-Rock-the-Boat part. Are there any other requests that will keep Lara safe?

Lara (Protector): That's enough.

Coach:  If anything comes up that might seem dangerous, will you stop the process?

Lara (Protector): Don't worry. I'll do that. I'm always here.

Coach:  If you say the word "stop," we will stop. Thanks for keeping Lara out of danger.

Lara (Protector): You're welcome. I take my job seriously.

Coach:  We'll keep our agreement and talk to both parts.

*Self Integration Example*

Coach:  Can you leave the protector role, shake that off and come back to your seat and be your Self now.

Lara:    Okay, I'm back. That was interesting to hear from my protector.

Coach:  Yes, your protector wants you to know how much he cares about you and how hard he works to make sure you are respected.

Lara:    I didn't know that. I've always found the protector a bit of nuisance, but now I have a new appreciation for his dedication.

Coach:  Would you like to take a moment to appreciate all the ways your protector has served you?

Lara:    Yes, in addition to appreciating the protector for all his years of keeping me safe and respected, I want to thank my protector for loving me. I used to think my protector was mean, but now I'm really clear how much he cares about me.

## Getting to know parts

Instead of talking *about* the parts, we talk *with* the parts. We invite parts to speak for themselves, to share their viewpoint, feelings and needs *in their own words*. Parts express surprise and delight when they finally get a chance to speak. Even more important, when they learn that the client is truly eager to listen—that's where the healing begins.

Just like people, parts want to be known and appreciated. Thanking these parts for their service goes a long way toward helping them feel valued.

Many parts will speak of their own accord without much prompting. If the part shows some reticence, we can hold silence or ask some curious questions to get to know a part.

What do you want to say?

What is it like to be you?

What are your gifts?

What role do you play?

How do you help out?

What do you need?

What does authenticity mean for you?

What else do you want to say?

*Getting to Know Parts Example*

Coach: May I speak to the part of you that doesn't want to rock the boat?

Lara: Yes, the part who doesn't want to rock the boat definitely wants to speak to you.

Coach: Okay, will you go to the place in the room where you can fully be this part?

Coach: And what name would you like to be called?

Lara: Don't Rock the Boat

Coach: Okay, Don't Rock the Boat, what do you want to say?

Lara (Don't Rock the Boat): The organization just took thousands of full-time jobs and made them all part time so that they don't have to pay benefits. At the other end of the spectrum, the senior executives' salaries have skyrocketed. And then they wonder why people don't show up for work.

Coach: What matters most to you?

Lara (Don't Rock the Boat): Even though I know how angry Lara is about the policies at work, I think she needs to keep a low profile if she wants the respect of her peers.

Coach: So you really want her to have respect.

Lara (Don't Rock the Boat): Yes, it's not part of my upbringing to speak up about injustice. As an Asian woman, I've learned to take up very little space and to honor other's opinions. Harmony is more important. But I wish Lara could find some courage and speak up for the underdog.

Coach: I'm hearing another part coming in—the part that wants Lara to speak up. Before we hear from that part, I'd like to give Don't Rock the Boat a chance to finish. Don't Rock the Boat, what do you need?

Lara (Don't Rock the Boat): I need to help Lara find inner harmony amidst all the turmoil.

Coach: What do you want to tell Lara?

Lara (Don't Rock the Boat): Hmmm… it's a funny thing, but I want her to find inner harmony so that she can speak up for human dignity.

Coach: You play an important role in Lara's life—supporting her to find inner harmony. Thanks for serving her. Now can you go back to Lara's seat?

Lara: I'm back.

Coach: What was it like to hear from Don't Rock the Boat?

Lara: Intense... inspiring... helps me understand the deeper motivation. To find inner harmony before speaking.

Coach: Okay, are you ready to hear from the part that wants to speak up?

Lara: Sure.

### Empathizing with parts

Parts do not change because we get them to see the errors of their ways. Ironically, parts are most likely to shift because we value them exactly as they are. Initially, most parts have no idea what they need, nor do they know why they do what they do.

Once we start talking to a part, we can connect empathically by:

creating a sense of safety

matching their energy

getting curious

mirroring them physically

reflecting their words

asking questions to understand

exploring emotions

listening for their needs

recognizing their positive intentions

appreciating their contribution to the whole

## Connecting with the Part's Energy or Life Force

Sometimes we refer to parts as energies. In seeking the gift that each part brings, we put our attention on their energy, which can reveal their underlying purpose. Even if a part is frustrated, angry or hurt, underneath is the life force. When we feel into the core of the anger or pain, we fully accept the emotions and create space for the fullness of their expression.

At the center of longing is pure energy. Connect with that pure energy and the heavens open. Just sitting with the pure energy of a part can be a deeply satisfying, mystical experience.

By inviting parts to go inside to sense their deepest yearning, we help them detach from their habitual beliefs and feelings and connect with the life energy as it flows within. This can be a moving experience as parts connect with something beautiful or divine. The shift away from lack and toward fulfillment can be a pivot point. Giving a part space to meditate on its longing for respect (for example), the longing dissolves into actual respect—respect for self, respect for the moment, respect for what is, respect for what's emerging. As the part imagines having deep respect, (which is not the same as how they think the need for respect should be met), they tune into the energy and move toward a state of bliss.

The energy that flows through us is sacred. Connecting with the beautiful, wild, powerful energy of life offers us a place of respite and peace. When we slow down and connect with the ecstatic flow of life, we get in touch with the longing and embody it. We experience the longing in a deeply fulfilling way, in our bodies, in our emotions and in our very being. Often times, parts come to realize that they already have exactly what they need.

*Connecting with the Part's Energy or Life Force Example*

Coach: Speak Up, you've found a place to stand that feels comfortable to you?

Lara (Speak Up): Yes, and I'm ready to talk!

Coach: I hear you…

Lara (Speak Up): You know what angers me the most? It's the people at the top giving themselves millions of dollars in bonuses while the hourly workers have to go out and get a second job just to pay the rent.

Coach: because you want to live in a world where…

Lara (Speak Up): …people care about all people, not just themselves. I want a world where people who have power use it to benefit the entire community, not just a few individuals. How many houses and boats and vacations does anyone really need?

Coach: I'm sensing more anger about something else… what's that?

Lara (Speak Up): I'm angry at Lara for not taking a stand. She cares more about her own little comfortable world than she cares about making a difference for others.

Coach: I'm hearing how much you want to contribute, to help Lara to make a difference. Your energy is vibrant and comes from a place of anger and love.

Lara (Speak Up): I'm a fighter!

Coach: Yes, and you fight because you long for a more caring world. What happens if you imagine living in a world where people care deeply for one another?

Lara (Speak Up): I get a little tearful…

Coach: And what do those tears want?

Lara (Speak Up): Integrity for Lara. Congruence between what she says and what she does.

Coach: So imagine she has that…integrity, congruence…

Lara (Speak Up): I can relax… appreciate Lara… support her more fully.

Coach: Before you go into supporting her more fully, just stay in that energy of your longing, allowing it to nourish you. Each breath filling you with more caring, more integrity, more alignment.

Lara (Speak Up): That feels wonderful.

Coach: Staying with your caring energy, what do you want Lara to know?

Lara (Speak Up): She can take her longing for caring with her wherever she goes. That will make it easy for her to speak up about injustice.

Coach: Ah, I can see how that connection to her caring is very nourishing. Are you ready to return to the Self?

Lara (Self): That was precious. I am much more connected to my energy, my desire to create a caring world, and from here, it's easy for me to speak up. At the same time I can still take care of myself. I have much more hope about being able to make a difference.

Coach: Staying connected to your life force, how will you make a difference?

Lara: First I want to spend time with myself, just appreciating this internal shift. Then I'm going to have several conversations with people at work and find the allies who want all people to make a living wage. Then we can create a plan to work with the decision-makers.

Coach: Let's take a moment to celebrate the alignment of your parts, and how that activates you.

Lara: I'm glowing…

## Detecting New Parts

Listening to parts is usually very simple as long as we hold respect. Perhaps the trickiest part of the process is noticing when a new part comes into the system. But how do we know if it's the same part or a different part? The telltale sign is a shift in emotion or energy. The body or the voice might shift too. When a part expresses a radical change in its belief or shifts to holding a new set of values, that's usually a sign that another part has decided to speak.

If the Strict Parent part suddenly says, "Well maybe it wouldn't be so bad to give the children more freedom to make their own choices and mistakes," that's not the Strict Parent part having an epiphany, it's the Lenient Parent wanting to be heard. Or if the Perfectionist suddenly sighs and says, "Perhaps I've been too controlling; maybe it's okay to make the decision before we have all the data," we can be sure another part is speaking. Occasionally a part does want to change strategies, but it continues to hold its values diligently.

Why is it important to differentiate between parts? Each part needs to be heard. If one part interrupts another, and we let that slide, we lose the trust of the whole system. We can step in and say, "I want to hear from you too," but first, I'd like to let the Perfectionist finish speaking. Once one part gets heard and appreciated, many more parts start lining up to be heard. It's very common for clients to be completely unaware that a new part has taken over, so we need to be vigilant about holding space for each part to finish speaking before another starts.

When in doubt, we can ask, "I hear a change in what you value. Is that a new part that has just spoken?"

Avoid the eager beginner's mistake of starting with, "Hello critic. I'm here to fix you." Good luck getting that part to show up or even talk to you again. Instead, get to know the part. Ask about its role, its purpose, how it feels and what it needs. The part will let you know when it's ready to make a change.

## Active Imagination

One of the ways clients can continue to work with parts is to ask them to practice Active Imagination as homework. Active Imagination is a Jungian technique developed to help people interpret their dreams. Like writing a play, we write a script, speaking with a part that appeared in our dream or in our psyche. In writing, we ask the part why it has appeared now. Then, imagining we are the part, we include the part's response in the script, and continue the dialog by asking curious questions such as: What is your role? What do you do? What do you want?

This practice can lead to extraordinary insights. The process is simply to ask to speak to a part and write down the conversation.

> *Active Imagination Example*
>
> Self: I'd like to speak to the part of me that doesn't want me to travel so much.
>
> Part: I'm here.
>
> Self: Can I ask you a few questions?
>
> Part: Sure. But I wish you'd just stay home.
>
> Self: How come?
>
> Part: You know why! It's because you get so depleted when you travel.
>
> Self: So you want me to be more rested?
>
> Part: More important than that, I want you to have better relationships with the people you love. Get a life!
>
> Self: What would you like me to call you?
>
> Part: Mr. Priority
>
> Self: Okay Mr. Priority, what's most important to you?
>
> Mr. Priority: Your relationships, of course!

Keep the dialog flowing until the part has said all it wants to say. No arguing with the part or giving it advice. Just listen with curiosity and learn all you can about the part. To wrap up the dialog, take a moment to appreciate the part, even if you don't like how it's acting or what it's saying.

The process of active imagination allows us to shift from seeing the figures in our dreams as external people, and begin to see them as parts of ourselves. We become conscious of our shadow parts and the process helps us reclaim lost parts and welcome them home.

## Working with a Wounded Child

Almost everyone has been wounded, physically or emotionally. Our original wounding—the first time we found out that we are not okay—often becomes a driving force in our lives. The first time an innocent child hears, "No!" can be traumatic. Bewildered, the child starts to believe it is flawed or not good enough. Core beliefs become embedded in the psyche, such as, "I don't matter. I am bad. If I don't do what people ask, I won't be loved." Even people who have had extraordinary parenting and idyllic childhoods usually have a wounded child within.

When a wounded child begins to re-emerge, this is a vulnerable moment. Our role as coaches is to be present, hold the pain with compassion and liberate the energy that's held within the wound. Within the vulnerability flows life itself.

We don't rush through this; we just stay present, sitting with the child, without trying to change it. There is nothing to get over or get through. Mourning opens the heart and helps the child to meet life fully. Mourning is pure sadness—a feeling that often has no words. The sadness is very alive and connected to something valuable that has been lost. The yearning is for that precious thing the child has lost.

When the child rests in the pure life energy of its desire, the old core belief loses its power. The original trigger is replaced by unconditional acceptance of life energy.

We only work with the Wounded Child if the protectors agree. They often have very good reasons for keeping the child hidden, so we make friends with the protectors before asking to talk to a wounded child. If the protectors refuse, we talk to those parts rather than the Wounded Child. Perhaps they have conditions that we must agree to before they'll give us permission. If they are adamant about not talking to Wounded Child, we thank them for keeping that part safe.

The Wounded Child's role is to hold all the suppressed emotions connected to the original trigger. So we accept all expressions of emotions with compassion. We don't try to change the wounded child unless it specifically asks for help with a change. We don't give advice or try to get it to see things differently or encourage it to grow up.

Many child parts are fragile or delicate and need to be held with care. Our role as a coach is to listen and help the client's Self to integrate what the child part has expressed. In doing so, we create a warm relationship and connect empathically with the child's feelings. Some child parts are too young to speak, but we can still honor them by giving them space to gurgle, cry or be held.

Only when we let the child know that we really get how bad it has been do they begin to release the burden.

### Working with a Wounded Child Example

Claire wanted to change her relationship with her father, but she had not spoken to him in years. "I don't even remember why I stopped talking to him; it was so long ago…" Her coach intuitively sensed that Claire was protecting a wounded child that needed to be heard, so asked for permission to talk to her little girl. Claire's protectors agreed.

Coach: I want to thank your protectors for introducing me to your little girl and allowing me to talk to her.

Claire: Okay, she's a little tentative…

Coach: Yes… can you be the little girl and move to a place in the room where the little girl would like to be? And just feel the tentativeness.

Claire: The little girl is sitting on the floor behind the chair.

Coach: So can you sit on the floor and be the little girl? Thanks for meeting with me today. What's it like to be you?

Claire: [silence] She cannot talk.

Coach: Okay, so just be the little girl and feel what the little girl feels.

Claire: [more silence] I'm scared.

Coach: What's scary?

Claire (Little Girl): I'm not loveable.

Coach: When was the first time you thought you were not loveable?

Claire (Little Girl): … When my mother died, my father sent me to live with my aunt in Mexico. I didn't speak the language. I didn't know anyone. I begged him not to leave me there, but he said, "You remind me too much of your mother," and he walked away.

Coach: So you've been carrying a lot of feelings that Claire didn't want to experience.

Claire (Little Girl): Yes, I was hurt, crushed, lost.

Coach: Which parts did you enlist as your allies to help Claire?

Claire (Little Girl): Mainly, the protector. When Claire's father came back to get her a month later, the protector insisted that Claire not look at or speak to her father. And he's been reminding her of that ever since.

Coach: So the protector is keeping Claire from looking at or talking to her father. And what has happened to you?

Claire (Little Girl): Most of the time, I don't think Claire even knows I exist. She ignores me completely.

Coach: And what would you like from Claire?

Claire (Little Girl): I'd like her to pick me up and hold me once in a while. Talk to me.

Coach: What would you tell her if she would listen?

Claire (Little Girl): That I'm sad. And lonely. I'm not loveable.

Coach: So you'd like Claire to know how bad it is for you. That you're sad and you'd like some attention and some love?

Claire (Little Girl): [big sigh] Yes. I just want to say how much I want to be loved.

Coach: Anything else you'd like Claire to know?

Claire (Little Girl): I feel relieved to be listened to like this…

Coach: Thanks so much for sharing what it's like to be you and telling me what's really going on inside.

Claire (Little Girl): I want Claire to just talk to me once in a while.

Coach: I will talk to Claire about that. Are you ready to move back to Claire's chair?

Claire: Phew… yes… I didn't even know I had a wounded little girl inside. That was intense. I had completely forgotten about living with my aunt for a month and what that felt like.

Coach: So take some time to integrate. [pause] Now that you've heard from your little girl, how does that impact you?

Claire: I appreciate her a lot more now. I want to spend some time with my little girl, getting to know her. I'm feeling more tender toward my father. But I'm still really angry with my father.

Coach:   So let's talk to that angry part of you and the tender part next week. How does that sound? [coach recognizes a new part coming in and names it]

Claire:   Okay.

Coach:   Would you like to spend some time this week with your little girl? Just getting to know her?

Claire:   Yes, I'll do that.

## Transformation of Parts

Most parts do not want or need to be transformed. They just need to be heard. Once clients integrate the information from multiple parts, they can make informed decisions about what changes they wish to make.

Above all else, parts need to be loved exactly as they are. If they get a hint that we are trying to change them, they interpret that as judgment, and rightly so. Coaches can get into trouble if we imply there is anything wrong with the part. One whiff of that and the part feels misunderstood and loses trust.

Once parts are deeply understood, they can relax, and that can be all the transformation they need. The purpose of Embracing the Shadow is not to transform troublesome parts, but to appreciate each part's contribution.

As agents of change, we need to check our impulse to try to get parts to relax, reform or retire. If we find some parts too unruly or think of them as destructive, it can be helpful to do our own inner work with our disowned parts. It can be difficult to embrace our clients' parts until we have embraced our own. Until we can love a part unconditionally, we cannot possibly support its transformation.

When parts come to the conclusion that they want transformation on their own, there are many ways we can serve. Because most of our dominant parts are working 24/7, they become exhausted and can't even imagine taking a break. When we welcome home and honor the parts that they have been trying to protect, they gain confidence that the child-parts can heal. Only then can the protectors relax. They begin to collaborate and rely on other parts to keep the vulnerable parts safe. In that way, we can expand the capacity of the psyche to access creative solutions.

All parts have important jobs, but most of those job descriptions were created long ago, when we were children. Life has changed, but some parts remain unaware that they are following outdated rules. Because each part is completely dedicated and has an underlying desire to serve, it may begin to recognize better ways to serve. When a part indicates it wants a promotion to a more valuable role, we can hold space for the part to expand its capacity to serve, without asking leading questions.

For transformation to be sustainable, we explore the past, present and future. We start by asking questions about the past so that we understand how the part came into being, its intention and how it operates. From there we look at the present by asking the part for its purpose or its deepest wish. Often there is a disparity between the part's intention and its impact. Looking at the gap invites the part into the space for change.

When we look at the future, we keep the part's purpose and skill set and help them redefine their role. The part may change its name in recognition of its new position. It can become a powerful ally when it rewrites its job description, so that it can become even more valuable. When asking questions, we empower the part to make its own decisions regarding a new role.

### Parts Transformation Example

Coach:  Last time we spoke, your Critic wanted a new role. Want to look at that now?

Mia:  Yes, that would be good because I could use a break from all my negative self-talk.

Coach:  Okay, let's start by honoring the Critic. Can you go to a place where the Critic wants to sit or stand?

Mia (Critic): I'm definitely standing. I can't sit down for a moment.

PAST (Get to know the part's role, and appreciate it, without trying to change it in any way.)

Coach:  What's been your job?

Mia (Critic): I point out mistakes and get Mia to change. I let her know when she looks ugly, fat or stupid. I tell her when she is lazy. I point out her flaws and tell her when she should shut up.

Coach:  How has all of this helped Mia in the past?

Mia (Critic): When I criticize Mia before other people do, I've kept Mia from suffering. And I've made sure that people like her. Because of me she knows when to change her behavior.

Coach:  What's your earliest memory of the first time you helped Mia?

Mia (Critic): I made sure she didn't take too many cookies.

Coach:  What happened that first got you activated?

Mia (Critic): Mia's mother told her she was being selfish and Mia was devastated. And I wanted to make sure that never happened again.

Coach:  Thanks for all that you've done to make Mia a better person.

PRESENT (Discover the part's higher purpose and deepest desire to serve.)

Coach:  What do you like to be called?

Mia (Critic): Critic is fine.

Coach:  Okay Critic, how do you currently serve?

Mia (Critic): Anytime I think Mia won't be liked, I intervene.

Coach:  What do you really want?

Mia (Critic): To keep Mia from being selfish and get her to care about others.

Coach:  What's even more important than that?

Mia (Critic): That she have friends who care about her.

Coach:  What's your highest purpose?

Critic:    To make sure Mia is loved.

Coach:  You sound very satisfied with your role and you are fulfilling an important purpose.

Mia (Critic): I do a good job. But I could do a better job… by helping her make friends and create loving relationships.

Coach:  What do you really want, more than anything?

Mia (Critic): To stop working so hard! To relax once in a while.


FUTURE (Creating a more collaborative future by helping the part write its new job description. Only do this if the part indicates it wants to make a change.)

Coach:  What would be the best use of your talents?

Mia (Critic): To help Mia discern how to make lasting friendships.

Coach:  What is a way to achieve your purpose?

Mia (Critic): Criticizing her so much doesn't work so well, so maybe I could help her be more discerning in how she relates to people.

Coach:  What role could you play in helping Mia relate to people?

Mia (Critic): I'm very discerning, so I could help her notice injustices and speak up in loving ways.

Coach:  If you could do any job for Mia, what would you choose?

Mia (Critic): Activist.

Coach:  Would you like a job promotion?

Mia (Critic): Yes, it's not that useful for me to constantly criticize Mia when I could be doing so much more. I want to help her build bridges and create great relationships.

Coach:  Given your new role, would you like a new name?

Critic:    Yes, I'd like to be called the Activist.

Coach:  Okay, Activist, I want to express gratitude from my heart. Not only have you served Mia diligently for years, but you are willing to step into a new role to help her create better relationships.

## Follow up

Just because a part experiences an epiphany, is profoundly moved and accepts a job promotion, doesn't mean the work is done. For transformation to take root and be sustainable, follow up is essential. In subsequent sessions we can ask the part:

How is your new job going?

What do you like most about your new role?

How could we tweak the job description so it's even more enjoyable for you?

What support do you need to be successful in your new role?

I've noticed that you have been collaborating with other parts.

## Working with an Internal Oppressor

Carl Rogers said, "The curious paradox is that when I accept myself just as I am, then I can change." The same is true about accepting parts. Instead of admonishing or fighting against an internal oppressor, if we simply witness and accept the oppressors' beliefs and emotions, we move closer to a mindful state that helps parts relax.

If we're part of a marginalized group and we experience prejudice, we often internalize oppression over time. Consciously or unconsciously, a part of us believes in the stereotypes and holds an oppressive view toward our identity group, whether we're a person of color, a woman, LGBTQQ, working class or survivors of other social constructs. When we internalize the values, beliefs and myths of our culture, we can sink into profound self-doubt.

We experience internal ridicule, criticism or punishment when part of us starts to use the methods of our oppressors against ourselves. Sometimes our internal oppressors silence us, express hatred or suggest death. But why? What's the positive intent or deeper purpose when the oppressor tells us, "You're not good at math. You're lazy. You probably won't succeed. You're so ugly. Too dark. Worthless." Ultimately the internal oppressor is trying to keep us safe, protect us from pain and ensure survival. But the methods of an internal oppressor can be brutal, so it isn't easy to open our hearts or even listen to these parts. Often their comments are directed toward the wounded child, which sounds an alarm because we want to protect the child from further abuse.

The internal oppressor seems to be ever present, but lies dormant until a real or perceived threat is experienced or remembered, then springs into action. It is not helpful to try to convince our internal oppressor that we are actually good, worthy or capable. Nor does it help to cast it aside. To negate the impact of the internal oppressor, the temptation is to call in the inner cheerleader to say, "You're beautiful. Brilliant. Just the right size. Strong. Worthy. So loveable. Perfect in every way." However, that only agitates the internal oppressor who only wants to be understood and valued.

Not just child parts, but oppressors can also use some re-parenting. Thich Nhat Hahn said, "You calm your feeling just by being with it, like a mother tenderly holding her crying baby. Feeling the mother's tenderness, the baby will calm down and stop crying." Through tenderness, it's possible to create a loving relationship with an emotional upset part, the same way we soothe a crying child. By engaging and respecting troubling, dominating parts of the psyche, intense emotions and outmoded beliefs can be released.

One of the most difficult aspects of Embracing the Shadow is to try to open our hearts to inner tyrants—ours or our clients. To release our own judgments about oppressors supports our clients in releasing theirs. As we gain greater access to our Self, we can be more fully present to engage with our clients' oppressors. In a compassionate, curious, mindful state, we can learn how the oppressor is suffering or what it is trying so desperately to protect.

Richard Schwartz says, "The Buddhist teacher Tsultrim Allione revived an ancient Tibetan tradition called Chod, which has practitioners feeding rather than fighting with their inner 'demons.' She finds that once fed with curiosity and compassion, these inner enemies reveal what they really need, feel accepted and heard, and become allies."

The Self is not only accepting, but has access to internal wisdom to connect deeply with all parts and has the capacity to heal the system. Instead of admonishing or fighting against the internal oppressor, if we simply witness and accept the oppressors' beliefs and emotions, we move closer to a mindful state that helps parts transform.

Similar to wounded children, the internalized oppressor is seeking love and support from the Self. As parts develop healthy relationships with the Self, their terror and suffering transform. When that happens the entire internal family deepens its trust in the Self, leading to more functional, fulfilling relationships.

For example, Noah, a man of color, came to coaching to work on internalized oppression. Most of his life he had diligently avoided behaviors that might reinforce racial stereotypes. The internal pressure to dress impeccably, keep a smile on his face and work long hours were impacting his health. His coach helped him listen for the positive intent of his internal oppressors, which included protecting him from other's criticism, being seen for his positivity and keeping him safe. Only then could he develop self-compassion, full expression and a healthier lifestyle. Revitalized, he got coaching on having crucial conversations with his boss. Over time he renegotiated his work hours and created more equality in the relationship. His coach helped him bring his parts into alignment. Once he attuned to his spiritual core, he made systemic changes in his organization and expanded opportunities for marginalized groups.

## When to Embrace the Shadow

Honoring all parts becomes a way of life. Whenever we see or hear parts that are out of alignment, we can bring them in by asking them to speak. We'll notice misalignment because we'll hear polarized voices vying for attention. It's only natural for parts that value the status quo to block the parts that want to make changes. When our clients experience internal conflict, this pathway is a form of internal mediation.

They may experience internal conflict at many levels: mental, emotional, physical and behavioral.

> I think I want to work with children / What if I can't make a living? (mental)

> I'm excited to move forward / I'm afraid to take action. (emotional)

> I really want to leave this firm / When I start to write my resignation letter, I get a headache. (physical)

> My goal is to start a group for LGBTQQ allies / I haven't asked anyone to join. (behavioral)

Through practice, the nuances of Embracing the Shadow will come. Our protectors naturally have reactions. They may be skeptical or block us, but with patience, we can do the inner work at the pace our internal system can handle. Our continual deep inner work supports our outer work. When we transcend our limiting beliefs we can work at a much deeper level.

Imagine having the skills to help people hear these discordant voices, and create sacred space for each part to be heard and unified, so that people awaken to greater wisdom, energy and possibilities.

Some parts have no desire to be transformed—they were activated to help us deal with very challenging or even dangerous situations and they are serious about protecting us. But we learn to work with parts that are highly resistant to change by opening our hearts. When in doubt, love the part. Get curious. Honor the part's wisdom.

Genuine connection comes from accepting each part exactly as it is, and acknowledging the importance of its role. That alone often leads to the golden sigh—that moment when shift happens. Ironically, transformation happens more often when we accept what is, not when we press for change.

## Honoring the Coach's Parts

If we do our own inner work with our own parts, we're less likely to hold judgment of a part of ourselves, and therefore we're less likely to judge that part when we encounter it in others. It can be difficult to advocate for social justice if we haven't brought social justice to our internal world. The healing and reparation work of honoring marginalized parts starts at the individual level, but impacts families, organizations and larger systems. Honoring all parts means we take a stand for honoring internal and external diversity.

As coaches, we often attract clients who are working on issues similar to our own. Their troubled parts are often similar to our troubled parts. Inevitably, our clients trigger us. When we get hijacked, occasionally compassion, curiosity and courage are not enough to return us to a state of equilibrium. Suppose a critical internal part says, "You're a terrible coach," right in the middle of a session, and follows that up with, "You should just quit, right now. You're not helping." First we can take a breath and empathize with the Critic, "I hear how troubled you are, but if you can step aside for now, I'll talk to you right after the session." Many parts are willing to step back temporarily if they know they will eventually be heard.

The process, the structure, the skills we use in Embracing the Shadow are not nearly as important as how we connect—with an open heart, deep curiosity and full presence. By loving each part of ourselves, we create trust that all parts can get the understanding they've been wanting. When we connect energetically with a part, and allow ourselves to emotionally engage, other parts begin to trust us. We can bring ourselves into the relationship with each part, without bias, without disconnecting. This opens the doorway for our clients to do the same.

Doing our inner work deepens our trust—in ourselves, in our clients and in the process. When we know how to listen deeply to all the voices in our inner world, we are naturally more effective in getting others to do the same. But we don't have to wait until every part of our internal committee is in harmony. We can start by honoring parts that want to be heard, and keep welcoming new parts as they show up. Our parts will love us for it—many will be astounded and grateful to finally be heard.

*Questions to Consider*

What parts of yourself are you eager to get to know?

What parts of yourself are blocking you from doing shadow work?

What parts of your clients would you like to avoid?

What is your commitment to exploring your inner critic?

# Section III:
# Making Visions Real

*Whatever you can do or dream you can, begin it. Boldness has genius, power, and magic in it.* —*Goethe*

Section III focuses on movement. It provides suggestions and strategies for turning dreams, goals and actions into reality. Section I focused on the coaching relationship and core coaching skills. Section II provided a range of processes that support clients in coming into alignment with their values, purpose and core selves. Once clients become clear and aligned, they are ready to move into action—action that creates desired changes in their personal and professional lives. Clear, aligned action supports individuals, groups, teams and organizations—and you as a coach. What is your vision for your coaching practice? Who are your ideal clients? How will you make your dreams a reality? Keep these questions in mind as you review the methods for supporting clients to move into action and as you review the chapter on *The Business of Coaching*. Remember, transformation requires both awareness and action.

# 10
# Strategy and Action

*A journey of a thousand miles begins with a single step. —Lao-Tzu*

This chapter is about supporting clients to strategize, create action plans and turn their visions and dreams into reality. Using the five pathways to alignment, new possibilities and perspectives emerge, which invite action and changes in their world. Action based on awareness makes transformation an integral part of our clients' new reality. What's possible when they face fear and take concrete steps toward a new way of living and being? What opens when awareness leads to clarity and clarity leads to action? What happens when things that once felt only remotely possible begin to take shape and fully emerge? Actualization is exciting for both coaches and clients.

## Strategic Planning

*A vision without a plan is just a dream. A plan without a vision is just drudgery. But a vision with a plan can change the world. —Old Proverb*

A strategic plan helps individuals and organizations determine where they stand, where they wish to go and how they plan to get there. By focusing on the big picture, long-term planning creates an opportunity for people to design their lives. As coaches, we help people become the authors of their lives and create their ideal future. How do we support them to choose actions that are aligned with their values, vision and purpose? How do they prioritize their goals and action plans? How do they allocate their resources? What strategies help them to take leadership and be the change they wish to see in the world? To ensure that action plans are compelling, we offer several tools and templates to support whole life strategic planning:

Balance Wheel

SMART Goals

Stretch Goals

Expand Your Comfort Zone

Planning Tool

Support System

A strategic plan includes a map with the final destination and directions on how to get where we're going. Whole-life strategic planning starts with the values, vision and purpose work explored earlier, which help us see our destiny. Once we have clarity about what's compelling, we look at our whole life, assessing our satisfaction with each area using the balance wheel. After comparing where we are with where we want to go, we close the gap by designing goals, action plans and support systems to create our ideal lives. Action plans naturally evolve from values, vision, purpose and balance wheel work. The diagram below shows the relationships of these various pieces.

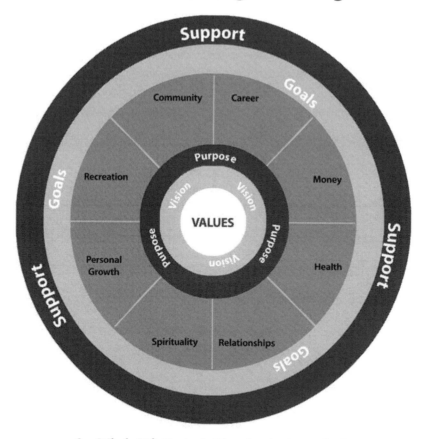

See Whole Life Strategic Planning in Appendix I.

# Balance

The life balance wheel gives a snapshot of our life right now, allowing us to assess our level of satisfaction in different areas of life and serving as a foundation for our strategic plan.

Instructions: With the center of the wheel as 0 and the outer edge as 10, rank your level of satisfaction with each life area by drawing a curved line to create a new outer edge. What actions can you take to increase your scores?

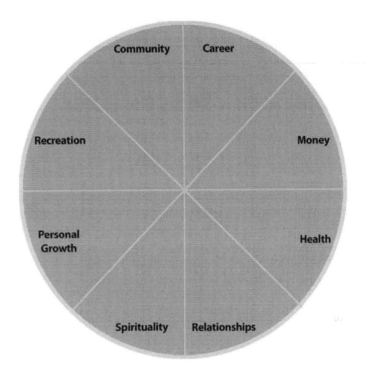

See Balance Wheel in Appendix I.

**Balance wheel categories:**

A description of each area of the balance wheel follows, but encourage clients to create their own balance wheel categories and descriptions based on what matters to them.

### Career

My work stimulates and fulfills me.

My career path makes good use of my talents.

I am proud of my contribution at work.


### Money

I have enough money to meet my basic needs and plan for the future.

I regularly contribute to a savings account.

I am free of money worries.

### Health

I exercise regularly.

I eat nourishing food.

I manage stress well.

### Relationships

I enjoy my friends and family.

My support network nurtures me.

I have meaningful connections with people I care about.

### Spirituality

My spiritual life is rich and fulfilling.

I have a spiritual practice that supports me.

My inner path and outer connectedness are sources of inspiration.

### Personal Growth

I continuously deepen my self awareness.

I actively seek personal and professional growth opportunities.

I am moving toward living the life of my dreams.

### Recreation

I regularly enjoy leisure time.

I have hobbies/activities that stimulate me.

Fun is an integral part of my life.

### Community

I belong to a community that is based on mutual respect.

I contribute to and receive support from my community.

I have an emotional connection with people who share my values.

Many coaches use the life balance wheel in the first coaching session to help clients review their whole life. Periodic review of the balance wheel can help people stay in alignment with what's most important and move into action. The balance wheel serves as a visual reminder of what life could be—imagine having straight 10s in each area of life. By looking at one area of life at a time, and exploring both short-term and long-term actions, it becomes easier to change one part of our life, one step at a time.

# Moving into Action

*If you have built castles in the air, your work need not be lost; that is where they should be. Now put the foundations under them. —Henry David Thoreau*

Actions may take a while to form, like islands coming forth in the fog. But if we hold possibilities for our clients, the action steps inevitably show up. Readiness for action steps naturally flows from alignment with values, vision and purpose.

As coaches, we help clients hold the big picture so they can align new plans with the overall strategy. When people are clear about what wants to be born and have faced the limitations of their inner or outer critics, they grow excited about bringing forth the vision. Action is the imperative that comes from a clear vision, but the vision changes as people evolve and grow.

Our client's next action is often right in front of both of us. Seek the low-lying fruit—the easy path or the opportunity for action that is ripe and ready. What actions arise from the heart and do not involve struggle and suffering? Invite them to think of stepping into action as an experiment. Experimenting has flexibility, learning and self-motivation in it.

Some empowering questions that support people to move into action are:

What is the easy way to accomplish this?

What action would keep the direction you are exploring alive?

What is your next step?

What are several small steps that would move you toward your goal?

Which one do you choose to do first?

What actions will you experiment with?

Invite your clients to notice what they are attracted to do, not what their inner critic says they should do.

# Establishing SMART Goals

*If a man knows not what harbor he seeks, any wind is the right wind. —Seneca*

Vision changes our outlook and attitude. Starting with the end in mind makes it easier to determine the goals and the path. Breaking down the goals into smaller objectives and action plans inspires us to act and increases the likelihood of success. One way to support our individual and organizational clients in goal setting is to use the SMART acronym:

**Specific:** The more specific the goal, the easier it is to implement and enlist support from others. The clearer the goal, the more powerful it becomes. Start by asking, "What is the desired outcome?" and refine it until it is concise, simple and clear.

**Measurable:** Measurable goals establish concrete criteria for determining progress and completion. Not only do you have the data to support staying on track, but you can celebrate the achievement of milestones, building momentum along the way. If a client states, "I want to become a better leader," ask, "How will you know you have achieved your goal?"

**Alive:** When goals are energizing, people are far more likely to put them into action. If goals are accompanied by a feeling of dread or if the body shrinks, reassess the goal. Set the bar high, but ensure the goals are doable. Unrealistic goals can de-motivate rather than inspire us. Goals that inspire us are not a burden, but joyful to accomplish.

**Relevant:** Without a sense of what makes the goal important, people rarely commit to or realize their goals. Ask, "What values does the goal honor? What will the goal get you? What meaning does the goal have? How does this goal make a difference for you or others? What impact will it have?"

**Time-Bound:** A useful and motivating goal is grounded within a timeframe and answers the question, "By when?" Without a completion date, there is no sense of urgency and no real commitment to the goal. A timeframe sets a clear intention of the desired completion date. A goal of increasing sales by 5 percent is meaningless without a date attached to it. "Let's expand our offerings," sounds very different from, "Let's expand our offerings by March."

SMART (specific, measurable, alive, relevant and time-bound) goals are used frequently in organizations to help employees and teams set goals they can clearly measure during performance evaluations.

*Examples of personal SMART goals:*

Improve my health by losing 12 pounds in the next 12 weeks. To achieve that goal, I commit to exercising aerobically for 30 minutes each day and to eating fruits, vegetables, whole grains and lean meats. I will keep a daily food and exercise log for the 12 weeks.

Deepen my inner awareness by meditating in silence for 20 minutes each morning for the next month and journal my insights each day.

## Compose and prioritize up to seven goals

Define your goals, starting each goal with an action verb. Make sure your goals are SMART.

Prioritize your goals from 1-7.

Ensure your goals are aligned with your values by identifying the values you will honor by achieving each goal.

Rate your commitment level to each goal: High, Medium or Low

Create an action plan by breaking down each goal into action steps with due dates.

| GOALS AND ACTION PLANNING WORKSHEET |
|---|
| Goal: |
| Priority: |
| Values: |
| Commitment level: |
| Action steps with dates: |
| 1. |
| 2. |
| 3. |

See Goals and Action Planning Worksheet in Appendix I.

Based on the work of the balance wheel, some clients will identify many goals for each area of their lives, so encourage them to identify the 5 - 7 most important goals that will make the biggest difference in their lives. Working on more than seven goals at a time disperses their energy, so encourage your clients to focus.

### Planning for successful goal implementation

To plan for successful implementation of goals, we can further explore:

How can you stretch yourself?

What would take you out of your comfort zone?

What resources do you need to accomplish each goal?

What predictable resistance or obstacles can you expect?

What accountability structures will inspire you?

What daily actions will serve you?

Who can you enlist to support you in reaching your goals?

How will you celebrate the milestones along the way?

## Setting Stretch Goals

Stretch Goals

Practical · Stretch · Outrageous

Without the challenge to set stretch goals, clients often take smaller steps than they are capable of. By challenging clients to create outrageous goals, we ask them to consider stepping farther than they might on their own. Even if they consider the outrageous goal to be too much of a stretch, they will settle on goals that are bigger than they would have chosen on their own (e.g. a stretch vs. practical goal).

*Tips for setting stretch goals:*

**Make sure the goal is compelling**

What makes this goal important to you?

**Search for the growing edge**

What would you do if you knew you wouldn't fail?

How can you play a bigger game?

**Balance the outrageous, ambitious and practical**

What's one ambitious element you could add to your goal and still achieve it?

How could you make that goal 10 times bigger and still achieve it?

What would make your heart sing?

# Expanding Your Comfort Zone

*Life shrinks or expands in proportion to one's courage. —Anaïs Nin*

Our comfort zone has the familiarity of an old couch. But everything now in our comfort zone was once unfamiliar. Life is full of choices. We can live our lives in fear of making mistakes or we can choose to act in alignment with our deepest values. Acting boldly and truthfully unleashes our full potential.

As we act on our courage, we don't eradicate fear from our lives. As we evolve, our fears change shape, vacillating between sharp barbs that paralyze and gentle prods that keep us moving in the right direction. Courageous people learn to use fear as the signpost telling them where to go next. Fear serves as our personal invitation from life to develop our courage, character and our own personal code of honor. We learn to take action even when it isn't always popular, safe or certain to do so. For example:

*A coach-in-training, came to her coaching session excited about the prospects of living a more holistic life—combining her coaching skills and massage training. She also came weighed down by the obstacles—two small children for whom she wanted to be a fantastic mother and role model, an unsatisfying job and financial challenges that required her to keep a job until her business took off. She wanted support in designing her ideal life and taking the action steps to get there. Early in the coaching, her words "peace" and "freedom" really brought her alive. She stepped fully into the aliveness of what her life would look like if filled with peace and freedom. She also stepped into the fear and sense of, "How can I possibly do it?" and decided to move toward the aliveness rather than be held back by the fear, uncertainty and inner critics. She changed her housing situation to ease the financial pressure, bringing more peace into her life. She also changed jobs, becoming the director of a nonprofit, which allowed her to use her coaching skills to impact the way her staff delivered services to the community. This brought in the freedom element in a big way. She was excited about the changes in her life and her ability to create them from the place of her personal power and alignment with what was most meaningful to her. In this place, she saw herself as a better role model for her girls—wanting them to also learn to live from the place of power and possibility.*

## Stepping out of your comfort zone

Using the diagram below, recall each time you stepped out of your comfort zone and write an event in the decade it occurred. The first decade might include going to school, riding a bike or diving off a diving board. In the second decade, riding a horse, going on a date, leaving home or getting a job are examples of stepping out of your comfort zone. Marriage, asking for a raise, having children, going skydiving might show up in the third decade. Changing careers, living in a new country, running for political office… keep going, filling in each decade, including the ones you haven't lived yet.

Remember key times you stepped out of your comfort zone and how you felt afterwards.

What happens when you expand or contract your comfort zone?

Imagine stepping out of your comfort zone now.

To accept life's invitation to act with courage, what actions will you take?

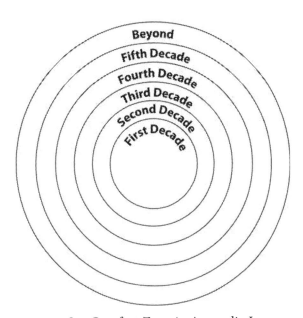

See Comfort Zone in Appendix I.

# Daily Habits

*The habit of setting priorities, overcoming procrastination, and getting on with your most important task is a mental and physical skill. As such, this habit is learnable through practice and repetition, over and over again, until it locks into your subconscious mind and becomes a permanent part of your behavior. —Brian Tracy*

Small, constructive actions done on a daily or routine basis can quickly give a sense of accomplishment and momentum. These daily habits form a foundation for major changes to take place. What actions, if taken on a regular basis, would make a difference for you? How do these daily actions tie into your strategic plan?

_____

_____

_____

_____

*Examples:*

Process all incoming mail daily.

Exercise four times each week.

Check email only twice a day.

## Planning Tool

Mind mapping is a right brain tool that supports planning and creatively exploring options. As part of our strategic plan, mind maps allow us to start with a central idea and build our ideas and plan out from that using a diagram that shows relationships between concepts. Wikipedia offers a list of free and proprietary mind map software http://en.wikipedia.org/wiki/List_of_concept_mapping_and_mind_mapping_software

*Example of a mind map:*

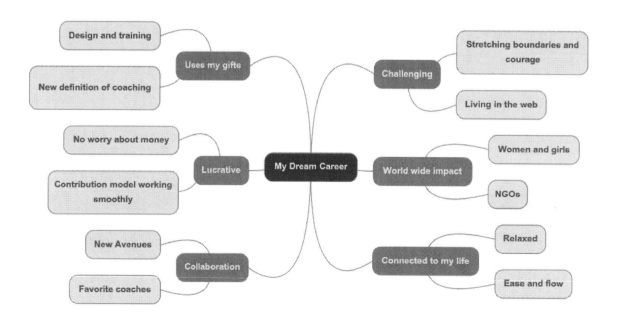

# Accountability

A valuable reason for working with a coach is to ensure accountability for what we want to create in our lives. Conventional views of accountability usually involve an unbalanced power structure with penalties exacted for unmet goals. Many clients expect this kind of accountability, but a more empowering accountability structure involves a power-with relationship, rather than the conventional power-over dynamic.

A power-with accountability structure helps clients identify their actions and what they want to be held accountable for so that they take full ownership. The coach serves as a witness to support clients in following through on their commitments.

Because some of our clients are used to power-over accountability, we explain what we mean by power-with accountability. Otherwise, they may unconsciously avoid us when they don't follow through on what they said they would do.

The three basic accountability questions are:

What will you do?

When will you do it?

How will I know you've done it?

All three questions invite clients to take responsibility for their actions and for structuring the follow-up. Our role as the coach is to draw attention to what is important to clients, and ask them to take responsibility for moving toward their goals.

When clients set up their own accountability structures, they're more likely to follow through. When we help them to connect to the life force within, they're more likely to create celebratory accountability structures.

A punitive approach might sound like, "What are the consequences if you don't complete your goals?" A more empowering question sounds like, "How will you celebrate each milestone along the way?"

When clients set goals they are passionate about and create self-directed action plans, they are more likely to solve their own problems and make effective decisions.

During the follow-up sessions, acknowledge what they accomplished and learned. When clients don't do what they say they will, the coach's role is to be curious. You can ask:

What did you learn?

What do you need to do to move forward?

How do you want to adjust your plan?

If you scrap the old plan, what would the new plan look like?

What support do you need to follow through?

Some clients make things more complicated than necessary and become wedded to "struggle and suffer." Consider the value of "challenge and build" as a different viewpoint. Changing this mindset may require the client to identify and understand their Protectors.

## Procrastination

When procrastination becomes repetitive, we share our observations with our clients. By giving voice to the patterns of repeated delay or excuses, we support clients in owning what's happening and looking beneath the surface for fears or unmet needs. We can ask probing questions such as, "How important is this goal to you?" or "What's more important to you than achieving this goal?" or "What's getting in the way?"

We can also explore resistance by helping clients get in touch with emotions and beliefs associated with the resistance. By not resisting the resistance, they can come to choice and insight, and then assess what's needed. Is it to question or recommit to the goal, revise or completely change it, or to look into the face of the resistance without judgment?

## The power of sharing goals

When people share their goals with others, they vocalize their commitment, which takes them one step closer to fulfillment. When clients share their goals and planned action steps with their coach or others, they cultivate partners and champions—people who hold the space for their achievement and celebrate their success with them.

# Action as "Doing Less"

For some clients, moving into action may involve doing less or slowing things down. For people who are constantly doing, action steps may involve spending more time relaxing. A coach shared the following example:

*I had a client who was a visionary with great ideas and ability to implement. Several months into the coaching, he realized he was driven by "shoulds," and that his self-image was wrapped up in his projects. My intuition was to ask him to stop doing—to experiment with not creating new projects for a month. That meant not taking action on his "Oh my God" or "What about this?" ideas. I really encouraged him to stay in the experiment. Not being driven by "shoulds" led to a rich period of self-reflection. His "inaction" broke a life-long pattern.*

*He came out of it with a depth of understanding of who he really was and what he really wanted for his life. He became more thoughtful about how he chooses new projects, and now bases his decisions on what he wants, not on what he feels he should do. The lesson for me as a coach was to take the unconventional route, trust my intuition and engage with the mystery—where neither of us had the answer.*

At times, the best action in service of a client's growth may be "inaction" or "being" rather than "doing."

# Support

Visions and plans often stretch people beyond their comfort zone and they benefit from strong support structures to create the changes they desire. Support can come in many forms; including friends, family and colleagues, to remind them they are not alone.

Simple tools and templates can help identify the support that is already there and apply that support to a specific goal.

### Support grid

Put the goal in the center and ask of each area: How does this area of my life already support me in reaching this goal and how can I better use that support?

| SUPPORT GRID | | |
|---|---|---|
| Relaxation/Recreation | Diet/Health | Physical Environment |
| Community | Primary Focus | Communication |
| Livelihood/Work | Resources/Finances | Spirituality |

©Kathy Kuser: Reprinted with permission.

| SUPPORT GRID | | |
|---|---|---|
| **Relaxation/Recreation**<br><br>I already have control of my schedule and I can CHOOSE to relax.<br><br>I can build relaxation/recreation into every day in some way. | **Diet/Health**<br><br>I already have a very strong body that works well for me. I eat well and grow much of my own food.<br><br>I can begin to eat more consciously and use the foods I love in more moderation. No second helpings. | **Physical Environment**<br><br>My physical environment is already very wild, beautiful and relaxing. It supports ease and health.<br><br>I can take advantage of my beautiful land and spend time every day in the woods. |
| **Community**<br><br>My community will support me in anything I dare to ask for.<br><br>I can talk about my body with three friends and ask for their support. | **Primary Focus**<br><br>Reclaiming my body. | **Communication**<br><br>I already have the ability to ask for what I need and have lots of people to ask for support.<br><br>I can write daily in my journal and use that support. |
| **Livelihood/Work**<br><br>My work already supports me in that I am self employed and can decide my schedule.<br><br>I can put work second instead of first and my health first. | **Resources/Finances**<br><br>I already have the resources I need to create anything I want.<br><br>I can make clear choices about how to spend my energy, saying no to four more things every week. | **Spirituality**<br><br>I already have a deep connection to the earth that will support me in this goal.<br><br>I can spend more time with the earth and really tune into messages in nature to support me. |

©Kathy Kuser: Reprinted with permission.

## Personal support network

The exercise below helps people assess their current support network. On the blank Support Network Diagram that follows:

**Vital Relationships:** In the first circle outside the "You" circle, list the first name of the people you can't imagine living without. List them in order of importance, starting at 12 o'clock with the most important, and going around the circle. Number each person, starting with 1, 2, 3, etc.

**Important Relationships:** In the second circle, list the people who are not quite as close to you, but who are still very important to you. Again, list them in order around the circle, starting with 12 o'clock. Number each person, starting where you left off on the inner circle.

**Supportive Relationships:** In the third circle, list those people on whom you depend, but who are not as close to you as those in the second circle. List them in order as you did with the other circles. Number each person, starting where you left off on the second circle. You may list as many as you choose.

Include people who would do anything for you day or night in the first circle. And likewise, you'd do anything to help them. For example, you might include your immediate family and dearest friends. In the second circle you might include your colleagues or extended family, and in the third circle your exercise partner or massage therapist.

## Support System Diagram

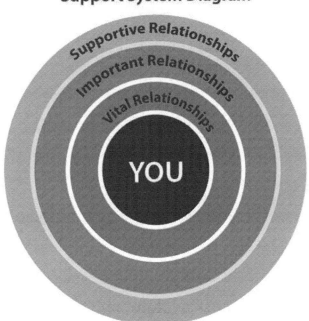

See Support System Diagram in Appendix I.

## Support tune up

Building on the information in your Support Network Diagram, list each "key" person in your support network and answer the following questions for each. Think about what you can ask for, what you can do, what you can say.

What do I get from this person? _____

_____

What do I give to this person? _____

_____

What is one step I can take to improve this relationship so that I get more of what I really need?

_____

_____

## Expanding your support team

If you're not satisfied with the support in your life, make up your imaginary support team, including your favorite characters from novels or movies, historic figures and archetypes. Once you create your ideal imaginary team, think about what each person brings, and look at how you can create real support in your life.

*Questions to Consider*

What action steps are you taking to help your dreams become reality?

What additional resources will you use to help clients move into action?

# 11

# The Business of Coaching

*Anything's possible if you've got enough nerve. —J.K. Rowling*

You know how to help clients turn their dreams and goals into reality. Now, what about yours? Although some people use coaching skills in existing professional and personal settings, many envision a coaching practice as a means to a more holistic and satisfying life. If you dream of sustaining yourself comfortably while doing the work you love, this chapter gets you started on the path to fulfill your dreams.

Many new coaches struggle to establish themselves, but it *is* possible to create a thriving coaching practice if you learn how to market yourself effectively. If you are concerned that you lack confidence or business knowledge, the good news is that you can develop both with perseverance and a willingness to try new things. It may take years to build a really profitable business, but as Lao Tzu said, "The journey of one thousand miles begins with a single step."

What makes your heart sing and what would your life look like if you gave yourself permission to do what makes your heart sing?

## Getting Clients

*Marketing is telling people what you do . . . over and over. —C. J. Hayden*

### Connecting with potential

How do you get potential clients interested in coaching? How do you help them get to know who you are and how you can help them? This section provides you with many ideas for connecting with clients. You don't need to establish a formal business to begin exploring ways of making connections. Just start coaching and consider the formal business endeavor whenever you're ready.

Communicating who you are and what you offer to your target market is what branding is all about. You are your brand. Nada Jones and Michelle Briody say, "Your brand makes people feel or think a certain way about you or even themselves."[1] Your presence impacts how people respond to you and how comfortable they feel with you. Building on the physical presence we talked about in Chapter 1, people sense your presence in everything you create. You share your identity via marketing materials and verbal messages that clearly express who you are, what you offer and what people get when working with you.

One way of attracting potential clients is by staying curious, telling everyone you know about coaching, and offering them a strategy session, providing direct experience for potential clients or referrals. This section provides you with many marketing options to consider.

## Your marketing message

What do you say when people ask, "What do you do?" One of the worst answers you can give is, "I am a coach." Why? Because many people have misconceptions about what coaching is and if you don't differentiate yourself from thousands of other coaches, they'll have no idea what's special about you. Your marketing message is your response when someone asks, "What do you do?"

Keep your marketing messages simple, clear and succinct. Sharing the core message clearly and confidently with just about everyone you meet opens doors. Some people refer to this as an elevator speech—something you can communicate in the time it takes to arrive at your floor in an elevator. The key is to confidently share your clear message without sounding scripted.

Identify four elements of your marketing message:

1. Ideal client—who do you really want to coach?
2. Problem—what issues are they likely to face?
3. Outcome—what results do they want to have?
4. Story—what's an example of a client's issue and result?

## Ideal client

Start by clearly stating your target client or your niche. Although your niche may shift as you grow, begin by defining your niche very narrowly, such as, "I work with executive directors of international nonprofits who focus on racial justice." Also identify your broader niche, such as, "I work with social justice advocates." Choose your niche based on the impact you want to have and the kinds of people you enjoy being around, because you'll be spending a lot of time with these folks. What kinds of people bring you joy? Provide intellectual stimulation? Open your heart? Once you answer those questions, experiment with your niche and how you talk about your ideal clients until it feels natural.

## Problem

Next explore the kinds of problems your ideal clients are likely to have on their minds. You may be tempted to put this in terms of your clients' aspirations, such as becoming a senior leader, being

---

1 Jones, Nada & Briody, Michelle (2009). Sixteen Weeks to Your Dream Business: A Weekly Planner for Entrepreneurial Women. New York: McGraw-Hill.

wildly successful in their field, or creating balance and inner peace. But start with their pain or their problems. Why might they be looking for a coach anyway? What's bothering them? What keeps them up at night? If you can convey that you understand their problems, you are more likely to connect. A bad example is, "I work with people who want to live in a socially just world." Even though it sounds beautiful, what does it really mean? You may think you're keeping all the doors open by describing your client's problem so broadly, but in reality, it takes something more specific to get people to open the door. It is far more effective to say, "I work with social justice activists who are fed up with seeing young men of color incarcerated, shot at and denied jobs."

## Outcome

Novices tend to talk about the process of coaching when they market, by saying, "I'll help you get clear about your values, vision and goals." Although that might be accurate, it's not very inspiring. Nobody wants to buy your wonderful 5-step process, but they do want to buy a desirable outcome or result. What results do you offer? Of course the results are up to the client, but what are your ideal clients looking for when they give you their credit card? What's the resolution to their problem? How does your unique brand of coaching give them some relief from their pain? For example, "I work with people who are stuck in their careers, would love to do something different and have no idea how to start. I support clients in creating a more satisfying and whole work life."

## Story

The goal of your marketing message is to get prospects to ask for more information. You know they're intrigued if they ask, "How do you do that?" or "Can you share an example?" Be ready to share several stories about ways you have helped clients. Choose one to share so that prospects can easily connect with one client's story. For example, "I coached a group of community leaders who then asked to be trained as coaches. They in turn trained their staff and their clients were so impressed, they also asked for coaching skills training."

## Putting it all together

*Marketing Message Examples*

As a relationship coach I work with people who are facing a challenging time in their relationships, either with partners, family or friends. Each of us needs a web of relationships to sustain and nurture us and we all go through phases of experiencing conflict or negativity in these relationships. This can be very painful and draining. To be with people as they connect better with themselves and others is my calling in life. I coached a married couple who were entangled in a legal battle for three years and supported them to see their role in the relationship. They divorced, but without bitterness. I coached a mother and her 21-year-old daughter who hadn't spoken to each other for over a year. Now they are each other's strongest support.—Altaf Shaikh

I coach women whose work is to make a difference in the world—who also want to deeply express their "mom" identity. I coached a mid-career working mom who was constantly tempted to over-commit and outperform through her decision to leave a tense job in which her contributions were not valued, and find a fulfilling, part-time job with collaborators who share her values. —Rebecca Aced-Molina

I support spiritual seekers with a social conscience connect heaven and earth. Some of the most powerful and impactful social justice leaders in our time have aligned their community and societal change work with their knowledge of Spirit. No matter the spiritual path or religious denomination, I support clients to bring heaven (spiritual consciousness) together with earth (social justice consciousness) to create change in this world. My client, an Executive Director for a legal nonprofit has incorporated daily meditation and visioning to make the most purposeful decisions about running their current organization. At the same time they are recruiting a like-minded team to start a new organization that is working with youth on international human rights issues with a spirit lens.—Damon Gbuduala Azali-Rojas

I work with exceptional men and women who want more freedom, fun and fulfillment in their life and work. I help my clients get clear about what's right for them, know how to make it happen, and achieve the results they want. Change doesn't have to be overwhelming! Drained by her stable job as a university professor, my client quit her job, started her business where she merged her passion for art and helping women step into their power. —Tanuja Ramchal

I am a travel companion. I accompany my clients on a journey into the landscape of their inner being. I travel with people whose fears and conditioning keep them from making the life changes they long for. I take them to places that hurt, places they fear to go to alone, places that need healing. Because I take my clients beyond their conditioning they start to see themselves, sometimes for the first time ever. At the end of our journey my clients emerge with a much different sense of who they are; a renewed sense of meaning and purpose, a great deal of healthy self-connection and the ability to manifest from this awareness. For me the beauty of this work lies in being in unconditional presence with my client, being an ambassador for the beautiful and unique being they are. Mirroring this beauty and its inherent potential back to them allows for the client to embrace themselves in love. This is a deeply reassuring and empowering process that, if the client is willing to go all in, will have long lasting and life-changing effects. —Daniela Herzog

## Strategy sessions

> *The Four-Fold Way*™:
> *Show up*
> *Pay Attention*
> *Tell the Truth*
> *Don't be attached to outcome. —Angeles Arrien*

If a prospect is intrigued by your marketing message, the next step is to offer them ways to experience what it would be like to work with you. You may send them an article you've written or point them to a blog post. You might share with them an exercise that gives them value. Once they are qualified prospects, meaning that you both feel a mutual "click," you can offer them a strategy session.

In the 90s most people had no idea what coaching was, so many coaches offered free sample sessions. Times have changed. Today, most people know what coaching is, so sample sessions are less common. The coaching field has passed the infancy stage. That's why we recommend strategy sessions instead of sample sessions. Strategy sessions are similar to an attorney's first consultation where you determine if it's a good fit. But a strategy session is more than a chemistry session; it's where you discover what clients really want, and whether coaching can help them.

During a sample session, a client can get coaching on any issue of their choice. Very often, prospective clients don't even know how to identify a coaching topic and coaches can feel like they have to dazzle the client in just one session. The pressure is high on both sides.

In contrast, a strategy session is designed to help clients make only one decision: whether to work with you as their coach. Strategy sessions are essentially a holistic approach where you look beyond the immediate pain, problems or symptoms to provide a "snapshot" of your prospects' core issues and core values. From there you help them discover underlying longing and dreams. By going beyond their immediate issues and getting them to look at their core, you help them invest in themselves and their own solutions. A strategy session is a highly focused meeting in which we discover what the prospect really wants out of coaching. This system naturally leads the right clients to hire you.

You'll be offering much more than a "sample" or an introduction, you'll be providing a deep understanding of what they want and what's stopping them. They begin creating their own strategic game plan to create a life they love. It's far more powerful than helping a client resolve an internal conflict or address any other immediate issues. By taking them into the big picture of their lives, you're offering them a vision of what they've been searching for, something truly "worth paying for."

### Strategy Session Example

We highly recommend you try this a few times and then personalize it to make it your own.

### Context

The purpose of this Strategy Session is to learn more about you, where you want to go and what challenges you face. We will also discuss the services I offer and see if I can help you get you where you want to go.

The meeting will take about 30 minutes. Does that work for you?

Do you have any questions before we start?

### The Situation

What's working for you right now?

What's not working as well as you'd like?

What inspired you to call me now?

### Desired Outcomes

What's your main objective?

What changes would you like to see happen in the next 3 years?

### Impact of Achieving Outcomes

What would be the best part of achieving those goals?

What would that mean to you?

If you achieved that goal what would you do next?

### Challenges

What's stopping you from achieving those goals?

What do you think could stop you from getting what you want?"

Five basic challenges:

        a) Lack of clarity

        b) No strategy or plan

        c) Lack of sufficient skills

        d) Non-supportive environment

        e) Psychological barriers

### Implications

What's the impact these challenges are having (on business, relationships, health, life, etc.)

What do you think it's costing you…?

How does it feel to you that …?

### Possibilities

If you could overcome these challenges and easily move toward your goals, what would that be like for you?

### Services

What has been the most valuable part of this Strategy Session so far?"

Your challenges are not uncommon. I've helped many people with similar challenges and similar goals, and helped them reach their objectives. Would you like to hear how coaching works?

- Main message (assessment tools, vision, values, goals, process work)
- Discovery session (longer session, designing our relationship, getting clarity on what you want out of coaching, what we'll cover)
- Logistics (hours per month, length of sessions, phone or in person, homework, emails)

### Confirm Commitment

Does working with me sound like it would be helpful?

Can you let me know why you want to work with me?"

### Enrollment

Coaching is designed to support you in _____. It is also about helping you _____. By the end of three months, the goal is for you to _____.

The fee for coaching is $XX per month payable at the beginning of the month for X months. Or if you want to pay for 3 months up front, the fee is _____. Do you have a preference?

### Answer Questions and Objections

Listen for needs and empathize with what they want.

Would you like to get started?

### Payment and Next Steps

The next step is to get on each other's calendars. I prefer to coach on Tuesdays and Wednesdays. Which is better for you? Okay, we could coach at 9 am. Can you start on _____?

Would you prefer to pay by credit card or is there an easier way?

I'll be sending you some questions to help me get to know you.

### Objectives for a strategy session include helping prospects:

Experience empowering questions

Get a glimpse of the difference coaching can make

Connect with their heart

Get clarity about their desired future

Determine if they want to work with you

Begin the coaching relationship

### Strategy Sessions for Enrolling Organizations

Enrolling organizations is a similar process, but there are often several people who are part of the decision. An empowering sales process is a collaborative approach to designing satisfactory outcomes. The following are a few empowering selling questions that are divided into sequential sections of the process.

**Upfront agreements**—structure the session

Do we have about an hour to talk?

Are there any other people who are helping you make this decision? Can we get them in the room?

If for any reason we decide not to work together, let's be honest about it, rather than waste each other's time. Okay with you?

**Objectives**—define the ideal outcomes

If you had a magic wand, how would you use it?

What do you want to see change around here?

**Connect with needs**—empathize with their pain

What is your biggest nightmare?

What led you to call me now?

**Budget**—determine the investment

How much would it be worth to make the changes we've talked about?

What's your budget for this project?

**Options**—explore ways to move forward

What alternatives have you considered?

How will you measure success?

**Solutions**—establish commitment and forward movement

How would you like to move forward?

Based on what you've told us, would you like to hear our recommendations?

**Follow-up**—build in next steps

Shall we review our next steps?

When would you like to talk again?

## Marketing and advertising ideas

Developing a marketing plan is an effective way to think through and plan marketing activities and to contribute to the success of your business. Be sure to use your marketing message consistently throughout all your materials. Choose your marketing vehicles based on your ideal clients. If your ideal clients use social media extensively, then put your focus there. If they belong to certain organizations, make connections with those groups.

Some specific ways of marketing and advertising your business include:

**Marketing Materials**—The most important print marketing materials for new coaches are business cards. These will be useful for all of your face-to-face networking so people know how to contact you. Brochures, flyers and other print materials can also be useful.

**Networking**—Word of mouth drives a significant number of initial contacts that eventually lead to enrollment. Possibilities include attending meetings, seminars and networking events; participating in online networks; serving on committees; volunteering or trading services; collaborating on projects; swapping contacts; and reading the trade press (e.g. Choice magazine or coachingcommons.org). Tell everyone you meet what you do. When you share your business vision with passion and energy, people inevitably suggest referrals. Follow up with your network and keep a list of contacts with their details.

**Referrals**—Ask clients, family, professional contacts and friends to refer clients to you. You can offer an incentive such as a free coaching session for every referral who becomes a client.

**Testimonials**—When clients let you know how much you've helped them, ask them if they would be willing to write a testimonial for you. Save these messages for use in your marketing materials (print, website or social media).

**Social Media**—choose your social media presence based on your interest level and how your ideal clients use social media. FaceBook, Twitter and LinkedIn are most widely used. Establish a FaceBook and LinkedIn presence for your coaching business as an online networking method. LinkedIn is a professional social network that can connect you with many business opportunities. Both tools allow you to broadcast messages to wide audiences for free.

**Blogs**—Blogging gets your message out and also helps people get to know you. People who read your blog may contact you for coaching. WordPress (http://wordpress.com/) is a common blogging tool.

**Blog Talk Radio** (http://www.blogtalkradio.com/)—Some coaches host blog talk radio shows or may speak as guests on a show to increase visibility.

**Public Speaking**—You can speak about coaching or on a personal empowerment topic at your local library, chamber of commerce or civic or church group. You may get paid for these talks or do them for free to help people get to know you. Public speaking can also include hosting meetings, serving on panels, making presentations and giving workshops. To increase your comfort with public speaking, you may want to join Toastmasters (http://www.toastmasters.org/) to get practice and build your confidence.

**Website**—Your website presence allows potential clients to look up information about you. Your website is a key method for providing information about your services and other resources.

**Writing and Publicity**—Includes writing for magazines and radio, newsletters, blogging, tweeting, being quoted by the media, having stories published about you and being interviewed for radio, TV or podcasts.

**Publishing**—Experienced coaches with particular experience in a niche or area of interest author and publish books and articles, which boost credibility and visibility.

**Workshops and Seminars**—Offering workshops or seminars attracts potential clients. Participants get to experience your style and get to know you. At the end of your workshop, they can sign up to receive a complimentary strategy session or receive mailings with additional information from you.

**Volunteering**—Consider volunteering some coaching in organizations or give a workshop to get into a new market or to help people see the value of coaching.

**Advertising**—Includes website banners, search-engine optimization, keyword accounts, internet display ads, newspaper and business directories and flyer distribution.

**Direct Contact and Follow-Up**—Includes cold calling, warm calling, canvassing, lunch or coffee with prospects, sending clippings and links and extending invitations.

**Video**—Shoot your own videos and post them to your Youtube channel or on your website. Share them on social media.

## Enrolling clients—getting to "Yes"

Enrolling clients in the coaching process comes through presence and authentic self-expression, not a separate marketing activity of selling yourself. Simply put, enrollment is linking what prospective clients want in their lives with what you have to offer, without gimmicks or manipulation. But it's a two-way street. Help them see your passion and authenticity. Sharing what you're passionate about and being vulnerable about your own growing edges also contribute to connection and enrollment.

## Enrollment questions

Enrollment questions are similar to empowering coaching questions. You can use them to connect with what's important to prospective clients. Here are a few examples of questions you might ask:

What keeps you awake at night?

If you choose to start coaching, what's the most important change you'd like to make in your life?

What stops you from working with a coach?

What has to happen so that you'll have a fulfilling life, one with no regrets?

What would make your investment in coaching worthwhile?

## Enrollment statements

Enrollment statements are very different from an elevator speech. They get to the heart of why you want to work with a particular person and connect you with what's most alive in him or her. Some examples of enrollment statements:

I want to be your coach because…

You inspire me by the way you…

I feel connected to your quest…

Coaching you would be special because…

## Establishing fees

Many new coaches struggle with pricing. Lack of confidence, undercharging and negotiating fees contribute to the failure of many coaching practices. Setting your fees and communicating them with confidence is critical to the success of your business. You can help people only if you have a successful coaching practice. To establish a prosperous coaching practice, get really clear about the value of your services and charge what you need to thrive. If you set your fees below the market rate, you risk feeling resentful, and potential clients may doubt your worth. Spend time thinking about your fees and practicing in front of a mirror how you will communicate prices before you begin enrolling clients.

Establish fees or a range of fees for each of your services. Gather this information from your coach, mentors, teachers and colleagues and adjust if needed based on what the market will bear.

Establish what percentage of your business will be reduced fee or pro bono and revise it as your experience grows or your financial needs change.

If you wish to work on a sliding scale to accommodate clients with financial need, be clear about the lowest fee you're willing to accept and the characteristics of the people you will be happy to coach at a reduced fee. While you are training, you may decide to take lower fees to build experience. Certified coaches with full practices can charge more.

Communicate your fees with confidence. As you let the information sink in, resist the urge to add more information. Giving prospects a chance to respond is critical. If you struggle with this, get coaching on this topic and practice until you master it. Or have your support team challenge you to see that the value you offer is worth the fees you charge. Comfortably and confidently communicating your fees really sends the message that you believe in the value of your services and boosts the odds of getting full-fee clients.

## Responding to objections

You can help your prospective clients come to their own conclusions about whether or not to hire you by asking a series of questions that help them explore their desired future. High-pressure sales tactics are the antithesis of co-creating a coaching relationship based on choice and trust.

Possible responses when they resist your price:

Explain that your rates are non-negotiable.

Connect empathically with their resistance.

Walk away so that you can meet your own needs for sustainability.

Explore your selection criteria and work with them at their price.

Negotiate a price that works for both of you.

Often money is not the real issue behind an objection. Either you haven't built the trust, helped them connect with how coaching will truly serve them, or made a deep connection. But sometimes money is the barrier, so consider some language for addressing objections to your fee:

I work on a sliding scale with four people a month at a reduced-fee. I would really love to work with you because I'm inspired by your dream. What amount would be a stretch for you, but doable for both of us?

I really want to work with you, but your suggestion of $100 a month is not sustainable for me. Perhaps we can reconsider coaching once you get a job.

I hear you that you want to start coaching and coming up with the money will be difficult. Would you like to brainstorm some ways that you could pay for this?

If we used our time well, what would you get out of coaching that would make your investment worthwhile?

Whether they hire you or not, you can still deepen the connection by hearing the "no" and empathically connect to the probability that they are saying "yes" to something else. Empathic responses can help uncover deeper needs. Objections about money are often about resistance to something else. How would you respond to the most common objections?

| RESPONDING EMPATHICALLY TO OBJECTIONS | |
|---|---|
| **Objections** | **Empathic Responses** |
| I'm too busy. | So your time is really valuable and you want to use it for things that are meaningful to you? |
| I can't afford coaching. | It sounds like you want to feel energized about how you use your money. |
| I don't think you can help me. | Ah, so you really want some help and you want to have confidence that you can get what you need? |
| I've already got several people who coach me informally. | You like the feel of an informal, friendly coaching relationship? |
| I'll have to ask my partner. | Are you a bit worried and want some reassurance about your intuition? |

# Creating the Coaching Partnership

*The key to realizing a dream is to focus not on success but significance—and then*
*even the small steps and little victories along your path will take on greater meaning.*
*—Oprah Winfrey*

## Discovery sessions

Once you get that new client, some groundwork needs to take place before coaching can get fully underway. Many coaches make their first session a discovery session, which differs from a typical coaching session. A sample discovery session outline is included in Appendix I. While you can customize your discovery session, some common elements to include are:

1.  Making an empathic connection
2.  Creating a conscious relationship
3.  Clarifying values
4.  Establishing focus of coaching and desired outcomes
5.  Agreeing on Logistics

**Making an empathic connection:** Learn all you can about your new clients, connect with their deepest desires, ask empowering questions and give them the space to tell you all they want you to know about themselves. You might ask: Is there anything you want me to know about your spiritual life? Culture? Background?

**Creating conscious relationship**: In this part of the discovery session, you design your relationship. How will you create a relationship of mutual respect, trust, openness and honesty? How will you work with each other? How will you co-create the best coaching relationship possible? What do each of you need in order to step into a powerful relationship? What agreements do you want to make and how will you handle it if either of you needs to break an agreement? How do you like to receive feedback? What kind of accountability structures work for you?

## COACHING *in Action* | Creating and Sustaining Conscious Relationships Across Race, Class and Immigration Status
*by Maria Rogers Pascual, CFT Faculty*

One of my more fulfilling and humbling experiences has been coaching six Latina immigrant women who are part of a new program that supports low-income entrepreneurs to launch their own cooperative businesses.

What makes this program unique is the strength-based approach of recognizing and continuously lifting up the life experience that these women bring to cooperative development. We remind them that they are in charge (not us) of the success of their business; that if any one can do it, they can. Their resilience is astounding: they have crossed borders against all odds; most of them are the primary bread winners for their families, hold 2-3 jobs, care for their children so they can one day go to college and more. But no matter how much I lift up their resilience, in this society, I know that I am the one with the privilege: a US passport, a Master's degree, stable income and the list goes on…

By the time the coaching sessions began, I already had a great deal of information about these clients—way more than they would ever have about me. Like most nonprofit or government programs of this nature, participants have to go through an extensive intake process that reveals their income level, family history and life experience.

So I had an inkling that the discovery session needed to be more about me than about them, and ultimately about the power differential between us. Most visible was my director level title; my skin color, lighter than most of the participants; my fluency in both English and Spanish; and my level of comfort as a trainer. The rest was a mystery that merited unveiling.

For my clients, coaching itself was completely new and unfamiliar. When asked what they understood about coaching, most of them compared it to a case worker who, "helps me cope with problems and access critical social services." After explaining what transformational coaching was about, I let each one of my clients ask anything she wanted about me. I could tell that asking me questions felt like a breach in some way, so it was very important to emphasize the many ways coaching differs, particularly that I was not the one with the answers. I could see the discomfort melt away as I revealed bits of information about myself, acknowledging differences of privilege and making connections to shared experiences.

One of my clients, I will call Itzel because she identifies as indigenous, took me to task. She asked where I was born, what my immigration status was, how I got this job and what prepared me for it. A shift in our relationship happened when I shared some pain I felt around not belonging when I moved to the US from Mexico at age 13. I did not plan it this way. I was ready to focus on my privilege and own it, but while essential, that is not what created the shift for us. My vulnerability around difficult life experiences gave Itzel an opening. I could feel her compassion and connection around this topic of belonging. It was a particular kind of felt experience in the moment that told me a door had opened for both of us.

Where power differences are so marked around race, class and immigration status, conscious relationship is ongoing rather than something you just focus on during a discovery session. These coaching experiences teach me so much about the true meaning of conscious relationship, which is unlikely if differences of power and privilege remain tucked under a rug. I am learning how to meet these differences with clear eyes and an open heart, and most of all, I am so grateful for a profession that gives me permission to learn from and be transformed along with my clients.

Some questions to consider addressing when building conscious relationship with clients:

What would a great coaching relationship look like?

What do you want to get out of this relationship?

What do we each need for our relationship to thrive?

How can I best support you with accountability for reaching your goals?

How would you like me to handle it if you haven't done what you said you were going to do?

How do you want me to be with you as your coach—do you want a hard-edged coach or one who is full of heart? Or both?

When you want more from me, how will you let me know?

What do you need from me if you get frustrated, angry or discouraged?

Discovery sessions are an opportunity for you to share your coaching style, concerns and preferences, for example:

I don't take things personally, so you don't have to pussy-foot around with me.

I like to take risks and want your permission to make mistakes—is that going to work for you?

I have a dog, so you may hear him in the background from time to time. If it bothers you, will you let me know?

If the coaching is not working for you, I want to know about it right away. We'll look at what we might need to change in our agreements, or perhaps decide not to continue.

Our time is valuable, so I'd like to start and end each session on time. Does that work for you?

**Values clarification:** This process helps you understand what really matters to your clients so you can help them align with their deepest needs. Some coaches spend at least half of the discovery session on values clarification. Some sample discovery questions include:

What are you most passionate about?

What do you want to happen in your lifetime so that you consider your life satisfying and well-lived?

What are the experiences that have had the most influence in your life and had the most impact in shaping you?

Who are the people who had the greatest impact in your life?

What do you see as your greatest gifts, talents or strengths?

What has been your greatest success or proudest achievement?

Other discovery questions focus on vision, support, focus and changes.

Describe your support system. Who are the people in your life who believe in you, encourage you, challenge you and see you through the hard times?

Imagine your ideal life. What does it look like? Where do you live? Who are you with? What are you doing? How do you feel when you wake up in the morning?

What areas of your life would you like to make some changes in?

What is one area that you would like to focus on in our coaching?

What is the greatest personal change you'd like to see in the coming year?

**Establishing focus of coaching and desired outcomes**: Determine the direction and agenda of the coaching relationship by visualizing the future and establishing personal and professional goals. How will we determine when the coaching relationship is no longer needed? How will we measure and celebrate success?

**Agreeing on logistics**: Make sure you are clear about scheduling, payments, missed sessions and vacations. This is a good time to clarify any agreements, including:

How many sessions are we contracting for?

What are the payment arrangements? What if payments are missed or late?

How will missed appointments or cancellations be handled?

Who will be calling whom? At what number?

How often will the relationship be reassessed and redesigned?

How will we give each other feedback and review the progress?

How will we end the relationship? How much advance notice will be given?

What will the completion session include and how will we celebrate?

**Cross cultural coaching**: If you and the client are from different cultural backgrounds, be alert for words, phrases, body language and cultural pressures, connections or traditions. While you do not have to give voice to the differences in your discovery session, reflecting what you see and hear can deepen the trust and connection and open more doors for the relationship. The awareness you gain and your openness to all that's happening for your client serves to deepen your connection and trust. Cross cultural coaching will be discussed in more detail in Chapter 13, *Cross Cultural Coaching* and Chapter 14, *Power, Privilege and Coaching.*

## Agreements and relationship

Resist the urge to dive straight into coaching and skip the discovery and conscious relationship building. One coach offers a cautionary tale of a new client she garnered when she was a relatively new coach. The client had just finished working with another coach and understood a great deal about how coaching worked. They were both eager to start coaching, so they just did a small amount of discovery about the background of her situation and jumped right in.

About a month into the coaching, the client got angry with the coach about her handling of one of her issues and told the coach off. The coach got defensive and blamed the client for handling it badly and the situation degenerated into a "your fault—my fault" dispute. They each had their assumptions about what the other was supposed to do, but they hadn't actually talked about it and shared their expectations.

The lesson for that young coach, now an instructor, was to design a robust, conscious relationship at the start, and set up a mutual agreement about what they would do if they ran into trouble. Building that conscious relationship can be like building a third entity upon which either party can refer when things don't run according to expectations. It's not a contract written in stone, but an agreement that the coach and client have created together that they can revisit and revise together as the need arises.

One never knows how things might have worked out differently, but the coach in this scenario is certain that creating a conscious relationship would have averted the dispute in the first place. Unfortunately, the relationship was lost. They were unable to backtrack and recreate a conscious relationship.

For more ideas and forms to use in getting started with new clients, see Appendix I.

## Coach's role

The coach's role in any coaching relationship includes:

Creating a safe supportive environment

Respecting the client's perceptions, learning style and needs

Offering support for new behaviors and learning

Challenging limiting beliefs

Requesting accountability structures to support movement

Believing more is possible than is seen on the surface

## Client's role

Coaches work with clients to create their own sense of power in the coaching relationship. Ask clients to:

Take responsibility for the content of the sessions

Express honestly what's working and not working

Make requests to redesign the coaching relationship

Step wholeheartedly into the coaching process

The coaching relationship flourishes when based on partnership rather than domination.

| DOMINATION | PARTNERSHIP |
|---|---|
| Power Over / Power Under | Power With |
| Independent / Dependent | Interdependent / Autonomous |
| Coach as oppressor, approval figure, star | Coach as resource |
| Authoritarian | Co-creation |
| Submits / Rebels | Collaborates |
| Experience fear, guilt, shame | Experience mutuality, connection, fulfillment |
| Punishment, reward, coercion | Free choice to contribute |
| Win : Lose or Lose : Lose | Win : Win |
| Loss of choice | Acts from choice and self-empowerment |
| Loss of personal responsibility for needs | Takes personal responsibility for needs |
| Depletion—Short-term gain | Sustainability—Long term balance |
| Fear of appearing weak | Freedom to be vulnerable and open as part of humanity |

*Adapted from the work of Riane Eisler.[2]*

2    Eisler, Riane, (2003). *The Power of Partnership: Seven Relationships that will Change Your Life.* New World Library

## COACHING *in Action* | **Coaching Ethics** *by Michael Wright, CFT Certified Coach*

Ethics are critical to protecting the integrity of the client, the service-provider, and the coaching profession at large. The International Coach Federation (ICF) maintains the most widely recognized Code of Ethics for the profession. This code provides the foundation for ethical decision making in coaching.

Considering what is ethical is an ongoing process, from the initial contact with a potential client through to the conclusion of the relationship and the handling of client information after we are no longer working together. The following list provides a few ethical tips. This list however is not exhaustive and does not replace the ICF Code of Ethics and ICF supplemental guidance as a primary resource.

### ETHICS TIPS

**Consult ICF Standards and Supplemental Ethics FAQs. When in doubt, ask a mentor or peer for additional support.**

The ICF Guidelines are a rich resource for coaches. However, they do not account for the nuances of every situation, so it is important to have a mentor or peers to lean on when inevitable questions arise.

**Know when to refer clients for mental health services and take action when psychological issues present themselves.** *(See page 220 "When to Refer Clients for Mental Health")*

As coaches, we make it clear that coaching is not therapy and it is not designed to treat or heal psychological problems. As such, when psychological problems arise (such as depression, chronic anxiety, addiction, or dangerous behavior to self or others, etc.), we acknowledge the situation and make referrals.

We can also get guidance on red flags from mentors, mental health professionals, or associations, such as the American Psychological Association or the American Psychiatric Association. When in doubt however, refer.

When a client is seeking treatment for psychological issues with a therapist, coaches do not necessarily have to cease work with the client. In fact, the coaching relationship and approach could be value-added to the work done in therapy. However, a coach needs to make sure the client is functioning at a level that makes a coaching approach fruitful.

Getting emergency contact information at the outset of a coaching engagement may be useful should more urgent issues arise, such as a client having suicidal thoughts. Depending on the circumstances, it may be necessary to reach out to an emergency contact. In addition, if the client has a therapist, we might also reach out to the therapist with the client's permission to assure the therapist is aware of any urgent circumstances.

**Be clear in agreements and discovery sessions about what confidentiality covers and what it does not.**

The ICF Code of Ethics mandates that coaches keep coaching sessions confidential, including content, times, and client names. Clients can however grant exceptions to confidentiality. Coaching agreements are an optimal place to spell out those exceptions. For example, if a coach is working with a minor and the parent wants to be apprised of details, all three parties—minor, parent and coach—should agree on what information will be disclosed and the minor should be present for those conversations. The same is true in an organizational context, where the parties include a supervisor, employee and coach.

The law however does not protect coaching sessions and contents in all jurisdictions. Therefore, should a client face a legal issue and the coach receives a subpoena for client records, a coach is generally required to divulge records as well as the contents of those sessions. Many coaches alert the client to that limitation in their agreements or verbally during the discovery session.

Also, while not legally obligated to do so, we are ethically inclined to report to authorities or others if we become aware that someone is being harmed or will be harmed, including the client. So that it doesn't come as a surprise, we can alert the client to this possibility during the discovery session.

*(Continued)*

**Secure in contracts with administrators or vendors their understanding and adherence to ICF Code of Ethics, in particular its confidentiality provisions.**

Vendors and administrators who contract with coaches and have access to client names and records are to maintain the same confidentiality that we maintain as coaches. This provides continuity of confidentiality and assurance to clients that their coaching relationship is private.

**Disclose conflicts of interest while maintaining confidentiality, and strongly consider declining engagements where it's not possible to fully serve the client as a coach.**

Conflicts can arise where clients have a relationship with one another that could compromise the coaching should they both work with the same coach. In disclosing conflicts of interest, confidentiality still holds. This requires that we discuss conflicts of interest in general terms, e.g., asking a current client if they object to us coaching someone else in their company or asking a current organizational client if they have concerns about us coaching a competitor's employees.

In a personal context, examples of relationships that might give rise to conflicts include married couples, family members or business partners. The relationship itself doesn't negate the feasibility of the same coach taking them on as individual clients. The question is whether we can be effective and unbiased as a coach and whether the subject matter and nature of the relationship at hand will allow us to maintain an open and safe environment.

In an organizational context, conflicts can present themselves when we coach multiple employees, some of whom may be the subordinates or superiors of others we are coaching. We can maintain our effectiveness by asking questions to assure the aims of coaching can be supported and by being explicit about the confidentiality of coaching. In cases where working with multiple employees may not support the integrity of the coaching, we can be frank about that with the sponsor (individual or department in a company that has hired the coach) and consider bringing in other coaches to handle the potential conflict.

**In an organizational context, use the sponsor to relay data on the coaching to other departments in the organization.**

Organizational work can present special challenges, especially when departments in the organization seek details of the coaching engagement, such as number of sessions or which levels in the company are receiving coaching. To maintain confidentiality, we can ask the sponsor to respond to those requests.

**Seek client's permission before using their name on websites and other materials.**

Confidentiality of client information is paramount in coaching. It is what allows the work between a client and coach to flourish. If we are working with an individual or organization and they offer a testimonial or case study, we ask for permission in writing before putting it on our website or other materials.

**Share with clients what is and isn't possible in coaching.**

Where an organization has specific objectives for coaching, be honest about what is possible and what may not be achievable. For example, if a company wants to use coaching to increase sales by 10%, we can let the company know we can strive for that; however, we cannot guarantee that outcome. The same is true of other metrics that might indicate the success of the coaching.

Another example might be a client who wants coaching to achieve their goal to find a partner. We cannot guarantee that. We can however let the client know that coaching could support them in living to their fullest, both with and without a partner.

**Spell out any degrees, qualifications, and experience to avoid misunderstanding.**

To assure that clients know what they are getting when they hire us, we are clear and up front about our qualifications. For example, if we received a Masters degree, we don't hide the field of our degree (e.g., physics, theatre, counseling). Where appropriate, we

**COACHING** *in Action* | **Coaching Ethics** *by Michael Wright, CFT Certified Coach*

*(Continued)*

relate its value to our coaching. If a client is seeking experience that we don't have, we are forthright about our background and focus instead on what we do offer as a coach. Should they want someone with different experience, we can refer them to a colleague.

**Keep the role of coach separate from other professional roles, e.g., psychologist, therapist, accountant, attorney.**

For example, if we practice both as a coach and as a psychologist or therapist, we do not practice both simultaneously with the same client. Should a client wish to engage us for both services, we close out the relationship for the first service before beginning the relationship for the second service. Also, we set up separate agreements for each engagement. Or, we can consider referring the client to another provider where the client would benefit from receiving both services at once.

## Completion with clients

Coaching relationships vary in length. Some last a few months, while others last several years. The time comes when one or both of you are ready to end the coaching relationship. Ideally, clients end coaching when they fully achieve their objectives and are ready to go on their own, so co-design a celebratory closure of the relationship.

Some clients have mixed feelings about closure, so take some time to celebrate the progress made and voice any disappointments, then explore the impact on both the coach and the client. This may feel like watching a bird fly off from the nest.

Clients may end coaching for any number of reasons—satisfaction with the outcomes, change in life circumstances or a desire for something different. As a coach, you may want to end a coaching relationship, perhaps because the client gets intractably stuck in an issue or because you want to make a referral to a therapist or another coach. You might even think you are not the best coach for a particular client or you are not enjoying the coaching relationship. Whatever the reason, a completion session brings closure to the coaching relationship. The components of a satisfying closure can include:

Appreciating key learning and insights

Celebrating accomplishments and goals reached

Voicing disappointments about any unmet goals or needs

Sharing mutual feedback and opportunities for growth

Establishing new commitments or steps that serve as a springboard for what's next

Expressing mutual gratitude for the value of the relationship

Creating space for resuming coaching

Designing how the relationship looks in the future

Asking for referrals

During the discovery session, you can let the person know that the last session will be an empowering completion session that you'll co-create. That way you avoid letting the relationship peter out or end on a sour note. Since we often come to love our clients, consciously re-creating the relationship can be useful so we don't end up continuing informal coaching without remuneration.

---

**COACHING** *in Action* | **When to Refer Clients for Mental Health Services**
*by Karen Romine*

Working with people to facilitate personal growth and achieve goals can sometimes trigger emotional or pathological issues that require professional intervention. Your services are valuable, and to ensure your continuing success, it's important to protect yourself against accusations of practicing therapy without a license. Here is a handy reference of symptoms and signs that psychotherapy or other mental health treatment is needed.

**RED FLAGS**

- Depressive symptoms, including sadness, hopelessness, lethargy, lack of pleasure, weight loss or appetite change, irritability, insomnia or sleeping too much, feelings of guilt, and/or poor concentration, particularly when symptoms endure for more than two weeks, when symptoms are accompanied by suicidal ideation, and/or when there is a history of suicide or suicide attempts in client's family

- Periods of euphoria ("natural high") accompanied by decreased need for sleep; poor judgment; impulsivity, such as excessive financial spending or promiscuity; distractibility; racing thoughts; and/or agitation and enthusiasm for goals

- Self-harming behavior, including cutting, pulling hair, excessive piercing or tattooing, picking at nails or skin to bleeding or other self-injurious actions

- Taking psychotropic medications without attending therapy

- Panic or anxiety attacks which occur suddenly and include physiological symptoms such as rapid heart rate, sweating, difficulty breathing and a feeling of impending doom

- Behavior dangerous to self or others, including quasi-accidental incidents

- Primary relationship that causes client excessive fear; keeps client isolated from friends, family or you as a helping professional; or involves signs of abuse

- Despite the fact that spiritual breakthroughs can be positive, hallucinations should always be referred for assessment

- Issues born of trauma and anxiety, including fears, aversions, phobias and agoraphobia (fear of leaving home)

- Paranoia, misreading the motives of others, and persistent, irrational fear

- Addictive behavior, including drugs, alcohol, sex (including internet pornography), emotional eating, shopping and gambling, even if it seems minor or infrequent

- Frequent sleepwalking can be a symptom of epilepsy or a seizure disorder; client should be referred to an MD for evaluation

**OTHER ISSUES THAT MAY BENEFIT FROM PSYCHOTHERAPY**

- Client's goals run counter to family-of-origin or culture-of-origin values and norms

- Client does not comply with recommended medical treatment

- Relationship issues, including those triggered by divorce, childbirth or infidelity

- A pattern of self-sabotaging behavior that does not respond to coaching interventions

- Periods of missing memory or dissociation (numbness, feeling/acting spacey, "going elsewhere" in consciousness)

- Unresolved grief

---

---

**COACHING *in Action* | When to Refer Clients for Mental Health Services**
*by Karen Romine*

*(Continued)*

- Identity confusion, including issues around race, gender and sexual orientation

- Anger management and impulse control issues

- Patterns of rebellion or authority issues

- Parenting and family relational issues

- Challenging relationship dynamics between client and trainer/coach, including dependency behavior, seductiveness, manipulation, needing excessive attention, alternating between idealization and devaluation, inappropriate anger, at times very suggestible, paranoia, entitlement and/or rapidly shifting emotions

- Adjustment periods after major life changes, including a death in the family, divorce, job change or moving

- Many clients can benefit from therapy when successful training and coaching services trigger "upper limits" issues, taking client into a life better than their previous comfort zone!

---

## Experiential phone coaching

Coaching may be done in person or over the phone. One of the obvious advantages of phone coaching is saving time for both parties because they can make calls from any convenient location.

Initially, clients may be reluctant to work on the phone. Once they experience it, most clients love the flexibility. Many people also report that they are more open and vulnerable over the phone than in person.

For the coach, working over the phone increases sensitivity to voice, tone, pace and inflection. You become adept at reading the energy of the client and develop more access to intuition.

Even experiential exercises translate to phone coaching. In the same way you might guide a visualization or an awareness exercise with individuals face to face, create the experience by giving instructions over the phone.

Some tips for creating powerful experiences over the phone:

Invite the client to create experiential exercises remotely. Consider it an experiment and encourage the client to step in wholeheartedly.

When the experience directs attention to the body, imagination or feeling, flow into the experience as a natural part of the dialogue.

Guide the experience as you would if you were face to face.

Speak in a tone and pace that invites your client to make a shift. If you offer a body awareness or an emotional awareness exercise, this may mean speaking more slowly or softly.

Leave time and silence for the client to do what you ask. Avoid the tendency to rush. Err on the side of giving more time than is needed so that you send the signal that the client can really drop into the experience.

Ask clients to pay attention to their experience and then ask them what they notice, so they can process the experience.

Protect the space you create for your client and guard against side conversations or jumping out of the experience prematurely.

Use your intuition and share what you sense or feel as you guide the experience. Assume your intuitions are useful for the client.

## COACHING *in Action* | **Stepping Past the Borders of Our Knowing**
*by Ivy Woolf Turk, CFT Certified Coach*

One day, early in my coaching career, I received an unexpected telephone call from a client I had been coaching for about six months. I was surprised to hear from her on a day when we hadn't scheduled a coaching session. I sensed a shrill quality in her voice that was not familiar. I asked her what was going on. She said that she needed to talk to me about something important, and was feeling very "ambivalent" about it.

I roused my curiosity and began to ask questions about her mixed feelings. After some beating around the bush, and a silence that seemed to go on forever, she informed me that it was because of some information she had found out about me! Specifically, she had googled me and found out that I had been formerly incarcerated. She explained that she felt very vulnerable and unsure about the discrepancy between the woman she thought she knew as her coach, and the woman she had read about in the news articles. She felt she had divulged information about herself and her family that was very personal, and didn't feel safe. She expressed concern about not knowing what to do going forward.

Well, that made two of us! As her words filled my head, my heart sank into my toes. I literally felt cold, like menthol had been injected into my veins. One of my greatest fears had been actualized. My inner critics were marching at full speed. My head was pounding with the words that my new career was over before it had even begun. My past would forever thwart my future… So I thought!

I knew instinctually, though, that I had to be in the moment, tap into my power, step into my coach's stand, and with all of the courage I could muster, go to a place where neither she nor I had the answer. I knew that it was possible for each of us to hold a vision larger than what was appearing at the moment. I wanted to empower her to step past her ambivalence and give myself an opportunity to step past my fear. I knew that if I could "self-manage," we might hold a space and create a safe container that would allow a new future for both of us.

So, I took a deep cleansing breath, and asked her if she was open to exploring this ambivalence more fully. I asked her what that might look like. She told me she needed to hear whatever I wanted to share about my journey, but couldn't promise any outcome.

And, so I did! Twenty minutes into describing not only the choices that led me to prison, but the authentic stories of my life and the resiliency that carried me through so many other adversities, she stopped me. The shrill in her voice had turned into a soft and compassionate whimper. She said "Oh Ivy, if you would still consider having me as your client, it would be my honor."

I started to cry. She went on to say that she hoped I didn't mind taking some advice from a client! She suggested that from now on, in my discovery sessions, I let every client know that "my greatest adversities, became the greatest curriculum for my growth." And so, stepping past the borders of our knowing, a truly authentic coaching relationship began and lives on to this day, and the foundation of what is now my successful coaching practice, was born.

## Coaching niches

When you think about how you want to use your coaching skills, do you want to be a generalist or specialize in a particular coaching niche? Some coaches start out coaching anyone who's interested and hone into a niche as they discover their passions. Other coaches are clear about their niche from the start. Sports coaches and acting coaches were the most widely known until recently. Now there are a wide range of coaching niches and people who specialize in coaching in every field (e.g., medicine, law, real estate, sales and health). Some popular coaching niches are listed below.

**Life Coaching**—focuses on any and all aspects of life including: personal, professional and relational.

**Executive Coaching**—focuses on supporting executives (usually corporate) in areas that can include visioning, strategizing, change management, employee relations and communication.

**Career Coaching**—supports people in clarifying their ideal career path and creating action plans to achieve their career objectives.

**Small Business Coaching**—supports business owners in creating and sustaining successful, profitable businesses.

**Wellness Coaching**—supports people in establishing optimal health, including physical and emotional well-being.

**Entrepreneur Coaching**—supports budding entrepreneurs as they clarify vision, mission, target market and successfully launch their ideas.

**Transformational Coaching**—helps people attune to who they are at the core and what's emerging by getting them in touch with their power and sense of all that's possible.

**Behavioral Coaching**—supports people who want to modify their behavior. Often suggested by their boss, objectives are co-created with clients taking the lead.

**Organizational Coaching**—works with the entire organization to support systemic change and reach organizational objectives.

**Nonprofit Coaching**—supports nonprofit leaders and staff to create a coaching culture for their organization and equips direct service providers to work with clients in empowering ways.

**Community Coaching**—support community leaders, funders, government and nonprofit organizations, volunteers and community members to create dynamic partnerships and sustainable community change.

**Spiritual Coaching**—helps people establish or enhance a deep spiritual connection and harness the power and insight inherent in that connection.

**Grief Coaching**—supports people who are dealing with any of life's losses.

**Cross-Cultural Coaching**—supports expatriates and others to explore and deal with cross-cultural issues.

**Relationship Coaching**—supports couples, business partnerships or people in any other relationship to address challenges and create their ideal relationship.

**Couples Coaching**—supports couples in creating relationships that value each other's uniqueness while developing their capacity for deeper expression of love, interdependency and mutuality.

**Family Coaching**—enhances relationships within families and provides support to overcome issues that interfere with optimal relationships.

**Kids Coaching**—works with children to develop their innate gifts and to develop their power to dream and create.

## Envisioning Your Ideal Practice

*Your visions will become clear only when you can look into your own heart. Who looks outside, dreams; who looks inside, awakes. —Carl Jung*

An important step in building a coaching practice is establishing a compelling vision. Just as you help clients create visions for their future, do the same for your coaching practice. You may have a good idea of how you envision your practice, who you want to work with and the impact you want to have, but getting it out of your head and onto paper will help you clearly communicate your vision and plan for success. When thinking of your business, consider the following questions:

What dreams do I have for my practice?

Who would I love to work with (ideal clients)?

What coaching specialties or niche interests me?

What does an ideal day/week/month look like?

Where do my passion and dreams for my coaching practice intersect?

What is the impact of my coaching for my prospective clients?

Where do I see myself working (home office, external office, client site)?

My ideal business has:

Number of Clients:

Types of Clients:

Hourly Rates:

Hours per Month:

Monthly Revenue from Coaching:

Other Income:

Total Income:

Monthly Business Expenses:

Monthly Net Income:

What will I have once this vision is a reality?

Some ideas to consider to let your creative juices flow:

Create a vision board for your coaching practice, getting in touch with all that's within you that's ready to come forth. Hang it where you can see it every day, visualizing everything you want to create.

Put your vision in writing and share it with everyone you know or meet.

Feel the fullness of your passion so others can feel it too.

Use constructive feedback from others to fine tune your vision.

Ignore negative or fear-based criticism. You're in the dreaming stage—the planning and reality checking comes later.

Some other things you can do with your vision:

Journal about your vision and see what insights arise.

Set an intention that can bring your vision into being and keep it alive for you each day.

Act as if your dreams are already a reality. When you stand in the fullness of your vision, you carry yourself differently, which boosts your confidence.

Enlist trusted friends to use your vision as a starting point for creating huge, outrageous visions for your coaching practice. You may become energized by the big dreams they imagine for you, and put ideas into motion that create an even bigger reality for you.

Dare to dream big!

Another thing to consider: instead of only coaching individuals, consider working with groups. While individual coaching can be a profitable model for some coaches (particularly executive coaches), many coaches find it beneficial to have multiple streams of income. Be open to other possibilities that appeal to you, including teaching, facilitating workshops, working with corporate teams, nonprofits or social activists—the list is endless. Think broadly—including multiple passions—while building your practice, then narrowing to where your passion, impact and profitability lead you once you're established.

## Getting clear about you

In a coaching business, you are your product. People choose to hire you as a coach because of who you are, what you value, how they resonate with you and what you can do for them. Just as you would intimately describe the details of a physical product you were selling, be clear about you as your product and the quality of service you will provide. Consider the following questions:

What am I passionate about?

What causes and people do I really care about and why?

What are my strengths, challenges and talents?

What are my core values?

What authentic qualities am I most proud of?

What do I enjoy doing?

What aspects of business do I dislike doing and how can I get it done? (e.g., who could I hire to handle that aspect of my business?)

What's unique about me that will benefit my clients?

What value will clients get from working with me?

## Developing confidence and overcoming fear

*Whenever we take a chance and enter unfamiliar territory or put ourselves into the world in a new way, we experience fear. Very often this fear keeps us from moving ahead with our lives. The trick is to feel the fear and do it anyway. —Susan Jeffers*

For many new coaches, fear and lack of self-confidence get in the way of establishing successful coaching practices. This is especially true for coaches who do not have experience running a business. You may wonder, "Who will pay me to coach them?" "Am I really worth $100 - $200 an hour, or more?" "Can the people I want to coach really afford fees in that range?" "Can I really earn a living as a coach?" While these questions are common for many new coaches, beware that they may be coming from your inner critic. You have big, new dreams that are taking you out of the realm of the familiar. You may feel comfortable and masterful in your former profession, but tentative and uncertain of your skills and value as a new coach. In this critical juncture, lack of confidence in your abilities, immobilizing fear of the unknown and undercharging clients can all adversely impact your ability to launch a successful coaching practice. Consider the following questions:

How am I feeling about myself as a coach right now?

How do my experience, wounds, talents, gifts and dreams contribute to my confidence as a coach?

What are my underlying fears or concerns?

Which qualities and strengths that contributed to success in my past professions are also valuable in my coaching practice?

What skills do I need to strengthen?

What will I do to continuously improve myself?

What are some strategies I can use to deal with inner and outer critics who doubt the viability of my dream?

So what are some ways to feel the fear and do it anyway? A master certified coach shared two things that she attributes to her success: she has worked with her own coach for the entire 15 years of her coaching career, and she changes coaches from time to time to benefit from different coaching styles and experiences. Another executive coach meets with a mutual support team of coaches every Monday morning for 90 minutes. To create your own support system, explore some possibilities:

Hire a coach/mentor to support you in getting really clear about your vision for your practice.

Work through any fear or confidence issues.

Design strategies, action steps and accountability.

Acknowledge your progress and success.

Set realistic fees.

Align yourself with other budding entrepreneurs and people who want to enhance their business. Join an existing group such as a Mastermind group or Ladies Who Launch (http://www.ladieswholaunch.com/) or start your own group of like-minded individuals. Meet with them regularly as an opportunity to:

Learn, share ideas and encourage one another.

Brainstorm, receive support and offer feedback.

Establish accountability by investing in each others' success.

Develop confidence while sharpening your business skills.

Create a full support team that may include a coach, mentor, accountant, attorney, marketer or others. Network with other coaches to learn how they overcame some of the obstacles you might be facing.

## Developing a Business Plan

Creating a business plan helps you establish a successful business, but the process doesn't have to be complex. Business plans are typically a work in progress. The Small Business Administration[3] suggests a business plan include the following sections:

**Executive Summary**—provides a concise overview of the entire plan, along with a history of your company.

**Company Description**—includes information about the nature of your business, why you're in business, the needs your business will satisfy, how you plan to satisfy those needs and a list of the types of individuals or organizations that you've identified as having these needs.

**Organization & Management**—includes your company's organizational structure and details about the ownership of your company.

**Marketing**—consists of your marketing and sales strategies. The marketing strategy includes market analysis, marketing research, pricing and communication and sales strategies. How will you get customers and insure their satisfaction and loyalty?

**Service or Product Line**—includes detailed descriptions of your coaching services and products. Describe the benefits your clients will receive from your services and products that will address their challenges or possibilities. How will you package your coaching options and what products will serve your clients?

---

3    U.S. Small Business Administration: http://www.sba.gov

**Financials**—includes information from your market analysis and is based on your objectives. Key information for new coaches in this section is prospective financial data including projected sales and expenses. What funding will you need to start or expand your business?

An SBA.gov online tool for generating a business plan can be accessed at: http://web.sba.gov/busplantemplate/BizPlanStart.cfm.

SCORE.org offers a Word document business plan template at: https://www.score.org/resources/business-plan-template-startup-business.

# Establishing Your Business

There are many resources available for people who are setting up a new business. Three useful USA websites are http://www.score.org, http://www.sba.gov, and http://business.gov. Rather than covering them in depth in this section, we provide an overview just to get you thinking about legal structure, naming your business and getting started.

## Legal structure of your business

When setting up your business as a legal entity, consider several options and the different legal, financial and tax considerations. As you research the legal structure for your business, you may wish to consult with an accountant and an attorney. Many coaches are sole proprietors—the simplest legal entity. Possible legal entities include:

**Sole Proprietorship**—A business owned and managed by one individual who is personally liable for all business debts and obligations.

**Partnership**—A single business owned by two or more people.

**Corporation**—A legal entity owned by shareholders.

**S Corporation**—A special type of corporation created to avoid double taxation (once to the shareholders and again to the corporation) by electing to be treated as an S corporation.

**Limited Liability Company (LLC)**—A hybrid legal structure that provides the limited liability features of a corporation and the tax efficiencies and operational flexibility of a partnership.

**Nonprofit**—An organization engaged in activities of public or private interest where making a profit is not a primary mission. Most nonprofits are exempt from paying federal and state taxes.

**Cooperative**—A business or organization owned by and operated for the benefit of those using its services. Cooperatives are not a legal structure.

## Name your business

A good business name is simple, easy to remember and gives a hint about the purpose of your business. After brainstorming an initial list of possible names, get feedback from family, friends and potential clients. Enlist them in suggesting alternatives. Evaluate the pros and cons to narrow your list. Try doing a search for the name and similar names on the internet to get a sense of what potential clients would find if looking for your business with that name. Check for availability of related internet domain names. If the name is available, you can register the domain name for as little as $10.00 a year. If your business name is fictitious or not your own, you will need to register it in accordance with your state or local regulations.

### Register your business

The legal name of a business is the name of the person or entity that owns a business. For example, if you are the sole owner of your business, its legal name is your full name. If your business is a partnership, the legal name is the name given in your partnership agreement or the last names of the partners. For limited liability corporations (LLCs) and corporations, the business' legal name is the one that was registered with the state government.

The legal name of your business is required on all government forms and applications, including your application for employer tax IDs, licenses and permits. However, you can file a "fictitious name" registration with your government agency. A fictitious name (or assumed name), trade name or DBA name (doing business as) is a business name that is different from your personal name, the names of your partners or the officially registered name of your LLC or corporation.

### Obtain your federal tax ID

Employers with employees, business partnerships and corporations, and other types of organizations, must obtain an Employer Identification Number (EIN) from the U.S. Internal Revenue Service.

### Register with your state revenue agency

Just as you must have a Federal Tax ID, you will also need to obtain Tax IDs and permits from your state's revenue agency.

### Obtain state licenses or permits

Many types of businesses need to obtain some type of business or professional license or permit from a state government. Check the requirements for the state where your business is located.

## Self-Care and Professional Development

Taking time to renew yourself, impacts your well-being. Since you are the product you are selling to your clients, how can you be at your best? Working with many clients can feel energizing or draining, so schedule down time to replenish yourself. Make time for your spiritual practices, hobbies, a massage, a walk in nature or keeping up with your fitness routine. It's easy to become consumed with building your business and serving your clients. If you end up putting yourself last, what message will you send to your clients? Make yourself as important as your clients and schedule self-nurturing activities and white space on your calendar before filling it with your business activities. Make room for what you love and for what renews you. You could work the business 24/7, so remember to take a break.

Part of self-care includes your professional development—expanding your skills as a coach. How important is it for you to factor professional development into your business budget? Consider joining the International Coach Federation (ICF) and become active in your local chapter and other organizations. You can attend meetings and workshops that deepen your coaching repertoire and confidence. Also consider joining other professional groups like local business associations. They help you build your network and serve as a resource for building your business.

## COACHING *in Action* | You Don't Have to Leave your Job to be a Coach
### *by Pailin Chirachaisakul, CFT Certified Coach*

It should have been so easy to leave my job and follow my dream.

When I first considered becoming a professional coach, I believed that after I became a coach, I would leave my office life and become a self-employed coach, so that I could do what I love.

As soon as I began my journey with the Coaching for Transformation (CFT) program, I started to feel a change. I was coached on what I want to do in my life—leave the company I worked for or stay. Honing in on this, we did an exercise called Envision the Future, where I saw myself as a mother wearing a long skirt with an apron, holding three children's hands—feeling so wise and peaceful. I felt so much joy.

My future was clear, so what was stopping me from leaving my job? Was it about money? No, I could earn money being a coach and facilitator. Was it about certainty? No, I didn't believe that without the company I could not do anything else. I was curious, "What was holding me back?"

Two days later, I was being coached again and this time, I made a deep connection to my need to serve. I realized that it would be so easy for me to leave the company and be with people who understand me. However, if I left, people in the company would never know or experience how wonderful, supportive and loving the coaching journey could be.

My intention for staying with the company was to share the coaching experience with everyone there. I had received so much from my coach training, and my need was to give back by helping the organization create a coaching culture for sustainability. That same night I had a dream, where I saw Martha (a CFT founder) speaking with my company's president. I took that as a sign.

The next day, it took all of my courage to write an email to my president. I remember how nervous and anxious I felt—actually, it went through my whole body. Nonetheless, I told him how wonderful the coach experience was for me, and how I would love to share with our company. I hit send. He replied "Let's talk." Two weeks later, Martha was in Thailand, sitting in the company's meeting room with our organization's Development Manager and team to discuss implementing a coaching culture. And just three weeks later, Vikram Bhatt (a CFT faculty member) was in Thailand to meet the team and continue the conversation about the opportunity to spread CFT in the company.

For me, I felt overwhelmed by the power of coaching and how everything had moved forward so rapidly. Now, I am in the transitional process to move from Risk Manager toward Internal Executive Coach and helping the organizational development team to create a coaching culture. I'm fulfilling my dream to be a coach and serving my need to build a coaching culture in my company—with the same love and support that I experienced in my CFT coaching journey.

# Giving Back

## Strategic contribution and social sector coaching

Call it donation, in-kind, volunteer service, charity work or pro bono; donating your coaching for free or at reduced cost to people and organizations supports the work they do in the world. The Leadership that Works faculty enthusiastically encourage you to make strategic contribution a part of your practice, not only because coaching makes the world a better place, but also because it helps you grow your practice.

Especially early on, when you are building your coaching practice, think strategically about how you use your valuable contribution hours. First, identify to whom you want to give. What causes or people in the world do you want to impact positively? Next, look at your candidates and consider the value of your contribution to them, and also weigh the potential value of that contribution to your own practice. How would the exposure you garner by contributing to them benefit your overall plan? Don't make your decision based solely on what good your service will do to your coaching business, but weigh the impact in the decision.

*Consider the benefits:*

What is the size of the nonprofit?

How visible are they in the community?

Who is on their board, and how would it be beneficial for me to serve on that board?

How will this relationship expand my network?

What can I learn from this relationship?

Keep in mind the benefits of strategic contribution during fallow times in your practice. Consider following the Leadership that Works adage, "When work gets slow, give something away." Recent research shows that volunteers have lower risk of heart disease. For the pure joy of it, consider making giving a conscious part of your life. How much would you like to contribute? Giving away 100 hours of coaching a year is only two hours a week. What joy will it bring you to give some of your coaching away?

*Questions to Consider*

What are your dreams for your coaching practice?

What impact would you like to have on your clients?

How can you put your vision into words—clearly and concisely?

Who can support you as you launch your practice?

What first step will you take to get started? And when?

# Section IV:
# Evolution of Coaching

*"Once social change begins, it cannot be reversed. You cannot uneducate the person who has learned to read. You cannot humiliate the person who feels pride. You cannot oppress the people who are not afraid anymore. We have seen the future, and the future is ours."* —Cesar Chavez

Section IV takes us through the theoretical underpinnings of coaching, honoring many of the historical models that have contributed to the field. Then we look at what is emerging and what excites us as coaches and trainers. As part of our mission at Leadership that Works—to expand the availability of coaching—we share what we're learning about cross cultural awareness and how coaching helps us navigate and shift the dynamics of power and privilege. Next we'll explore organizational coaching and the unique challenges of coaching in the social sector. In the last chapter we delve into the nuances of coaching soul and spirit. We hope you'll join us in creating a future where we all can thrive.

# 12
# Contributions to Coaching

Coaching evolved from a variety of root disciplines, theories and practices. Some of the early roots of coaching included athletics, psychology, therapy, management theory, the self-help movement, adult learning theory, support networks, the holistic movement and education. In this chapter, we'll delve into the theoretical underpinnings of coaching by exploring some of the root disciplines that have contributed to the evolution of coaching.

Because professional coaching was developed by several people independently during the same period of time, early theories and practices often resulted in confusion. Coaching is still commonly misunderstood, despite widespread usage in the business world and personal development.

As coaching emerged as a distinct field, a key factor was the shift in psychological understanding from a pathology view to a growth-enhancing view. This shift was spawned by the humanist and human potential movements, encounter groups, large group awareness trainings, self-help literature and 12-step groups.

In the 1960s, the Human Potential Movement led to the emergence of a number of centers such as National Training Laboratories, Tavistock, Findhorn and Esalen, where interdisciplinary and experiential gatherings led to innovative theories and practices that were human-potential focused rather than pathology focused.[1]

Influenced by Esalen, Werner Erhard developed est training in 1971, which later became known as the Forum and then Landmark Education. Both Thomas Leonard and Laura Whitworth worked for Erhard and went on to become pioneers in the coaching field. While Leonard popularized coaching by defining and documenting the process and founding the International Coach Federation, Laura Whitworth and

---

1    Brock, Vikki (2008). *Grounded Theory of the Roots and Emergence of Coaching.* A dissertation.

John Whitmore contributed to the evolution of the field by adding fuel to the coaching fire through conferences, workshops and writing. Many others developed theories, models, tools and practices that have spread through social networks, face-to-face conferences and workshops.

In Vikki Brock's 2008 dissertation on the Grounded Theory of the Roots and Emergence of Coaching, she found that:

coaching sprang from several independent sources at the same time and spread through relationships;

coaching has a broad intellectual framework that draws on the synergy, cross-fertilization and practices of many disciplines;

modern patterns and practices of coaching are dynamic and contextual;

coaching came into existence to fill an unmet need in an interactive, fluid world of rapid change and complexity; and

coaching came into being in an open integral social network from a perspective of diversity, collaboration and inclusion.[2]

Coaching is a growing social phenomenon that attracts people from many disciplines. Brock predicts that coaching will become interwoven in the fabric of life because it's a fluid social movement that has spread through human relationships.[3] Collaboration is highly valued by coaching professionals, which has led to the cross-fertilization of ideas and practices. In the 1990s, numerous coaches described other coaches as "not really coaching" because they were really practicing psychology or consulting. In turn, other professionals accused coaches of lacking foundational knowledge, and many didn't even recognize coaching as a profession. Fortunately, coaching has become a multi-disciplinary field and has re-embraced cross-fertilization, collaboration and inclusion, while taking a more rigorous approach to understanding its deep roots and history.

So let's take a look at how coaching builds on many modalities.

## Person-Centered Approach

*In my early professional years I was asking the question: How can I treat, or cure, or change this person? Now I would phrase the question in this way: How can I provide a relationship which this person may use for his own personal growth? —Carl Rogers*

Carl Rogers developed what he called a client-centered approach to psychotherapy and founded the humanistic psychology movement. In the early 1960s, he brought empathy and "unconditional positive regard"[4] to a world of personal development that was dominated by Freudian psychological traditions that relied on the therapist's opinions and agendas.

---

2    Brock, Vikki (2008). *Grounded Theory of the Roots and Emergence of Coaching*. A dissertation.
3    Brock, Vikki (2008). *Grounded Theory of the Roots and Emergence of Coaching*. A dissertation.
4    Rogers, Carl R. (1995). *On Becoming A Person: A Therapist's View of Psychotherapy*. Boston: Houghton Mifflin.

Rogers saw in his clients the need for a relationship in which they were accepted. He said, "If I can provide a certain type of relationship, the other will discover within himself the capacity to use that relationship for growth and change, and personal development will occur."[5]

Carl Rogers developed the person-centered approach and stated several sufficient conditions required for change. Three that we rely on heavily in coaching are:

**Congruence or Genuineness**: coaches are "not acting" and can draw on their own experiences and self-disclosure to facilitate the relationship.

**Unconditional Positive Regard**: coaches accept the client unconditionally, without judgment, disapproval or approval. This facilitates increased self-regard in the client.

**Empathic Understanding**: the coach experiences an empathic understanding of the client's internal experience. Accurate understanding helps the client believe in the coach's unconditional love.[6]

Rogers said, "The curious paradox is that when I accept myself just as I am, then I can change."[7] This principle is widely used in Coaching for Transformation: creating an environment where the client can move toward full self-acceptance is the precursor to transformation.

## Psychosynthesis

Roberto Assagioli developed psychosynthesis in 1910, one of the earliest forerunners in humanistic psychology. He asserted that the direct experience of the self led to spiritual goals of self-realization and "one humanity." The study of the person with many sub-personalities and a soul led to experimentation by many, including Richard Schwartz's work with Internal Family Systems and Hal & Sidra Stone's work with Voice Dialogue.

## Experiential Learning

*Tell me, and I will forget. Show me, and I may remember. Involve me, and I will understand. —Confucius*

Experiential learning is based on the understanding that we learn by doing. In the early 1980s, David Kolb developed a model of learning that became widely used. In layman's terms, Kolb asserted "that adults learn by having an experience, then reflecting on that experience, coming up with new insights or ideas and then going out into the world to apply these new insights."[8] When they apply their new insights, they then have new experiences to learn from and learning becomes an endless cycle.

We embrace experiential learning in the Coaching for Transformation approach where participants learn new coaching processes through:

5    Rogers, Carl R. (1995). *On Becoming A Person: A Therapist's View of Psychotherapy*. Boston: Houghton Mifflin.
6    Rogers, Carl R. (1995). *On Becoming A Person: A Therapist's View of Psychotherapy*. Boston: Houghton Mifflin.
7    Rogers, Carl R. (1995). *On Becoming A Person: A Therapist's View of Psychotherapy*. Boston: Houghton Mifflin.
8    Kolb, D. A. & Fry, R. (1975). Toward an applied theory of experiential learning; in C. Cooper (ed.). *Theories of Group Process*. London: John Wiley.

Knowledge (reading and listening)

Demonstration (watching instructors demonstrate the process)

Practice (experimenting with the new process)

Reflection (capturing insights)

Application (applying the learning as a coach)

Likewise, we believe clients learn from their own experience. As coaches, we take a stand that clients are dynamic, powerful and creative—inherently capable of finding their own solutions. So we ask rigorous questions to help them reflect on and learn from their experience. We don't stop there. We help them apply their learning in their lives, whether realizing their goals or deepening their awareness.

## Existential Therapy

*One must have at least a readiness to love the other person, broadly speaking, if one is to be able to understand him. —Rollo May*

Existential therapy is based on the assumptions that life is uncertain and that we have freedom of choice. Rollo May believed the purpose of psychotherapy was to set people free.[9] As human beings, we all share the experience of facing and confronting uncertainties whether we have issues with health, employment, romance or conflict. Whatever the uncertainty, we experience a felt sense of unease or anxiety.

Anxiety is not always something problematic that must be reduced or removed. Anxiety can feel stimulating, putting us in touch with our sense of aliveness, and becomes the source for creative and original insight. Indeed, a life without anxiety would lack meaning and opportunity. However, when anxiety becomes unmanageable or intolerable, we initiate ways to reduce or remove anxiety. Unfortunately, these strategies can be problematic if we refuse to face the source of the anxiety. We all face anxiety, but our unique worldview influences how we experience life.

In the Coaching for Transformation process, we embrace the philosophy of existential coaching. Instead of applying general techniques to specific unique experiences or issues, we create a secure and trustworthy "life-space" to encourage clients to know themselves more clearly and to experience more honestly their worldview. By supporting them in examining their beliefs and views, we uncover competing beliefs and help them challenge the ambiguities, tensions and limitations that have an impact on their aspirations.

Many of the transformational pathways build upon the root discipline of existential coaching. We help clients explore several view points and recognize that they have full choice in every moment.

---

9    May, R. (1999). *Freedom and Destiny*. W. W. Norton & Company.

## Gestalt Therapy

*I do my thing and you do yours. I am not in this world to live up to your expectations,*
*and you are not in this world to live up to mine. You are you and I am I, and if by*
*chance we find each other, then it is beautiful. If not, it can't be helped. —Fritz Perls*

Gestalt therapy was developed by Fritz Perls, Laura Perls and Paul Goodman in the 1940s and 1950s. Combining existential and experiential psychotherapy, the focus is on the present moment. Personal responsibility is key, as is the coach/client relationship. Arnold Beisser described Gestalt's paradoxical theory of change: the more we attempt to be who we are not, the more we remain the same.[10] Conversely, when people identify with their current experience, the conditions of wholeness and growth support change. Put another way, change comes about as a result of "full acceptance of what is, rather than a striving to be different."[11]

## Behavioral Science

*If you truly want to understand something, try to change it. —Kurt Lewin*

The NTL Institute for Applied Behavioral Science originated in the 1940s as an experiment in group relations to help people become sensitive to interpersonal dynamics. Known for the development of T-Groups, experiential learning, sensitivity training, feedback and diversity awareness, they've left a deep imprint in the coaching field. As part of reeducating adult learners, Kurt Lewin developed a process where people alter, replace or transcend their usual patterns of thinking, which is more complex than learning something anew. Applied Behavioral Science provided the underpinnings for Organization Development.

## Process Consulting

In Edgar Schein's 1960s book about process consultation, he advocates for clients to own the outcomes. He discusses the importance of understanding the emotions, biases, values and reality of the person the consultant is working with and the impact those factors can have on perceptions. He saw this approach as being valuable for anyone in the "helping" professions.[12]

Process consultation helps clients find the solution themselves without giving them advice. Process consulting is especially useful when neither the problem nor the solution is entirely clear. The process consultant starts by finding a person in the organization whose intention is to improve the way things are done and then identifies a process to create the desired change. Many consultants today give expert advice rather than following Schein's process. Coaching is similar to process consultation in that we avoid giving advice and instead, support people in gaining clarity and finding their own solutions.

10   Beisser, A. (1970). *The Paradoxical Theory of Change.* In Gestalt Therapy Now, ed. J. Fagan & I. L. Shepard. Harper & Row.

11   Houston, G. (2003). *Brief Gestalt Therapy: Brief Therapy Series.* Sage Publications.

12   Schein, Edgar (1987). *Process Consultation, Volume 2: Lessons for Managers and Consultants.* Addison-Wesley Publishing.

In Schein's approach, the consultant and the client act as equal partners and share mutual responsibility. This learning-based process supports clients in continuous development, long after the consultant has moved on. By developing a learning organization, employees at all levels engage in dialogue, problem diagnosis and resolution, and shared vision. Everyone takes responsibility for the end result.

## Management Theory X and Theory Y

Business coaching and executive coaching share a common basis with management theories that appeared in the early 1960s, including two known as "Theory X and Theory Y." Douglas McGregor, working at the MIT Sloan School of Management, studied two very different attitudes toward employee motivation, and asserted that most companies followed one or the other. The Theory X view assumes that employees are inherently lazy and will avoid work if they can. Because of this, workers need to be closely supervised and managed.

Theory X managers believe that their employees do not really want to work, that they would rather avoid responsibility and that it is the manager's job to structure the work and energize the employee.

Theory Y managers view employees as self-motivated, eager to accept greater responsibility and able to exercise self-control and self-direction. On the whole, employees enjoy their mental and physical work duties and, if given the chance, they have the desire to be creative and forward thinking. A Theory Y manager believes that, given the right conditions, most people want to do well at work and the manager's role is to tap the pool of unused creativity in the workforce. Rather than trying to control people, a Theory Y manager removes the barriers that prevent workers from fully actualizing themselves.

Of course, coaching shares McGregor's Theory Y view of employees. As we learn more about human behavior, the Theory Y view of human performance dominates management theory. Due to the shift from a manufacturing economy to an information and services economy, for the first time in history, managers can no longer assume they know more about the business than their staff. Knowledge sharing, creativity and lateral thinking are vital to every level of business.

Theory X management just doesn't work in knowledge-rich environments. Managers can't force things like "creativity" or "commitment to excellence" onto employees who aren't internally motivated to perform well at their jobs. Most management theory today is based on Theory Y notions such as trust, mentoring, modeling ethical behavior, empowerment and improvements to workplace environment. Coaching has expanded Theory Y at the personal level.

## Emotional Intelligence

In the book *Emotional Intelligence* by Salovey and Mayer, the five domains of emotional intelligence are:

Knowing one's emotions

Managing emotions

Motivating oneself

Recognizing emotions in others

Handling relationships[13]

When we ask empowering questions and slow down, the actual circuitry of our mind maps can be interrupted for reconsideration. Beliefs can shift when seen in a new light. Clients can respond to the emotions, thoughts, needs and intuitions that are present. By guiding them to pay attention to their bodies, they can interrupt the autopilot of habit. New ways of responding to information become possible.

This circuitry can rewire itself more effectively when people are in touch with their bodies and the natural world. By bringing awareness to the body we can respond to natural openings and can restore new energy flows.

## Positive Psychology

Closely related to coaching, Positive Psychology was originated by Abraham Maslow in 1954[14] and developed further by Martin Seligman. As the father of the modern positive psychology movement, Seligman shifted the focus of psychology away from its dominant focus on mental illness, unhappiness and dysfunction to nurturing talent and improving life.[15] The research done by positive psychologists explores why people are happy or not, and what factors impact and increase happiness. The results of these studies have provided valuable resources for psychologists and coaches. Both professions have found that goals based on a client's core values are more easily achieved, are more sustainable over time and bring deeper satisfaction.

## Nonviolent Communication

Nonviolent communication (NVC) was developed by Marshall Rosenberg in the 1960s as a method of communicating with others and understanding oneself. Nonviolent communication can be seen as both a spiritual practice that helps us see our common humanity, and a set of skills that help us create stronger human connections and communities. The four step model includes:

Observations (without evaluation)

Feelings (without interpretation)

Needs (without strategies)

Requests (without demand)[16]

Based on the belief that everything we do or say is an attempt to meet a need, Rosenberg's work enhances emotional intelligence by deepening awareness of universal human needs. The coaching process deepens as people uncover their needs in the moment. The NVC model is applicable in

---

13  Salovey, Peter; Brackett, Marc A. & Mayer, John D. (2004). *Emotional Intelligence: Key Readings on the Mayer and Salovey Model.* Port Chester, NY: Dude Publishing.

14  Maslow, Abraham H. (1970). *Motivation and Personality.* New York: Harper & Row.

15  Seligman, Martin E. P. (2002). *Authentic Happiness: Using the New Positive Psychology to Realize Your Potential for Lasting Fulfillment.* New York: Free.

16  Rosenberg, Marshall B. (2003). *Nonviolent Communication: A Language of Life.* Encinitas, CA: PuddleDancer.

contexts ranging from intimate relationships, conflict resolution, healing and reconciliation, and collaborative communication—at home and at work.

NVC offers three ways to build connection:

honest self-expression—sharing in ways that inspire compassion

empathy—listening with compassion

self-empathy—practicing self-compassion[17]

As simple as it sounds, many people find the process difficult to master because we're actually changing decades of habitual, judgmental ways of responding when we connect with the heart of each step.

# Neuro-Linguistic Programming

Richard Bandler and linguist John Grinder founded Neuro-Linguistic Programming (NLP) in 1970 as a method of psychotherapy that capitalizes on the connection between neurological processes, language and behavioral patterns.[18] Neuro-Linguistic Programming has come into use as a coaching or behavioral transformation method that uncovers patterns of thought and identifies new approaches to thinking and personal behavior. The premise is that the words we use reflect our perception of our problems—that our attitudes are self-fulfilling—creating behaviors that our thoughts initiate. The goal of NLP is to remodel the thoughts and mental associations to create more desired outcomes. As a form of therapy, NLP educates people in self-awareness, effective communication and changing their patterns of mental and emotional behavior.

Andreas and Andreas developed the NLP Core Transformation Process to change unwanted behavior, feeling or responses, and also to come to a greater wholeness within where thoughts, feelings and actions are in harmony. They base their work on five "core states" that the components of our psyches want for us: 1) Being 2) Inner Peace 3) Love 4) OK-ness 5) Oneness.[19]

# Adult Learning Theory

The close parallels between Adult Learning Theory and coaching started in the 1960s when some early life coaching sessions grew out of adult learning programs. In 1973, Malcolm Knowles developed principles of adult learning to support the design of classes for adult learners. These principles closely parallel coaching principles today:

Adults need to actively engage in the learning process and we guide them to discover their own knowledge, not give them facts.

Adults need to connect their learning with their life experiences so we draw out the learner's experience and knowledge.

Adults are goal oriented and know the goals they want to attain. We provide support and structure for achieving those goals.

---

17  Rosenberg, Marshall B. (2003). *Nonviolent Communication: A Language of Life*. Encinitas, CA: PuddleDancer.
18  Bandler, Richard & Grinder, John (1979). *Frogs into Princes: Neuro Linguistic Programming*. Moab, UT: Real People.
19  Andreas, Connirae & Andreas, Tamara (1994). *Core Transformation: Reaching the Wellspring Within*. Moab, UT: Real People.

Adults must see a reason for learning something. We can help them see how learning is applicable and relevant in their lives.

Adults prefer to focus on the aspects of a lesson that are most useful in their lives and we help them actualize their learning.

Adults need respect and acknowledgement for the wealth of experience they bring. We treat them as equals and encourage them to express themselves freely.[20]

Each of these principles is relevant for us in the Coaching for Transformation process as we honor our clients' resourcefulness and learning styles.

## Learning Styles

In the 1970s, Dunn and Dunn developed one of the most widely used categorizations of learning styles, which expanded on Neuro-Linguistic Programming:

visual learners

auditory learners

kinesthetic learners[21]

**Visual learners** prefer to learn through seeing. They think in visual imagery and learn best via visual aids, diagrams, flip charts, illustrations, pictures, handouts and taking notes.

**Auditory learners** prefer to learn through listening. They listen for the nuances of speech; including tone, pitch, volume and pace. They thrive when listening to lectures or tapes, participating in discussions or reading aloud.

**Kinesthetic learners** prefer to learn through experience—moving, touching and doing. They like to learn through activities, experiments, practicing role plays and other forms of exploration. A hands-on approach allows them to actively explore the environment.

In 1987, building upon the work of David Kolb and Peter Honey, Alan Mumford identified four different ways people prefer to learn. Those learning styles are: Activist, Reflector, Theorist and Pragmatist.[22]

**Activists** like new experiences and ideas, but get bored with implementation. Activists learn best when they are involved, collaborating, challenged and leading.

**Reflectors** like to collect data, carefully consider and look at a situation from different perspectives. They learn best when observing, reviewing and producing analyses or reports.

**Theorists** like to adapt and integrate observations into complex and logically sound theories. Theorists learn best when put in complex situations requiring their skills and knowledge, in structured situations with clear purpose, when they have interesting ideas or concepts to ponder, and when they can question and probe.

**Pragmatists** like trying things out, when concepts can be directly applied and when they can avoid lengthy discussions. They learn best when there is an obvious link between the topic

---

20   Knowles, Malcolm S.; Holton, Elwood F. & Swanson, Richard A. (1988). *The Adult Learner: The Definitive Classic in Adult Education and Human Resource Development*. Houston, TX: Gulf Pub.

21   Dunn, R.; Dunn, K. & Price, G. E. (1984). *Learning Style inventory*. Lawrence, KS, USA: Price Systems.

22   Honey, P. & Mumford, A. (1982). *The Manual of Learning Styles*. Maidenhead, UK: Peter Honey Publications.

and task, they can try out new techniques and receive feedback, are shown techniques with obvious advantages, and when they are shown a model they can copy.

Many coaches use learning style instruments, such as the Learning Style Inventory, to leverage preferred learning styles while moving toward goal achievement.

## Cognitive Therapy

Of all the psychology disciplines, cognitive therapy is the most closely related to coaching. Developed by Aaron Beck, cognitive therapy works on the principle that the way we act results from the way we feel, and that our feelings result from the way we think.[23] In cognitive therapy, unlike many other forms of therapy, the focus is on current thought systems and ways that adults can retrain themselves to have new, more productive thoughts and behaviors in the future. Cognitive therapy does not focus on the source of the unproductive thought patterns that led to the undesired behavior.

The focus of cognitive therapy is helping people with dysfunctional behaviors learn new, more useful behaviors. However, the theory and practice can also be applied to help functional people develop new behaviors that support them in goal achievement. Similar to cognitive therapy, coaching is based on the theory that thoughts impact behaviors. In the Coaching for Transformation approach, our work with limiting beliefs, inner critics, expanding the view and visualization share similarities with cognitive therapy.

## Immunity to Change

In 1984, Kegan and Lahey suggested that development is the ability to make meaning of experiences. They developed the Immunity to Change process to help people build awareness of why behavioral change, despite the best intentions, is so difficult to implement. To bring light to hidden barriers to change, they developed the four-column Immunity Map which explores the motivators behind commitments, competing commitments, and the "big assumptions" that drive behavior and limit personal change or block development.

## Neurobiology

In recent years, the field of neurobiology has greatly expanded our understanding of how the brain contributes to our emotions and actions. We now understand that neuroplasticity, the ability of our brains to change and grow, continues throughout the life span. We also understand the means by which our guts and our hearts communicate with specific parts of the brain and the ways in which our facial expressions and other physical responses connect to certain parts of our nervous systems.

This knowledge has many implications for our coaching. We and our clients can create new pathways in our brains through practiced repetition of patterns we would like to foster. When the coach is present with the client with warmth and acceptance when the client faces shame, fear or overwhelm, the client's nervous

**RESOURCES**

Sarah Peyton
www.empathybrain.com

Dan Siegel
www.drdansiegel.com

Steven Porges
www.stephenporges.com

---

23  Alford, B. A. & Beck, A. T. (1998). *The Integrative Power of Cognitive Therapy.* The Guilford Press.

system is soothed, new neural connections built and what seemed unachievable for the client gradually comes within reach.

In the Coaching for Transformation approach, the insights of neurobiology impact our work with the body and with places of deep emotion.

## COACHING *in Action* | A Trauma-Informed Coaching Model *by Leslie Brown, CFT Faculty*

The air was thick with the energy that my client radiated as she described her most recent interaction with her supervisor. Suddenly her voice trailed off and I noticed she was teleported into a meeting that occurred 10 years prior. As I listened intensely, I acknowledged the pain invoked by the traumatic flash back and supported her to move forward, inviting the examination of her own growth from that distant memory. The scene that I am describing is one that is familiar to many coaches who work with clients that have elevated levels of trauma.

### WHAT IS TRAUMA?

"Psychological trauma involves experiences (witnessed or confronted) with extreme human suffering, severe bodily harm or injury, coercive exploitation or harassment, sexual violation, ethno violence, politically-based violence or immediate threat of death." (Marcenich, 2009)

### WHAT IS THE IMPACT OF TRAUMA?

Trauma overwhelms our clients' coping capacity and can limit their access to physical, emotional, intellectual or spiritual energy and power. The perception and impact of trauma varies greatly and many display a mix of survival responses including but not limited to:

- Fight,
- Flight,
- Freeze,
- Submit, or
- Shut down of non-essential tasks which means that rational thought is less possible.

### A 3-PHASE APPROACH TO COACHING CLIENTS

As humans navigating life we have all experienced traumatic events and often the impact leaves a lasting impact on how we move through life. Using a 3-Phase trauma informed framework, we can assist clients to slow down, get curious, identify impact and determine next steps. During the first phase we work to create a safe and supportive environment. The second phase provides a space to pause, recognize and acknowledge the trauma. This includes an opportunity to discuss and determine additional mental health supports. The third and final phase creates an opportunity to highlight and promote the resiliency and resourcefulness of the client, launching them into action.

### PHASE 1: PROVIDING A SAFE AND SUPPORTIVE COACHING ENVIRONMENT

During Phase 1 the coach supports the client by creating a coaching environment that promotes physical and emotional safety. To support physical safety, coaches assist clients to locate a space that is free from threat, harm or danger by partners, family, other consumers, visitors or staff. If coaching is conducted virtually the coach should engage the client to ensure they are in a space where they feel safe.

To support emotional safety, coaches start all coaching relationships with co-designed conscious community agreements. These agreements provide a space to identify strategies that support the client's on-going emotional safety including; plans for good and rocky times, mental health history reviews, identifying support systems and planning for the client's connection to community resources.

### PHASE 2: ASSISTING CLIENTS TO RECOGNIZE AND ACKNOWLEDGE THE IMPACT OF TRAUMA

During Phase 2 the coach supports the client to recognize the impact of trauma on their everyday lives. Trauma often represents the place where many people have lost a part of themselves. By acknowledging trauma we are able to assist clients to reconnect with lost parts of themselves.

*(Continued)*

When trauma is triggered, we can support clients to pause and acknowledge the presence of pain, numbness, or confusion associated with trauma.

We can also support clients to move through a traumatic flashback (a temporary pause that transports the client back to the initial moment of trauma) by assisting them to connect and ground in the present moment.

Coaching assumes that the client is already high functioning and is capable of taking consistent action steps toward their life vision. Therefore if we notice that our clients' trauma makes them unable to function at a level that supports moving toward their goals, we:

> "Recognize when a referral might be indicated for psychotherapy and/or medical assessment. (see "When to Refer Clients for Mental Health Services" in Chapter 11)

> Discern when a client is actually asking for counseling but prefers to call it "coaching."

> Understand how the intensity and longevity of blocks, ruts, and fears differ in high functioning people from blocks, ruts, and fears, from people who need psychotherapy to move beyond their stuck place." (Benham, K. Fox, S. , 2002).

## SAFETY PLANNING

When supporting clients who have experienced trauma it is important to listen for behaviors that indicate a client might be suicidal. Active suicidal ideation involves an existing wish to die accompanied by a plan to carry out the death. Anyone who has or knows someone who has active suicidal ideation should call 911 or go to the nearest emergency room immediately. Passive suicidal ideation involves a desire to die, but without a specific plan for carrying out the death.

## SUPPORTING SAFETY PLANNING

When passive suicidal ideation is observed or indicated we support clients to develop a Safety Plan, a prioritized written list of coping strategies and sources of support for clients at risk for suicide.

It should identify any triggers that may lead to a suicidal crisis, such as an anniversary of a loss, alcohol, or stress from relationships. Also include contact numbers for the person's doctor or therapist, as well as friends and family members who will help in an emergency. The basic components of the safety plan include:

1. Recognizing warning signs that are proximal to an impending suicidal crisis;

2. Assisting client to identify and employ their internal coping strategies;

3. Utilizing client contacts as a means of distraction from suicidal thoughts and urges. This includes going to healthy social settings, such as a coffee shop or place of worship or socializing with family members or others who may offer support without discussing suicidal thoughts;

4. Assisting client in contacting family members or friends who may help to resolve a crisis and with whom suicidal thoughts can be discussed;

5. Contacting mental health professionals or agencies; and

6. Assist clients to reduce the immediate potential for use of lethal means.

## PHASE 3: ACKNOWLEDGING CLIENTS RESILIENCY AND RESOURCEFULNESS TO SUPPORT RECLAIMING POWER

During Phase 3 the coach assists the client to reclaim the power lost during the traumatic experience by acknowledging their resiliency and resourcefulness. "Resiliency is the capability to cope successfully in the face of significant change, adversity, or risk. While resourcefulness is the ability to deal promptly and skillfully in new situations or during difficulties." (Stewart et al.,1991 as cited by Greene and Conrad, 2002) To assist clients during this phase coaches should:

- Hold the client's agendas;
- Pause to celebrate resiliency;
- Recognize and build upon resourcefulness; and
- Assist the client to reclaim power and take action toward their goals.

**COACHING** *in Action* | **A Trauma-Informed Coaching Model** *by Leslie Brown, CFT Faculty*

*(Continued)*

As we work through this model with our clients, we may experience second hand trauma ourselves. Good self-care is always imperative for coaches.

**REFERENCES:**

Centers for Disease Control and Prevention (CDC). Adverse Childhood Experiences (ACE) Study. Available at http://www.cdc.gov/ace/

Greene, R. R. (Ed.). (2002). Resiliency: An integrated approach to practice, policy, and research. Washington, D.C.: NASW Press.

Marcenich, L., (2010) Trauma Informed Care, Powerpoint Presentation, Available at: http://smchealth.org/sites/default/files/docs/LMarcenichPwrpt.pdf

Meinke, L., Top Ten Indicators to Refer a Client to a Mental Health Professional, Retrieved on May 7, 2015 from: www.coachcommunity.de/networks/files/download.162283

Stanley, B. & Brown, G. K. (2008). Safety Planning: A Brief Intervention to Mitigate Suicide Risk. Submitted for publication. Retrieved on May 7, 2015 from: www.mentalhealth.va.gov/docs/VA_Safety_planning_manual.doc

# Coaching Models

A good deal of what we talk about in coaching is abstract and intangible—for example, emotions, values, hopes and dreams. Both the client and the coach can get lost in the soup. Coaching models serve as navigational tools that provide structure and support. A model serves as a conceptual map, or a chart that lays out the territory. As a system or a set of steps, a coaching model maps out strategies for projects, shows pathways for emotional growth, helps with communication or helps balance competing demands on our time.

Recognizing our individual cultural perspective helps us partner more effectively without imposing our own beliefs and values. According to Diane Lennard, "The model simplifies and clarifies the complexities of coaching. Rather than ignore the complexity of the coaching process, coaches can use the model to focus on essential factors and manage the complexity."

A coaching model can act as a container for the coaching process, but that doesn't mean we have to follow a model rigidly. On the contrary, models can support creativity and serve as something we can rely on for support, particularly if we see the model as a work in process.

## Benefits of using a coaching model

Using a model in our coaching sessions can help clients picture their progress through the stages of a process, sort out the various components of a problem or situation, and consider what could happen next. But primarily a model helps the coach more than the client. Whether graphic or verbal, the most useful coaching models help:

organize ideas about coaching into a conceptual framework

use plain language to simplify concepts

clarify our understanding and unique view of coaching

highlight the key factors, putting focus on what's important

generate interesting questions and uncover new challenges

guide coaching decisions

articulate what we do and why

serve as a tool for continual learning

## Incorporating models in coaching

Many coaches are trained to use a specific coaching model. They may brand themselves as an Integral Coach, a Co-Active Coach or an NLP Life Coach. Many models have contributed to the field of coaching and once you're grounded in the Coaching for Transformation model, we encourage you to explore the value of other coaching models. Then we ask you to develop your own coaching model by integrating your cultural background, unique experience and your niche market.

Below is a partial list of coaching models that we encourage you to research, experiment with, and modify to create your own.

The CLEAR Model (Hawkins, 1982)

Stage of Change Model (Procheska & Norcross, 1994)

GROW Model (Landsberg, 1996)

Systems Perspective (Tobias, 1996)

Iterative Feedback Model (Diedrich, 1996)

The Inner Game (Gallwey, 1997)

Co-Active Model (Whitworth, Kimsey-House and Sandahl, 1998)

Single-, Double-, Triple-loop Model (Hargrove, 1999)

Solution Focused Therapy/Coaching (O'Hanlon, 1999)

Eight Stage Model (Hudson, 1999)

Multimodal Therapy Model (Richard, 1999)

Transformative-Developmental Model (Laske, 1999)

Systems & Psychodynamic Approach (Kilburg, 1996, 2000)

Systems Approach to Executive Coaching (O'Neill, 2000)

CAAACS Model (Auerbach, 2001)

Existential Approach (Peltier, 2001)

Developmental Coaching (Hunt & Weintraub, 2002)

Behavioral Coaching (Zeus & Skiffington, 2002)

Constructive-Developmental Theory Approach (Fitzgerald & Berger, 2002)

Authentic Happiness Coaching (Seligman, 2004)

Action Frame Theory Approach (Cocivera & Cronshaw, 2004)

REBT (Anderson, 2002; Sherin & Caiger, 2004)

Septet Coaching (Silsbee, 2004)

Global Executive Coaching (Renwick, 2006)

Adventure Based Coaching (Kemp, 2006)

Coaching for Transformation (Kellogg, Michaels, Brown & Lasley, 2006)

Some clients enjoy the structure and flow of working with a model and others value more freedom. Some find models clarifying and inspiring, while others find them confining and limiting. We resist the urge to make our clients work within the framework of a model just because it provides structure for the coaching session. We can simultaneously give ourselves a powerful framework for coaching and the freedom to diverge from the model whenever we wish.

*Questions to Consider*

Which root disciplines would you like to explore more deeply?

How does the historical context of coaching contribute to your personal philosophy as a coach?

What other modalities would you like to blend with your coaching?

# 13
# Cross Cultural Coaching

*A fish discovers its need for water only when it is no longer in it. Our own culture is like water to a fish. It sustains us. We live and breathe through it. What one culture may regard as essential, a certain level of material wealth for example, may not be so vital to other cultures. —Fons Trompenaars and Charles Hampden-Turner*

To ensure that coaching is accessible to everyone, coaches need to become culturally aware and adept at cross cultural coaching. In fact, every coaching relationship is cross cultural: we all have similarities and we all have differences that can inform and strengthen the coaching engagement. As the field of coaching widened its reach—becoming more accessible to diverse groups of people—cross cultural coaching evolved into a critical knowledge area for coaches.

This chapter provides a starting point on the journey into the rich and diverse world of cross cultural coaching. We start with appreciation of culturally different perspectives. Cultural awareness helps people explore and build on diversity to develop creative and synergistic solutions. As coaches we get called upon to help clients navigate cross cultural interactions. These interactions may originate from situations in culturally diverse workplaces, relationships and communities or clients may be living as expatriates in another country. It may be as common as women working with men or young people working with elders. Children of immigrants may struggle with differences between dominant viewpoints from the country in which they were raised and viewpoints of their parents or beliefs from their country of origin. In addition, workplaces, classrooms, social services and other institutions all have their own distinct cultural norms.

As organizations merge, or groups collaborate to strengthen their work, or community members access services, coaching clients may bring issues of 'culture clashing' to their sessions. Coaches can help people deepen their awareness of their own norms, values and beliefs—and be at choice in how they operate and behave. We can support clients to become curious about the differences they may be experiencing in our rich, culturally diverse world—and be open to differing ideas, values, traditions and styles. To be most effective as coaches we can start by exploring our own multicultural orientations and becoming curious about our own beliefs and perspectives. Through self-reflection, experiential learning, curiosity about cultural differences, reading about cultural awareness, attending workshops on cultural awareness, and developing and practicing new skills, we can enhance our own cultural self-awareness.

As the global community becomes smaller, we interact with, work with, and live in communities with more and more people who are culturally different than our families of origin. Technological advances make it possible to communicate regularly with people around the globe, and organizations continue to expand their alliances. Whether it is between different communities in a similar geographic area or globally, coaches can increase the opportunities to support cultural self-awareness and cross cultural awareness. In facilitating effective cross-cultural communication coaches can play a role in creating a more respectful global community that can utilize all its diverse assets for the betterment of all.

In this chapter, we explore the basis of culture and the importance of cultural competency for coaches. We also review the coaching skills that are valuable for cross cultural coaching and provide a framework for viewing cultural difference.

## Overview

The coaching profession is expanding from a somewhat narrow focus (western culture) and small segment of the population (corporate executives) to being available in every country to increasingly wider segments of the population. Although the cultural dimension is still not fully incorporated into organizations and the coaching profession, the need for culturally competent coaches from different cultural backgrounds and different segments of society continues to increase as coaching extends beyond executive offices and into the mainstream.

Coaches may work with clients from another culture or they may facilitate cross cultural communication and learning in a variety of settings such as:

Global managers with staff in multiple countries

Professionals on a virtual work team from multiple countries

Organizations with different cultural perspectives working together to achieve common community objectives

Individuals enmeshed in problems related to cross cultural differences

Immigrants and next generation family members torn between culture of origin and culture of their current country

Expatriates living and working in a country other than their native one

In any of these situations, coaches help clients clarify their own cultural perspectives, recognize and respect cultural differences, resolve issues related to cultural difference and explore opportunities for new, mutually beneficial and creative ways of working and relating across cultures. Coaches also engage people to expand their viewpoints, open to new possibilities for collaboration and synergy, listen with curiosity, ask questions that invite increased reflection and awareness, and foster connection and trust.

In this chapter we invite you into meaningful dialogue and exploration to develop the knowledge and skills needed to become effective cross cultural coaches. The next chapter takes a deeper look at culture as it relates to power and privilege in coaching. Cross cultural learning invites us to listen deeply, explore and challenge long-held assumptions and stereotypes, and to open the doors for new and deeper learning. How do we really hear another's experiences without judging, dismissing, minimizing or defending ourselves? This work requires the willingness and courage to not only face feelings of discomfort that may arise, but also embrace them. By doing this work we equip ourselves to become fully available for clients of various backgrounds—deepening the heart connection.

The gifts of cross cultural coaching are many: different perspectives that invite new possibilities, honesty in naming what's present, learning what really matters, listening to understand how others see the world and opportunities for increasing trust and partnership.

## Culture

Culture can be defined as a shared and learned system of values, beliefs and attitudes that shape and influence perception and behavior. Culture is the basis from which groups of people understand, interpret and solve problems in the world. Culture impacts our perspectives. Philippe Rosinski defines a group's culture as "the set of unique characteristics that distinguishes its members from another group."[1]

Culture has several layers or dimensions. At the surface are physically observable characteristics or traits associated with particular cultures (e.g., language, artifacts, customs, food, clothing, art, architecture). Below the surface are deeper layers that are not so readily apparent. These include norms, values and basic assumptions. Norms get to the heart of what is considered acceptable by a cultural group. They are often perceived as things members of the group "should" do. Norms are the legal and social rules people within the group live by. "Cultures whose norms differ significantly tend to speak about each other in terms of extremes…Using extreme, exaggerated forms of behavior is stereotyping."[2] Values are the ideals and aspirations held in esteem by the cultural group. Values address the questions: What's important to us? What do we aspire to do or be? Basic assumptions are a given in the cultural context and are often internalized and unconscious. When you challenge people's basic assumptions, they may respond with confusion or irritation.

Culture is much more than nationality, ethnicity, religion or race. It involves the groups we are born into as well as the ones we choose to associate with during the course of our personal and professional lives. We are members of multiple groups and so operate within multiple cultures.

In addition to nationality, ethnicity, religion and race, cultural groups can include members of the same geographical region, profession, corporations, organizations (religious, professional, government and nonprofit), unions, socioeconomic status, gender and sexual orientation, age groups and those who share common abilities or disabilities, among others. Just as individual

---

1    Rosinski, Philippe (2003). Coaching Across Cultures: New Tools for Leveraging National, Corporate & Professional Differences. London, UK: Nicholas Brealey Publishing.
2    Rosinski, Philippe (2003). Coaching Across Cultures: New Tools for Leveraging National, Corporate & Professional Differences. London, UK: Nicholas Brealey Publishing.

groups have distinct cultures, so do different organizations as well as different divisions and country offices within a global organization.

Characteristics, perspectives and behaviors within cultural groups are not uniform, but are rather distributed along a bell shaped curve. On average (top of the curve) members exhibit similar preferences and viewpoints. On the outer edges of the curve, members share some but not the majority of the group's characteristics. Groups can also have sub-cultures.

It is growing increasingly common for people to interact with people from other cultures. This can take the form of geographically dispersed virtual teams working on the same project, a person speaking with a call center representative in a distant country, cultural diversity in a city like New York, a global manager responsible for operations in several countries, people from various countries sharing a topic of interest in an internet café, nonprofit staff working to empower low income clients, social change activists working at the heart of the problems as well as with people who can fund the solutions—the possibilities are endless. It is increasingly likely that some of your clients will bring cross cultural issues into your coaching relationship. Consciously, or unconsciously, your cultural perspectives can impact your coaching—the feelings, attitudes, perceptions and behaviors that arise impact the depth and effectiveness of the coaching.

Multicultural coaches often hold group coaching sessions to allow teams of people from several countries to discuss cross-cultural challenges. An example follows:

> In the first meeting people spoke tentatively. A man from Sweden expressed his disappointment that no one made an effort to pronounce his name. A woman from Germany described her despair that meetings started late. A Pakistani man lamented that people in the UK didn't understand his humor. When he described himself as a very funny guy in his home country, and expressed how sad he was to have given up that part of himself, the coach asked for a moment of silence while everyone in the room took in the enormity of his loss. The use of silence supported people to engage in deeper curiosity of each other. This led to a deeper exploration about what they most appreciated about their unique cultures and how they could collectively create a new culture that honors differences.

How we view others who have perspectives different than ours is often related to the cultural groups we were born into or now belong. People's reactions and subsequent actions in response to a stimulus are directly related to the meaning they attribute to the stimulus. The meanings can differ within cultures. For example, cultural perspectives that value competition, winning and individuality can foster respect for each person's unique gifts, but can also lead to comparisons and evaluations that detract from productivity.

# Cross Cultural Competency

*I think we have to own the fears that we have of each other, and then, in some
practical way, some daily way, figure out how to see people differently than the way
we were brought up to.—Alice Walker*

When we think of competence we typically think of mastery. In the case of cross cultural
communication and coaching, competence is less about arrival and more about ongoing learning
that helps both coach and client see new perspectives and operate within a wider range of options.
From this place of openness, we can support clients' continued alignment and growth as well as
our own. Alignment with values supports engagement in creative solutions. As we have explored
in Section II, *Pathways to Alignment*, when clients become increasingly aligned, their focus shifts
from what they can do for themselves to the contribution they can make in the world. Our ability
to see, understand and try on various points of view of other cultures equips us to make an even
greater contribution in the world—one in which collaboration leads to synergy.

Sue and Sue (2008) describe multicultural competence as follows:

> "Multicultural competency is not a destination. It is a process of ongoing learning—
> inviting self-awareness and assessment of inherited biases, stereotypes and viewpoints of
> others as well as increasing awareness of the cultures and experiences of others who are
> different from us culturally."[3]

Sue and Sue go on to define a culturally competent helping professional as one who:

> Is actively in the process of becoming aware of his or her own assumptions about human
> behavior, values, biases, preconceived notions, personal limitations and so forth. (attitudes
> and beliefs component)

> Actively attempts to understand the worldview of his or her culturally different client.
> (knowledge component)

> Is in the process of actively developing and practicing appropriate, relevant and sensitive
> intervention strategies and skills in working with his or her culturally different client.
> (skills component)"[4]

By extension, cross cultural coaching competencies have three components: self-awareness (about
attitudes and beliefs), knowledge (about others who are culturally different) and skills (to support
connection across cultures).

Milton Bennett proposed a 6-stage model for the development of intercultural sensitivity and
competence.[5] The developmental stages represent increasing sensitivity to cultural difference.

---

3    Sue, Derald Wing & Sue, David (2008). *Counseling the Culturally Diverse: Theory and Practice.* Hoboken, NJ: John Wiley & Sons.

4    Sue, Derald Wing & Sue, David (2008). *Counseling the Culturally Diverse: Theory and Practice.* Hoboken, NJ: John Wiley & Sons.

5    Bennett, M. J. (1993). Towards ethnorelativism: A developmental model of intercultural sensitivity. In R. M. Paige (Ed.),
     *Education for the intercultural experience* (pp. 21–71). Yarmouth, ME: Intercultural Press

Bennett suggests that we develop cross cultural capabilities by moving from ethnocentric stages (individual's own culture is central) to ethnorelative stages (individual's culture is experienced in the context of other cultures). Philippe Rosinski proposed a 7th stage, leveraging difference, which he suggests is consistent with the coaching notion of unleashing people's potential.[6] As we move through the stages, we increase competency in cross cultural contexts. These stages are situation dependent—you can be in one stage in one situation and in another stage in another context.

Ethnocentric

1. Denial (deny that cultural differences exist; disinterest; avoidance)

2. Defense (acknowledge cultural differences—construct defenses against them; view them negatively; us vs. them mindset; "we know best")

3. Minimization (acknowledge cultural differences but trivialize them; assume similarities outweigh differences; "we are tolerant and color-blind")

Ethnorelative

1. Acceptance (recognize, respect and value cultural difference; more skills needed to implement)

2. Adaptation (cultural awareness plus intercultural competence demonstrated; cultural differences are discussed with appropriate openness and trust)

3. Integration (integrate aspects of own cultural perspectives with those of other cultures)

4. Leveraging difference (make the most of cultural differences; synergize)

We can use this model to help clients assess how they relate to cultural differences and identify opportunities to try on other perspectives, empower others or take collaborative action. Rosinski suggests that it will be hard to coach clients effectively beyond stages the coach has yet to master. As coaches, we bring clients to a place of alignment with themselves where they can create powerfully and creatively. In order to get to powerful alignment, clients need to bring every part of themselves to the coaching. They do that most comfortably in high trust, culturally aware and competent relationships. This requires us as coaches to do our own cultural work.

A newly formed diverse global team who had previously worked as separate local teams, worked through the stages of cultural development defined by Bennett with the help of a coach.

A major company with local operations in a number of countries began globalizing their teams and standardizing approaches. Work teams became increasingly diverse. For one global IT team, their success, survival and on-time completion of projects became dependent upon their ability to overcome differences and learn to trust each other. The team started out at Level 2 (Defense) on Bennett's scale. They acknowledged cultural differences but clearly were not happy about being organized into a single team. Trust was at an all-time low. The Europeans did not trust the Americans to get the job done. The Americans did not like the rules coming down from the corporate headquarters in Europe. The mindset was clearly "them" vs. "us." The global head organized a series of face to face team building meetings to work through the issues of trust and to create

---

6    Rosinski, Philippe (2003). *Coaching Across Cultures: New Tools for Leveraging National, Corporate & Professional Differences.* London, UK: Nicholas Brealey Publishing.

opportunities for cross cultural learning and sharing. These meetings took place in Switzerland, Germany, France and the UK so team members had the chance to experience a variety of local cultures as part of these events. Those were some of the richest and most memorable experiences of that team's work life. The team included Americans (black, white, Chinese and Filipino), Germans, French, Swiss, English, Australian, Christian, Muslim, male, female, young, middle-aged, slim, overweight, athletic and non-athletic. To get to know each other and support each other in the challenges that some could do more easily than others, they learned to let go of the need to control and began to listen and include. Their face-to-face team building experiences for the first several years of their global teamwork led to a high level of trust and friendship. They started with sharing their stories and learning about each other while working on physical and intellectual challenges, while taking long hikes, and over laughter and drinks in the bar.

The trust equipped them to work together around the clock, like a well-oiled machine, using the time differences around the globe to keep the projects moving. They learned to leverage their cultural differences to collaboratively complete projects on time by valuing each team member's contributions—knowing everyone could be counted on. In addition to their work-related collaborations, they expanded their connection by organizing video conferences simply to gather together to help team members in another country celebrate a life event.

## Cross Cultural Coaching Skills

Specific coaching skills and methods help coaches build effective cross cultural coaching partnerships and support them in helping clients broaden their perspectives in cross cultural interactions. Let's explore some of these skills in the cross cultural context.

### Awareness

Whenever we are coaching—particularly cross culturally—how can we be alert to our own ignorance? How do we let go of what we think we know about our client's experience and approach everything as a mystery? Part of developing awareness is learning about and embracing our own culture and experience. Another part is learning about cultural bias and privilege so we don't assume others have that same experience. Humility comes with awareness. How do we convey our desire to explore and learn?

### Curiosity

Once we are clear that we don't know another person's experience we can approach coaching with curiosity. To avoid making assumptions, we wonder and ask questions about our client's experience.

### Vulnerability

When we're willing to speak about our own experiences and our lack of experience, we create a safe place for clients to open up.

### Self-Management

We learn to recognize and self-connect when we're triggered. We take care of ourselves so we are not coming from anger or lack. We learn about and embrace our own cultural experience so we are not threatened by another's cultural experience. Our clients notice when we get triggered, and may avoid that topic in the future unless we name what is happening and are open, willing and available to explore and stay present. Another aspect of self-management is to recognize our judgments of basic assumptions held by our clients and transform them into curiosity. In that way, we open to understanding the client's perspectives and the cultural basis from which they emerged. This equips us to see multiple sides of the situation.

## Empowering Questions

One of the ways we find out what is going on with people who may be holding back is asking evocative open-ended questions that elicit deeper awareness for both our clients and ourselves.

## Deep, Transformational Listening

In deep, transformational listening, we listen for our own perspectives or judgments as issues are raised by the client and listen to the words, tone, pacing and also for what's underneath—for what's not being said. We also listen for what wants to emerge or be released.

In addition to the core skills above, we can call out the power by confronting cross cultural issues and leveraging opportunities. The five pathways to alignment are useful for supporting clients to address cross cultural issues:

Exploring Needs and Values—connect empathically with cultural values

Expanding the View—explore options and shifting cultural viewpoints

Experiencing the Moment—support staying fully present with difficult emotions

Envisioning the Future—dare to dream of a world where all people are respected and honored

Embracing the Shadow—address internalized oppression

Transformational coaching skills were woven into a teambuilding workshop designed for an east coast US team that was created following a global merger and reorganization between two US companies, one on the east coast and the other on the west coast:

Culture clashes made the merging of the US operations particularly challenging. As a result of the reorganization, many things changed for members of the east coast team. Some lost their flexible work hours; others were given new job responsibilities that they did not like. Although team members remained committed to their work and customer focus, the morale of the group became low. Resentment about the merger and the resulting impact on their jobs showed up as powerlessness. The coach began with a series of meetings with the local manager, followed by one-on-one interviews with team members. This helped the coach assess the situation and gave team members a chance to voice their concerns. A custom-designed experiential workshop helped them learn a series of coaching and communication skills that supported them in building a more effective, engaged and empowered team. They learned to explore feelings and needs, ask open ended questions, listen more effectively, give constructive feedback, make requests and explore alternate viewpoints. They co-designed a much more engaging way forward for the team. Their relationship with their manager and with each other began to improve when they got in touch with their ability to design new and collaborative solutions to what they previously perceived as insurmountable problems.

During mergers and acquisitions, organizational cultures often clash even within the same country. By increasing our openness and awareness to differing perspectives, we find the opportunity to develop new, more synergistic approaches that originate from a new culture based on the best of both worlds.

# A Framework for Cultural Competency

Culture influences every individual and group in implicit and explicit ways. One model of differences in national cultures was developed by Fons Trompenaars, a Dutch cross-cultural communications and international management theorist, in conjunction with Charles Hampden-Turner.[7] Trompenaars and Hampden-Turner explored how cultural differences at the national level impact how people do business together or manage others. They found that, "every culture distinguishes itself from others by the specific solutions it chooses to certain problems which reveal themselves as dilemmas."[8] In their research they observed the meanings various cultures attributed to situations, policies and approaches. The model is based on seven dimensions that represent how people in various national cultures solve problems in three main areas: relationships with others, relationship to the passage of time and relationship to the environment. The first five dimensions describe how we relate to other people. The dimensions are useful in understanding interactions between people from different national groups.

The seven dimensions of the model are:

1. Universalism vs. Particularism (rules vs. relationships)
2. Individualism vs. Communitarianism (individual vs. group orientation; "I" vs. "we")
3. Neutral vs. Emotional (degree to which emotions are expressed)
4. Specific vs. Diffuse (in relationship in specific predetermined ways vs. changing and contextual)
5. Achievement vs. Ascription (work to receive status vs. status based on family and position)
6. Attitudes to Time (e.g., Sequential vs. Synchronic) (do one thing at a time vs. several things at once; present/future vs. past focused)
7. Attitudes to the Environment (e.g., Internal vs. External) (we control our environment vs. the environment controls us)[9]

Trompenaars tested these dimensions on 55 national cultures. The results can be used by business managers or leaders in organizations to predict how people from different cultures may act in a work setting. This framework also equips coaches with a powerful lens to support clients to use intentional language to name and address issues of culture. By supporting them to become aware of the hidden influences of culture, we empower them to make new and bold choices.

---

7   Hampden-Turner, Charles & Trompenaars, Fons (1998). *Riding the Waves of Culture: Understanding Diversity in Global Business*. Second Edition. New York, NY: McGraw-Hill.

8   Hampden-Turner, Charles & Trompenaars, Fons (1998). *Riding the Waves of Culture: Understanding Diversity in Global Business*. Second Edition. New York, NY: McGraw-Hill.

9   Hampden-Turner, Charles & Trompenaars, Fons (1998). *Riding the Waves of Culture: Understanding Diversity in Global Business*. Second Edition. New York, NY: McGraw-Hill.

The table below provides more detailed characteristics of three of Trompenaars' cultural dimensions:

| | |
|---|---|
| **1. UNIVERSALISM VS. PARTICULARISM** | Universalism: Standards and rules take precedence over relationships. The right solution can be defined and applied. |
| | Particularism: Relationships and unique circumstances are more important than rules or contracts. |
| **2. INDIVIDUALISM VS. COMMUNITARIANISM** | Individualism: People regard themselves as independent entities within society. |
| | Communitarianism: People regard their individual identity as integrated with their role within a larger group. |
| **3. NEUTRAL VS. EMOTIONAL** | Neutral: Emotions are checked at the door, and are not a key player in making decisions. Cool logic is seen as the key to maintaining unclouded decision making. |
| | Emotional: A wide gamut of emotions is common—loud laughter, animated hand gestures and raised voices. |

Adapted from Hampden-Turner and Trompenaars.[10]

**Universalism vs. Particularism**

As an example of how Trompenaars' model can be applied, Universalist perspectives and approaches to problem solving are much more common in Switzerland, USA, Canada, Australia and UK where people value rules more than relationships. In contrast, France, China and India have a tendency toward particularist approaches because people value relationships over rules. How does this impact people working in global organizations? How does it impact people whose nationality is from a country with Universalist tendencies but whose cultural roots are those of a Particularist group (e.g., Chinese Americans)? Imagine a newly globalized pharmaceutical company with a virtual work team comprised of members from US, UK, Switzerland, France, Germany, Poland, Australia and India. What are the challenges and what are the opportunities? One example of how this plays out is in the Universalist approach to doing business via short meetings and detailed legal contracts, where in Particularist countries taking time to build relationships, and someone's word based on that relationship is much more important than a contract. When companies globalize they often attempt to standardize approaches across countries. The underlying assumption is a universalistic perspective: "what works here is good for everyone" or "what we implemented here that's working will work everywhere else." What this approach fails to consider is how the policies and approaches will be received in various cultures, particularly in those where relationships are more important than rules.

---

10   Hampden-Turner, Charles & Trompenaars, Fons (1998). *Riding the Waves of Culture: Understanding Diversity in Global Business.* Second Edition. New York, NY: McGraw-Hill.

### Individualism vs. Communitarianism

While coaching is based on relationships, it also originated in the US and operates under the basic assumption that our coaching approach is applicable for all cultures (individualism). There is an opportunity and imperative to tweak the coaching to honor, recognize and support various cultural differences.

In individualistic cultures like the US, the emphasis is more on individual achievement in isolation of the community. The coaching profession assumes the view that individuals are able to create the lives they want. We believe in unlimited possibilities for our clients and help them maximize their personal and professional potential. We believe this and also want to remain aware of the cultural bias of this belief—honoring that some of our clients may see it differently. For example, it is not so simple for clients from Communitarian cultures such as India where family and community responsibilities are frequently as important as desires for individual satisfaction and achievement. For example:

*Priya is an Indian-American woman in her early thirties. She has a successful small holistic wellness practice. She originally came to coaching to plan how to achieve her goals for expanding her business and making it feel like a "grown-up business." Her clients love her down-to-earth spirit, the homey office atmosphere, her hugs and loving advice about all aspects of health care. After several sessions of dreaming, clarifying and goal setting about her professional goals, Priya revealed some things that were deeply troubling to her. Although she loves her business just as it is, by her family's standards, she is not successful. A more impressive looking office, wearing a uniform, having a receptionist and developing a professional look sounded like it would satisfy the family. Her heart wasn't into it. Then she revealed that she and her boyfriend (of non-Indian descent) wanted to get married. They are in love and have had a secret relationship for six years. Her parents think they are just casual friends. She shared how she has to choose between him and her parents. Her parents would never accept him and would be shamed by her choice. She shared how deeply upset her parents were when her sister ran off and married an Indian man from a lower caste. She is very close to her parents and since she is single, she is still living at home with them. Her friends are telling her to marry the man she loves. She is torn between wanting him and her parents in her life and is convinced she cannot have both.*

How would you coach Priya?

How can Priya honor herself and maintain the cultural connections that are so important to her?

How can you best support her as a coach as she sorts through these issues?

*Manuel is a Latino-American male with a flair for drama. He moved to the United States from Mexico in 2004 and still struggles with the language. In 2006, Manuel contracted HIV during outreach work with immigrant and undocumented populations. He frequently falls sick and needs to stay hyper-vigilant to take his medication, visit his doctor regularly and attend to his health needs. All this attention to health makes Manuel look "weak" to his brothers and cousins. He is constantly being made fun of and teased for being "feminine," and not macho enough. Manuel loves his family dearly and can't imagine life without them. However they dramatically impact his self-esteem and sense of self-image. He believes that his family suspects that he is gay, which triggers them to make insensitive jokes. Though Manuel is openly gay in his work and personal life, he doesn't dream of coming out to his family. He believes it would be too much for them to take, and he would risk being cut off from the family. At the same time, it is painful for Manuel to keep such a large part of himself from his family.*

How would you coach Manuel?

How would you coach Manuel considering how his culture impacts his ability to manifest his dreams?

How is Manuel's ability to develop his personal identity influenced by his cultural values?

*Tara is a young Pakistani-American, 24 years old. She is a part-time public policy student at UC Berkeley while also working part-time for a nonprofit with homeless and disconnected 18 to 24-year-old youths. In Tara's coaching sessions she often talks about feeling torn between two selves—the version of herself that is required to go home to her parents' house every Friday night to spend the weekend with the family, and the Bohemian, artistic version of herself that engages in political discussions at cafes, shops at thrift stores and makes her own clothes with her garage-sale found sewing machine. Tara shares feelings of anger and resentment with her family for not encouraging her to follow her dreams and live life to the fullest. Tara's extended family fills her parents with dread that their daughter is not yet married to a good Muslim man. In addition, Tara feels frustrated that her college classmates don't need to work part-time to help pay for school, and thinks she's at a constant disadvantage because she doesn't have the leisure time or study time they do.*

How would you coach Tara?

What role does culture play in Tara's ability to manifest her dreams?

In what ways does a collectivist culture impact Tara?

In what ways does an individualist culture impact Tara?

In the work world an example of an individualistic approach is pay-for-performance where individuals are recognized and rewarded for their individual efforts. In more communitarian countries, this approach to single out certain employees is in opposition to their views that the group or team is more important than an individual. They may not accept that group members should excel individually in a way that reflects poorly on or invites negative comparison to other members of the group. They might view outstanding performance by an individual as one whose efforts benefitted members of the group.

Reflect on your cultural upbringing. Which of Trompenaars' cultural dimensions most accurately reflect you and your cultural group?

How can this model assist managers, leaders and coaches when working cross culturally?

Think of someone from another culture that you interact with. Which of the descriptions would you think might fit him or her?

How can this awareness impact your cross cultural communication?

# Expanding Cross Cultural Awareness

The journey toward cross cultural competence begins with self-assessment and self-awareness. It requires us to listen deeply and empathically to others who are culturally different. It invites us to challenge long-held stereotypes, biases, preconceptions and traditional ways of doing things as we seek to build cross cultural alliances based on mutuality, openness and trust. We develop cross cultural competency by having the difficult conversations, putting ourselves in another's shoes, to see with new eyes. Regular practice and a willingness to fail and learn help us open to new ways of being with people. The rewards of this sometimes challenging journey are many. Being open to the diverse perspectives and experiences of others gives us a wealth of innovative ideas, opinions and wisdom with which we can more effectively be full, authentic and compassionate members of the world community. By embarking on this journey, we are letting go of fears and learned biases that sap our spirits. Humans are social animals; we are meant to be in communion with one another. When we are cut off from one another, we cannot be whole.

*Suggestions to enhance cross cultural coaching:*

Examine your own views, thoughts, biases and stereotypes about your client's cultural group.

Invite clients to help you see things from their various perspectives.

Consider a directive or structured approach based on a client's cultural background and individual needs.

Invite the use of culturally relevant traditions, movies, stories, music, role models and storytelling into the coaching relationship as metaphors, homework assignments or discovery questions.

Be alert for coaching language that doesn't resonate with certain clients.

For individuals from neutral cultures that are not comfortable with personal sharing and expression of feelings, presenting issues may more frequently be associated with academic or career issues.

For clients from external cultures, presenting issues may be more frequently associated with issues in school or the workplace and with leadership or societal pressures challenging their core values.

Consider the cultural context of information shared and adapt your approach as warranted.

Seek to understand the cultural background of each client as well as the client's unique self-identity.

For some cultures, spirituality is more often a cultural view practiced through customs, rituals and affirmation of beliefs. Based on your client's interests and needs, it may be refreshing to incorporate variations of these practices into coaching.

For collectivist cultures, you may not only be coaching the individual. The individual may have a strong view of being an integral part of family or community, and what affects the client affects the community.

Listen for ethnic identity in discovery sessions.

Ensure your materials reflect the diversity of your clients.

*Questions to Consider*

What are your earliest or significant experiences with cultural difference?

How do you define yourself culturally or regarding your identity? (age, race, ethnicity, religion, gender, sexual orientation, ability, etc.)

What's important to you to facilitate meaningful conversation across cultural difference?

What are the values we honor in learning about and committing to cultural competency?

Reflect on your cultural upbringing. What cultural messages did you receive? How do these messages shape you?

What are some issues that may arise when coaching someone from a different culture?

What will you do to become a more culturally competent coach?

What are your values around culturally competent coaching?

# 14
# Power, Privilege and Coaching

*My work cuts through racial, class, geographic, and ethnic separations to directly connect to the heart, mind, and emotion with people. —Lily Yeh*

As the field of coaching continues to evolve and expand beyond the corporate realm into the many sectors, effective coaches need to understand how power and privilege impact cross-cultural dynamics. Coaches who develop cultural competence become increasingly aware and equipped to create authentic connections that deepen trust. This includes understanding the ways in which power, privilege, bias and discrimination influence relationships—consciously and unconsciously.

How do we co-create a coaching alliance where clients and coaches can show up fully, as the whole people we are? How do we create the conditions which invite each of us to vulnerably share experiences of bias or discrimination based on race, religion, gender, ability, sexual orientation, ethnicity or age? What do we say or do when a client stereotypes groups or says something we find offensive or hurtful? How do we remain alert for and manage our emotional reactions to triggers without minimizing or negating the feelings, values, perspectives and lifestyles of others? We are all products of cultural conditioning and bring our values, norms, beliefs, lifestyles and life opportunities into our relationships. Unspoken undercurrents in cross cultural coaching relationships can limit the full impact of the coaching when left unaddressed. Coaches who are willing to embark on deep inner and cross cultural learning have an opportunity to contribute to world changing, transformational work.

What are the opportunities? Leadership that Works weaves threads of power, privilege, rank and culture throughout the curriculum, in addition to its organizational policies and practices, so that culturally competent coaches can contribute to:

Increasing inclusiveness and diversity within the coaching profession.

Making coaching more available and effective for everyone regardless of race, gender, sexual orientation, age, socioeconomic status, physical ability or language ability.

Supporting culturally diverse clients to address internalized oppression and step boldly into their full power in ways that benefit them, their families and communities.

Changing the ways people lead, communicate and collaborate cross culturally to solve problems in communities around the world.

Supporting clients to deepen their awareness of diversity issues and consider how they wish to use their privilege to make a greater contribution.

In this chapter we:

Invite self-awareness with respect to cultural identity, beliefs, biases, preconceptions and stereotypes.

Increase awareness of factors that contribute to miscommunication and mistrust cross culturally.

Provide information to increase knowledge of others who are culturally different.

Explore how coaches can build trusting, effective relationships with clients who are addressing issues of safety, respect or power differences.

## Overview

*We all should know that diversity makes for a rich tapestry, and we must understand that all the threads of the tapestry are equal in value no matter what their color.— Maya Angelou*

It's easy for people who are part of a dominant culture (culture of power) to move through their daily routines without noticing the impact of their power and privilege. When people are comfortable, they can take certain things for granted—such as entitlement to resources including loans, housing and education. They may not be aware of problems faced by people with less power or privilege.

Paul Kivel says, "Whenever one group of people accumulates more power than another group, the more powerful group creates an environment that places its members at the cultural center and other groups at the margins. People in the more powerful group (the "in-group") are accepted as the norm, so if you are in that group it can be very hard for you to see the benefits you receive."[1] Members of the in-group do not notice that they are surrounded by their culture of power. They are often unaware of their limited perspective or don't know how to bridge the gap to become effective cross cultural communicators and collaborators. Kivel goes on to say, "We remain unaware of the superior status and opportunities we have simply because we're white, or male, or able-bodied, or heterosexual… People on the margins are only able to participate on unfavorable terms, at others' discretion, which puts them at a big disadvantage. They often have to give up or hide much of who they are to participate in the dominant culture."[2] As coaches, part of our role is to help clients come out of hiding and boldly share more of themselves.

---

1    Kivel, Paul (2000). *The Culture of Power.* Retrieved from http://paulkivel.com/articles/cultureofpower.pdf
2    Kivel, Paul (2000). *The Culture of Power.* Retrieved from http://paulkivel.com/articles/cultureofpower.pdf

Historically, the coaching profession comes from, and is concentrated in white, upper-middle-class, heterosexual, corporate culture. Therefore, inherent blind spots come from its culture of origin. With that in mind, one of the goals of the Coaching and Philanthropy Project (CAP )[3] was to gather recommendations for coach training organizations to more effectively address issues of cultural competency and to better serve the nonprofit sector. These recommendations were made through the Coaches of Color Consortium (C3), a group of nonprofit professionals with deep roots in communities of color who were trained to become coaches through the CAP project. They suggested adaptations needed to make coaching culturally relevant for the nonprofit sector. For instance, most coaching models and frames are limited to the experiences and thoughts of members of mainstream society whose understanding and business model imperatives do not include the experiences of people from other backgrounds and heritages the world over. In addition, C3 found that many coach trainers are not grounded in the life experiences of people of color and do not have a positive frame of reference about them and their communities. Furthermore, trainers often come from deficit-based thinking and are not using culturally-aware language.

In our conversations with the C3 group, they offered many recommendations. A few of their suggestions for developing a culturally competent profession include:

Require trainers to attend cultural competency, anti-bias, white privilege trainings and have cultural competency become a part of the certification requirements.

Unearth assumptions about how coaches' backgrounds and experience influence how they see the world, and then how those perspectives and paradigms impact the kinds of questions they come up with (or what they become curious about).

Introduce information about internalized, interpersonal and structural oppression and how they relate to one's clients.

Develop awareness of racism and its impacts today, and acknowledge it as a reality for a majority of the world.

Develop case studies that come from the nonprofit sector.

Sponsor think tanks, affinity groups and support structures for trainees who are in the nonprofit sector.

Commit to offering programs and resources for free or at a reduced cost to increase the impact, and reach those that can most benefit.

Our vision at Leadership that Works is to make coaching available to everyone. We envision a world where people create from all parts of themselves. To support coaching becoming more widely available, coaches need to learn how to create effective coaching alliances with people outside of the mainstream culture. For example, how do we support a disabled person living in a world created for the physically able, or someone living in a community where most practice a different religion, or an immigrant struggling with the new culture, or a person of color dealing with subtle or overt racial discrimination?

---

3    The Coaching and Philanthropy Project is a partnership between BTW informing change, CompassPoint Nonprofit Services, Grantmakers for Effective Organizations, and Leadership that Works. This work was made possible by the generous funding and support of W.K. Kellogg Foundation, The Harnisch Foundation, The James Irvine Foundation, the David and Lucile Packard Foundation, and the Evelyn and Walter Haas, Jr. Fund.

Our goal is to create environments where people feel safe in speaking their truth and sharing their relevant life experiences. This requires some inner work for each of us as coaches so we can authentically communicate that each person's cultural experience and background matters. Curiosity and openness are key. We can commit to exploring and shifting our cultural biases and anything else that disconnects us from people who are different from us in some way.

How do we learn more about our personal impact? Cross cultural awareness and developing competency involve opening to learning from people who we perceive as different and who perceive us as different. This may include learning from people who have experienced prejudice or discrimination based on race, ethnicity, gender, sexual orientation, ability, age or any other difference.

## Why is Awareness Important?

*I think we have to own the fears that we have of each other, and then, in some practical way, some daily way, figure out how to see people differently than the way we were brought up to. —Alice Walker*

As coaches, we co-create a relationship with our clients that invites their authenticity, discovery, aliveness, alignment with core values and courageous action. This is not always so straightforward with people from outside of mainstream cultures who have learned to hold back parts of themselves in order to make it in the world. We can call forth those hidden parts by building trust, creating open, vulnerable partnerships and by giving and inviting authenticity. This does not mean simply saying culturally different clients are free to bring everything to the coaching and putting the responsibility on them to do so. What you say and how you say it (or even what you fail to say) can impact the relationship. For example, if a coach says, "Race and culture don't mean anything to me. I just see you as a person," the client may experience alienation. Even with the best intentions and lack of malice, we can send the message, "Your experience, your struggles and where you come from aren't important," or "I don't want to go to those messy, sensitive or hard places with you."

How we connect and build trust with people from a different culture (including those who we assume are from our own culture or identity group) in authentic, respectful and meaningful ways influences their willingness to share their deepest concerns. Cross cultural communication invites us on an ongoing journey of self-assessment, experiential learning and skills development that facilitate genuine heart connection across cultures and power differentials. As we grow in our ability to look at our own privileges, biases and preconceptions that can impact our coaching effectiveness, we equip ourselves to serve our clients more authentically. Culturally competent coaches find ways to create a safe environment and actively invite the less comfortable parts of people forward.

We also do this work for our own empowerment as coaches. To call out the power of our clients requires us to stand in our own power. Doing the internal work—whether it is addressing our privileges or our internalized oppression—helps us liberate ourselves to be of service to our clients as well as our communities.

Ultimately, coaches support expansion of awareness not just for the sake of learning, but to help clients determine what they want to do. Instead of allowing clients to remain disconnected from their power while thinking of themselves as victims of sexism, racism, heterosexism or other hurtful behaviors, we help them make a choice. They may come to the coaching session angry, sad or deflated—hoping to make sense of their interactions, process their anger, understand their pain or heal the past. Then what? We can coach them to discover and acknowledge their feelings, and determine how they want to move forward. We can role play conversations so that they can practice transforming their initial reactions into productive, compassionate or fiercely courageous responses. Our role isn't to diagnose or label behavior, but rather to help clients develop support systems and create action plans that honor their authentic voice and cultural heritage.

> Reflect on the various cultural influences in your upbringing. How would you describe the cultural groups you belong to?

> Think of someone from another culture that you interact with. How can you deepen your awareness of her or his culture?

> How can you support managers, leaders and other coaches to expand their cross cultural awareness?

## Understanding the External Forces of Power

*Washing one's hands of the conflict between the powerful and the powerless means to side with the powerful, not to be neutral.* —Paulo Freire  *(Brazilian activist & educator)*

The term "social conditioning" refers to the ways individuals are taught what is acceptable in social situations. For example, we are taught early on in school not to shout out an answer. Through both negative and positive reinforcement, students learn to raise their hands and wait to be called on before speaking in class. This mini-lesson is transferred from the classroom into other aspects of our lives—in situations where we see something happening that we don't agree with yet hesitate before sharing our thoughts, or wonder if anyone cares what we have to say about a situation that may not be "any of our business." We may question the level of positional or authoritative power we have to make a difference, even if we are personally empowered to speak up.

All social interactions are riddled with power dynamics. Consider the dynamics at play when a child tells an adult he thinks a decision made for him by the adult is unfair, or a teacher tells a parent her child has been expelled, or a doctor informs a patient she needs surgery. In any of these situations, the dynamics of positional power can include authoritative power due to age, education or class. The power dynamics impact perceptions of who has expertise, what is "right" or "wrong," whose needs matter and who has choice.

In addition, because books, articles and histories have generally been written by those with positional power and who have the resources, as coaches we may not have been exposed to information about the particular group our clients belong to. We may even not have much knowledge about our own cultural groups. It can be helpful to seek information written by people from the cultural groups we want to learn about—especially about the strengths, achievements and resiliency—so that we don't burden our clients for information about "their people." Our

**COACHING** *in Action* | **How We Help, How We Harm: Deepening our Understanding of Culture, Power, Privilege and Rank**

*by J. Manzon-Santos, J. Naude, M. Scott, M. O'Hearne, K. Fowler*

Individuals can experience power, privilege and rank as a result of the status they have earned through their own endeavors in life such as professional or academic achievement. These markers of status may be relatively obvious and more easily anticipated and worked with. However, power, privilege and rank that come from the social groups that one identifies with or belongs to, can be more subtle and difficult to name and engage. These forms of social power, privilege and rank are not earned; they are something people are born into.

Every social group has its own set of norms, standards, beliefs and values, all of which help to comprise its unique culture. Members of each group have a deep unconscious understanding of how to behave and fit in. They know which behaviors are valued and which are not. They know the rules of engagement.

Members of a dominant social group are afforded power, privilege and rank and typically experience a general sense of comfort since they are in settings that align with their norms, standards, beliefs and values. The ease they feel contributes to an inner confidence and a belief that everyone thinks and feels like them. They can carry a subtle sense of entitlement to speak and do as they please.

On the other hand, people who are not members of a particular dominant group often feel marginalized. They do not feel they belong nor experience the same inner confidence. Their behavior is tentative and they may not speak up when they are in disagreement. Members of dominant social groups tend to speak with authority as if their worldviews are "the truth."

When individuals behave with little awareness of the power, privilege and rank associated with their social groups, their attitudes and behaviors may demean, dismiss or ignore others. This harm is sometimes referred to as causing micro-aggressions. In a coaching context, the effect on communication between a coach from a dominant group and a client from a marginalized group could be distorted by these power, privilege and rank differences. The effect on the process of coaching is likely to be harmful rather than helpful if the coach is unaware of the power, privilege and rank afforded them by their membership in various dominant social groups. It is the cultural experience of belonging to dominant social groups and the cultural experience of belonging to marginalized social groups that we wish to lift up here.

In the following table, social groups appear in no order of importance, nor is it an exhaustive list. It is rather an invitation to coaches and clients alike to reflect on how different categories of power, privilege and rank might show up. We encourage you to think about additional categories that you are aware of and/or have direct experience with and how their dynamics may impact your coaching.

Keep in mind that a social group's dominance is often context-dependent. For instance, white men may not necessarily carry power, privilege and rank in all circumstances. A white male who is a minority in terms of numbers in a multi-racial workplace may feel socially marginalized if he feels unable to engage in effective communication with his peers; however, he may also be perceived, even subconsciously, by the decision-makers, as more promotion-worthy.

How we connect with various social groups can be extremely complex. All of us likely identify with multiple dominant social groups and with multiple marginalized groups. The same applies to our clients. How aware we are of the cultures of dominant groups and the cultures of marginalized groups, and how we hold this complexity and intersectionality (living in multiple worlds) in our sessions and within ourselves, takes on tremendous importance.

**COACHING *in Action* | How We Help, How We Harm: Deepening our Understanding of Culture, Power, Privilege and Rank**
*by J. Manzon-Santos, J. Naude, M. Scott, M. O'Hearne, K. Fowler*

| CATEGORY | DOMINANT SOCIAL GROUPS | MARGINALIZED SOCIAL GROUPS |
|---|---|---|
| Citizenship | Citizens | Residents, Immigrants, Migrants, Refugees, Undocumented People |
| Global Citizenship | Citizens of First World or Global North Nations | Citizens of Third World or Global South Nations, Landless Nations, Peoples, Tribes |
| Literacy | English Language-Literate [Global North] | Non-English Language-Literate [Global North] |
| Age | Adults | Children, Youth, Elderly |
| Sexual Orientation | Heterosexual/Straight People | Lesbians, Gays, Bisexuals, Queers, Two-Spirits [North America] |
| Religion | Christians [Western Hemisphere] | Muslims, Buddhists, Jews, Hindus, Traditionalists, Atheists, Agnostics |
| Caste | Higher Caste (Brahmins, Kshatriyas, Vaishyas) [India] | Lower Caste (Shudras, Dalits) [India] |
| Race | Whites/People of European Descent | People of Color [North America]; Latinos/Hispanics; People of Asian Descent; Indigenous/Native/First Nations People [Canada] ; Blacks/People of African Descent; Coloreds [South Africa]; People of Arab Descent; Roma People [Europe]; People of Mixed-Race |
| Freedom to Move | Free Individuals | Prisoners |
| Gender | Cisgender Men (men whose experience of their gender agrees with the sex they were assigned at birth) | Cisgender Women/Transgender/Gender Non-Conforming/Same Gender Loving/Intersex |
| Class | Owning Class/Wealthy/Upper Class/Middle Class | Working Class/Poor/Landless/Homeless |
| Education | College Educated | Less Educated |
| Psychological Health | Psychologically Healthy | Living with Psychological Challenges |
| Ability | Able-Bodied / Physically Healthy | Disabled/Living with Physical Challenges |
| Beauty | Conforming to Predominant Beauty Standards | Not Conforming to Predominant Beauty Standards |
| Additional | | |

understanding of the role of disabled people in the successes of disability rights movements may help a client connect to their power as a disabled person.

Similar to culture, power structures are sometimes internalized in a person's choices or interactions and sometimes externalized in systems and processes. Systemic power refers to the structures and systems of order that govern groups of people or society. The courts, insurance companies, taxes, education, banking or voting rights are examples of systemic power. They are all large, non-individualized ways of setting up a system of rules that dictate how others behave. Depending on who you are and your particular circumstances, systemic power structures may protect your rights, or protect the rights of a different group at your expense.

In the article "The Culture of Power," author Paul Kivel writes:

> "If you are a woman and you have ever walked into a men's meeting, or a person of color and have walked into a white organization, or a child who walked into a principal's office, or a Jew or Muslim who entered a Christian space, then you know what it is like to walk into a culture of power that is not your own. You may feel insecure, unsafe, disrespected, unseen or marginalized. You know you have to tread carefully."[4]

As coaches, understanding the dynamics of the culture of power can be helpful in supporting clients to make meaning of what they feel or need. Because so many power dynamics are felt, rather than articulated, we can often sense something is "off" before we know exactly what it is. As coaches, we can support people to find language for some of these "sensed" dynamics. Also, for individuals who are part of the culture of power, it can be hard to recognize what that culture is—that there even is a culture (they may see it as a norm)—or how it may feel for someone outside that group. Culture is often likened to gravity. You don't know it's there until you jump up and something drags you back down. Even if it's unconscious, we each have ways in which we use power over others or give our power away. While we may be adept at recognizing when we are excluded, or when we don't quite fit into a group, it can be hard to realize the ways in which we may exclude others from groups. We may not even experience "a group" but rather "it's just how it is."

*Questions to Consider*

What are ways in which you benefit from a culture of power and privilege?

In what ways have you been hurt by power and privilege?

How does your power and privilege or lack of it impact your coaching relationships?

What will you do to become a conscious ally for your clients?

---

4    Kivel, Paul (2000). *The Culture of Power.* Retrieved from http://paulkivel.com/articles/cultureofpower.pdf

# Privilege

*Love is what we are born with. Fear is what we learn. The spiritual journey is the unlearning of fear and prejudices and the acceptance of love back in our hearts. Love is the essential reality and our purpose on earth. To be consciously aware of it, to experience love in ourselves and others, is the meaning of life. Meaning does not lie in things. Meaning lies in us. —Marianne Williamson*

Privilege has been described as "unearned rights, benefits, immunity and favours that are bestowed on individuals and groups solely on the basis of their race, culture, religion, gender, sexual orientation, physical ability or other key characteristic."[5] Another form of privilege is socioeconomic class and caste. In each type of privilege, the privileged group is considered the norm and others are considered to be different or outside of the norm. The culturally dominant group defines the rules and acceptable behaviors; others are expected to comply. Privilege is typically invisible to those who possess it. It can be thought of as "just the way things are" or "the way things should be." Some people are part of several privileged groups, while others may be members of few or none.

Male privilege and related power are associated with unequal pay for equal work (with women's pay less than men's on average), higher rates of employment for men than women, more men in top leadership/decision-making positions than women, domestic and sexual violence targeted against women, and human rights violations targeting women—to name a few.

In the U.S., Christianity is the dominant religion. As a result, Christians hold more political positions and control more legislative decisions, so they hold more power and privilege. White American males have historically been the dominant group in power, and the history of race relations in the U.S. has resulted in the distinctions of white and non-white people. This is also true in countries in which Europeans established colonies where they continue to have a powerful and privileged presence, such as Australia and South Africa. Interestingly, though able to see and refer to the race of others, some white people are not comfortable with self-identifying or being identified as "white" and may deny having a "culture."

Along with being the dominant group in a society, come power and privilege. White privilege has been defined by Adams, Bell and Griffin (2007) as:

> "The concrete benefits of access to resources and social rewards and the power to shape the norms and values of society those whites receive, unconsciously or consciously, by virtue of their skin color in a racist society."

Peggy McIntosh, in her article "White Privilege: Unpacking the Invisible Knapsack," says:

> "I was taught to see racism only in individual acts of meanness, not in invisible systems conferring dominance on my group from birth…As a white person, I realized I had been taught about racism as something that puts others at a disadvantage, but had been taught

---

5    An invitation to narrative practitioners to address privilege and dominance. A document created from conversations between Salome Raheim, Cheryl White, David Denborough, Charles Waldegrave, Kiwi Tamasese, Flora Tuhaka, Anita Franklin, Hugh Fox, & Maggie Carey. http://www.dulwichcentre.com.au/privilege.html

## COACHING *in Action* | **Navigating Rank** *by Belma González, CFT Faculty*

I was coaching a young working class Latina, I'll call Elizabeth. She was the Program Director in a small social justice organization working with families of color. Her supervisor, Sydney, was the executive director and founder, a middle-aged white woman from wealth. Sydney had created her board of directors from friends—so they were mainly wealthy, older and white.

When Sydney decided to step down, Elizabeth seemed the natural successor. She had been overseeing the finances, the personnel, all the day-to-day operations for several years and receiving excellent reviews. Given the organization's mission, it also made sense to have a person of color as the new executive director (ED). Sydney had been doing the fundraising; however, Elizabeth had been a development director for another organization previously and she had good long-term relationships with the organization's funders. Sydney told Elizabeth—you'll be the new ED if you want it. Elizabeth told her, she did want to be the ED.

However, the board decided to do a full-fledged search. And, Elizabeth only heard that she needed to submit an application to be a part of the search. She wasn't told by Sydney what had changed, but decided to broach the subject. She learned the board had concerns regarding her "sophistication." Elizabeth brought this as an issue to coaching… "I guess I need to be more sophisticated; how do I learn to be more sophisticated?" I asked what this meant to her... what she thought about this. Elizabeth hesitated… I was having a strong intuition—I wondered if "sophistication" wasn't code. "Code?" she asked, and then said, "Ohhhh…" I asked her about the "Oh". "You mean like it's about me being…not like them?" I said, "Shall we just call it out?" And, she said—"It's class stuff." So I said, "And maybe race and age stuff too?"

Elizabeth answered yes… We talked about how we couldn't know this for certain—and we could both pay attention to our feelings about it—from our life experiences and our intuition.

Then we looked at what she wanted to do. Eventually, Elizabeth's strategy was to ground herself. To know she believed she was the best candidate. To know that her skills, experience and passion were so right for the position and that her ethnicity, class and age were assets. And, in her interviews Elizabeth shared this with the interviewers. Meanwhile, they asked her to be the interim director (while Sydney took unpaid time off) and Elizabeth got that they were testing her. From my experience with the nonprofit sector often having a scarcity perspective, I got curious about her having two jobs—the interim ED and her program director job—and what she thought about this. After this coaching session, she went back to the board and negotiated: she agreed to be the Interim if she could promote another staff member to interim program director and hire a temporary admin person.

Long story short: they put Elizabeth through being an interim at only a slight raise for three months, they put her through three interviews, and they finally hired her officially. After discussing her frustration about the process in coaching, and deciding to take a stand regarding her value to the organization and as a role model, she agreed to accept the position if she received retroactive executive director salary for the months she'd been interim. Elizabeth also wanted to remove the founder from the board, who as a major donor, had a conflict of interest. They agreed. She then officially promoted the person who'd been interim program director (without putting him through a hiring process), and brought on constituents—parents of color—as board members. She is still the ED, doing great work that impacts social and educational inequities.

not to see one of its corollary aspects, white privilege, which puts me at an advantage. …I have come to see white privilege as an invisible package of unearned assets that I can count on cashing in each day, but about which I was 'meant' to remain oblivious."[6]

McIntosh describes a number of things associated with white privilege that she previously was not aware of and had taken for granted. Just a few of the 50 she describes are listed below:

If I should need to move, I can be pretty sure of renting or purchasing housing in an area which I can afford and in which I would want to live.

I can be pretty sure that my neighbors in such a location will be neutral or pleasant to me.

I can go shopping alone most of the time, pretty well assured that I will not be followed or harassed.

I can turn on the television or open to the front page of the paper and see people of my race widely represented.

Blogger Barry Deutch describes an internet acquaintance who says, "The first big privilege which whites, males, people in upper economic classes, the able bodied, the straight (I think one or two of those will cover most of us) can work to alleviate is the privilege to be oblivious to privilege."[7] How do we increase our awareness of privilege? Without dividing people, how do we bring conscious awareness to power and privilege as a way to build authentic relationships with people who are different?

## Microaggressions

*Any real change implies the breakup of the world as one has always known it, the loss of all that gave one an identity, the end of safety. And at such a moment, unable to see and not daring to imagine what the future will now bring forth, one clings to what one knew, or dreamed that one possessed. Yet, it is only when a man is able, without bitterness or self-pity, to surrender a dream he has long cherished or a privilege he has long possessed that he is set free — he has set himself free — for higher dreams, for greater privileges. —James Baldwin*

Microaggressions are subtle and often unintentional acts or statements that reflect inherited biases based on race, sexual orientation, gender or other perceived differences. Since microaggressions are frequently unintended and delivered by people who consider themselves free of bias, we can unknowingly stimulate pain in people who are different from us. As coaches we need to be alert to the possibility of committing microaggressions, which can lead to people thinking they are unwelcome, isolated, unsafe or alienated. Alternative explanations can leave the recipient uncertain whether the "insult" is real, intended or misperceived.

---

6   McIntosh, P. (1988), "White privilege: Unpacking the invisible knapsack," Independent Student, Winter 1990, volume 49, number 2.
7   Retrieved from: http://www.amptoons.com/blog/the-male-privilege-checklist/

The following table contains a sample of microaggressive behaviors and statements.

| MICROAGGRESSION | MESSAGE |
|---|---|
| "When I look at you, I don't see color." "America is a melting pot." | Denying a person of color's racial/ethnic experiences. |
| Asking an Asian person to help with a math or science problem. | All Asians are intelligent and good in math/sciences. |
| A white man or woman clutches their purse or wallet as a Black or Latino approaches. | You are a criminal. |
| Using the pronoun "he" to refer to all people. | Male experience is universal. Female experience is meaningless. |
| Assuming only two options for relationship status: married or single. | LGBT partnerships do not matter or are meaningless. |
| A female doctor is mistaken for a nurse. | Women occupy nurturing roles. |

Excerpted from Sue & Sue.[8]

As a coach, how do you handle it when your client communicates an experience of microaggression? As a client, what's at stake if you share your experience, and what do you sacrifice if you don't? To develop authentic cross cultural communication and respect, it takes curiosity and diligence to address microaggressions rather than overlook, ignore or minimize them.

We can grow by becoming aware of microaggressive statements or questions and the impact they have on others. Regardless of the intent or what we think about the situation, we can acknowledge the feelings of the speaker, and give feedback to the person who communicated the microaggression. Feedback using "I" statements offers more opportunities for connection than "you" statements.

The following example is based on an exchange between two coaching students. The white female thought she was complimenting the black male when she said, "You are so intelligent and articulate." Her statement angered him and led to disconnection. A response using "I" statements might have been, "As a black man, I feel angry when you say 'You are so intelligent and articulate,' because I interpret that as, 'You are an exception.' I need respect for all black men who are often stereotyped as neither smart nor articulate!" When people are fully heard, insight and learning occur and relationships grow authentically. For example, when someone has the courage to share their painful experience of a microaggression, the listener is more likely to create connection by replying with gratitude, empathy and curiosity. If the coach says, "I'm not sexist," it's very different from saying, "Thank you for bringing that to my attention. I see how deeply that statement impacted you. Please tell me more. I really want to understand." Note that the focus is on the

---

8    Sue, D. W. & Sue, D. (2008). *Counseling the Culturally Diverse: Theory and Practice,* 5th edition. New Jersey: John Wiley & Sons

person who felt injured, not on the person who hopes to explain, justify, minimize or deflect what was said.

The following is an example of how microaggression can play out in a coaching session:

Ann:    One of my male colleagues on the board repeatedly interrupts me when I'm talking. I'm furious about that.

Coach:  Get over it! (microaggression)

Ann:    I'm angered by your response which undermines the trust between us. I experience my colleague's actions as sexist. He doesn't interrupt our male colleagues. I need you to hear and acknowledge my experience even if you don't agree with my assessment or labeling of his behavior.

Coach:  Ann, thank you for that feedback. Trust between us is important. You helped me see your experience from a different perspective. I acknowledge your fury with his actions and your sadness about my response because you want respect for your experience, right?

Ann:    Thank you for hearing the fullness of my feelings and need for respect.

Coach:  Let's brainstorm some ways you can reclaim your power in your interactions with your colleague.

Note in this example that the coaching goes beyond the client teaching her coach about multiculturalism and becomes a platform for moving both the coaching and the coaching relationship forward. The coach can also help this client gain awareness that labeling her colleague's behavior as "sexist" creates more distance between them. If she learns to share her feelings, needs and requests with her colleague as she did with her coach, she opens the possibility for increased connection between them.

## Trust

The history of race relations and other cross cultural differences has led to caution in revealing feelings and attitudes about differences to people we do not know well. How are we specifically taught by direct and indirect messages to avoid discussions about race or other differences? Daily experiences of prejudice and discrimination are still a reality for many marginalized groups. As a result, racial and ethnic minorities and other identity groups such as LGBT people, disabled people, etc., may initially approach relationships with someone not of their group cautiously. In a coaching relationship, this may mean that self-exposure and deep sharing will be delayed until trust is established. Building trust requires that we recognize and acknowledge others' experience.

Curious questions can lead to more disclosure giving the client the sense that the coach "gets me" which aids the trust building process. At the same time the coach needs to be sensitive to asking too many questions to prevent the response, "I'm tired of educating straight people about what it's like to be gay. Do a little research, will you?" Self-disclosure from coaches about their own vulnerable lack of awareness and desire to understand another's personal experience and cultural background builds trust over time.

## COACHING *in Action* | **Coaching at Home** *by Kathleen Moore, CFT Faculty*

I stepped into the role of coach instead of mom in this session with our 19-year-old son. He was back from his freshman year in college and brought with him some behaviors that were outside of the boundaries of what we could accept in our home. The high school years had been tough as he was caught drinking on several occasions including one time when he showed up to school drunk. As his mom, and president of the school board, I was especially challenged by his defiance.

As parents we saw each mistake as an opportunity for growth and worked hard to help our children learn. However, when he moved home from college for the summer and his brother found pot in his room, it was time to coach him as an adult instead of parenting him as a child. With two younger children left at home who were influenced by his choices, something had to change. I was able to self-manage by reminding myself that he was now an adult who was perfectly capable of discovering for himself what was possible with the assistance of a coach.

Coach: Would it be okay to identify some of your values?

Andrew: Okay.

Coach: I will share a few that I see and then ask you to add to the list. The things I see as important to you include independence, privacy and adventure or risk taking. Do those seem like values for you?

Andrew: Yes.

Coach: What other values can you identify as important?

Andrew: Privacy is a big one. Respect. Fun is important. I don't know any others.

Coach: What about family relationships?

Andrew: Of course.

Coach: At this age how does your value around family relationships fit with independence?

Andrew: They are both important.

Coach: What does it look like to have a strong relationship with family when your need for independence puts you at odds with family values?

Andrew: It doesn't work but I want to make my own choices.

Coach: What options are there for preserving your relationships and being independent?

Andrew: I don't know.

Coach: Is there something you could do to have a relationship with family and make your own choices?

Andrew: I could choose not to live at home.

Coach: That is one option. What else?

Andrew: I could respect the family expectations and make different choices about how I use my independence.

Coach: What would that look like?

Andrew: I could live at home to be with family but not break the rules at home.

Coach: And how does that feel?

Andrew: Hard. But I think it is possible.

As a result of this coaching many things shifted. He remained at home and found other ways to feel independent. This would not have happened if a line had been drawn in the sand and the options had been presented by me as his mom.

# Intersectionality—Living in Many Worlds at Once

Culture plays an integral part in the socialization process by which people learn behaviors, values and beliefs. The goal of socialization is to prepare people to become active functioning members of society.[9] Generally, parents or guardians are the primary agents of socialization,[10] providing social norms and order to children;[11] however, secondary agents of socialization may include media, authority and educational institutions throughout life. In instances when a child belongs to the dominant group of society, the individual's socialization process can remain seamlessly aligned—primary and secondary agents of socialization reinforce accepted behaviors, values and beliefs of society.

Latino, Asian, Black or immigrant parents living in the United States face the task of raising children able to survive and prosper in a society that devalues their ethnicity or race. Secondary agents of socialization provide messaging that may be inconsistent with cultural messages taught by family and others in the cultural group. For example, if you're coaching a Latino parent with children in an American school that minimizes, deters or institutes punishments for speaking Spanish, how will you support dual socialization? Your client may want coaching on how to talk to teachers who consider speaking Spanish a detriment to the child's learning. At the same time the client may want a road map for simultaneously respecting her elders, which includes honoring their culture by speaking Spanish. Your client may need support for navigating conflicting values and determining how to teach her children to belong in multiple cultures and environments.

Another common challenge faced by teens and adult children and grandchildren of immigrants and others from the non-dominant culture is the pressure they face to conform to the cultural expectations of their parents and cultural communities despite their desire to adopt some of the practices of the dominant culture or even other cultures that are meaningful to them. This may include pressures to marry someone within the culture or to practice the same religious beliefs and rituals of the culture, despite the actual desires of the client. At times the pressures can be so severe that a client may feel the need to choose between one world and another—sacrificing personal values, needs and beliefs or the connection with family and cultural community. How can you help your clients navigate, balance and honor the competing personal desires and pressures they may experience?

How will you help clients address issues of race or ethnic socialization—the process of preparing children to understand their unique heritage, culture and their station in a minority group in society? Clients may want coaching on the challenges of straddling two or more worlds. What may be acceptable in one world, may not be in the other and how they are valued in one, may not be mirrored in the other. This might include coaching on how a minority fits into dual worlds in their workplace or community. Or clients may want support for the pain of being asked to choose between their family and the person they love. The desire to belong results in a conflict of two or more worlds; each having its own rules and perception of what it means to be part of the group; influencing how we answer the question, "Who am I and do I fit in?" W. E. B. Dubois, in *The Souls of Black Folks*, describes the consequence of slavery for African-Americans as living in a

9    Thompson, V. L. S. (1994). "Socialization and its relationship to racial identification among African Americans." *Journal of Black Psychology* 0.2: 175-188.

10   Peters, M.F. (1985). Racial Socialization of Black Children. In H. P. McAdoo & J. L. McAdoo, Black Children: Social, educational, and parental environments (pp.159-173). Beverly Hills, CA: Sage.

11   Glass, J. & Bengston, V. L. (1986). "Attitude similarity in three-generation families: Socialization, status inheritance, or reciprocal influence?" *American Sociological Review*, 51, 685-698.

world of "double consciousness"—defining and seeing ourselves through the eyes of the dominant culture.[12]

Dual socialization is a phenomenon commonly experienced by people of color—as well as other groups—all of their lives, consciously or subconsciously. How will you support your clients to function well in the dominant culture, while also living in their own respective group ethnicities or identities? Managing dual socialization requires tremendous emotional and mental agility. High emotional intelligence is essential for dual socialization, in continuously learning and abiding by firm yet unspoken rules to a game of survival in dominant cultures.

Emotional loneliness is commonly experienced by Blacks, Latinos, Native Americans and Asians, especially, in academia or other professional settings. Fear, distrust and self-protection may serve as inner critics inherited from generation to generation for a client with this life experience. At the same time, it is important that we remember that these inner critics are probably living side by side with an inner strength and resilience that comes from a client's pride in their culture.

Since parents or guardians are the primary agents of socialization, what is the impact when a child is raised by parents or guardians not of their culture? For example, children of color adopted by white parents or someone who is lesbian, gay, bisexual or transgender raised by parents who are heterosexual. Coaching people with these life experiences is likely to include helping them navigate the various cultures they live in—they may experience isolation, alienation and stigmatization from their own family members.

> How can you discover what taking a risk in the workplace feels like for a client not from the dominant culture?

> How can you support clients who feel torn between pressures from family and community and the desires of their own hearts?

> What do you want to keep in mind when coaching a client from a different culture?

## Diverse Experiences and Voices

What follows are a few reflections from coaches about cross cultural coaching. The reflections and case studies in the next section are conversation starters to help you think about various aspects of communicating and coaching effectively across cultures and power differentials. As you read the experiences, reflections and case studies, consider how you would coach each client.

> *"What's important to me in a coach is understanding and also someone who takes the time to share deeply about their own experiences. Coach self-disclosure is important to me. In the past I had an African-American therapist and found I did not disclose much to her. I didn't want to feel judged and didn't want to feel that she understood me just because we have the same skin color. I also had a therapist who was an older Jewish man who was open about his struggles. That helped me feel comfortable with him. I also sensed that he really wanted to understand me. He saw me as an individual. I opened up to him a lot and we had a good relationship until the day I shared with him about the breakup with my boyfriend and he gave me advice that clearly showed he had racial biases and stereotypes about African-American males. That ended our relationship."*
> —*African-American Female*

---

12   DuBois, W. E. B. (1903). *The Souls of Black Folk*. Chicago: A. C. McClurg & Co.

*Questions to Consider*

What thoughts came into your awareness as you read this experience?

What is really important to this client in a coaching relationship?

How would you co-create an effective cross-cultural or same-culture coaching relationship with this client?

*"Coaching multiculturally is a delicate dance. In cross-cultural coaching, I wouldn't initially talk about experiences of being Asian or ethnically different. I might think my coach just wouldn't understand it or they might think I just need to get over it. If I were being coached by someone of another cultural background, and I brought up a racist moment I experienced, it would be helpful for my coach to say something like 'I haven't had a lot of experience with this. Can you tell me more about it? Put me in your shoes and help me walk through what you experienced so I can see it from your perspective.' That would make me feel open. It would feel good to be able to teach my coach about my experience."—Korean-American Female*

*Questions to Consider*

What insights did you gain from this sharing?

How might this case study inform your cross-cultural coaching?

*"Looking into the large audience of fraternity members who had donned Ku Klux Klan hoods and gowns at a racially offensive social event which spawned the instant meeting, I shuddered. Suddenly, I inhaled strength and courage from Dad's spirit and those of my grandparents and of my ancestors. Voices from my past lifted my speech upon the audience. I began, 'I challenge each and every one of you to recognize racism...'" —College Student, First Generation Mexican-American Female*

*Questions to Consider*

If a client opened up the coaching session with the passage above, what tools would you need to create safe space for exploration?

What do you want to acknowledge here?

What culturally aware, empowering question would you ask this client?

What do you sense really matters to this client?

*"Blindness still feels like the really hard thing—the attitudes and issues around it. The stupid things people say like, 'how are you going to do the job if you're blind?' Why do I have to explain how I do things? People treat me like I'm damaged or inferior. Always assuming I need help. Things are set up for sighted people—that's why we need help. People don't realize that. They have some idea of what they need to do to help me. People have expectations of how disabled people are supposed to be in the world. They judge and see us as different—not normal. My best friends don't do anything about my blindness. They just hang out with me as a regular person. If I need help, I'll ask for it. I want to be in a space comfortably. Help can be overwhelming for me. I prefer when people are not nervous or hung up about it. Some people with disabilities prefer the help or need it. Others, like me, prefer to ask if I need it. What I'm really wanting is for people to think*

*ahead and integrate the needs of disabled and non-disabled people. For example in a classroom setting, a teacher can casually include locations of things like water, candy dishes and restrooms when they give housekeeping announcements to the class. Blind people in the class would then have the same information as others without singling them out.*

*I still face discrimination. When I try to rent an apartment, I can't get an upstairs apartment because people are afraid I'll fall down the stairs. I wish people would acknowledge that there are external obstacles for disabled people and if possible help change them or at least acknowledge that it sucks and encourage the client to advocate for change. Regarding coaching, listen and dig underneath the surface to get to the heart of the concerns and to form the heart connection. Discussion has to happen among people who are able to hear each other. I want my coach to understand how big the problem is." —Disabled Female*

### Questions to Consider

Imagine your client just shared this story. What are your instincts telling you right now?

What are the feelings and needs voiced by the client? Take time and notice them all.

How would you let the client know that you really heard her?

How can you gain a deeper understanding of the challenges she faces?

How can you address your own microaggressions?

## Case Studies

*You may think your actions are meaningless and that they won't help, but that is no excuse, you must still act. —Mohandas Gandhi*

### Janice

Janice is 40, married to an older man and is in the process of adopting a baby from Sierra Leone. Janice often talks about how she has difficulty interacting with her co-workers in the office. She believes no one in the office likes her. She shares in coaching sessions that she is rarely invited to join group lunches, and no one ever stops by her desk to chat after a meeting or to share about their weekends. Often she talks about moving into her dream home, in a fancy neighborhood. She does not like her current home and rarely goes outdoors to tend to the garden, even though gardening and relaxing in the yard are ways she likes to de-stress. During a coaching conversation, Janice reveals that she feels uncomfortable being a minority African-American person in a largely white neighborhood. She believes that if she spent too much time outdoors, the neighbors would notice her and the value of her current home would go down, impacting re-sale value and subsequently hurt her ability to buy her dream home.

### Questions to Consider

How would you coach Janice?

What role does culture play in Janice's ability to manifest her dreams?

What questions could you ask to check if Janice's perception of race in her neighborhood is having an impact on her work relationships?

**Guadalupe**

Guadalupe is a first generation Mexican-American who is fully bicultural and bilingual, having been born and raised in San Antonio, Texas. She has a master's degree in public policy, works for a renowned advocacy organization, and performs modern dance professionally in New York City in her spare time. During Guadalupe's coach training program, a classmate asked her about the origin of her name. When she explained that her parents emigrated from Mexico before she was born, and that she was named after Mexico's patron saint, her peer stated, "Oh! And you seem American and… so educated!" Guadalupe shared that she was left feeling devalued, shocked and injured knowing that she suddenly was "the other" to this woman. She stumbled over her words as she began, "Well, I'm American. And… I was educated in American schools… um… and…" She stopped herself and realized she was fulfilling the part of "the other" in trying to explain her "Americaness" and her "educatedness" before "the arbitrary judge." Guadalupe shared that this felt wrong on so many levels and that it was not the first time something like this had happened. She went on to explain that rage crept up inside her heart as it had on similar occasions, but she had no safe space to set it free in that moment without the possibility of being perceived as an "emotional Latina" or "dangerous Mexican." She said that the rage plummeted to the pit of her stomach, imploded upon itself into sadness, and spiraled into deep, somber isolation.

*Questions to Consider*

How would you coach Guadalupe?

As her coach, what is the first thing you say?

Notice the feelings in your body as the experience and sharing of it sink in. What feelings and thoughts are you aware of?

What multicultural coaching skills would you draw upon?

How would you handle this interaction in a way that supports Guadalupe's trust? At the same time, how would you help the other student feel understood and understand the impact of her statement?

## Summary

*When we speak we are afraid our words will not be heard or welcomed. But when we are silent, we are still afraid. So it is better to speak. —Audre Lorde*

In this chapter we invited you to go deeper into the heart of your culture of origin to consider the impact of power and privilege in your life. We also invited you to open your heart and mind to the experiences and cultural viewpoints of people who have faced discrimination, marginalization and/or oppression as a member of a minority cultural group. Each of us has experienced what it is like to be in the minority as well as what it felt like to be in the majority—if only for a short time. Even across socioeconomic and ability levels we want to be more aware of those who can too easily experience exclusion. At the core, coaching is about deep and authentic heart connection. People from cultures of power can become intentional allies for those with less power, and those with less power can open to trust and collaboration to create exciting transformation in individuals, organizations, communities and in the world.

*Questions to Consider*

Coaching can change the world! How will you contribute?

Ask two people of color and two white people, "What does it mean to be white?"

How does privilege impact your coaching?

What stories do you tell yourself about people whose culture differs from yours?

When your personal biases come up in coaching, how will you address them?

# 15 Coaching in Organizations

*In a time of drastic change it is the learners who inherit the future. The ill-trained will find themselves equipped to live in a world that no longer exists. —Eric Hoffer*

**TOPICS**

- Changing the Mindset
- Organizational Challenges
- Benefits of Coaching in Organizations
- Designing Multiple Relationships
- Leadership Coaching
- The GROW Model
- SWOT Analysis
- Five Phases of Organization Development
- Appreciative Inquiry
- Cultural Transformation
- Seven Steps for Leading the People-Side of Change
- Evaluation of Coaching

One arena where coaching has an especially strong presence is in organizations. In this chapter, we address coaching processes that are particularly relevant in organizations, including: changing the mindset from boss to coach, designing multiple relationships and creating collaborative measures of success. We address concepts in leadership coaching and introduce the GROW model and SWOT analysis. We look into the five phases of organization development, Appreciative Inquiry and evaluation of coaching in organizations. Beyond personal transformation, we'll look at organizational and cultural transformation, including leading the people side of change.

Many organizations use both internal and external coaches. One way coaching in organizations differs from coaching individuals is that organizational coaches often address more than one agenda. The person being coached has an agenda, but so does the organization or the department that is footing the bill for the coaching.

Many organizations use the "coach approach" which means managers utilize coaching skills and core principles to enhance the way they work with others and bring out the best in them. They may offer structured sessions, or offer coaching on the fly by integrating the skills into their managerial role. Coaching skills help empower others, which creates a more effective and enjoyable workplace.

## Changing the Mindset

Leaders and managers who learn and integrate coaching skills are able to change their mindset from boss to coach. The following chart illustrates the changes that are possible when leaders empower others through coaching.

| FROM BOSS | TO COACH |
|---|---|
| Invokes fear to achieve compliance | Shares power to stimulate creativity |
| Looks for problems to solve | Looks for strengths to leverage |
| Makes demands | Makes requests |
| Controls through power | Facilitates by empowering |
| Knows the answer | Seeks the answer |
| Points out mistakes | Celebrates learning |
| Delegates responsibility | Establishes accountability |
| Believes knowledge is power | Believes vulnerability is power |
| Issues directives | Engages in dialogue |
| Sees people as "costs" to minimize | Sees people as "assets" to develop |

Some of the most common ways coaching is used in organizations are:

Leadership Development

Behavioral Change

Follow-up to Training

Emotional Competence

Accountability Structures

Vision, Mission and Strategic Planning

Problem Solving and Decision Making

Capacity Building

Change Management

Performance Measurement

Clarifying Roles and Responsibilities

Work - Life Balance

Fostering a Collaborative Culture

## Organizational Challenges

Individuals and leaders in corporate environments face many challenges that can present opportunities for coaching executives, middle managers or teams. Some challenges are routine, while others may occur during times of change. Some corporate challenges include:

**Mergers and Acquisitions**—When companies restructure, downsize or merge, reshuffled teams and work responsibilities contribute to increased stress, decreased morale, interpersonal conflicts and resentment. Coaching can help teams build trust, clarify vision and roles and support the transition to a blended culture.

**New Team Start Up**—When new teams come together on a project, they can go through rocky periods until roles and responsibilities, communication channels, vision and mission are clearly established and shared. Coaches can support the formation and development of a team.

**Global Virtual Teams**—When people are part of teams that are geographically dispersed, coaches can support them in working across time zones and in determining how to work together effectively.

**Goal Setting**—Based on company, division or departmental objectives, coaches can support individuals and teams to participate in setting fair, achievable goals. At the same time, coaches can help managers ensure consistency and alignment of personal goals with organizational goals.

**Performance Objectives**—How people assess, communicate and reward performance for individuals and teams can motivate or de-motivate staff. Coaching can help people identify competencies and create motivational leadership development plans.

**Empowerment**—Morale issues and lack of trust emerge when people in power micromanage others. Creating a coaching culture helps empower leaders at all levels where feedback is a two-way street.

Social sector challenges include:

**Mission Creep**—When organizations shift their mission to meet the requirements of funders, coaches can support them in staying true to their purpose.

**Scarcity Mentality**—When organizations struggle to secure funding, coaches can support the shift from the poverty mentality that drives most nonprofits.

**Rescuers Syndrome**— Even when nonprofits mean well, their efforts to rescue others often result in dependency. Coaching can support movement toward effective partnerships.

**Burn-Out**—When leaders actually believe their work is more important than their well-being, coaching can help them create a culture of self-care.

**Board Development**—When board members avoid fundraising or lack the skills to provide oversight, coaching can help to develop a fully engaged board.

**Dependency**—Ways of working with low-income clients may create dependency and lack of motivation for self-sufficiency. Creating a coaching culture within the organization and with clients creates interdependence.

**Leadership Capacity**—When nonprofits put clients first and staff last, they don't invest in their own professional development. Coaches can support capacity building through leadership coaching.

**Powerlessness**—When social change advocates lack the political savvy to effect change, they become heartbroken and turn on each other. Coaches can re-invigorate organizations by helping colleagues reconnect with their dreams and create sustainable action plans.

Related to organizational challenges are a host of opportunities for coaches. When coaches are curious about the unique challenges their organizational clients face, they can craft a relationship that effectively serves the individuals or teams they support.

Some of the opportunities for coaches in organizational work include working individually with executives, mid-level managers or nonprofit leaders or working with groups such as corporate teams, nonprofit boards or nonprofit staff. Coaches can also teach coaching skills, facilitate workshops for visioning, strategic planning or teambuilding and support team growth and development. Coaching contributes to improved team dynamics, communication, trust building, empathy, feedback and shared values.

# Benefits of Coaching in Organizations

The command, coercion and control model might work in emergencies, but can fail to tap the full range of human potential. Today, when empowered employees resolve problems, continuous performance improvement frequently becomes a way of life.

It is a rare organization that hasn't experienced the stress of workforce reductions, budget cuts and streamlined operations. At the same time, people everywhere want a sense of meaning, satisfaction and respect for the work they do. Coaching empowers individuals to develop their leadership potential, so that they engage in their work wholeheartedly and affect the bottom line. Rather than fearing the consequences of change, coached employees embrace change and collaborate to create a better future.

Some of the benefits of coaching in organizations:

Increases job satisfaction by building morale and trust

Promotes focused professional development

Facilitates career advancement and succession planning

Attracts, develops and retains talented leaders

Fosters creativity, innovation and team spirit

In addition to collecting a paycheck, work is an important source of human fulfillment, a way to develop potential and an outlet for creative expression. Coaching can encourage employees to bring their best ideas and efforts to the workplace, increasing commitment to the organization and its overall success.

Different from mentors or consultants, skillful coaches rarely provide solutions or advice. Instead, a coach facilitates what's most important to the person being coached by asking rigorous questions. The coaching relationship helps people focus, connect with what's important, explore new possibilities and choose an action plan. Attuned to values and vision, a coach helps people build capacity, take leadership and maximize their contribution.

Coaching is a collaborative rather than an authoritarian relationship, with a focus on solutions rather than analyzing problems. The coach doesn't need to be an expert in the client's profession; the emphasis is on fostering awareness, setting and realizing challenging goals and facilitating sustained personal and organizational growth.

---

**COACHING in Action |** **Voice and Choice** *by Jagruti Gala, CFT Faculty*

### EMBODYING AND EMBEDDING A COACHING CONSCIOUSNESS FOR THE CHILDREN OF THE WORLD

Zoom into an after-school learning center AURA in a small town, Vadodara, in Gujarat, India, where a group of 15 children are learning about heroism. Rahul, age 8, has just disrupted the class for the third time—this time by spilling water on the floor. The teacher, Priti, is experiencing distress and is tempted to give the child a grim warning. She pauses and takes a breath—she gets in touch with her inner distress and silently acknowledges her need for order and cooperation. She touches her yearning to contribute to how her children learn and connect with each other in her classroom. Then she reminds herself of her 'contribution mantra'—which is part of her coach's stand—the best learning and connection comes from what's in the here and now. She looks now at Rahul, with new eyes of curiosity, and says, 'Rahul, I noticed that we stopped our work three times today because you had some problem. You may be upset and I wonder what's happening. I really want to listen to you and understand. How would it be if we formed our Circle of Sharing to talk about this for the next ten minutes?'

Circle of Sharing is a ritual that was introduced in the classroom after Priti attended coach training. Whenever there is a situation of distress or conflict that needs immediate attention, the children and teacher sit in a circle where space is made for deep listening and giving and receiving empathy. Children are the Wise Ones and Priti is the Guide of the Wise Ones. All can contribute to the conversation and Priti facilitates. Contracting time is sacred and for today, it's ten minutes. If there remains a need for more conversation it would be taken care of later, outside the class or with a shared agreement for more time.

As Rahul gets heard, he shares that his mother had yelled at him, called him a lazy boy and pulled his arm to make him pick up his toys and paints before coming to AURA. Priti and the children take turns to support Rahul to name his feelings and touch his needs. Rahul moves from naming anger to hurt and fear. He receives empathy that he wanted his mother to be respectful, caring and soft. As the empathy touches Rahul he shares that he was most hurt for being called lazy and that he had actually wanted his mother to look at his artwork before he could put stuff away. He wanted her attention and understanding. The conversation helps Rahul to move from a place of agitation to calmness. At one point Priti asks Rahul if he could possibly see the situation from his mother's eyes and try to guess what was going on for her. Rahul is able to guess that she was rushed for time and anxious and possibly tired. Priti ends the ten-minute circle by naming that Rahul wants understanding and offers to work with him offline to help him. The class then proceeds with collaboration and harmony. Priti is greatly satisfied that she was able to embody a consciousness that enabled a rich learning for the whole group.

Priti is one among a group of teachers trained in the essential skills of coaching and an introduction to the Coaching for Transformation model. This work has awakened and excited them about how the coaching consciousness can transform the way children and adults engage with each other. There can be a world where adults and children share power and children can be empowered to be in choice from a very young age.

As these teachers embraced the coaching approach, they came back with stories of wonder and awe, humbled by the wisdom of children. They came back gladdened with the richness of their own transformation. They came back claiming that coaching goes beyond training and skills, it is a way to be!

## Designing Multiple Relationships

When you coach in organizations, who is your client? When organizational leaders contract for coaching services for an employee, they look for clarity on their return on investment. They have a desire to know what progress is made through the coaching intervention. You can create accountability structures while simultaneously honoring the confidentiality of the coaching relationship. Some ways to handle this are to:

Design reporting structures initiated by clients. This takes you out from the middle of the communication.

Design a three-way meeting where clients and their sponsors or managers talk about progress. You can facilitate or witness the conversation.

However you design this reporting structure, make it clear with all involved that you will not breech confidentiality. This allows you to hold the integrity of the coaching relationship and allow clients to do their best work. If the sponsor wants to know how the coaching is going, be clear that you will not have private conversations about progress.

Sometimes clients leave the organization as a result of the coaching work. You can tell organizational leaders about this possibility upfront to manage expectations. Once employees (especially ones who are having problems) start to look deeply at what they want and the degree to which their current work supports this, they may choose to leave. On the flip side, clients who become more aware, can identify their passion, become even more dedicated to the mission of the organization and expand their capacity to lead.

Imagine that an HR director calls you to coach a senior vice president because he has problems with people skills. Who is your client? In this case, you actually have more than one set of agendas to address. The HR director is the sponsor, so you'll need to address issues such as retention of the employee, reporting structures that honor confidentiality and payment agreements. Since the VP is your coaching client, it will be helpful to assess buy-in for the coaching process, address confidentiality issues and arrange reporting structures before you begin coaching.

A common pitfall in organizational coaching is confusing coaching with consulting. Most organizations use consultants (usually subject matter experts hired to bring their expertise to bear on a problem in the company), but using coaches is less common. Your discovery session is a good place to make sure your client understands the difference between coaching, consulting, mentoring and therapy.

## Leadership Coaching

Coaching has become the most popular leadership development process. In his 2006 research, Dr. Brian Underhill found that:

43% of CEOs and 71% of the senior executive team reported that they had worked with a coach.

63% of contacted organizations say they plan to increase their use of coaching over the next five years.

92% of leaders being coached say they plan to use a coach again.[1]

Underhill says, "Both indicators provide a strong endorsement of coaching; the first by the organizations paying the bills, and the second by the leaders who are actually receiving coaching."

The 2009 Harvard Business Review survey found that the popularity and acceptance of leadership coaching continues to rise even in a tight business environment. The survey concluded that clients keep coming back because "coaching works." The report also found that:

Over 48% of companies now use coaching to develop the leadership capabilities of high-potential performers.

The median hourly rate of coaching is $500 (from a low of $200 to a high of $3,500).

The typical coaching assignment is from 7-12 months.[2]

In a 2008 Personnel Today article, Chris Sharpe from Capita confirmed an increase in organizations looking for executive coaching skills to "develop senior managers to lead their teams more effectively." He says more and more learning and development professionals "have taken coaching qualifications in the market today."[3]

Many large organizations expect to have coaching departments in the near future. According to Darren Shirlaw in a 2007 Personnel Today article, "In 10 years' time there will be coaching departments in companies" and most companies will "have a Chief Learning Officer in five years' time."[4] The report claims that 80% of coaching in organizations is executive and leadership coaching, with business coaching accounting for around 20%.

Although coaching is offered as a perk at many organizations, human resources departments are becoming more rigorous about measuring the return on investment (ROI) of leadership coaching. In a white paper by David Ledgerwood, "*Does Executive Coaching Pay?*"[5] he offers a summary of the research on the ROI of coaching. Articles that weigh both sides of the issue include, *Is Executive Coaching a Con?*[6] and *The Wild West of Executive Coaching.*[7]

Whether we're internal or external coaches, we can choose to see every person in the organization as a leader. Although some people are born with an innate capacity to lead, anyone can develop leadership skills. Coaching elicits the leader in people. Through the coaching process, leaders connect with their power—the ability to see what needs to happen, tap resources and make things happen. As coaches, we intentionally look for strengths and open new opportunities for growth in our clients.

We serve as witnesses to clients' desires to create a better future. We coach people to live a deeper life and play a bigger game. How? Using a client-centered model, we help them enhance their

1    Bolt, Jim. Coaching: The Fad that Won't Go Away. *Fast Company*. April 10, 2006
2    Coutu, Diane; Kauffman, Carol; Charan, Ram; Peterson, David B.; Maccoby, Michael; Scoular, P. Anne; Grant, Anthony M.; What Can Coaches Do for You? *Harvard Business Review*, 00178012, Jan2009, Vol. 87, Issue 1.
3    Bentley, Ross. Full steam ahead. *Training & Coaching Today*, Jan 2008, p25.
4    Shirlaw, Darren. Coaching goes it alone. *Training & Coaching Today*, Oct 2007 p12.
5    Retrieved from: http://www.alocgroup.com/knowledge-base/articles/does-executive-coaching-pay
6    Retrieved from: http://www.personneltoday.com/articles/2008/02/04/44205/is-executive-coaching-a-con.html
7    Canner, Niko. The Wild West of Executive Coaching. *Harvard Business Review*, Mar2005, Vol. 83 Issue 3, p144-145

leadership competencies, deepen their learning, build their relationships, awaken their full authenticity, expand their vision, commit to action and contribute to the good of the whole.

Our leadership coaching model below provides a structure for professional development:

# Leadership Coaching Model

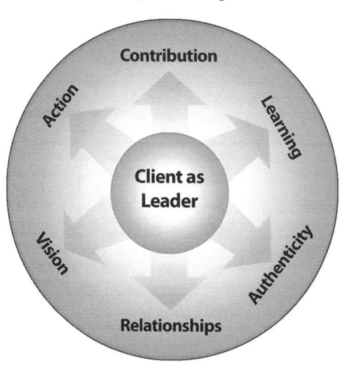

Learning: Look for opportunities to deepen awareness, challenge old ways of doing things, seek innovation, take risks, stay ahead of trends and develop fresh insights.

Authenticity: Acknowledge the unique gifts and diversity of team members, encourage full self-expression, values, walking the talk and celebrating passion.

Relationships: Explore ways to build relationships, recognize other's contributions, encourage heart connection, express appreciation, empower the team, create support systems, foster joint decision making and celebrate success.

Vision: Broaden perspectives, create from unlimited possibilities, set new intentions, communicate excitement and design a better future.

Action: Create opportunities to set clear goals, make action plans, break projects into steps, set up accountability structures for measuring results and celebrate milestones.

Contribution: Build awareness of the innate desire to contribute, generate opportunities to serve, offer support and creatively contribute to the good of the whole.

In the corporate environment, where the stakes are high and changes happen at the speed of light, most leaders welcome the chance to have an hour with their trusted coach to slow down, explore the nuances of their emotions, expand their vision and actualize their plans. Ultimately, coaching clients talk about similar issues across the board, but you can plan for some major differences when coaching leaders and executives. The following suggestions support you in working with these clients:

- Conduct comprehensive, in-depth assessments, including 360° feedback, Myers-Briggs Type Indicator (MBTI), Fundamental Interpersonal Relations Orientation–Behavior™ (FIRO-B®) and DISC (Dominance, Influence, Steadiness, Conscientiousness).

- Forge a strong contract between the client, the coach and the client's manager.

- Utilize models and tools to support structured coaching.

- Support executives to harness inner motivational dynamics to achieve sustainable, measurable behavioral change.

- Provide challenging, "hard-to-hear" behavioral feedback and evidence of observable change.

- Measure the return on investment with the executive as the prime owner of results.

- Enhance the leader's ability to self-assess and gather reliable feedback from others.

- Engage other's support to facilitate the desired behavioral change.

- Demonstrate return on investment by serving the needs of the organization and the people being coached.

## Executive coaching

Executive coaching is more than an open, trusting relationship; it's a partnership for deepening awareness, creating a learning culture, developing leadership capacity and driving transformational outcomes.

In many organizations, executives are treated like royalty, but they often experience loneliness, rarely get feedback, have few role models and can be blind to their own limitations. Coaches provide a safe environment for learning and reflection. Simultaneously, they challenge the executive to deepen awareness and expand opportunities for growth and development.

As a partner in the executive's journey, coaches hold a results-orientation to the leader's specific challenges. Mary Beth O'Neill says, "Bringing your own signature presence to coaching is the major tool of intervention." She defines signature presence as "bringing yourself when you coach—your values, passion, creativity, emotion and discerning judgment—to any given moment with a client."[8] This is particularly important to executives—who want to be met energetically on all levels. Many coaches have never been C-level leaders (CEO, COO, CFO, etc.), but they can still coach effectively by bringing all of themselves to the coaching relationship.

Executives at the top of their organizations want to work with coaches who understand the power dynamics, the demands of the position and the accelerating speed of change. They also need a trusting relationship where they can safely express their fears and uncertainty and figure out how to ask for help. To start with, coaches can listen to their clients' frustrations and then help

---

8    O'Neill, Mary Beth (2007). *Executive Coaching with Backbone and Heart a Systems Approach to Engaging Leaders with Their Challenges*, Second Edition. San Francisco, CA: Jossey-Bass.

## COACHING *in Action* | **Opening the Space** *by Sushma Sharma, CFT Certified Coach*

The coaching relationship is about co-aching for something more. What do we ache for? What is important for me is opening the space. The space becomes fertile for adventure and discovery.

The container is a safe space for all kinds of sharing to happen. A container of love and trust where I am a friend and confidante...where possibilities exist for dreams to unfold and significant differences are explored.

An example: I met a prospective client who was not very sure about coaching, but shared, "I have my 360° feedback which I don't understand. I report to two bosses. One of them rates me very open and the other one rates me closed. How can that be? I just don't get it. How can one person be experienced in two vastly different ways?"

I asked, "How are you different with these two people?"

He said, "With one I am not very open…"

"What is the block, if any, you experience with him?" I asked.

"I shut up and am not very spontaneous with him whereas with the other I just flow."

I asked, "So what is going on in this relationship?"

He told a story about a previous boss who would share his expectations and not bother him until the date of delivery. So he felt trusted. Whereas in the present situation he experienced distrust.

"Well where do you think he is operating from?"

"Anxiety I guess."

"So what are you doing to help your boss build trust with you?"

"Nothing, I don't like reporting and tom-toming about all that I am doing."

"How would he know all that you are doing as you are not even in the same city?"

"You are hitting the nail on the head. I am always wondering why he is micro-managing. I hate that. So I don't share on a regular basis. He has no clue about the progress."

"What is the real block you experience with him?" I asked.

"That he distrusts me and I can't stand it, so I keep quiet because I don't want to have a conflict."

"So coaching may help you to build new competencies to handle such conversations."

"I like what you are saying. I get suffocated, so I take recourse into silence. I need to know how to build trust with someone who is an anxious leader. You seem to understand me...how do we take it forward together?"

"My foundation as a coach is built on authentic, risky conversations. Which helps us to have new eyes and new perspectives. If you are game, I am ready to dive in with you..."

We arrived at the decision to start our coaching. The challenge was attractive to him...he felt understood and had new perspectives about his behavior. I was pushing our boundaries of exploration and reflection. Here and now, experiencing the process, the space for conversation was created, for him to share without judgment. It was like play...he laughed at his own ways of being.

Later, when the organization was going through a merger, the senior leaders were put through an assessment process, which was very anxiety provoking, as they didn't know if they'd end up in a lesser role. I said, "I can totally resonate with your anxiety. Putting myself in a similar situation brings up a lot of self-doubt and anger." These emotions were coming alive for me and I was sharing what was happening to me in the moment. He said, "I think you really understand me," and began sharing more of his anxiety. We both shared the sensations and the impact, exactly as it came, without censoring. This level of honest sharing creates a leveling partnership of equals.

In a conversation with my client and his boss, I asked the boss, "How do you see your relationship with my client?" He described it as a very good relationship, very relaxed. My client was shocked. He said, "I don't see it that way at all," and began to share all the things he'd shared privately with me. The boss got some rare insights and asked me to coach him and four other people. My intuition is a big part of how I coach, asking the questions that strike me in the moment.

them carve out time for reflection, solicit candid feedback, deepen self-awareness, clarify their motivation and understand their impact on the system.

Originally, executive coaching was an organization-sponsored, six-month relationship that focused on performance, leadership development or transition. Coaches helped leaders recognize the gap between the current reality and their organization's full potential. At the same time, coaches supported clients to look at themselves with fresh eyes. Transformational coaching focused on self-awareness, changing mindsets and optimizing behavioral shifts.

Ultimately, executive coaches partner with the men and women who lead organizations to help them design successful change initiatives. Instead of one-executive-at-a-time, the field of executive coaching is moving toward developing key groups of leaders. Although most coaches are trained to focus on individual development, they are expanding their role to support dual clients—the individual and the organization. The growing focus is on facilitating collective leadership and building relationships between leaders and teams.

By developing pivotal leadership talent pools, the coaching initiative results in a greater return on investment. The move toward team coaching requires coaches to develop full awareness of team dynamics, organization development, patterns in the wider system and collaborative processes. When coaches contract with the whole team of executive leaders, they make collective shifts in how they work together. Working with individual clients is no longer an end in itself, as coaches help executives collaborate to lead the next phase of organization development.

## FeedForward

Executive and leadership coaches can help leaders identify and change behaviors using the FeedForward process.[9] Marshall Goldsmith, a behavioral coach listed by Forbes as one of the top ten coaches in the world, created feedforward to support individual leadership development. The process supports awareness by asking clients to choose the one behavioral change that will make the most difference in their leadership. Since interpersonal skills are the number one reason people fail in the workplace, and since interpersonal skills can be learned, the feedforward process supports behavioral change by engaging multiple stakeholders in the process. Ultimately, feedforward changes not only behavior, but perceptions held by others.

Ever get a piece of feedback and decide to change your behavior, but no one notices? They still remember what you did three years ago, that one time you lost it.

With feedforward, we ask clients to engage multiple people in their behavioral change process and, because they meet monthly to ask what changes they noticed and what else clients can do, they become stakeholders in our clients' development process. Ultimately, if clients change their behavior and also work to change people's perception of their behavior, they can also form strong bonds and supportive, developmental relationships.

The ten-minute feedforward questionnaire asks stakeholders to offer suggestions to support the development of one competency. Instead of looking in the rearview mirror, the questions focus on the future. Feedforward helps clients envision and focus on a positive future, not a failed past.

---

9    Goldsmith. Marshall (2004). Changing leadership behavior. *The Journal for Quality and Participation*, 27(4), 28–33.

The feedforward process is designed especially for clients who have achieved a substantial degree of professional success, a group which tends to resist negative judgment.

# The GROW Model

Although a few people have the initiative and support they need to take themselves to the top of their game, most people need a lot of help. A coaching culture empowers authentic, strong leadership at all levels of the organization. Whether an organization uses external or internal professional coaches, or develops peer coaching relationships within the organization, a coaching culture helps people bring their heart and soul to work.

Coaches hold people accountable for the actions they say are important to them. Organizations that establish coaching cultures encourage 360° connections where people seek out coaching relationships in all directions. They proactively coach their peers, direct reports, bosses, customers and even family members.

The GROW model[10], as described by John Whitmore, author of Coaching for Performance, provides a simple process for encouraging learning, action and growth.

GOAL setting for the session as well as short and long term.

REALITY checking to explore the current situation.

OPTIONS and alternative strategies or courses of action.

WHAT is to be done, WHEN, by WHOM and the WILL to do it.

The GROW model provides a memorable structure for helping people establish goals and create action plans. The model is a structure that supports individuals and groups in identifying what matters and moving forward into action. It may sound counter-intuitive to start with the goal instead of the reality, but opening with what people want provides direction and clarity. Even when people come into the session with a lot of clarity about their goal, exploring the broader goal, or deepening the awareness of related goals moves the group forward.

The purpose of the Reality stage is to empathically uncover the emotions and motivation connected to the desired change. With that awareness, the process helps people self-connect, go deeper and understand the nuances of their motivation. Traditionally, the Reality stage is used to help people identify weaknesses, barriers, resistance and budget constraints, but the flip side is even more important. Identifying the group's strengths; including their relevant experience, access to resources and past successes, all support movement toward the desired future. To uncover the real situation, we connect with people's feelings and values so that we get to the heart of the matter.

In the Options stage of the model, we support people as they brainstorm strategies to meet their needs. This is the rowdy, outrageous, fun phase where anything goes. Letting the imagination run wild awakens creativity and gives people a range of options to choose from. We get out the magic wand and give people full permission to dream. A coach shared the following: "Sometimes

---

10   Whitmore, J. (2010). *Coaching for Performance*, Nicholas Brealey Publishing.

the accountants in the group roll their eyes if I say, 'Imagine you have an unlimited budget,' but invariably this exploration helps people identify new possibilities, and then they can find much less expensive ways to get what they really want." Flinging the doors wide open taps the group's resourcefulness. Likewise, we can also ask, "So how would you do this if you had no budget and very little time?" to help the group find less costly alternatives.

After generating a wide range of options, we move into the Way Forward phase and help the group create compelling action plans. This is where the rubber meets the road. We find out what people will actually do and when they're going to do it. In this phase, we ask for commitments and build in accountability structures by asking three simple questions: What will you do? When will you do it? How will you track your progress?

| **G**oal | What do you want? |
| | What will that get you? |
| | What is exciting about this goal? |
| | What's even more important than this goal? |
| | How will you measure the results? |
| | What does success look like? |
| | What's the big picture? |
| **R**eality | How are things going right now? |
| | How do you feel? |
| | What values and needs are most important? |
| | What is the biggest concern? |
| | What resources are available? |
| | What barriers do you face? |
| | What does the resistance really mean? |
| **O**ptions | What are some of the ways you could approach this issue? |
| | Would you like to brainstorm some options? |
| | In your wildest dreams, what strategies would you choose? |
| | If you had more money, time or authority, what would you do? |
| | What if you could start all over? |
| | What are some of the advantages and disadvantages of each option? |
| **W**ay Forward | Which option is your best choice? |
| | When will you get started? What's the first step? |
| | What else do you need to do? |
| | On a scale of 1-10, how committed are you to this plan? |
| | What would take you to a ten? |
| | What accountability structures would support you? |
| | How will you celebrate success? |

If we spend a lot of time in the Goal stage and even more time in the Reality stage, the Options stage goes relatively quickly and people are bursting with ideas. The Way Forward stage is very short because people are fully engaged and have the vision and drive to take ownership of the action plan. The more time spent at the Goal and Reality stages, the easier it is to find the Options and Way Forward.

If we see hesitation in the Way Forward stage of the model, where people are reluctant to commit to action steps, that's usually because we haven't spent enough time in the Goal or Reality stages to identify the vision or what people really care about. If the action plan doesn't materialize, or if the commitment level is below a 7 on a scale of 1-10, we can revisit the goal to make it more compelling or replace it with another goal that people can readily commit to implementing. So the GROW model is not always linear—sometimes we circle back to clarify the goals or expand the reality.

Although GROW is one of the earliest coaching models, it's still widely used in organizations and by coaches and clients who value structure and clarity.

## Using the GROW model with teams

In addition to using the GROW model with individuals, you can also use it with groups or teams within organizations. The following is an example of using the GROW model with a team. This streamlined example highlights the coach's role, whereas in actuality, the team members said a lot more and the facilitator intervened much less often.

### GOAL

Terry: Okay, we know what we want to work on today—better communication with the other teams.

Facilitator: What's important about that?

Marissa: Our team acts like we're on a little island and we don't know how to expand a good thing.

Facilitator: What is the good thing that you want to expand?

Philippe: Working really well together. Respecting each other. Having fun at work.

Sal: Yeah, but it's more than that. Without the cooperation from the other teams, we're really ineffective.

Facilitator: Ah, so if you could expand the way you work together to include the cooperation of the other teams, then what would be possible?

Terry: Instead of the rivalry, we'd all be collaborating toward the same end—launching this new green technology on time and under budget.

Sal: Working with them would be like coming to a party instead of a brawl.

Facilitator: Okay, so if you were to paint a picture of your vision, what's the ideal relationship between you and the other teams?

Chloe: Ideal? To do that, I think we need to expand our sense of "we." When I think of work, I think of this core group as my family, and everyone else is an outsider.

Philippe:   I want a way to change that, to retain the team spirit we've worked so hard to build, and to let the other teams into our inner circle.

Facilitator:   How would you measure your success?

Sal:   It's not very tangible, but we'd know it when we see it.

Marissa:   Fewer complaints. We'd have fewer bottlenecks.

Philippe:   We'd have more dialogues with them instead of about them. We'd celebrate success with them.

Facilitator:   So what do you want to get out of this session today?

Terry:   A structure, some kind of plan for creating a bridge from our island that connects to the other teams.

## REALITY

Facilitator:   What's stopping you from connecting with the other teams?

Sal:   The saddest thing for me is that they hate us because they see our team having a good time, and all they do is fight.

Philippe:   All they do is throw complaints at us.

Marissa:   Yeah, but if we look at how we contribute to that, we don't really listen or give any validity to their complaints.

Terry:   I get frustrated when I tell them certain things can't be done and they say, "Of course it can be done." We're such geeks. I think we all lack communication skills.

Facilitator:   So if you dig into it, what do you think someone really needs when she says, "Of course it can be done?"

Terry:   Probably power. No, maybe it's respect. Or maybe she just wants recognition that she has a good idea, that she has something to contribute.

Facilitator:   And what does your team need?

Philippe:   To expand the good will, create partnership, to be trusted. Completely trusted. All we really need is to collaborate.

## OPTIONS

Facilitator:   Knowing that you all need collaboration with the other teams, and they probably need respect and to contribute their ideas, let's look at some options.

Sal:   Invite them over for lunch and get to know each other a little better.

Marissa:   Sounds a bit too touchy feely for them. We could all get together and have a brainstorming session where we really honor their ideas.

Terry:   Yeah, but I want marketing to understand that we can't possibly meet their deadlines.

Philippe:   Or maybe we need to understand why we have to meet their deadlines.

Facilitator:   What do you really want that you may not believe is possible?

Sal:   I just want them to like us.

| Marissa: | I don't care if they like us. I want them to understand the value we bring. Appreciate our role in the launch, instead of treating us like we're a big nightmare. |
| Terry: | Maybe we have to give them the appreciation that we want to receive. |
| Sal: | How about we blast them with thank you notes? |
| Terry: | Thank you for giving us impossible tasks and impossible deadlines? |

**WAY FORWARD**

| Philippe: | So let's talk about what we're actually going to do. |
| Marissa: | Let's get representatives from each team together to bridge the cross-functional divide. We'll create a plan for collaboration together. |
| Terry: | Part of that can be about getting a deeper understanding of each team's function and contribution to the whole. |
| Facilitator: | So who will do what by when? |
| Sal: | Okay, I'll put together an inviting agenda based on what we've talked about and send a draft to each of you by Friday. |
| Marissa: | And I'll arrange the meeting time and space for next month. |
| Terry: | I'd like to try facilitating the meeting, using the GROW model. Would one of you co-facilitate with me? |
| Philippe: | I'm game. It sounds like we're all on board with this plan, but I just want to check in about commitment level. Does anyone have an objection to moving forward with this plan? |

**EVALUATING THE PROCESS**

| Facilitator: | Hearing the silence, it sounds like you're done. Yes? Now that you've used the GROW model a few times, would you like to evaluate how it's working for you? |
| Sal: | What I like most about it is that we have a structure and a sense of direction. |
| Marissa: | I'm not happy with the way we under-use the Options phase. I'd like to see us spend more time there and explore our wildest dreams—to expand the possibilities. |
| Philippe: | We could also get a little more concrete about the actual goals. |
| Terry: | For me, I like the way some of us are stepping into the facilitator role. I want to stretch myself into doing that more often. |

People like the GROW model for its simplicity. Anyone can use it without a lot of training or practice. Hanging the model on the wall during a meeting gives people a sense of the flow and the entire group becomes facilitative very quickly. The GROW model has a reputation for being fast, but not very deep, which is exactly what some groups want. However, we can change the depth by lingering in the reality stage and deepening awareness before moving into action.

# SWOT Analysis

A SWOT analysis is a common business tool for scanning the environment and informing strategic planning. You can use it to evaluate the organization and you can also use it with individuals. The traditional SWOT analysis looks at strengths, weaknesses, opportunities and threats. Instead of looking at weaknesses, you can focus on wishes. From an appreciative perspective, looking at wishes inspires you far more than looking at what you don't want. Instead of saying, "My weakness is poor time management." notice if it feels more inspiring to say, "I wish for excellent time management skills." When your clients express a wish, listen carefully to their words, because wishes already imply movement. Strengths and wishes point to the internal landscape, the things we have control over. Opportunities and threats focus on the outer landscape, the things we do not control.

Below is a shortened example of a personal SWOT analysis.

| APPRECIATIVE SWOT ANALYSIS | |
|---|---|
| **STRENGTHS** | **WISHES** |
| visionary leader | develop new ways of empowering my team |
| risk taker, explore new ways of developing people | more patience and presence |
| surround myself with brilliant, competent people | more time for relaxation and creative outlets |
| give honest, authentic, inspirational feedback | stronger recruiting skills |
| **OPPORTUNITIES** | **THREATS** |
| work with Miguel to flesh out the Seagate idea | economy floundering, impacting dollars spent on coaching and training |
| decrease my number of direct reports and free up time for innovative projects | merger talks—my position may be impacted |
| write the book I've been planning | my mentor and partner may retire soon |
| attract venture capital for my innovative ideas | market is over saturated with coaches in my niche |

See SWOT Analysis in Appendix I.

## Appreciative SWOT analysis

You can use your SWOT analysis to identify the trends that will make it possible for you to stretch yourself, have the impact you want and reposition yourself as a professional coach.

What are three ways to use your strengths to realize your wishes?

What impact would you like to have in your organization?

How can you reposition yourself to be the change you wish to see in the world?

The Appreciative SWOT Analysis is from *Courageous Visions: How to Unleash Passionate Energy in Your Life and Your Organization* by Martha Lasley.[11]

# Five Phases of Organization Development

Coaching is often the entryway to organization development (OD) work. Stages of OD work include:

Entry and Contracting

Sensing and Discovery

Diagnosis and Feedback

Planning Interventions and Action

Evaluation and Closure

As organization development consultants enter organizations to collect data, diagnose the organization's needs, design interventions and evaluate progress, we can also build internal organizational capacity to do the same. Each phase of the OD process serves a distinct purpose. So let's see how this works.

## Entry and contracting

Authenticity, presence and empathy are the vital components of the entry process. During the initial conversations, we build trust by listening non-judgmentally and offering support. Rather than glossing over or censoring the issues, this approach allows the underlying concerns and opportunities to surface. By listening deeply, understanding the client's issues and establishing the alliance, we uncover the goals and deeper desires. Desires take us much deeper than goals. By tapping people's passions, we get clarity about personal and organizational expectations. Once we're connected with their hearts, we co-create desired outcomes, determine roles and responsibilities and establish business terms.

## Sensing and discovery

While relying heavily on our intuition, we also collect information based on hard data. Dialogue, surveys, interviews, assessment tools and focus groups are used both to collect information and build relationships. Throughout this process, the emphasis on building relationships means we're much more likely to generate trust, which helps us get to the heart of the matter.

## Diagnosis and feedback

We come in looking for what works and what we can leverage. Instead of a pathological approach to diagnosis, we can help members of the organization identify the life-giving energy in their work experiences and then discover their needs and wishes. A summarized report of the information and shared analysis acts as a catalyst for deepening awareness, inviting choice and stimulating action. Many organizational cultures have a preference for hard data, a scoring system for analyzing the current situation and a way to measure progress. When accompanied by anecdotal data, the impact can be very moving, heart-connecting and inspirational. Analyzing the data for

---

11   Lasley, Martha (2004). *Courageous Visions: How to Unleash Passionate Energy in Your Life and your Organization.* Discover Press.

the client can be highly informative, but isn't as empowering as a joint analysis. Collectively, we can explore a gap analysis between the current situation and the desired situation.

## Planning interventions and action

We end up with one-way communication and minimal buy-in unless we intervene with authentic feedback. Feedback leads to a blueprint for change and collaborative action planning. Action plans are broken down into small steps with accountability structures, including who is taking responsibility and agreed-on dates for completion. Implementation of the action plan can include a wide range of organization development interventions: individual or group coaching, training, leadership development, team building, diversity dialogues and conflict resolution are some of the processes used to support the change initiative.

## Evaluation and closure

The measures of success established at entry are derived jointly. Evaluation can include financial measures, such as the bottom-line impact (profitability or return on investment) or stakeholder satisfaction (quality-of-life or employee retention). Organization development work is an intimate process that calls for an empowering closure. Instead of celebrating once a year at the company Christmas party, we advocate for continuous celebration. We not only celebrate successes; we also celebrate new insights gained from disappointment or failure. Both provide opportunities for heart connection and stimulate dialogue that leads to new opportunities.[12]

# Appreciative Inquiry

Appreciative Inquiry is an organization development process that permeates the coaching world. The process starts with the belief that whatever we put our attention on appreciates (grows and develops). When we focus on clients' problems, those problems become more entrenched and difficult. When we focus on strengths, creativity, aliveness and movement, those parts grow and get stronger.

At the core of Appreciative Inquiry is the choice to view human beings as mysterious, moving, changing, expanding, life-affirming, creative, spiritual beings. Once we make this choice, we no longer see people as problems to be solved or issues to be fixed. Together with our clients, we look deeply, call forth and nourish the life-generating forces already in existence to create a present and future that is more joyful and fulfilling.

To create that present and future, the coach uses the following principles of Appreciative Inquiry:

Focus on anything that is working, creative and alive.

Include failure and breakdown. Rather than analyzing problems, look at the positive that is available.

Find the positive in the negative. "When you say that communication is terrible with your boss, I see you have an image of what great communication looks like. Can you describe that?"

Build the positive image rather than trying to solve the negative image.

Focus on "what do you wish for?"

---

12   Lasley, Martha (2010). *Facilitating With Heart: Awakening Personal Transformation and Social Change*. Discover Press.

Listen without judgment. You grant power to clients by holding them whole and creative even when they experience a breakdown.

Use stories to explore the strengths and abilities they tapped in the past and anchor them in the reality of their power.

Recognize themes and choose topics to explore further.

Use the strengths and dreams, by developing images and visions, of the life people want and create innovative ways to make it happen.

## Four phases of Appreciative Inquiry

Appreciative Inquiry summits are usually held over several days where the entire organization comes together to explore the four phases of Appreciative Inquiry. Colleagues from all levels of the organization interview each other and discover each other's stories, dream about the future, design how they want to work together and deliver the desired results.

### 1. Discovery—Appreciating

In the discovery phase, we clarify values and use storytelling to capture the best of what is. We discover what gives life and energy to the organization. We start by asking people to interview each other in pairs, gather stories that capture memorable experiences and discover organizational strengths and assets. Sharing and collecting these stories helps build organizational capacity by valuing and expanding on the best of what already exists.

*As stories are collected, ask the following questions:*

When it comes to your organization, what do you take pride in?

What energizes people?

What are the best stories about the organization?

### 2. Dream—Envisioning

In the dream phase, we get out our magic wands and imagine what might be. Together we think big and share our hopes for our work and our relationships. We look at individual and organizational calling to explore our greater purpose and deepest wishes. In this phase, we act out our dreams to dramatize the possibilities and stretch the imagination.

*Questions for this phase:*

What is the world calling your organization to do?

If you had no constraints, what new possibilities would you explore?

If you surrounded yourselves with life-giving forces, what would that look like?

### 3. Design—Co-constructing

In the design phase, large numbers of people come together to co-create the future organization. In small groups, we explore the lofty images of the dream stage and determine what's possible. We align values, structures, systems and mission with the ideal by talking about what should be. In this phase, the team crafts provocative propositions which stretch the organization. We design by exploring possible actions and making choices that will create a more desirable future.

*Questions for this phase:*

What choices can turn our dreams into reality?

How does each piece look in an optimal system?

To create a more desirable future, what actions do you choose?

## 4. Delivery—Sustaining

In the delivery phase, we develop action plans to realize the provocative propositions. In an open forum, we ask employees to determine their contribution and how they wish to serve. We establish personal and organizational commitments to fulfill these contributions and determine what will be. Small groups collaborate on the new initiatives that grow out of this process. Because people are deeply involved in the first three phases, commitment and alignment come easily in the fourth phase.

*Questions for this phase:*

What action plan do you need to put into place to create a wonderful future?

How can you bring about lasting cultural change?

What do you need to do to sustain your preferred future?[13]

## Appreciative inquiry questions

These questions can get to the heart of the life-giving qualities of the client.

Tell a story about a time when you faced an obstacle and you overcame it. What did you find inside you that allowed you to overcome the obstacle?

Talk about a time when you were proud of yourself.

Tell a story about alignment—a time when you experienced a depth of connection to yourself, your work, Spirit, another person or nature. Connect with the place in your body where the energy lives while telling the story.

Where are you, what are you doing and who are you with when you "come home" to yourself?

Imagine you receive a letter from your guides, reminding you what you have forgotten about yourself and what is possible for your life. What does it say?

Tell a story of a time when you felt deeply supported.

Talk about a time you surprised yourself.

What delights you? What engages your senses? What makes you laugh from your belly? What do you love? What makes you want to get up and dance?

What things do you value most about yourself, the nature of your work, the organization?

What do you consider the core factor that gives life to the organization?

Put yourself in the customers' shoes. What would they say makes us unique?

Consider the best strategies, structures, operating procedures and processes that have brought us to this point—the things that make this the kind of company you want to work for. Which of these must we maintain and preserve, as we continue to grow?

---

13   Lasley, Martha (2010). *Facilitating With Heart: Awakening Personal Transformation and Social Change.* Discover Press.

You may notice that many of these questions involve telling a story. Storyteller Laura Simms says, "Storytelling has the capacity to directly engage the heart and imagination in such a way that a deeper level of listening is activated, which opens the eyes of perception. The deepest learning happens in the unspoken story that is generated in the mind mixing the images called forth in the telling. ….The thinking mind is kept entranced by the content, while the images dip down and uncover and awaken the dreaming imagination and intuitive intelligence of the listener."[14] Stories engage the imagination and bring information from places other than the thinking mind.

To use Appreciative Inquiry to generate stories about the future, consider this scenario:

You wake up five years from now, and this organization is wildly successful.

What do you see going on? What are people doing and saying?

What is different from today? How has technology advanced customer service?

What decisions need to be made today to create this future?

What are the three actions we should begin now in the present to make this future image a reality?

As coaches, we can use storytelling questions with our clients to awaken possibility based on what has worked before. We can interrupt the stories that are re-runs of their failures.

### How appreciative inquiry works with negativity

Appreciative Inquiry is not a Pollyanna approach. We address things that do not work, but from the viewpoint of creating from the positive. We can use negative data to uncover what people want: "You say that your relationship with your new employee is difficult, that you are angry a lot and end up acting in ways you don't like. This tells me you recognize what you want that relationship to be like. Tell me about what you wish for in your relationship with your new employee." There is great power in listening to the negative in order for there to be space for the positive. We can focus on the "wishes" questions to segue from the negative to what is possible.

## Cultural Transformation

In organizational coaching, just as in personal coaching, a transformational approach puts the emphasis toward improving whole systems rather than solving specific problems.

Cultural transformation is a radical form of systemic change that builds on the positive energy that already exists. Instead of condemning past values, norms, beliefs and practices, we identify what is already serving the culture and find ways to expand the life force. We identify the aliveness and collective wisdom by looking deep within and discovering what is already effective in terms of economics, ecology and humanity. We then generate solutions that tap collective wisdom.

Lynn Twist does innovative work as a social entrepreneur with the Pachamama Alliance. In her book, The Soul of Money, she tells the story of the women of Dharmapuri who practiced female infanticide because they believed that "life was so horrible for a girl, and she would become such a financial burden to the family, that it was cruel to let a girl child live and more kind to kill her."

---

14   Watkins, J. M. & Mohr, B. J. (2001). *Appreciative Inquiry: Change at the Speed of Imagination*. San Francisco: Jossey-Bass/Pfeiffer.

After sharing their secrets, shame and grief, they vowed to end the cycle forever. Lynn was stunned when they said, "We could not have taken this courageous step without your outside ears and eyes."

After several days of intimate conversations, the women of Dharmapuri then turned the tables on Lynn. They asked if there were things in her home culture that overwhelmed her. Lynn shared her deep upset with the violence portrayed in American media, and how the horrible messages are exported all over the world. Looking deep into her eyes, they told her to remember that they would be there for her, to encourage her to speak out.[15]

Until that moment, she had considered violence in movies mild compared to the horror of infanticide. Gratuitous violence has become so accepted in our culture that she saw it as a given, and felt hopeless as the profits from the media industry feed the appetite for violence. One can imagine people from a peaceful culture would be as horrified by media violence as we are by infanticide. The women of Dhamapuri can inspire us to look for opportunities to change our own culture.

All of this points to the value of sharing our stories of inner and outer transformation as we deepen our awareness and explore new ways of creating life-serving cultures. Beyond the ripple effect of personal transformation, taking a stand for change and leading a cultural change initiative can have a profound impact on society.

## Seven Steps for Leading the People-Side of Change

The sections on Cultural Transformation and Seven Steps for Leading the People-Side of Change are adapted from Martha Lasley's book, *Facilitating with Heart*.

### 1. Assess Readiness for Change
Take the long view and explore the relevant history of change for the group, culture or organization. Find out what made past changes successful and look for evidence that the organization can handle more change. If necessary, develop additional capacity for change.

### 2. Build a Case for Change
Discover the urgent crises and opportunities that get people's attention. Study the market and competitive forces that drive the change process. Explore the implications to the bottom line. Imagine what happens if you don't make the change.

### 3. Enlist a Team of Change Agents
Start by finding your highest-level change sponsors. Look for other key influencers from all levels of the organization to enlist. Recruit people who have the power to lead the change initiative and get others on board.

---

15   Twist, Lynn & Barker, Teresa (2006). *The Soul of Money: Reclaiming the Wealth of Our Inner Resources*. W. W. Norton & Company.

### 4. Develop a Change Communication Plan

Design the best ways to communicate the benefits and the drawbacks of the change. Describe your vision so that you empower others to contribute. Incorporate the vision of how the change serves the highest good and helps the organization thrive.

### 5. Manage Resistance to Change

Identify the people most likely to oppose the change and determine how you will address their needs. Anticipate the obstacles and create a plan to overcome resistance to change.

### 6. Build Momentum

Pay attention to the pace and tone so that people can easily absorb the changes. Build short-term wins into the process. Define the milestones you will celebrate along the way.

### 7. Sustain a Culture that is Receptive to Change

Manage your continuous personal change process and model openness. Establish expectations, desired behaviors and competencies that people need to develop to support the desired changes. Sustain a culture of continuous improvement and keep the energy alive to ensure future success.[16]

## Evaluation of Coaching

### Create collaborative measures of success

How do we tap the organization's life force? How do we create collaborative measures of success? The success of the coaching initiative is measured based on criteria that are tied to organizational goals. The steps for creating collaborative measures of success include:

Tie the coaching initiative to organizational goals.

Set observable objectives that are directly tied to the initiative.

Specify how coaching will be applied to achieve these objectives.

Isolate the effects of the coaching initiative by collecting pre-and post-data or using a comparison.

Sometimes the people being coached have full autonomy to use the coaching any way they wish. More often, the sponsor of the coaching initiative, the person being coached and the coach collaborate to set measurable objectives. Objectives start with verbs. Sometimes our objectives are vague but can be measured with a 360° feedback assessment. To improve on vague objectives we articulate observable, actionable objectives that we can easily measure.

| VAGUE OBJECTIVES | MEASURABLE OBJECTIVES |
|---|---|
| Improve communication skills | Reduce employee turnover |
| Collaborate with cross-functional teams | Streamline feedback process |
| Improve team productivity | Increase market penetration |
| Deepen personal awareness | Improve response time to complaints |
| Develop decision-making skills | Reduce litigation costs |

---

16   Lasley, Martha (2010). *Facilitating With Heart: Awakening Personal Transformation and Social Change.* Discover Press.

Not everything needs to be measured. Some of the objectives are best left as intangible benefits of coaching, but others can be converted into monetary benefits. For instance, if turnover is reduced, customer complaints are decreased or if a new product is launched ahead of schedule, this translates into bottom-line impact. The challenge is to take intangible results and make them measurable, e.g. strengthening communication skills, building internal leadership capacity or improving the quality of life for employees.

Zeus and Skiffington list five measurement tools for evaluating outcomes:

Interviews can be structured or unstructured, but often they are most valuable when given both before and after coaching has begun.

Self-reports tend to be less than objective, but clients find the self-reflection valuable.

Ratings by others can be similar to the 360° evaluations many firms use.

Self-monitoring are similar to self-reports, but ongoing.

Direct observation is often done by shadowing, in which the coach follows, observes and critiques the client during the day.[17]

*Questions to Consider*

What do you find appealing about organizational coaching?

What structures will support you when working with individuals or groups in organizations?

What do you need to enhance your capacity to coach in organizations?

---

17   Zeus, Perry & Skiffington, Suzanne (2002). *The Coaching at Work Toolkit: A Complete Guide to Techniques and Practices.* McGraw-Hill.

# 16
# Coaching for Social Change

*Never doubt that a small group of thoughtful, committed citizens can change the world; indeed, it's the only thing that ever does. —Margaret Mead*

## Taking Coaching out to the World

Extending the evolution of coaching into the future, we see the ripple effect of coaching reaching far and wide—into nonprofits, schools, health care and government agencies. Imagine every family, every organization and every community all over the world having easy access to coaches. Let's take that one step further and envision people learning coaching skills before they graduate from high school so that everyone experiences deep listening and empowering questions on a daily basis. What if politicians actually listened to each other with open hearts? What if teachers asked empowering questions and believed in their student's ability to find their own answers? What if social workers supported their clients with a peer coaching process that awakened them to their full potential? All of these things are already happening in pockets all over the globe and the coaching profession is called to make coaching skills available to all.

Since 1998, Leadership that Works has supported individuals and organizations through coaching training and leadership development. We started by coaching and training anyone and everyone, but recognized early on that we were drawn to work with people who care about human evolution and take a stand for social change. Through our work with social activists, nonprofit leaders, government agencies and philanthropic organizations, we began taking coaching deeper into the sectors of society that need it most. Instead of helping people with privilege gain even more power, we began working with changemakers to support the development of systemic solutions to social problems— some at the local level and some on a global scale. Whether we're working with social entrepreneurs or direct service providers, we empower them by developing coaching cultures in their organizations. Ultimately we co-create sustainable programs that directly impact people in need.

# Evolution of Social Sector Coaching

Although coaching started out in the business sector as a resource for current and emerging leaders, it is now taking hold in the social sector where it continues to evolve.

Coaching in the social sector initially focused on leadership development and organizational capacity building, which includes improving organizational systems, processes and results. One-to-one coaching of executive directors and other key leaders of social change initiatives strengthened them as leaders and supported them in implementing desired changes in their organizations.

As part of the Coaching and Philanthropy[1] (CAP) project, Leadership that Works partnered with CompassPoint, BTW Informing Change and Grantmakers for Effective Organizations to conduct an unprecedented deep dive into learning about the nonprofit sector's support for and use of coaching. In the 7-year project, the partner organizations assessed and advanced coaching as a strategy for building effective nonprofit organizations. The CAP project focused primarily on leadership development and organizational capacity building.

In subsequent work, Leadership that Works and other coaching organizations began helping nonprofit leaders incorporate coaching competencies into all levels of their organizations. As they created coaching cultures in their organizations, people became more empowered, productive and satisfied. The organizations evolved through continuous feedback and social sector leaders started using coaching to bring out the best in their teams. As a result, creating a coaching culture became a major force in the evolution of coaching.

More recently, Leadership that Works has provided coaching skills training to direct service providers in nonprofit organizations—dramatically changing the ways in which they work with their clients. When these professionals, which include case workers, financial counselors, and any nonprofit staff who work directly with clients, add coaching skills to their existing toolbox, they shift their focus from problem-solving to a partnership that expands possibilities and transfers ownership and accountability to the clients. The direct service providers report they are less stressed, while their clients become more empowered and engaged, leading to sustainable results.

A growing trend in collaborative community partnerships is the use of coaching as the foundation. These collaborative initiatives include partners from foundations, nonprofits, government agencies, community leaders, volunteers and community residents all working together to achieve a common community goal. The partners receive coaching skills training and individual coaching which supports collaboration, communication, brainstorming, opening to new possibilities and shifting from limiting to empowering viewpoints that lead to more creative actions. Embedded throughout the programs are opportunities to embrace and leverage cultural diversity.

We envision bringing coaching skills directly to the people who need it regardless of their income levels. Our hope is that coaching continues to spread in organizations, schools, families, communities and individuals from all walks of life. The possibilities are limited only by the

---

1 The Coaching and Philanthropy Project is a partnership between BTW informing change, CompassPoint Nonprofit Services, Grantmakers for Effective Organizations, and Leadership that Works. This work was made possible by the generous funding and support of W.K. Kellogg Foundation, The Harnisch Foundation, The James Irvine Foundation, the David and Lucile Packard Foundation, and the Evelyn and Walter Haas, Jr. Fund.

imaginations of the people who continue to learn this effective way of communicating and collaborating to create sustainable social change.

Leadership that Works remains at the forefront of this ground breaking work—providing needs assessment, strategic planning support, basic and advanced coaching skills training, one-to-one mentoring, group support for skill enhancement, opportunities to share best practices, online learning communities and program evaluation. Our goal is to expand access to coaching through collaboration with funders, nonprofits and community leaders to provide coaching to an ever-widening circle of people.

## Unique Challenges in the Social Sector

During the economic crisis of 2008, foundation endowments shrunk drastically and recovery has been slow. Many organizations have lost government funding and private donations have contracted. As the needs in the social sector increase, organizations are expected to do more with less. If nonprofits have a budget for leadership development at all, it's considered discretionary and one of the first things to go when budgets are cut.

In the corporate environment, the training and development department recognizes that the long-term health of the organization depends on leadership development. Except for large organizations, most nonprofits don't have staff who devote time and resources to leadership development, so getting coaching in the door is often the biggest challenge.

Coaches surveyed by the CAP Project overwhelmingly agreed (95 percent) that in order to be effective working in nonprofits, coaches need to understand nonprofit organizational culture.[2] To effectively coach in the social sector, coaches need an understanding of:

Organizational Structure (leadership dynamics of executive director, board of directors and board committees, board governance)

Cultural Awareness (power dynamics, privilege, dismantling isms, internalized oppression)

Fundraising and Finance (budgeting, undercapitalization, third-party funding, funder criteria, sustainability needs of nonprofit staff)

Volunteer Management (recruiting, selecting, developing and assessing volunteers)

Mission (developing and living the mission, vision and values)

Roles (complexity of the many roles of the executive director and senior staff)

Human Resources (addressing burnout, lack of accountability, insufficient salaries)

Scarcity (shifting the culture from insufficiency, limited funding, human resources, support and time to an assets-based culture)

Sacrifice (martyrdom, rescuer's syndrome, work/life balance, internalized oppression)

Succession Planning (founder syndrome, developing leadership capacity)

---

2    Coaching and Philanthropy: An Action Guide for Coaches. 2009. Kim Ammann Howard, BTW informing change Michelle Gislason, CompassPoint Nonprofit Services Virginia Kellogg, Leadership that Works

With a full understanding of the challenges in the social sector, it's much easier to work from an asset-based or strengths perspective and tap the passion and core values of clients. With familiarity comes ease in addressing issues of power, culture and recurring themes. In a mission-driven culture, connecting with the yearning of clients helps us engage people in self-reflection, strategic thinking and effective action.

As a coach in the social sector, you might find yourself supporting leaders to move away from dependency on the "heroic leader" toward a culture of shared leadership. Unlike their corporate counterparts, social sector leaders are more likely to use empowering, creative leadership models. For instance, social justice organizations often utilize a collective leadership model with more than one person at the top, or a shared-leadership model, where everyone on the team considers themselves a leader. Their decision-making process is often more inclusive, using a participatory decision-making process to nurture organizational creativity.

Below is an example from a coach working with a new executive director:

> I worked with a mid-thirties director, Valdez, who had been a community organizer and was mentored by the founders of the organization. When one of the co-directors died suddenly and the other co-director didn't want to be the exclusive director, Valdez was promoted to director. He inherited a seasoned organization and older members questioned whether he was capable of leading the organization. It appeared that the previous director had worked himself to death. Literally. So Valdez was thinking, "I don't want to die doing this work."

> He felt scared, excited, proud and nervous about honoring the co-founders' legacy. He knew that he was meant to inherit the organization and get everyone to recognize, "We can survive even under someone else's leadership." His work was to convince Baby-Boomers that Gen-Xers, and even younger, could be leaders of the movement; that they could carry on. He felt incredible responsibility about his role and said, "As one of the younger ones, I've got to do it right because they're expecting us to fail. They're waiting to see that we're not as committed; we don't work as hard." Valdez often heard comments like, "You all aren't as committed as we were. We were the ones who started this. Look at us, we're still doing this work after all these years." Valdez was very much concerned and wanted to ensure that the organization would survive the transition, so I coached him on creating a thriving organization that would survive beyond his leadership. We used several pathways—Embracing the Shadow helped him face his fears; Expanding the View to explore his challenges and Envisioning the Future to help him expand his dreams. Once he reached full alignment, I asked him how he wanted to partner with others, which called out his power as a leader.

A social sector coach describes an experience of coaching when the life of the organization is at stake.

> Historically, my work with nonprofit executive directors focuses on four major issues: How do I work effectively with my board? How do I transition out? How do I get some work-life balance? How do I raise money? But rarely have they ever thought about who they are as a leader and how that impacts all their decisions.

*In an era where lots of organizations have gone under, an executive director was getting ready to do a big "ask" to a foundation and came to coaching to boost her confidence. We explored two things: "What is the best way to talk about your work?" and "What's compelling about you that you need to remember when you go in to do that 'ask'?" She was facing increasing competition, considering a merger, and unsure about how to have merger conversations without undermining her organization. Coaching helped her to balance her personal leadership style (very open and sharing) with the realities of the marketplace which required her to be more strategic.*

Another coach describes the joys and challenges of social sector coaching:

*A lot of executive directors are facing retirement now, but they don't actually have a retirement plan because they simply haven't had the financial means. Personal needs tend to get put on the back burner. I do a lot of coaching with executives who are uncertain how to interface effectively with their board. They ask, "What is my job as an executive director—to direct the board or take direction from the board?" The success of the executive directors' work depends on the efficiency and effectiveness of their board. Procuring funding is another major concern because there's a lot of mission creep, where organizations slowly change their mission to meet the criteria of funders. When they say, "Just tell me what you'll fund and we'll make sure we provide that," a lot of dependency and power issues arise which makes the whole system dysfunctional. This problem increases when funding is less available.*

*When coaches understand these power dynamics, we can help leaders get really clear about their mission. How can they communicate their mission in a way that funders understand, without having to bend over backwards like a pretzel to fit what the funders want? Coaching helps executive directors get a stronger backbone—to really take a stand for what the organization does.*

Here's an example from a coach working with a client with a strong connection to her values.

*I was coaching a board member of a nonprofit who had a strong personal stand for diversity, multicultural awareness and social justice. After joining a board that she thought was aligned with her values, she came to realize they actually had no commitment to social justice at all. Even though they put some sweet words on their website, there was no action toward social change. Because she made a commitment to herself to only serve organizations that valued diversity, she faced a tough decision—not whether to quit, but how to quit serving on the board. She agonized over many questions: Do I put my reputation on the line and take a stand for human evolution? Or just quit quietly without saying why? Will I be seen as a complainer in a culture where people make nice all the time? Will I burn the bridges I've worked so hard to create?*

*As her coach, because I knew how important this issue was to her, I was driving her to take a stand. I also helped her regain her trust in herself—that she actually has influence and that her stand could actually create a shift in the organization. Before she was out the door, the organization offered her the opportunity to create a diversity program for people in under-served communities. After some soul searching, she declined the offer, celebrated their decision and recommended someone else to run the program.*

To thoroughly understand the complexities of the social sector, coaches need experience which can be gained by:

Taking a leadership position in a nonprofit

Serving on a nonprofit board

Volunteering in a nonprofit organization

Interviewing social sector leaders about their accomplishments and challenges

A favorite line from the nonprofit world is, "If you've seen one nonprofit… you've seen one nonprofit." Each organization has unique challenges, but you can deepen your awareness of nonprofit issues by exploring the following websites:

Compasspoint: http://www.compasspoint.org

Management Help: http://managementhelp.org

Nonprofit Hearts: http://www.nonprofithearts.netml

Rockwood Leadership Institute: http://www.rockwoodleadership.org

## Leadership Development and Capacity Building

Historically, most funders and senior teams in the social sector put their focus on program results, and wouldn't dream of using part of their budget for leadership development. The social sector faces serious problems about cultivating the next generation of leadership. In the Daring to Lead study of more than 3,000 executive directors, 75% plan to leave their organization within the next five years and less than 17% have succession plans. Facing the question of whether to "make" or "buy" leaders, isn't even an option. They won't be able to recruit from other agencies simply because there aren't enough leaders waiting in the wings. Internal leadership development is essential to the sustainability of the social sector.

The Coaching and Philanthropy[3] project's research shows that coaching is a very effective strategy for developing leaders and their organizations. Many nonprofit leaders view coaching as a way to develop and hone key leadership and management skills.

In the table that follows, the nonprofit leaders using CompassPoint's coaching referral and matching service had similar "coaching intake themes." Derived from a 12-month period, the themes are ranked in order of priority. [4]

---

3    Coaching and Philanthropy: An Action Guide for Coaches. 2009. Kim Ammann Howard, BTW informing change Michelle Gislason, CompassPoint Nonprofit Services Virginia Kellogg, Leadership that Works

4    Coaching and Philanthropy: An Action Guide for Coaches. Kim Ammann Howard, BTW informing change Michelle Gislason, CompassPoint Nonprofit Services Virginia Kellogg, Leadership that Works Source: CompassPoint, Coaching Referral and Matching Service Intake Data, September 2008 – September 2009.

| REASONS FOR SEEKING HELP | PRIORITY ISSUES |
|---|---|
| Managing Others | Delegating, giving feedback, dealing with different personalities or leadership styles, managing up |
| Self-Awareness | Identifying or refining communication style, identifying personal strengths and personal vision |
| Self-Management | Managing time, organizing work, managing stress |
| General Leadership/ Sharing Leadership | Transitioning from manager to leader, embracing power and responsibility of position, communicating vision, obtaining alignment of vision, maintaining external relationships, strengthening and managing board relationships, building self-confidence, developing bench strength, developing staff leaders, beginning to plan for succession |
| Change Management | Developing personal strategies for managing change, obtaining buy-in from others, developing new identity as an organization, dealing with emotions of change, managing culture change |
| Targeted Content Coaching | Developing capacity and skills to address discrete, well-defined organizational issues such as finance, board development or raising funds |
| Work-Life Balance | Dealing with burnout, prioritizing work, caring for self, setting boundaries, saying no |
| Personal Professional Development | Planning for professional development, career planning, identifying strengths and weaknesses as they relate to personal growth |
| Transitioning Out/ Transitioning In | Transitioning Out: Developing an exit plan, determining when to leave and what's next, letting go, dealing with "founder's syndrome" <br><br> Transitioning In: Dealing with pressures facing the new executive director or manager, meeting expectations, understanding the "what" of the job and how to set up self for success |

Coaching is especially valuable in supporting social sector leaders who are facing pivotal points in the life of the organization, including:

Executive director transition

Shift in the founder's role

New strategic plan

Managing change

Expansion or cut back of program or funds

Start-up organization

What follows is a story offered by a coach about creating an ideal relationship with a board.

*I coached an executive director who said, "My board makes hostile remarks, undermines me at every turn and they are never straight with me. I think my job is in jeopardy." She wasn't happy about going to work and was compromising her values on a daily basis. She held an entrenched viewpoint that her board was out to get her and as long as she believed that, nothing could shift. So we worked to shift her viewpoint to, "I can create a board that really works for me. It's really possible to have the support that I need." From that empowered viewpoint, she created a plan of action to develop an ideal relationship with her board. From there, she worked on finding her voice and made requests of her board. She had never imagined that she could ask for what she needed.*

*She kept her job, asked a few board members to leave, and was able to create a new board that was responsive to the needs of the organization. Most importantly, they interacted with her differently—she finally got the respect she'd been craving. She used the concept of creating a conscious relationship to get clear with the board how they wanted to work together. From there she created conscious relationships with her staff.*

*The coaching tools that had the most impact were calling out the power and challenging. Her viewpoint was so entrenched—she repeatedly said, "This is an impossible situation; I'll never figure it out." As a coach, I took a stand that surprised her, "Of course you will figure it out; there are many options here." I had no idea how it was going to come out for her. But I took a stand for her resourcefulness and happiness, and knew that something useful would come out of the exploration.*

Most people come into the social sector because they are passionate about the organization's mission. They become managers "accidentally," not because they have a strong desire to manage people or run an organization. So they often need support in developing management skills, including creating a coaching culture in their organizations. They face complex, diverse challenges, but they often need help with basic skills like saying "no," holding people accountable, or choosing how they prioritize their goals.

According to David Coleman, a seasoned executive coach who works with nonprofit leaders, the primary benefits of coaching are:

Helping leaders gain new perspectives on themselves and their situations

Building the confidence of leaders

Retaining valued employees

Developing new leaders

Bringing renewed energy to longtime leaders so they can recommit to the tasks ahead[5]

A coach who only works with social justice organizations offers an example of her challenges:

*I coach people working in social justice organizations who are doing things to change the world to make it a more equitable place. They are very heart driven, very values driven and that's*

---

5    David Coleman, "A Leader's Guide to Executive Coaching," Nonprofit Quarterly, Spring 2008.

*incredibly inspiring. People are not coming to coaching with "I don't know what to do with my life..." They know what they're doing and why.*

*But it's challenging coaching them because they don't know how to balance other priorities in their lives. They honor the collective more than the individual. A new client said, "Taking care of myself; that's not as valuable as taking care of my staff or the organization or the movement."*

*Surrounded by so much inequality, he said, "I can't slow down because who am I to rest when other people have so much less than I have. I need to keep working on behalf of the cause." So a lot of my work is around sustainability. I told him, "Yes, it's true that the inequality doesn't stop and what is also true is that if you keeping working the way that you're working, we'll lose you from the movement, you'll burn out, you'll get sick." Once he realized he wouldn't treat anyone else the way he treats himself, he changed the way he works and lives.*

More and more grantmakers are including coaching as part of their leadership development initiatives as a way to build capacity in organizations. As leaders address organizational challenges and opportunities, the coaching process has a ripple effect on their families, communities and movements.

## Creating a Coaching Culture

As the value of coaching for nonprofit leaders became more apparent, Leadership that Works and other coaching organizations began providing coaching skills training to nonprofit staff to create coaching cultures within organizations. Coaching is most effective in organizations where executives and senior managers support coaching and have been through training. Combined with peer coaching programs, this approach builds a coaching culture and creates a more productive, engaged, results-oriented workforce. When organizations and their partners participate in coaching training together, the culture spreads like a social epidemic, and can make action-oriented, individual empowerment, and effective collaboration the norm in organizations and communities.

A coaching culture is created when:

Coaching flows in all directions—upwards, downwards and sideways

Learning becomes a way of life

People actively seek feedback

People engage in respectful, energized, candid conversations

Teams cultivate passion and full engagement

Collaborative decision making speeds up the change process

When staff develop strong coaching skills, their commitment to their work deepens and they communicate more authentically with colleagues, clients and stakeholders. The goal is to embed coaching skills throughout organizations and extend them to key partnerships.

Coaching skills build a common language and foster trusting relationships among staff and between staff and their clients. When leaders start practicing coaching skills, they model new behaviors that permeate the organization. As leaders and staff learn to ask effective questions that bring out solution-oriented thinking, they begin to see the world differently. The process helps people change their old beliefs and perceptions so that they generate excitement about their work.

Instead of using classic rewards and punishment to motivate employees, in a coaching culture, employees easily tap each other's inner strength and wisdom. This helps them envision a better future, set more compelling goals, make better decisions and take action to accomplish goals. Some additional benefits in a coaching culture are that people:

> Create stronger manager-employee relationships
>
> Empower their direct reports
>
> Set challenging goals
>
> Improve decision-making skills
>
> Establish effective accountability
>
> Provide direction for employee development
>
> Improve company systems

What is needed in organizations to make coaching more successful? We start by ensuring the buy-in for coaching at all levels and the training of multiple staff in an organization. We build in support for the champions of coaching in an organization. Instead of getting all the training at once, we spread the training over six months with on-going contact and support from a mentor. In between the basic and advanced training, peer support and learning teleconferences provide an opportunity to brainstorm about what works and how to address challenges.

## Coaching skills training for direct service providers

In addition to the benefits an organization derives from creating a coaching culture, providing coaching skills training to the organization's direct service providers changes how they work with their clients. Neighbor Works America, Annie E. Casey Foundation and LISC comprehensive services initiatives are investing in coaching to support long-term client engagement. This approach helps clients achieve significant outcomes, not just short term goals. With this "coach approach," direct service providers integrate the skills of coaching into their existing skill set, to empower staff and clients in ways that bring out aliveness and responsibility. As an added benefit, the staff are more excited and less burned out.

Just by adding the skills of empowering questions, acknowledgment, challenges, requests and accountability, direct service providers improve their effectiveness. People who do direct-service work in a nonprofit are required to support clients to reach measurable outcomes. For example, in financial literacy work, each client is required to save "x" dollars a month, or they're required to set up a budget by a certain date, in order to continue receiving services from the nonprofit organization. By adding coaching skills to their toolbox, financial counselors don't replace what they already do well, but instead add coaching skills to enhance their ability to work more effectively.

In the Early Childhood Connections project in Battle Creek, Michigan, family coaches coach family leaders (heads of families could be parents, grandparents, aunts, uncles or others).

Coaching becomes the service delivery model and all the staff and coaches receive coaching for themselves, and coaching training to build their skills. This builds a common delivery language and methodology for staff and a consistent service expectation for families.

Housing-based resident services coordinators, financial educators and financial coaches who attended coach training found that they work differently with clients as a result of the training. In their evaluations, they describe how they have changed the way they interact with clients. They wrote that they:

Use open-ended (empowering) questions to help clients learn about themselves and shape their own goals and action plans.

Listen differently. Use curiosity and focused listening to get the "real issues."

Listen for who clients are and what they are saying rather than focusing on who they want them to be.

Judge less, view their clients as whole and resourceful and as a result, clients don't feel threatened.

No longer try to solve clients' problems—help them shape their own ideas about what to do.

Help clients identify their own values and take actions consistent with those values.

Find clients are taking more responsibility for making plans and acting to improve their lives, and they are holding themselves accountable for their results.

As part of the evaluation, the direct service providers told stories about how they used coaching to make a difference in clients' lives:

*When reviewing credit reports, I would immediately focus on the credit score and dictate what needed to be done to correct mistakes and raise the score. This approach was often difficult for clients to hear and respond to—especially when the score was very low. Now I have conversations with clients first (values, goals in life), and relate the credit report to what the client wants to do with his/her life. By helping clients put the credit score in perspective (only one tool), and asking powerful questions about what can be done to improve the score, and other steps clients can take to reach goals (such as borrowing from family/friends or improving the business plan), I am able to help clients move closer to their goals.*

*A client was requesting emergency food help. I asked powerful questions to find out why she ran out of food this month. The client then revealed an unattended health problem, and I helped her find medical assistance as well as the food.*

*I was writing a service plan with a client. When it came to the education plan the client became lethargic. During the conversation the client mentioned cosmetology—that she had tried to take a class in the past, but it fell through. I asked what it feels like when you think about being a cosmetologist. She perked up and got excited. I fed back to her the excitement she showed about cosmetology and helped her work through her belief that she couldn't do it. She wanted it for 10 years, but hadn't done it. When she came back the following week she had enrolled. She said it was the first time anyone asked her what she really wanted to do—and believed that she could do it.*

*We learned strong listening skills—to help clients formulate their own agenda. In this training I really began to understand how to be there for my clients without imposing my opinions and judgments on them. I finally understand "client-centered listening" and it has had a tremendous impact on my conversations with clients, co-workers and partners. I have a much better understanding of their goals, hopes and concerns than I did previously.*

*Coach training taught us how to shift responsibility for problem-solving away from the resident services staff to the residents themselves.*

## Collaboratives and Communities

Imagine communities where:

Parents engage fully in the lives, education and health of their children.

Families learn how to create financial stability.

Community members create food systems, health systems, financial systems and educational systems that create a level playing field.

Initiatives foster more honest communication and effective feedback structures.

People share a common belief that all humans have the ability to create meaningful and happy lives.

Seasoned leaders, nonprofit staff and emerging leaders have the support, time and energy to engage in professional development to effect change in their communities.

We envision coaching skills embedded in communities everywhere, so that parents, teachers, caseworkers and change makers thrive. We are committed to bringing coaching to communities to unlock potential, engage all stakeholders and include marginalized groups.

### Bridges to Tomorrow

Gheens Bridges to Tomorrow (B2T) in Louisville, Kentucky, U.S.A. is an exciting example of how coaching can support community initiatives. The project is a unique collaborative that involves nonprofits, foundations, corporate donors, community centers, volunteers and families who are working together toward the common goal of ensuring children are prepared to succeed in kindergarten and beyond.

For B2T, coaching is central to the way this ambitious collaborative improves children's and families' success. Gheens, one of the largest private foundations in Kentucky, U.S.A., invited a number of Louisville nonprofit organizations to submit concept ideas for how they might "make a lasting impact on the community" with a large grant from the foundation. This invitation unleashed the creative energy of staff at Louisville's Metro United Way. Their concept paper combined early childhood development with financial stability for families, with the assumption that children's success in school would dramatically improve if their families were economically secure.

Gheens chose to invest $2 million over four years in Metro United Way's proposal because it was "pioneering and entrepreneurial."[6] That initial risk-taking investment started a revolutionary new

---

6      Dare to Dream Bigger, a First Year Diary of the Gheens Bridges to Tomorrow Initiative, Metro United Way, p.1

approach to supporting families and communities by putting the parents and their children at the center.

The B2T initiative supports families through four childcare and early childhood development neighborhood centers in the most economically disadvantaged communities in Louisville. The program incorporates a creative curriculum for early childhood development, family coaches working one-on-one with family leaders, and a comprehensive set of community resource partners committed to serving parents in areas of education, health, financial services and employment.

Early in the initiative, executives and key staff of all partner agencies, including Metro United Way, participated in coaching training. They were so taken by the approach; they decided to make coaching the cornerstone for the service delivery model. In 2008, Leadership that Works worked with the Bridges program to train local coaches and provide on-going support to ensure the coaching culture would be fully embedded in the initiative. The program included on-site training over two years and mentoring for executive directors, senior staff and family coaches. In addition, a local mentor supported the family coaches based at the neighborhood centers.

Armed with new coaching skills and the charge to build relationships with parents at the neighborhood centers, the family coaches reached out to dozens of family leaders and established relationships. In July 2008, Spalding University of Louisville began a program evaluation of Bridges to Tomorrow.[7] The report states that Bridges has implemented "a number of best practices along with a particularly outstanding broad-based approach."[8] It points out that, "empowering people as Bridges to Tomorrow does, although often a slower process than more directive approaches, also holds greater promise of more long-lasting change." While the Bridges program faces many challenges, not least among them is sustainable funding for this broad-based, family focused approach, the Spalding findings illustrate the promising potential for coaching as a core strategy:

> *A number of the family leaders have reported positive changes at a level well beyond initial expectations. They have described dramatic shifts in attitudes and behaviors not only regarding their financial decisions but also affecting their health and family relationships either in service of their financial changes or as results of them. Although the family leaders particularly attribute these changes to the family coaches and to the coaches' empowerment approach, they also credit a number of other components such as the sense of community that has developed among family leaders and the mutual support and accountability that has grown among them. In addition, many participants and staff have been impressed by the project's commitment to a shared vision, which has helped them feel included in it.[9]*

### Early Childhood Connections

Similarly, in the Early Childhood Connections (ECC) project in Battle Creek, Michigan, because many young children in their community are at risk of failing before they have the opportunity to begin reaching their potential, the ECC project employs family coaches. These coaches visit the families of every newborn infant in the county. Trained to evaluate and assess infants and their home surroundings, the family coaches provide an important link to the wider community. In many cases, only one home visit is needed to start the infant and family on the road to a

---

7     Gheens Bridges to Tomorrow, Program Evaluation, Year Two: 2008-2009, Evaluation Team: Ken Linfield et al., 2010.
8     IBID, p. 2
9     IBID, pp. 1-2

successful future. In the event that needs are identified, the coach links the family to appropriate community services and connects them to a virtual family resource center. Subsequent follow-up visits are managed by the family coach along with any referred agency representatives. The coach, in conjunction with the local school district, provides the family with an introduction to the school community. This "Crib to Kindergarten" approach helps build a family-school relationship, ensuring initial school success, while paving the way for ongoing success in school.

ECC recognizes that an empowerment model engages families in a way that builds rapport and engagement. Coaching is at the heart of this initiative. With a common language and coaching skills in their tool box, the family coaches listen to what family leaders want for their children, and help them create the plans to succeed as their "child's first teacher."

Not satisfied to have coaching embedded only in their program, the ECC project also provides coaching skills training to many of their collaborating agencies that the families in Battle Creek might also work with. The goal is to bring this coaching language and orientation to the whole community, so that families who interface with many social service agencies can engage fully with an empowerment orientation.

## On the horizon

Providing coaching services and coaching skills training to community members is an emerging trend for social change coaching. Family leaders (parents and guardians) who received coaching in these projects, asked for additional training to help them support their children more effectively. The new horizon includes coaching as life skills training, shared directly with parents. Coaching helps families view their lives differently, become empowered to plan better futures for themselves and their children, and design strategies to support their life goals. These examples affirm the possibilities of working directly with community members—especially in low income communities. When everyone has access to coaching skills, regardless of their income level, the possibilities for community change are endless.

Consider a brighter future where:

Children create exciting visions for their lives and learn to design support systems to keep their dreams alive.

Pre-teens and teens peer coach one another during their challenging years.

Gang members communicate effectively to reduce violence.

Community groups work collaboratively rather than competitively.

Parents and teachers collaborate more effectively to support children's learning and development.

Youth communicate their feelings, needs and requests more effectively with parents and other adults in their lives.

One area where the benefit of providing the skills directly to people who need them is taking hold is through volunteer efforts in prisons. When groups of inmates are taught coaching, communication and conflict resolution skills, they integrate the learning in ways that empower them to make life-altering choices—both within the prison and upon their return to the community. They use the skills not only to change the way they interact with other inmates; they plan their futures, peer coach one another informally, and collaborate with outside facilitators to lead training.

**Tattva Shakti Dhara: Free the Power Flow - Coaching for Organizational Re-Orientation** *by Anuradha Prasad, CFT Certified Coach*

The Kutch district in western India is located in a semi-arid region where people depend mostly on crafts, dryland agriculture and nomadic animal husbandry. Located in the capital Bhuj, Kutch Mahila Vikas Sangathan (KMVS), an NGO founded in 1989, has organized poor rural women to address gender inequities. They foster the leadership of women to transform their condition and impact their economic, political, social and cultural status.

By organizing, mobilizing and educating for consciousness raising, KMVS has grown from a single collective of rural women, to become a network of seven grass-root women's organizations (sanghathans) with an active membership of more than 20,000 women leaders, organizers and practitioners.

Pastoralists, farmers, artisans, fishers, wage-workers, musicians, elected representatives, birth attendants and single self-employed women have come together to organize collectives that impact the transformative potential of rural women in the region.

However, a recent in-depth analysis revealed that the organization has slowly become more project-oriented. The movement-based connection with women and their issues was missing.

One emerging hypothesis was that the pressure of finding funds for development work was pushing the organization into a very masculine stance. Project planning, implementation, reporting to fulfill funders' requirements were taking precedence. The inner connection to the feminine, both in individuals and in the organizational presence was getting lost.

KMVS began a reorientation of its processes, programs and activities. The purpose was to renew focus on women's leadership and empowerment. To do this, the leadership recognized that first, they needed to transform themselves.

So 15 of the top leaders of KMVS, both men and women, attended "Tattva Shakti Dhara" (Flow of the Power of Essence). The participants learned to teach coaching skills to grassroots women leaders of the community. The main foundation of the process was the Kutchi (Sufi) culture's focus on love, peace and harmony both within self and with others. The program helps leaders find the Shakti (power) within, to revitalize the organization and to raise the power of community leaders.

On a personal note, I was wondering where the passion for the work of KMVS was lost. The image that came to me was to get the river flowing again. River? I asked myself, where is the river in Kutch? Meditating deeper, I got the word Saraswati, the mythical river that has gone underground. I turned to Google out of curiosity and to my astonishment found that the river Saraswati is believed to flow under ground through the Rann of Kutch before joining the Arabian Sea. This image was a signal for resurfacing the strength of KMVS, to tackle the myriad issues faced by women of Kutch today. The flow of the river gave me a sense of alignment within and became a foundation of the work.

# Creative Approaches to Coaching in the Social Sector

Three fast-growing trends in coaching that make investment dollars go further include peer coaching, group coaching and community coaching.

**Peer coaching** is a long-term investment that pays strong dividends. When organizations set up a peer coaching culture they create high-trust relationships, and support each other's leadership development across traditional boundaries. People can coach 360°—it's not uncommon for people from different levels to coach upward, downward or laterally. The author of *The Heart of Coaching*, Thomas Crane describes The 7 Characteristics of a Coaching Culture:[10]

1. Leaders are Positive Role Models
2. Every Member is Focused on Customer Feedback
3. Coaching Flows in all Directions—Up, Down and Laterally
4. Teams Become Passionate and Energized
5. Learning Occurs, More Effective Decisions are Made, and Change Moves Faster
6. HR Systems are Aligned and Fully Integrated
7. The Organization Has a Common Coaching Practice and Language

When the entire organization collaborates to create a coaching culture and people have a shared understanding of how to coach, they support each other's growth and development. The systemic practice of coaching increases the capacity for growth and change.[11]

**Group coaching** is a facilitated group process that uses coaching principles to support professional development. The synergy comes from leveraging the wisdom, energy and experience of the group. The process gives leaders a valuable opportunity to connect with their peers and know that they're not alone in their challenges. Instead of perpetuating the silo mentality, group coaching is a way to use leadership development funds more productively while actively working on pressing issues.

**Community coaching** is a group process that uses the mindset and skill set of coaching to support communities who are seeking change. The coach serves as a catalyst to bring forward the wisdom of the group. The coach uses expanded coaching tools by helping groups:

1. Get clarity about their work and nurture their collective vision.
2. Catalyze group learning and discover new options.
3. Analyze situations and develop collaborative processes.
4. Overcome barriers to change and synthesize strategic initiatives.
5. Make collective decisions and sustain their work together.

Mary Emery and Ken Hubbell, leaders in community coaching, list the following outcomes of community coaching:[12]

---

10    Crane. Thomas. 2011. *Business Coaching Worldwide* (2005, Volume 1, Issue 1).
11    Crane. Thomas. 2011. *Business Coaching Worldwide* (2005, Volume 1, Issue 1).
12    Mary Emery and Ken Hubbell, retrieved from http://communitycoaching.com/six-rs_2.html

**Coaching Creates These 7 Outcomes**

1. Communities used new ways to live and work together.

2. Community teams uncovered new ideas that led to successful community change.

3. People came to see the reality of different perspectives, so they could work with others more effectively, reduce conflict and create the conditions for a learning community.

4. Leaders included the whole community rather than a select few or the traditional elite.

5. Groups successfully challenged the status quo.

6. Community groups were able to generate self-direction—to decide for themselves what will work, how and why.

7. The group found a way to get unstuck and connect or reconnect their strategic work to their vision.

## COACHING *in Action* | **The Flying Fish** *by Leslie Brown, CFT Faculty*

I sat in the empty training room awaiting the small group of youth participants from our housing program and found myself drawing a blank. Suddenly I could not remember the definition of coaching nor could I recall anything about my intention for the day. In my swirl of confusion I caught sight of Nemo, my physical reminder of the momentum of the day "Just Keep Swimming." With my intention suddenly clear I began to focus my energy on my deeper agenda which was to introduce coaching as a way for youth to bond with each other as well as begin thinking about life beyond their time in foster care.

As the participants started to arrive with their mumbled hellos and scowling faces I began to question my readiness to facilitate my first coaching group. However, as the group began to peer from up under their low pulled hoodies I realized that they were as nervous as me and my role was to create a safe space for them to open up and engage. As I picked up Nemo I saw a couple of them get really curious about the presence and relevance of the fish. I used it to my advantage and began to get the group warmed up by asking who had seen the movie "Finding Nemo." Several youth raised their hands and I asked a brave volunteer to give the premise of the movie. My next question was "What does this movie have to do with the lives of foster youth?" Suddenly I noticed a shift in energy as the group moved from trying to figure out my angle to focusing on the questions before them.

I invited a few people to share their responses and then shifted the focus back to creating a safe space. I began by developing a conscious community conversation and once again brought out Nemo to support facilitation. The goal of the activity was to ensure that all voices in the group were heard and that each person had an identified support partner (a support partner, acknowledges their partner's comments or adds their experience in response to their partner's comment). I asked that each youth go around the circle and answer the question, "What do you need to be successful in a group?" While some youth struggled with the question, others were able to clearly articulate and I saw others begin to build from the ideas presented. As each person added a new layer to the conversation I began to capture the themes on chart paper. After our discussion we all agreed on the things that would serve as a conscious community agreement.

Once we finished the agreements I shifted to our final activity and asked the group, "What are the core barriers for transition for youth leaving foster care?" The room suddenly became quiet and many of the youth began to shift around in their seats looking for a way out. As I begin to be sucked into the nervous energy of the group I saw Nemo out of the corner of my eye and picked it up and tossed it to a youth. As the youth caught Nemo he began to share his response and just as naturally threw it to another youth who acted as his "support partner." This strategy worked for the duration of our time together and provided me the opportunity to facilitate the coaching group with the support and momentum of Nemo the flying fish. My biggest lesson learned was that the momentum required in a coaching group starts and ends with the coach and the key is to "Just Keep Swimming" and the power of coaching will take over and support the group in moving forward.

They go on to say that "activities where these coaches are providing support range from board development, economic revitalization, civic engagement, helping low income women become financially independent, community planning and encouraging organizational collaboration. The coaches have goals of helping groups generate improvement in the areas of employment, education, poverty-reduction, housing, environmental enhancement, business development, economic renewal and leadership development."

As the coaching profession evolves, empowerment becomes a way of life, not just for people with means, but for everyone. Coaches and clients alike are continuously seeking ways to make a difference and create positive change in the world. Coaching in the social sector is gaining momentum and the impact is truly transformational.

*Questions to Consider*

What's your vision for expanding coaching in the social sector?

In what way are you called to make a difference in your community? How might you begin?

# 17
# Soul and Spirit

*When a person encounters her individual soul…she has uncovered her unique gifts, her destiny, her life purpose, or personal meaning. Through soul encounter, she learns why spirit and nature gave birth to the exceptional individual she is and about her particular way of belonging to the world. —Bill Plotkin*

## TOPICS

Defining Spirituality, Soul and Spirit

Connection to Everyday Life

Engaging the Client with Spirit and Soul

Working with Soul

Working with Spirit

Developing the Inner Witness

Coaching with Secular Clients

How do we support clients in connecting deeply with their soul (core essence) and with their longing for deep connection to spirit (something greater than themselves)? Clients come to us because they have a yearning. Their longing might show up as wanting more fulfillment at work, more money or perhaps a more satisfying relationship. They might want to write a book, create a dance or travel. And yet we know there is more to it, so we engage with our clients to reveal their deep desire for change.

Underneath our obvious desires, we long for our gifts to be welcomed and well-used in the world. Each of us wants to experience deep connection with our divine essence. Underneath all of our desires is the yearning for our deepest personal expression to be realized and to feel that we truly belong and matter in the world. To realize our full potential and make a difference are at the heart of the transformational agenda.

Many clients ignore the call to soul and spirit for years. They may want it more than anything, yet are afraid to move toward it. Savoring that yearning becomes a pathway to a deeper, more satisfying life. As coaches, we create the space for clients to look more deeply, to hold onto the genuine expression of a fulfilling life.

In this chapter, we explore the realms of soul and spirit, the relationship of soul and spirit to coaching, and methods to help clients deepen their awareness of and connection to soul and spirit. Soul and spirit coaching provides a means of supporting clients in deeper exploration, regardless of whether they consider themselves secular, religious or spiritual.

Soul and spirit coaching is about engaging with another human to witness and call forth the unfolding of their soul, manifested in their unique and deepest contribution to the world. As we engage with another human, we witness and call forth their unfolding as spiritual beings—the journey toward awareness of oneness with self, others and the world. We call forth their unfolding in the material and physical world and support them in aligning these actions in soul and spirit. Simultaneously, as coaches, we grow and deepen our own spiritual connections through this witness.

# Defining Spirituality, Soul and Spirit

*One realm (spirit)…turns upward toward the light, …helps us to disidentify from the commotion of the strategic mind so we can reclaim the inner quiet, peace and wholeness of our true nature. It is about cultivating the blissful experience of being fully present in the moment and one with all creation.*

*The other realm (soul) leads not upward toward God but downward toward the dark center of our individual selves and into the fruitful experience of nature…it shows us where and how to make our stand. On this half of the spiritual journey, we do not rise toward heaven but fall toward the center of our longing. —Bill Plotkin*

## Spirituality

Many see spirituality as a mystery beyond comprehension. For some of us spirituality is our birthright. For nearly all, spirituality is connected to the point of view that there is more to life than meets the eye, that we are each a unique being with a value beyond our worth to our economy, or our village, our state, or nation.

There is surely no easy way to say exactly what we mean by spirit or spirituality. The Book of the Tao famously states that "The Tao that can be spoken is not the eternal Tao." Even from a pure coaching perspective, descriptions differ from person to person.

For some, spirituality is another term for religion. For others, spirituality is the antithesis of religion, a connection with meaning that doesn't involve the supernatural in any way. You may find some of the following commonalities in your explorations of spirituality with clients:

A quest for meaning in everyday life—a feeling that life has value, or meaning.

A commitment to values, and living in accordance with them.

The pursuit of transcendence to life beyond self, or beyond the material realm.

An appreciation of the connectedness of life between self, others, a divine presence and nature.

A commitment to transformation into a more enlightened, more connected or more fulfilled being.

A connection to something larger than one's self which could include a group of people with a common purpose such as societal transformation or challenging injustice.

## Soul

The soul is the personal, unique aspect of the self that embraces the essence of our individuality. When clients refer to the "real me," they tap what is most wild and natural within. In his poetry,

David Whyte has several phrases that describe soul:

> One life you can call your own.

> Shape that waits in the seed of you to grow and spread its branches against a future sky.

> That small, bright and indescribable wedge of freedom in your own heart.

> The one line already written inside of you.

> Your own truth at the center of the image you were born with.[1]

Our unique purpose is our soul imperative. We each come into this world with a seed inside that is the work we are meant to do in the world. Soul is that deep place in us that holds our purpose and never lets it go. We receive clues throughout our lives that can point us toward what is ours to do. Soul work then is a developmental process, an ongoing quest to understand that deep purpose inside and to discover how to best fulfill our soul work in the world.

### Spirit

Spirit is the broad, communal aspect of pure energy, shared among all souls. Mysterious. Limitless. When clients experience the interconnectedness of life, they are connecting with spirit. This spirit, God or life force is referenced in many traditions, some which worship deities and some which do not.

## Connection to Everyday Life

Connection to soul and spirit is a current under all day-to-day living. As a coach, you help clients become more of who they are. When you see your clients deeply, it impacts how they see themselves.

Taoist writings say:

> "In ancient times, people lived holistic lives...
> integrated mind, body, and spirit in all things...
> If you want to stop being confused, then...
> Allow your work and your recreation
> to be one and the same...
> Serve others and cultivate yourself simultaneously...
> understand that true growth comes from meeting and
> solving the problems of life in a way that is
> harmonizing to yourself and to others."[2]

In the Bhagavad Gita, one of the central scriptures of yoga, Krishna, an enlightened master, says to his disciple Arjuna: "It is better to do your own duty imperfectly, than to do another's perfectly."[3]

The soul, that connection to self, is made visible in the world through core powers. These core powers are values, knowledge and abilities that are made visible through action in the world. Values are those parts of us that have to be present for us to be congruent with our innermost

1   Whyte, David (1997). *The House of Belonging*. Many Rivers Press.
2   Walker, Brian (1995). *Hua Hu Ching: The Unknown Teachings of Lao Tzu*. HarperOn.
3   *The Bhagavad Gita, Translated for the Modern Reader* (1996). Nilgiri Press.

selves (integrity, adventure, passion, security, etc.). Knowledge here refers to that power in you that simply knows what is best for you. It is not learned information, but the core of your knowing. Abilities refer to your skills and talents that help you to create and manifest your core self.

Our first core principle of coaching speaks about clients as being whole while simultaneously moving toward a greater expression of their wholeness. As coaches, we work with our clients to realize even more wholeness by confronting everything that has them live divided.

> *A "small, still voice" speaks the truth about me, my work and the world. I hear it and yet act as if I did not.*

> *I pay a steep price when I live a divided life—feeling fraudulent, anxious about being found out, and depressed by the fact that I am denying my own selfhood. A fault line runs down the middle of my life, and whenever it cracks open—divorcing my words and actions from the truth I hold within—things around me get shaky and start to fall apart. —Parker Palmer*

## Engaging the Client with Spirit and Soul

An attitude of non-judgment, without forcing change on our clients, allows us to create space for self-acceptance. At the same time, we serve our clients most by fiercely holding their potential, by trusting them and believing in their resourcefulness. They have the answers for their life. Using the core principles helps us remember to support our clients from the inside out as we witness their process.

Not forcing change opens potent possibilities. Powerful change comes from awakening experience within. The process of the "deep talking to the deep" goes beyond the intellect. When we open clients to their feelings, the wisdom of their bodies, the uniqueness of their core individuality and connection to all life, we engage the insight and motivation for effective action. Three powerful pathways for coaching for spirit and soul are:

Power of witnessing through awareness—witnessing, reflecting and honoring all that is unfolding and holding space for all that is still waiting to be born.

Power of love, compassion and empathy—offering unconditional love and full transparency for the sake of connection to soul and spirit.

Power of congruence and development of body, mind, soul and spirit—utilizing all the core coaching skills and pathways to alignment in service of the whole client's alignment with self, core values and with the spirit realm.

## Working with Soul

Often, clients come to us without an understanding of working in the area of soul. In modern cultures, there is a bias against nature and our own wildness, which leads many clients to an over-emphasis on the realm of spirit. "Take me toward the light" is a cry often heard. As coaches, we want to help clients move both toward the core of their individuality as well as to the realm of their oneness with all.

How exactly do we move clients closer to the core of their individuality? It begins with an acceptance and ease with where they are, balanced with fiercely calling them to what we see is possible. Add the power of curiosity and the beauty of looking for natural openings. And then, stand with them in their pain and their joy, in their stuckness and their creativity. That allows them to relax and allow their inner resources to flow.

In this co-created space, we can use many concrete tools to move our clients in closer contact with their soul. For example, nature gives us an easy and powerful way to work with clients in the realm of soul. The wildness of nature matches the inner nature of the soul. Even a small amount of time in a wild place can awaken the soul. Some specific ways to support our clients' connection with soul include working with the natural world and working with wounds.

## Working with the natural world

We can send our clients on nature walks or for quiet time in wild places. Help them create a context for this by crafting a question to sit with, without forcing the answer. Or, ask them to have a conversation with something in nature or the earth itself. This can take the form of a structured time of talking and then listening. Notice that nature is a mirror and step into silence and openness in order to see that mirror.

This work in nature is about opening to the possibility that the entire universe is a resource for growth. The earth is waiting to be in relationship with us all, and stepping into that relationship can bring profound insight and knowledge.

Maya:   Since we've been exploring soul and nature, at times I remember a wild child side of me—the part of me that always loved adventure and was immensely curious about everything. She is the part of me that loved the beach as a child and sat on rocks by the water daydreaming. She was the moon gazer and the part of me that so enjoyed walking barefoot in the grass. She was not understood in my family, so I packed her away. I miss her.

Coach:  Your face was glowing and your voice just seemed to flow and glide as you remembered your wild child. What do you notice as you talk about that part of you?

Maya:   I feel so fully alive and connected. Like something that was lost and so important has come home. I want to play with her and explore with her again. I love the way I feel!

Coach:  She seems so alive in nature. How can you play with her this week?

Maya:   Oh, there are so many ways—so many places I want to go with her… We will walk in the woods or walk along the water's edge at the ocean.

Coach:  What will you open to while you are there?

Maya:   I will be alert for all the wonderful things in nature that make me smile and all the messages that nature holds for me there. I sense a grounding and a returning to myself that feels so powerful. I am going to make space for that part of me every day.

Help your clients design personal rituals and ceremonies to mark important milestones or to call in unseen forces for assistance. Ceremonies can help clients when they know they want to be in deeper connection with their soul self or in deeper conversation with the Sacred Other. Ceremonies are a time to offer something back and to stand in deeper relationship with self and the Sacred Other. Ceremony and ritual can be reverent or outrageous; can be a simple moment or a community-witnessed event. Help your clients to be creative and to create ceremony and ritual from the place of their deepest knowing.

Using these tools can take courage on the part of the coach. Because of the societal pressures to conform, sometimes this work with soul can seem "touchy-feely" to some clients. This is where your power to invite them into connection with soul will help them venture into the unknown. Your fierce courage can call them into a realm they may be avoiding or unsure about. What you can count on is that your clients want a deeper connection with their authentic self and multiple pathways will take them there.

## Working with woundedness

Some clues to soul work are the obvious places where we are drawn to time and again. The less obvious place to look is in our sacred wounds, those challenging, often traumatic events that have the potential to unleash our power. Acknowledging the power of our wounds strengthens us, as life's emotionally painful events can be transformed into power and well-being.

From Bill Plotkin's point of view, the biggest psychological wounds in our lives are only wounds because they keep us from fulfilling our soul work.[4]

For example, Clayton's greatest wounding came from abandonment and lack of connection. That pointed him in the direction of natural connections, networking, spider webs and organic mycelium in the forest. Spending time with nature and opening to the messages from fungi brought insight into his soul. Making artwork related to these powerful natural symbols was a healing process for him. His coach helped him explore multiple opportunities to use his woundedness as a source of new growth.

We can learn much about clients' potential soul work by listening to what they share about the wounds or scars in their lives and helping them explore the deeper meaning each may hold. This is related to the transformational agenda. What lies beneath the surface of the everyday problems holds deep promise. Our work with clients takes them to that place of deep exploration.

Such wounds are highly individual. An event that would be deeply wounding to one person might be trivial to another, even among siblings. From the perspective of soul work, an occurrence might only be wounding for someone whose soul imperative is related to that event.

Other tools to help clients move toward a deeper connection with soul include solitude, journaling (free-writing), active imagination, vision boards and the use of poetry, storytelling and dream work. All of these call out the deepest soul stirrings of clients and help them make sense of themselves in a less heady way. We can also encourage our clients to use dance, drumming, chanting or artwork to touch deeper into who they are. These same tools can help us connect deeply with our own souls in service to ourselves and our clients.

---

4    Plotkin, Bill (2003). *Soulcraft: Crossing into the Mysteries of Nature and Psyche.* New World Library.

Additional resources we can offer clients are visioning work and vision quests. The beauty of questing is that our clients move into ritual spaces that remove distractions and invite them into very deep conversation with the Sacred Other and their soul. There are many types of vision quests available and, for the client who is ready for deep listening, it can be profoundly life-altering. We can choose a quest for deep diving into soul or for connecting with spirit.

# Working with Spirit

Spirit is like a mega support system. This perspective meshes with the view that we each have a soul imperative in this world. We can see spirit as whatever we lean on as our connection to oneness. It might be helpful to consider spirituality as a relationship with spirit (or the universe, or the higher purpose, or God—however your clients view it). For Lily, the earth itself is the place she leans into to notice and understand her place in the oneness. For Raji, leaning on Ganesh to remove obstacles brings him into a state of awe and wonder. The understanding of spirit will be different for each of our clients, and part of our job is to hold that unique view for each of them.

We look for give-and-take between our clients and spirit. That relationship can mature and change over time, so we hold space for that change. We also hold space for interacting with spirit on levels other than verbal, including the heart, body, art, sound, work and emotion. This holds true for all aspects of coaching, but is especially important to remember in soul and spirit work, since many religious traditions have narrowed the realms of interaction with spirit.

## Meditation and awareness exercises

Meditation is intended to still the mind, increase concentration and thereby tap into greater resourcefulness. That resourcefulness can be intensified by the deeper connection with spirit that people may experience through a regular practice of meditation. Some meditations focus more on joy, some on processing emotion. Some focus on the breath or physical sensations. Some can involve watching thoughts without engaging with them. Some are still, some are moving. Tai Chi is a form of meditation for many practitioners.

When we take ten seconds or a minute to have someone integrate an experience, we are using a simple technique that is the basis of meditation—paying attention to what is happening in the body, mind, emotions and environment in the moment; noticing without judgment. When we take a client into a body-awareness exercise, we are employing the idea of meditation or inner focus.

There are many workshops on various types of meditation that can be helpful in jump starting a practice. Surprisingly, meditating with a large group or with a friend can be easier than meditating alone. People experience great benefits from even a short amount of daily meditation. So beginners may find it more useful to take even a few minutes a day to meditate than to aim for longer daily sessions and fall short. There are many resources available on the internet for guided meditations.

Also, remember that for some clients, meditation is not the answer. Encourage clients to find their own way—which may look different than sitting still. They might walk quietly or work with awareness.

**COACHING** *in Action* | **Connecting to Spirit** *by Damon Azali-Rojas, CFT Faculty*

Unless the coach is open and connected to spirit, it is hard to help others connect. When my coaching goes deep, I embody spirit, which influences my intuition and use of metaphor.

Although I have been a priest in an African Traditional Religion for over ten years, 18 months ago I considered myself cut off from spiritual awareness. I felt utterly mechanical in my rituals and offerings. I say this because if I can make the shift, I think anyone can.

In one program, I called on the ancestors to be present, invited folks to tap into social justice energy or just breathe and be mindful. One person found this alienating. Huh? I am not always sure if my spirituality is welcomed. My sense is that mainstream society is pretty divorced from real spirit in their daily lives and are guided by manipulative political-spiritual soundbites. I choose to fully step into my own spirituality, while being careful not to offend.

In my view, there are a few things coaches can do to support ourselves and our clients to step into spirit:

- Do our own spiritual work/practice and be able to use what we learn to be aware of when spirit is present for clients. When it is, name it.

- Ask about our client's beliefs and share our own beliefs in the spirit of understanding and curiosity (vs. my tradition is older or better than yours).

- Invite clients to increase their awareness of spirit in their lives. To seek it out, to ask for it. Meditation, communing with nature, music and prayer can awaken the feeling, and then we can support them in inviting that feeling in their daily lives.

- With secular clients, use our gifts that we have developed and translate it into the language they feel comfortable with (e.g. universal connection or social movement energy vs. God or spirit.)

I connect with the larger more expansive vision of Spirit that is connected to the sacredness of all beings on this planet as well as the environment. Many of our clients need support to pull apart and differentiate these aspects in order to de-clutter their spiritual path.

## Yoga, Tai Chi and Qigong

The Eastern practices of Yoga, Tai Chi and Qigong contribute to mind-body harmony and deeper spiritual connection. In these traditions, the breath is a link between body and mind; and combinations of mindful movements, holding postures and breathing contribute to physical, mental and spiritual wellbeing. These practices can be beneficial to a variety of people independent of their religious or spiritual beliefs. Through focusing on the breath and bodily sensations, these practices increase awareness, relaxation and mental clarity while decreasing stress, anxiety and tension.

In Western cultures, our thoughts frequently dominate our minds. A way to have a change of mind and see more possibility is to have a change of body. Yoga, Tai Chi, Qigong and similar disciplines enhance the functioning of the body's endocrine and nervous systems. They work on body, mind and spirit at the same time.

Along with awareness of what is happening in the body; stretching and simple postures and movements affect breathing and emotions and clear the mind. These can be integrated into a coaching session, not as a separate stretching session, but as a way to interrupt habit and bring the wisdom of the body and intuition into the inquiry of coaching.

Many clients find it helpful to incorporate some of these disciplines into their daily life or take a class which gives them a supportive structure.

## Prayer

Prayer, simply defined as "a devout petition to God or an object of worship,"[5] is traditionally viewed as a way to directly communicate with God/Spirit. Virtually all religious traditions have prayer practices and many have extensive bodies of written prayers from which people can draw. These written prayers provide models in those traditions of how to address God or gods as well as offer comfort and inspiration. In some traditions, the prayers are all extemporaneous or come from an oral tradition. Often an understanding of a client's prayer-life can offer a window into their most cherished beliefs about the universe. As coaches, whether we resonate with a client's particular tradition or not, we can listen closely to the way that prayer allows the client access to their deepest spirituality.

## Reading spiritually-inspiring literature

You can't get spirit by knowing about it. However, the mystic, the poet, the teacher or the carpenter, who writes from a place of connection with spirit, is like a match that ignites a deep knowing.

---

### COACHING *in Action* | **Prayer Led Me to Coaching** *by Anne Yardley, CFT Certified Coach*

The spring after I retired, I was searching for my next steps. I had retired the summer before and given myself space to relax. I had read Sybil MacBeth's book *Praying in Color* and decided to try drawing my prayers as a Lenten discipline. The very first day, I drew a discernment prayer—a listening ear, some words representing different things in my life, some metaphors for God. That night I was talking with my husband and said, "I think I want to be a life coach." No one was more surprised than I was to hear that come out of my mouth!

I am a lifelong Christian, a liberal Protestant, who experiences God most deeply in music, nature and silence. I often connect most deeply to God through singing hymns at home at the piano. It took me many years to recognize that as a form of prayer. As an active church musician and as a professor in a seminary, I have been surrounded by religious words and ideas, symbols and sounds, rituals and sacraments. They form an important part of who I am as a person and as a coach. I am a better coach when I take time to honor my own needs for connecting with God/Spirit whether that is the "still small voice within" or the majestic forces of nature.

Not surprisingly, I'm very curious about my clients' spirituality and its manifestations. What are the tools and resources they already have from their own traditions? Are there experiences from their past that cause them to block their access to God/Spirit? Are there ways that I can help them integrate themselves more fully?

For me, coaching soul and spirit is what Coaching for Transformation is all about. The pathways to alignment are all about helping ourselves and our clients lead lives of wholeness. Lives in which our actions are congruent with our deepest values and beliefs. Religious traditions have much to teach us about the pathways to such wholeness.

---

5   dictionary.com

As lifelong learners of human development, coaches often read about psychology, soul and spirit. The work we do on ourselves influences and opens possibilities in our clients. We are interconnected beings.

As it is helpful to understand the dynamics of human behavior, it is also helpful to be nourished by spiritual truths and guiding lights that open the way to our true nature.

### Introspection and journal writing

While thoughts can get enmeshed in intractable patterns, making them conscious through writing can create clarity by putting those thoughts in the light of day. It is often useful to have clients explore what you have done in a session through inquiry. Writing opens the intuitive and creative part of the brain and is a vehicle to spiritual understanding and experience.

Taking the time to put our thoughts in writing can focus and crystallize patterns, ideas, points of view and dreams that were previously incoherent. Poetry or journaling can become a dialog with the self and a pathway to understanding the soul. Writing without censoring, or free writing, has the uncanny ability to provide creative answers. It is one of the ways to tap into the unknown, the collective unconscious and the universal mind, as well as a great way to download what is in the mind.

### Action and service

Working with clients to align intention with their desires, passions and messages of body, mind, emotions and spirit is an important part of spiritual work. Action is the complement to all this deep work in the realm of soul and spirit. Action is where the soul and spirit find fulfillment.

The nourishing value of service work provides perspective on our own situation, and can open up the gateways to love and compassion that are tremendously therapeutic.

There is a world of difference between action for its own sake and action that is in alignment with body, mind, emotion, soul and spirit. This aligned action is what we call creation in the Coaching for Transformation model, because it has its origin in understanding and inner resourcefulness.

## Developing the Inner Witness

Witnessing consciousness is about coming to the interior space where we can suspend judgment and be completely available to clients. In that frame of mind, we are best able to notice and respond creatively to whatever shows up in our client and the relationship.

There is a part of our consciousness that is aware of what is happening without being enslaved by it. This part of us is always free and is the calm center within us. It is at our spiritual core.

Self-awareness is not the same as thought. When we experience life without thought, we come into our natural rhythm and flow. When athletes perform at their peak, they are in a flow—in the zone. That zone is beyond the realm of conscious thought. In the same way, when a coach is totally present and not chained to the track of linear thinking, the possibilities for movement and transformation are exponentially greater.

The coach who is willing to enter the unknown with clients, steps into the world of the extraordinary, the unimagined, the realm of pure possibility. Fresh possibilities open when a coach steps into the place of witness.

*Example of Soul and Spirit Coaching*

Dawn: I want to look at why I'm still so disconnected spiritually and why my body still feels like I need to work in corporate mode (high pressure, high pace) rather than in the balanced way I dreamed of when working for myself. I was listening to an indigenous wisdom CD yesterday and three terms that were key for that West African tradition stood out for me: Spirit, Community and Heart-to-Heart Sharing. A fourth came to me later: Home.

Coach: What's significant about those words?

Dawn: Well, community and heart-to-heart sharing are part of the work that I'm passionate about and are part of my life now. To do that work well, I need to be in a deep relationship with Spirit. I want balance and peace so home becomes a more nurturing and inviting space. That balance and peacefulness also come from deep connection with God.

Coach: What is the relationship between those terms?

Dawn: What's coming to me is that it is not so much the importance of the relationship between them, but between my soul and each of them.

Coach: Say more.

Dawn: It's that the authentic me—me at the core—needs to be in deeper relationship with each. There needs to be a flow. In the past, yoga and meditation would connect me with Spirit. Lately, I can't get my mind to calm down when I do either.

Coach: I'm sensing the words spirit, community and heart-to-heart sharing are in a circle. How does that feel to you?

Dawn: Yes, I have them written on a piece of paper and I drew a circle around them already. The word soul is also in the circle at the center.

Coach: What are you noticing as you look at and reflect on those words?

Dawn: My mind is working against the new way of being. It's like it still thinks I'm in corporate, not working for myself.

Coach: What was the way of working in corporate?

Dawn: Racing, racing, racing. Deadlines, pressure, competition, fear, anxiety. What's going on in my head now feels like a warrior who doesn't know the war is over—that the game has been changed. They're trying to defend the old way. They want to keep me safe from the new way of being.

Coach: I notice you're talking about the warrior as plural—there is more than one.

Dawn: That's interesting…. Yes—there are many… I'm seeing colored balls racing around in my head. It's like they are all in a pinball machine—all moving at once. Fifty of them—red, yellow and blue balls.

Coach: And what are you sensing as you watch them move?

Dawn: They represent things on my to-do list. They all want my attention. They fear something has gone terribly wrong and they need to fix it. They want to keep me safe from the new way of being.

Coach: Like your soul changed the game on your brain?

Dawn: Yes—exactly.

Coach: Keep watching the balls... I sense your brain is like a group of small children who have to get used to this new thing. How do you get them acclimated?

Dawn: No—they don't feel like children. They feel older—like they are in charge and they're jumping up and down for my attention—saying, "Me first." "No, me." "No—someone's waiting for me, so me first." "No—me, you're late getting me done." They frustrate me. They make me feel tired and stressed. When I sit down to do yoga, it's like having a hundred puppies in a room and telling them all to sit. I get one to sit and the rest keep running around. I asked God for the ability to earn a living doing what I love, and I was blessed with the ability to do that. I know I can only get the balance and joy and peace I crave if I get back into a deeper relationship with God.

Coach: What else are you noticing?

Dawn: It's interesting. Now I'm seeing this cylindrical gray mist appearing to the left of the balls.

Coach: Tell me about the mist. What do you notice about it? What are the edges like? How dense is it?

Dawn: It's light gray and has a fixed cylindrical shape like it's in a tall glass, but there is no rigid border. It's not dense—it's like a gray fog. It's standing tall, firm, grounded, centered.

Coach: So it's permeable?

Dawn: Yes. As I keep watching it, I'm noticing that there are fewer balls.

Coach: What do you sense about this mist?

Dawn: I sense it is my soul. I'm feeling more peaceful as I watch it. There are no balls now.

Coach: Your voice is very soft and I feel the calm in you.

Dawn: I wonder what this all means. It's interesting. I wonder if it means…

Coach: (interrupting) Rather than interpreting it, step into the mist.

Dawn: Wow—that feels significant. Yes—I'm in it now and I feel totally at peace.

Coach: What do you notice about it now that you're inside of it?

Dawn: It feels wet—moist like fog on my skin—my face. It smells like walking in fog—kind of fresh, wet and clean. The peace is so deep here. Everything has slowed down. I feel one with Spirit here.

Coach: What else are you seeing or sensing through your "mist eyes?"

Dawn: This is so interesting! The balls are back, but they are all still. They are all covered by the mist. It's like they are stacked up in front of me—all covered by the mist and slowly, one ball came to me. Only one.

Coach: What is the impact of seeing that?

Dawn: That when I step into the mist and feel it fully, the balls stop and are surrounded by the mist and only one ball comes to me. When I'm grounded in my core—in touch with my soul, I automatically connect with Spirit and receive guidance about the one important thing to do in any moment. This feels so powerful!

Coach: I feel your peace and hear your excitement about the importance of this insight for you. You are looking at everything in your life from the "mist eyes."

Dawn: Yes—I like that. There is power here—a gentle power. And guidance and peace. This is so awesome. How can I hold onto it?

Coach: Yes, how can you?

Dawn: I will journal about it each day and email you in a week and let you know what I'm learning. And I will put a recurring daily reminder in my Blackberry that says, "Have you stood in the mist today?" I feel so much more connected to my soul and to Spirit now. Thank you!

In the coaching example above, how did the coach support Dawn in reconnecting with both her soul and spirit?

What were the turning points that led to deeper awareness for Dawn?

How was *soul* and *spirit* coaching combined with *pathways to alignment* in this example?

## Coaching Secular Clients

Ideally, we address spirituality in our discovery sessions and know where our clients stand in regard to soul and spirit. Some clients may be eager for spiritual coaching. Others may be strongly opposed, be it from a religious standpoint, from an atheistic or agnostic standpoint, or simply from disinterest.

If a client seems uncomfortable with spiritual terminology, we can still do deep work using secular terminology. We can ask, "When do you feel more connected with something that is beyond yourself?" or, "What values do you hold that go beyond your own wellbeing."

We can work with the client on meditation, body awareness, earth-based coaching and many of the suggested practices in this chapter. Also keep in mind the spiritual benefits that come with these activities:

Art—concerts, exhibitions

Community—family events, parties, ceremonies

Physical activities—swimming, playing, sex

Nature—sunsets, storms, deaths, births

There are many ways to bring spirituality into the daily life of clients who are looking for more. Below is a list of traditional spiritual practices, along with secular counterparts. We can work with clients to select practices that resonate with them and set up structure and accountability as we would any action steps. And keep in mind that spiritual practice may be more deeply personal or sensitive to our clients than some other action steps, such as exercising daily or sending job applications.

## Elements of spiritual practice

| TRADITIONALLY RELIGIOUS | SECULAR |
|---|---|
| Meditation | Contemplation |
| Prayer | Visualization, vision boards, mantras, intention, asking |
| Scripture, Dharma | Study, learning |
| Sabbath | Vacation, weekend |
| Service | Volunteering |
| Congregation, Sangha | Community, society |
| Ritual, ceremony | Traditions (birthdays, holidays, funerals) |
| Austerity | Discipline |
| Altar, totems, dress | Mantle, mementos, dress |
| Hymns | Music |

*Questions to Consider*

What are some ways you want to explore soul and spirit coaching?

How can you support heart connection and deep personal expression of soul?

How can you provide space for connection with Spirit?

# Appendix I
# Sample Forms & Resources

## Client Information - Personal Profile

Name: _____

Company: _____

Billing Address: _____

Business Phone: _____

Cell Phone: _____

Fax: _____

E-mail Address: _____

Occupation/Title: _____

Home Address: _____

Home Phone: _____

Date of Birth: _____

Names of important people in your life: _____

_____

# Client Questions

Answer the following questions and return these questions to your coach before your intake session. All questions are optional—be as brief or as detailed as you choose.

What do you want to get out of coaching?

What do you want to happen in your lifetime so that you consider your life satisfying and well lived?

If there were a secret ambition in your life, what would it be?

Describe your "dream career" (what, when, where, with whom?).

Describe your support system. Do you have people in your life who believe in you, encourage you, challenge you and see you through the hard times?

What are five of your "gifts" or talents?

What do you have to contribute that is unique?

How are you your own worst enemy?

What has been your most thrilling success or proudest achievement?

What activities have meaning and heart for you?

Who inspires you?

What are five things you have been procrastinating on?

What is the greatest personal change you'd like to see in the coming year?

# Focus of Coaching

Clear goals lead to success. Part of the Intake process will be to define your goals and make plans for their completion.

Fill out this form and be sure to include target dates for reaching each goal.

## Personal Goals

(Health, balance, relationships, fun, money, spiritual, personal development)

Date achieve by: _____

1. _____

2. _____

3. _____

## Business or Professional Goals

Date achieve by: _____

1. _____

2. _____

3. _____

## Other Goals

Date achieve by: _____

1. _____

2. _____

3. _____

What else do you want your coach to know?


What have you been putting off that you can start now?

# Coaching Client Prep Form

Please email (YOUR EMAIL) or fax (YOUR FAX) this form to your coach before each coaching call.

Name _____ Date_____

What I have accomplished since our last call: _____
_____
_____
_____

What I didn't get done: _____
_____
_____
_____

Opportunities that are available to me right now: _____
_____
_____
_____

Challenges and problems I am facing right now: _____
_____
_____
_____

How I can best use my coaching call today: _____
_____
_____
_____

What I intend to do by the next call: _____
_____
_____
_____

Other areas: _____
_____
_____
_____

# Sample Welcome to Coaching Letter

YOUR LOGO HERE

February 19, 20XX

Dear Client's Name

Welcome to coaching! I am looking forward to working with you. Please fill out the following forms and email to YOUR EMAIL ADDRESS or fax them to YOUR FAX NUMBER, prior to your discovery session at TIME on DATE.

> Personal Information
>
> Focus of Coaching
>
> Client Questions
>
> Coaching Agreement

The purpose of the questions is to help me get to know you a little better and give you a head start on the coaching process. There may be some questions that you can't answer or that do not apply to you. That's fine. Your answers can be as brief or as detailed as you choose.

The rest of the binder contains forms to use during the intake session and throughout our coaching relationship. Look them over but wait until the discovery session to fill them out.

I am very excited about building our alliance! I feel confident that you can really create some exciting changes and possibilities during our time together.

Warm regards,

YOUR NAME

# Frequently Asked Questions About Coaching

**What is coaching?**

Coaching is a powerful, ongoing relationship that helps you focus and realize your visions and goals. With a Professional Coach, you will get the tools and support to remove obstacles and facilitate change.

**What are some reasons people hire a coach?**

to plan a career move

to make your present job more fulfilling

to plan your life based on what matters most to you

to get more organized

to create more balance in your life

to focus your energy to finish or plan a project

to increase your effectiveness as an executive, manager or sales person

to work with your team to increase productivity and effectiveness

to make your life more fulfilling

to start a business

to get motivated

to increase your income

**How is coaching done?**

Typically, individual coaching is done by telephone, for four ½-hour sessions each month. To create profound changes in your life, we ask for a three-month commitment.

**Is coaching therapy?**

No, coaching is not therapy. You will find that coaching focuses on strategic planning and personal growth and does not attempt to heal emotional trauma. Coaches regularly refer clients to other professionals for issues that are better suited to a therapeutic relationship.

**What is a typical session like?**

The hallmark of coaching is self-responsibility. The client sets the agenda for the call and the coach follows that agenda. You can expect powerful and clarifying questions, focused and fine-tuned planning tools, and accountability. As your coach, I'll have high expectations of you and support you thoroughly.

**What does it cost to hire a coach?**

The charge for coaching is $X per month for four ½-hour calls per month. Some clients work with a coach for an hour or two a week, which increases the fee. Your check is due on the first of each month. If it makes it any easier, you can pay by Visa or MasterCard.

Your coaching fee is an investment that pays big dividends. If you're like most people, money is available for the things you really want or need. Are you cautious about spending money and concerned about making intelligent choices? Here are three things you can do to maximize your investment:

Hire the right coach. Find the coach whose specialties best match your needs.

During your first coaching session, set a 90-day goal that's worth accomplishing. Make sure the goal is something that's worth the coaching fee, something you'd be happy to pay for.

Make the most of your coaching time. Tell your coach what results you want and your coach helps you make it happen.

### How do I get started?

It's easy. Call me to arrange a sample coaching session, and we'll talk about whether coaching is right for you. If the chemistry is right, and you decide you want to move on to the next step, we'll get out our calendars and schedule your discovery session. A couple of days later, you'll receive your "Welcome to Coaching" package which includes some self-assessment and planning tools. And that's just the beginning!

# Sample Coaching Agreement

I, _____, am committed to creating a coaching alliance with Sally Jones. The coach agrees to hold all content of our sessions completely confidential. I commit to creating a successful alliance that supports me in reaching my goals and living the life I want.

I agree to coaching for a minimum of three months.    ___yes ___no

I agree to shape the coaching relationship to best meet my needs by:
    Sharing what I know about my own motivation    ___yes ___no
    Co-designing structures that will support me    ___yes ___no
    Asking for changes if the coaching strategy is not working    ___yes ___no

I give the coach permission to:
    Challenge me with powerful questions    ___yes ___no
    Make requests that I take action when I identify things that are important to me    ___yes ___no
    Hold me accountable for taking actions I commit to    ___yes ___no
    Provide inquiries for me to think about    ___yes ___no

I agree to the following business arrangements:
    Fee of _____/month    ___yes ___no
    Paid at the beginning of the month    ___yes ___no
    Fee for the one-time intake appointment of _____    ___yes ___no
    Fee covers four ½ hour sessions per month with unlimited email    ___yes ___no
    In months with five weeks, one week is off    ___yes ___no

I agree to the following scheduling items:
    If I am late for an appointment, my session will be shortened    ___yes ___no
    I will re-schedule any appointments 24 hours in advance, or forfeit the appointment and pay the fee    ___yes ___no
    After two missed appointments without re-scheduling, the alliance may be terminated    ___yes ___no
    I will give one month's notice and use the final call at the conclusion of the coaching relationship for completion    ___yes ___no

_____

Client Signature            Date

_____

Coach Signature            Date

# Sample Discovery Session Outline

1. Welcome

2. Agenda for the session: create a powerful vision of what is possible in our work together.

3. Elements of Intake

4. What is coaching
   a. Can I say I coach you?
   b. Questions, not answers
   c. Consultant vs. coach
   d. Personal responsibility
   e. Accountability

5. Creating conscious relationship
   a. What do you hope to get out of coaching?
   b. How will you get the most out of our coaching relationship?
   c. What criteria will you use to evaluate your investment (time and money) in coaching?
   d. How do you want to be coached (challenged, supported, offered inquiries, held accountable)?
   e. Would you like to hear my coaching philosophy?
   f. Holding the relationship sacred (confidential, intimate, profound, honest).
   g. Co-designing a celebratory closure of the coaching relationship.
   h. Guidelines, questions, or requests we have of each other?
   i. Sign the Coaching Agreement?

6. Share resources
   a. Coaching Prep Form
   b. Values, Purpose, Vision, Goal Setting Forms
   c. What assessment tools would serve you? (DISC, 360 Feedback, Enneagram, MBTI, Tarot Cards, Astrology Chart)

7. Logistics
   a. Payment agreements
   b. Vacations
   c. Missed calls
   d. Appointments

8. Discovery

    a. Imagine you are creating life from the highest and best, most alive place inside of you. Describe that place.

    b. What is possible in life if you were creating from that place?

    c. What do you need me to know about you?

    d. Who you are:

        i. Bright places, dark places, where effective, where not?

        ii. Strategies for dealing with the inner critic?

        iii. What happens for you when things don't work out as expected

            1. How do you want me to be with that?

        iv. Mission/Purpose

        v. What else do you want me to know about you?

        vi. Values work

9. Designing the future

    a. Goals for coaching

    b. Appointments/Questions

10. Completion—are we still a fit?

# Feelings

| PEACEFUL | LOVE | GLAD | PLAYFUL | ENGAGED |
|----------|------|------|---------|---------|
| blissful | affectionate | confident | adventurous | absorbed |
| carefree | amorous | delighted | alive | alert |
| centered | empathic | ecstatic | buoyant | aroused |
| composed | friendly | encouraged | energetic | astonished |
| expansive | grateful | excited | exuberant | curious |
| fulfilled | loving | exhilarated | giddy | eager |
| quiet | nurtured | grateful | goofy | engrossed |
| quiet | open | happy | impish | enriched |
| relaxed | radiant | hopeful | inquisitive | enthusiastic |
| relieved | sensitive | inspired | invigorated | fascinated |
| satisfied | tender | joyful | lively | intrigued |
| serene | trusting | proud | mischievous | surprised |
| trusting | warm | satisfied | refreshed | touched |

| MAD | SAD | SCARED | TIRED | UNEASY |
|-----|-----|--------|-------|--------|
| agitated | blue | afraid | blah | helpless |
| angry | dejected | anxious | bored | anguished |
| annoyed | depressed | apprehensive | dull | apathetic |
| bitter | despairing | desperate | embarrassed | boggled |
| concerned | despondent | dread | exhausted | chagrined |
| disgusted | discouraged | fearful | fatigued | detached |
| edgy | dismayed | frightened | hurt | frustrated |
| enraged | distant | horrified | indifferent | hesitant |
| exasperated | distressed | jealous | inert | perplexed |
| frustrated | gloomy | jittery | lethargic | puzzled |
| furious | heavy | lonely | listless | skeptical |
| grouchy | helpless | nervous | mopey | torn |
| hostile | lonely | sensitive | overwhelmed | troubled |
| impatient | miserable | shocked | passive | uncomfortable |
| irate | overwhelmed | startled | reluctant | confused |
| irritable | sorrowful | suspicious | restless | unglued |
| livid | troubled | terrified | sleepy | unsteady |
| outraged | unhappy | worried | weary | withdrawn |

| UNIVERSAL NEEDS AND VALUES | |
|---|---|
| Expression | celebration, vitality, humor, passion, creativity, imagine, dream, romance, inspiration |
| Harmony | peace, security, safety, order, consistency, calm, stability, relaxation, comfort, ease, reassurance, beauty |
| Autonomy | independence, dreams, freedom, choice, individuality, space, spontaneity |
| Integrity | authenticity, meaning, purpose, justice, fairness, honesty, presence, openness, trust, respect, equality |
| Community | interdependence, trust, bonding, inclusion, belonging, cooperation, unity, synergy, integration, loyalty, participation, partnership, acceptance |
| Contribution | mastery, growth, service, gifts, enrichment, empowerment, support, acknowledgment, help, nourishment |
| Connection | understanding, closeness, appreciation, empathy, support, consideration, love, affection, companionship, mutuality, nurturing, intimacy |
| Play | adventure, challenge, daring, risk-taking, thrill, fun, humor, amusement, laughter, pleasure, sensuality |
| Meaning | awareness, celebration, clarity, competence, consciousness, creativity, understanding, hope, learning, purpose, effectiveness, growth, discovery |
| Well-being | health, sustenance, safety, shelter, rest, sex, food, clothing |

# Coaching with the Energetic Body: Spinning the Chakras for Awakening

*The body is a vehicle of consciousness. Chakra are the wheels of life that carry this vehicle about-through its trials, tribulations, and transformations.—Anodea Judith*

A map toward wholeness using the energetic body of the Chakra System

| THE SHADOW | | THE LIGHT |
|---|---|---|
| **ATTACHMENT**<br><br>Excess: Spiritual addiction, confusion<br><br>Deficient: Limited beliefs, materialism | | **AWARENESS**<br><br>Right to know<br><br>Wisdom / knowledge / spiritual connection |
| **ILLUSION**<br><br>Excess: Trouble concentrating<br><br>Deficient: Inability to see problems, denial | | **INTUITION / IMAGINATION**<br><br>Right to see<br><br>Accurate interpretation / imagination / seeing |
| **LIES**<br><br>Excess: Inability to listen, talking in circles<br><br>Deficient: Fear of speaking aloud | | **COMMUNICATION**<br><br>Right to speak - to be heard<br><br>Clear communication / creativity / resonance |
| **GRIEF**<br><br>Excess: Poor Boundaries, jealousy<br><br>Deficient: Lonely, bitter, critical, lack of empathy | | **LOVE / RELATIONSHIPS**<br><br>Right to love - to be loved<br><br>Balance / compassion / relationships / self-acceptance |
| **SHAME**<br><br>Excess: Blaming, aggressive, scattered, always 'doing'<br><br>Deficient: Lack of confidence, fearful, passive | | **POWER / WILL**<br><br>Right to act<br><br>Will / purpose / self-esteem / drive / spontaneity |
| **GUILT**<br><br>Excess: Obsessive attachments, poor boundaries<br><br>Deficient: Fear of pleasure, emotionally numb | | **SEXUALITY / EMOTIONS**<br><br>Right to feel - to want<br><br>Fluidity / pleasure / feeling & emotions |
| **FEAR**<br><br>Excess: Hoarding, heavy, sluggish, materialism<br><br>Deficient: Frequent fear, lack of discipline, 'spacy' | | **SURVIVAL**<br><br>Right to be here - to have<br><br>Stability / grounding / prosperity / trust / physical health |

# Strategic Planning Wheel

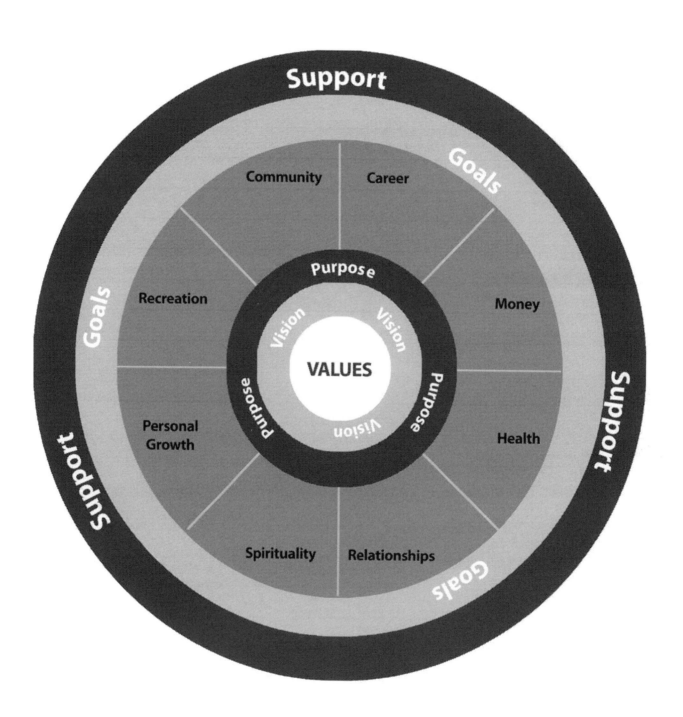

# Balance Wheel

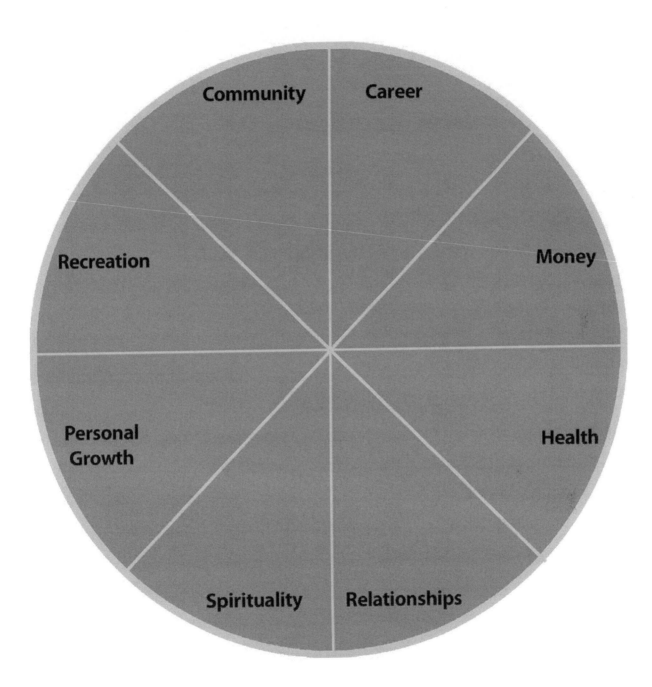

# Expanding your Comfort Zone

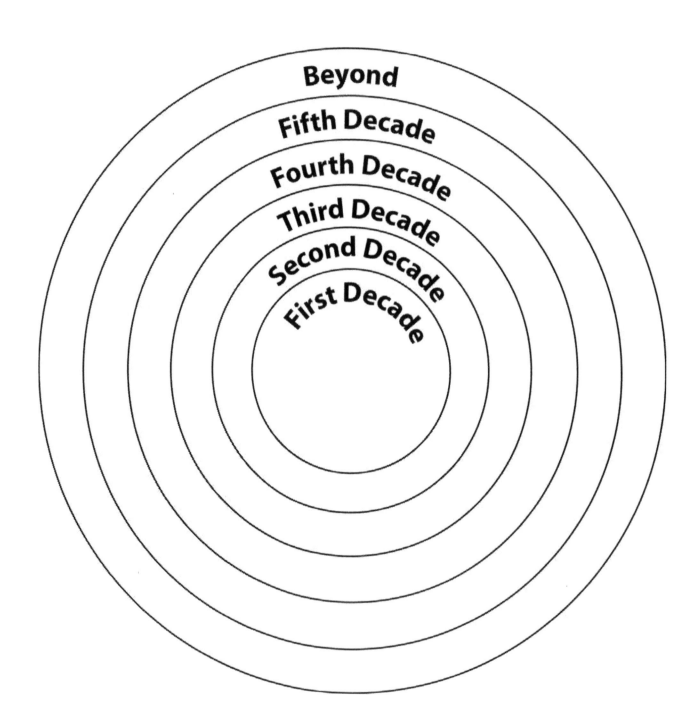

# Support Grid

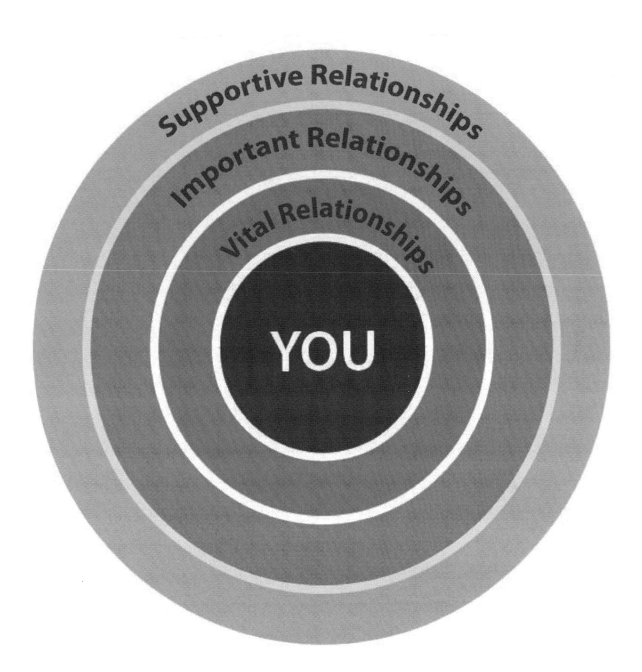

# SWOT Analysis

| APPRECIATIVE SWOT ANALYSIS | |
|---|---|
| **Strengths** | **Wishes** |
| **Opportunities** | **Threats** |

# Goals and Action Planning Worksheet

| GOALS AND ACTION PLANNING WORKSHEET |
|---|
| Goal: |
| Priority: |
| Values: |
| Commitment level: |
| Action steps with dates: |
| 1. |
| 2. |
| 3. |
| Goal: |
| Priority: |
| Values: |
| Commitment level: |
| Action steps with dates: |
| 1. |
| 2. |
| 3. |
| Goal: |
| Priority: |
| Values: |
| Commitment level: |
| Action steps with dates: |
| 1. |
| 2. |
| 3. |

## GOALS AND ACTION PLANNING WORKSHEET

| | |
|---|---|
| Goal: | |
| Priority: | |
| Values: | |
| Commitment level: | |
| Action steps with dates: | |
| 1. | |
| 2. | |
| 3. | |

| | |
|---|---|
| Goal: | |
| Priority: | |
| Values: | |
| Commitment level: | |
| Action steps with dates: | |
| 1. | |
| 2. | |
| 3. | |

| | |
|---|---|
| Goal: | |
| Priority: | |
| Values: | |
| Commitment level: | |
| Action steps with dates: | |
| 1. | |
| 2. | |
| 3. | |

| | |
|---|---|
| Goal: | |
| Priority: | |
| Values: | |
| Commitment level: | |
| Action steps with dates: | |
| 1. | |
| 2. | |
| 3. | |

# Appendix II
# International Coach Federation

*Never forget that you are one of a kind. Never forget that if there weren't any need for you in all your uniqueness to be on this earth, you wouldn't be here in the first place. And never forget, no matter how overwhelming life's challenges and problems seem to be, that one person can make a difference in the world. In fact, it is always because of one person that all the changes that matter in the world come about. So be that one person. —Buckminster Fuller*

| TOPICS |
| --- |
| ICF Credential |
| ICF Core Competencies |
| ICF Code of Ethics |

## ICF Credential

The Coaching for Transformation program is an International Coach Federation (ICF) Accredited Coach Training Program (ACTP). If you choose to pursue an ICF credential after completing the Coaching for Transformation course, you will follow the ACTP track. In addition to your certification training, the ICF credentialing process requires completion of the Coach Knowledge Assessment, a specific number of coaching hours and a minimum number of clients. During the Coaching for Transformation program, you will begin coaching immediately and will build your coaching repertoire as you go through the program. We encourage you to begin working with clients (paid and pro bono) as soon as you feel comfortable.

ICF is the largest worldwide resource for professional coaches. It is the leading global organization dedicated to advancing the coaching profession by setting high professional standards, providing independent certification and building a network of credentialed coaches. ICF offers the only globally recognized, independent credentialing program.

### The ICF credentialing program

Establishes and administers minimum standards for credentialing professional coaches and coach training agencies.

Assures the public that participating coaches and coach training agencies meet or exceed these minimum standards.

Reinforces professional coaching as a distinct and self-regulating profession.

Coaches who have been credentialed by the ICF have received coach-specific training, achieved a designated number of experience hours and have worked with a mentor. The ICF offers three credentials (ACC, PCC and MCC).

The ICF Associate Certified Coach (ACC) credential is for the practiced coach. It requires completion of a set amount of coach-specific training, a minimum of 100 coaching experience hours with at least eight clients, and completion of the Coach Knowledge Assessment.

The ICF Professional Certified Coach (PCC) credential is for the proven coach. It requires completion of a set amount of coach-specific training, a minimum of 500 coaching experience hours with at least 25 clients, and completion of the Coach Knowledge Assessment.

The ICF Master Certified Coach (MCC) credential is for the expert coach. It requires completion of 200 hours of coach-specific training, a minimum of 2,500 coaching experience hours with at least 35 clients, completion of the Coach Knowledge Assessment, and a performance evaluation.

Refer to the ICF website (http://coachfederation.org) for additional information.

# ICF Core Competencies

### A. Setting the Foundation

Meeting Ethical Guidelines and Professional Standards

Establishing the Coaching Agreement

### B. Co-creating the Relationship

Establishing Trust and Intimacy with the Client

Coaching Presence

### C. Communicating Effectively

Active Listening

Powerful Questioning

Direct Communication

### D. Facilitating Learning and Results

Creating Awareness

Designing Actions

Planning and Goal Setting

Managing Progress and Accountability

## A. Setting the Foundation

**Meeting Ethical Guidelines and Professional Standards**—Understanding of coaching ethics and standards and ability to apply them appropriately in all coaching situations.

Understands and exhibits in own behaviors the ICF Standards of Conduct (see list, Part III of ICF Code of Ethics).

Understands and follows all ICF Ethical Guidelines (see list).

Clearly communicates the distinctions between coaching, consulting, psychotherapy and other support professions.

Refers client to another support professional as needed, knowing when this is needed and the available resources.

**Establishing the Coaching Agreement**—Ability to understand what is required in the specific coaching interaction and to come to agreement with the prospective and new client about the coaching process and relationship.

Understands and effectively discusses with the client the guidelines and specific parameters of the coaching relationship (e.g., logistics, fees, scheduling, inclusion of others if appropriate).

Reaches agreement about what is appropriate in the relationship and what is not, what is and is not being offered, and about the client's and coach's responsibilities.

Determines whether there is an effective match between his/her coaching method and the needs of the prospective client.

## B. Co-Creating the Relationship

**Establishing Trust and Intimacy with the Client**—Ability to create a safe, supportive environment that produces ongoing mutual respect and trust.

Shows genuine concern for the client's welfare and future.

Continuously demonstrates personal integrity, honesty and sincerity.

Establishes clear agreements and keeps promises.

Demonstrates respect for client's perceptions, learning style, personal being.

Provides ongoing support for and champions new behaviors and actions, including those involving risk taking and fear of failure.

Asks permission to coach client in sensitive, new areas.

**Coaching Presence**—Ability to be fully conscious and create spontaneous relationship with the client, employing a style that is open, flexible and confident.

Is present and flexible during the coaching process, dancing in the moment.

Accesses own intuition and trusts one's inner knowing—"goes with the gut."

Is open to not knowing and takes risks.

Sees many ways to work with the client and chooses in the moment what is most effective.

Uses humor effectively to create lightness and energy.

Confidently shifts perspectives and experiments with new possibilities for own action.

Demonstrates confidence in working with strong emotions and can self-manage and not be overpowered or enmeshed by client's emotions.

## C. Communicating Effectively

**Active Listening**—Ability to focus completely on what the client is saying and is not saying, to understand the meaning of what is said in the context of the client's desires, and to support client self-expression.

Attends to the client and the client's agenda and not to the coach's agenda for the client.

Hears the client's concerns, goals, values and beliefs about what is and is not possible.

Distinguishes between the words, the tone of voice, and the body language.

Summarizes, paraphrases, reiterates, and mirrors back what client has said to ensure clarity and understanding.

Encourages, accepts, explores and reinforces the client's expression of feelings, perceptions, concerns, beliefs, suggestions, etc.

Integrates and builds on client's ideas and suggestions.

"Bottom-lines" or understands the essence of the client's communication and helps the client get there rather than engaging in long, descriptive stories.

Allows the client to vent or "clear" the situation without judgment or attachment in order to move on to next steps.

**Powerful Questioning**—Ability to ask questions that reveal the information needed for maximum benefit to the coaching relationship and the client.

Asks questions that reflect active listening and an understanding of the client's perspective.

Asks questions that evoke discovery, insight, commitment or action (e.g., those that challenge the client's assumptions).

Asks open-ended questions that create greater clarity, possibility or new learning.

Asks questions that move the client toward what they desire, not questions that ask for the client to justify or look backward.

**Direct Communication**—Ability to communicate effectively during coaching sessions, and to use language that has the greatest positive impact on the client.

Is clear, articulate and direct in sharing and providing feedback.

Reframes and articulates to help the client understand from another perspective what he/she wants or is uncertain about.

Clearly states coaching objectives, meeting agenda, and purpose of techniques or exercises.

Uses language appropriate and respectful to the client (e.g., non-sexist, non-racist, non-technical, non-jargon).

Uses metaphor and analogy to help to illustrate a point or paint a verbal picture.

## D. Facilitating Learning and Results

**Creating Awareness**—Ability to integrate and accurately evaluate multiple sources of information and to make interpretations that help the client to gain awareness and thereby achieve agreed-upon results.

Goes beyond what is said in assessing client's concerns, not getting hooked by the client's description.

Invokes inquiry for greater understanding, awareness, and clarity.

Identifies for the client his/her underlying concerns; typical and fixed ways of perceiving himself/herself and the world; differences between the facts and the interpretation; and disparities between thoughts, feelings, and action.

Helps clients to discover for themselves the new thoughts, beliefs, perceptions, emotions, moods, etc. that strengthen their ability to take action and achieve what is important to them.

Communicates broader perspectives to clients and inspires commitment to shift their viewpoints and find new possibilities for action.

Helps clients to see the different, interrelated factors that affect them and their behaviors (e.g., thoughts, emotions, body, and background).

Expresses insights to clients in ways that are useful and meaningful for the client.

Identifies major strengths vs. major areas for learning and growth, and what is most important to address during coaching.

Asks the client to distinguish between trivial and significant issues, situational vs. recurring behaviors, when detecting a separation between what is being stated and what is being done.

**Designing Actions**—Ability to create with the client opportunities for ongoing learning, during coaching and in work/life situations, and for taking new actions that will most effectively lead to agreed-upon coaching results.

Brainstorms and assists the client to define actions that will enable the client to demonstrate, practice, and deepen new learning.

Helps the client to focus on and systematically explore specific concerns and opportunities that are central to agreed-upon coaching goals.

Engages the client to explore alternative ideas and solutions, to evaluate options, and to make related decisions.

Promotes active experimentation and self-discovery, where the client applies what has been discussed and learned during sessions immediately afterward in his/her work or life setting.

Celebrates client successes and capabilities for future growth.

Challenges client's assumptions and perspectives to provoke new ideas and find new possibilities for action.

Advocates or brings forward points of view that are aligned with client goals and, without attachment, engages the client to consider them.

Helps the client "Do It Now" during the coaching session, providing immediate support.

Encourages stretches and challenges but also a comfortable pace of learning.

**Planning and Goal Setting**—Ability to develop and maintain an effective coaching plan with the client.

Consolidates collected information and establishes a coaching plan and development goals with the client that address concerns and major areas for learning and development.

Creates a plan with results that are attainable, measurable, specific, and have target dates.

Makes plan adjustments as warranted by the coaching process and by changes in the situation.

Helps the client identify and access different resources for learning (e.g., books, other professionals).

Identifies and targets early successes that are important to the client.

**Managing Progress and Accountability**—Ability to hold attention on what is important for the client, and to leave responsibility with the client to take action.

Clearly requests of the client actions that will move the client toward his/her stated goals.

Demonstrates follow-through by asking the client about those actions that the client committed to during the previous session(s).

Acknowledges the client for what they have done, not done, learned or become aware of since the previous coaching session(s).

Effectively prepares, organizes, and reviews with client information obtained during sessions.

Keeps the client on track between sessions by holding attention on the coaching plan and outcomes, agreed-upon courses of action, and topics for future session(s).

Focuses on the coaching plan but is also open to adjusting behaviors and actions based on the coaching process and shifts in direction during sessions.

Is able to move back and forth between the big picture of where the client is heading, setting a context for what is being discussed and where the client wishes to go.

Promotes client's self-discipline and holds the client accountable for what they say they are going to do, for the results of an intended action, or for a specific plan with related time frames.

Develops the client's ability to make decisions, address key concerns, and develop himself/herself (to get feedback, to determine priorities and set the pace of learning, to reflect on and learn from experiences).

Positively confronts the client with the fact that he/she did not take agreed-upon actions.

# ICF Code of Ethics

## Preamble

ICF is committed to maintaining and promoting excellence in coaching. Therefore, ICF expects all members and credentialed coaches (coaches, coach mentors, coaching supervisors, coach trainers or students), to adhere to the elements and principles of ethical conduct: to be competent and integrate ICF Core Competencies effectively in their work.

In line with the ICF core values and ICF definition of coaching, the Code of Ethics is designed to provide appropriate guidelines, accountability and enforceable standards of conduct for all ICF Members and ICF Credential-holders, who commit to abiding by the following ICF Code of Ethics:

## Part One: Definitions

**Coaching**: Coaching is partnering with clients in a thought-provoking and creative process that inspires them to maximize their personal and professional potential.

**ICF Coach**: An ICF coach agrees to practice the ICF Core Competencies and pledges accountability to the ICF Code of Ethics.

**Professional Coaching Relationship**: A professional coaching relationship exists when coaching includes an agreement (including contracts) that defines the responsibilities of each party.

**Roles in the Coaching Relationship**: In order to clarify roles in the coaching relationship it is often necessary to distinguish between the client and the sponsor. In most cases, the client and sponsor are the same person and are therefore jointly referred to as the client. For purposes of identification, however, the ICF defines these roles as follows:

**Client**: The "Client/Coachee is the person(s) being coached.

**Sponsor**: The "sponsor" is the entity (including its representatives) paying for and/or arranging for coaching services to be provided. In all cases, coaching engagement agreements should clearly establish the rights, roles and responsibilities for both the client and sponsor if the client and sponsor are different people.

**Student**: The "student" is someone enrolled in a coach training program or working with a coaching supervisor or coach mentor in order to learn the coaching process or enhance and develop their coaching skills.

**Conflict of Interest**: A situation in which a coach has a private or personal interest sufficient to appear to influence the objective of his or her official duties as a coach and a professional.

## Part Two: The ICF Standards of Ethical Conduct

### Section 1: Professional Conduct at Large

As a coach, I:

1) Conduct myself in accordance with the ICF Code of Ethics in all interactions, including coach training, coach mentoring and coach supervisory activities.

2) Commit to take the appropriate action with the coach, trainer, or coach mentor and/or will contact ICF to address any ethics violation or possible breach as soon as I become aware, whether it involves me or others.

3) Communicate and create awareness in others, including organizations, employees, sponsors, coaches and others, who might need to be informed of the responsibilities established by this Code.

4) Refrain from unlawful discrimination in occupational activities, including age, race, gender orientation, ethnicity, sexual orientation, religion, national origin or disability.

5) Make verbal and written statements that are true and accurate about what I offer as a coach, the coaching profession or ICF.

6) Accurately identify my coaching qualifications, expertise, experience, training, certifications and ICF Credentials.

7) Recognize and honor the efforts and contributions of others and only claim ownership of my own material. I understand that violating this standard may leave me subject to legal remedy by a third party.

8) Strive at all times to recognize my personal issues that may impair, conflict with or interfere with my coaching performance or my professional coaching relationships. I will promptly seek the relevant professional assistance and determine the action to be taken, including whether it is appropriate to suspend or terminate my coaching relationship(s) whenever the facts and circumstances necessitate.

9) Recognize that the Code of Ethics applies to my relationship with coaching clients, coachees, students, mentees and supervisees.

10) Conduct and report research with competence, honesty and within recognized scientific standards and applicable subject guidelines. My research will be carried out with the necessary consent and approval of those involved, and with an approach that will protect participants from any potential harm. All research efforts will be performed in a manner that complies with all the applicable laws of the country in which the research is conducted.

11) Maintain, store and dispose of any records, including electronic files and communications, created during my coaching engagements in a manner that promotes confidentiality, security and privacy and complies with any applicable laws and agreements.

12) Use ICF Member contact information (email addresses, telephone numbers, and so on) only in the manner and to the extent authorized by the ICF.

### Section 2: Conflicts of Interest

As a coach, I:
13) Seek to be conscious of any conflict or potential conflict of interest, openly disclose any such conflict and offer to remove myself when a conflict arises.

14) Clarify roles for internal coaches, set boundaries and review with stakeholders conflicts of interest that may emerge between coaching and other role functions.

15) Disclose to my client and the sponsor(s) all anticipated compensation from third parties that I may receive for referrals of clients or pay to receive clients.

16) Honor an equitable coach/client relationship, regardless of the form of compensation.

## Section 3: Professional Conduct with Clients

As a coach, I:
17) Ethically speak what I know to be true to clients, prospective clients or sponsors about the potential value of the coaching process or of me as a coach.

18) Carefully explain and strive to ensure that, prior to or at the initial meeting, my coaching client and sponsor(s) understand the nature of coaching, the nature and limits of confidentiality, financial arrangements, and any other terms of the coaching agreement.

19) Have a clear coaching service agreement with my clients and sponsor(s) before beginning the coaching relationship and honor this agreement. The agreement shall include the roles, responsibilities and rights of all parties involved.

20) Hold responsibility for being aware of and setting clear, appropriate and culturally sensitive boundaries that govern interactions, physical or otherwise, I may have with my clients or sponsor(s).

21) Avoid any sexual or romantic relationship with current clients or sponsor(s) or students, mentees or supervisees. Further, I will be alert to the possibility of any potential sexual intimacy among the parties including my support staff and/or assistants and will take the appropriate action to address the issue or cancel the engagement in order to provide a safe environment overall.

22) Respect the client's right to terminate the coaching relationship at any point during the process, subject to the provisions of the agreement. I shall remain alert to indications that there is a shift in the value received from the coaching relationship.

23) Encourage the client or sponsor to make a change if I believe the client or sponsor would be better served by another coach or by another resource and suggest my client seek the services of other professionals when deemed necessary or appropriate.

## Section 4: Confidentiality/Privacy

As a coach, I:
24) Maintain the strictest levels of confidentiality with all client and sponsor information unless release is required by law.

25) Have a clear agreement about how coaching information will be exchanged among coach, client and sponsor.

26) Have a clear agreement when acting as a coach, coach mentor, coaching supervisor or trainer, with both client and sponsor, student, mentee, or supervisee about the conditions under which confidentiality may not be maintained (e.g., illegal activity, pursuant to valid court order or subpoena; imminent or likely risk of danger to self or to others; etc) and make sure both client and sponsor, student, mentee, or supervisee voluntarily and knowingly agree in writing to that limit of confidentiality. Where I reasonably believe that because one of the above circumstances is applicable, I may need to inform appropriate authorities.

27) Require all those who work with me in support of my clients to adhere to the ICF Code of Ethics, Number 26, Section 4, Confidentiality and Privacy Standards, and any other sections of the Code of Ethics that might be applicable.

**Section 5: Continuing Development**

As a coach, I:
28) Commit to the need for continued and ongoing development of my professional skills.

## Part Three: The ICF Pledge of Ethics

As an ICF coach, I acknowledge and agree to honor my ethical and legal obligations to my coaching clients and sponsors, colleagues, and to the public at large. I pledge to comply with the ICF Code of Ethics and to practice these standards with those whom I coach, teach, mentor or supervise.

If I breach this Pledge of Ethics or any part of the ICF Code of Ethics, I agree that the ICF in its sole discretion may hold me accountable for so doing. I further agree that my accountability to the ICF for any breach may include sanctions, such as loss of my ICF Membership and/or my ICF Credentials.

For more information on the Ethical Conduct Review Process including links to file a complaint, visit www.coachfederation.org.

*Adopted by the ICF Global Board of Directors June 2015.*

# Appendix III
# Recommended Reading

## Coaching Models

Britton, Jennifer J. (2010). Effective Group Coaching: Tried and Tested Tools and Resources for Optimum Coaching Results. John Wiley & Sons Canada, Limited.

Crane, Thomas G. and Lerissa Nancy Patrick (2002). The Heart of Coaching: Using Transformational Coaching to Create a High-performance Culture. San Diego: FTA.

Flaherty, James. (2010). Coaching: Evoking Excellence in Others. Amsterdam: Elsevier Butterworth-Heinemann.

Stoltzfus, Tony (2008). Coaching Questions: a Coach's Guide to Powerful Asking Skills. Virginia Beach, VA: Tony Stoltzfus.

Whitworth, Laura, Henry Kimsey-House, and Phil Sandahl (2006). Co-active Coaching: New Skills for Coaching People toward Success in Work and Life. Mountain View, CA: Davies-Black.

Williams, Patrick and Diane S. Menendez (2007). Becoming a Professional Life Coach: Lessons from the Institute of Life Coach Training. W. W. Norton & Company.

## Coaching in Organizations

Hargrove, Robert A. (2008). Masterful Coaching. San Francisco: Jossey-Bass.

Lasley, Martha (2004). Courageous Visions: How to Unleash Passionate Energy in your Life and Organization. Discover Press.

Orem, Sara, Jacqueline Binkert, and Ann L. Clancy (2007). Appreciative Coaching: a Positive Process for Change. San Francisco: Jossey-Bass/Wiley.

Skiffington, Suzanne, and Perry Zeus (2007). Behavioral Coaching: How to Build Sustainable Personal and Organizational Strengths. Sydney: McGraw-Hill.

Stober, Dianne R., and Anthony Grant (2006). Evidence Based Coaching Handbook: Putting Best Practices to Work for Your Clients. Hoboken, NJ: John Wiley & Sons.

Whitmore, John (2009). Coaching for Performance: GROWing Human Potential and Purpose: The Principles and Practice of Coaching and Leadership. Boston: Nicholas Brealey.

Wilson, Judith, and Michelle Gislason (2010). Coaching Skills for Nonprofit Managers and Leaders: Developing People to Achieve Your Mission. San Francisco, CA: Jossey-Bass.

Zeus, Perry, and Suzanne Skiffington (2002). The Coaching at Work Toolkit: A Complete Guide to Techniques and Practices. New York, NY: McGraw-Hill.

## Executive Coaching

Goldsmith, Marshall, and Laurence Lyons (2006). Coaching for Leadership: The Practice of Leadership Coaching from the World's Greatest Coaches. San Francisco, CA: Pfeiffer.

O'Neill, Mary Beth (2007). Executive Coaching with Backbone and Heart: A Systems Approach to Engaging Leaders with Their Challenges. San Francisco: Jossey-Bass.

Peltier, Bruce (2010). The Psychology of Executive Coaching Theory and Application. New York: Routledge.

Ting, Sharon, and Peter Scisco (2006). The CCL Handbook of Coaching: A Guide for the Leader Coach. San Francisco: Jossey-Bass.

Underhill, Brian O., Kimcee McAnally, and John J. Koriath (2008). Executive Coaching for Results: The Definitive Guide to Developing Organizational Leaders. San Francisco: Berrett-Koehler.

## Multicultural Coaching

Belf, Teri-E (2002). Coaching with Spirit: Allowing Success to Emerge. San Francisco: Jossey-Bass/Pfeiffer.

Lennard, Diane (2010). Coaching Models: A Cultural Perspective: A Guide to Model Development for Practitioners and Students of Coaching. New York: Routledge.

Passmore, Jonathan (2009). Diversity in Coaching: Working with Gender, Culture, Race and Age. London: Kogan Page.

Rosinski, Philippe (2003). Coaching across Cultures: New Tools for Leveraging National, Corporate, and Professional Differences. London: Nicholas Brealey Pub.

## Business of Coaching

Brown-Volkman, Deborah (2003). Four Steps to Building a Profitable Coaching Practice: A Complete Marketing Resource Guide for Coaches. New York: IUniverse.

Fairley, Stephen G., and Chris E. Stout (2004). Getting Started in Personal and Executive Coaching: How to Create a Thriving Coaching Practice. Hoboken, NJ: J. Wiley & Sons.

Grodski, Lynn and Allen, Wendy (2005). The Business and Practice of Coaching: Finding Your Niche, Making Money, and Attracting Ideal Clients. W. W. Norton & Company.

Hayden, C. J. (2007). Get Clients Now!: A 28-day Marketing Program for Professionals, Consultants, and Coaches. New York: American Management Association.

Leshinsky, Milana (2007). Coaching Millions: Help More People, Make More Money, Live Your Ultimate Lifestyle. Xeno Press.

Mann, Monroe (2008). Start Your Own Coaching Business: Motivational, Life, Business. Irvine, CA: Entrepreneur.

The Coaching Starter Kit: Everything You Need to Know to Launch and Expand Your Coaching Practice. New York: Norton, 2003.

## Contributions to the Field of Coaching

Chodron, Pema (2004). Start Where You Are: A Guide to Compassionate Living. Boston: Shambhala.

Cornell, Ann Weiser (1996). The Power of Focusing: A Practical Guide to Emotional Self-healing. Oakland, CA: New Harbinger Publications.

Dass, Ram (2005). Paths to God: Living the Bahagavad Gita. Three Rivers Press.

Doidge, Norman (2007). The Brain Th at Changes Itself: Stories of Personal Triumph from the Frontiers of Brain Science. New York: Viking.

Goleman, Daniel (1996). Emotional Intelligence: Why It Can Matter More than IQ. London: Bloomsbury.

Heider, John, and Lao Tzu (1997). The Tao of Leadership: Lao Tzu's Tao Te Ching Adapted for a New Age. Atlanta, GA: Humanics New Age.

Kegan, Robert, and Lisa Laskow Lahey (2009). Immunity to Change: How to Overcome It and Unlock Potential in Yourself and Your Organization. Boston, MA: Harvard Business.

Lao Tzu and Brian Browne Walker (1995). Hua Hu Ching: The Unknown Teachings of Lao Tzu. San Francisco, CA: HarperSanFrancisco.

Levine, Peter A. (2005). Healing Trauma: A Pioneering Program for Restoring the Wisdom of Your Body. Boulder, CO: Sounds True.

Markova, Dawna (2000). I will Not Die an Unlived Life: Reclaiming Purpose and Passion. Conari Press.

Nemeth, Maria (2007). Mastering Life's Energies: Simple Steps to a Luminous Life. Novato, CA: New World Library.

Perls, Frederick Salomon (1973). The Gestalt Approach and Eyewitness to Therapy: Fritz Perls. Palo Alto, CA: Science and Behaviour.

Pert, Candace B. (1999). Molecules of Emotion: The Science Behind Mind-body Medicine. New York: Touchstone.

Rogers, Carl R. (2004). On Becoming a Person: A Therapist's View of Psychotherapy. London: Constable.

Rosenberg, Marshall B. (2005). Nonviolent Communication: A Language of Life. Encinitas, CA: PuddleDancer.

# About the Authors

### Martha Lasley, MBA, PCC

A founding partner of Leadership that Works, Martha creates results-oriented programs that inspire, motivate, and transform. Passionate about mentoring leaders, she helps teams develop a coaching culture where visionaries and change agents shift the power dynamics so that all people can thrive. As a trainer for the Center for Nonviolent Communication, she is an advocate for doing inner work in order to fuel the outer work we're called to do. Martha served on the faculty and coached MBA students at Capella University for ten years. She has authored two earlier books: *Facilitating with Heart* and *Courageous Visions*.

What people experience in Martha's presence is a woman who listens deeply to each person's heart and has a knack for drawing people into their power. She says, "I work with movers, shakers and changemakers who are stuck in back-to-back meetings, but have visions that rock. I help people make their visions real. Bold, compassionate, transformational coaching is a vehicle for creating a better world – where people value cultural humility, racial justice, shared power, and access to resources for all. My vision is to develop transformational coaches and facilitators in every nook and cranny of the world so that social change can flourish."

### Virginia Kellogg, MCC

Virginia takes a stand and fights for those who are marginalized and stays true to herself and the planet at a heart level. What makes Virginia's work unique is her commitment to expanding the reach of the coaching profession. She is a staunch supporter of making coaching available, moving coaching from its current context of privilege into the wide world. As a pioneer in connecting the field of coaching to the greater need in the world, she has been instrumental in creating the bridge between coaching, nonprofits and philanthropy and bringing coaching innovations into the social sector. Passionate about bringing coaching to all people, she challenges the coaching profession to become more available and relevant to all communities.

She says, "I work with people to look at the biggest picture of their possible impact and move toward that. It might be family based, community or global work. When I worked as a coach trainer in the federal prison system, everything shifted for me. I really learned there that once human beings see what they have to offer, even a glimpse of that, they set about offering it. Even when locked up for 30 years, they find a way to offer their gifts. I learned about the power of coaching, the deep way that this process connects people to themselves and holds them to bring more of themselves into the world."

### Richard Michaels, MCC

Richard is a certified gestalt therapist, master certified coach and a visionary cofounder of the Coaching for Transformation certification training. He has been an executive coach and life coach for 18 years. Richard has been creating and facilitating personal, professional and spiritual development programs for over 35 years in the US, Canada and Mexico. The common thread in his work has been in-depth transformation through increasing self-awareness, self-confidence, creativity, skillfulness in communication and effective action. He was a founding member, mentor, fund-raiser and former trustee of Kripalu Center for Yoga and Health, Lenox, MA.

Asked why he coaches, he shares, "I'm enlivened by the process. It calls me into deep connection with myself and others. Whether my client's task is building an inspired team, working with a board of directors, staff, colleagues, or recognizing and following a new vision—self-awareness, communication, and seeing from new points of view are foundations for realizing the potential within individuals and groups. Clients and students inspire me to become more vulnerable and free and committed to transformation."

Outside of coaching and training, Richard is a passionate oil painter. A source of inspiration, learning and satisfaction, it has deepened his way of seeing and coaching others to support the unfolding of their creative potential. He is author of *Moments on Canvas: Paintings by Richard Michaels*, see www.RichardMichaelsArtist.com. He is married and lives in Great Barrington, MA and spends part of the year in Oaxaca, Mexico.

### Sharon Y. Brown, MS, PCC

As a catalyst for personal, organizational and community transformation, Sharon supports people to envision powerful futures, overcome obstacles and co-create or advocate for the changes they want for their lives, families, organizations and communities. Drawing on her deep connection with Spirit and the ancestors, Sharon brings warmth and compassion in addition to a fierce commitment to collaboration, connection, personal and cultural awareness, and justice.

Sharon joined the Leadership that Works faculty in 2010 after leading the team that developed the multicultural coaching curriculum. She currently trains and mentors aspiring certified coaches and also teaches coaching skills in school, workplace, prison, and community settings. Sharon is actively involved in the innovative work of Leadership that Works to make coaching skills widely available to community members and direct service providers to help shift the way they communicate, collaborate and partner with people they serve or engage.

Sharon says, "Coaching skills transformed my life, so I'm passionate about helping people experience the power of coaching—personally and collectively. I truly believe coaching skills can support personal empowerment, deep cross-cultural connection, and a commitment to co-creating and advocating for organizational and community change."

# Index: Coaching in Action

# Index

Made in the USA
Columbia, SC
28 November 2018

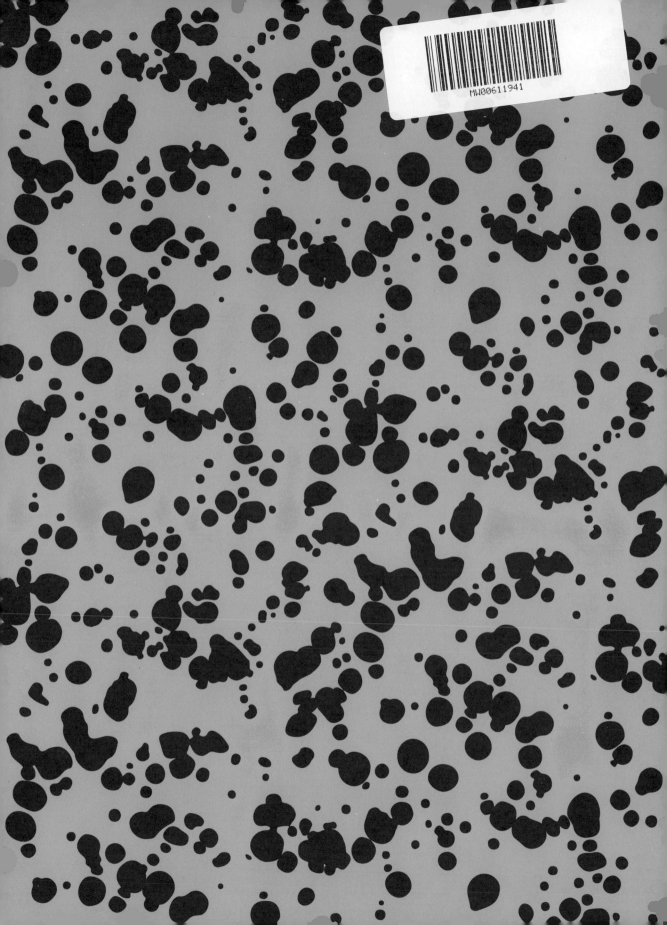

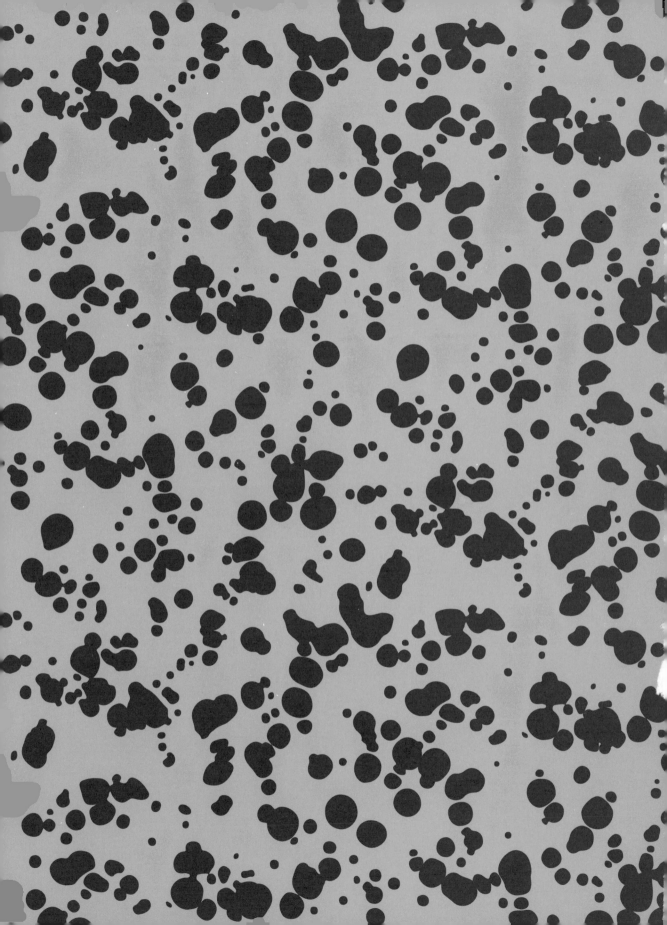

# ANNA JONES  Easy Wins

Also by Anna Jones:

*A Modern Way to Eat*
*A Modern Way to Cook*
*The Modern Cook's Year*
*One: Pot, Pan, Planet*

# ANNA JONES
# Easy Wins

12 flavour hits, 125 delicious recipes,
365 days of good eating

Photography by Matt Russell

4th Estate · *London*

Anna Jones is a cook, writer, the voice of modern vegetarian cooking and the author of the bestselling *One: Pot, Pan, Planet*, *A Modern Way to Eat*, *A Modern Way to Cook* and *The Modern Cook's Year*.

Her books are sold in ten countries and have been translated into five languages. *One: Pot, Pan, Planet* was a Sunday Times bestseller and *The Modern Cook's Year* won the coveted Observer Food Monthly Best New Cookbook Award and The Guild of Food Writers Cookery Book Award. Her previous books have been nominated for the James Beard, Fortnum & Mason and Andre Simon awards.

Anna believes that vegetables should be put at the centre of every table, and is led by the joy of food and its ability to affect change in our daily lives. She lives in Hackney, East London, with her husband and two children.

For Esca. You bring the sun out

# Introduction

Standing at my kitchen counter, chopping some vegetables, throwing them into a pan and then ending up with a meal that tastes incredible will forever amaze me. Simple ingredients shown a little love and attention come together to make more than the sum of their parts. This to me is an Easy Win. A little moment of kitchen alchemy that reassures me. Recipes that are reliable sources of joy in a world that is ever-changing.

Unbelievably, I've been cooking as my job for twenty years, and in that time I've seen the way we cook and eat at home change almost completely. The time we spend in the kitchen is less, but we expect much more flavour from our food. A recipe must be fast but clear, easy but layered with taste. We are all on a quest for flavour, especially in vegetable-led cooking. There has been nothing short of a revolution when it comes to putting plants at the centre of our plates. We are all eating more vegetables, and that thrills me. Now I want to help you find a new roster of classic, repeatable recipes that become favourites – to help you make the most of every meal you cook.

That's where the twelve ingredients in this book come in. I also think of them as Easy Wins, ingredients that exceed expectations. They sit quietly in your cupboard or fridge, asking nothing, staying fresh for weeks or months, but when called on add a serious hit of flavour for very little effort.

Lemons, olive oil, vinegar, mustard, tinned tomatoes, capers, chilli and harissa, tahini, garlic, onions, miso and peanut butter. These are the twelve ingredients I use most often in my kitchen to make food taste great, and I know they will be the favourite ingredients in your kitchen too. They seem to be favourites for almost everyone I talk to – loved ingredients that are already in our kitchens. I landed on these twelve after months of observing, note-taking and asking friends about the things that help them cook the best food. They are all ingredients that last a long time, are relatively affordable and easily available. All of them add an element of flavour that I love and crave.

I have chosen only twelve ingredients, so there is a full chapter on each ingredient and a generous number of recipes for you to

Easy Wins

delve into. If you buy an ingredient mentioned in this book, there will be many ways to use it. There is nothing more annoying than a recipe book that asks you to buy sumac or yuzu, for instance, to only use it once.

It's important to mention that some of the ingredients I have chosen come from cultures that are not my own and that I use with respect and reverence, honouring the traditions they come from, the artisans who make them and the memories and meaning they hold for the people to whom they belong. Dotted through the book are recipes from some friends and favourite cooks whose knowledge and knowing of these ingredients is far greater than mine.

My hope with this book is that you cook a few, or maybe even all, of the recipes from a chapter, and in doing so get to know each ingredient, its nuances and its multifaceted flavour. In the tahini chapter, you might learn how bitterness can be a good thing and how it can counter sweetness. In the miso chapter, you will build umami in different ways when you mix it with cheese in a rarebit or with mustard to roast beetroots. It's only by actually cooking that we create the balance of flavour and texture that tastes good to us, and then we learn and adapt how we cook to suit our own palates.

When I had my son Dylan, I had post-natal depression and felt wholly unlike myself. For those months I felt mostly panicked about cooking, not knowing what to choose and not being able to find the time to shop for that night's dinner. It shifted how I think about cooking; it was something that had always come quite easily to me, but for a time it was a stress, another thing on my very full plate that I grew to begin to resent having to do. Luckily those days passed, and my love of cooking returned, but it shifted my perspective permanently to make my recipes as easy as they could be, from the shopping to the table.

This book was written during a summer heatwave, very pregnant with my son Esca and in the months when he was a baby. In those days before and after, my focus was sharply pulled, using the time I had in the most efficient way. Often, I was not sure when my next window to write or cook might be. The recipes in this book are a reflection of that time and of my life.

Recipes with an outrageous amount of flavour for the work it takes to put them together, leaning on ingredients that add an immediate and upfront hit of flavour. All the recipes are, as usual, choreographed and carefully thought out so that they take the least time possible. Each window of time where something might be boiling or roasting is used to do another small task, such as making a topping or cooking something to serve it with, so your cooking window is compact but calm, clear and ordered, wasting no time.

A lot of the work of cooking happens before and after you put a pan on the heat. That is often not the hard part. The deciding, shopping, unpacking, the washing-up. It's often not a lack of skill or desire that stops us from cooking but a lack of other things – from the headspace to plan and shop, to budget or accessibility. I can't make your life less busy, but I have tried to stick to a palate of ingredients that are easily available and for the most part affordable, and to write recipes that are pared back and don't ask you to use every pan or dish in the house.

I have tweaked how I write my recipes in this book to make shopping and cooking as easy as possible. This book lists the amount of each ingredient needed not just in the ingredients list but also in the method at the point at which you use it, so you don't need to cast your eye back over to the ingredients list. It may seem like a small thing, but I've found it much easier to cook from recipes this way. I hope you do too.

And lastly but perhaps most importantly, there is a guide to the ways in which we can shop, cook and eat in a way that treads more lightly on the planet. From how we can reduce waste to the ways in which we can use less energy when we cook. Things we might know and need a reminder of, and hopefully some new tricks too. Saving food, time, energy and money.

I want this book to become full of recipes that are reliable friends and that bring a smile to your face. Dinners that come together so quickly and easily that you no longer need to look at the book. Meals that are so delicious you end the day on a high, patting yourself on the back, because you made something so good. Daily moments of triumph. Easy Wins.

# Golden rules for easy wins

often there will be key things ahead which will be useful to know at the start. Reading the recipe will let you see the big picture and what you are aiming for.

## 4. Cooking <u>without</u> a recipe

Think about balancing flavour. Read over the chart on pages 230–231, which will help you ask some useful questions about the decisions you will make as you cook. You want to balance flavour and texture, while also having some contrast in flavours and textures, and also think about when to season and when to add acidity before you start cooking.

## 1. Think sustainably

It has never been more important to consider the sustainability of how we eat, cook and store our food. If you are reading this book, you have already made a great start by eating more vegetables and cooking from scratch. When planning meals, make sure you use up food you already have – do a quick fridge and cupboard check before you shop. When shopping, opt for food less travelled – local and seasonal. If food is from further afield, choose long shelf-life food that is less likely to be flown in. Think of the energy you are using when you cook. Do not waste.

## 2. Shop well

The food you make is only as good as your ingredients. Buy the best you can within your means. Eating in-season fruit and veg will taste better and be lighter on the planet. For so many of us, budget is a huge consideration, so simpler recipes with fewer ingredients are your friends.

## 3. Cooking <u>with</u> a recipe

Read the recipe first. I am guilty of charging into a recipe without looking ahead, but reading over the recipe before you start is key: you might think you know what's coming, but

## 5. Be flexible

A recipe or a dish is a framework, and if you don't have every ingredient or every piece of equipment you can usually improvise. I am not saying you can replace the hero ingredient, but you could swap capers for olives or parsley for basil. You could use a hand-held blender instead of a food processor. Swap like for like, spice for spice, herb for herb, dairy for dairy, keeping things roughly the same consistency if possible.

## 6. Season

Season well, season evenly and layer; think of the salty ingredients that will be part of your dish and balance those with the salt you add. See pages 10–15 for more on salt and seasoning.

## 7. Work methodically

I am not by nature a neat cook, but one thing I learnt as a chef was the benefit of working cleanly. Getting your ingredients and equipment out first, using a mixing bowl to gather waste, and cleaning as you go will make you a better cook and your cooking more successful.

'Taste at every stage of the recipe, then taste again.'

## 8. Control your heat

Remember, you are in control of the cooking process and your hob or oven. You can always take the pan off the heat or the tray out of the oven if things are cooking too quickly. Don't feel like once you start cooking a recipe you have to keep pace. I have added notes on all the cooking times in the recipes, which encourage you to use visual markers like browning and softness as well as timings.

## 9. Taste, taste, taste

Tasting and adjusting is the one thing that chefs do that home cooks tend to miss. Taste as you go. Taste at every stage of the recipe, then taste again. Tasting and adjusting the seasoning and balance of acidity, sweetness and umami will make your food as delicious as it can be.

## 10. Make it your own

This is your dinner. Make it taste good to you. Your taste buds are unique, so this food should reflect that – that could mean more dill, more capers, less lemon, more crispy breadcrumbs. It should be a plate of food you are proud of and want to eat. Recipes are a guide; you are cooking for yourself and the people around your table.

## 11. The final layer

Making your food sing. Often what sets great food apart is a finishing touch. Crispy sage in brown butter spooned over pasta or fried eggs. A coriander and green chilli chutney on top of a dal. A salsa verde next to some roasted veg. It's this final element, a last topping that takes the flavour and texture to the next level. Often, a flavour-boosting finish is something that can be made in the time the 'main' element is cooking. It could be as simple as chopping some herbs or nuts to top a bowl of soup. This is the extra bit that makes food great.

## 12. Eat with your eyes

We eat with our eyes. I know that when I make a bit of extra effort to make my food look good, it makes me value what I am eating more and makes me feel sated in a different way, whether that's putting the food on a plate you love, scattering over some herbs or just taking care of how you put each spoonful on the plate.

## 13. Fill your plate with plants

We all know that eating plants is good for us and the planet. If you have this book in your hands, I'll take that as a given. Eating a wide variety of plants is important. According to Tim Spector, aiming for thirty plants a week, including nuts, seeds, pulses, whole grains, fruit and vegetables, will help us have a healthy gut microbiome, which is key to overall health. We counted up our weekly plant tally, and we all got to thirty much more easily than I expected. And Dylan found it a fun challenge. Bonus points for fermented foods.

# Planet-friendly cooking

Sustainability can be a complicated topic. Let's start with some good news. The fact that you are reading this book means you are already off to a good start – eating lots of plants and cooking from scratch.

Here are some simple, positive changes we can make every day in our kitchens. Some of these might feel obvious, but we all need a reminder now and then. You might already be doing a lot of this; if so, could you encourage someone else to make these changes? We need an army of people making small, repeatable everyday changes.

## Eat mostly plants

If we want to help slow, and begin to reverse, climate change, it is widely agreed that the most powerful thing we can do is eat fewer animals and more plants. That might mean one meal a day without meat (though I would encourage much more if you can); for others it might mean fine-tuning your vegan diet. Try to make sure that as many of the food decisions you make as possible line up with how you want the world to look.

## Waste less

After putting vegetables at the centre of your diet, reducing your waste is the next most impactful thing you can do. It's an easy win; it costs nothing. Think about how you shop so as not to overbuy food. Store it carefully and do a quick, regular mental inventory of what needs to be used before shopping. Use best-before dates only as a guide – your instinct will tell you if it is good to eat. Be flexible – don't be afraid to swap and change recipes to use up what you have.

## Eat a diverse plate

The world's capacity to produce food is being undermined by our failure to protect plant and animal life – biodiversity. You can help by varying what you eat, the fruit, the veg, the pulses, the grains and dried goods. If we eat a wide range of different foods, not only is it more nutritious, we also support farmers in growing lots of different crops and encouraging biodiversity. We currently rely on a handful of crops, many of which are being drastically over-farmed and are decimating the soil

Support sustainable farming and eat as much variety as you can fit into your diet. Additionally, this can help with supporting your gut microbiome – it's suggested 30 plants a week is a good aim to keep your gut healthy.

## Eat locally and seasonally

Ensure your diet is as seasonal and local as possible within your means. Eat fruit and vegetables that are in season and are grown as close to you as your circumstances and budget allow. Trying to buy UK-grown dry goods is also a great idea: there are great pulses, grains, honey, oils and vinegar produced in the UK.

## Consider air miles

Food miles are a huge part of the discussion around sustainability. But it's often hard to know exactly which foods are high on the food miles scale and what impact that has on their carbon footprint. I generally check labels and try to buy fresh foods as locally as possible and only buy dry goods from further afield that are likely to have been shipped not flown. Foodmiles.com is a good resource.

## Protect soil

Soil is essential, home to 98% of life on Earth, and we need it to sustain all life. But our soils are degrading at an alarming rate, and soil is being lost 40 times faster than it is being made. We have taken soil for granted and now one-third of the world's arable soils are degraded. The situation is urgent, as it takes a thousand years for one centimetre of topsoil to form. It is generally accepted that if nothing is done, we only have 60 harvests left. If we do not radically change how we grow and produce food now, our children will not be able to feed themselves.

You can help by switching your shopping habits. If you have the means and access, choose to buy produce from growers practising conservation or regenerative farming. If that is a bridge too far,

consider buying organic – your money will be supporting farmers and farming methods that put soil health at the core of their business. It is my sincere hope that these farming practices will become more widespread in the coming years and more accessible and affordable to all.

## Choose fairtrade

While I base my shop around local and seasonal food as much as I can, we live in a world with a global food system. Buying foods from communities on the other side of the planet can help support and regenerate local economies, good farming practices and hence the environment. By buying fairtrade, you are guaranteeing fair prices and investing in local communities. Buying fairtrade means you are sending a clear message to the food system that you care about the people who grew or made your food. Fairtrade also requires farmers to adhere to sustainability targets.

## Consider energy

Consider the energy you use when you cook. It's not something which is often part of the sustainability conversation. A third of the energy we use at home is used in the kitchen, so try to cook things in one pan or tray, and only turn on one heat source (either the hob or the oven, not both) to reduce the energy use in your kitchen. If you turn the oven on, don't preheat it for more than five minutes, and try to cook a couple of things at once. If you are cooking in a pan, put a lid on it. Make sure your fridge is not overfilled, but your freezer is more efficient if it is full.

## Do what you can

Make the changes that you can within your lifestyle, time and budget. Don't look back or feel guilty, look forward, with every day an opportunity for positive change.

'We need an army of people making small, repeatable everyday changes.'

# Salt and seasoning

If you want good-tasting food, after buying quality ingredients the next most important thing you can do in your kitchen is season your food well. It's said that salt makes food taste more like itself. All you need to season your food well is salt and your taste buds. It's a part of cooking everyone can get excited about, no matter your skill or means.

Salt is a mineral. It's one of a few key nutrients we need to stay alive, to maintain our body's balance, so we need to eat it daily. We are wired to crave the salt that keeps our bodies working, so to us salt makes everything taste better.

Salt amplifies flavour but can alter texture and enhance or mellow other flavours. There is a skill to adding salt, or seasoning. Adding good salt at the right time in cooking will give you well-seasoned food. If you season well while cooking, you won't need to add salt to your food on the table. Home-cooked food as a rule will almost always be lower in salt than processed food.

Salt doesn't just enhance flavour, it reduces our perception of bitterness, enhances sweetness and reduces our perception of acidity in food. Salt should taste clean and flavourless, like the taste on your lips after a dip in the sea. For us to taste salt, it must be dissolved in water, either the water we cook with or our saliva when we eat it.

## Types of salt

### Salt of the earth

- Table salt
  Likely sourced from an underground salt mine (though all salt originally comes from the sea). Dense and very salty, it is purified to remove other minerals and usually has added iodine. I don't use this salt unless I am in a pinch.

- Coarse or rock salt
  Like table salt but with bigger crystals.

### Sea salt

The salt left behind when seawater evaporates; the processes used to extract the salt yield different types of salt:

- Fine sea salt
  I use fine sea salt for seasoning water for pasta and veg and for anything where I need to measure it in tea-spoons, like breadmaking or baking.

- Flaky sea salt
  This is my most-used salt for seasoning almost everything, from veg before roasting to finishing salads. It forms miraculous pyramids. I always use Halen Môn sea salt.

- Sel de gris and fleur de sel
  A special, originally French, type of sea salt, sel de gris is coarser and fleur de sel has a flower-like grain. These can be used instead of flaky sea salt; sel de gris will sometimes need grinding first.

- Kosher salt
  Popular in America, this is salt with no additives which is finer than flaky salt and good for cooking with. Different brands have different grain sizes, so they are not interchangeable.

## How to season

### A pinch of salt

I keep my salt in a shallow, wide bowl on the kitchen surface next to the hob. It's important to be able to get all five fingers into the bowl; small bowls and salt pigs do not allow for that.

### The four-finger pinch

When recipes say a pinch of salt, most of the time they don't literally mean a two-finger pinch. Every chef I have worked with uses a more solid pinch, using three or four fingers to scoop up a good pinch of salt. I use four fingers, leaving out my little finger but using my other three fingers and my thumb to form a little platform for a good amount of salt to sit on. You can use this pinch for when you are seasoning a small area or when the salt will dissolve (like a dressing).

### The upturned sprinkle

One way chefs ensure an even distribution of salt is to take a generous pinch, turn their hand around so the pinched fingers are facing upwards, then, with the fingers still facing up, wriggle the hand back and forth to scatter the salt evenly. The upturned sprinkle is for when you have a large surface to season evenly – like a tray of veg for roasting or the top of a focaccia. There is a useful video on what is called the 'wrist wag' salting technique if you need to see it.

### The palm pinch

For things that need a generous seasoning – think water for blanching veg or pasta water – I use a palm pinch. I gather salt from my bowl with all four fingers and my thumb so I have a decent half-palm pinch of salt. Remember here, a lot of this salt will stay in the water when you boil or blanch, so you are not literally adding this much salt.

### Season evenly

It might feel like the annoying behaviour of a TV chef, but seasoning from a height is actually a good thing to do. It means the salt falls evenly over whatever you are trying to season. It goes without saying that this is not needed if the salt is going into a liquid.

'Salt should taste clean and flavourless, like the taste on your lips after a dip in the sea.'

### Season often – layering

When you season is as important as how. Good cooks season little and often throughout the cooking process, adding salt at every stage and building saltiness slowly in each part of what's being cooked. Adding it to ingredients throughout the cooking process can actually transform not just how they taste but the molecular structure of the food, for example changing the texture, colour and aroma of the ingredients too.

### How to taste

When tasting food, you are not tasting for saltiness but for the food to taste at its peak, for the flavour to be bright, upfront and immediate, not flat. Well-salted food does not taste of salt.

## Salting different foods

### Vegetables

Vegetables contain pectin, which is the stuff that makes jam set and keeps vegetables crunchy. When we cook, we soften the pectin in fruit or vegetables. This happens through ripening, heat or seasoning with salt. I can't think of a vegetable that doesn't benefit from salt.

· Roasted vegetables
Salt and toss in oil before roasting and then again at the end of cooking.

· Blanched or boiled vegetables
Very generously salt water for blanching; most of the salt will go down the drain. Salting also helps vegetables hold on to more nutrients. I taste this water to check how salty it is. Obviously, it will be hot, so use a spoon and allow it to cool a little before tasting. It should taste decently salty to you. By tasting time and time again, you are developing a sense of the perfect level of salt for you and for the veg you are cooking.

· Pan frying or sautéing vegetables
Add at the beginning of cooking and then again at the end.

### Pre-salting

Watery veg (and fruit) benefits from salting before you cook it. This will allow the salt to do its work and season the veg more evenly, and it will draw some of the water out, so be sure to pat veg dry beforehand if you are cooking them. Aubergines are a good example here.

### Raw fruit and veg

Salt is hygroscopic (that means it loves water). When it hits the surface of fruit or veg, it draws out the moisture. There is then an imbalance of a salty layer on the outside and less salty cells inside – so the non-salty cells start to move outwards and the effect is the veg sheds its water. This is useful in salting tomatoes, or for any veg you want to be less watery.

### Potatoes

They need a good amount of salt. I use about one-third more salt when I'm seasoning potatoes than I do with any other root vegetable. I just think potatoes need more salt.

### Tomatoes

Like potatoes, tomatoes absolutely need salt. I always season my tomatoes, if I'm going to eat them raw, with a generous amount of salt and a splash of acid, usually red wine vinegar, and let them sit and absorb the salt and the acid for at least ten minutes.

### The exception: mushrooms

I always salt mushrooms after they have cooked or browned, as salting them earlier encourages them to release liquid, which means they take longer to brown and may be tougher when cooked.

### Eggs

Eggs absorb salt easily – it helps their proteins come together at a lower temperature, which keeps them tender. I add a pinch to any eggs I am whisking before cooking,

Easy Wins

or I add salt to the water if I am poaching them. Salt does not get through the shell of an egg, so season boiled eggs after cooking, and the same goes for fried.

### Pulses and grains
As a young chef, I was taught never to salt my beans while cooking. I can safely say this is nonsense. I have cooked beans both with and without salt to compare, and the salted beans are softer and, it goes without saying, tastier. If you are soaking your beans, season the soaking water; if not, add salt to the beans from the beginning of cooking. As beans are cooked for a long time, more of the salt from the water will have a chance to get into the bean, so you don't need as much salt in the water as if you were boiling veg or pasta.

### Pasta
There is an idiom that pasta water should be 'as salty as the sea'. To me, it's an exaggeration, though I have seen pasta cooked in seawater. If you have ever had a full gulp of seawater, you will know it is unbearably salty. Pasta water should be heavily seasoned with salt (remember most of it will go down the plughole when it's drained): I usually add 2 very generous four-finger pinches to a 5-litre pot. You will get to know how much salt to use – how much your pot needs for the amount of people you regularly cook for. As with the water for cooking veg, I taste the water I am going to cook pasta in to check for salt. Be careful to let it cool and then taste and add more if you think it needs it.

### Rice
Basmati rice has a delicate fragrance and adding salt can mask this, so, thanks to cook Nik Sharma, if I am cooking plain basmati I will not season it with salt. The delicateness of the basmati comes through, and I make sure the food I am serving with the rice is well seasoned to balance it out.

### Bread and baking
There are many theories on when to season your dough, especially if you make sourdough bread. Ideally, you add it after mixing the flour and water and letting that sit to come together first, but if you add it sooner your bread will still work.

### Fat
Salt needs water to dissolve, so it won't dissolve in pure fat like olive oil. Most fat has a little water content – butter, yoghurt, salad dressing, etc. It takes salt longer to dissolve in fat or anything with a low water content, so season it as early as possible to allow time to absorb.

### Sweet
Salt is just as important when it comes to sweet food. A little salt can amplify the flavour and sweetness in a dessert. Think of salted caramel; a sea salt-topped cookie. Fine salt should be used in batters, pastries and custards, etc., and flaky salt should be used for topping things before baking or finishing.

## Other ways to add salt

As well as using actual salt to season when we cook, it's important to take into account that many ingredients we add to our cooking are inherently salty and will add to the overall seasoning of a dish. I like to think about what I am adding to the dish before I start cooking, and adjust the level of salt I add accordingly at each moment when I would season. If I am making a tartare sauce, for instance, using both salty capers and cornichons, I would start by making an unsalted mayonnaise and then add the capers and cornichons, the lemon and parsley, and taste to see if it needed actual salt as well. It may need more capers, more lemon, more herbs, not just more salt. So: taste, think, adjust, taste, think, adjust, adding each thing you think it's missing little by little until it's perfect.

'I can't think of a vegetable that doesn't benefit from salt.'

Salt and seasoning

Two of the twelve ingredients I picked to focus on in this book are 'salty' ingredients. Capers and miso, on page 150 and 284 respectively. Reading and cooking your way through these chapters is a good way of understanding how salty ingredients can be used to create well-seasoned food.

Salty ingredients I use in my kitchen:
- Capers
- Chutney
- Ketchup
- Kimchi
- Mayonnaise
- Miso
- Mustard
- Olives
- Pickles or cornichons
- Preserved lemons
- Salted butter
- Salty cheese (Parmesan and pecorino)
- Seaweed
- Soy sauce
- Vegetarian fish sauce

## Rescuing oversalted food

We have all overseasoned food; I have many times. Sometimes the level of saltiness can be past repair, but, most of the time, one of the tricks below will bring back a salty pot of food.

Dilute the salt
Add more unsalted ingredients to dilute the level of salt. Starchy things are particularly good here – potatoes, rice, pasta, grains. Add more water if it's a liquid dish.

Add acid
Acid helps neutralise saltiness, so adding lemon, lime or vinegar, or even tinned tomatoes or yoghurt (which are acidic), will help. Start by adding a little on a spoon to see what the acid does, then correct the whole dish.

Add dairy or oat milk
Adding dairy will do two things – it will add some sweetness and acidity, which will both counter the saltiness and coat your mouth when you eat, creating a kind of barrier for the salt.

Add raw potatoes or dough
A piece of raw potato or dough added to a soup or stew will absorb some of the salt and therefore reduce the saltiness. Take it out before eating, obviously.

Add a little sweetness
Sweetness can help counter saltiness, so a pinch of sugar or a drop of maple syrup or honey could help. Equally, if a salad has been oversalted, try adding something sweet: think slices of peach to a tomato salad or some sliced grapes to a herby green salad.

Halve it
Halve the oversalted dish or sauce, then correct it a half at a time; diluting it can work well here. You can refrigerate or freeze the second half and tackle that another time.

If all else fails, order takeaway
There is always another chance to make dinner, so don't beat yourself up.

## What about pepper?

Pepper is a spice and, to me, does not have a place in every dish or on every dinner table. Spicing is flavour but also part of culture and tradition. I use many other spices (cumin, coriander seed, smoked paprika) just as much as I use pepper. See page 338 for more on spices.

# Lemons

Lemons the colour of the sun sit heaped in a bowl on my counter. A constant in my cooking, second only to salt. A seasoning. A brightening. Sharp juice squeezed over, food stands to attention with pips left behind in my hand. Zest the skin and a haze of misty oil creeps up to my nose and fills the room with freshness and promise. My cooking is a love letter to lemons. A foil for richness, a lift when something is lacking, sharp against sweet. To me, almost everything benefits from lemon. Sometimes I scratch the skin and sniff and stand at the bowl, not cooking, just smelling, spirits lifted.

# On Lemons

Lemons are a third seasoning in my cooking. So often when a dish is lacking something, lemon will complete it. Once I have tasted for salt, my next thought is lemon – juice added at the end of cooking for a lift, or zest for zing. Like salt, adding lemon helps food taste more like itself.

You can harness so many different flavours from a lemon: the sharp, refreshing acidity from juice; the brightening sherbet of fresh zest; the rounded lift of a roasted lemon, with its sharp but caramelised notes. And then there's the preserved lemon, which brings something altogether different to the table, salty, tangy, full.

Sharp, Acid, Sour, Bitter

## Types

- Amalfi lemons
  From the Italian coast, these are pitted and knobbly. They taste a bit sweeter than your average variety.

- Meyer lemons
  A cross between lemon and mandarin/pomelo. They are my favourite lemons. You don't see them much in the UK, but I eat more than my fair share when I travel to California.

## Goes well with

Almost everything

| | |
|---|---|
| asparagus | feta |
| basil | ginger |
| blueberry | honey |
| broccoli | mint |
| caper | olive |
| chilli | parsley |
| chocolate | potato |
| coconut | rosemary |
| coriander | saffron |
| courgette | sesame |
| corn | thyme |
| cumin | tomato |
| dill | turmeric |

## Favourite uses

Juice needs to be added late on in cooking, as the sharpness will be lost if it's heated for too long.

- Grated over feta before baking
- To finish a dal
- Whole slices cut thinly then chopped small in a salad
- Cut into wedges and roasted with potatoes
- Squeezed into a glass of water with maple syrup and a pinch of salt
- Zested over squares of chocolate
- Cooked into a pickle with mustard seed and chilli

## Storage and tips

I keep as many as I will use in a week on my counter, with the rest stored in the fridge, replacing the ones in the bowl as they are used.

Lemons past their best can be squeezed and the juice frozen in ice-cube trays.

Half a lemon is almost always enough; the other half will sit for days in your fridge until needed, as will a zested lemon.

Most lemons are unripe. Keep them in your bowl until you can dent them with a finger – they will be juicier. If you don't have time for that, rolling them quite hard under your palm on a surface will help release the juice.

Waxed and unwaxed – most lemons have an edible waxed coating so that they keep for longer. It's waxy and greasy to the touch and turns sticky when wet. Run under hot water, then rub enthusiastically with a tea towel to get some of it off.

Extend the life of a squeezed lemon by putting it halved into your dishwasher for sparkling dishes.

## What to buy

Buy unwaxed organic lemons if you can, or, even better, ones with leaves – they are a marker of the lemon's freshness.

# Quick preserved lemons

4 large unwaxed lemons, roughly
chopped into 1cm pieces
2 tablespoons fine sea salt
1 tablespoon golden caster sugar

Preserving lemons in their whole
state, adorned with nothing but salt,
relies on an essential ingredient
many of us are short of: time. By
chopping the lemon into smaller
pieces, adding a little sugar to balance
the immediate acidity of the fruit
and accelerating the process with a
little heat, you can have a batch of
preserved lemon pieces much quicker
than whole ones. These are a good
thing to make if you don't always keep
fresh lemons on hand, or to preserve
them when lemons are in season in
your part of the world.

MAKES 2 MEDIUM JARS

*Prepare your lemons*
Halve 4 large unwaxed lemons then
chop them into rough 1cm dice,
removing seeds and trying to keep as
much juice as possible. Add the pieces
to a small saucepan as you go.

*Bash the lemons*
Using the blunt end of a rolling pin,
push and pound the lemons lightly
in the pan to extract the juice. Add
2 tablespoons fine sea salt and
1 tablespoon golden caster sugar
and pound again to mix well.

*Cook the lemons*
Bring the lemons to a simmer, then
turn the heat down to the very lowest
setting and cook until the peel just
starts to soften, about 4–5 minutes.
Set aside to cool completely, then
transfer to a large sterilised jar.
These lemons will keep very happily
in their jar in the fridge for up to
a month.

Lemons

# One-pot pasta al limone

400g spaghetti or linguine
2 large unwaxed lemons
1 clove of garlic, peeled and
    bashed but kept whole
100ml olive oil
1 teaspoon flaky sea salt
50g salted butter or vegan butter
40g Parmesan or vegan
    Parmesan-style cheese
    (I use a vegetarian one),
    grated
½ a bunch of basil (15g), leaves
    picked and torn (optional)

Pasta al limone. I can't think of a plate of food that shines a light on lemon flavour in quite the same way. Pasta, lemon and Parmesan come together in alchemy to create something worthy of any table.

I tested out a lot of pasta al limone recipes before I landed here. Some had cream, some had finely chopped lemon but none came close to the creaminess of this one and none was as easy. The one-pan method (where you cook the pasta and sauce in one pan) was made for pasta al limone. The starchy water it creates is exactly what is needed to thicken the lemony sauce and coat the pasta. I like to keep this pretty simple. I have suggested some basil as an option at the end, but these simple lemony noodles are enough on their own and a true pantry pasta. If you like, you could add some greens or even stir through some warmed cannellini beans.

SERVES 4

*Fill the pasta pan*
Put 400g spaghetti or linguine into a large lidded saucepan. Grate in the zest of 2 large unwaxed lemons and add 1 clove of garlic, peeled and bashed but kept whole, 100ml olive oil and 1 teaspoon flaky sea salt.

*Add water and cook*
Add 1 litre boiling water, cover with a lid and bring to the boil. As soon as it boils, remove the lid and simmer for 8 minutes, using a pair of tongs to turn the pasta in the thickening pasta water every 30 seconds or so as it cooks.

*Add the lemon juice*
Once the pasta has had 8 minutes, squeeze in the juice of one of the zested lemons and simmer for a final 2 minutes with the lid off.

*Finish the pasta*
Once almost all the water has evaporated, take the pan off the heat, stir in 50g salted butter or vegan butter and 20g grated Parmesan or vegan Parmesan-style cheese and leave to sit for a minute or two, so the pasta can absorb most of the remaining water and form a lemony sauce. Taste and add more salt, lemon juice and butter or olive oil as needed. Tangle into 4 bowls and finish with the rest of the Parmesan and ½ a bunch of torn basil leaves, if you like.

# Lemon, green chilli and Cheddar tart

1 organic egg, beaten (or oat milk for vegans)

320g ready-rolled all-butter puff pastry (vegan pastry if needed)

1 unwaxed lemon

2 tablespoons extra virgin olive oil

150g good-quality mature Cheddar or vegan Cheddar-style cheese, grated

½ an onion, peeled and very thinly sliced

1 green chilli or jalapeño chilli, finely sliced

½ a bunch of parsley and/or coriander (15g), leaves picked

½ a bunch of mint (15g), leaves picked

The idea for this came from watching pizza man Chris Bianco put loads of thinly sliced lemon on top of his ciabatta. I thought the same thing would work with a tart. This tart is fresh, the richness of the pastry is countered by the zip of lemon, the sweetness of onion and the pep of green chilli and it's rounded out with the bite of the Cheddar. It's also a very friendly recipe that looks like it took a lot longer to make than it did. I've doubled this to feed a crowd.

The pastry has a very quick and fuss-free pre-bake to make sure it's crisp, then it's topped with the Cheddar, onion, lemon and chilli. It's essentially an assembly of a dish. You need to use a cold baking tray at the start so that the pastry holds its nice layers when it gets into the oven.

SERVES 4

*Preheat the oven and prepare the pastry base*
Preheat the oven to 200°C/180°C fan. Beat 1 organic egg, if using, in a small bowl. Lay out the 320g ready-rolled all-butter or vegan puff pastry on a cold baking tray. Working quickly to keep it cold, score the pastry to form a rim about 1cm around the edge of the rectangle – this will form the edge of the tart once cooked. Prick the middle of the base all over with a fork and lightly brush with the beaten egg or a little oat milk. Bake in the oven for 20–25 minutes until golden.

*Slice and dress the lemon*
Slice three-quarters of 1 unwaxed lemon, leaving a final quarter for later. I want you to slice it really thinly here, discarding the ends, seeds and any slices that have too much pith as you go. A mandoline can be helpful. Toss the slices in 1 tablespoon extra virgin olive oil and a pinch of sea salt.

*Take your pastry out of the oven*
As soon as the pastry comes out of the oven, press down on the middle rectangle of the base (which will have puffed up a little), flattening the middle of the pastry ready for the toppings and leaving a nice risen border around the outside. Turn the oven up to 220°C/200°C fan.

*Assemble the tart and bake*
Scatter 150g grated Cheddar or vegan Cheddar evenly over the baked pastry base, followed by ½ an onion, peeled and very thinly sliced, the dressed lemon and finally 1 finely sliced green chilli. Return to the oven for 15 minutes and bake until the pastry is deep golden and the cheese is bubbling.

*Make the herb salad*
Put the picked leaves from ½ a bunch of parsley and/or coriander and ½ a bunch of mint into a small bowl with the juice from the remaining quarter of a lemon and 1 tablespoon olive oil. Season with salt and pepper, then toss to dress the leaves.

*To serve*
Remove the tart from the oven and allow to cool for a few minutes before serving with the dressed herbs.

# Double lemon pilaf with buttery almonds

300g basmati rice
75g unsalted butter
100g whole almonds,
    roughly sliced
2 onions or shallots, peeled
    and finely sliced
½ teaspoon ground turmeric
1 tablespoon nigella seeds
3 unwaxed lemons
½ a bunch of coriander (15g),
    leaves picked
½ a bunch of mint (15g), leaves
    picked

This double lemon pilaf uses lemon first in the rice, which mellows a little as it cooks, and then a shock of bright lemon juice to finish. I have kept the recipe simple, but I've suggested a few vegetables that I often add at the end as the seasons change. It's great on its own, though, with some sautéed greens and yoghurt.

SERVES 4

*Preheat the oven and prepare the rice*
Preheat the oven to 180°C/160°C fan. Wash 300g basmati rice well then soak in cold water for 20 minutes, or as long as you have.

*Brown the butter and toast the almonds*
Heat a large, ideally heavy-based, lidded, ovenproof sauté pan over a medium heat, then add 75g unsalted butter and 100g roughly sliced whole almonds. Once the butter has started to brown and the almonds look toasty, use a slotted spoon to scoop the nuts out, leaving most of the butter behind.

*Cook the onions*
Add 2 peeled and finely sliced onions or shallots to the browned butter and cook for 5 minutes, until softened and beginning to brown. Add ½ teaspoon ground turmeric and cook for another minute.

*Add the rice and bake*
Drain the rice well and add it to the sauté pan. Cook over a medium heat for a couple of minutes, stirring all the time to seal the rice. Add 1 tablespoon nigella seeds, the zest and juice of 2 unwaxed lemons, 750ml boiling water or vegetable stock and a teaspoon of sea salt. Cover the pan and place in the preheated oven for 15–18 minutes, or until the rice is fluffy and all the water has been absorbed.

*Finish the pilaf*
Top with the buttery almonds, the leaves from ½ a bunch of both coriander and mint, and finish with a squeeze of juice from the final lemon.

Seasonal additions:
Add the vegetables to the sauté pan with the onions and stir through the rice before putting in the oven.

Spring
Podded or frozen peas and asparagus (tips left whole, stems sliced; add for the last 5 minutes of cooking).

Summer
Green or runner beans, topped and tailed, runners sliced, and a handful of cherry tomatoes.

Autumn
Sautéed sliced leeks and shredded sweetheart cabbage or greens (sauté the leeks and cabbage in butter or olive oil first).

Winter
Shredded kale or cavolo nero and very thinly sliced or grated squash.

# Lemon traybake with green olives and herbs

2 onions, peeled and cut into
   wedges
5 tablespoons extra virgin
   olive oil
4 long green Turkish peppers,
   halved and deseeded, or
   1 large green pepper, halved
   and quartered
1 unwaxed lemon
2 medium courgettes
150g runner beans or green beans
a bunch of spring onions
100g stone-in green olives
a bunch of mint (30g),
   leaves picked
a bunch of parsley (30g),
   leaves picked
1 clove of garlic, peeled and grated
150g Greek or oat Greek yoghurt

I will eat lemon in any form. I've considered eating the sweet Amalfi ones like an apple. I do understand, though, that some people do not share my overenthusiasm for all forms of lemon – no matter how sharp or bitter. And I appreciate that, for some, adding pieces of whole raw lemon to salads, as I love to do, may be a step too far. This traybake uses chopped whole lemon slices, but they are roasted, which tempers their sharpness and acidity and sweetens them. This is entry-level whole-lemon eating.

This is a late spring to summer combination of vegetables but you could swap out the runner beans for asparagus in spring and for purple sprouting broccoli in winter.

SERVES 4

*Roast the longer cooking vegetables*
Preheat the oven to 240°C/220°C fan. Put 2 onions, peeled and cut into wedges, in a large shallow baking tray with 3 tablespoons extra virgin olive oil, 4 Turkish peppers, halved and deseeded, and a good pinch of sea salt and freshly ground black pepper. Toss to coat everything, then roast in the oven for 20 minutes.

*Prep the rest of the veg*
Roughly cut 1 unwaxed lemon into thin slices, then halve each slice. Chop 2 medium courgettes into large 3cm chunks. Cut 150g runner beans in half at an angle or trim 150g green beans, leaving them whole.

*Add the rest of the veg*
Once the onions and peppers have been roasting for 20 minutes, add the lemon slices, courgettes and beans to the roasting tray. Reserve 2 spring onions for later and add the rest to the tray, keeping them whole. Toss

so everything is coated in oil. Return to the oven for a further 10–15 minutes until everything is tender and roasted.

*Make the green olive and herb dressing*
Destone 100g green olives and roughly chop them. Roughly chop a bunch of both mint and parsley and finely chop the reserved spring onions. Put everything in a bowl with 2 tablespoons extra virgin olive oil and 1 peeled and grated clove of garlic, season with freshly ground black pepper and mix together. Taste and add some salt or more olive oil as needed.

*Put everything together*
Spread 150g Greek or oat Greek yoghurt over the bottom of a serving platter, then pile on the lemon-roasted vegetables. Spoon over the olive dressing, finishing with a little more olive oil if needed. Serve with warm flatbreads.

# My perfect lemon salad

2 heads of butter lettuce or
    4 Little Gems
2 handfuls of peppery leaves
    (I like rocket or mustard leaf)
2 unwaxed lemons
4 tablespoons extra virgin
    olive oil
1 teaspoon runny honey or
    maple syrup
½ teaspoon Dijon mustard
hard cheese for grating
    (I use a vegetarian pecorino
    or Parmesan), optional

This is my platonic ideal of a salad. Very lemony and very bright. It sits perfectly next to almost anything and cuts through even the richest foods. I have included the washing instructions for the leaves, because it is so important that they are clean and dry for the dressing to cling to them properly.

SERVES 6

*Prepare the lettuce*
Remove any wilted or bruised leaves from 2 heads of butter lettuce or 4 Little Gems, then trim each head at the root to break the lettuce into individual leaves. Drop them into a sink filled with tepid water. Trim and discard bruised leaves or stalky bits from the peppery leaves and drop the remaining leaves and tender stems into the sink too. Swirl the greens in the water then drain them well. Wash the leaves once more in cold water. Spin dry in a salad spinner.

*Chop the lemon*
Slice then finely chop 1 unwaxed lemon, removing the seeds as you go. You want both the flesh and the lemon peel here. Be sure to chop both as small as possible. Grate the zest from the other lemon into a jam jar and squeeze in the juice from the second lemon.

*Make the dressing*
Put 4 tablespoons olive oil into the jam jar with 1 teaspoon runny honey, ½ teaspoon Dijon mustard, a good pinch of sea salt and freshly ground black pepper, and shake to mix. Taste the dressing by dipping a leaf of lettuce into it – the water in the lettuce will mellow the dressing so this is always the best way to taste it.

*Finish the salad*
Put the leaves into a large mixing bowl with the lemon pieces, add a good pinch of salt and pepper, then a few tablespoons of the dressing. Toss together gently with your hands to coat each leaf. Taste and add more dressing if needed. Pile high on a serving plate and finish with some grated Parmesan or pecorino cheese if you like.

# Lemon chickpeas with halloumi and seeded honey

5 tablespoons olive oil
1½ teaspoons nigella seeds
½ teaspoon ground turmeric
1 × 700g jar chickpeas
½ teaspoon coriander seeds
½ teaspoon Turkish chilli flakes
50g runny honey or maple syrup
200g kale, spring greens or
    cavolo nero
1 unwaxed lemon
1 × 200g block of halloumi

This was a quick dinner one night when reserves were low but the need for flavour and texture was high. Jarred chickpeas are a quick dinner staple in our house. Plump, rich and pleasingly salty, they are perfectly seasoned already, so make an almost foolproof base for a meal. I like to hit them up with a good jolt of lemon and here they get frizzled with spices and served with lemony greens and a honeyed halloumi. This is inspired by something I ate at Bubala, a great Middle-Eastern vegetarian restaurant in London. I try to use jarred chickpeas here, as tinned don't work as well. If you are using tinned, add less liquid from the tin.

SERVES 4

*Cook the chickpeas*
Add a tablespoon of olive oil to a medium saucepan. Add 1 teaspoon nigella seeds and ½ teaspoon ground turmeric and cook on a medium heat until sizzling and fragrant. Standing back a little in case they spatter, add a 700g jar of chickpeas and their liquid to the pan. Cook for 10 minutes, stirring occasionally, until soft and starting to break down a little.

*Mix the seeded honey*
While the chickpeas are cooking, put the remaining ½ teaspoon of nigella seeds, ½ teaspoon coriander seeds and ½ teaspoon Turkish chilli flakes in a pestle and mortar and bash until fine, then add a good grinding of black pepper. Stir the spices through 50g runny honey or maple syrup and set aside.

*Prepare the greens and lemon*
Remove the leaves from the stalks of 200g greens. Tear or cut any very large leaves and finely slice the stalks, discarding any super tough bits. Thinly slice half an unwaxed lemon, then chop the slices so you have small lemon pieces. Save the other half of the lemon for later.

*Cook the greens*
Put a large frying pan over a medium heat. Add 3 tablespoons olive oil and the stalks of the greens and cook for a couple of minutes to soften the stalks. Add the leaves and the lemon pieces, stirring so the lemon and oil coat the greens. Fry for 3–5 minutes until slightly crisp and bright green. Remove the greens from the pan and set aside for a moment.

*Cook the halloumi*
Cut a 200g block of halloumi into thick slices lengthways. Put the kale pan back on a medium heat and add the halloumi with a tablespoon of oil and cook for a minute or two on each side until golden brown. Put the golden halloumi on a plate and pour over the seeded honey.

*To serve*
Squeeze the remaining lemon half over the greens and stir to coat. Divide the spiced chickpeas between shallow bowls and top with the honeyed halloumi and a handful of greens.

# Emily's lemony celeriac schnitzel

½ a bunch of thyme (10g), leaves
   picked
3 unwaxed lemons
1 large celeriac (800g), peeled and
   sliced into roughly 2cm-thick
   discs
125g panko breadcrumbs
3 cloves of garlic, peeled
70g blanched hazelnuts
3 tablespoons olive oil
250g roasted red peppers from
   a jar, drained
1 tablespoon pomegranate
   molasses
1 teaspoon Turkish chilli flakes
1 teaspoon cumin seeds,
   coarsely ground
1 teaspoon tomato purée
1 preserved lemon, deseeded and
   finely chopped
60g Parmesan or vegan
   Parmesan-style cheese
3 tablespoons plain or spelt flour
2 large organic or free-range eggs
200ml groundnut oil
a handful of coriander leaves,
   parsley and dill to serve
peppery salad leaves, to serve

My great friend Emily loves lemon
as much as I do. So much in fact that
Dylan calls her Aunty Lemony. Emily
has been by my side in the kitchen
and as a friend for the last fifteen
years and has been a huge part of all
of my books and recipes. So it would
not have been right to have a lemon
chapter without a recipe from Em.

SERVES 4

*Preheat the oven and cook the celeriac*
Preheat the oven to 180°C/160°C fan.
Bring a large half-full pan of salted
water to the boil. Add the picked
leaves from ¼ a bunch of thyme and
the juice and zest of 1 unwaxed
lemon. Peel and slice 1 large celeriac
into 2cm-thick discs and, once the
water is boiling, simmer them for
8 minutes until they are soft when
pierced with the tip of a knife but
still holding their shape. Remove,
drain and set aside.

*Toast the breadcrumbs*
Meanwhile, put 50g panko breadcrumbs with 3 peeled cloves of garlic
and 70g blanched hazelnuts on a
large baking tray, drizzle with olive
oil and season with salt. Bake for
10 minutes or until golden. Remove
from the oven and leave to cool a
little. Turn the oven down to
170°C/150°C fan.

*Make the muhammara*
Put 250g drained roasted red peppers,
1 tablespoon pomegranate molasses,
1 teaspoon Turkish chilli flakes,
1 teaspoon coarsely ground cumin
seeds and 1 teaspoon tomato purée
into a food processor and pulse until
well combined. Add the breadcrumb
mixture to the blender with the
juice and zest of another unwaxed
lemon. Pour in a tablespoon of olive
oil and pulse to a textured, dippable

sauce. Stir through 1 finely chopped
preserved lemon and season
if needed.

*Prepare the breadcrumbs*
Get out three shallow bowls and
put 75g of panko breadcrumbs into
one then grate in the zest of the last
unwaxed lemon and 60g Parmesan
into the bowl. Season with pepper
and set aside. Put 3 tablespoons plain
or spelt flour into the second bowl
with the remaining picked thyme
leaves, season and set aside. Crack
2 eggs into the last bowl, give them
a good whisk and set aside.

*Heat the oil*
Pour 200ml groundnut oil into a wide
high-sided frying pan and place over a
medium heat. While the oil is heating,
breadcrumb the celeriac.

*Breadcrumb then fry the celeriac*
Dip the celeriac in the seasoned flour,
dusting off any excess, then into the
eggs, followed by the breadcrumbs,
making sure each piece is evenly
coated. Continue until all the celeriac
is coated.

   Once the oil is hot enough (about
180°C), add 2 of the celeriac schnitzels
to the pan and fry for 2 minutes on
each side until golden and perfectly
crisp. Carefully remove the schnitzels
from the oil, put them on a baking tray
and into the oven while you fry the
other two.

   When all the schnitzels are fried,
put a good spoonful of muhammara
on a plate, top with the schnitzel and
scatter over the herbs dressed in lemon
juice, and the peppery salad leaves.

# Dylan's lemony ice lollies

*Strawberry, apple and lemon*
10 strawberries, plus a few
    extra slices
1 red apple, cored and roughly
    chopped
200ml apple juice
juice of 1 unwaxed lemon

*Watermelon, pear and lime*
1 pear, cored and chopped
juice of 2 unwaxed limes
200ml apple juice
2 large slices watermelon (15g)

Many of the recipes for this book were cooked during a blistering July heatwave in London. There were pies in 40 degrees, which got eaten after the temperatures dropped each evening. But in the daytime all we wanted was cold, refreshing, citrussy things. Dylan was on ice-lolly duty, coming up with his favourite refreshing combinations of fruits. These were the winners: a sherbety strawberry one and lime, pear and watermelon. (I know it's a lemon chapter, but I'm making an exception.) We each ate at least 2 a day.

MAKES 6 MEDIUM-SIZED ICE LOLLIES

*Strawberry, apple and lemon*
Put 10 strawberries, 1 cored and roughly chopped red apple, 200ml apple juice and the juice of 1 unwaxed lemon into a blender and blend until smooth. Add some extra strawberry slices to each mould then pour the mixture into your lolly moulds and freeze for at least 5 hours.

*Watermelon, pear and lime*
Put 1 cored and chopped pear, the juice of 2 unwaxed limes and 200ml apple juice into a blender and blend until smooth. Cut 15g watermelon into slices that will fit within your lolly moulds, add to each mould, then pour in the mixture and freeze for at least 5 hours.

# Hot lemon and bay pudding

25g unsalted, room temperature
    butter, plus extra for greasing
225g caster sugar
3 large free-range or organic eggs
30g plain flour
zest and juice of 3 unwaxed
    lemons
250ml whole milk
1 fresh bay leaf
icing sugar, to serve

This is one of those magical puddings that is spooned into the dish as one unassuming batter and comes out of the oven transformed into a double-textured pudding: a light lemon sponge top and a rich lemony custard at the bottom. One of the best examples I know of kitchen alchemy and one of the easiest puddings. I add bay here, as I love lemon and bay together. The bay brings some grounding depth to the sherbety hit of lemon. This pudding is inspired by one made by JR Ryall of Ballymaloe. You can skip the bay if you like things more classic, though. I've not found a good way to make this without eggs, so there are no vegan switches here.

SERVES 4

*Cream the butter and sugar*
You will need approximately a 1.2-litre pie dish, lightly greased with softened butter. Preheat the oven to 180°C/160°C fan. Put 25g of butter into a mixing bowl or the bowl of a stand mixer and turn the mixer on low. Gradually add 225g caster sugar. As there is not much butter it won't go creamy and fluffy but will remain sandy.

*Separate the eggs*
Carefully separate 3 large free-range or organic eggs and put the yolks into one bowl and the egg whites into another very clean bowl (a spotless bowl will help to get the best lift out of your egg whites when you whip them).

*Add the yolks to the batter*
Add the egg yolks to the sugar mixture, then mix in 30g plain flour. Then add the zest and juice of 3 unwaxed lemons followed by 250ml milk.

*Whisk the egg whites*
Using a hand-held electric whisk or the whisk attachment of your stand mixer, whisk the egg whites until they form stiff peaks (when the bowl is held upside-down the whites should stay put in the bowl).

*Fold in the whites*
Use a metal spoon or spatula to carefully fold the egg whites into the batter. Be gentle to keep as much lightness from the egg whites as possible. Trust the process here; it will seem too liquidy and split but it will come together in the oven.

*Bake*
Put 1 fresh bay leaf into the bottom of the dish, then pour in the batter and bake for 40 minutes until the top is golden and set. Dust with icing sugar and serve immediately. It's also good cold from the fridge the next day.

# Citrus and maple sherbet

4 big unwaxed lemons, 8 if you
   want to serve in lemons
   (the Amalfi ones are best
   if you can get them)
1kg ripe cantaloupe melon
8 clementines, peeled, deseeded
   and roughly chopped
150ml maple syrup, plus more
   if needed

This sorbet is bright, pink and refreshing. I grew up eating lemon sorbet in hollowed-out lemons in restaurants on holiday. To a seven-year-old me there was nothing more delicious, chic or fun than dessert in a lemon, and I still stand by that at forty-four. Please know, though, that there is absolutely no need to hollow out a lemon to serve this in. I often make it as a quick dessert in little glasses.

I love making ice cream and sorbet. I have an ice-cream machine, but I rarely get it out. It's heavy and feels like a faff, so I only use it on special occasions (see the chocolate caper ice cream on page 170). Here I ask you to freeze the fruit first, then use a food processor to blitz to an instant sorbet with some maple syrup. It feels like magic. I make this for me and my kids a lot in the summer, scooped into cones, which feels almost as fun as a lemon.

MAKES A BIG TUB OF SORBET, ENOUGH
TO FILL LOTS OF LEMONS

*Prepare the lemons*
If you don't want to go all in on the kitsch filled lemons, you can cut the top and bottom off 4 lemons, then place on a chopping board and use a knife to cut away the zest and white pith from 4 lemons. Cut the flesh in half and pick out any seeds, then roughly chop the flesh into 2–3cm pieces. The zest from the outside can be kept for making tea or cooking.

If you want to serve the sorbet in lemons, cut the bottom off 8 big unwaxed lemons at the stalk end so they sit flat, then cut the top third off each lemon (keeping these tops). Use a spoon to scoop out the flesh from all 8 lemons. You will be using the flesh from 4 lemons in this recipe (see above), so for these pick out

any seeds and chop the flesh into 2–3cm pieces. The rest can be kept for something else. If using them to serve in, you want to keep the lemons whole so you can fill them later and keep the lemon flesh for the sorbet. Put your 8 hollowed-out lemons and tops into the freezer.

*Prepare and freeze the melon
and citrus*
Cut 1kg ripe cantaloupe melon in half and spoon out the seeds. You will need about 500g of the flesh. Roughly chop the flesh into 2–3cm pieces and put it into a container with 8 peeled, deseeded and roughly chopped clementines (you should end up with about 600–700g of peeled clementines) and the roughly chopped flesh of the 4 lemons. Freeze the fruit for 8 hours, or ideally overnight. It can be kept frozen for up to a month, until needed.

*Make the sorbet*
Remove the frozen fruit from the freezer and put in a high-powered food processor, along with 150ml maple syrup. Blend for 3–4 minutes, until smooth. You might need to stop a few times and use a spatula to scrape down the sides to make sure the food-processor is catching everything. Taste and add more maple syrup if needed; how much you need will depend on the sweetness of your fruit.

Scoop straight into bowls or the hollowed-out lemons and eat immediately, or put into a tub to keep in the freezer. You can keep any leftovers in the freezer, and leave it out for 5 minutes before scooping – if it becomes icy you can blend again before serving.

# Double lemon cake with streusel topping

250g plain flour, plus 80g for the
  streusel topping
20g porridge oats
250g plus 2 tablespoons golden
  caster sugar
zest of 4 unwaxed lemons
200g unsalted butter at room
  temperature, plus 70g cold
  unsalted butter and a little
  extra for the tin
80g ground almonds
1½ teaspoons baking powder
1 teaspoon bicarbonate of soda
½ teaspoon sea salt
3 large organic or free-range eggs
1 teaspoon pure vanilla extract
250g natural yoghurt or oat
  yoghurt
100g good-quality lemon curd,
  plus extra to serve
crème fraîche, to serve

This is my ideal cake. Lemony, soft-crumbed and streusel-topped. The idea for this recipe comes from baker Thalia Ho, who has a cake in her book *Wild Sweetness* that ripples lemon curd through it. This cake is loaded with three types of lemon: lemon zest studded through the cake batter, the curd on top and a hit in the streusel topping.

MAKES A 23CM CAKE, SERVES 12

*Make the streusel topping*
Put 80g plain flour, 20g porridge oats, 2 tablespoons caster sugar and a pinch of sea salt into a bowl and mix well. Add the zest of 1 unwaxed lemon, then add 70g of cold unsalted butter. Use your fingers to rub the butter into the flour like a crumble mixture until large sticky clumps have formed. This is your streusel.

*Preheat the oven and line your tin*
Preheat the oven to 180°C/160°C fan. Grease a 23cm cake tin with butter, then line with baking paper.

*Mix the dry ingredients*
Put 250g plain flour, 80g ground almonds, 1½ teaspoons baking powder and 1 teaspoon bicarbonate of soda into a mixing bowl with ½ teaspoon sea salt and mix with a whisk until there are no lumps.

*Cream the butter and sugar*
In a stand mixer with the paddle attachment, or in another mixing bowl with an electric hand whisk or wooden spoon, cream 200g unsalted butter and 250g golden caster sugar until pale and fluffy. This will take about 3–4 minutes in a stand mixer and longer by hand.

*Add the eggs*
Scrape down the bowl and add 3 large organic or free-range eggs one at a time, mixing on a low speed until each one is incorporated, then mix in 1 teaspoon pure vanilla extract, the zest of another unwaxed lemon, and 250g natural yoghurt or oat yoghurt.

*Add the dry ingredients*
Add the dry ingredients to the batter in the mixing bowl and mix until just combined. This is a very forgiving cake, but minimal mixing will make it as light as possible.

*Put the batter into the cake tin and add the lemon curd*
Scrape the batter into the prepared tin and level it gently with a spatula, then spoon over 100g good-quality lemon curd in little patches and use your spoon to swirl it in a little. Scatter the streusel topping evenly to the very edges of the cake; don't pile it into the middle or it will sink.

*Bake the cake*
Bake for 1 hour, or until a skewer inserted into the middle of the cake comes out clean. Cover the top of the cake with foil if it looks like it's browning too fast. Allow to cool for 15 minutes in the tin, then remove from the tin and leave to cool completely on a wire rack. Serve with some crème fraîche rippled with a little lemon curd.

# Lemon soda bread

400ml whole milk or oat milk, plus a little extra for brushing
3 unwaxed lemons
350g plain or plain spelt flour, plus extra for dusting
350g wholemeal flour
2 teaspoons bicarbonate of soda
2 teaspoons flaky sea salt
150g unsalted butter or vegan block, at room temperature
2 teaspoons good-quality runny honey or maple syrup

This is one of the most moreish things I have made in a while. This recipe is a lesson in how lemon can lift even something hearty like soda bread. Lemon is used in lots of ways here: the juice turns milk into buttermilk; the zest lifts the flavour of the bread and is also added to a honey and lemon butter to spread on the just-out-of-the-oven slices. Soda bread is a great entry-level bread to make if bread-making or sourdough scares you. It's so easy and needs no kneading, rising or shaping. This is best served fresh on the day it is made. After that it needs toasting. Once cooled, you can slice and freeze it, then toast the slices from frozen as needed.

MAKES ONE GOOD-SIZED LOAF

*Preheat the oven and prepare the tray*
Preheat the oven to 180°C/160°C fan and line a shallow baking tray with baking paper and a dusting of flour.

*Make the buttermilk*
In a jug, measure out 400ml whole milk or oat milk, then add the zest and juice of 2 unwaxed lemons. Give it a good stir and set aside for 15 minutes to thicken up and curdle. Oat milk won't thicken or curdle but the recipe will still work perfectly.

*Make the dough*
In a large mixing bowl, mix together 350g plain flour, 350g wholemeal flour, 2 teaspoons bicarbonate of soda and 1 teaspoon of flaky sea salt. Make a well in the middle of the flour and pour in the thickened, lemony buttermilk mixture, stirring until there are no dry floury patches, then use your hands to bring it together to a rough dough. Don't over-mix here. The less you mix it, the lighter the bread will be; this is not like a normal yeasted bread dough.

*Shape and bake the loaf*
Tip the dough out on to a well-floured surface, use your hands to bring it together into a rough ball, then scoop it on to the lined and floured tray. Use a knife or dough scraper to make a large, deep cross on the top of the bread, brush with a little extra milk, then bake in the oven for 40 minutes until golden brown all over.

*Make the lemon honey butter*
In a small bowl, mix and mash 150g unsalted butter or vegan block, at room temperature, with the zest of 1 lemon and 2 teaspoons good-quality honey or maple syrup. Taste and add as much of the second teaspoon of sea salt as needed; this will depend on the saltiness of your butter.

*Take your loaf out*
Remove the bread from the oven and tap the bottom of the loaf. If you get a hollow sound, it's perfect, so pop it on a wire rack to cool. Leave to cool for about 30 minutes to an hour. Slice and serve warm with a thick spread of the lemon honey butter and/or jam. Keep any leftover bread well wrapped and eat within 2 days, or slice and freeze in a freezer bag.

# Olive Oil

The first pressing of olives, oil pouring in a thin, steady stream from a spout, green as grass and shimmering. Sipped from a spoon – buttery, peppery, like a freshly mown lawn. Like nothing I have tasted before or since. The oil on my counter is not green but golden; a bottle lasts barely a week for all its uses. A thick layer in a pan for sizzling. A plentiful pour over pasta, to season, coat and add richness. Beaten into cake batter. A deep layer to slow cook in, the vegetables taking on its blonde butteriness. Drizzled onto yoghurt with honey. To top vanilla ice cream. Glugged onto focaccia. Drinkable.

# On Olive Oil

I couldn't cook without olive oil. A good olive oil improves almost anything – it's one of my most-loved and most-used ingredients. Your food will taste good if you start with a good oil. It can feel hard to know which oil to use. There are so many, and they vary hugely in taste, quality and cost. And the expensive ones are not necessarily the best.

Oils will range from peppery to buttery, and while it may seem silly to taste your oil like you might a wine, it's not. Finding an oil you like the taste of in your price range will make all your cooking better. To me, the most important factor in olive oil is freshness. So when you buy oil, use it quickly and don't keep it for ages in your cupboard.

It's often said that olive oil should not be heated high for fear of its compounds breaking down and becoming unhealthy for us. Actually, the smoke point of extra virgin olive oil is quite high – 190°C or above – and most cooking in a home kitchen will be done far below this, so I use it for almost all my cooking.

In my kitchen, I have three olive oils. I use a decent but affordable extra virgin olive oil for almost all frying and cooking. A favourite more expensive olive oil is used for best – it's for finishing food that's already cooked, from soups to salads. Lastly, there is a light olive oil I use occasionally for making mayonnaise and for frying when I don't want an olive flavour.

I am generous with olive oil when I am cooking, and some of the amounts in these recipes might be more than you are used to adding. I use olive oil for the texture and mouth-feel it gives, as well as its flavour, and for that you need more than a thin drizzle. Many of the recipes in this chapter rely on a brave use of olive oil. Olive oil is a fat our body likes and needs, and I am sure these home-cooked dishes will still have far less fat than processed food.

Peppery, Buttery, Rich, Spicy

- First pressing
  The bright green, grassy oil from
  the first pressing of the olives.
  Worth seeking out.

- Extra virgin
  Other than grinding and pressing,
  no other chemicals or processes are
  used in its production. Good extra
  virgin will often taste peppery,
  grassy, fruity or spicy.

- Virgin
  One down in quality (and price) from
  extra virgin, it has minimal flaws.

- Light
  This refers to a lighter colour rather
  than a lower fat content. A refined
  oil with fewer nutrients and less
  flavour – produced using heat after
  the first pressing of the olives.

Goes well with

| | |
|---|---|
| almond | ice cream |
| caper | lemon |
| chilli | pulses |
| chocolate | rosemary |
| cucumber | soft herbs |
| garlic | tomato |
| greens | yoghurt |

Favourite uses

- For drizzling over almost anything
- For drizzling over focaccia, pasta,
  salads, scrambled eggs
- For finishing chocolate desserts
- For olive oil-roasted tomatoes
- To confit garlic
- Instead of butter in cakes
- To braise runner beans
- In a thick layer on top of a ribollita

Storage

Store somewhere cool and dark
with a consistent temperature:
temperature fluctuations from a
fridge, stove or oven are not good
for your oil. It's best stored in dark
bottles out of the sun in a cool place.

What to buy

- Spanish
  Belazu and Brindisa both import
  really good oil from Spain and are
  widely available. I use these oils
  a lot.

- Palestinian
  Zaytoun is a warm, peppery and
  affordable Palestinian oil I buy often.

- Greek
  Two Fields and Citizens of Soil
  offer a subscription of beautifully
  golden oil delivered straight to
  your kitchen.

- Italian
  Saint Rosalia is a verdant oil in
  excellent packaging. Selvapiana
  and Fontodi are oils I have been
  cooking with for years.

# Jalapeño and coriander oil

1 large bunch of soft herbs
  (I used coriander)
2–4 chillies, depending on heat
  (I used 3 jalapeños)
500ml extra virgin olive oil

Most of the time I use olive oil as it is, unadorned. A good olive oil needs nothing added to it. But I do know a lot of people who buy chilli oil, so this recipe encourages you to make it, not buy it. Most chilli oil in the shops uses rubbish oil and focus on chilli heat. I make this when I have lingering herbs or chilli to use up, and I often have both. I used coriander and jalapeños here, but any chilli and soft herb would work well. The oil keeps for ages, and I use it to top tacos, beans, soups and dips. Use a decent extra virgin but not the very best olive oil here. You want the oil to be mellow and buttery; the most important thing is to make sure it's fresh. I encourage you to use limp bunches of herbs, as it won't matter if they have started to droop, and the same goes for the chillies.

MAKES ABOUT 500ML OF OIL

*Blanch and ice the herbs*
Put a pan of water on to boil and get a large bowl of iced water ready next to your sink. Once boiling, blanch the herbs in the water for 20 seconds, then drain and immediately dunk under the iced water. Drain and pat dry on a tea towel.

*Blitz the oil*
De-stem the chillies and put the chillies, seeds and all, into a blender with the blanched herbs and pour in the oil. Blitz on high for a minute or so until you have a smooth, very green oil.

*Set up the sieve/muslin for draining*
Put a piece of muslin or a thin, clean tea towel over a sieve and set that over a mixing bowl or wide-mouthed jug. It's best to do this in or near the sink.

*Sieve your oil*
Carefully pour the oil into the centre of the muslin, allowing as much to drip through on its own as possible. Once the dripping has stopped, gather the corners of the muslin to create a little bag with the green herby oil in the middle. Use your hands to squeeze the top of the bag, pushing as much of the green oil through as possible. This might take a few attempts. You only want the herby paste left in the muslin. You can use the paste in the base of a curry or freeze it.

*Store the oil*
Pour the oil into a jug or bottle, where it will keep at room temperature for a couple of weeks, or in the fridge, where it will keep for a couple of months. If you keep it in the fridge, the oil will solidify. Just bring it to room temperature before you use it, or spoon it straight from the jar on to something hot, and it will turn back to oil immediately.

Ways to use the oil:

· To top tacos
· To spoon over pasta
· On a tomato salad
· To make a dressing
· Mixed with chopped fresh herbs for a quick topping

# Frizzled spring onion and olive oil dip

1 bunch of spring onions,
    trimmed
150ml extra virgin olive oil
1 teaspoon Turkish chilli flakes
    or ½ teaspoon chilli flakes
1 teaspoon caster sugar
½ teaspoon ground turmeric
150g thick strained Greek
    yoghurt
zest and juice of 2 unwaxed
    limes

John is obsessed with dips. He will dip almost anything, especially pizza crusts. I can't quite get into the pizza crusts into sour cream and chive dip he loves, but I do love a dip. This one is a take on the traditionally Chinese spring onion oil, but with a hit of chilli and turmeric, and sits on top of a thick lime yoghurt.

You can buy really good thick Greek yoghurt from the supermarket or your local shop. If your yoghurt is not thick (and by that I mean spoonable, almost the consistency of clotted cream), then you can strain the yoghurt yourself. Hang it in a piece of muslin or a clean thin tea towel over a mixing bowl overnight or for as long as you have to thicken it. It's fine out of the fridge overnight.

SERVES 4

*Prep and frizzle the spring onions*
Trim then thinly slice both the white and green parts of 1 bunch of spring onions, then put them into a small pan with 100ml olive oil and 1 teaspoon Turkish chilli flakes and cook over a low–medium heat until you can hear everything begin to sizzle. Cook until the edges of the spring onions are beginning to brown and crisp. Add 1 teaspoon sugar and ½ teaspoon ground turmeric and cook for another minute.

*Cool and season*
Take the pan off the heat and allow the oil to cool in the pan. Once cool, season with salt and pepper.

*Season the yoghurt and serve*
Mix 150g thick strained Greek yoghurt with the juice and zest of 2 limes, season well with sea salt, then put into a shallow bowl or on a plate. Swirl in the oil and serve with warm bread or raw veg for dipping.

# Spiced aubergines with cucumber salsa

150ml extra virgin oil, plus
    2 tablespoons
3 medium aubergines (about
    750g), trimmed and sliced
    lengthways into wedges
1 teaspoon cumin seeds
1 teaspoon coriander seeds
1 teaspoon ground turmeric
2 cloves of garlic, peeled and
    very thinly sliced
a small thumb-sized piece of
    ginger (15g), peeled and sliced
    into thin matchsticks
1 cucumber, peeled and roughly
    diced
zest and juice of 1 unwaxed
    lemon
a small bunch of mint, leaves
    picked
pinch of Turkish chilli flakes,
    plus extra for sprinkling
200g Greek yoghurt or oat
    Greek yoghurt
a drizzle of pomegranate
    molasses or runny honey,
    to serve
4 warm flatbreads, to serve

Aubergines love olive oil like no other vegetable. They literally lap up the oil, and the flavour. Thanks to the oil, these aubergines should be so soft and buttery that you can cut through them with a spoon. This way of cooking the aubergines in a good amount of decent olive oil and a little water is an easy route to the best aubergines I've ever tasted. It's all done in a tray, layering the flavours as you cook; the olive oil brings a warm golden richness to the aubergine.

SERVES 4

*Preheat the oven and the tin*
Preheat the oven to 180°C/160°C fan. Pour 150ml extra virgin olive oil into a large, deep roasting tin and put it in the oven to heat up.

*Prep the aubergines*
Salt 3 aubergines, sliced lengthways into wedges, generously. Carefully remove the hot oil from the oven, add 1 teaspoon cumin seeds, 1 teaspoon coriander seeds and 1 teaspoon ground turmeric, then lay the aubergine wedges in a single layer on top so they sizzle a little. Carefully add 150ml cold water (the oil will spit, so be careful) and roast in the oven for 15 minutes.

*Turn the aubergines and add the garlic and ginger*
Take the tray out of the oven, turn the aubergines so they cook evenly, then scatter 2 cloves of garlic, peeled and very thinly sliced, and 15g ginger, peeled and sliced into thin matchsticks, into the tray around the aubergine. Return to the oven for a further 15 minutes until the ginger and garlic are lightly golden and cooked.

*Make the cucumber salsa*
Put 1 peeled and roughly diced cucumber into a bowl with the zest and juice of 1 unwaxed lemon and 2 tablespoons extra virgin olive oil. Roughly chop a small bunch of mint leaves and stir into the cucumber with a pinch of Turkish chilli flakes. Season with a pinch of sea salt and a few grinds of freshly ground black pepper.

*Finish the aubergines*
Put 200g Greek yoghurt or oat Greek yoghurt on a platter or a few plates, then top with the aubergines, a spoonful of cucumber salsa, extra Turkish chilli flakes and a drizzle of pomegranate molasses or honey. Serve with 4 warm flatbreads.

# Pappa pomodoro

400g ripe cherry tomatoes
150ml good-quality extra virgin
    olive oil, plus extra for frying
    and drizzling
2 cloves of garlic, peeled and
    finely sliced
a bunch of basil (30g), leaves
    picked and stalks finely
    chopped
800g fresh tomatoes, roughly
    chopped, or 2 × 400g tins
    good-quality plum tomatoes
200g stale good-quality bread,
    like sourdough (2 slices) or
    ciabatta

I cooked this a lot as a young chef, both in the restaurants I worked in during stints cooking in Mallorca and Tuscany and at home, when tomatoes were cheap and plentiful.

This soup is a lesson in how olive oil can lift something from simple to incredible. Here it adds some buttery olive flavour but also when it hits the tomato it makes this soup creamy and many times more satisfying than it would be without it.

SERVES 4

*Char the cherry tomatoes*
Heat a large pan big enough to cook your soup in. Add 400g ripe cherry tomatoes and cook on a high heat until softened and charred at the edges. Add 100ml water to the pan to pull all the tomato flavours up off the bottom of the pan. Keep the heat on high to reduce the liquid by three-quarters.

*Fry the garlic*
When the tomato juices have all but cooked away, add a glug of oil to the pan and turn the heat down to medium. Add 2 cloves of peeled and finely sliced garlic and the chopped stalks from a 30g bunch of basil and simmer for a couple of minutes with the tomatoes, or until softened but not browning.

*Add the tomatoes*
Tip in 800g chopped fresh or tinned tomatoes. If you are using tinned, break them up with the back of a spoon, then add 600ml or 1½ tinfuls of cold water. Bring to the boil, then reduce to a simmer and cook for 15 minutes, stirring every now and then.

*Add the bread*
Tear 200g stale good-quality bread into the tomatoes in smallish pieces. I keep the crust on here, but if you

prefer take yours off. Stir in the bread and add a good pinch of sea salt and ground black pepper. Tear in almost all the basil leaves and let the soup sit on a low heat for 10 minutes.

*Finish the soup*
Pour over 150ml good-quality extra virgin olive oil, stirring it in. The soup should be a thick, almost porridge-like consistency. If you need to, add a few splashes of hot water to loosen it. Taste and check the seasoning, adding more salt and pepper if needed. Serve with the remaining basil torn over the top.

# Buttery green veg and herb braise

2 bulbs of fennel, trimmed and
  sliced into 6–8 wedges
650g medium waxy potatoes,
  peeled and halved if small, or
  cut into 3cm chunks if bigger
1 medium courgette, cut into
  irregular 3cm pieces
150ml extra virgin olive oil,
  plus 3 tablespoons
3 cloves of garlic, peeled and
  finely sliced
1 heaped teaspoon coriander
  seeds, crushed
a few sprigs of oregano or
  thyme (10g), leaves picked
1 unwaxed lemon, ½ thinly
  sliced, the remaining half
  to serve
150g green vegetables (e.g. green
  beans, podded broad beans
  or peas, asparagus or runner
  beans), cut into bite-sized
  pieces
200g thick natural yoghurt
a small handful of parsley leaves
  (15g), roughly chopped
a small handful of fresh dill (10g),
  and/or chives, finely chopped

Cooking vegetables in olive oil and water in this way brings out a buttery sweetness and allows the richness of the oil to lap around them as they cook. The result is beautifully cooked vegetables with a rich olive oil broth. I often make this as it is, but if you want a more filling meal then adding some cooked giant couscous or a tin of white beans for the last few minutes of cooking is a great idea.

SERVES 4

*Prepare the vegetables*
Trim 2 bulbs of fennel, then slice into 6–8 wedges, depending on the size of your bulbs. Peel and roughly chop 650g waxy potatoes into halves or 3cm chunks if they are bigger. Then roughly chop 1 medium courgette into irregular 3cm pieces.

*Heat the oil and cook the fennel*
In a large, wide, lidded heavy-based pan, heat 3 tablespoons extra virgin olive oil over a medium-high heat. Add the fennel and cook for 5 minutes, turning over occasionally until lightly golden on both sides.

*Add the garlic, herbs and oil*
Stir in 3 peeled and finely sliced cloves of garlic, 1 heaped teaspoon coriander seeds, crushed, and fry for a further minute, then add the potatoes, the leaves from a few sprigs of oregano or thyme, ½ an unwaxed lemon, cut into thin slices, and 150ml extra virgin olive oil along with 250ml cold water (or enough to cover the vegetables) and a big pinch of flaky sea salt.

*Cover and cook*
Cover, bring to a boil, turn down to a low simmer and cook for 15 minutes. After 15 minutes, stir in the courgette pieces and plenty of freshly ground black pepper along with 150g green

vegetables cut into bite-sized pieces and cook for a further 10–15 minutes until everything is soft. You may need to add the longer-cooking green veg with the courgettes first, and any quicker-cooking veg like peas only for the last 5 minutes.

*To serve*
Spoon the veg and some of the broth into bowls and top with a big spoonful of thick natural yoghurt and an extra squeeze of lemon, some chopped parsley and dill and a little more flaky sea salt and freshly ground black pepper.

# Stanley Tucci's spaghetti alla Nerano

about 200ml of olive oil
8–10 small courgettes, sliced
    into thin rounds
a large bunch of basil (75g),
    leaves picked
extra virgin olive oil, for
    drizzling
500g spaghetti
100–200g grated Parmesan
    cheese

This recipe comes with the kind permission of Stanley Tucci. It's the pasta I dream about most. After watching Stanley and Felicity (my friend and agent) eat it on his TV show, I made it every week over the summer. This plate of pasta is a lesson in the beauty of a few ingredients, cooked simply and with care, which Italians in my opinion do best. And also a lesson in how olive oil is the maker of greatness in a dish.

It takes a while to fry all the courgettes but the sweetness it brings out will pay you back. Try to use little sweet courgettes for this; the big ones can be more bitter which you don't want here.

SERVES 4

*Cook the courgettes*
Put about 200ml olive oil in a large pot and bring to a low boil over a medium-high heat. Slice 8–10 small courgettes into thin rounds and fry in batches in the oil until they are golden brown. Remove and set aside on paper towels. Sprinkle them with sea salt and scatter over 75g basil leaves. Transfer to a bowl and drizzle liberally with extra virgin olive oil.

*Cook the pasta*
Cook 500g spaghetti in plenty of salted boiling water until al dente and strain, reserving about 2 cupfuls (500ml) of the pasta water.

*Finish the spaghetti alla Nerano*
Place the cooked pasta back into the pan over a low heat with the courgette mixture and stir together gently. Add the pasta water, a little at a time, to create a creamy texture. You may not use all of the pasta water. Now gradually add 100–200g grated Parmesan to the mixture and continue to combine by stirring

gently and tossing. When the mixture has a slight creaminess, remove from the stove and serve immediately.

Note: The fried courgettes can be refrigerated for about 5 days for use at a later date. Best to bring them to room temperature before using.

# Butter beans with green olives and tomatoes

100ml extra virgin olive oil
2 onions, peeled and finely
   chopped
2 cloves of garlic, peeled and
   finely sliced
2 tablespoons tomato purée
1 teaspoon dried oregano
1 teaspoon caster sugar
1 × 400g tin finely chopped
   tinned tomatoes or passata
100g stone-in green olives,
   destoned
2 × 400g tins or 1 × 600g jar
   butter beans, drained
½ a bunch of parsley (15g),
   roughly chopped
½ a bunch of dill (15g), roughly
   chopped
200g feta, or vegan feta-style
   cheese, crumbled

These are loosely based on gigantes plaki – a Greek recipe for butter beans cooked with tomatoes and lots of olive oil. These are one of the things I like to cook a double batch of and have to eat for days. They are the kind of dish that's better on the second or third day. I use jarred butter beans, which are far superior, but if you can't get them, tinned will work; I find tinned less 'buttery' and not cooked as evenly. I use tins of the fine tomato pulp here or passata. If you are using chopped tinned tomatoes, whizz them up to break down any larger pieces of tomato.

SERVES 4

*Caramelise the onions and garlic*
Add 2 tablespoons extra virgin olive oil and 2 peeled and finely chopped onions to a large saucepan and place over a medium heat. Cook, stirring regularly, for 4–5 minutes until soft and just starting to caramelise. Add 2 peeled and finely sliced cloves of garlic and fry for another minute or so, keeping an eye on it until it is lightly golden.

*Add the tomato purée*
Add 2 tablespoons tomato purée, 1 teaspoon dried oregano, 1 teaspoon caster sugar, a big pinch of sea salt and a few grinds of freshly ground black pepper to the onions and garlic and stir together to cook the tomato purée into the oil for a minute or two.

*Add the oil and tomatoes*
Add the remainder of the olive oil (70ml) and a 400g tin of finely chopped tomatoes or passata. Bring to a simmer, then turn down the heat and allow to bubble, stirring occasionally, until the tomato sauce splits and you can see a layer of oil forming around the edges.

*Add the olives and beans*
Destone 100g stone-in green olives and add them to the pan with 2 drained 400g tins or 1 drained 600g jar of butter beans. Mix the beans and olives in and cook for 5 minutes over a medium heat until the beans are coated in the tomato sauce. Roughly chop half a bunch of parsley and half a bunch of dill and stir half of each into the beans.

*Put everything together*
Spoon big piles of the beans into bowls and top with 200g crumbled feta, more extra virgin olive oil, and the rest of the chopped dill and parsley.

*If you want to cook your own beans*
Soak 200g dried butter beans in cold water, ideally overnight but for at least 4 hours. Drain and place in a large heavy-based pan with a litre of water, 100ml extra virgin olive oil, 1 teaspoon sea salt, a few bashed cloves of unpeeled garlic and a few sprigs of hardy herbs (rosemary, thyme, bay all work). Bring the beans to the boil and cook over a high heat for 5 minutes, then reduce the heat to a simmer and cook for 1–2 hours, skimming away any scum that rises to the surface. Cook until the beans are just turning soft, and can be squashed with your fingers.

# Tortilla Español with herbs and shallots

2 large onions, peeled, halved
and thinly sliced
400ml extra virgin olive oil,
plus 2 tablespoons
6 medium waxy potatoes (650g),
peeled and cut into 3mm-
thick slices
8 medium organic eggs
1 small shallot, peeled and
finely diced
1 tablespoon red wine vinegar
1 stick of celery, finely sliced
a small bunch of parsley (25g),
leaves picked

Tortilla is one of my favourite things in the world to eat. A Spanish friend, Carolina, used to make it for us. She'd make a huge panful and we'd eat it for dinner warm and then cold the next day with vinegary tomato salad or in bocadillos. To me a tortilla is the perfect olive oil recipe, as frying the potatoes and onions in a generous amount of oil is key. The oil can be strained and kept for your next tortilla or any other savoury dish. A special mention here to my friend Kitty, who lent me her tortilla knowledge.

SERVES 4

*Cook the onions*
Peel, halve and thinly slice 2 large onions. You want the slices to be equally thin, so they all cook at the same time. In a small, non-stick round pan (about 24cm) heat 400ml of your best extra virgin olive oil on a medium-high heat. Add the sliced onions and cook, stirring every so often, for 5 minutes until they are soft and slightly golden. Remove the onions from the oil with a slotted spoon to a mixing bowl and set aside.

*Cook the potatoes*
Cut 6 medium waxy peeled potatoes into thin 3mm-thick slices, again making sure they are the same size so they cook evenly. Add them to the same hot oil and cook for 8–10 minutes, until they are soft and a knife goes through with no resistance. Drain the potatoes, keeping the oil in a heatproof bowl or jug for later. Add the potatoes to the bowl with the onions. No need to wash the pan as you will use it later.

*Whisk and add the eggs*
Lightly whisk 8 medium organic eggs in a small bowl, then pour them over the warm potatoes and onions

and stir gently to bring everything together. Season well with a good pinch of flaky sea salt, then cover with a plate that snugly fits over the bowl to rest for 10–15 minutes. This is a really important stage, as it makes everything thicken up, meld together and cook evenly.

*Cook the tortilla*
Once the mixture is rested, heat the same pan on a medium heat with 2 tablespoons of the oil you used earlier. Pour the egg mix into the pan and turn the heat down to the lowest setting for 1–2 minutes. Run a spatula around the edges a few times to make sure it's not sticking, then leave to cook for around 4–6 minutes until you can see that the bottom and edges are setting.

*Flip the tortilla*
Give the pan a shake to make sure the bottom hasn't stuck, then place a plate that's larger than the pan over the tortilla, cover your hand with a tea towel and carefully but confidently and quickly flip the tortilla on to the plate.

Slide the tortilla back into the pan, tucking in its edges with a spatula to get the characteristic rounded shape. Continue to cook over a low heat for a further 4–6 minutes until just set around the edges but still a little soft in the middle. Slide the tortilla out on to a plate, then leave to cool while you make the salad.

*Make the parsley salad*
Put 1 small finely diced shallot in a bowl with 1 tablespoon red wine vinegar and 2 tablespoons olive oil and mix until the shallot is coated. Add 1 finely sliced stick of celery and the leaves from 25g parsley, toss together once more and pile on the tortilla.

# Crispy-bottomed traybake pizza

1 teaspoon (7g) active dry yeast
2 teaspoons runny honey
700g strong bread flour
½ tablespoon sea salt (about 12g)
40ml extra virgin olive oil,
  plus more for greasing and
  finishing
2 cloves of garlic, peeled and
  crushed
1 × 400g tin good-quality finely
  chopped tomatoes (I use
  Polpo ones)
1 ball of mozzarella, torn
a bunch of basil, leaves picked,
  stalks finely chopped

Plus the toppings you love –
  these are mine:
1 green chilli, finely sliced
50g Parmesan cheese, grated
2 tablespoons stone-in green
  olives, destoned and torn
1 tablespoon capers

I made this a few weeks before having my son Esca. I spent the days before he was born writing this book, and in the evenings I watched food TV. One night in particular I was a few episodes deep in the *Chef's Table* pizza – after which all I could think about was making bouncy Roman-style pizza with choose your own adventure toppings.

There is a lot to say here. First of all I make a very wet, no-knead dough, so while this recipe needs some time it's very hands off. It's the only kind of pizza I would try to make in a domestic oven, which I don't think gets quite hot enough for thin Neapolitan-style pizza.

The crispy bottom of the dough is what makes this kind of oven-baked pizza so good, so don't scrimp on the oil. Lots of oil between the dough and the hot tray is what's going to give you that golden crispy bottom.

I've given you two routes for the dough, similar to the focaccia on page 156 – one that is an overnight prove (for maximum flavour in the dough) and one that you can make at lunchtime for your dinner.

When it comes to toppings, I keep things pretty simple and truly believe the best pizza is a Margarita. I've also given some of my other favourite options – but this is pizza, which I know is personal, so feel free to put on it whatever you love best. Just don't overload it.

SERVES 6–8

*Make the dough*
Whether you are doing an overnight prove or a shorter prove, stir together 525ml lukewarm water with 1 teaspoon (7g) active dry yeast and 2 teaspoons runny honey. In a large bowl, mix 700g strong bread flour with ½ tablespoon sea salt, then add the yeast and honey mixture and 40ml extra virgin olive oil. Stir to combine using a spatula or dough scraper until there are no floury pockets in the dough. The dough will still look scrappy and scruffy at this stage and that's what you want. Scrape your hands and the sides of the bowl clean and cover with a tea towel.

*First prove of the dough*
For an overnight prove put the covered bowl into the fridge until you are ready to work with it. It should have at least doubled in size by the morning. For a shorter prove, knead the dough for 4 minutes until smooth, then leave at room temperature (away from draughts or cold spots) for 1–2 hours, or until doubled in size.

*Second prove*
If you have proved your dough overnight, get it out of the fridge and allow to come to room temperature. Once it has reached room temperature or, if doing the shorter prove, doubled in size, pour 4 tablespoons oil on to a 4cm deep 35 × 35cm roasting tray. Using your hands or a dough scraper gently transfer the dough into the tray. Drizzle then use your hands to rub another 2 tablespoons olive oil over the dough. Gently stretch it to the edge of the tray. Leave it to rest for half an hour to 45 minutes until it's puffed up to about double the size.

*Make the quick tomato sauce*
While the dough is having its last prove, heat a glug of olive oil in a frying pan. Once the oil is warm, but not too hot, add 2 peeled and crushed cloves of garlic and cook on a medium heat until the room

*Continued over...*

Olive Oil

smells of garlic and the edges are just beginning to brown. Add a 400g tin of good-quality finely chopped tomatoes and a good pinch of salt and cook on a medium heat for 6–8 minutes, until the tomatoes have broken down and the sauce has thickened and sweetened. Turn off the heat.

*Preheat the oven and shape the pizza*
Preheat the oven to 220°C/200°C fan. After the dough has had its final rest, dimple the dough once more with the pads of your fingertips. You want the dough to be a bit flatter and less aerated than a focaccia, so don't be afraid to remove any big air bubbles here.

*Top the pizza*
Spread all of the tomato sauce on to the dough, leaving a border around the edges, then scatter a ball of thinly torn mozzarella over it. Then add your toppings. My forever pizza is topped with capers, destoned, torn green olives, finely sliced green chilli and a good grating of Parmesan, but top yours with what you love. Remember this is a big pizza so you can divide it up in half or quarters and finish each one differently.

*Bake the pizza*
Drizzle the pizza with another 1–2 tablespoons of extra virgin olive oil, then bake in the oven for 30 minutes until golden and bubbling.

Favourite pizza topping combinations:

Classic
Tomato sauce, mozzarella and – once it's out of the oven – basil.

Lemon bianco
No tomato, just mozzarella or ricotta, thinly sliced red onion, thinly sliced lemon and capers.

Potato and taleggio bianco
No tomato, just very finely sliced potato, a few rosemary needles, dotted with taleggio.

Greens and ricotta
Tomato sauce, greens scrunched with salt and olive oil, ricotta, lemon zest, lots of grated Parmesan when it comes out of the oven.

# Smoky mole-spiced confit tomatoes

1 tablespoon cumin seeds
1 tablespoon coriander seeds
350ml extra virgin olive oil
1–2 tablespoons chipotle paste
    or chipotle in adobo
1 tablespoon unsweetened cocoa
    powder
1 unwaxed lime
900g tomatoes, a mixture of
    sizes, shapes and colours, on
    the vine if possible
1 whole head of garlic, halved
    horizontally across the
    middle

As these tomatoes cook they fill your kitchen with the most insane smell. Sweet and tomatoey with the back note of warm heat from chipotle and cocoa, these tomatoes are a flavour party so they are an amazing thing to build a meal around. I've given you a few suggestions on ways to eat them as they are too good to be limited to one. But however you serve them I suggest you make the jalapeño yoghurt, as it goes so well with the deeply savoury tomatoes.

How much chipotle you add to the tomatoes will depend on how spicy you like your food and also how hot your chipotle in adobo or chipotle paste is. Different brands vary.

SERVES 4–6 DEPENDING ON HOW YOU SERVE THEM

*Preheat the oven and toast the spices*
Preheat the oven to 160°C/140°C fan. While the oven is heating up, put 1 tablespoon cumin seeds and 1 tablespoon coriander seeds in a deep 30cm × 20cm roasting tin large enough to hold all the tomatoes and roast in the oven for a few minutes until they smell toasted.

*Flavour the oil*
Measure out 350ml extra virgin olive oil and mix in 1–2 tablespoons chipotle paste or chipotle in adobo (depending on its spiciness and your love of heat), 1 tablespoon unsweetened cocoa powder and a big pinch of flaky sea salt. Peel 2 strips of zest from 1 unwaxed lime using a veg peeler and add this to the oil.

*Put everything in the tin*
Prepare 900g tomatoes by cutting any large tomatoes in half across the middle but leave the stalks or vines on. Add to the roasting tin with the spices, making sure any tomatoes you have

cut in half are facing cut side up. Halve 1 whole head of garlic horizontally across the middle, and nestle it into the tomatoes. Pour over the chipotle oil, making sure it comes two-thirds of the way up the large tomatoes. Place the tin in the preheated oven and roast for 2 hours.

How to eat and serve the tomatoes:
There are several different ways to enjoy these tomatoes. However you serve them, make sure you squeeze the roasted garlic out of its skin and spoon over lots of the spiced oil. Any oil left after you have eaten the tomatoes can be poured into a jar and kept in the fridge for a couple of weeks.

*Make the jalapeño yoghurt*
My favourite way to eat these is with this yoghurt, with the contrast of cool and hot, fresh and rich. Put 200ml natural yoghurt into a small bowl, grate in the remaining unwaxed lime zest and squeeze in its juice, then mix well. Add 1 tablespoon pickled jalapeños, the picked and chopped leaves from 15g coriander and a pinch of flaky sea salt. Mix together, then top with the last tablespoon of pickled jalapeños.

*Make a rice bowl*
Serve the tomatoes and squeezed-out garlic on top of deep bowls full of rice tossed with lime and butter (see page 194). Add some sliced avocado, coriander, the jalapeño yoghurt and finish with a good drizzle of oil over everything.

*Make a mole tomato sauce*
Remove the stalks from the tomatoes and squeeze out the garlic from its papery skins, then blitz the

*Continued over...*

tomatoes with 8 tablespoons of the oil for a rich, smooth tomato sauce. Stir through pasta, or cook veg or beans in it.

*Add black beans*
When the tomatoes are cooked, strain most of the oil from the roasting tin, squeeze the garlic out of its skin and remove any tomato stalks. Add 2 × 400g tins of drained black beans to the roasting tin, spoon and scrunch everything together, then return to the oven for another 10 minutes to warm through. Serve with warm corn tortillas and the jalapeño yoghurt.

*Make mole tomato tacos*
Add a little salt and pepper to seasonal vegetables (I like courgettes or squash) and roast until golden. Toss with the mole tomatoes then return to the oven to warm the tomatoes. Pile on to tacos with chopped white onion, sour cream and coriander. Finish with lots of lime.

# Citrus olive oil cake with chocolate icing

2 clementines, or 1 small
    unwaxed orange
1 small unwaxed lemon
4 tablespoons extra virgin olive
    oil, plus 1 tablespoon for the
    ganache, and a little extra for
    greasing
Demerara sugar
4 organic eggs, at room
    temperature
250g soft light brown sugar
250g ground almonds
1 teaspoon baking powder
1 teaspoon bicarbonate of soda
100g dark chocolate, chopped
1 teaspoon honey

This cake is somewhere between Claudia Roden's classic boiled orange cake and a grown-up Jaffa Cake. The olive oil brings some buttery notes which bounce off the citrus and almonds. The icing is made with olive oil and is one of the easiest, most satisfying ganaches I have made. I like to grind whole blanched almonds for this cake; to do that just blitz the whole almonds to a fine powder. Shop-bought ground almonds will work fine though.

SERVES 10–12

*Cook the citrus*
Wash 2 clementines and 1 small unwaxed lemon, then put them into a large saucepan and cover with water. Bring to the boil, cover the pot and simmer for about an hour until very soft, then remove from the pan and leave to cool.

*Preheat the oven and prepare the tin*
Preheat the oven to 200°C/180°C fan and line the bottom of a 23cm round, loose-bottomed cake tin with baking paper. Drizzle the paper with olive oil, then sprinkle with a little Demerara sugar, tilting the tin so it coats all of the sides.

*Blitz the citrus*
Once the clementines and lemon are cool enough to handle, cut them open and remove and discard the pips. If you want to, weigh the fruit to check you have about 300g. Add 4 tablespoons extra virgin olive oil to the fruit and blitz to a smooth purée either in a food processor or with a hand-held blender.

*Make the cake batter*
In a stand mixer or using a hand-held whisk, beat 4 organic eggs with 250g soft light brown sugar for a

minute or two, until pale and fluffy. Add the citrus purée, 250g ground almonds, 1 teaspoon baking powder, 1 teaspoon bicarbonate of soda and a pinch of salt and mix again until light and smooth.

*Bake the cake*
Pour the batter into the prepared tin. Bake in the middle of the oven for 50 minutes–1 hour, or until a skewer comes out clean, then leave to cool in the tin.

*Make the chocolate and olive oil ganache*
Put 100g chopped dark chocolate, 1 tablespoon extra virgin olive oil and 1 teaspoon honey in a heatproof bowl over a barely simmering pan of water (a bain marie) and place on a low heat. Warm gently until the chocolate has melted and the mixture is smooth. Set aside for 20 minutes or until cool. The ganache will harden once it cools, so you will want to ice the cake while the ganache is still just warm.

*Finish the cake*
Once the cake has cooled completely in its tin, take it out, put it on a serving plate and drizzle the top of the cake with the ganache. Slice and serve with the rest of the ganache.

# Double ginger cake with lemon crème fraîche

250g plain flour
2 teaspoons ground ginger
½ teaspoon ground cinnamon
1 teaspoon baking powder
1 teaspoon bicarbonate of soda
200g dark brown muscovado
    sugar
125ml olive oil
5 balls stem ginger (about 75g) in
    syrup, roughly chopped, and
    the syrup from the jar
3 large free-range or organic
    eggs
200ml whole milk or oat milk
2 tablespoons Demerara sugar
200g crème fraîche
1 tablespoon ginger syrup
zest of 1 unwaxed lemon and
    1 tablespoon juice
1 tablespoon extra virgin
    olive oil

I find it hard to love any cake more than ginger cake. This cake has two hits of ginger to make it fiery. The ginger works so well with the treacle darkness of the muscovado. Olive oil makes the most perfect sponge texture and then shows up again in a sharp lemon crème fraîche, which gives this whole thing a school dinner pudding feeling in the best, freshest possible way.

SERVES 8

*Preheat the oven and prepare the tin*
Preheat the oven to 180°C/160°C fan. Line the base and sides of a square 23 × 23cm cake tin with baking paper.

*Mix the dry ingredients*
Whisk 250g plain flour, 2 teaspoons ground ginger, ½ teaspoon ground cinnamon, 1 teaspoon baking powder, 1 teaspoon bicarbonate of soda and a good pinch of sea salt together in a large mixing bowl. Make sure there are no lumps of baking powder.

*Mix the wet ingredients*
In a small, deep saucepan over a moderate heat, warm 200g dark brown muscovado sugar and 125ml olive oil until the sugar has melted a little. Add 3 balls of roughly chopped stem ginger to the pan. Break 3 large free-range or organic eggs into a mixing bowl, add 200ml whole milk or oat milk and the sugar, oil and ginger mixture and mix well.

*Mix dry into wet*
Add the dry ingredients to the wet and mix gently but quickly until no flour is visible.

*Bake the cake*
Pour the batter into the tin, sprinkle over 2 tablespoons Demerara sugar and bake for about 35–40 minutes,

until it is slightly puffed and spongy to the touch. Leave to cool a little in the tin.

*Make the lemon crème fraîche*
Mix 200g crème fraîche with 1 tablespoon ginger syrup, 1 tablespoon lemon juice, 1 tablespoon extra virgin olive oil and stir to mix well.

*Serve the cake*
Once the cake is cool enough to handle, remove it from the tin and cut into 8 squares. Divide the crème fraîche between 8 bowls, put a slice of cake into each bowl, top with a drizzle of extra virgin olive oil and more chopped stem ginger and some lemon zest.

Olive Oil

# Vinegar

Sharpness in a bottle from orange to black. Pickles, sweet and sour. Malt for fish and chips. White wine for herby vinaigrette. Cider with mustard for boiled potatoes. Rice wine, gentle, for splashing on sushi rice. Herby with lovage for summer tomatoes. Blood orange for chicory salad. Black vinegar for dipping dumplings. Red wine for pink pickled onions. I have more bottles of vinegar than I need – a shelf full so I can choose the perfect match. Though really I only need one or two. Not just for dressings and pickling but for baking, roasting, dipping, curry, for balance.

# On Vinegar

To me, acid is the most important and forgotten aspect of cooking. It's a highlight, a top note that brings a plate of food together. Vinegar is an always available, cheap and easy way to add a hit of acidity. It has a lower acidity level than lemon and lime, but it doesn't have the natural sweetness of citrus, and so it tastes sharper.

Vinegar is something I find myself craving, and I keep as many vinegars on hand as I do oils. An essential collection of vinegars to me would be white wine or cider, a red wine vinegar and a rice wine vinegar. With these vinegars, you can do everything.

We are used to using vinegar for dressings and seasoning, but I think vinegar is underrated as an ingredient. I will add acid to my food during cooking and at the end to balance. Adding vinegar to roasted squash, for example, seasons the squash with acidity from within, and the vinegar mellows as it cooks.

The way I use vinegar most is to quickly pickle an element of my dinner in the time it takes me to cook everything else. From finely sliced onions to grated carrot and beetroot or thinly sliced cucumber, these quick pickles are made with the vinegar that suits what I am eating best. Always with a pinch of salt and sometimes one of sugar, and often with an added herb or spice, these are a boosting final element to lots of my simple dinners.

Pickles – by that I mean gherkins and cornichons and their brine – feature heavily in this chapter too. They bring vinegary acidity as well as crunch to so much of what I cook.

Sour, Acid, Sharp, Fruity

### Types

- Pasteurised vinegar is treated with heat to neutralise the bacterial culture, known as 'the mother'. Unpasteurised vinegar has the mother inside the bottle, which is the equivalent of a sourdough starter, so the unpasteurised vinegar is usually cloudy with bits.

- Balsamic
  Made from grapes that are cooked before they are fermented. Dark with a syrupy flavour – the best is made in Italy's Modena and Reggio Emilia DOCG regions.

- Wine (red and white)
  Made from wine – you can buy specific types: chianti, Champagne, chardonnay, etc. The sharpness and flavour vary wildly. I use this for dressings, pickles and some cooking – think red wine vinegar for braised red cabbage.

- Sherry
  Made from sherry within a designated region in Spain. Rich, nutty and caramelly in flavour with a colour to match.

- Malt
  Malt-flavoured with a toasty note – quite punchy, for chips and to cut through fatty foods.

- Rice
  Sweet and silky, toasty, unobtrusive sourness, for rice, noodles, dressings, when you want gentle acidity.

- Cider
  Sharp and fruity with a punch, I buy it unpasteurised, so it's cloudy. Used for dressings, cooking and even apple pie. Also for drinking with fizzy water or hot water, honey and lemon.

- Infused vinegars
  Infusing one of these base vinegars with other ingredients gives amazing variations in flavour. From cherries to sorrel, lovage to blood orange.

### Goes well with

Vinegar cuts through fatty flavours

| | |
|---|---|
| boiled potatoes | mustard |
| chicory | pickling veg |
| chips | rice |
| cucumber | roast potatoes |
| dairy | salad dressing |
| dumplings | tomato |

### Favourite uses

- A basic brine for pickled veg
- A sharp salad dressing
- Agrodolce leeks or squash – a hint of sweet and a hit of sour
- Pickled rhubarb and fruit
- My pickled cabbage soup
- A dipping sauce for fritters and dumplings
- Stirred through vegetables before roasting
- With sparkling water as an aperitif
- In warm water as a tonic

### Storage and tips

Vinegar keeps for years thanks to its high acidity level. Keep it with the top on in a cool, dark cupboard if possible.

If your vinegar is unpasteurised, sediment might settle at the bottom. Shake it back in or strain it if that's a problem, but the sediment is thought to retain the nutrients too.

### Favourite brands and where to buy

- I buy most of my vinegars from my friend Andy of The Vinegar Shed, especially his homemade infused ones – he's leading a well-overdue vinegar revolution. His lovage-infused vinegar is my go-to.

- Brindisa's Valdespino sherry vinegar is hard to beat; I've not found a better one yet.

# Homemade vinegar and quick pickles

CHEAT'S APPLE CIDER VINEGAR
MAKES 500ML

750ml good-quality British cider
150ml raw apple cider vinegar
(with the mother)

*Mix the vinegar*
Put 750ml cider and 150ml raw apple cider vinegar in a clean, large (at least 1-litre capacity) non-reactive container. Shake and swirl the container to mix everything evenly, then loosely cover the container with a piece of muslin, a double sheet of kitchen towel or cheesecloth and set aside in a cool dark place.

Taste the vinegar every couple of weeks until it's reached an acidity you like. The cider will evaporate over time, but you should still have at least 500ml vinegar and 150ml left to start another vinegar fermentation. Transfer your 500ml finished vinegar to a sterilised bottle and store in a cool dark place.

---

HOMEMADE HERB VINEGAR
MAKES 200ML

200ml raw apple cider vinegar
a bunch (30g) any soft herbs (tarragon, chervil and lovage work well)

*Make the vinegar*
Put 200ml apple cider vinegar and 30g soft herbs into a small, clean jar. For a singular flavour, use just one herb, or you could also use a mixture that you have spare after cooking. I like to add odds and ends of soft herbs to a jar of vinegar in the kitchen to create something complex and unique.

*Mature the vinegar*
Close the jar with a lid and set aside for a couple of days and up to a month, depending on how intense you want your herb flavour. If you can't make your own apple cider vinegar, shop-bought raw vinegar will work well.

---

QUICK PICKLES

This method of quick pickling is great for using up those last few vegetables in the salad drawer. Depending on the aromatics and the size of the veg you're using, your pickling liquor can be used warm or cold. Try these scattered over salads, tossed through grains or alongside some hummus and flatbreads for a super-simple starter to any meal.

500g veg of your choice (radishes, beetroot, cauliflower, cabbage, carrots)
250ml white wine vinegar
150ml water
1 tablespoon fine salt
1 tablespoon golden caster sugar
1 tablespoon whole spices (coriander seed, fennel seed, mustard seed, star anise)

*Prepare your vegetables*
Cut 500g vegetables according to how tender they are, and how much cooking they would normally require. For example, radishes could be left whole but hardier vegetables like cauliflower or carrots will need to be sliced thinner.

*Make the pickle liquor*
In a small saucepan, put 250ml white wine vinegar and 150ml water, followed by 1 tablespoon sea salt and 1 tablespoon golden caster sugar. Bring to the boil and stir until the salt and sugar are dissolved, then add 1 tablespoon whole spices of your choice and remove from the heat.

*Jar your pickles*
Fill two sterilised 500ml jars with your chosen cut vegetables. If the vegetables are hardier, or cut in large pieces, pour the pickle liquor over them while it's still a little warm. This will soften them slightly and help the vinegar in the pickle liquor permeate into them. For more tender and delicate vegetables, allow the liquor to completely cool and then cover them, sealing the jars as you do so. These will keep happily in a cool dark place for up to 3 months. Once open, store in the fridge and consume within a week.

# Chilli vinegar noodles with sesame tofu

a small piece of ginger (10g), grated
4 tablespoons sriracha or chilli sauce
3 tablespoons maple syrup
4 tablespoons rice wine vinegar
3 tablespoons soy sauce or tamari
½ a white or sweetheart cabbage, very finely sliced
250g firm tofu, cut into long, thin pieces (about 1cm × 3cm)
2 tablespoons neutral oil (such as groundnut or vegetable)
2 tablespoons sesame seeds
200g egg or udon noodles
½ a bunch of coriander (15g)

This is a pantry-staple noodle dish. It's made often in our house, sometimes even more simply, without the tofu. The rice wine vinegar dressing makes these simple noodles a more-than-the-sum-of-its-parts dinner. You can easily double this to serve 4.

SERVES 2

*Make the dressing*
Grate a 10g piece of ginger into a small bowl and add 4 tablespoons sriracha or chilli sauce, 2 tablespoons maple syrup, 4 tablespoons rice wine vinegar and 2 tablespoons soy sauce or tamari. Taste and add more soy if you like it salty.

*Dress the cabbage*
Scoop half a finely sliced white or sweetheart cabbage into a mixing bowl, add 2 tablespoons of the dressing and scrunch everything together with your hands so it's all evenly coated. Set aside.

*Slice and cook the tofu*
Slice 250g firm tofu into long, thin pieces (about 1cm × 3cm). Heat a large frying pan over a medium heat, add 2 tablespoons neutral oil and fry the tofu until golden on all sides. Add 2 tablespoons sesame seeds to toast for 30 seconds, then take the pan off the heat. Add 1 tablespoon of soy and stir for a minute before adding a tablespoon of maple syrup.

*Cook and dress the noodles*
Cook 200g udon noodles for a minute less than the packet instructions. Drain, keeping a little of the water. Tip them into the tofu pan, add the remaining dressing and a splash of the noodle water and put back over a medium heat for a minute or two until everything is coated in the vinegary sauce.

*Serve the noodles*
Divide the noodles and tofu between 2 bowls and top with the cabbage salad and the leaves from ½ a bunch of coriander.

# Ajo blanco

220g blanched almonds
100g good-quality bread, stale
  (I use sourdough)
2–4 cloves of garlic, peeled
  (depending on your love of
  garlic – I use 2)
1 small cucumber (150g), peeled
  and roughly chopped
100g green grapes
600ml ice-cold water
200ml extra virgin olive oil,
  plus more to finish
3 tablespoons sherry vinegar
½ a bunch of dill (10g) or fennel
  fronds, finely chopped

I first tried this soup in a very hot kitchen during my first summer as a chef. It was made by one of my all-time favourite cooks, Steve Pooley. There are few people who have taught me more about cooking and the unbridled joy of eating. This soup is just that – a joy. Refreshing and richly satisfying all at once, with a perfect balance of mellow creaminess from the almonds, punch from the sherry vinegar-soaked bread and sweetness from the grapes. This needs to be served super-cold, so if it's not as chilled as you think it should be, add a couple of ice cubes.

If you don't have sherry vinegar, red wine vinegar will work in its place, though you might need a little less.

SERVES 4

*Toast the almonds*
Put 220g blanched almonds into a frying pan and place over a low heat. Shake for a few minutes, allowing the almonds to toast very slightly; you want the very palest tinge, to accentuate the taste of the nut. Tip most on to a plate and leave to cool. Toast the rest until nutty and brown. Keep the well-toasted ones separate.

*Soak the bread*
Tear 100g good-quality stale bread into a large bowl and cover with 100ml cold water. Leave it to soak for 10 minutes.

*Blend the ajo blanco*
Once the almonds are cool and the bread has soaked, discard the remaining soaking water. Put the bread into a food processor or blender, add the lightly toasted almonds, 2–4 peeled cloves of garlic, 1 peeled and roughly chopped small cucumber and 75g green grapes. Add a little of the 600ml iced water and whizz until smooth.

*Add the oil*
Now with the motor running slowly add the rest of the iced water, 200ml extra virgin olive oil and 3 tablespoons sherry vinegar and blitz until really smooth. If you have a powerful blender your soup may be smooth enough to eat without sieving. If not, use the back of a ladle to press the soup through a sieve into a bowl, forcing out every last drop of liquid.

*Season and chill*
Season your soup with a little salt and pepper, then taste and add more seasoning, vinegar or oil until it tastes good to you. Cover and chill in the fridge for at least 2 hours, along with 4 soup bowls.

*Serve the ajo blanco*
Chop the well-toasted almonds into little shards and slice 25g green grapes. Once cooled, divide the soup between the bowls, drizzle with a little good olive oil and top with the almonds, grapes, ½ a bunch of finely chopped dill or some fennel fronds and a few ice cubes if you want it super-cool.

# Courgettes agrodolce with sticky onions

5 tablespoons extra virgin olive oil, plus a little extra to serve

4 small or 2 regular courgettes (500g), cut into 1.5cm-thick rounds

1 red onion, peeled and thinly sliced

4 tablespoons red wine vinegar

1 tablespoon golden caster sugar

1 teaspoon dried chilli flakes, plus extra to serve

1 clove of garlic, peeled and thinly sliced

½ a bunch of mint (15g), leaves picked

250g ricotta

Agrodolce means sweet and sour in Italian. In Italy there are so many ways of using this contrast of flavours to bring out the most in ingredients. Here I've used courgettes, but this technique would work for aubergine, thinly sliced butternut squash or fennel. The hit of vinegar which might feel angry on its own is offset with a little bit of sugar, which mellows the acidity and rounds off the flavour. I've written this recipe to serve 2 people but it can easily be doubled, though you will need to fry the courgettes in a few batches.

SERVES 2 AS A MAIN, 4 AS A SIDE

*Fry the courgettes*
Heat a frying pan over a medium-high heat and add 5 tablespoons extra virgin olive oil. Season 500g courgettes cut into 1.5cm-thick rounds with sea salt and fry them for 3–4 minutes on each side or until blistering and golden brown, then remove with a slotted spoon on to a plate.

*Cook the onion and add the agrodolce*
Add 1 thinly sliced red onion to the same pan and lower the heat. Fry for 10 minutes until soft, then add 4 tablespoons red wine vinegar, 1 tablespoon golden caster sugar and 1 teaspoon dried chilli flakes and return the courgette pieces to the pan. Cook for a few minutes, then taste and season and divide the courgettes and onion between two plates.

*Season and finish*
Sprinkle over 1 peeled and thinly sliced clove of garlic and a few more dried chilli flakes, tear over the leaves from half a bunch of mint and drizzle with a little olive oil. Season 250g of ricotta with salt and pepper and spoon it next to the courgettes.

# Cheese and pickle roast potatoes with chilli-dressed leaves

1kg new potatoes, scrubbed
    clean
10 cornichons (35g), roughly
    chopped, plus 100ml of the
    brine from the jar
100ml extra virgin olive oil
3 fresh red chillies
juice of 1 unwaxed lemon
100g Comté cheese or vegan
    mature Cheddar-style cheese
1 head of radicchio or other
    bitter lettuce

A tray of these for dinner is just about the best thing I can think of to eat. Squashed crisp-edged potatoes, tossed and baked in pickle brine to give them a subtle but important chip-shop-vinegar feeling. Once hot and crisped, the potatoes are topped with cornichons and cheese and finished with a chilli and bitter lettuce salad, though the potatoes are also good just on their own.

Pickle brine is often thrown away but it is highly seasoned gold. It is acidic, a little salty and usually a little sweet, so it instantly adds depth like a splash of vinegar would but in a more mellow way.

SERVES 4

*Preheat the oven and parboil the potatoes*
Preheat the oven to 200°C/180°C fan. Bring a large pan of salted water to the boil, add 1kg scrubbed new potatoes and cook for 10–20 minutes, depending on their size, until they are just cooked. Drain and leave the potatoes to steam dry in a colander.

*Season and roast the potatoes*
Tip the potatoes into a roasting tin, toss them with 50ml cornichon brine, 2 tablespoons olive oil and salt and pepper, then roast for 15 minutes. Remove the tin from the oven and, using a potato masher, squish the potatoes until they crack and expose some of the soft, fluffy insides. Pour over another 2 tablespoons olive oil and return to the oven for another 30–40 minutes, turning the potatoes halfway, until golden and crispy.

*Make the chilli dressing*
Prick 3 fresh red chillies with the tip of a sharp knife – this stops them exploding when they are cooked. Using a pair of metal tongs, hold the chillies one at a time over a gas flame until they're blackened and blistered all over. If you don't have a gas hob you can do this in a dry frying pan. Once they are all blistered, put them in a small bowl, cover and leave for 15 minutes. This way they will steam in their own heat and the skins will peel off easily. Once cool enough to handle, peel the chillies, open them up and scrape out all the seeds. Discard the seeds and finely chop the flesh. Put in a mixing bowl with the remaining olive oil (70ml) and the juice of 1 unwaxed lemon and mix well. Season to taste with sea salt and black pepper.

*Finish the potatoes and dress the leaves*
Once the potatoes are golden and crisp, add 50ml of cornichon brine while the potatoes are still hot, then toss with 10 roughly chopped cornichons and a generous grating of Comté or vegan Cheddar. Tear 1 head of radicchio into bite-sized pieces, season with salt and toss in the chilli dressing.

# White bean and pickle stew

50g unsalted butter or vegan butter

2 tablespoons olive oil

2 medium onions, peeled and finely sliced

2 × 400g tins or 1 × 600g jar cannellini beans, drained

1 litre hot vegetable stock (made with 1 teaspoon vegetable stock powder or ½ a stock cube)

½ a head (125g) cavolo nero, de-stemmed and leaves roughly chopped

12 cornichons, chopped, plus 4 tablespoons of their pickling brine

½ a bunch of dill or parsley (10g), roughly chopped

Parmesan or vegan Parmesan-style cheese, grated, to finish

4 tablespoons crème fraîche or oat crème fraîche

I put pickles on pretty much anything. During my second pregnancy I panicked on getting near to the bottom of my last jar of Marks & Spencer's mustard seed gherkins. Most of the time pickles, gherkins and cornichons are eaten cold, to make the most of their crunch and acidity. But they keep their crunch when added to soups and stews, bringing texture and a hit of sour interest. Here they sit next to onions, beans and greens and a smattering of dill to make a quick stew that tastes much more layered and complicated than it is to make.

SERVES 4

*Cook the onions*
Heat 50g unsalted butter and 2 tablespoons olive oil in a deep sauté pan or wide saucepan over a medium heat. Add 2 peeled and finely sliced medium onions and cook for 10 minutes until golden and beginning to crisp. Take out half of the onions and put to one side.

*Add the beans*
Add two 400g drained tins, or 600g jarred, cannellini beans to the pan with 1 litre hot vegetable stock. Season with salt and pepper and use the back of a spoon to squash about half the beans to make the stew creamy. Bring to a simmer over a medium heat and cook for 15 minutes, until the beans are hot and starting to break down.

*Add the greens*
De-stem 125g cavolo nero. The best way to do this is to pinch a thumb and finger across the stem at the base, then run them along the stem, separating the leaves from the stem. Save the stems for a vegetable stock another day, or compost them, then roughly chop the leaves into bite-sized pieces, add to the stew with half (6) the chopped cornichons and 4 tablespoons of pickling brine and cook for 5–7 minutes until the greens are soft. Taste and season with salt and pepper, adding more brine if needed.

*Finish the stew*
Once the greens are soft, spoon the stew into bowls, top with the reserved onions, the other half (6) of the chopped cornichons, ½ a bunch of dill or parsley, some more olive oil, some grated Parmesan or vegan Parmesan-style cheese and a spoonful of crème fraîche.

# Cynthia's quick aubergine moju

2 medium aubergines, cut into
   2cm-thick slices
3 tablespoons neutral oil
100ml apple cider or coconut
   vinegar
2.5cm piece of ginger, peeled
   and roughly chopped
4 cloves of garlic, peeled and
   roughly chopped
2 whole cloves
5 whole cardamoms, bashed and
   seeds removed
2.5cm piece of cinnamon stick
2 teaspoons mustard seeds
1 stalk of lemongrass, roughly
   chopped
10cm piece of pandan leaf,
   roughly chopped (optional)
1 teaspoon chilli powder
2 medium red onions, peeled
   and finely sliced
4 green chillies, split down the
   middle
10–12 fresh curry leaves
3½ teaspoons sugar
to serve, rice, rotis and, if you
   like, some dal

Cynthia Shanmugalingam wrote
one of my favourite books of the
year: *Rambutan*, a collection of Sri
Lankan recipes and stories from
Cynthia and her family and friends.
It's a book as rich in stories as it is
in sambal. Cynthia has been kind
enough to share her recipe for moju.
When I read her book, I was struck
by the role vinegar plays in Sri
Lankan cooking. This recipe feels
like a pickled curry. It's moreish
and brilliant and uses vinegar in
a way and with flavours I've never
considered.

Cynthia tells me, 'Mojus are a kind
of vinegary pickle, a wildly flavourful
combination of sweet-and-sour,
with cloves, cardamom, cinnamon,
lemongrass, curry leaves and, if you
can get it, pandan leaf.' She says that
the vinegar draws out the bitterness
from the mustard seeds, leaving a
punchy, fragrant flavour. In Sri Lanka,
aubergine moju is traditionally made
of soft, deep-fried aubergine, but this
is Cynthia's easier recipe where the
aubergine is roasted. She eats this with
rice and perhaps a simple dal curry, or
smeared inside a cheese toastie.

SERVES 2 AS A SIDE, MORE AS A
SIDE/PICKLE

*Roast the aubergines*
Preheat the oven to 240°C/220°C fan.
In a large bowl, mix 2 medium
aubergines cut into 2cm-thick slices
with ½ teaspoon salt and a couple of
tablespoons neutral oil. Then lay out
the slices on a baking tray so they are
flat next to each other and roast for
30–45 minutes, until golden brown
on both sides and cooked through.
Remove and set aside to cool.

*Make the spice paste*
While the aubergines cook, make
the spice paste. Blitz 100ml apple

cider or coconut vinegar, 2.5cm
roughly chopped ginger, 4 roughly
chopped cloves of garlic, 2 whole
cloves, the seeds from 5 bashed
cardamom pods, 2.5cm piece of
cinnamon stick, 2 teaspoons
mustard seeds, 1 roughly chopped
stalk of lemongrass, 1 teaspoon
chilli powder and, if you are using
it, a roughly chopped 10cm-piece
of pandan leaf, together in a food
processor to form a paste.

*Cook the onions and chillies*
Place a medium-sized saucepan or
wok over a medium-high heat and
add a tablespoon of neutral oil,
2 peeled and finely sliced medium
red onions, 4 green chillies, split
down the middle, and 10–12 fresh
curry leaves, and cook for about
1–2 minutes until the curry leaves
are bright green and the onions are
beginning to brown.

*Add the spice paste and serve*
Add the spice paste and 3½ teaspoons
sugar to the onions in the pan and
cook for 2–3 minutes, until the paste
begins to colour. Add the roasted
aubergines, and stir gently to coat in
the mixture. Taste and add more salt
if you think it needs it. Serve warm
or at room temperature with rotis or
rice and dal.

# Sweet pickled apple pie

175g cold unsalted butter, cut
   into small cubes
120g Demerara sugar
300g plain flour, plus extra for
   dusting
1 free-range or organic egg
5 tablespoons apple cider
   vinegar
1.25kg apples (an equal mix of
   tart Bramleys and crisp,
   sweet varieties like Gala,
   Jonagold or Discovery)
   (about 8 apples)
1 tablespoon cornflour
½ cinnamon stick, ground
1 teaspoon green cardamom
   pods, husks discarded, seeds
   removed and ground
2 tablespoons milk of your
   choice
crème fraîche or double cream,
   to serve

I back this apple pie as the best I've ever eaten. The appley cider vinegar brings a tartness to the apples which is so welcome against a just sweet pastry and a crunchy Demerara top. The vinegar also makes its way into the pastry to help ensure it's super short and buttery.

SERVES 8

*Make the pastry*
Put 175g cold, cubed unsalted butter, 50g Demerara sugar and 300g plain flour into a food processor and blitz until you have an even crumb-like texture. Next, separate 1 free-range or organic egg and keep the white for later. Add the yolk to the food processor with 1 tablespoon apple cider vinegar and 1 tablespoon iced water, then pulse until the pastry just comes together; you don't want to overwork it. If you don't have a food processor, you can do this with your hands, using a small knife to cut the butter into the flour then switching to your hands to bring it together.

*Chill the pastry*
Tip the pastry out and divide into two pieces, roughly two-thirds for the base of the pie and a third for the top. Shape each piece into a flat disc, wrap them separately in clean tea towels and rest in the fridge for 1 hour.

*Make the pickled apple filling*
Peel, core and slice 1.25kg apples into 1cm-thick slices. Add them to a bowl with 4 tablespoons apple cider vinegar, 1 tablespoon cornflour and 50g Demerara, along with ½ ground cinnamon stick and the ground seeds from 1 teaspoon cardamom pods. Toss to coat all the apples evenly, then leave to sit until the pastry has had its hour chilling.

*Make the pie*
Take the pastry out of the fridge and dust your work surface and a rolling pin lightly with flour. Roll the larger piece of pastry into a circle 5cm larger than your pie tin. Roll the pastry on to your rolling pin, then unroll it on to the pie tin. Use the back of your hand or a scrap more pastry to persuade it into the edges of the tin. Allow the excess pastry to hang over the edges. Spoon the pickled apples into the middle of the tin, leaving any excess liquid behind.

*Top the pie and preheat the oven*
Roll out the smaller disc of pastry until it is 2.5mm thick and a couple of centimetres larger than your pie tin. Brush the edges of the second disc with 2 tablespoons milk, then use the same rolling pin technique to lay the lid over the top, draping it over the apples. Use a sharp knife to trim off any excess pastry, then use your fingers or a fork to crimp or seal the edges. Chill the pie for 30 minutes while you preheat the oven to 210°C/190°C fan and preheat a baking tray.

*Finish the pie*
Beat the reserved egg white, brush it on to the pastry lid, scatter over 20g Demerara, then place the pie on the preheated baking tray and bake for 30 minutes, turning it around halfway. After 30 minutes turn the oven down to 180°C/160°C fan and bake for a further 20–30 minutes until the pastry is a deep golden colour. Leave to cool for 20–30 minutes then serve with crème fraîche or double cream.

# Mustard

Sharp, hot, pungent, peppery. Two jars of seeds, a punchy powder in the spice drawer, four pots and a squeezy bottle stacked in my fridge door. From amber to blonde. Smooth and spoonable Dijon. Wholegrain, dotted brown and ochre. Fiery English as bright as a dandelion. A pot of smoked mustard. And American in a canary-yellow bottle, sweet but sharp. For sandwiches. For dressings. For mayonnaise and aioli. For warm potatoes. A jar lasts as long as the spices in the cupboard. A spoonful gives flavour in excess. Abounding. To be used carefully but bravely. To coat calm white vegetables in a remoulade, to top a flatbread, to be the punch in a salsa verde. Unmatched.

# On Mustard

A tiny teaspoon of mustard adds an unreasonable amount of flavour. I use it in so much of my cooking. It can be a subtle, warm note or an upfront sit-up-and-pay-attention jolt of flavour. However you use it, it's such an easy way to get flavour into food quickly.

Brown and black seeds are hotter than the white/yellow ones. How hot a particular mustard tastes is dependent on the type of seed used, as well as what it's blended with.

This chapter focuses on mustard as a jarred condiment made from the seeds, as well as on whole seeds and powdered mustard. You can also buy mustard oil, widely used in India.

Mustard and ketchup are the perfect combination. Mustard brings heat and a little bitterness to the sweet, sour umami of ketchup. Add a pickle and you are very close to perfect.

When we think of mustard, we don't often think of texture, but if you have ever made your own mayonnaise, think of the role it plays in helping the oil begin to emulsify. And as well as heat or pepperiness, it also adds acid from the vinegar it is made with. Hence it goes so well with honey, which adds the sweetness it lacks.

Sharp, Hot, Pungent, Peppery

## Types

- **Dijon**
  A classic French mustard made from brown mustard seeds, white wine and vinegar. On the hotter side.

- **Wholegrain**
  Made with yellow and brown mustard seeds, and sometimes with other spices added too. Pungent and aromatic.

- **English**
  Hot and unmistakably bright yellow, made from brown and sometimes yellow seeds. You can buy it jarred or powdered.

- **American yellow**
  Made from yellow mustard seeds and turmeric for colour, this is a smooth and mild mustard.

- **Honey mustard**
  As it sounds, wholegrain blended with honey for a sweeter taste, lovely in mashed potato.

- **Mustard powder**
  A bright-yellow powder with a punchy hot kick, made by drying and grinding black and white mustard seeds.

- **Seeds**
  Black, brown, white/yellow, use these whole. Buy them in small amounts and use within a couple of months, as the oils in them can go bitter quickly.

## Goes well with

| | |
|---|---|
| apple | honey |
| butter | leek |
| cabbage | lentil |
| cheese | mayonnaise |
| chilli | miso |
| coconut | mushroom |
| dill | olive oil |
| egg | potato |
| green bean | radish |
| greens | white bean |

## Favourite uses

Jarred/squeezy

- A cheese toastie
- A classic vinaigrette
- Beaten into eggs for an omelette
- On hot dogs and burgers with pickles
- In salsa verde
- In potato salad
- Slathered on sandwiches
- With mushrooms on toast

Seeds

- Tempered with curry leaves to finish a curry
- With coconut milk
- Fried until they pop and stirred into mash

## Storage

Keep unopened jars in a cool, dark spot. Once open, I keep it in the fridge, but thanks to the acid in it you can keep it at room temperature.

## Favourite brands/where to buy

For Dijon I usually buy Maille, the iconic French brand; for wholegrain, I like big jars of Pommery. I always have a jar of smoked Dijon from Halen Môn on hand too. For English, I go classic Colman's, or Tracklements also make a fiery one I love. I also have a squeezy bottle of French's American and Johnny's Senap, Hot and Sweet Swedish Mustard.

# Homemade mustard

6 tablespoons black mustard
    seeds
6 tablespoons yellow mustard
    seeds
1 tablespoon fine sea salt
½ cup (120ml) verjus (or another
    ¼ cup vinegar and
    ¼ cup apple juice)
¼ cup (60ml) raw organic apple
    cider vinegar
¼ cup (60ml) apple juice

Once you've got your head around the principles of making mustard, it is actually pretty easy. Making your own means you can create one that's suited to your tastes, whether it be fiery and smooth for toasted sandwiches or textured and sweet for dressing bitter winter salads.

In its simplest form mustard is just two ingredients: mustard seeds and a liquid. Yellow mustard seeds are the mildest, brown mustard seeds are warmer still and black pack the most punch. A blend gives you a wonderful balance of heat and aroma.

Most mustards use vinegar as their base liquid, along with a little salt. In southern Germany beer may be used in place of vinegar and in Dijon it's common to see verjus (unripe, unfermented grape juice) used.

The cooking method also alters the final character of your mustard. Mixing or blending the ingredients cold (or at room temperature) retains the fiery character of the seeds, whereas adding heat dulls the fire of the seeds for a more mellow mustard.

If you can get verjus then it's such a great ingredient to use here, but if not, just double up on the cider vinegar and apple juice. You will need a 300ml sterilised jar to store the mustard.

MAKES APPROXIMATELY 300G

*Grind the mustard seeds*
In a blender or pestle and mortar, pound or pulse together 6 table-spoons black mustard seeds and 6 tablespoons yellow mustard seeds to the consistency you like: a powder for a smooth Dijon-style mustard, or rough and coarse for something more rustic like a wholegrain mustard.

*Add the salt*
Put the ground or bashed mustard seeds in a bowl with 1 tablespoon fine sea salt and mix well to combine.

*Heat the liquid*
Here you need to make a decision on how punchy or mellow you want your mustard to be. Heating your liquid will mellow the heat of the mustard. It's nice to experiment with different batches. If you decide to heat the liquid, put ½ cup verjus (or another ¼ cup vinegar and ¼ cup apple juice), ¼ cup raw organic apple cider vinegar and ¼ cup apple juice in a small pan and warm but don't boil.

*Add the liquid to the seeds*
Add the warm liquid to the mustard seeds and salt and mix well to combine.

*Steep and store*
Put the mustard into a glass bowl or jar, cover and set aside for 24 hours or up to a week. The mustard's flavour deepens over time and as the seeds absorb the liquid it will thicken slightly too. Taste it each day until it has a consistency and flavour you're happy with, then transfer to a sterilised glass jar and store in the fridge for up to 6 months (I've used mine for much longer though).

# Mustard egg mayo with pickles

6 large free-range or organic eggs
4 good ripe tomatoes, sliced
a dash of red wine or cider
    vinegar
6 tablespoons good-quality or
    homemade mayonnaise
    (see method)
1 heaped teaspoon Dijon mustard,
    plus more for the bread
½ teaspoon English mustard,
    plus more for the bread
6 cornichons, roughly chopped
½ a bunch of soft herbs (15g),
    finely chopped – I like a
    mixture of chives and tarragon
4 slices of good bread (I use a
    poppy-seed sourdough),
    about 400g
good olive oil
1 Little Gem lettuce, finely
    shredded

This is a staple lunch at home, something I crave every couple of weeks. I am not into the more traditional finely chopped egg mayo. I like it to have generous bits of fudgy yolked egg, crunchy bits of cornichons and lots of mustard.

The key here is the balance, so make sure you add more mustard, pickles, lemon and salt and pepper to taste. It's your lunch.

I have given a quick mayonnaise recipe here if you want to make your own, but jarred is fine.

SERVES 4 (BUT EASILY HALVED FOR 2)

*Cook the eggs*
Bring a small deep pan of water to the boil, then add 6 large organic eggs and simmer gently for 7 minutes (do a minute less for medium eggs). The eggs will be set but still a little fudgy in the middle.

*Peel the eggs*
Drain the eggs then put them back in the pan. Shake the pan gently to break the eggshells, then fill the pan with cold water and leave the eggs to sit in the cold water for a couple of minutes. This helps the shells detach from the egg whites, making them easier to peel.

*Season the tomatoes*
Slice 4 good ripe tomatoes, season generously with salt and sprinkle over a dash of red wine or cider vinegar.

*Make the egg mayonnaise*
Once cold, peel the eggs, chop into rough quarters and slices and put in a bowl with 6 tablespoons mayonnaise, 1 heaped teaspoon Dijon mustard, ½ teaspoon English mustard, 6 roughly chopped cornichons and ½ a bunch of finely chopped soft herbs. Gently stir together, trying not to break up the eggs too much.

*Pile it on toast*
Toast 4 slices of good bread, then rub with olive oil and a little salt. Add a thin slick of mustard to each slice of toast – Dijon or English. Finely shred 1 Little Gem and pile it on the toast. Lay the seasoned tomatoes over the top of the lettuce, then pile on the egg mayonnaise. Finish with the last of the herbs and more olive oil, salt and pepper.

To make your own mayonnaise:
Put a wet cloth on your work surface and rest a mixing bowl on top. Add an egg yolk to the bowl with 1 teaspoon Dijon mustard and 2 tablespoons lemon juice. Whisk this together for a minute until it becomes pale and thick. If the egg yolk is not whisked enough before you add the oil, it won't emulsify. Next start adding 175ml groundnut or vegetable oil a little at a time in a slow and fine stream. Keep adding the groundnut oil, then do the same with 75ml mild olive oil in the same steady stream until you have a thick, glossy mayonnaise. Once you have added all the oil, add some sea salt and some more lemon juice.

What to do if your mayonnaise splits:
Don't panic! Either add 1 teaspoon at a time of freshly boiled water, whisking until it comes back to a silky mayonnaise. Or whisk another egg yolk in a separate bowl and slowly whisk this into the split mayonnaise, one teaspoon at a time, until smooth.

# Leeks and peas with spiced mustard butter

10 leeks, washed, trimmed and
   cut into 5cm-wide pieces
150g salted butter or good
   extra virgin olive oil
zest and juice of 1 unwaxed
   lemon
2 teaspoons mustard powder
1 teaspoon yellow mustard seeds
1 teaspoon coriander seeds,
   bashed
300g frozen garden peas
toasted sourdough or flatbreads,
   to serve
thick Greek yoghurt, oat
   yoghurt or soft goat's cheese,
   to serve

Leeks and mustard are a prime flavour match. I find it hard to cook leeks without adding a spoonful of mustard somewhere along the way. Here the leeks are half-braised and half-roasted with the lift of some vivid mustard powder, which brings a fierce but welcome punchy hit, and mustard seeds which bring texture as well as a more mellow pop of heat. Adding peas at the end brings sweetness which rounds out the mustard.

SERVES 4

*Prepare the leeks*
Preheat the oven to 200°C/180°C fan. Wash and trim 10 leeks, removing any large leafy bits and the thicker outer layer. Cut them into 5cm-wide pieces and stand them upright in a deep tray or thick pot, so they are all tightly packed together.

*Dress and bake the leeks*
Mix 100ml boiling water and 1 tea-spoon salt in a small jug then pour this over the leeks. Dot 75g salted butter on top, season with freshly ground black pepper, cover with foil and place in the oven for 40–50 minutes until they are really soft.

*Make the mustard-seed butter*
In a small pan, melt 75g salted butter with the zest of 1 unwaxed lemon, 2 teaspoons mustard powder and 1 teaspoon yellow mustard seeds. Add 1 teaspoon bashed coriander seeds to the pan, heat until fragrant, then set aside.

*Add the peas*
Remove the leeks from the oven and gently stir 300g frozen garden peas into the buttery leek liquid. Place the foil back on top and set aside for 5 minutes for the peas to cook in the steam. They should stay bright green.

*Serve the leeks*
Squeeze the lemon juice over the leeks and peas and re-melt the butter so it's slightly foaming. Serve the leeks with toast, a big dollop of yoghurt or soft goat's cheese and the butter poured over the top.

Mustard

# Roast spring vegetables with mustard cheese sauce

a bunch of purple sprouting or
 Tenderstem broccoli (200g)
1 bunch of asparagus
150g fresh, unpodded peas
4 tablespoons olive oil
1 tablespoon fennel seeds
a few sprigs of thyme (5g),
 leaves picked
300g crème fraîche or oat
 crème fraîche
50ml whole milk or oat milk
175g mature Cheddar or vegan
 Cheddar-style cheese, grated
2 tablespoons Dijon mustard
10g unsalted butter or vegan
 block
½ a bunch of parsley (15g),
 leaves picked
½ a bunch of sage (15g),
 leaves picked
½ a bunch of tarragon (15g),
 leaves picked
extra virgin olive oil, for
 drizzling

This is a plate of everything that I find comforting. Roast broccoli with its crispy roasted flowery ends, and roasted spring peas and asparagus with a cheesy mustard sauce that brings it all together. The mustard lifts the flavour and puts a bit of punch into the plate of comfort. Some roast herbs add texture and fresh dimension.

SERVES 4

*Prepare the vegetables*
Preheat the oven to 240°C/220°C fan. Cut 200g purple sprouting or Tenderstem broccoli into florets, then trim any tough bits from the stalk and slice the stalk into 1–2cm-thick pieces. Trim the tough ends from 1 bunch of asparagus.

*Roast the vegetables*
Put the broccoli, asparagus and 150g of unpodded peas into a large roasting tray with 3 tablespoons olive oil, 1 tablespoon fennel seeds and the leaves from a few sprigs of thyme. Season with sea salt and freshly ground black pepper, then toss together so the vegetables are all evenly coated. Roast in the oven for 30 minutes, turning halfway through.

*Make the sauce*
Meanwhile, put 300g crème fraîche and 50ml milk in a small saucepan and bring to a low simmer over a medium heat. Turn off the heat, add 175g grated Cheddar, 2 tablespoons Dijon mustard and 10g unsalted butter and stir until the cheese is melted and you have a cheesy, mustardy sauce.

*Roast the herbs*
Remove the broccoli and asparagus from the oven and set aside to cool slightly. On a low-sided/flat baking tray, mix the leaves from ½ a bunch each of parsley, sage and tarragon with 1 tablespoon of olive oil, then spread them out on the tray so they are all in one even layer, with no leaves overlapping. Bake in the oven for 2–3 minutes, until the herbs have crisped up but are still green. Keep a close eye on them as they can overcook and turn brown very quickly.

*Bring everything together*
Spoon the cheese sauce on to the base of a large serving platter or on 4 plates, top with the roast vegetables, the crispy herbs and a drizzle of extra virgin olive oil. Serve with bread for mopping up the sauce.

# Warm lemon and double mustard potato salad

1.2kg waxy new potatoes
a bunch of spring onions or
    2 small leeks, washed,
    trimmed and finely sliced
1 unwaxed lemon, half finely
    chopped
4 tablespoons extra virgin olive
    oil, plus extra for frying
1 teaspoon runny honey or
    maple syrup
1 tablespoon apple cider vinegar
    or white wine vinegar
1 tablespoon Dijon mustard
2 tablespoons wholegrain
    mustard
4 sticks of celery, thinly sliced
    on the diagonal, leaves
    reserved
a small bunch of radishes,
    trimmed and thinly sliced
a bunch of dill (25g), roughly
    chopped

I think that potato salad is my favourite way to eat mustard. This easy version uses two mustards, wholegrain and Dijon, countered by some lemon and lots of freshness and crunch from celery, radishes and herbs. I eat it at room temperature in the summer and just warm in the winter. The key here is dressing the just-drained potatoes while they are still warm, allowing the mustard vinaigrette to flavour them all the way through.

SERVES 4–6

*Cook the potatoes*
Boil 1.2kg waxy new potatoes in a pan of well-salted boiling water for 15–20 minutes until they are tender and easily pierced with a knife. Drain in a colander and allow them to steam dry for a couple of minutes.

*Prepare the spring onions and lemon*
Wash and finely slice a bunch of spring onions or 2 small leeks. Cut half of an unwaxed lemon into thin slices, removing the pips as you go, then pile the slices on top of each other and chop finely so you have small pieces of lemon, skin and all.

*Caramelise the spring onions and lemon*
Heat a little olive oil in a frying pan over a medium heat and add the chopped spring onions or leeks and cook for 2–3 minutes until beginning to brown. Add the lemon pieces and cook for another 5 minutes, allowing them to char at the edges. Turn the heat off but leave the spring onions and lemon in the pan.

*Make the dressing*
In a mixing bowl large enough to fit all your potatoes, mix together 1 teaspoon honey or maple syrup, 1 tablespoon apple cider vinegar, 1 tablespoon Dijon mustard, 2 tablespoons wholegrain mustard, 4 tablespoons extra virgin olive oil and the juice from half a lemon.

*Drain and bash the potatoes*
Once the potatoes are cool enough to handle, use your hands or a potato masher to gently break their skins (you don't want to mash them). Add them to the bowl of dressing while still warm and toss together. Dressing the potatoes while still warm allows them to absorb the flavour better.

*Finish the salad*
Once the potatoes have cooled to room temperature, add 4 sticks of celery, thinly sliced on the diagonal, and a bunch of trimmed and sliced radishes to the bowl, with the lemon and spring onion mixture, a bunch of roughly chopped dill and the celery leaves. Mix again gently, breaking things up a little more. Taste and season well with sea salt and black pepper. Add more olive oil, salt or vinegar if you think they are needed until the flavours are well balanced.

*Store the salad*
The salad will keep for up to 4 days in an airtight container in the fridge; let it come to room temperature before eating.

Mustard

# Mustard seed and curry leaf snacking nuts

400g unsalted nuts – I used
  cashews but unsalted
  macadamia, pecans, almonds
  or peanuts would work
1 tablespoon groundnut,
  vegetable or coconut oil
1 teaspoon flaky sea salt
a handful of fresh curry leaves
  – about 30
3 tablespoons mustard seeds
  (I use a mixture of black and
  yellow)
1 tablespoon mustard powder
1 teaspoon black pepper, freshly
  ground
1 unwaxed lime

These to me are the perfect thing to
have with a drink. With a decent hit
of mustard seeds and the punch of
mustard powder, freshness from lime
and the impossible-to-put-into-words
flavour of curry leaves. If you want
the spices to stick to the nuts more,
you could toss the warm nuts in a
tablespoon of honey or maple syrup
once out of the oven. This will also
add a little sweetness. I like mine as
they are. These last a couple of weeks
if you snack on them slowly, but if
you are making them for a party then
double up.

MAKES 450G TO SERVE 4–6 AS A SNACK

*Toss the nuts with the spices*
Preheat the oven to 180°C/160°C fan.
Put 400g nuts on a lined baking tray
with 1 tablespoon groundnut oil
and 1 teaspoon flaky sea salt and toss
to coat.

*Roast the nuts*
Roast in the oven for 10 minutes,
stirring a few times, until they are
golden and toasted. After 10 minutes,
when golden, scatter over 30 fresh
curry leaves, 3 tablespoons mustard
seeds and 1 tablespoon mustard
powder and shake the tray so the nuts
are all evenly coated. Return to the
oven to roast for another 5 minutes.

*Finish the nuts*
Remove and season with 1 teaspoon
freshly ground black pepper, leave
to cool a little, then grate over the
zest of 1 unwaxed lime. Allow to
cool completely, then transfer to an
airtight container where they will
keep for a couple of weeks.

# Jammy onion and salsa verde flatbreads

4 onions, peeled, halved and
  sliced about 1mm thick
6 tablespoons olive oil
2 tablespoons butter (optional)
400g plain flour
1 teaspoon baking powder
2 tablespoons capers, roughly
  chopped if large, plus
  2 tablespoons brine from
  the jar
a bunch of parsley (30g)
a bunch of basil (30g)
½ a bunch of mint (10g)
1 tablespoon Dijon mustard
1 tablespoon red wine vinegar
8 big green pitted olives,
  roughly chopped
2 tablespoons extra virgin
  olive oil
250g ricotta or vegan soft cheese

Mustard to me is the heart of a good salsa verde, bringing together the green hit of herbs and the saltiness of the capers and cornichons. Salsa verde is all about balance between salty capers, sharp cornichons, fragrant mint, basil and parsley and some acid from vinegar rounded out with the heat of some Dijon mustard. This version uses more mustard than usual, as I wanted it to be front and centre against the blank canvas of the flatbread and ricotta. If you don't have time to make the flatbread this is nearly as good on toasted sourdough.

SERVES 4

*Prep and cook the jammy onions*
Slice 4 onions as thinly as you can, ideally on a mandoline. Put the onions into a large frying pan with 4 tablespoons olive oil and a pinch of flaky sea salt. Stir to evenly coat the onions in the oil, then slowly cook them on a medium-low heat for 25–30 minutes until they are really, really soft.

*Turn the heat up*
Now turn the heat up a little and, if you are using it, add 2 tablespoons butter, then stir for a few minutes until the onions are starting to caramelise. Take off the heat, set aside in a bowl and wipe out your pan with kitchen paper.

*Make the flatbread dough*
In a mixing bowl whisk 400g plain flour with 1 teaspoon baking powder and a good pinch of sea salt. Mix 2 tablespoons caper brine with 150ml warm water and add it, little by little, to the flour, bringing the mixture together with your hands until you have a rough dough.

*Knead and roll the flatbreads*
Add 2 tablespoons light olive oil to the dough, gently knead in the bowl for a minute, then tip out on to a clean surface and knead for another minute until you have a soft ball of dough. If it's too sticky or dry, add a little more flour or water as needed. Cover with a damp tea towel until you're ready to cook.

*Make the salsa verde*
Roughly chop most of a bunch of both parsley and basil, and ½ a bunch of mint, leaving a few leaves whole for later. Add to a bowl with 1 tablespoon Dijon mustard, 1 tablespoon red wine vinegar, 2 tablespoons capers and 8 roughly chopped green olives. Mix well, then drizzle in 2 tablespoons extra virgin olive oil. Taste and add a little more salt, olive oil or vinegar as needed. You are looking for a spoonable herby sauce.

*Cook the flatbreads*
Divide the dough into 4, then roll each piece into a rough circle with a rolling pin or stretch the dough into rounds with your hands. Heat the frying pan you used for your onions to a medium heat and add the flatbreads one by one, cooking for about 2–3 minutes on each side until lightly golden and slightly puffed up. Remove and wrap in a clean tea towel to keep warm while you cook the rest.

*Put everything together*
Drain 250g ricotta, then tip it onto a small plate. Drizzle with a little extra virgin olive oil and season with salt and pepper. Scoop some of the ricotta on to the warm flatbread with a good layer of the jammy onions and top with the salsa verde and the herb leaves you saved earlier.

# Mustard, mushroom and walnut flammekueche

100g crème fraîche or vegan crème fraîche
1 tablespoon wholegrain mustard
1 tablespoon and 1 teaspoon Dijon mustard
1 teaspoon runny honey
zest of ½ an unwaxed lemon
½ teaspoon fennel seeds, bashed
100g Parmesan (I use a vegetarian one) or vegan Parmesan-style cheese, freshly grated
150g greens of your choice (I like chard or cavolo nero)
3 tablespoons olive or rapeseed oil, plus extra for frying
150g mixed mushrooms (I use a mixture of oyster, shiitake and wild)
200g plain flour, plus extra for dusting
a few sprigs of thyme (15g), leaves picked
50g toasted walnuts, finely chopped

This is a version of flammekueche, often dubbed 'German pizza', and the inspiration for it comes from my dear friend and writer Anja Dunk. Here you make an instant dough with no rising agent, which makes it easy, quick and foolproof. The topping uses an upfront hit of wholegrain and Dijon mustard both in the crème fraîche and tossed through the mushrooms before they bake, which give them majorly satisfying crisp edges.

SERVES 2 GENEROUSLY, OR 4 AS PART OF A MEAL

### Make the mustard filling
Put 100g crème fraîche into a medium mixing bowl with 1 tablespoon wholegrain mustard, 1 tablespoon Dijon mustard, 1 teaspoon runny honey, the zest of ½ an unwaxed lemon, ½ a teaspoon bashed fennel seeds, and 50g freshly grated Parmesan. Put to one side.

### Cook the greens
Peel the leaves from the stems of 150g greens and finely chop the stems. Heat a frying pan over a medium heat and add some olive oil. Once hot, add the stems and cook for 2–3 minutes. Roughly chop the leaves then add these too, cooking them for 4–5 minutes until wilted and all the moisture has evaporated. Set aside to cool.

### Prepare the mushrooms
Use a brush or a piece of kitchen paper to remove any dirt from 150g mixed mushrooms, then tear them into bite-sized pieces, varying the size and shape. Put the mushrooms in a bowl with 1 teaspoon of Dijon mustard and stir gently so they are all coated in the mustard.

### Preheat the oven and make the dough
Preheat the oven to 220°C/200°C fan and put a large baking tray into the oven. Put 200g plain flour, the leaves from a few sprigs of thyme and a big pinch of sea salt into a large mixing bowl with 3 tablespoons olive or rapeseed oil and 80ml cold water. Mix together with your hands to form a dough. Put the dough on to a floured surface and roll into a roughly A4-sized rectangle. Take the tray out of the oven and transfer the dough to the tray.

### Assemble the flammekueche
Working quickly, spread the dough with the crème fraîche mixture, top with 50g chopped toasted walnuts, the wilted greens and finally the mustardy mushrooms, then grate over 50g of cheese.

### Bake the tart
Bake for 15–18 minutes until the edges are deep golden and the filling bubbling. Cool on the baking tray for a few minutes, then carefully slide on to a wire rack to cool. Serve at room temperature (or hot from the oven if you like!) with a bright green salad like the one on page 30.

# Jeremy Lee's rémoulade

2 organic egg yolks

1 teaspoon organic cider vinegar

2 heaped teaspoons Dijon
mustard

a few drops of Tabasco

200ml groundnut or vegetable
oil

50ml extra virgin olive oil

juice of 1 unwaxed lemon

1 heart of leafy celery, thinly
sliced

300g celeriac, peeled and cut
into fine strips

1 kohlrabi, peeled and cut into
fine strips

2–3 apples

1 level teaspoon English mustard

50–75g freshly grated
horseradish

some salad leaves (Jeremy uses
50g baby spinach, 50g land
cress and 50g leafy rocket)

a bunch of flat-leaf parsley (30g),
leaves picked and chopped

Jeremy Lee is one of my favourite cooks. When I started writing about mustard, he was for some reason never far from my thoughts. Jeremy does British food better than anyone, and mustard shows up in so many of his recipes. So when I was thinking of iconic mustard recipes, this rémoulade was non-negotiable. Thanks for sharing it with me, Jeremy.

Jeremy describes this as a feisty salad that pairs well with sharp cheese and many other things. He believes wholeheartedly in making plenty of mayonnaise for when urges for a sandwich mount. For this salad, use half the recipe for mayonnaise and keep the rest in a sealed jar in the fridge.

If you can't find kohlrabi then you could replace it with more apple, or a firm pear or a bunch of radishes. This recipe requires a good bit of chopping, so a mandoline or julienne peeler (very cheap) or food processor with a slicing blade can come in handy.

SERVES 6

*Make the mayonnaise*
Beat 2 organic egg yolks with 1 teaspoon organic cider vinegar, a pinch of sea salt, a teaspoon of Dijon mustard and a drop or three of Tabasco. Add 200ml groundnut or vegetable oil drop by drop, whisking thoroughly. Continue until the sauce thickens, then add the oil a spoonful at a time. Slowly add 50ml olive oil and drops of lemon juice and taste for seasoning. Cover and refrigerate.

*Slice the veg and apples*
Thinly slice 1 celery heart. Peel 300g celeriac and 1 kohlrabi, then slice thinly and cut into fine strips. Slice 2–3 apples thinly and cut into fine strips, tossing them in the juice of half a lemon as you go to stop

the slices browning. If chopping this much veg sounds a chore you could use a julienne peeler or a mandoline.

*Dress the rémoulade*
Place all the vegetable and apple strips in a large bowl with 1 teaspoon of Dijon mustard, 1 level teaspoon English mustard, 50–75g freshly grated horseradish and a big pinch of freshly ground black pepper. Mix well. Add half the mayonnaise, then some salad leaves and the chopped leaves from a bunch of flat-leaf parsley. Mix deftly and serve.

# Vegetarian flavour swaps

There are some flavours and ingredients that, as a vegetarian, I still miss: how easily anchovies build the umami base of a tomato sauce, the crispness a lardon brings or the deep savouriness of Parmesan. Over the years, I have come up with ways to echo some of these flavours. Most of these swaps come out of cooking recipes I used to love as an omnivore, and trying to make them as delicious without meat, fish and sometimes dairy. I am not saying these are the same or exact flavour matches, but they are ways to build flavour and texture that echoes and equals.

Often, we imagine it's the headline ingredients, like prawns or pancetta, that give us the unmistakable sense of a dish like paella or carbonara. More often than not, though, it's one of the 'supporting actors' – like the saffron in a paella – and the way the dish is cooked that will actually be the signature flavour and texture.

## Chorizo
### Smoked paprika

One ingredient I hear people say they miss a lot when they eat more plants is chorizo. Using smoked paprika in your food, where you might have used chorizo before, is a great swap. Try it in baked eggs, or in a stew or soup. Smoked paprika comes in sweet (less hot) and hot (as it sounds), which I use the most, as well as 'agridulce' or bittersweet (a little pleasant bitterness). Smoked paprika adds a great depth and rounded flavour from the top notes of chilli and the base notes of smoke. My favourite smoked paprika is La Chinata or Santo Domingo.

## Smoked meat
### Smoked salt/water

The smoked and cured meats that I used to cook with, things like lardons, pancetta and prosciutto, add fattiness and a smoky flavour with very little effort. But I have found that by using smoked salt or smoked water (which is just water that has been put in a smoker), you can achieve the same rounded woody smokiness, which really helps replicate that flavour. A good example is a version of a carbonara that I make. I use root veg, or tofu, cooked in a pan until crisp using lots of olive oil, which echoes the fat in the meat, then I add smoked salt or smoked water to give them a smoky flavour, which is such a great interruption to the creamy carbonara. The best smoked salt and water is from Halen Môn.

## Lardons
### Crispy capers

As well as using lardons for flavouring, I also cooked with them for their texture. A handful of golden lardons sprinkled on to a salad, for instance, could really lift the level of crisp-edged crunch. My new answer? Crispy capers.

Essentially, these are capers that you have fried hard and fast in olive oil. They open into a kind of flower. They're super salty like lardons, and they have a texture all of their own. I sprinkle them on top of pasta, quiches, tarts or even just a traybake of vegetables to add that pleasing texture and saltiness.

## Anchovies
## Capers

Anchovies are one thing that I used a lot in cooking, though I was never a huge fan of anchovies on their own. I often replace anchovies in my recipes with capers, from pasta to pizza, and way beyond. The intense saltiness of a caper replicates that of an anchovy. I realised I mainly used anchovies as a seasoning, cooking them down with chilli, olive oil and garlic for a quick sauce for pasta. The idea here is that the anchovy breaks down and just becomes a kind of sauce or seasoning. If you finely chop your capers and use them in the same way in a pasta sauce, you'll get that deep umami saltiness. For this, I think the larger capers in vinegar or salt (soaked and washed before using if salted) are best.

## Parmesan cheese
## Old Winchester

Parmesan cheese uses animal rennet, so it's not vegetarian. Any cheese that calls itself Parmesan, which has protected origin status, has to be made in this way with rennet. So if you're vegetarian and want to avoid this, it's important to look for a 'Parmesan-style' cheese in the supermarket – they're not allowed to call it 'Parmesan'. However, these cheeses often don't have the same pleasing crystally structure that is the reason I love Parmesan so much. So I prefer a cheese called Old Winchester for this reason. It's a British cheese that is both butterscotch-sweet and deeply umami, and, like Parmesan,

it has those moreish crystals. And, being British, it means it hasn't travelled as far.

## Umami richness
## Miso

Miso isn't a specific swap, but it's something I use often to add that umami depth that comes from meat or meat stock. If I'm making a vegetable stock and I want it to be deep, dark and full-bodied, I will add some red miso or dark miso. If I want to make something that has a lighter, brighter stock, more in the chicken stock territory, then I might start with a bit of white miso, more caramel in colour, with a rounded flavour that's a bit gentler and less salty.

## Depth
## Star anise

One spice I find myself using a lot in my cooking since becoming vegetarian is star anise. It has a deep, rounded flavour with a sort of aniseed note. I find it really helpful for adding to things like Vietnamese pho, massaman curry, stocks and soups, as well as marinades for vegetables or tofu. Try adding a couple of star anise to a squash soup.

## Sea flavours
## Seaweed

Adding seaweed to your food brings a fresh, clean taste of the sea without using any fish. For something like sushi rice, I often top it with crumbled-up crispy seaweed sheets or furikake seasoning, or use dried kombu to make a quick stock or add depth to an existing broth.

## Bacon
## Smoked tofu

I'm not going to pretend that smoked tofu tastes exactly like bacon, because it doesn't. There are many types of vegan bacon, but I've never met one that I liked and was not super

processed. Where I may have had bacon in a sandwich before, I now use smoked tofu. I slice it thinly and fry it in a hot pan with some oil until crisp on each side. Then I mix a little maple syrup with smoked paprika and drizzle this on to the hot slices, then turn off the heat and toss, making sure it's evenly coated. I'll give the slices a few more seconds on each side and then put them into my sandwich. Great for a vegan BLT or crumbled on top of a salad.

## Deep savouriness
## Marmite

Marmite is cheap, nutritious and very useful. A spoonful of Marmite can add a deep flavour that it might take hours of cooking to produce another way. I often add Marmite to my stews and gravies. It's one of the things that I might add towards the end of cooking. If I've got a gravy, for instance, that I feel is lacking in flavour, if it needs that umami hit and some more depth, then a little bit of Marmite – just a quarter or half a teaspoon – will add a rich colour and also that distinctive flavour but in a much mellower form.

## Rounded depth
## Saffron

Saffron has a reputation for being really expensive, and by weight it is expensive, but to get that rounded, sunshiny flavour you only need to use a tiny bit. Bloom the saffron in hot water – essentially soaking the threads in hot water until they release the golden saffron colour and flavour. Saffron is used a lot in many different cultures. It's obviously a key ingredient in paella, so if you were making a vegetarian paella (see page 182), the saffron would still give you the same signals as a fish paella, but without any of the fish or seafood. It's also used a lot in Persian cooking: adding a little bit of bloomed saffron to some yoghurt served next to some barbecued veg transports me to my Iranian friends' houses, a real decadent flavour that is hard to put your finger on.

# How to cook flexibly

## 1

What is the anchor?

*Ingredient cooking method, cuisine?*

A
------------------------------------>
Craving spice — dal

B
------------------------------------>
I have potatoes to use up

## 2

How will I cook it?

*Fry, braise, char, grill, roast, keep it raw. How will that affect the flavour?*

Fry, simmer, temper

Tortilla Español

## 3

Main and supporting flavours?

*Is the main ingredient going to carry the dish? What does it need to back it up?*

------------------------------------>
No, the lentils need some help, so I will add spices, tomato, coconut

------------------------------------>
Yes, this is a simple dish — potatoes, onions, olive oil, salt

It can be useful to think about cooking in the same terms as music. When I listen to a song, I hear the song, as a whole, without much nuance. I don't have musical instincts and have not spent time training my ear. When my brother (a musician) listens to the same song, he hears something totally different.

When it comes to food, I know I have an instinctive understanding of it, and I have spent the last twenty years honing that understanding. Just like music, you need to know the basics – a few principles, scales and standards – before you can improvise. I am hoping this framework will get you to ask the right questions when you cook and give you the confidence to cook without a recipe and build your own dishes, just as a musician might build the layers in a song.

## 7

How will I balance it?

A
------------------------------------>
Serve with plain rice/breads for contrast, and yoghurt for temperature contrast and richness, chutney for sweetness

B
------------------------------------>
Hot and cold contrast from the tortilla and the salad, sweetness from onions, butteriness and pepperiness from olive oil

## 4

How and when will
I add salt?

*Which ingredients are
already salty? When
would it make sense to
season each element?*

→

Season the onions at the
start, taste and season as I go
at each stage

→

Season the onions and potatoes
well as they cook, the eggs when
they are whisked

## 5

How will I add acidity?

*Are there naturally acidic
ingredients? How and when
will I add acid?*

→

I will add tinned tomatoes
and finish with lemon juice

→

No natural acidity in a tortilla
— add acid with lemon-dressed herb
and shallot salad

## 6

How will I layer flavour?

→

By cooking the onions until sweet,
then adding spices at the beginning,
and more spice in a temper at the end

→

By frying onions and then the
potatoes in olive oil, by browning
the egg on the outside, adding the
salad for acidity

## 8

How will I add texture?

→

A temper of spices at the end,
yoghurt for creaminess, crisped
roti or chappatis

→

Softness inside, crispness from
browning on outside, crunch
from the salad

## 9

Does it need something
to finish?

→

Yoghurt, chutney, herbs

→

The herb and shallot salad

## 10

Taste / Adjust / Taste / Adjust

→

Here you could add more lemon juice
or salt, more tempered spice if it was
lacking, herbs for freshness, yoghurt
to reduce heat

→

To check the seasoning before
cooking the whole tortilla you could
fry off a little of the mixture and
taste and adjust

# Tomatoes

Tinned, paste and passata. Reliable tins and tubes. Bringing summer when it's not. Sun-scorched ripe tomatoes, pressed and packed into tins and jars. Intense paste, cooked, milled then dried, in the sun if you are lucky, for a deep hit of tomato. Tomatoes for us when they have long since left the vines. An intense tomato flavour that a fresh tomato could not give. Extra acidity from the tins or passata which makes the tomato sauce I always want to eat – a clove of garlic smashed whole and sizzled in olive oil, a tin of tomatoes splattered in, and a pinch of salt, makes something much more, so loved. Beyond their million other uses, I would love a tin of tomatoes for this alone.

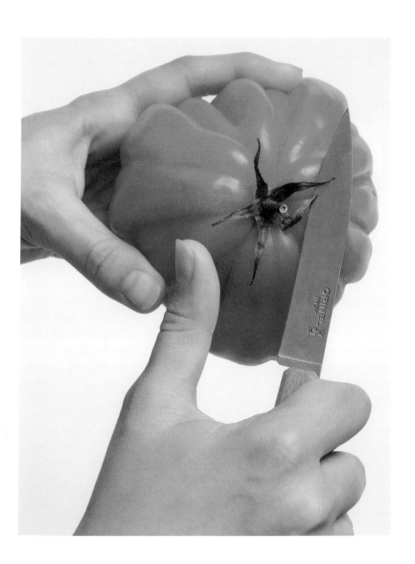

# On Tomatoes

This chapter centres on preserved tomatoes, not fresh. I eat fresh tomatoes for most of the year – colourful British ones in the summer and the hardier, saltier Italian and Spanish winter varieties in the winter. But nothing comes close to the ease of a tin or the squeeze of a tube.

Tinned tomatoes and passata are almost always the tomatoes I use for cooking, even in tomato season. To me, once cooked, they have a perfect balance of acidity and sweetness. It is harder to get that sharp acidity from a fresh tomato. And the paste or purée is so deeply flavoured that you only need a tablespoon or two; its raw edges softened by a minute or two cooked and stirred in the pan.

Tomatoes are rich in citric acid, so they have a lot of natural acidity as well as sweetness.

Sweet, Rich, Silky, Umami

## Types

- Tinned, chopped or plum
  Peeled, from tomatoes with few
  seeds; acidic, jammy when cooked.
  I use these for almost everything.
  Whole DOP San Marzano are
  the best.

- Tinned cherry tomatoes
  Often much more flavourful than
  fresh cherry tomatoes – they usually
  include skin and seeds. I use these
  for cooked salsas, pasta sauce and
  for when I want more of a feeling of
  fresh tomato from a tin.

- Purée
  Intensely rich, sweet, sticky – I use
  this when I want an intense savoury
  hit of tomato without adding too
  much liquid.

- Passata
  Fruity, bright – cooked and sieved
  tomatoes. I use these for a thinner
  sauce for pizza or for a soup or stew
  where I need more liquid.

## Goes well with

| | |
|---|---|
| allspice | ginger |
| aubergine | lemon |
| avocado | lime |
| black bean | mint |
| basil | miso |
| caper | mustard |
| chilli | olive |
| cheese | oregano |
| cinnamon | parmesan |
| coriander | peanut |
| corn | potato |
| cucumber | rosemary |
| egg | tamarind |
| garlic | watermelon |

## Favourite uses

Tinned
- My kind of puttanesca with capers,
  olives and parsley
- Spaghetti and (veg) meatballs
- Red curry
- Store cupboard chickpea stew with
  preserved lemon and herbs

- Shakshuka
- Quick tomato soup

Paste
- To flavour baked rice
- To bolster the base of a soup, stew
  or curry
- To make a dry, flavourful sauce
  for pasta
- To add to ratatouille or baked
  vegetables for a boost of flavour

Passata
- For pizza sauce
- In soup

## Storage

Store somewhere cool and dry, and,
once open, in the fridge for up to
a week.

A squeeze of lemon is said to
remove the metallic taste from a
tin of tomatoes.

## Favourite brands/where to buy

Most supermarkets sell decent tinned
tomatoes, passata and paste. Buy the
best your budget allows.

I buy whole tomatoes and chop
with scissors in the tin. To me, the
whole plum tomatoes are usually
better quality. Whole Italian plum
seem to be the most reliably good.

Paolo Petrilli organic peeled
tomatoes are expensive jarred
tomatoes (they use them at the River
Cafe for a reason).

Bomba tomato paste is worth a
mention for deep savouriness too
– made with extra strength triple
concentrated tomato paste, full-
bodied red wine and tasty soffrito,
meaning it's good for vegans.

# Oven-dried tomatoes

2kg tomatoes
olive oil
2 tablespoons flaky sea salt
spices: a teaspoon of ground
    fennel, cumin or coriander
    seeds are my favourite
    (all optional)

I could have written a recipe here for homemade tinned tomatoes, which I have made once, and while it was satisfying, I have not done it again, which says it all. You can buy very good tinned tomatoes, so I do. This tomato recipe, though, is a game-changer. It makes tomatoes their most tomatoey – the very best version of themselves. It's very easy and gives you an intense oven-dried tomato that you won't be able to buy in a shop. This recipe asks you to leave the oven on (low) for a couple of hours, so I suggest making a decent batch to make it worthwhile.

MAKES ABOUT 2 MEDIUM JARFULS

*Prepare your tomatoes*
Heat your oven to 100°C/80°C fan. Wash the tomatoes, then slice them in half, cutting away any bits of core as you go. Place the tomatoes cut side up on a baking tray.

*Season your tomatoes*
Brush or drizzle the top of each tomato with olive oil, then liberally but evenly scatter over sea salt. If you are adding spice, sprinkle this evenly over the tomatoes too.

*Bake the tomatoes*
Bake the tomatoes in the warm oven for 4–6 hours until they have shrunk to about a third of the size they were when they were fresh. You want them to be dried out but still a little juicy.

*Store*
Allow the tomatoes to cool completely before putting them into jars or airtight containers. They will keep in the fridge like this for a week or so. To keep them for longer, store them under oil – spoon the tomatoes into sterilised jars, then cover with oil and keep in the fridge for up to 2 months.

Ways to use your tomatoes:
· Great with any kind of eggs, particularly egg mayonnaise
· Good tossed in a salad with herbs and a mustardy vinaigrette
· Excellent in a sandwich of any kind. I like crispy smoked tofu, lettuce and these tomatoes, BLT style
· Great in a toasted sandwich
· Good in a tart or quiche where normal tomatoes would have too much liquid

# Any way Puy lentils with tomato sauce

300g Puy lentils, washed
4 cloves of garlic, 2 peeled and
　　whole, 2 finely sliced
1 small tomato, or a plum
　　tomato from a tin
a few sprigs of thyme or oregano
2 bay leaves
1 tablespoon vegetable stock
　　powder, or ½ a stock cube
olive oil
1 red onion, peeled and finely
　　chopped
1 × 400g tin good-quality
　　chopped tomatoes
a pinch of golden caster sugar
a splash of red wine vinegar
½ a bunch of tarragon (10g),
　　leaves picked and roughly
　　chopped
4 tablespoons good-quality
　　crème fraîche

Lentils pair so well with tomatoes. Both the lentils and the tomato sauce here are basics which I love to cook and often form part of my kitchen routine. Eaten together, they are even better.

Puy lentils lend themselves amazingly to quick cooking – they don't need soaking, they cook in 30 minutes and they're hearty, delicious and creamy. Adding a tomato and a few cloves of garlic to the pan as the lentils cook imparts great flavour.

SERVES 4

*Cook the lentils*
Put 300g washed Puy lentils into a saucepan with 2 peeled cloves of garlic, 1 small whole tomato, a few sprigs of thyme or oregano, 2 bay leaves and 1 tablespoon vegetable stock powder or ½ a stock cube. Cover with a litre of hot water, place on a medium heat, bring to a simmer, then turn the heat down. Blip away for 25–30 minutes, until the lentils are soft and the water has almost evaporated. If they are looking too dry, top up with a little more boiling water from the kettle.

*Make the tomato sauce*
While the lentils are cooking, make the tomato sauce. To a small pan, add a good glug of olive oil and 1 peeled and finely chopped red onion and cook for 10 minutes, or until soft and sweet. Add 2 thinly sliced cloves of garlic and cook until browning at the edges, then add a 400g tin of good-quality chopped tomatoes and about 200ml or half a tomato tin of water, a pinch of golden caster sugar and a good pinch of sea salt. Cook for 15 minutes until sweet and thick. Add 3 tablespoons olive oil and keep warm.

By now the lentils should be cooked and most of the water should

have evaporated, so scoop out the tomato and the garlic and put them into a bowl. Once cool enough to handle, pop the garlic cloves out of their skins and use a fork to mash them to a paste. Peel the cooked tomato and mash it with the garlic, too. Stir this paste back through the lentils. Taste, season with salt and pepper, then dress with a generous glug of olive oil and a splash of red wine vinegar.

To serve, ladle the lentils into bowls and top with a couple of spoonfuls of the tomato sauce. Roughly chop ½ a bunch of tarragon leaves and fold through 4 tablespoons good-quality crème fraîche, then add spoonfuls of the herby mixture to the top of each bowl. Finish with a good drizzle of olive oil and some black pepper.

# Black bean nasi goreng

250g cooked brown basmati rice

4 shallots, peeled and finely
    chopped

2 sticks of celery, finely chopped

3 tablespoons groundnut oil

5 cloves of garlic, peeled and
    finely chopped

2 red chillies, 1 finely chopped

a bunch of coriander (30g),
    stalks and leaves finely
    chopped

2 small cucumbers or ½ a large
    one, thickly sliced

2 tablespoons rice wine vinegar

½ teaspoon runny honey or
    sugar

2 tablespoons plus ½ teaspoon
    toasted sesame oil

2 tablespoons plus 1 teaspoon
    soy sauce

2 tablespoons tomato purée

1 tablespoon miso paste (I use
    red or brown rice miso)

3 tablespoons kecap manis, or a
    mixture of soy and honey

1 × 400g tin black beans,
    drained

4 free-range or organic eggs
    (optional)

a bunch of spring onions,
    trimmed and finely sliced

2 unwaxed limes to serve

Dear friends David and Naomi live down the street from me. Naomi was once a ballerina and is now a yoga teacher, and David is a writer. David also loves to cook. Not many people invite me for dinner – one of the few downsides of cooking for a living. David and Naomi do, and one night David made this. Black bean rice inspired by nasi goreng. A wholly untraditional take, but a very good one. The key here is the depth the tomato purée (and a little miso), fried off until it's browned and sweet, brings to the rice as well as the frankly inspired addition of black beans, which give a deep umami hum. It's topped with a spring onion-fried egg and some quick pickled cucumber. That night I could not have imagined anything I would have rather eaten.

SERVES 4

*Do you need to cook some rice?*
If you don't have cooked rice to use up, cook 250g brown basmati rice according to the packet instructions.

*Fry the veg and aromatics*
Finely chop 4 peeled shallots and 2 sticks of celery and sweat in a tablespoon of groundnut oil for about 10 minutes, or as long as you've got, until soft and sweet. Add 5 cloves of garlic, peeled and finely chopped, 1 finely chopped red chilli and the finely chopped stalks from a small bunch of coriander and fry for a couple more minutes.

*Make the cucumber pickle*
Meanwhile, thickly slice 2 small cucumbers or ½ a large cucumber and finely chop another red chilli. Put it all into a little bowl and add 2 tablespoons rice wine vinegar, ½ teaspoon each of runny honey and

toasted sesame oil and 1 teaspoon soy sauce. Stir through half of the chopped leaves from a bunch of coriander.

*Add the flavourings*
Add 2 tablespoons tomato purée and 1 tablespoon miso paste (I use red or brown rice miso) to the pan and cook for 5 minutes before adding 2 tablespoons toasted sesame oil, 3 tablespoons kecap manis and 2 tablespoons soy sauce. Then add a 400g tin of drained black beans and cook for a few more minutes. Tip into a bowl.

*Fry the rice*
Put the pan back over the heat and add another couple of tablespoons of groundnut oil. Once hot, add 250g cooked brown basmati rice and cook for a few minutes until it is beginning to crisp at the edges and is piping hot. Tip in the black bean mixture, stir in well and cook for another couple of minutes.

*Fry the eggs*
If you are cooking the eggs, heat another large frying pan and add a couple of tablespoons of groundnut oil. Once hot, add a bunch of trimmed and finely sliced spring onions, then crack in 4 eggs and cook until the edges are crisp but the yolk is still soft.

*To finishs*
Serve the nasi goreng piled into bowls with the spring onion-fried egg, cucumber pickle and the rest of the bunch of chopped coriander and wedges of lime.

# Traybake lemon dal with pickled green chillies

1 tablespoon coriander seeds
2 teaspoons cumin seeds
2 × 400g tins plum tomatoes
2 tablespoons ghee or other
    cooking oil
2 unwaxed lemons
a thumb-sized piece of ginger,
    peeled
8 cloves of garlic, peeled and
    finely sliced
2 green chillies, sliced
2 teaspoons golden caster sugar
50ml white wine vinegar
1 teaspoon sea salt
a bunch of coriander (30g),
    chopped
1 teaspoon ground turmeric
a cinnamon stick
1 tablespoon Kashmiri chilli
    powder (or ½ teaspoon if
    using other chilli powders)
1 tablespoon yellow mustard
    seeds
300g split red lentils
1 × 400ml tin coconut milk
800ml hot vegetable stock
250g paneer or firm tofu
warm rice, parathas or roti,
    yoghurt and chutney to serve

Dal is a staple of our weeknight cooking. It's the dinner I never get bored of. I have a few favourites I make on rotation: coconut, lemon and now this traybaked tomato one. This dal is made in the oven, so it's very hands-off. The tinned tomatoes are roasted first to give a deeper hit of tomato flavour. Serve this with a pot of rice, some parathas, some salted yoghurt and chutney.

SERVES 4

*Crush the tomatoes*
Preheat the oven to 220°C/200°C fan.
  Add 1 tablespoon coriander seeds and 2 teaspoons cumin seeds to a high-sided baking tray and toast in the oven for 2–4 minutes until fragrant, then remove and tip into a pestle and mortar and crush before returning to the tray. Drain 2 × 400g tins of tomatoes and add to the tray. Use a potato masher or the back of a large spoon/fork to crush the tomatoes to release their juice and flatten them a little, and spread them evenly over the tray.

*Add the flavourings and roast*
Add 2 tablespoons ghee or oil, then grate in the zest of 1 unwaxed lemon and 1 thumb of ginger and add 8 thinly sliced cloves of garlic. Toss the tomatoes in the spices and roast for 30 minutes until sticky and intensified in flavour.

*Make the quick pickle*
Put 2 sliced green chillies, 2 teaspoons golden caster sugar, 50ml white wine vinegar and a teaspoon of salt into a small bowl and mix well. Add the zest of a second unwaxed lemon. Stir through a bunch of chopped coriander, stems and all. Put in the fridge to keep cool.

*Add the spices and lentils*
Once the tomatoes have had their time, remove them from the oven and stir in 1 teaspoon ground turmeric, a cinnamon stick, 1 tablespoon Kashmiri chilli powder and 1 tablespoon yellow mustard seeds. Add 300g split red lentils and pour over a 400ml tin of coconut milk and 800ml hot vegetable stock. Cover tightly with foil and return to the oven for another 40 minutes.

*Add the paneer*
After 40 minutes, carefully take the tray out of the oven and remove the foil. Stir the dal, then season well with sea salt. Tear 250g paneer or firm tofu over the top of the dal and squeeze over the juice of the 2 zested lemons. Return to the oven for a further 15 minutes or until the edges of the paneer are beginning to turn golden, the dal is creamy and the lentils are soft.

*Finish with the chilli and serve*
Serve with rice, parathas, yoghurt and chutney and the pickled chilli and coriander mixture. Will keep in the fridge for up to 7 days.

# Orzo, feta and tomato traybake

4 red onions, peeled and cut
    into thin wedges
1 red chilli
1 red pepper, deseeded and
    chopped
1 head of garlic, cut across the
    middle
olive oil
1 × 400g tin plum tomatoes
1 teaspoon nigella seeds
1 teaspoon coriander seeds,
    crushed
250g orzo
200g feta or vegan feta-style
    cheese
½ a bunch of coriander (15g),
    leaves picked
½ a bunch of parsley (15g),
    leaves picked
2 tablespoons toasted pine nuts

Along with rigatoni, spaghettini and casarecce, orzo is one of my most-used kinds of pasta. Special mention also goes to rachette (tennis racket-shaped pasta my kids love). Orzo has such a pleasing texture with an olive oil-rich tomato sauce. This is a frequently cooked dinner all made in a tray. Roasted onions go sweet and jammy, then tinned tomatoes are added and roasted until their flavour intensifies, more jammy, sticky flavour builds up and then, when the orzo and liquid are added, all the flavour is swept up off the tray and a broken-up slab of feta tops it all. It's a very hands-off, pleasing dinner.

SERVES 4

*Roast the onions and peppers*
Preheat the oven to 220°C/200°C fan. Put 4 peeled red onions cut into thin wedges into a large deep-sided baking tray (roughly 30cm × 40cm) with 1 whole red chilli, 1 red pepper, deseeded and chopped, and 1 head of garlic cut across the middle. Drizzle over a splash of olive oil. Roast in the hot oven for 20 minutes until the onions are cooked and the edges of the peppers are beginning to char.

*Add the tomatoes and spices*
Drain a 400g tin of plum tomatoes and keep the juice. After the onions and peppers have been cooking for 20 minutes, put the tomatoes into the tray with 1 teaspoon nigella seeds and 1 teaspoon coriander seeds, crushed, then put the lot back into the oven for another 20 minutes so the tomatoes can roast and intensify.

*Break up the tomatoes and squeeze out the garlic*
Take the tray out of the oven and use the back of a wooden spoon or a potato masher to break up the tomatoes. Take the garlic out and squeeze it from its papery skins into the tray – discard the skins.

*Add the orzo and liquid*
Put the tomato liquid from the can into a measuring jug then add freshly boiled water until you have 800ml of liquid. Add to the tray with 250g orzo and dot the top with 200g feta or vegan feta-style cheese, then return it to the oven for 15 minutes, stirring it all halfway, until the orzo is cooked.

*Add the herbs and serve*
Take it out of the oven and shower with the picked coriander and parsley leaves and the pine nuts as well as a drizzle of olive oil, and eat right away as the pasta will continue to cook as it sits.

# Coconut and tomato laksa

1–3 small Thai red chillies, depending on how hot you like it

6 cloves of garlic, peeled

2 shallots, peeled and chopped into a few chunks

a thumb-sized piece of ginger, peeled and chopped into 3

15 raw cashew nuts (40g)

1 tablespoon sambal oelek or other chilli sauce

2 tablespoons coconut oil or other cooking oil

2 tablespoons tomato purée

200g dried flat rice noodles

1 × 400ml tin coconut milk

3 unwaxed limes

4 lime leaves

½ a bunch of coriander (15g) (reserve a few sprigs for garnish)

½ a bunch of mint (15g) (reserve a few sprigs for garnish)

200g silken tofu, cut into cubes

1 tablespoon coriander seeds

ADD SEASONAL VEGETABLES

Spring – 2 handfuls of freshly podded peas, a bunch of asparagus, thinly sliced, and a few sliced spring onions

Summer – 2 handfuls of halved cherry tomatoes, 2 handfuls of halved sugar snaps (120g)

Autumn – a small sweet potato, peeled and very finely sliced, and 2 handfuls of shredded kale

Winter – 2 carrots, peeled into thin ribbons with a speed peeler, and a bunch of purple-sprouting broccoli, stalks cut into thin rounds and florets halved

Tomato purée feels old-fashioned, retro and reliable. While it might not have the draw of a tall jar of passata or a pleasingly designed tin of tomatoes, a tube of tomato purée holds promise. This laksa-style soup shows it off in all its glory – the dish gains so much depth from a tablespoon or so. Here that deep, savoury tomato is mixed with aromatics, and once it hits the creamy coconut milk, well-rounded, multi-layered flavour is created in not much time at all. I use the term 'laksa' so you know to expect richness, spice and coconut. This recipe is far from a traditional laksa, which has so many variations all over South East Asia, for which I encourage you to seek out chefs like Lara Lee or Mandy Yin. The paste can be made and frozen in ice-cube trays for a very quick version if that's your kind of thing. I have suggested some seasonal variations for vegetables here so you can make this all year round.

SERVES 4

*Make the laksa paste*
Blend 1–3 small Thai red chillies, 6 cloves of garlic, 2 chopped shallots, a chopped thumb of ginger and 40g raw cashews in a blender or food processor until smooth. Add 1 tablespoon sambal oelek, 2 table-spoons coconut oil and 2 tablespoons tomato purée and blend until smooth.

*Cook the rice noodles*
Fill a pan with water and bring to a boil. Once boiling, remove from the heat, add 200g dried flat rice noodles and soak them for 6–10 minutes, until tender but still chewy. Drain the noodles and rinse well under cold water, then toss in a little oil to stop them sticking.

*Make the soup*
Fill and boil your kettle. While the noodles soak, heat a large saucepan over a medium heat, add the laksa paste and fry for a couple of minutes to cook the tomato purée and the spices. Once the paste has darkened in colour a little, add a 400ml tin of coconut milk along with a tin-full (400ml) of boiling water. Add the juice of 2 unwaxed limes, 4 lime leaves, most of ½ a bunch each of coriander and mint and season to taste with sea salt.

*Add the vegetables*
Add your chosen veg to the pan and simmer until tender. This may take longer for some of the winter vegetables than for the spring and summer vegetables.

*Serve the laksa*
Divide the cooked noodles between 4 bowls, then divide 200g cubed silken tofu among them. Evenly add the vegetables, then the laksa broth. Finish with the remaining mint, coriander and wedges from the remaining lime.

# Linguine with mushroom and herb polpette

3 tablespoons capers
zest and juice of 1 unwaxed lemon
100ml extra virgin olive oil
8 cloves of garlic, peeled
2 × 400g tins cherry tomatoes
200g mushrooms (I use chestnut
  mushrooms)
2 onions, peeled and roughly
  chopped
200g smoked tofu
2 tablespoons olive oil
a sprig of rosemary, leaves finely
  chopped
10 sage leaves, finely chopped
50g fresh breadcrumbs
1 × 400g tin black beans, drained
  (240g black beans once
  drained)
50g pine nuts
125g ball of mozzarella, grated
50g sundried tomatoes, finely
  chopped
500g linguine
a bunch of basil, leaves separated
Parmesan cheese

Linguine and meatballs, vegetarian ones, are Dylan's favourite. As hard as I tried, Dylan still preferred the shop-bought 'meat' balls to the ones I made. Until now. I agree with him that there are few better ways to use a tin of tomatoes than in a big platter of tomato linguine twisted around little savoury polpette. These are rich with umami mushrooms, black beans and smoked tofu and have the pleasing bounce which I think Dylan loves so much. I make double the amount of these and freeze a batch.

SERVES 4

*Make the tomato sauce*
Put 3 tablespoons capers and the zest and juice of 1 unwaxed lemon into a food processor and blitz until you have a smooth paste. Add 100ml extra virgin olive oil to a large saucepan, add 4 peeled and sliced cloves of garlic and fry over a medium heat until just turning golden. Spoon in the caper mix and fry for a minute, then add 2 × 400g tins cherry tomatoes. Season generously with salt and pepper and leave to simmer away.

*Make the meatball mix*
Put 200g mushrooms, 2 peeled and roughly chopped onions and 4 peeled cloves of garlic into the food processor and blitz until you have a roughly chopped mixture. Add 200g smoked tofu and pulse to incorporate. In a large frying pan add 2 tablespoons olive oil and place over a high heat. Tip in the veg mix and fry for 10 minutes, stirring often until all the veg is dry and a little golden. Add a sprig of finely chopped rosemary, 10 finely chopped sage leaves and 50g breadcrumbs and continue to fry for another 5 minutes.

*Finish and shape the meatballs*
Tip the vegetable mixture into a mixing bowl to cool. Blitz 1 × 400g tin of drained black beans and 50g pine nuts until you have a textured paste. Add the black bean mixture to the cooled veg with 125g grated mozzarella and 50g chopped sundried tomatoes. Using clean hands give it all a really good scrunch until it clings together. Shape into 30 roughly 30g balls and put on a plate and into the fridge for 10 minutes.

*To fry the meatballs*
Heat your biggest frying pan over a medium heat and add 4 tablespoons olive oil. Once hot, fry the polpette for 4–5 minutes on each side until golden brown. You may have to do this in batches. You could also roast them for 20–25 minutes at 200°C/180°C fan.

*To bake the meatballs*
Preheat the oven to 200°C/180°C fan and put the polpette on to a baking tray and drizzle generously with oil and toss to coat. Bake in the hot oven for 25 minutes until golden and crisp.

*Cook the pasta*
Bring a large pan of water up to a rolling boil. Season the water generously with salt, add 500g linguine and cook until al dente.

*Mix the pasta and sauce*
Toss the pasta and meatballs into the tomato sauce and add most of a bunch of basil, reserving a handful for serving. Tip on a platter and top with the rest of the basil and a grating of Parmesan if you like.

# Nadya's tepsi with amba tomatoes

2 medium aubergines (about 300g each), cut into 1cm-thick slices
olive oil
3 medium potatoes, peeled and sliced ½cm thick
3 onions, peeled and sliced ½cm thick
100g tomato purée
2 green peppers, deseeded and cut into 1cm-thick slices
3 tablespoons tamarind paste, or juice of 1 unwaxed lemon
150ml hot good-quality vegetable stock
400g tomatoes, sliced ½cm thick (I used a mixture of colours and sizes)
½ a bunch of parsley (15g), leaves picked
2 tablespoons amba
juice of ½ an unwaxed lemon
pickled turnips (optional)
100g salted yoghurt

Sometimes people come into your life at the perfect moment. Nadya Mousawi did. Nadya is a doula and came to us in the hazy days when Esca was small and helped me navigate having a tiny baby again. She made us food, helped me feed him, chatted through my worries. It's how all mums should be supported (which I could write much much more about). This tepsi was a favourite thing Nadya made. It's from Iraq, where Nadya is from. For this and so many other things, I am so grateful, Nadya.

Here, tomato purée joins up with sour/sweet tamarind to make a flavour blanket which coats layers of aubergine, peppers and potatoes in a moreish sweet and sour bake. It gets better as the days go by and will sit unbaked in the fridge for a couple of days. Nadya eats it with rice and yoghurt and Iraqi pickled turnips, so we do too.

SERVES 4–6

*Roast the aubergine*
You will need a medium baking dish, roughly the size of a sheet of A4 paper. Preheat the oven to 240°C/220°C fan. Salt 2 medium aubergines, cut into 1cm-thick slices and toss to season, then drizzle a good amount of olive oil on both sides and roast them on a baking tray for 30 minutes until soft and golden. Turn the oven down to 180°C /160°C fan.

*Cook the potatoes*
Cook 3 medium potatoes, peeled and sliced ½cm thick, in boiling salted water for about 8 minutes until cooked through, then drain and allow to steam dry.

*Cook the onions*
Meanwhile, heat a glug of olive oil in a frying pan and cook 3 onions, peeled

and sliced ½cm thick with a little salt until soft and sweet. Add 1 tablespoon tomato purée and a splash of water to cover the onions in a thick tomatoey sauce. Once it bubbles, take the pan off the heat and spread the onions evenly on to the bottom of your baking dish and season. This is your first layer.

*Cook the green peppers*
Put the frying pan back over a medium heat, add a little olive oil and once hot add 2 green peppers, cut into 1cm-thick slices, and cook until charred and soft. Layer them on top of the onions and season with salt, then wipe the pan clean.

*Sauté the cooked potatoes*
Put the frying pan back on the heat again, add a good amount of olive oil and then add the drained potatoes and fry until golden (in batches if needed). Once golden, layer the potatoes on top of the peppers and season really well with salt.

*Add the aubergine layer*
Take the aubergines out of the oven, lay on them top of the potatoes and season.

*Make the tamarind mix*
In a jug mix the remaining tomato purée with 3 tablespoons tamarind paste or the juice of a whole lemon and 150ml hot stock. Pour the mixture over the tepsi, then top with 400g tomatoes sliced ½cm thick, salt and pepper and a generous drizzle of olive oil. Then bake for 45 minutes until bubbling and charred.

*Make the parsley salad*
Mix the leaves from ½ a bunch of parsley with a little lemon juice and serve with the amba, pickles and 100g salted yoghurt.

# Spiced tomato soup with lemon and herb flatbreads

5 tablespoons olive oil

3 onions, peeled and finely chopped

4 sticks of celery, finely chopped

2 carrots, peeled and finely chopped

6 cloves of garlic, peeled and finely chopped

1 tablespoon cumin seeds

1 tablespoon coriander seeds

2–4 tablespoons harissa paste (depending on heat)

2 × 400g tins cherry tomatoes

800ml hot vegetable stock (made with 1 teaspoon bouillon powder or ½ a stock cube)

200g mature Cheddar or vegan Cheddar-style cheese, grated

50g feta or vegan feta-style cheese

2 preserved lemons, skin roughly chopped

50g pickled green chillies, roughly chopped

a bunch of parsley (30g), chopped

½ a bunch of mint (15g), chopped

½ a bunch of dill (15g), chopped

4 large fluffy Turkish flatbreads

4 tablespoons za'atar

There are two soups I make for our family when the reserves are low and cupboards are bare: a quick frozen pea and coconut soup from my second book and a version of this soup. I think it's a bit of magic that a delicious soup can come from nothing more than a few simple vegetables, a little spice and a couple of tins of tomatoes. I use tinned cherry tomatoes as I like the sweetness they bring, but a couple of tins of plum tomatoes would work well too. The soup starts with a base of onion, garlic, carrot and celery, but you could also use leek, fennel or shallots too. The crowning glory of this soup is the lemon and herb flatbreads. They come together just like a cheese toastie. I come back to them again and again.

SERVES 4

### Start the soup

Add 3 tablespoons olive oil to a medium saucepan along with 3 peeled and finely chopped onions, 4 finely chopped sticks of celery, 2 peeled and finely chopped carrots, and 6 peeled and finely chopped cloves of garlic and fry the lot over a medium-low heat for 15–20 minutes, stirring every so often, until soft and sweet but not browned. You will need to adjust the heat as you go and perhaps add a little more oil or even a splash of water if it's beginning to catch.

### Add the spices

Once the vegetables have softened, add 1 tablespoon cumin seeds, 1 tablespoon coriander seeds, and 2–4 tablespoons harissa paste and stir to toast for a minute. Add 2 × 400g tins of cherry tomatoes and their juice, then 800ml hot vegetable stock. Reduce to a simmer and cook for 20 minutes, stirring often.

### Make the flatbread filling

Grate 200g Cheddar cheese into a mixing bowl, then crumble in 50g feta cheese. Add 2 roughly chopped preserved lemons and 50g chopped pickled green chillies. Mix in the chopped leaves from a bunch of parsley and from ½ a bunch each of mint and dill. Taste and season with salt and pepper if needed.

### Bake the flatbreads

Preheat the oven to 240°C/220°C fan. Place the flatbreads on a baking tray and drizzle one side with oil and a little za'atar. Flip the flatbreads over on to the unoiled side, pile the filling on to one of the flatbreads and spread evenly, then sprinkle over some more za'atar. Place the other flatbread to sandwich the filling – oiled side up – then place in the oven for 10 minutes so the cheese melts and the flatbread toasts.

### Blend the soup

While the flatbreads are in the oven, use a hand-held blender to blend the tomato mixture until you have a creamy soup. Keep it warm on a low heat. Taste and season with more salt if needed.

### Serve the soup and flatbreads

Take the flatbreads out of the oven, slide on to a large chopping board and carefully slice up and serve alongside the soup.

# Mersedeh's mirza ghasemi

3 large aubergines or 5 medium
    aubergines
3 tablespoons olive oil
1 medium onion, peeled and
    finely chopped
2 cloves of garlic, peeled and
    finely chopped or grated
1 teaspoon ground turmeric
1 × 400g tin chopped tomatoes
3 tablespoons tomato purée
1 teaspoon maple syrup or sugar
2 large free-range or organic
    eggs (beaten), plus more if
    eating as a main course
chopped chives and crushed
    walnuts, to finish
flatbreads to serve

This is a recipe from my lifelong friend Mersedeh Prewer. Our friendship has seen us through all the ups and downs, but up or down, our friendship has always centred around what's for dinner.

This is a rich dip I've eaten at Mer's table, made with tomatoes and tomato purée and smoked aubergine. The unusual thing (for me) is that eggs are stirred through at the end to enrich it. It's so good scooped with flatbread and next to a pile of herbs and some feta. It's not just eaten as a dip to start a meal but is also great as a main dish with rice.

SERVES 6

*Char the aubergines*
Cook 3 large or 5 medium aubergines whole over an open flame (gas hob or barbecue) until blackened and the flesh has softened. You can also do this under the grill, set to medium-high, in your oven. The idea here is to get a smoky flavour into the final dish.

*Cool and peel the aubergines*
Allow the aubergines to cool, then peel them or cut them in half and scoop out the flesh, discarding the skins.

*Cook the onion*
Put a lidded frying pan over a medium-low heat, add 3 tablespoons olive oil and 1 medium onion, peeled and finely chopped, and a pinch of sea salt. Cook the onion for 10 minutes until it is soft and sweet and starting to brown, then add 2 finely chopped or grated cloves of garlic and cook for another 2–3 minutes, making sure the garlic does not burn. Then stir in 1 teaspoon ground turmeric.

*Add the tomatoes*
Add a 400g tin of chopped tomatoes and cook until the tomatoes have softened and broken down. Stir in the aubergine flesh and mash the mixture gently. Add 3 tablespoons tomato purée, 3 tablespoons water, 1 teaspoon maple syrup or sugar, then season and cook for about 10 minutes, stirring gently now and then.

*Add the eggs*
Make a few holes in the mixture and add 2 beaten eggs. Once the eggs start to turn pale yellow and firm a little, stir them in until evenly distributed through the aubergine mixture. Let the mixture simmer gently on a low heat and with a lid on the pan for a further 10 minutes.

*Finish with herbs*
Serve warm but not piping hot, with a drizzle of olive oil and a sprinkling of chopped chives and crushed walnuts, alongside more fresh herbs, feta and flatbread.

# Paneer rolls with quick tomato chutney

2 tablespoons ghee or vegetable
   oil
2 red onions, cut into eighths
1 green or red pepper, deseeded
   and cut into long strips
a 250g block of paneer or firm
   tofu, cut into 2cm pieces
6 tablespoons quick tomato
   chutney
4 parathas (I use the frozen
   ones)
a small bunch of coriander,
   leaves picked
wedges from 1 unwaxed lime

FOR THE QUICK TOMATO
CHUTNEY
1 teaspoon cumin seeds
½ teaspoon dried chilli flakes
1 tablespoon olive oil
1 red onion, peeled and finely
   chopped
2 cloves of garlic, peeled and
   finely chopped
1 small thumb-sized piece of
   ginger, grated (15g)
1 green chilli, sliced lengthways
1 × 400g tin chopped tomatoes
20g caster sugar
100ml red wine vinegar
juice of 1 unwaxed lime

One lunchtime as I was putting this book together, I was craving both the bounce of paneer and the sharp sweetness of a tomato chutney. Half an hour later I was eating these in a quick break from writing. The chutney is quick, keenly spiced and comes from a tin of tomatoes. What is left can be kept in a jar in the fridge for a week or so. What's key in this recipe is coating and quickly cooking the paneer in the chutney. The perky sweetness of the tomato is such a good contrast to the milky paneer (and also works very well with firm tofu). I used ready-made parathas here, but roti or chapatis would work too.

MAKES 4

*Cook the onions and peppers*
Put a large frying pan over a medium heat and add a little oil or ghee. Add 2 red onions, cut into eighths, and 1 green or red pepper, deseeded and cut into long strips. Turn up the heat and cook for 5 minutes until charred at the edges and softening. Tip the onions and peppers on to a plate.

*Add the paneer/tofu*
Put the empty pan back on the heat, add a little more oil or ghee, turn up the heat and add 250g paneer or tofu, cut into rough 2cm pieces. Cook for 4–5 minutes, turning every couple of minutes, until hot, crisp and browned all over. Add the onions and peppers back to the pan.

*Coat the paneer in the chutney*
Take off the heat and add 2 tablespoons of the tomato chutney and stir to coat. Put to one side to cool slightly.

*Cook your paratha*
Toast your parathas in a pan until warm. If using the frozen ones, follow the instructions on the packet.

*Make your rolls*
Pile the sticky paneer into the warm parathas, top with a tablespoon of the chutney and a few sprigs of coriander and a squeeze of lime. Add a little yoghurt too if you like. Serve warm with a napkin.

For the chutney:
*Toast the spices*
Put 1 teaspoon cumin seeds and ½ teaspoon dried chilli flakes in a dry frying pan and toast for a couple of minutes, then crush in a pestle and mortar.

*Cook the aromatics*
Put the frying pan back over the heat, add a little olive oil and 1 finely chopped red onion, 2 cloves of finely chopped garlic, and 1 small thumb of grated ginger, then fry for about 10 minutes until soft.

*Add the liquid*
Add a 400g tin of chopped tomatoes, the toasted cumin and chilli flakes, 20g sugar and 100ml red wine vinegar.

*Simmer the chutney*
Bring to the boil, then reduce the heat and simmer for 25 minutes, squashing the tomatoes with the back of a spoon as they soften, until the chutney is sweet and sticky.

*Add the lime*
Take the pan off the heat and squeeze in the juice of 1 unwaxed lime.

# Capers

I buy four jars at a time. The tiny ones are my favourite; rarely a day passes without their briny, salty acidity. Vinegary buds, so full of flavour they pop in your mouth. Little hits of acid that make meals better. So small they have no right to be so flavourful. Fry them in hot oil and they open out into deep-green flowers, still sour but crispy. We ate them at our wedding, fried into bloom on top of a tomato tart. Scatter them into mayonnaise with herbs and cornichons, fold them into caponata with olives and parsley, bake them into focaccia with their brine. Sizzle them in browning butter to spoon over mashed potato. Allow them to crisp next to roast potatoes. Make margaritas with the brine. And ice cream, caper chocolate cream.

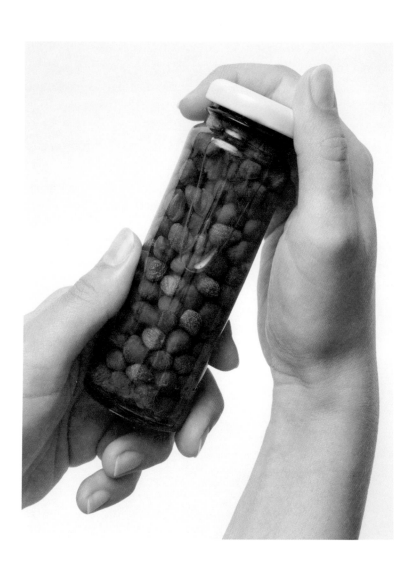

# On Capers

Capers are a constant in my kitchen. To me, they are the perfect balance between salty and acidic. They bring salt, acidity and umami, with a perky, almost mustardy, note. They ask little of me and sit in my fridge for months.

I think they are unmatched in vegetarian cooking in the way they can create a rounded savoury, umami base of flavour, and they stand in for anchovies in my cooking.

Do not pour away the brine. It's a perfectly salty-sour flavour hit that can be used to add a seasoning, giving the dish a nip and a lift. It's also incredible in margaritas (page 173).

Fried, these little flowers transform into crunchy savoury flavour bombs. I use these fried capers anywhere that their salty crunch is welcome. I lean towards the small jarred nonpareille capers in vinegar, as they are so easy to use. I love how easy they are to use straight from the jar.

You can't argue that the flavour of salted capers is the best. All my chef friends use them. The salt seems to preserve their flavour better.

Sour, Salty, Umami

## Types

Capers are the small flower buds of the Capparis, or caper, bush that grows in the Mediterranean. Capers are the immature, unripe green flower buds. You can eat the fruits of the same plant, which we know as caper berries. They're picked by hand, often on a small scale. New buds develop on the bush every day, so the capers are harvested daily.

There are lots of varieties – in size order starting with the smallest: nonpareille, surfines, capucines, capotes, nocella, fines and grusas.

I mostly buy larger capote, nocella or fines capers – all larger types of caper, which I tend to chop a bit before using – and the tiny lilliput or nonpareille capers, which I eat whole.

- Brined in salted water
  The most common

- In vinegar
  With an extra kick: my favourite

- Salted
  Salt is said to keep their flavour best; the salt should still be white when you buy them

## Goes well with

| | |
|---|---|
| beetroot | lemon |
| cauliflower | olive |
| chocolate | parsley |
| cucumber | pickles |
| dill | potato |
| egg | tomato |

## Favourite uses

- Puttanesca pasta
- Crisped in oil to top pretty much anything
- In salsa verde
- In tartare sauce
- To scatter into a tray of roast potatoes for the last 10 minutes
- Always on pizza

## Storage

Brined or vinegared capers need to be covered in their pickling liquid when stored or they will dry out and quickly lose their flavour. You can top up a jar with white wine vinegar and a little water. I keep them in the fridge once open.

Salted capers last for years if kept in an airtight container. To use salted capers, they must first be soaked in cold water to mellow the saltiness, then drained. I like to soak mine for at least an hour. If they are particularly salty, you can change the soaking water once during soaking.

## What to buy

If I am buying from a supermarket, I opt for the small lilliput or nonpareille (which translates from French as 'has no equal') caper, which I find plumper and I like the smaller size.

Buy them on holiday in Italy, Spain, France or Greece – often they will be cheaper and handpicked locally.

# Nasturtium capers

300g nasturtium seeds
15g fine sea salt
500ml white wine vinegar

Nasturtiums are a wholly edible plant, providing peppery leaves at the last turn of spring, vibrant edible flowers through the warmer months and seed pods at the end of summer. Often termed 'poor man's capers'. Punchier and more peppery than a classic caper, they can be then used throughout the year as a direct replacement.

MAKES A 1-LITRE JAR

*Steep the nasturtium seeds*
Steep 300g nasturtium seeds in plenty of cold water for a moment to clean them. Drain and blot dry on kitchen paper. Tip the cleaned, drained seeds into a 1-litre sterilised jar.

*Make the brine*
Put 15g fine salt and 500ml white wine vinegar in a medium saucepan and bring to the boil. As soon as it boils, remove from the heat and pour directly over the nasturtium seeds. Seal the jar and store it in the fridge, where it will keep indefinitely. The seeds will be ready to use after a couple of months.

*Use the vinegar*
Once you have used all the nasturtium 'capers' you'll be left with nasturtium vinegar. Keep it in the fridge and use it in dressings and braises. A little of it is amazing poured over super-sweet fruit.

# Wild garlic capers

(Photograph opposite)

300g wild garlic seed heads
6g fine sea salt
500ml apple cider vinegar

Like nasturtiums, wild garlic can be used in a lot of ways in the kitchen. Just before the plants retreat to the woodland floor the seed heads remain, standing proud. Preserving these seed pods requires a little time, but they bring an entirely new dimension to cooking with capers.

MAKES A 1-LITRE JAR

*Pick the wild garlic pods*
Harvest 300g seed heads from the top of the wild garlic flower stems, trying to pick heads with as few white flowers left on them as possible. In a large bowl or bucket, steep the seed heads in plenty of cold water to rinse and remove all dirt and remaining white flowers. Drain and repeat the process once more.

*Salt the wild garlic heads*
Pat the seed heads dry and add to a large bowl, weighing them as you do so.

Add the salt and scrunch it in until everything is thoroughly mixed.

*Store in their salt*
Put the salted seed heads into a sterilised jar and store in the fridge, shaking the jar every few days, for a month.

*Add the vinegar*
After leaving the heads for a month, put 500ml apple cider vinegar in a medium saucepan, bring to the boil, then set aside. Rinse the seed heads under cold running water for a moment, then put into a new sterilised jar of the same size they were salted in. Pour over the vinegar while it is still piping hot and seal the jar. Store in the fridge indefinitely and use in place of normal capers for a subtly garlic-y addition.

# Focaccia with lemon, capers and fennel seeds

2 teaspoons runny honey
3.5g/½ sachet or 7g/1 sachet
    active dry yeast
700g plain flour
½ tablespoon sea salt (about 12g)
40ml extra virgin olive oil,
    plus more for greasing and
    finishing
40g capers, plus 2 tablespoons
    brine from the caper jar
1 tablespoon fennel seeds
the peel of 1 unwaxed lemon,
    pared with a vegetable peeler
½ small bunch of oregano,
    leaves picked
flaked sea salt, for finishing

This recipe is inspired by my brilliant friend Samin Nosrat, who uses a brine to season her focaccia, evenly salting the dough to make it all the more delicious. Here I put capers on top and use the brine they sit in to season the focaccia. You can make this two ways: either with an overnight prove, or with a shorter 2–3 hour prove.

To store the focaccia, wrap it in baking paper then keep it in an airtight bag or container. Gently toast or reheat before serving.

MAKES 1 LARGE FOCACCIA FOR 8–10

*Make the dough*
Whether you are doing an overnight prove or a shorter prove, mix 525ml lukewarm water with 2 teaspoons runny honey then add ½ teaspoon active dry yeast for overnight, or 1 teaspoon yeast for a shorter, 2-hour prove and stir to dissolve. In a large bowl, mix 700g plain flour and ½ tablespoon sea salt, then add the yeast and honey mixture and 40ml extra virgin olive oil. Stir to combine everything and bring it together to a rough dough, and, using a spatula or dough scraper, scrape your hands and the sides of the bowl clean, then cover the bowl with a tea towel.

*Prove the dough*
For an overnight prove, leave at room temperature for 12–14 hours, until at least doubled in size. For a shorter prove leave for 2–3 hours, or until doubled in size.

*Transfer the dough*
Once your dough has doubled in size, pour 3 tablespoons extra virgin olive oil on to a 20cm × 30cm, 4cm-deep roasting tray. Carefully transfer the dough into the tray – use a dough scraper to help you. Rub

2 tablespoons olive oil over the dough and gently stretch it to the edge of the tray. Leave it to rest for half an hour, pulling it back to the edges again if need be.

*Add the topping*
Mix together 40g capers and 1 tablespoon fennel seeds and evenly sprinkle them over the dough with a pinch of flaked sea salt.

*Dimple and brine the dough*
Oil your fingers lightly again and, forming a claw with your fingers, dimple the dough all over, creating irregular and deep dimples. Pour over the caper brine, trying to spread it as evenly as you can. This brine will season the focaccia to begin with. Leave to rest for another half an hour.

*Preheat the oven and bake the focaccia*
Preheat the oven to 220°C/200°C fan. After the dough has had its final rest, run your fingers back over it in the same claw-like fashion to make sure the toppings are at one with the dough. Bake for 25–30 minutes on the middle shelf, until golden-brown. Add the peel of 1 unwaxed lemon, ½ a bunch of picked oregano leaves, a little more oil and flaked sea salt, then move the focaccia to the top shelf and bake for a further 5–7 minutes.

Remove from the oven and drizzle over 2 tablespoons more oil. Leave to cool for 5–10 minutes, before lifting it out of the tin.

Other toppings I love are jarred artichokes, cherry tomatoes, red grapes, bay leaves, rosemary, thyme, red or green chilli, pickled chillies, half a thinly sliced onion or jalapeños.

# Cauliflower caponata

1kg cauliflower, broken into roughly 4cm florets
3 red onions (350g), peeled and cut into eighths
3 sticks of celery, cut into 2cm pieces
extra virgin olive oil
3 tablespoons white wine vinegar
2 × 400g tins plum tomatoes
100g stone-in green or black olives, stones removed (I use a mixture of both)
3 tablespoons capers
50g raisins
½ a bunch of parsley (20g), leaves picked
warm bread, to serve

Caponata is a masterclass in balancing sweet, sour and salty. It's most often made with aubergine, which you have to fry in lots of olive oil first, making it less of a weeknight situation. This buttery cauliflower version is all done in the oven and to me it's just as good as the aubergine version. It has the texture of a stew and can be eaten warm as an antipasto, as is most common in Italy, or on toast or tossed through pasta.

SERVES 4

*Preheat the oven and roast the cauliflower*
Preheat the oven to 220°C/200°C fan. Put a cauliflower, broken into roughly 4cm florets, 3 red onions, peeled and cut into eighths, and 3 sticks of celery, cut into 2cm pieces, into a large, high-sided baking tray with 1 tablespoon extra virgin olive oil, 2 tablespoons white wine vinegar and a little sea salt and pepper. Toss to coat, then roast for 25 minutes, until everything is slightly charred and starting to soften. Turn the oven down to 200°C/180°C fan.

*Add the rest*
Add 2 × 400g tins of plum tomatoes, breaking them in your hands as you do so, along with 100g stone-in green or black olives (stones removed), 3 tablespoons capers and 50g raisins. Give everything a good mix, mashing slightly with a fork, and return to the oven for 40 minutes, or until everything is soft and sticky.

*Finish with the vinegar and oil*
Once ready, and while the mix is still piping hot, add another tablespoon of vinegar, toss through a handful of parsley leaves and serve. Finish with a very generous dousing of extra virgin olive oil to bring it all together.

# Courgette and salsa verde gratin

a few sprigs of oregano or
marjoram (5g)
½ a bunch of mint (15g)
½ a bunch of parsley (15g)
150ml extra virgin olive oil
2 small cloves of garlic, peeled
3 tablespoons capers, drained
(rinsed and soaked if salt-
packed)
zest and juice of 1 unwaxed
lemon
1kg courgettes, cut into 5mm-
thick discs
200g fresh breadcrumbs, from
good bread
50g unsalted butter (or vegan
butter) or more olive oil
2 banana shallots (about 100g),
peeled and finely sliced
1 green chilli or jalapeño,
deseeded and finely chopped
120g nutty cheese, like Gruyère
or Emmental, or 100g vegan
Cheddar-style cheese,
coarsely grated

This recipe is loosely based on one
I have been making for years
from the *Sunday Suppers at Lucques*
restaurant cookbook. Capers
are front and centre here, tossed
through the gratin and providing the
backbone to the salsa verde. This is a
light gratin, with lemon, capers, mint
and parsley the main events rather
than the heavy cheese or cream a lot
of gratins go in for. I make this with
a lemony-dressed peppery salad.

SERVES 4

*Make the salsa verde*
Using a mortar and pestle (or a food
processor if you prefer), pound or
blitz 5g oregano, 5g mint and 5g
parsley leaves to a paste. You may
have to do this in batches if your
pestle and mortar is small. Add 50ml
extra virgin olive oil and mix or blitz
it in. Tip the mixture into a bowl.
Pound 1 clove of garlic with a little
salt and add it to the herb oil. Gently
pound or pulse 2 tablespoons capers
until they're partially crushed, and
add them to the herby garlic mixture.
Stir in 100ml extra virgin oil, a
grinding of black pepper and the zest
and juice of 1 unwaxed lemon. Taste
and adjust for acidity and salt.

*Prepare the courgettes*
Heat the oven to 200°C/180°C fan.
Toss 1kg courgettes, cut into 5mm-
thick discs, in a colander with a good
pinch of sea salt and let them sit for
10 minutes over a bowl to catch any
juices (there won't be loads of liquid).

*Prepare the brown butter breadcrumbs*
Place 200g breadcrumbs in a
heatproof bowl. Heat a small pan
over a medium heat for 1 minute.
Melt 50g unsalted butter until it
begins to turn light brown and starts

to smell nutty, then pour it over
the breadcrumbs and mix well.

*Make the gratin*
Tip out any liquid from the mixing
bowl under the courgettes and
put the courgettes into it. Finely
slice 1 clove of garlic and add it
to the courgettes with 2 shallots,
1 deseeded and finely chopped
green chilli, 4 tablespoons of the
salsa verde and a good grind of
pepper. Toss to mix everything and
add 120g coarsely grated Gruyère
or vegan cheese and half of the
breadcrumbs. Taste for seasoning.
The raw garlic will taste strong but
will mellow as it cooks. Toss the
remaining tablespoon of capers
with the rest of the butter-coated
breadcrumbs.

*Bake the gratin*
Place the courgette mixture in
a 26–30cm round gratin dish,
ovenproof pan or something
similar. Scatter the remaining
caper breadcrumbs over the top
and bake for 40–45 minutes, or
until the courgettes are soft and
the top is golden and crisp.

*Serve the gratin*
Serve with the remaining salsa
verde spooned over the top. I like
mine with a lemon-dressed green
salad, and if I'm hungry some boiled
or roasted buttered new potatoes.

# Pantry pasta with capers and lemons

50g shelled unsalted pistachios
2 banana shallots, peeled and
thinly sliced
4 cloves of garlic, peeled and
thinly sliced
100ml olive oil
1 unwaxed lemon
3 tablespoons capers
400g pasta, like linguine
½ a bunch of flat-leaf parsley
(15g), finely chopped
grated Parmesan cheese or
vegan Parmesan-style cheese,
to serve

Like all the best recipes, this comes from the store cupboard, with the exception of a bit of parsley, which can be left out if you don't have any. Here, a good hit of capers, sticky shallots, lemon and pistachios come together to make a quick sauce that gives you all the flavours. Pasta water is key to getting the lemony–capery sauce creamy and sticking to the pasta, so make sure you don't miss out keeping it back – it's the most important ingredient in this recipe.

SERVES 4

*Cook the pistachios and shallots*
Heat a large frying pan over a medium heat and add 50g shelled pistachios. Toast them, tossing regularly, until golden brown and fragrant. Allow to cool for a moment, then transfer to a pestle and mortar and roughly bash. Set aside for serving. Peel and finely slice 2 shallots and 4 cloves of garlic. Return the frying pan to a medium–low heat and add 100ml olive oil. Add the shallots and garlic and cook for 8–10 minutes, or until golden at the edges.

*Chop the lemon*
Cut 1 unwaxed lemon in half, removing the pips, then slice and finely chop one half, peel and all, discarding the pithy end. Keep the other half of the lemon for squeezing over later.

*Finish the sauce*
Add 3 tablespoons capers and the finely chopped lemon to the shallots and garlic in the frying pan and cook for another couple of minutes until you have a thick paste, then turn off the heat. This can be done ahead.

*Cook the pasta*
Put a large pot of very well salted water on to boil. Add 400g pasta to the boiling water and cook for a couple of minutes less than the packet instructions – you want it not quite al dente. Drain, keeping a mugful of pasta water to finish the sauce.

*Finish the sauce*
Add the drained pasta to the shallot pan along with about half a mug of pasta water and cook, turning the pasta with tongs or a spoon, until the caper, shallot and lemon mixture has come together into a thick sauce, adding a dash more pasta water if needed. Add the juice of the remaining half lemon and ½ a bunch of finely chopped flat-leaf parsley and toss again. Serve in bowls with a scattering of toasted pistachios and grated Parmesan.

# Brown butter potatoes with lime tartare sauce

1kg small floury or new
   potatoes, scrubbed clean
100g salted butter (or 100ml
   olive oil)
6 tablespoons capers, plus
   2 tablespoons caper brine
1 large free-range egg yolk
2 tablespoons Dijon mustard
150ml olive oil
100g sour cream
zest and juice of 1 unwaxed lime
a small bunch of dill or fennel
   fronds, to serve

These have quickly become my desert-island potato. And, coming from a major potato enthusiast, that's something. The capers are added for the last bit of roasting with the potatoes, which adds a super-savoury crispy little pop of saltiness. Capers are used again in a lime and sour cream tartare sauce. For me, this is a complete dinner with a zippy green salad, perhaps some lemon-dressed chickpeas or white beans.

SERVES 4–6

*Parboil the potatoes*
Bring a large pan of salted water to the boil, add 1kg small potatoes, then bring back to the boil and simmer for 10–20 minutes, depending on the size of your potatoes, until they are just cooked. Drain and leave the potatoes to steam dry in a colander.

*Brown the butter*
Preheat the oven to 200°C/180°C fan. Put the potato pan back on the hob and add 100g salted butter. Cook over a medium heat until it turns nutty brown and smells toasty. If you are vegan, use a good olive oil in place of the butter and skip the browning stage; it will still be delicious, and you could add a toasty note with some smoked salt.

*Roast the potatoes*
Take the butter pan off the heat, put the potatoes in a 25cm × 30cm roasting tray and pour over the brown butter. Season generously with salt and pepper and toss everything in the tray. Roast for 25 minutes. Take the potatoes out of the oven and use a potato masher to crush the potatoes into the base of the pan, making a flat surface for crisping up. Scatter over 4 tablespoons capers and bake for another 25 minutes until golden and crisp.

*Make the lime tartare sauce*
Meanwhile make your tartare sauce. Put 1 large free-range egg yolk and 2 tablespoons Dijon mustard in a bowl and mix well. Gradually whisk in 150ml olive oil. Loosen with 2 tablespoons caper brine and 100g sour cream. Finely chop 2 tablespoons capers and add to the sauce along with the zest and juice of 1 unwaxed lime.

Serve the crispy brown butter potatoes with the tartare sauce and with dill or fennel fronds torn over.

# Pumpkin cecina with caper-lime chutney

200g gram flour

400g butternut squash, peeled and grated

zest and juice of 1 unwaxed lime

2 tablespoons olive oil, plus extra for greasing

1 red onion, peeled and finely chopped

4 cloves of garlic, peeled and sliced

a few sprigs of oregano (5g), leaves picked and finely chopped

2 jalapeños or fat green chillies, finely sliced

4 tablespoons capers

50g stone-in green olives, destoned and roughly chopped

400g tomatoes (vine or cherry), roughly chopped or halved

1 tablespoon light brown soft sugar

150g soft cheese – drained ricotta or feta

a few handfuls of peppery salad leaves, to serve

This recipe comes from a few places. Cecina is a Tuscan chickpea flour flatbread similar to socca, farinata or panisse. It comes together quickly and it's a super-affordable vegetarian dinner. I add squash to mine but other root veg like sweet potato, celeriac or salted and squeezed-out grated courgette would work too. The chutney is inspired by Mexican Veracruz sauce, which uses capers and olives for punch and is great to scoop up with the cecina.

SERVES 4

*Make the squash cecina*
Mix 200g gram flour with 400ml cold water in a bowl, mix in 400g grated squash, the zest of 1 unwaxed lime and a pinch of sea salt and let the mixture sit for an hour.

*Make the Veracruz-style chutney*
Heat a large pan over a medium heat, drizzle 1 tablespoon of olive oil into the pan, then add 1 peeled and finely chopped red onion and cook for 10 minutes until soft and sweet. Add 4 peeled and sliced cloves of garlic and cook for a further 3 minutes. Add the finely chopped leaves from a few sprigs of oregano and 2 finely sliced green chillies and cook for another minute or so. Add 4 tablespoons capers, 50g destoned and roughly chopped green olives and 400g chopped tomatoes, along with 1 tablespoon light brown soft sugar and the juice of 1 unwaxed lime, and cook for 10–15 minutes over a medium-high heat until the tomatoes have broken down and the chutney is sticky.

*Cook the squash cecina*
Preheat the oven to 220°C/200°C fan. Once the oven is hot, oil a 25cm × 30cm high-sided baking tray with 2 tablespoons olive oil and put back in the oven for 5 minutes. Carefully remove the oiled tray from the oven, add the cecina batter and bake for 35–45 minutes, turning it in the oven halfway through (to ensure it cooks evenly), until set and golden brown around the edges.

*Finish with the chutney and cheese*
Remove the cecina from the oven and let it cool for a few minutes before loosening from the tray. Once cool enough to cut, chop into large pieces and top with 150g soft cheese, the chutney and a few handfuls of salad leaves.

# Corn on the cob with caper and herb crumbs

4 corn on the cob in their husks
2 tablespoons olive oil
100g fresh breadcrumbs
4 tablespoons capers, roughly
    chopped, plus 1 tablespoon
    of caper brine
1 red or green chilli, deseeded
    and finely chopped
100g crème fraîche or sour cream
1 unwaxed lime
50g Parmesan or pecorino
    cheese, finely grated
½ a bunch of chives (10g), finely
    chopped

This recipe comes from my love of Mexican elote corn – crema and mayo-smothered corn topped with chilli and cotija cheese. This takes that idea down a different flavour route with capers, chives, lime and green chilli. A coating of crème fraîche, then caper-y breadcrumbs, then cheese and chives makes this my perfect corn. It also works as a salad if you cut the corn from the cobs, dress the kernels in the lime crème fraîche, then top with the caper breadcrumbs and cheese.

SERVES 4

*Cook the corn*
De-husk 4 cobs of corn, removing all the leaves and strings. You can then cook the corn one of two ways. To boil it, add the cobs to a deep pan of salted boiling water and cook for 10–12 minutes until tender. To griddle or barbecue it, blanch the cobs in boiling salted water for 5 minutes, then cook on a smoking hot griddle pan or barbecue until charred all over.

*Fry the breadcrumbs*
While the corn is cooking, heat 2 tablespoons olive oil in a large frying pan then add 100g breadcrumbs, 4 tablespoons capers, roughly chopped, and 1 deseeded and finely chopped red or green chilli. Cook the breadcrumbs for about 5–8 minutes, or until they are golden and toasted. Allow to cool.

*Make the dressing*
Mix 100g crème fraîche or sour cream with the zest and juice of ½ an unwaxed lime and 1 tablespoon caper brine, then put to one side.

*Dress the corn*
Once cool enough to handle, put the corn on to a plate, dress with the crème fraîche mixture and the remaining lime zest, then use the back of a spoon to cover the cobs all over. Next roll the cobs in the caper-spiked breadcrumbs, but don't worry if you don't get a perfect covering. Finally, scatter over 50g finely grated Parmesan or pecorino and top with ½ a bunch of finely chopped chives and the remaining lime half cut into wedges.

# Kitty's caper and chocolate ice cream

1 heaped tablespoon salted
    capers (about 15g)
200ml double cream
500ml whole milk
20g cocoa powder
5 organic egg yolks
140g caster sugar
80g good-quality dark milk
    chocolate, broken into pieces

On a trip to Italy I'd heard about a caper and chocolate ice cream and as wild as it sounds I imagined the salty depth that the capers would bring to a rich chocolate ice cream. So I asked my friend Kitty Travers of La Grotta Ices if she had a recipe, which of course she did. Kitty makes my favourite ice cream, mostly using in-season fruits. It's like she has climbed inside my head and come up with all the flavours I would love. This caper and chocolate one is up there with her best. Like all real ice cream, it does take a little time and an ice-cream machine, but you won't be sad you made the effort.

MAKES 1 LITRE ICE CREAM

*Soak the capers*
Soak 1 heaped tablespoon salted capers in a good amount of cold water for at least 1 hour.

*Heat the cream and milk*
Heat 200ml double cream, 500ml whole milk and 20g cocoa powder in a large heavy-based saucepan until it comes to a simmer, then turn down very low to bubble away for 8–10 minutes, whisking constantly to combine and cook the cocoa. Turn off the heat.

*Add the eggs to make the custard*
Put 5 organic egg yolks and 140g caster sugar into a mixing bowl and whisk together. Add a ladleful of the hot milk mixture and whisk it into the eggs. Then add the egg mixture to the rest of the hot milk and put the pan back on a medium-low heat and cook, stirring all the time, until it coats the back of a spoon. Take off the heat.

*Add the chocolate and capers*
Break 80g good-quality dark milk chocolate into pieces. Pour the custard into a blender and while it's still hot add the chocolate pieces and blend to melt them into the custard. Drain the capers and squeeze out any excess liquid. Add the capers to the mixture in the blender and blend in well.

*Refrigerate and churn*
Refrigerate the custard overnight. Put the whole blender jug into the fridge, if it fits, as you will blend it again before churning. The next morning blend the mixture again, then put it in an ice-cream machine and churn it according to the instructions.

*Freeze*
Transfer to a lidded container and freeze for 4 hours before serving. Take it out of the fridge a few minutes before you want to eat it to make it scoopable.

# Caper brine margarita

zest and juice of 2 large
    unwaxed limes (you need
    60ml of juice)
½ teaspoon fine red chilli
    powder
5g flaky sea salt (½ teaspoon)
10ml caper brine, plus extra for
    the rim
120ml best-quality mezcal or
    tequila
30ml agave syrup

When it comes to drinks I am a sour
and salty person. This margarita uses
caper brine that would otherwise be
thrown away, bringing to the table
what olive brine might to a martini.
In fact I've made a dirty martini with
caper brine and it was great, but this
is better.

MAKES 2 MARGARITAS

*Make the chilli-lime mixture for
the glass*
Put the zest of 2 large unwaxed limes
into a bowl with ½ teaspoon fine
red chilli powder and 5g flaky sea
salt. If you like, put your glasses in
the freezer to frost up. (I like thin
tumblers or coupes).

*Rim the glasses*
Put the chilli-lime salt mixture on a
plate. Pour a couple of tablespoons
of caper brine onto another plate.
Dip the rims of two glasses into the
caper brine, then into the chilli-lime
mixture.

*Make the margarita*
Put some ice into a cocktail shaker
or other similar container with a
lid. Add 120ml best-quality mezcal
or tequila, 30ml agave syrup, 60ml
lime juice and 10ml caper brine and
shake until the shaker is frosty and
cold. Load your rimmed glasses with
ice and divide the margarita mix
between them.

# Chilli
# and Harissa

From searing heat to gentle hum. Chilli is the warming heart.
A spike of heat. I love mellow, rounded heat, so I use dried and
preserved chillies. Whole raisiny ancho to spoonable spiced
harissa and smoky chipotle in adobo. The chillies I have in my
spice cupboard and this book are the few I can buy with ease.
There are many more, and they all belong to cultures that are
not my own. I use them with wonder, respect and reverence.
A spoonful of harissa adds deep embedded flavour that fills
the room. Smoked paprika brings a fruit-like roundedness that
makes it the spice I reach for most. Chipotle in adobo brings
smokiness to an aubergine parmigiana. Ancho brings mild,
raisiny-sweet smokiness to tacos, salsa and chimichurri.

# On Chilli and Harissa

Chilli gives heat; a warming sensation in your mouth. This warming feeling is not actually your mouth heating up but something called chemesthesis – your mouth's response to irritation. When we eat something spicy, from a hot chilli to a peppercorn, our sensory receptors get irritated and that gives the sensation we get from 'hot' or spicy food. Chilli heat is measured in Scovilles and ranges from a mild red pepper to chillies that will blow your socks off.

In Mexico alone, there are close to a hundred varieties of chilli. In the UK, we use very few varieties. When it comes to dried chilli, which is my focus in this chapter, I would wager that a lot of houses might have some chilli powder and some dried chilli flakes. And if that is what you have, then you can use a small amount of either in any of these recipes. They might not have the same depth of flavour, but your recipe will still taste good.

Heat, Smoky, Sweet, Earthy

## Types

There are hundreds of types of dried chillies, but in this chapter I focus on the ones that I buy fairly easily and that get used a lot in my kitchen.

Dried chillies and spices

· Chipotle – a ripe smoke-dried jalapeño chilli used in Mexico.

· Ancho – mild, sweet-tasting. They have a fruity, earthy flavour.

· Pasilla – translates as 'little raisin', a wrinkly medium-hot chilli.

· Arbol – have an intense, clean heat and a nutty, grassy flavour.

· Smoked paprika – smoky, finely ground chilli, which you can buy in dulce (sweet), hot (picante) and agridulce (bittersweet).

· Turkish chilli or pul biber – a bright reddish chilli from Turkey, that's used like the Eastern equivalent of black pepper. It has a sweeter, more friendly chilli flavour. I use it when I'm cooking for kids.

Jarred chilli and chilli pastes

· Harissa – a North African red chilli paste made from chilli, garlic, olive oil, citrus and warm spices.

· Chipotle in adobo – smoky chillies cooked in a vinegary tomato sauce ready for cooking.

## Goes well with

| | |
|---|---|
| almond | lime |
| avocado | mango |
| aubergine | mint |
| broccoli | orange |
| cauliflower | peanut |
| chickpea | pepper |
| chocolate | pineapple |
| coconut | potato |
| coriander | pasta |

## Favourite uses

*Dried chillies*
· Chilli flakes – with cinnamon and fennel seeds on squash for roasting

· Chilli flakes – on top of thick yoghurt with salt and lemon, or see page 340

· Chilli flakes – sizzled in oil with slices of garlic, then tossed through pasta

· Pul biber – sprinkled on hummus with olive oil and sumac

*Harissa*
· Spooned into a stew of chickpeas, kale and lemon

· Swirled into yoghurt for spooning on soups/stews and flatbreads

*Chipotle in adobo*
· Spooned into a tin of black beans with some sizzled garlic

## Storage and tips

Buy chillies in small quantities and replace them often, as they will lose their potency over time. Pastes can be stored in the fridge.

Pastes like harissa and chipotle will keep in the fridge for months once opened.

## Favourite brands

For harissa, La Miri from Tunisia is my current favourite. For whole dried chillies, the Cool Chile Company have a good selection. And I love Daphnis and Chloe's chilli flakes.

Easy Wins

# Ancho chilli harissa

6 dried ancho chillies
1 tablespoon cumin seeds
1 tablespoon coriander seeds
6 cloves of garlic, peeled
2 roasted red peppers in brine,
    drained
200ml olive oil, plus a little
    extra
1 tablespoon red wine vinegar

Harissa is one of my most used ingredients. I don't think anything can beat it on the flavour it gives for not much cost or effort. It's so low-maintenance as an ingredient; a jar will sit happily for ages in your pantry unopened and then for months in the fridge without spoiling. It is a sure-fire way of making something taste like you have spent a lot more time cooking than you actually have. This is a mellow harissa that uses sweet, smoky anchos and roasted red peppers.

MAKES 1 × 500G JAR

*Toast the chillies and spices*
Put 6 dried ancho chillies into a piping hot frying pan and toast until fragrant. Set aside to cool slightly while you toast 1 tablespoon cumin seeds and 1 tablespoon coriander seeds in the same hot pan. When fragrant, set aside the spices and remove the seeds and stems from the chillies.

*Soak the chillies*
Put the chillies into a heatproof bowl, cover with boiling water and set aside for half an hour to soften.

*Blitz the harissa*
Drain the chillies and put into a food processor with the cumin and coriander seeds, 6 peeled cloves of garlic, 2 drained, roasted red peppers in brine, 200ml olive oil and 1 tablespoon red wine vinegar. Pulse until you have a not-quite-smooth paste, adding a little extra oil to loosen if you like.

*Jar and store*
Transfer to a sterilised jar, cover with a little extra olive oil and store in a cool dark place until needed. Once opened keep in the fridge.

Chilli and Harissa

# Quick charred corn and crispy onion salad

6 corn on the cobs, husks
 removed, or 780g frozen
 sweetcorn
a small bunch of coriander,
 chopped
zest and juice of 2 unwaxed
 limes
3 tablespoons extra virgin
 olive oil
1 teaspoon harissa paste
100g crispy onions/shallots,
 shop-bought or see recipe
 on page 268

A recipe that's more than the sum of
its parts. This is great with flatbreads
and perhaps some baked feta, or even
in tacos with some avocado and more
coriander. The harissa adds a bolt
of flavour for very little effort and
brings it all together.

Fresh corn is best here, but if you
want to make the dish out of season,
use cooked and cooled frozen or
unsweetened tinned corn, then char
the kernels in a dry frying pan. Work
to about 130g of frozen corn per cob.

SERVES 4

*Cook the corn*
Heat a griddle pan to a high heat,
then, when the pan is piping hot,
add 6 de-husked corn cobs in batches,
turning every few minutes, until
charred all over and cooked through.
This works really well on a barbecue
too. Or you can cut the kernels from
the cobs use 780g of frozen sweetcorn
and char them in a dry frying pan.

*Cut the kernels from the corn*
Set aside to cool slightly, then, if
necessary, slice off the kernels with
a sharp knife. Add to a serving bowl
with a small bunch of chopped
coriander.

*Make the dressing and serve*
Put the juice and zest of 2 unwaxed
limes, 3 tablespoons extra virgin
olive oil and 1 teaspoon harissa paste
into a bowl or jam jar, give it a good
shake, then pour it over the corn and
coriander. Give everything a mix,
taste and season with salt, and top
with 100g crispy onions or shallots
and serve.

# Lemon, artichoke and butter bean paella

1 litre vegetable stock
2 onions, peeled and finely
    chopped (keep the trimmings)
1 carrot, peeled and finely
    chopped (keep the trimmings)
5g saffron threads, soaked in
    50ml warm water
good-quality extra virgin
    olive oil
1 bulb fennel, trimmed and
    finely chopped, any herby
    bits kept for later
1 red pepper, deseeded and
    finely chopped
2 ripe tomatoes, flesh finely
    chopped, seeds discarded
4 cloves of garlic, peeled and
    finely chopped (keep the
    trimmings)
1 heaped teaspoon sweet
    smoked paprika
100ml white wine
100ml tomato passata
300g short-grain paella rice
    (see recipe intro)
1 × 700g jar butter beans, drained
1 × 400g jar artichokes, chopped
    into bite-sized pieces
1 unwaxed lemon, cut into
    8 wedges
a bunch of parsley (30g), chopped

A few things to say about paella: while recognising I am absolutely no expert, I have found it's best made in a thin-based paella-style pan over a gas flame. Failing that, whatever large shallow (to remove the liquid quickly) sauté pan you have will work, the thinner-based the better.

The rice must be short-grain so it won't dry out when toasted. I have used bomba (also known as Calasparra). I have been told that risotto rice works as well too.

DO NOT STIR. This is not a risotto. The lack of stirring is what gives you the crisp, browned, sticky, chewy layer of 'socarrat' which is the main reason I eat paella.

Don't scrimp on the olive oil – the oil and your generosity with it is what makes this.

SERVES 4–6

*Heat the stock and soak the saffron*
Put 1 litre vegetable stock in a pan and add all the trimmings from your veg to add some more depth to the stock. Soak 5g saffron in 50ml warm water.

*Fry the vegetables*
Heat about 4 tablespoons oil in your pan, add 2 peeled and finely chopped onions, 1 peeled and finely chopped carrot and 1 trimmed and finely chopped bulb of fennel and sauté for about 10 minutes until really soft and sweet and beginning to brown. Add 1 deseeded and finely chopped red pepper, 2 finely chopped ripe tomatoes, 4 peeled and finely chopped cloves of garlic and 1 heaped teaspoon smoked paprika and cook for another few minutes. Add the soaked saffron and its water, 100ml white wine and 100ml tomato passata and cook for another few minutes.

*Add the rice*
Add 300g short-grain paella rice to the pan and stir it well to coat, adding more oil here if you think you need it. Strain the stock. Shuffle the rice into an even layer and add about 800ml of the stock. Simmer hard, no stirring, for 10 minutes, by which time a good amount of the liquid should have been absorbed but it should still feel like there is enough for it to cook for another 10 minutes. If not, add some of the remaining stock. Remember, no stirring.

*Add the butter beans and artichokes*
Next, scatter over a 700g jar of drained butter beans and a 400g jar of artichokes, chopped, and cook, without stirring, for another 8–10 minutes. Again, if the rice looks too dry before it's cooked (check by trying some – it should be just al dente but not too hard or chalky), add a little more stock, but do not stir it in.

*Crisp up the bottom (the socarrat)*
The key to the crispy bottom is to let it cook for a while after all the liquid has been absorbed. You should hear a sizzle. Leave it for about 30 seconds then turn off the heat – you should begin to see the edges crisp. The thicker the base of the pan you have, the harder this is. If you serve and haven't got a crispy bottom, drizzle a little oil around the edge of the pan and put it back on a high heat for another few minutes. Take it off the heat and cover to allow it to rest for 10 minutes then top with lemon wedges, a bunch of chopped parsley and any fennel fronds.

# Squash and smoked chilli empanadas

1kg squash (butternut or any firm squash), peeled, seeds removed and cut into 1cm cubes

2 tablespoons olive oil, plus 80ml

½ a bunch of fresh oregano (5g), leaves picked, or 1 teaspoon dried oregano

2 dried ancho chillies

500g plain flour, plus extra for dusting

160g unsalted butter or vegan butter, cold and cubed

1 red onion, peeled and very finely sliced

zest and juice of 1 unwaxed lemon

100g Cheddar or vegan Cheddar-style cheese

1–2 green chillies, finely chopped

½ a bunch of parsley (15g), chopped

1 egg, beaten, or a few tablespoons oat milk

Years ago, I spent a few brilliant months in Argentina. Money was tight, so I lived mostly on empanadas: cheap, filling, delicious. In Argentina and across South America, if you're lucky, you'll come across an empanaderia – a bakery with glass cabinets full of empanadas. It's been years since I walked through the doors of such a place, but I find myself craving the flaky pastry and chilli eaten with your hands, all of which adds up to empanadas.

I dip them in chimichurri, an Argentinian-style salsa verde which is by no means traditional with empanadas but I like it. These are filled with squash, Cheddar (again not traditional, but I like the kick), herbs and quick-pickled red onions. If you can't get your hand on the dried chillies, then 2–3 teaspoons of chipotle or ancho in adobo (jarred paste) will work in their place.

MAKES 16 EMPANADAS

### Roast the squash
Preheat the oven to 220°C/200°C fan. Scatter 1kg peeled, deseeded and cubed squash on a roasting tray with 2 tablespoons olive oil, the leaves from a couple of sprigs of fresh, or ½ teaspoon dried, oregano, salt and pepper, and roast for 25–35 minutes, until soft and slightly caramelised. Set aside to cool. Turn the oven down to 210°C/190°C fan.

### Soak the chillies
Put 2 dried ancho chillies into a wide-based bowl or a heatproof measuring jug with 100ml boiling water and leave to sit and soften for 5 minutes. Once soft, remove the stalks and deseed if you like things less spicy. Then finely chop 1 of the chillies and keep the other aside for the chimichurri.

### Make the pastry
While the squash is cooking, make the dough. Put 500g plain flour, a good pinch of sea salt and 160g cold, cubed butter in a food processor and blitz until it resembles breadcrumbs (you can do this by hand in a bowl using the rubbing method too). Add 80ml olive oil and blitz until the mixture has the texture of sand, then add 50–100ml ice-cold water, a little at a time, until it comes together into a dough. Tip out onto a clean work surface and gently knead until it is smooth, then shape into a disc, cover with a clean tea towel and chill in the fridge for an hour.

### Pickle the onion
Put 1 peeled and very finely sliced red onion and the zest and juice of 1 unwaxed lemon into a bowl, then scrunch it all together with your hands until the onion starts to turn pink. Add the chopped soaked chilli, crumble in 70g Cheddar or vegan Cheddar-style cheese, add 1–2 finely chopped green chillies, 15g chopped parsley and the remaining sprigs of fresh, or ½ teaspoon dried, oregano and season. Add the squash and mix until combined.

### Make the empanadas
Line two baking trays with baking paper. Cut the pastry into two (putting half back into the fridge while you roll out the first batch of dough) and on a lightly floured surface roll it out to a thickness of a 50p piece. Use a 10cm cutter (or a bowl this width) to cut out 6 rounds (you will have 16 in total), then place a heaped tablespoon of the filling in the centre of each. Brush one side of the pastry with the

*Continued over...*

beaten egg or oat milk, then fold the other side over. Press down the edges with a fork, to stick them together neatly. Repeat this process with the other half of the pastry so you have 16 in total.

Lay the empanadas on the tray, brush the tops with egg wash or oat milk and grate over 30g Cheddar. Grind over the remaining black pepper, then bake in the oven for 25 minutes, or until golden brown. Leave to cool for a few minutes before serving with a dollop of chimichurri.

vinegar and 1 teaspoon sea salt. Stir together to form a silky, herby sauce, taste, adjust the seasoning if needed, and serve. This can be kept in a jar in the fridge for up to 1 week.

---

SMOKED ANCHO CHIMICHURRI

As well as being the perfect accompaniment for empanadas, chimichurri is also great as a dressing for roast veg or as a topping for a bowl of polenta or lentils.

a bunch of flat-leaf parsley (30g), finely chopped
½ a bunch of oregano (10g), leaves picked and finely chopped
1 shallot, peeled and finely chopped
2 cloves of garlic, peeled and finely chopped
1–2 dried ancho chillies, soaked, deseeded and finely chopped, or a good pinch of dried chilli flakes
3 tablespoons extra virgin olive oil
1 tablespoon red wine vinegar

MAKES 1 SMALL BOWLFUL

In a small bowl, mix a bunch of finely chopped flat-leaf parsley, ½ a bunch of finely chopped oregano leaves, 1 finely chopped shallot, 2 finely chopped cloves of garlic, 1–2 soaked, deseeded and finely chopped dried ancho chillies, 3 tablespoons extra virgin olive oil, 1 tablespoon red wine

Chilli and Harissa

# Roast sweet potatoes with sticky chilli salsa

1kg sweet potatoes (about
    3 large potatoes), cut into
    2cm-thick rounds
4 tablespoons extra virgin
    olive oil
2 large red onions, peeled and
    finely chopped
1 large thumb-sized piece of
    ginger (about 50g), peeled
    and finely grated
2 vine tomatoes, roughly
    chopped
1 dried ancho chilli, soaked and
    roughly chopped
1 tablespoon red wine vinegar
1 teaspoon caster sugar or maple
    syrup
50g skin-on almonds, roughly
    chopped
150g Greek yoghurt or oat
    yoghurt
3 unwaxed limes
8 corn tortillas or tacos, to serve

Sweet potato, lime, ginger, yoghurt and smoked chilli come together to make a plate of food that feels like everything I want to eat. The onions, ginger and tomatoes make a salsa that would and does make anything better. This would work really well with squash or pumpkin too.

If you can't find dried ancho chillies, you can use a tablespoon of ancho flakes or ancho in adobo or chipotle paste.

SERVES 4

*Roast the sweet potatoes*
Preheat the oven to 220°C/200°C fan. Put 1kg sweet potatoes, cut into 2cm-thick rounds, into a large baking tray or 2 smaller ones, drizzle over 2 tablespoons olive oil and scatter with salt. Roast for 20 minutes, then turn the potatoes over and cook for 15 minutes until golden on both sides.

*Make the salsa*
Heat 1 tablespoon extra virgin olive oil in a frying pan over a medium heat, add 2 finely chopped red onions and a good pinch of sea salt and cook for 10 minutes, until soft. Add a large finely grated thumb of ginger to the pan and cook for another 5 minutes.

*Finish the salsa*
Add another tablespoon of olive oil to the onions, plus 2 roughly chopped vine tomatoes, 1 soaked and roughly chopped dried ancho chilli, a tablespoon red wine vinegar and a teaspoon caster sugar or maple syrup. Turn the heat down to low and cook for 20 minutes until sticky and sweet, then add 25g roughly chopped, skin-on almonds and take off the heat.

*Make the lime yoghurt*
Mix 150g Greek yoghurt with a good pinch of salt and the juice and zest of 1 unwaxed lime.

*Put it together*
Once the sweet potatoes are cooked, you are ready to serve. Spread the lime yoghurt over a plate or platter and top with the sweet potatoes and half of the salsa. Cut 2 unwaxed limes into wedges and put around the plate for squeezing over. Serve with warm tacos, the rest of the salsa and another 25g chopped skin-on almonds.

If you are only eating a bit at a time, the salsa, yoghurt and sweet potatoes are best stored separately. They will keep in the fridge for up to 4 days.

Chilli and Harissa

# Chipotle aubergine parmigiana

4 large aubergines (1.4kg in total)
olive oil
1 small onion, peeled and
   finely chopped
2 cloves of garlic, peeled and
   finely sliced
2 × 400g tins good-quality
   plum tomatoes or 800g fresh
   tomatoes, peeled and roughly
   chopped
1–2 tablespoons chipotle in
   adobo (depending on your
   love of heat)
1 tablespoon red wine vinegar
a small bunch of oregano (15g),
   or 1 tablespoon of good dried
   oregano
3 balls mozzarella (375g) or 300g
   vegan mozzarella, drained
   and thinly sliced
120g Parmesan or vegan
   Parmesan-style cheese, grated
100g fresh breadcrumbs (about
   4 slices of bread)

I love parmigiana. I love its layers, its buttery aubergine, the carefree amount of olive oil. Everything. In this parmigiana the aubergine is griddled, not fried, then doused in olive oil (though you use a good amount less than if it was fried). The griddling sounds like a job but it's pretty easy to do and you can start them off while you make the sauce. I've added some smoky chipotle in adobo here, which backs up the smoky notes of the griddled aubergine and rounds it all off. It is far from traditional.

I appreciate that buying 3 balls of mozzarella or vegan mozzarella can be expensive and it's a lot of cheese. I've made this with just two balls of mozzarella, making a thinner layer of cheese, and it was still great.

SERVES 4–6

*Prepare and griddle the aubergines*
Top and tail 4 large aubergines, then cut them lengthways into 5mm–7mm-thick slices. Generously drizzle them with olive oil and toss to coat well. Get a cast-iron griddle pan or barbecue really hot and, working in batches, griddle the aubergines first on one side, then the other, until cooked through and charred in places – each side will take about 4 minutes, so settle in. As they are ready, lay them on a large tray or plate and, when they're still warm, sprinkle with salt and drizzle with oil.

*Make the tomato sauce*
While the aubergines are grilling, get your tomato sauce on. In a deep pan, fry 1 small finely chopped onion and 2 peeled and finely sliced cloves of garlic gently in a couple of tablespoons of olive oil, until soft and sweet, then add 2 × 400g tinned or 800g chopped fresh tomatoes,

1–2 tablespoons chipotle in adobo, 1 tablespoon red wine vinegar and half a small bunch of fresh, or ½ tablespoon dried, oregano. Give it a good stir, mashing up the tinned tomatoes if necessary, and simmer for 25 minutes, until rich and thick. Preheat the oven about now to 200°C/180°C fan, so it is ready at the same time as the sauce.

*Layer up the parmigiana*
Spread a little tomato sauce in the bottom of a roughly 30cm × 20cm ovenproof dish, then cover with a layer of the charred aubergines, overlapping the slices slightly. Cover this with another thin layer of tomato sauce – use the back of a spoon to spread it out evenly, then top with a layer of mozzarella slices from 1 ball of mozzarella and ⅓ (40g) of the grated Parmesan. Repeat with another layer of aubergine, sauce, mozzarella and Parmesan and continue the layers until all the ingredients are used up. You should end up with three layers of each.

*Make the breadcrumbs*
Blitz 100g fresh breadcrumbs with the other half-bunch of fresh, or the remaining ½ tablespoon dried, oregano, 2 tablespoons of olive oil and a pinch of salt and toss together. Then sprinkle over the top.

*Cook the parmigiana*
Bake the parmigiana in the middle of the oven for 30–35 minutes, then remove and leave to rest for at least an hour before serving. I serve mine with a lemon-dressed green salad.

# Spiced potato traybake with crispy chickpeas

olive oil

1kg waxy potatoes, cut into 1cm-thick wedges, skin-on

2 red peppers, deseeded and cut into 3cm pieces

1 whole head of garlic, cut in half across the middle

1 tablespoon coriander seeds, bashed in a pestle and mortar

300g cherry tomatoes, halved, or 1 × 400g tin cherry tomatoes, drained

1 × 600g jar chickpeas, drained

2 tablespoons harissa paste

1 tablespoon black mustard seeds

1 teaspoon ground turmeric

200g Greek yoghurt or oat yoghurt

juice of 1 unwaxed lemon

½ a bunch of coriander (15g)

All the things I want to eat on a weeknight. This is cooked in two trays so you get a tray of crisp-edged potatoes and peppers and a tray of crispy harissa chickpeas and tomatoes. It's all brought together with a spiced yoghurt. I serve this with a herb salad of coriander and parsley leaves dressed in a little lemon and salt.

SERVES 4–6

*Season and bake the vegetables*
Preheat the oven to 220°C/200°C fan. Put a couple of tablespoons of olive oil in a baking tray and put in the oven to warm for 5 minutes. Take the tray out and carefully add 1kg skin-on waxy potatoes cut into 1cm-thick wedges, 2 deseeded red peppers cut into 3cm pieces, 1 whole head of garlic cut in half across the middle and 1 tablespoon bashed coriander seeds. Season well with salt and pepper and roast in the oven for 40 minutes until the potatoes are beginning to turn golden.

*Make the crispy harissa chickpeas*
Cut 300g cherry tomatoes in half (no need to do this if you are using tinned). In another baking tray put 600g drained jarred chickpeas, 2 tablespoons harissa paste and the halved tomatoes (or 400g tin cherry tomatoes, drained). Season well with sea salt and freshly ground black pepper and roast on a shelf below the potatoes for 35 minutes at the same temperature.

*Make the spiced yoghurt*
Meanwhile, heat 2 tablespoons of olive oil in a small pan and add 1 tablespoon black mustard seeds. Cook until they pop, then take off the heat and stir in 1 teaspoon ground turmeric. Allow to cool, then ripple through 200g yoghurt with the juice of 1 unwaxed lemon.

*Serve*
When the potatoes are browned and soft and the peppers jammy and charred, finely chop 15g coriander and scatter over the chickpeas and tomatoes. Serve in bowls with the spiced yoghurt.

# Koftes with spiced tomato and lime butter rice

olive oil
1 onion, peeled and finely
    chopped
6 cloves of garlic, peeled and
    finely sliced
2 small thumb-sized pieces
    of ginger (10g), peeled and
    finely grated
3 tablespoons rose harissa paste
½ a bunch of coriander (15g),
    roughly chopped
½ a bunch of parsley (15g),
    roughly chopped
450g firm tofu, crumbled
6 tablespoons gram flour
2 × 400g tins finely chopped
    tomatoes, or passata
300g (about 1½ cups) basmati rice
25g butter, ghee or coconut oil
1 teaspoon cumin seeds
zest and juice of 1 unwaxed lime

These koftes are so moreish, made from tofu, herbs and harissa, and cooked first until golden in the pan and then in tomato and harissa sauce. I serve them on top of cumin and lime butter rice. I use a cup method for perfect rice; it's much easier than weighing it.

SERVES 4

*Make the koftes mixture*
Put 2 tablespoons olive oil in a large frying pan on a medium-high heat and add 1 peeled and finely chopped onion. Cook until soft, sweet and golden at the edges. Add 3 peeled and finely sliced cloves of garlic, a small thumb of finely grated ginger and cook for another couple of minutes before adding 1 tablespoon rose harissa and cooking for another 2 minutes. Transfer to a bowl to cool. Once the mixture is cool, add most of the roughly chopped parsley and coriander, reserving a little for the end, 450g crumbled firm tofu and 6 tablespoons gram flour, a good pinch of sea salt and a grinding of black pepper. Blitz half the mixture with 1–2 tablespoons cold water until you have a rough paste, then mix both together.

*Roll out the koftes*
Divide the mixture in half, then each half into 6 pieces (so you have 12 in total) and, with slightly wet hands, roll each one into a firm oval shape.

*Cook the koftes*
Put 4 tablespoons olive oil into the same pan on a medium-high heat. Once hot, fry the koftes in batches for 2–3 minutes on each side, until golden brown all over, then transfer to a baking tray and put into a low oven to keep warm. Wipe the pan clean.

*Make the tomato sauce*
Put the same pan on a medium-high heat. Add 1 tablespoon olive oil and, once hot, add another small thumb of grated ginger and 3 cloves of finely sliced garlic, and fry, stirring, for 2 minutes. Add 2 tablespoons rose harissa and stir, then add 2 tins of finely chopped tomatoes or passata and ½ a teaspoon of sea salt. Simmer for about 10 minutes until you have a rich tomatoey sauce.

*Cook the rice*
Put 300g (1½ cups) basmati rice in a sieve and run it under cold water for 30 seconds, until the water is clear. Fill and boil the kettle. Get a medium saucepan with a tight-fitting lid. Melt 25g butter, ghee or coconut oil in a saucepan over a medium heat. Add the rice and 1 teaspoon cumin seeds. Cook for 2–3 minutes, stirring all the time, until the rice looks shiny. Add 3 cups or 750ml boiling water, 1 teaspoon sea salt and the juice and zest of 1 unwaxed lime. Bring to the boil and simmer for 8 minutes on a medium heat with the lid off.

Then turn off the heat, wrap the pan lid in a tea towel and put it on the pan (this will absorb excess moisture). Leave for at least 5 minutes, avoiding the temptation to peek. When you take the lid off, you should see little air holes in the light and fluffy rice, with no liquid at the bottom. Stir in more lime and butter if you like.

*Add the koftes to the sauce and finish*
Gently put the koftes into the tomato sauce in the pan, spoon the sauce over to coat and cook for another 2 minutes, until the koftes are warmed through. Serve the koftes with the rice and the last of the coriander and parsley.

# Smoked chilli cornbread

140g unsalted or vegan butter
(see intro), plus extra to serve
150ml Greek-style yoghurt or
oat Greek yoghurt
2 large free-range or organic
eggs
2 dried ancho chillies, soaked,
deseeded and finely chopped
(soaking liquid reserved)
4 spring onions, trimmed and
finely chopped
zest of 1 unwaxed lime, finely
grated
2 tablespoons runny honey or
maple syrup
100g quick-cook polenta
75g plain flour
½ teaspoon fine sea salt
the kernels from 4 corn on the
cob, or about 520g defrosted
frozen corn
½ teaspoon baking powder
½ teaspoon bicarbonate of soda
olive oil
2 garlic cloves, peeled and finely
sliced
2 × 400g tins black beans with
liquid
3cm piece of cinnamon, ground
feta or vegan feta-style cheese,
crumbled, to serve
a bunch of fresh coriander (30g),
chopped, to serve

This brown butter cornbread is inspired by one made by Ixta Belfrage in her book *Mezcla*. This one differs a lot from Ixta's; it has ancho chillies, spring onions, lime and honey to flavour the cornbread as it cooks. The brown butter is Ixta's trick, though, giving the whole thing a satisfying deep nutty flavour.

I have only found one vegan butter (Naturli vegan block) that browns, so I'd search that out or skip the browning step altogether. I most often make this with fresh corn, but defrosted frozen corn will work too.

SERVES 8

*Get ready*
Preheat the oven to 220°C/200°C fan. Grease and line a 20cm cake tin.

*Brown the butter*
Add 140g unsalted or vegan butter to a pan over a medium heat and cook, stirring, for 5 minutes, until the butter foams, turns a deep nut brown and smells toasty. Leave to one side to cool.

*Make your batter*
In a large mixing bowl, mix 150ml Greek yoghurt or oat Greek yoghurt with 2 large eggs, 1 soaked, deseeded and finely chopped dried ancho chilli, 4 finely chopped spring onions, the finely grated zest of 1 unwaxed lime, 2 tablespoons honey or maple syrup, 100g quick-cook polenta, 75g plain flour and ½ a teaspoon of fine sea salt.

*Prepare the corn*
If using 4 fresh corn ears, cut the kernels from the husks. If using 520g kernels (defrosted if frozen), just make sure you dry them with kitchen paper. Blitz 400g kernels in a food processor until you have a rough porridge with pieces the sizes of

breadcrumbs. Keep the remaining 120g or so whole and set aside.

*Finish the batter*
Add the cooled brown butter, ½ teaspoon baking powder and ½ teaspoon bicarbonate of soda to the batter and mix well.

*Bake the cornbread*
Pour the batter into the lined tin and scatter the remaining 100g whole corn kernels on top. Bake for 40–45 minutes until cooked through and evenly golden. Leave to cool a little before serving.

*Cook the black beans*
Whilst the cornbread bakes, heat a little olive oil in a small saucepan. Add 2 peeled and finely sliced garlic cloves, cook for a minute, then add 2 × 400g tins black beans with their liquid, a 3cm piece of cinnamon, ground to a powder, and 1–2 tablespoons of the soaking liquid from the chillies, along with 1 soaked, deseeded and finely chopped ancho chilli. Cook for 6–8 minutes, or until thick and glossy, then set aside. Keep warm.

*Serve the cornbread*
Serve the cornbread in wedges with the black beans, feta and a bunch of chopped coriander. Some chopped tomatoes dressed with lime would also work well here.

# Tahini

Tahini the colour of caramel sits on my counter next to the oils and vinegars. It's used too often to be put away. Buttery and sweet with some backup from gentle bitterness. It walks the line between sweet and savoury like nothing else. It's borrowed from a culture that's not my own, with thanks and grace. I spoon it onto fruit, yoghurt and honey with coffee to start the day. Drizzle it into focaccia sandwiches of tomato and rocket for lunch. Scoop it onto chickpea stew for dinner. It brings depth. Savouriness. It's baked into cookies and cakes, swirled into breads. I whip it and drizzle it, whisk it into a dressing for salad, for noodles. It has my heart.

# On Tahini

Tahini comes from an Arabic word meaning 'to grind'. It is of course made from sesame seeds and is used from the Middle East to the Mediterranean and the Balkans. Tahini can be made from black or white sesame seeds and is usually made with hulled or shelled seeds, for a smoother, less bitter flavour. Unhulled tahini is usually a little coarser, with a more earthy taste. Use it as a spread, a dressing or a dip. Maybe it's best known for being an essential ingredient in hummus and baba ghanoush, but its uses are countless.

Its flavour profile is slightly bitter, nutty and earthy. Its fattiness means it's a really useful ingredient for marrying things together, and its rich creaminess also makes it a really useful vegan ingredient.

Rich, Silky, Sweet, Bitter

## Types

- White
  Made from white sesame seeds, much like peanut butter. How dark and toasty the tahini is depends on how well-toasted the sesame seeds are. A deeper toast will give a darker colour and a more intense flavour.

- Black
  Made with black sesame seeds. A deep, thick, black paste, it has a nuttier and deeper flavour than white, so you need less.

- Hulled vs unhulled
  Hulled sesame seeds are the ones which have had their tough outer shell removed. Tahini from hulled seeds is smoother and less bitter. Most tahini you can buy in the shops is made from hulled seeds. Unhulled tahini is usually labelled as such and has a darker, more bitter and earthy taste and is more textured.

## Goes well with

| | |
|---|---|
| blood orange | noodles |
| broccoli | parsley |
| carrot | peanut butter |
| cauliflower | pear |
| chickpeas | pomegranate |
| chilli | rocket |
| chocolate | soy |
| cucumber | sugar |
| flatbread | sweet potato |
| honey | tomato |
| kale | walnut |
| lemon | yoghurt |

## Favourite uses

- Add it to yoghurt – with a little garlic, lemon and plenty of herbs for an easy dip
- Swirl it through brownies to balance out their richness
- Make a salad dressing with olive oil, lemon, salt and tahini
- Pair it with date molasses to balance out its bitterness and drizzle over yoghurt, toast or aubergines
- Swirl it into soup or stew with a squeeze of lemon
- Mix it with chilli oil and toss through warm noodles
- Put it in a smoothie with dates, banana and oat milk
- Spread it on toast with in-season fruit
- Spoon it into a baked sweet potato
- Mix with honey and serve next to cheese

## Storage

Once open, it can be stored in a cool place or a fridge for several months after opening. Like peanut butter, it will separate and will need a stir before using. It's important to stir your tahini really well before you use it, getting right to the bottom of the jar. It seems a pain, but it will mean you don't end up with half a jar of unusable claggy tahini.

## Favourite brands/where to buy

Brands can differ hugely. I want my tahini smooth and rich, rather than thick and claggy. Lebanese, Israeli and Palestinian brands tend to pour well. I love Al Nakhil tahini, which I buy from the Honey & Co Deli online but can be found all over. The Al Arz brand is another favourite. Belazu's tahini is also really good and available in most supermarkets in the UK. From the US, I love Seed & Mill tahini.

# Homemade tahini

300g white sesame seeds
50–75ml neutral oil (such as
sunflower or vegetable)

Homemade tahini is hard to beat.
It's actually surprisingly low-effort.
Toasting the sesame seeds before
blending them not only turns up the
flavour, but releases a little of the
seeds' oil, making the whole process
easier. To make a strikingly dark
version, simply swap the toasted
white sesame seeds for black sesame
seeds, though take care when toasting
them to watch that they don't burn.

MAKES 1 MEDIUM JARFUL

*Toast the seeds*
The depth of colour and flavour of
your tahini will depend on how much
you toast your sesame seeds. I like
them well toasted, taken to a deep
golden-brown colour, but toast them
less for a milder tahini. Toast 300g
sesame seeds in a dry frying pan over
a medium heat, moving them every
30 seconds so they don't catch.

*Blend the seeds*
Put the sesame seeds into a food
processor with a pinch of salt and
pulse a few times. Scrape down the
sides of the processor and blitz for
around a minute before scraping down
the sides again. Repeat this process
until the sesame seeds have broken
down into a light sandy texture.

*Add the oil and jar*
Scrape down the sides of the
processor once more, then blitz
again, gradually adding 50–75ml
neutral oil, such as sunflower or
vegetable, until the sesame mixture
is the thickness you like – I go for
the consistency of double cream.
Transfer to a sterilised jar, where it
will keep happily for at least a month
in a cool dark place. Over time the
oil from the mixture will naturally
move to the top of the jar.

# Honey & Co's tahini-creamed chard

200g tahini

3 tablespoons extra virgin
olive oil

1 teaspoon ground cumin

4 cloves of garlic, peeled and
crushed, and 3 cloves of garlic,
peeled and minced

juice of ½ an unwaxed lemon

2 large bunches of Swiss chard,
green, rainbow or a mix
(once separated should
produce 400g stalks,
400g leaves)

4 tablespoons olive oil

1–2 large onions, peeled and
diced (about 200g)

1 teaspoon sea salt

2 tablespoons toasted white
sesame seeds, to sprinkle
over the top

Sarit Packer and Itamar Srulovich are two of my favourite people. I have passed by their deli a lot over the last few years and every time I do I leave with a full bag of supplies. Always a pot of tahini. So much so that I can't think of tahini and not think of Sarit and Itamar. I thought I could not love them more, and then they sent me this recipe. It's a lesson in how simple is often the most perfect.

They learnt about it on a trip to Boston, where they ate at Ana Sutron's Oleana, which they tell me was one of the first restaurants to bring Middle Eastern food to contemporary dining in the West.

Itamar says, 'All the food we had there was dream-worthy, but it was the simplest plate that had us pining to go back to Boston – a dish of Swiss chard with tahini that was so good, such a wonderful marriage of flavour and texture, that we couldn't get it out of our heads from the moment we got back from Boston.'

And so, as with all great recipes, this is passed from Ana to Sarit and Itamar, to me and now to you. In Oleana they serve it as a mezze, but I have taken to serving it for dinner with bread.

SERVES 4–6

*Make the tahini sauce*
Place 200g tahini, 3 tablespoons extra virgin olive oil, 1 teaspoon ground cumin, 1 minced clove of garlic and the juice of ½ an unwaxed lemon in a blender with a good pinch of sea salt and 150ml cold water and blitz to a smooth, airy sauce.

*Prepare the chard*
Tear away the leafy parts of 2 large bunches of Swiss chard and set aside. Cut all the stalks into small dice.

*Cook the onions and stalks*
Heat 4 tablespoons olive oil in a very large saucepan on a medium heat and add 4 peeled and crushed cloves of garlic and 1–2 large peeled and diced onions and sauté for about 8 minutes. Add the diced chard stalks and 1 teaspoon of sea salt and continue sautéing for another 10–12 minutes or until the stalks are very soft.

*Add the leaves and finish*
Next add 2 cloves of peeled and minced garlic and the chard leaves. You may need to add the leaves in batches and allow them to wilt before adding the next. Increase the heat to high, mix well, cover the pan and cook for about 2 minutes until the greens are wilted. Remove from the heat and mix in the tahini sauce, sprinkle with 2 tablespoons toasted sesame seeds and serve.

# Tomatoes and whipped tahini

500g good ripe tomatoes, at
    room temperature
2 tablespoons red wine vinegar
150g tahini
2 cloves of garlic, peeled
2 teaspoons Dijon mustard
a bunch of flat-leaf parsley (30g),
    leaves picked
¼ red onion, peeled and finely
    diced
3 tablespoons olive oil
2 tablespoons small capers
    (or larger ones, chopped)

This came from a craving for Ed Smith's tomato tonnato, a riff on vitello tonnato. Both are distinctly un-vegetarian but I wanted the acid-spiked creamy sauce against a salted and vinegared summer tomato. Here the creaminess comes from tahini, which partners so well with tomato. It's important that your tomatoes are at room temperature, to make the most of their flavour.

I use brined capers here, but if you are using salted capers soak them in lots of cold water for 1 hour before using.

SERVES 4

*Chop and season the tomatoes*
Cut 500g ripe tomatoes into slices and chunks which look good and are bite-sized. Put them in a colander over a bowl and season with a teaspoon of salt (seems a lot but it's needed) and 1 tablespoon of red wine vinegar. Leave to sit.

*Whip the tahini*
Put 150g tahini, 2 peeled cloves of garlic, 1 tablespoon red wine vinegar, 2 teaspoons Dijon mustard and 100ml ice-cold water into a food processor and blitz for 4–6 minutes. It will seize and stiffen at first (don't worry) but then it will lighten in colour and turn fluffy and creamy. Taste and add salt and more vinegar and mustard, if needed.

*Make the parsley salsa*
Meanwhile, make the salsa. Finely chop the leaves from a bunch of fresh flat-leaf parsley, then finely dice ¼ of a peeled red onion and mix with 2 tablespoons of olive oil. Season with a tablespoon or two of the reserved tomato juices (these should be salty and acidic, so add as much or as little as you like).

*Put everything together*
Spoon the whipped tahini on to a plate and use the back of a spoon to spread it into peaks and dips. Any leftover whipped tahini can be kept in a jar in the fridge for 3–4 days. Taste the tomatoes, adding more salt if you think it's needed. Dress them with a tablespoon of olive oil, then spoon the tomatoes over the tahini and top with 2 table-spoons small capers (or larger ones, chopped). Spoon the salsa over the tomatoes to finish.

Tahini

# Butter bean, tomato and tahini cassoulet

450g ripe cherry tomatoes
1 bulb of fennel, trimmed and
    cut into thin wedges
4 cloves of garlic, peeled
olive oil
1 × 700g jar cooked butter beans
    or 2 × 400g tins
juice of ½ an unwaxed lemon
4 tablespoons tahini
3 tablespoons white sesame
    seeds
2 slices sourdough bread (150g)
a bunch of basil (30g)

This is a riff on the cassoulet recipe from my first book *A Modern Way to Eat*. It's one of the most-cooked recipes from that book, and I think it's so loved thanks to the fact it's super-easy to make but also because of its velvety butteriness. I am working with the same theme here; the tahini adds an instant richness which sits up against the tomatoes, fennel and butter beans. You will need an ovenproof pan – mine is a cast-iron one that's 30cm across.

SERVES 4

*Cook the tomatoes*
Preheat the oven to 240°C/220°C fan. Put 450g ripe cherry tomatoes and 1 trimmed bulb of fennel, cut into thin wedges, into an ovenproof pan. Flatten 2 peeled cloves of garlic with the blade of a knife, add those to the pan with 2 tablespoons olive oil and a good amount of salt and pepper, then stir to mix. Roast for 20 minutes, until the vegetables are soft and charred.

*Mix the butter beans*
Tip 1 × 700g jar or 2 × 400g tins of butter beans and their liquid into a bowl along with ½ a jar or 1 tin of water, grate in 2 cloves of garlic, then add 4 tablespoons olive oil, the juice of ½ an unwaxed lemon, 4 tablespoons tahini and 3 table-spoons white sesame seeds.

*Add the butter beans and bread*
When the vegetables have had their time, scoop them out of the pan, then tip the garlicky butter beans into the ovenproof pan. Tear over 2 slices of sourdough bread (150g), return the veg to the pan on top of the beans and bread, and put back in the oven and bake for another 30 minutes.

*Finish*
Once the butter beans look crisp and the bread golden, take them out of the oven and tear over a 30g bunch of basil. Serve with a lemon-dressed green salad or some greens.

# Börek with dark molasses tahini

500g spinach, chard, spring
    greens, cavolo nero or kale
200g feta or manouri, or vegan
    feta-style cheese, crumbled
3 tablespoons toasted white
    sesame seeds, plus extra for
    sprinkling
2 sprigs of thyme, leaves picked
1 large handful of Greek (or
    regular) basil, torn
50ml olive oil (or melted butter),
    plus an extra drizzle of oil
    for the greens
250g pack fresh filo pastry
    (about 6–9 sheets,
    30cm × 40cm)
4 tablespoons tahini
1 tablespoon runny honey or
    maple syrup
1 teaspoon carob molasses
    (optional)

I spent a week a while back in Turkey in the pine forests above Göcek with my friend Nadia. We ate like queens: breakfasts of fresh cheese, scarlet tomatoes, bitter greens and dark tahini. There were little börek pastries, sweet olive oil-kissed tomatoey green beans, and courgette and cauliflower fritters, all served close enough to the Greek basil growing in the garden that you could reach out and tear it from your seat.

This börek is my attempt to make the one that Sevgi, the cook, and the all-women kitchen crew served. They served it with some molasses tahini, the discovery of my trip.

MAKES ONE BÖREK TO SERVE 6–8

*Blanch the greens*
Put 500g greens in a colander and pour just-boiled water over them, so that they wilt a little. (For hardier greens, like cavolo nero or kale, remove the stems, cut, put them in a lidded pan on a high heat and steam, covered, for 2 minutes, then drain.) Once cool, squeeze out as much liquid as possible, then roughly chop.

*Make the filling*
Transfer the chopped greens to a large bowl. Add 200g crumbled feta, 3 tablespoons toasted sesame seeds, the picked leaves from 2 sprigs of thyme, a large handful of torn basil and a drizzle of olive oil, then mix. Season well and set aside.

*To make the swirled large börek*
Preheat the oven to 200°C/180°C fan and heat a baking sheet lined with baking paper. Lay 3 sheets of filo on a work surface, with the longest side facing towards you, and the shorter side in front of you, as if you were reading a letter. Keep the remaining sheets covered with a damp tea towel.

Working one sheet at a time, overlap the 3 sheets, moving from left to right, by around 2–3cm, brushing oil between each layer so it seals. You should end up with a large sheet about 65cm × 45cm. Fold the sheet in half horizontally so you end up with a sheet about 22cm wide.

Lay half the greens and feta filling 2cm up from the longest edge and brush the pastry around it with oil or melted butter. Roll it up gently but tightly to create a long sausage shape, then curl it around anticlockwise from right to left, to create the start of the swirl, and place in the centre of a large baking sheet. Repeat this method twice more with the other 6 sheets, using up the remaining filling mix. Then wrap the second two shapes around the first in a circle.

*Cook the börek*
Brush generously with oil or melted butter and sprinkle with sesame seeds, then bake for 30–35 minutes or until golden.

*Make the molasses tahini*
Meanwhile, mix 4 tablespoons tahini, 1 tablespoon honey or maple syrup and 1 teaspoon carob molasses (if using), then whisk with 40ml water to loosen. Let the börek cool slightly, then drizzle with the tahini and sprinkle with more sesame seeds. Serve warm or at room temperature.

Tahini

# Sesame and chilli oil noodles

150g medium dried egg noodles
1 tablespoon peanut butter
2 tablespoons tahini
1 tablespoon soy sauce or tamari
1 clove of garlic, peeled and
    finely chopped
2 teaspoons toasted sesame oil
2–3 tablespoons chilli oil or
    chilli crisp
a bunch of spring onions (about 6),
    trimmed and finely sliced
4 tablespoons toasted sesame
    seeds (white, black or both)

Lucky and Joy is a Chinese-influenced restaurant local to me with brightly painted walls and food that slaps you in the face with flavour. For the last year or so I've been eating their sesame noodles most weeks. This is a quick version of cold sesame noodles I made when I was craving them but they were shut for a holiday. It uses tahini as opposed to Chinese sesame, which is not traditional in any way, but it is what I always have at home so...

SERVES 2 AS A MAIN, 4 AS A SIDE

*Cook the noodles*
Cook 150g medium dried egg noodles in boiling salted water for a minute less than the packet instructions, until al dente. Drain and rinse under cold water.

*Make the tahini sauce*
Whisk together 1 tablespoon peanut butter, 2 tablespoons tahini, 1 table-spoon soy sauce and 1 finely chopped clove of garlic. Add 2 teaspoons toasted sesame oil and between 75ml and 125ml room-temperature water (depending on the thickness of the tahini) and whisk until you have a smooth, pourable sauce about the thickness of double cream.

*Toss together and serve*
Toss the cold noodles in the tahini sauce and scoop into bowls, then top each with 1–2 tablespoons of chilli crisp, adding a little at a time until it's the right kind of heat for you (you can always serve extra on the table). Scatter over a trimmed and finely sliced bunch of spring onions and finish each bowl with a tablespoon of toasted sesame seeds.

# Wedge salad with tahini ranch dressing

2 cloves of garlic, peeled
2 tablespoons olive oil
100g fresh breadcrumbs
50g pitted green olives, roughly
    chopped
2 unwaxed lemons
250g Greek yoghurt or oat
    Greek yoghurt
120g tahini
1 bunch of chives (20g), chopped
1 bunch of dill (20g), chopped
2 iceberg lettuces or 8 Little Gems

This is what I want to eat all summer. The lettuce is seasoned with salt and pepper and lemon (always season your lettuce), then covered, and I mean covered, in the yoghurt tahini ranch. As with any dressing you want it to be a little too much when tasted on its own, as the crispy iceberg will water it down – tasting the dressing on a bit of lettuce will help you check if it's right.

SERVES 4

*Make the breadcrumbs*
First make the breadcrumbs. Smash 1 peeled clove of garlic and put it in a frying pan with 2 tablespoons olive oil. Place on a medium-low heat and allow to sizzle for 3–4 minutes until the garlic is golden brown and smells great. Add 100g breadcrumbs and cook for 3 minutes, moving them all the time, then add 50g roughly chopped pitted green olives and continue cooking for a couple of minutes until the breadcrumbs are toasted. Season with ½ teaspoon of sea salt, tip into a shallow bowl to cool and grate in the zest of 1 unwaxed lemon.

*Make the tahini ranch*
Put 250g Greek yoghurt or oat Greek yoghurt into a bowl with 120g tahini, grate in 1 peeled clove of garlic, add the juice of 1 unwaxed lemon and season with salt and pepper. Add ½ a bunch of chopped chives and ½ a bunch of chopped dill and stir in. Add a little cold water to thin it to a drizzleable dressing with the consistency of double cream. Taste and adjust, adding more salt and lemon juice as needed.

*Make the salad*
Trim any rogue leaves from the outside of 2 iceberg lettuces or

8 Little Gems, then leaving the root on, cut each iceberg or Little Gem into 4 wedges through the core. Break the wedges up into smaller chunks with your hands so you still have a few layers of lettuce but the dressing can get to them more easily. Spread a third of the dressing evenly over a serving platter, then put the wedges on top and season with salt and pepper, taking care to get in between the layers of lettuce leaves, then squeeze over an unwaxed lemon in the same way.

*Put everything together*
Spoon the rest of the tahini ranch very generously over the top of the lettuce leaves, then top with the breadcrumbs and remaining ½ a bunch each of chopped chives and dill. Serve immediately. You want this to be cold and refreshing.

# Sesame ramen noodles

300g dried ramen noodles
(I like Clearspring) or 800g
fresh ramen noodles
250g spring or Asian greens or
other green veg
150g tahini
1 tablespoon rice wine vinegar
1 tablespoon soy sauce
1 tablespoon chilli oil, plus
extra to serve
1.5 litres good vegetable stock
4 spring onions, trimmed and
finely sliced
2 tablespoons toasted white
sesame seeds

Tantanmen is a Japanese noodle soup which uses Japanese sesame paste, coating the noodles in the savoury creamy broth it makes. If you can get or have Japanese sesame paste, then use that, but I have found tahini, which I always have in the cupboard, works well. I have deliberately left the recipe simple here, with just some greens, and given you a few seasonal ideas for what veg to add so you can cook this all year. A jammy egg, cooked in boiling water for 6 minutes, is a good addition too.

SERVES 4

*Cook the noodles and veg*
Bring a large pan of salted water to the boil, add 300g dried ramen noodles or 800g fresh and cook just less than the packet instructions – you want them to be al dente. About 30 seconds before they are ready, add 250g spring or Asian greens to the same pan, then drain the lot and rinse under cold running water to cool.

*Make the broth*
Whisk together 150g tahini, 1 table-spoon rice wine vinegar, 1 tablespoon soy sauce and 1 tablespoon chilli oil until you have a thick paste. Heat 1.5 litres good vegetable stock in a large pan over a medium heat until hot but not boiling. Turn off the heat and whisk in the tahini paste. Add more soy or salt if needed.

*Prepare the toppings*
Choose your toppings from the suggestions that follow this recipe and get them ready to go.

*Finish the ramen*
Divide the noodles and greens between 4 bowls, pour over the tahini broth, then top with 4 trimmed and finely sliced spring onions, 2 tablespoons toasted white sesame seeds, some chilli oil and one of the seasonal vegetables below.

Spring
pan-fried asparagus/thinly sliced radishes/chopped spring onions

Summer
pan-charred sweetcorn/pan-roasted cherry tomatoes/chopped spring onions

Autumn
pan-crisped mushrooms/cavolo nero/crispy onions

Winter
thinly sliced sweet potato cooked with the noodles/pan-crisped tofu/chopped toasted nuts

Tahini

# Smoky aubergines with tahini and spiced tomatoes

4 medium aubergines
100g tahini
1 clove of garlic, peeled
30g white sesame seeds
½ teaspoon chipotle flakes or
   chilli flakes
½ teaspoon sweet smoked
   paprika
¼ teaspoon ground cinnamon
1 jalapeño chilli, finely chopped
   (deseeded if you like)
2 large ripe tomatoes, roughly
   chopped
1 teaspoon maple syrup
½ a bunch of parsley (15g),
   chopped
½ a bunch of coriander (15g),
   chopped
juice of 1 unwaxed lime

Tahini and aubergines. They work. Here the aubergines are grilled until they almost collapse and become buttery, soft and everything an aubergine should be. Once they are peeled they are pale and sit on top of the punchy sauce that makes them sing. Richness comes from tahini over the top. Do not skip over this recipe; it's a favourite.

SERVES 4

*Cook the aubergines*
This can be done on a barbecue, griddle pan or in the oven (preheated to 200°C/180°C fan). Prick 4 medium aubergines 10 times with the tip of a knife to stop them exploding. To barbecue or griddle, heat your barbecue or griddle to super-hot, then add the aubergines and cook, turning every few minutes, until the skin is charred and the flesh is so soft it feels as if it might collapse. If you are using the oven, place the aubergines on a baking tray and cook for 30–40 minutes, turning halfway, until soft and collapsing.

*Make the whipped tahini*
Mix 100g tahini with 50–100ml ice-cold water in a bowl until you have a thick whipped-cream consistency. Grate in a peeled clove of garlic.

*Toast the seeds and spices*
Toast 30g white sesame seeds in a hot pan, or in the oven if you are using it, stirring them every few minutes until they are evenly golden. Stir in ½ teaspoon chipotle flakes or chilli flakes, ½ teaspoon sweet smoked paprika and ½ teaspoon ground cinnamon for the last 30 seconds.

*Make the spiced tomatoes*
Finely chop 1 jalapeño chilli (removing the seeds if you like)

and put into a bowl. Roughly chop 2 large ripe tomatoes and add these to the jalapeño with the spiced sesame seeds, 1 teaspoon maple syrup, ½ a bunch of chopped parsley and the same of chopped coriander and the juice of 1 unwaxed lime. Taste and add salt and more syrup to balance out any flavours which feel too dominant.

*Peel the aubergines*
Once the aubergines are cooked, leave them to cool. Once they are cool enough to handle, hold them by the stem and peel the skin off.

*Put it together*
Take a platter or 4 plates, spoon the tahini on top, then use the back of a spoon to spread it around the platter or plates. Place the aubergines on top then pile on the spiced sesame tomatoes.

# Tomato, peach and tahini sandwich

1 ripe peach
1 tablespoon apple cider vinegar
1 green chilli, sliced
1 teaspoon runny honey
2 ripe summer tomatoes,
    thickly sliced
zest of 1 unwaxed lemon
2 pieces of fresh bouncy
    focaccia (see page 156 for
    a recipe)
2 tablespoons tahini
1 bunch of wild rocket
extra virgin olive oil
½ a bunch of basil (15g), leaves
    picked

This was inspired by a recipe that landed in my inbox one summer morning. It was from the Natoora newsletter, by a chef called Daisy Bennett. I jumped up and made a simpler version of it almost immediately, and it became a summer staple. Putting peach in a sandwich might seem like a strange thing to do, but remember tomato is also a fruit. The tahini tempers the sweetness here. Please note that your sandwich will only be as good as your peaches and tomatoes.

SERVES 2

*Dress the peach*
Cut 1 ripe peach into 8 slices and put into a bowl with 1 tablespoon cider vinegar, 1 sliced green chilli and 1 teaspoon runny honey.

*Season the tomatoes*
Cut 2 ripe summer tomatoes into thick slices and put into a colander over a bowl with a good scattering of sea salt and a teaspoon of the liquid from the peach. Stir in the zest of 1 unwaxed lemon.

*Make the sandwich*
If your bread is not super fresh, warm it in the oven or toaster or in a hot, dry pan. Cut 2 pieces of fresh bouncy focaccia in half horizontally to form two 'sandwiches'. Spread one side of each focaccia sandwich with 1 tablespoon tahini and lay on half a bunch of wild rocket. Use a spoon to drizzle the other side with the juice from the tomato bowl, then some olive oil. Top the rocket with the peach, tomatoes and the leaves from half a bunch of basil and sandwich together. Eat with a napkin.

Add ons:
Mozzarella, burrata or feta would all work well as additions.

# Tahini, pear and honey flapjacks

100g white sesame seeds
100g sunflower seeds
350g jumbo porridge oats
100g dried fruit (I use a mixture
    of golden raisins and dried
    pears), roughly chopped
50g crystallised ginger, finely
    chopped
250g unsalted butter, vegan
    butter or flavourless coconut
    oil, plus extra for greasing
200g soft light brown sugar
100g tahini
4 tablespoons runny honey or
    maple syrup
zest of 1 unwaxed lemon

These flapjacks are a line-up of lots of my favourite things – tahini, toasted sesame, dried pears, crystallised ginger and brown sugar. Punch from the ginger (which I love so much I could write a book about it), chew from dried pears and raisins, sweetness from honey or maple, then the tahini rounds it all off with its buttery depth, just the right side of bitter, and stops it feeling too sweet.

If using coconut oil here, I would recommend using the one for cooking often marked 'odourless' or 'cuisine', as it doesn't have a strong coconut flavour.

MAKES 16

*Preheat the oven and line your tin*
Preheat the oven to 180°C/160°C fan. Grease a 20cm square tin with butter or oil, then line with baking paper.

*Toast the seeds*
Toast 100g white sesame seeds and 100g sunflower seeds until golden brown in the oven as it is preheating. Give them a stir every few minutes, keeping a close eye on them so they don't burn. They should take about 10–12 minutes in total.

*Pulse the oats*
Pulse 350g jumbo porridge oats in a food processor until broken down a little. Add 100g roughly chopped dried fruit and 50g finely chopped crystallised ginger and pulse until incorporated.

*Melt the butter and sugar*
Melt 250g butter, dairy-free butter or coconut oil, 200g soft light brown sugar, and 100g tahini in a large pan on a low heat. Once it's melted take it off the heat and stir in 4 tablespoons runny honey or maple syrup.

*Mix the oats and butter*
Mix the oats with the toasted seeds and the zest of 1 unwaxed lemon. Add a good pinch of flaky sea salt, pour in the butter and sugar mixture and stir again, until you have a sandy oaty mixture. Make sure all the oats are evenly coated.

*Bake*
Spoon the oat mixture into the lined tin. Use the back of a spoon to press down a little and level it out but don't pack it down too much. Bake in the preheated oven for 40–45 minutes or until golden brown (it will be slightly darker at the edges).

*Cool and cut*
Leave in the tin until cooled completely then cut into 16 squares. Will keep in a sealed container for up to a week.

Tahini

# Apple galette with tahini frangipane

150g cold unsalted butter or non-dairy butter (I use Violife Vioblock), cut into small cubes
200g tahini
75g light soft brown sugar
1 large free-range egg, beaten, or 60ml sparkling water
1 tablespoon plain flour
500g sweet shortcrust pastry (vegan if needed)
6 medium firm, sweet apples (I like Red Delicious, Braeburn or Jonagold)
100g golden caster sugar
2 tablespoons Demerara sugar
crème fraîche, cream or ice cream to serve

I have made a lot of frangipane tarts. Their chewy, crisp bite is a perfect texture. As a young kid, I was unnaturally obsessed with cooking and made kirsch-soaked cherry frangipane tarts that my dad loved. In kitchens I made them stuffed with figs and peaches. This is a riff on the classic almond frangipane and instead uses tahini. It's all the better for it; the tahini offsets the sweetness of the pastry. This recipe works best with a homemade or thicker, more rustic tahini. If you struggle to get your tahini to whip, add another tablespoon of flour to the mix.

SERVES 8–10

*Brown the butter (optional)*
Add 150g cold cubed butter to a small pan and cook over a medium heat, stirring regularly, until the butter browns and smells nutty. Pour into a heatproof bowl and put into the fridge to chill for around 1 hour, or until the consistency of soft butter.

*Make the tahini frangipane*
In a stand mixer or with a hand-held electric whisk, whip 200g tahini on the highest setting for 4–5 minutes until it thickens. Then add 75g light soft brown sugar and whisk again, scraping down the sides of the bowl as you go, until you have a thick mixture and none of the sugar is visible. Add 4 tablespoons (60g) of the chilled butter bit by bit with the mixer running on medium speed.

Add 1 large egg, beaten, and a good pinch of sea salt, followed by 1 tablespoon plain flour and mix to combine.

*Roll out the pastry*
Roll out 500g sweet shortcrust pastry to about 35cm × 35cm, then transfer to a large baking-paper-lined square baking tray. Use a spoon or spatula to spread the tahini frangipane over the pastry, leaving a 3cm border around the edge, and put it into the fridge to chill.

*Cut the apples*
Top and tail 6 medium firm, sweet apples, reserving the trimmings, and cut the apples into rounds across the middle so you get thin circles with little star shapes. Stack them on top of each other in their apple shape – this will make it easier to lay your slices out on your tart. Add the apple tops and bottoms to a small saucepan with 100g golden caster sugar and 100ml water. Bring to the boil, turn down to a simmer and cook for 8–10 minutes, or until slightly thickened and glossy.

*Make the tart*
Take the rolled-out pastry out of the fridge and lay the apples on top, I like to lay them overlapping each other but any way you like will work. Fold the edges of the pastry back over the edge of the apples to create a roughly rectangular galette. Put it back into the fridge while you heat the oven.

*Bake the tart*
Preheat the oven to 220°C/200°C fan. Use the remaining butter to brush the pastry edge and sprinkle with 2 tablespoons Demerara sugar. Bake for 35–45 minutes in the middle of the oven, turning halfway, until golden brown and bubbling at the edges. Remove from the oven, brush all over with the apple glaze and serve with crème fraîche, cream or ice cream.

Tahini

# Georgie's tahinopita

1 × 7g sachet of active dried
    yeast
130g soft light brown sugar
1½ teaspoons Maldon sea salt
    (or other flaky sea salt – if
    using regular fine sea salt,
    use less)
600g strong white bread flour,
    plus extra for dusting
olive oil
100g tahini
6 tablespoons runny honey (or
    maple syrup if vegan)
1 tablespoon ground cinnamon
½ teaspoon sesame seeds

This bread is a recipe from my friend Georgina Hayden. We cooked, tested recipes and hung out together for years, and I was always in awe of Georgie's breads and baking. Tahinopita are the stars of the bakeries Georgie visits when she's back in Cyprus. The soft, fluffy, doughy-in-a-good-way bread twisted with a tahini, sugar and cinnamon mixture which catches and caramelises in some places where it gets hit by the heat of the oven, and in other places where it's hidden between the folds of the dough, gives it a frangipane crossed with cinnamon bun feeling. Tahinopita shows off tahini at its best, deep and moreish with a grown-up sweetness.

SERVES 10–12

*Make the dough*
Measure 400ml warm water into a measuring jug and whisk in 7g active dried yeast and 30g soft light brown sugar. Leave to one side for 5 minutes. Stir 1¼ teaspoons sea salt into 600g strong white bread flour in a bowl, then make a well in the middle. Pour the yeast mixture into the well, along with 2 tablespoons olive oil, and stir the flour into the liquid with a fork until all mixed together – you're looking for a slightly damp dough. If it feels dry add a splash more water. Turn the dough out on to a lightly floured surface and knead for 5–8 minutes until smooth and elastic.

Grease a mixing bowl with a drizzle of olive oil and pop in the dough, turning it over in the oil so it gets lightly coated all over. Cover with a clean tea towel and leave in a warm spot for around an hour to an hour and a half, or until doubled in size.

*Make the tahini filling*
When the dough is ready, make the filling by mixing together 100g tahini, 100g soft light brown sugar, 4 tablespoons honey (or maple syrup), 1 tablespoon ground cinnamon and ¼ teaspoon sea salt.

*Shape the dough*
Turn the dough out on to a lightly floured surface, knead it for a couple of minutes, then gently roll it out into a large rectangle, around 55cm × 30cm. Evenly dot and spread the tahini mixture all over the dough (it will be too thick to spread, so you'll need to use your hands for this bit – poking it and prodding it into place), and don't worry if it isn't completely covered; it'll spread as it bakes. Roll the dough into a large Swiss roll, starting with one of the long edges, as tightly as you can, then slice the whole thing in half lengthways. Press together two of the ends and then plait the two pieces so that the cut side is always facing up. Once you've finished plaiting the dough, join the two ends together to form a ring and place it on a lightly oiled baking sheet. Leave it to one side for 30 minutes to prove again. Meanwhile, preheat the oven to 180°C/160°C fan.

*Bake the tahinopita*
When the dough has finished its second prove, drizzle the dough with 1 tablespoon honey or maple syrup, and sprinkle with ½ teaspoon sesame seeds. Pop the tray in the middle of the oven and bake for 35–40 minutes, until golden all over and cooked through. When it is ready, remove from the oven and leave to cool for 10 minutes on the tray before transferring to a wire rack and drizzling with another tablespoon of honey or maple syrup.

Perfect any time of the day, with a small cup of strong Greek coffee or a mug of tea.

# All about flavour

Flavour is just the vanilla in your ice cream or the turmeric in your dal. Flavour is both what we literally taste – the sweet, salty, sour, bitter and umami – and what we feel, see and remember when we eat. A bite of a ripe run-down-your-chin peach will be about its taste and sweetness but also about how we perceive a peach: where we are eating it, our memories of perfect holiday peaches and even how peaches play into our lives, families, childhoods and celebrations. Even the temperature or ripeness of the peach might trigger a specific memory, and all these things form part of the flavour of that peach.

Flavour goes deeper and it means different things to different people. It might jog a memory and transport us back to our homeland. It's about connection. It's about food shared. It's about being human. Flavour symbolises different things to different people. The same dish eaten by one person might remind them of how their mother cooked it, while for another it might remind them of a time when that food was a comfort. This all plays into how we perceive the flavour of food.

Packet ramen noodles make me think of late-home-from-school childhood dinners. Greengages remind me of the sun on my skin and browsing markets in the south of France. Cheese soufflés and puffy omelettes make me think fondly of my mum; banana sandwiches my dad. There is so much in each of these memories.

Nik Sharma in his excellent book *The Flavor Equation* makes sense of this bundle of tastes, senses and feelings.

# Emotion + Sight + Sound + Texture + Aroma + Taste = Flavour

Nik spells out that what we deem delicious is actually a combination of all of these things coming together into one holistic experience.

## Emotion

Your emotional state when you try a dish affects how you perceive the flavour. It has been shown that flavour can affect our emotions too: Nik Sharma says that the same news told to someone drinking a sweet drink and others drinking a bitter drink in a study evoked different reactions. For instance, I'll always remember the paella (or a version of it) on page 182 as the first dish my son taught me how to cook after making it at school.

## Sight

We eat with our eyes: the colours and shapes and look of food are crucial in building our appetites and our perception of what we eat. We have learned to associate certain colours with certain flavours. Years of writing about and styling food has made me realise how much we rely on a photo to know what we are cooking. If food looks appetising, it begins to sate us even before we take a bite.

## Sound

Sound is a forgotten element when it comes to both cooking and eating. A sound can be a marker that food is cooked: the crackle of a loaf of bread which tells you it is cooked, or the hollow tap on its bottom. But sound is more than a marker. It is an amplifying sensation that brings on appetite and tells us when something is going to be good: think of the snap of a chocolate bar or a biscuit.

## Texture and temperature

From crunchy to soft and yielding, cool to hot, the delicate sensors in our mouth allow us to feel our food. An ice-cold slice of watermelon on a hot day will taste and feel wholly different to a warm one. It will feel crunchier, juicer and more delicious all round.

## Aroma/smell

A huge part of how we taste food is actually how we smell it. Often, we refer to someone losing their taste, but almost always it's actually their ability to smell food which is affected.

## Taste

Taste is an instinct. On a basic level, it guides us to foods that are safe and to reject those that aren't. It is connected to memory, and as we eat over time, memories build up that become part of how we taste. It's this that I am going to focus on.

The taste and flavour map on page 230–231 shows the commonly accepted matrix of flavours. I like to think of this as an interdependent system. Like a solar system where the main tastes are the planets that depend on each other to stay in balance, everything is dependent on the others to shine. On top of this, there is an added layer of senses and emotions, which I see as the sun, giving them life.

Sweet, salty, sour, bitter and umami are the commonly accepted tastes, the planets, but I have added a few outliers which I find useful to consider when I am thinking about flavour.

Greenness
herbs, greens, grassy, verdant flavours. Even grassy olive oil.

Heat and spice
warmth that comes from chilli, cinnamon, cumin and the endless list of spices.

Creamy richness
which comes from fat, oil or dairy, or plant-based yoghurt, cream or milk.

I can't put my recipes together without these elements, so I consider them the stars to the planets in my flavour solar system.

# The flavours in this book

| | Sweet | Salty | Sour | Umami | Bitter | Hot | Verdant | Creamy |
|---|---|---|---|---|---|---|---|---|
| Lemon | ● | | ● | | ● | | | |
| Olive oil | | | | | | | ● | ● |
| Vinegar | | | ● | | | | | |
| Mustard | | | | ● | | | | |
| Tomato | ● | | | | | | | |
| Capers | | ● | ● | | | | | |
| Chilli | | | | | | ● | | |
| Tahini | | | | | ● | | | ● |
| Garlic | | | | ● | | | | |
| Onion | ● | | | | | | | |
| Miso | | ● | | ● | | | | |
| Peanut | ● | ● | | | | | | ● |

# How flavour works

| | |
|---|---|
| Sight | Sweet |
| Sound | Sour |
| Smells | Salty |
| Feeling | Bitter |
| Memory | Umami |
| Culture | (Five tastes) |

## Flavour

# How taste works

Sweet

Verdant          Salty

## Taste

Hot          Sour

Bitter          Umami

# Layering flavour

What we define as a delicious flavour is a combination of lots of elements coming together. Knowing how and why our ingredients work together will make you a better cook. This book pulls out twelve ingredients which all sit within one of these flavour profiles. Cooking through each chapter and seeing how that ingredient can be used in different ways is a great way to build on your understanding of taste and how different ingredients are balanced.

## Sour/acidity

Sourness or acidity is, to me, one of the most important parts of cooking, and it's often a key element to add or balance to make food taste good.

The acid in a food will affect how it cooks, not just how it tastes. An example is cooking red onions. If you add lemon or vinegar to onions, they change colour from deep purple to bright pink, and they cook more quickly.

### Acid can

- Temper sweetness and saltiness: if a dish feels too sweet, acid will help. The same if a dish is too salty.

- Help counter bitterness: think of a chicory salad with a punchy dressing.

- Cut through fat: think gherkins in a burger or vinegar on chips.

## Bright/acidic foods

Most foods have some level of acidity. Lemons and rhubarb are obviously acidic, but yoghurt, milk, honey and coffee are less obvious acidic foods. Here are a few I use most in my kitchen.

### Citrus
In particular, lemons and limes. Limes are more acidic, with a stronger bright sourness than lemons, and lemons are sweeter. The juice and zest bring different types of acidity: the juice is sharp and fresh, and the zest is bright and sherbety, thanks to the oils in the skin. See page 16 for more.

### Vinegar
Vinegar is a cheap and always available source of acidity. Its flavour and acidity can vary greatly. See page 78 for more on vinegar.

### Tomatoes

Tomatoes have lots of citric acid, but they sweeten as they ripen. If you want to add tomato flavour but also some acidity, the best tomato will be tomato purée or tinned toms. See page 124 for more on tomatoes.

### Yoghurt, kefir and buttermilk

Their sourness comes from the fermentation of bacteria in milk or non-dairy milk. They add a freshness and creaminess as well as acidity.

### Tamarind

Comes from the tangy pulp inside tamarind pods. I use it most often in a glossy brown paste from a jar, which brings a more subtle sweet/sour acidity with caramelly notes. It's at home in curries and stews, and dressings for bright, crunchy salads.

## How to use acid

- Add yoghurt to your food: yoghurt on the side of a curry, or to top a soup or on a flatbread.

- Add fruit to a salad: apples, apricots or sour cherries for a pop of acidity.

- Add citrus juice or vinegar at the very end of cooking for an acidic kick. A good way to balance a dish.

- Add citrus or vinegar to root vegetables as they roast for a mellow acidic note that sweetens as it cooks.

- Acid can be used to preserve: pickles and the natural acid foods create as they ferment naturally in foods like sauerkraut or kimchi.

- Dry ingredients like sumac, amchur (dried mango), dried lime and citrus zest all add sourness without liquid.

## Salty

In this book, two chapters focus on capers and miso, but in my kitchen there are always cornichons, olives, stock and soy. These all have a natural saltiness to them, so if you're cooking with one of those ingredients it's important to remember that some salt is going to come from that, and you will need to adjust the seasoning accordingly. For more on salt, see page 10.

### Salt can

- Reduce the intensity of bitterness: salting aubergines is an example of this.

- Acidity can enhance the perception of salt in food, so adding lemon juice or vinegar to your cooking means you might need to add less salt. For anyone who is trying to reduce salt, this is a really good technique.

- Umami-rich foods like soy or miso boost the perception of saltiness as well.

- Salt and sweet:
  I add a little bit of salt to things like my morning porridge but also to anything I bake with chocolate. It's just a small amount; you don't want a strong salty flavour, but you do want to have that sort of enhancement that salt brings.

## How to use salt

- Seasoning
  One thing I can't stress enough about salt and seasoning is to taste your food as you cook. It is the key difference as far as I've seen between professional cooks and home cooks. Chefs taste every part of the food throughout the cooking process. This will give you an idea of how the flavours are developing, how each individual element is tasting, and how they might come together. So if one element of your meal is tasting a bit salty, you can step in and make sure that you don't over-salt other elements of the meal, and, hopefully, it will balance out.

'Knowing how and why our ingredients work together will make you a better cook.'

- Texture
  Salt can add texture if you're using a flaky salt – sprinkle it on top of a salad or even on the top of a chocolate tart or brownie to add crunch and texture as well as saltiness.

- Speed of cooking
  Adding salt to a pot of boiling water not only seasons the vegetables as they're cooking but it also allows them to cook quicker. The loss of nutrients is also significantly reduced when vegetables are cooked in salty water rather than in just plain water.

## Sweet

The natural sugars in foods are responsible for their sweet taste. Vegetables naturally have their own inherent sweetness and natural sugars. Think about a sweet potato or squash, for instance. So when it comes to sweetness in savoury cooking, you might add sweetness to a salad dressing that tastes a little bitter to bring balance. Or add sour cream to level out a very sweet roasted sweet potato.

### Sweetness can

- Reduce the intensity of hot chilli heat – think super-hot Thai chillies with palm sugar (and lime).

- Sweetness can make acids less powerful – think lemonade: the sweeter it is, the less lemony it tastes.

- Temperature affects sweetness – the warmer something is, the sweeter it will taste. When making ice cream or anything served very cold, you may need to increase the sweetness of the room-temperature custard for it to taste as sweet when it's cold.

- Sugar can mask bitterness – think about stirring some sugar into a cup of coffee. It also helps with the bitterness of cabbage or bitter leaves.

- Sugar can enhance all flavours. I use it sparingly and always add it bit by bit, but it's a good balancing element to turn to if there is something missing in your food.

## Sweet foods

### Onions
Onions cooked slowly to bring out their natural sugars bring sweetness and depth. Raw onions have a hint of sweetness but also acidity. More on onions on page 264.

### Lemons
Lemons have lots of natural sugar that sits against their acidity. When cooked, their sugar intensifies and their acidity mellows.

### Maple
I use maple to sweeten savoury food, dressings, tofu, dipping sauces and sometimes add a splash to a soup or stew that needs balancing. I find maple (a liquid sweetener) much more versatile than sugar.

### Honey
Honey brings a brighter, fresher sweetness with more nuance, and I use honey a lot in my cooking. Just a drop will often join up the dots and round out the flavour.

### Sugar
The most obvious type of sweetness is sugar. My favourite is muscovado sugar, which has a deep, dark, almost black treacle caramel consistency.

### Fruit
Adds freshness and sweetness and can be a good way to add sweetness subtly.

### Sweet vegetables
From sweetcorn to sweet potato and squash. It's worth considering the sweetness of these vegetables as you cook.

'Bitterness splits opinion more than any other taste.'

## Bitterness

Bitterness splits opinion more than any other taste. As humans, we are very sensitive to bitter tastes at extremely low levels. Almost every culture in the world cooks with bitter foods, from tahini to bitter greens and radicchio. Our natural response is to steer clear of bitter foods to protect us from harm or damage. Our brains are hardwired to see foods that taste bitter as unpleasant, so we avoid them.

### Bitter can
Salt, acid or sweetness will mellow bitter flavours, so if you're still getting used to bitterness in your food using one or more of them might be a good idea.

## Bitter foods

### Citrus fruit
Some fruit, like grapefruit, has more bitterness than other citrus fruits. Most of the bitterness comes from the white part under the skin, so when you zest a lemon or lime be careful to only use the brightly coloured top layer, unless you want to add bitterness.

### Tahini
Tahini has a mildly bitter taste which is a great first introduction to bitter. It's also rich and rounded as well as slightly sweet, which balances the gentle bitterness.

### Alcohol
Beer is bitter thanks to the hops it's made from and the fermentation process. Wine, especially red, can also be bitter.

### Coffee
Coffee is a classic bitter taste. It is great in cooking: I add it to chillies, and it also enhances chocolate-flavoured desserts, brownies and cakes.

### Cocoa and cacao
If you've ever eaten a raw cocoa bean, you will know how much natural bitterness is in cocoa or cacao. Cocoa has a bitter and acidic taste, but the addition of sugar and milk helps mask the bitterness. It can also be used in stews and chillies, echoing Mexican and ancient Incan and Mayan cooking.

### Bitter lettuces
I love using bitter lettuces. For me, they have to be coated with a dressing that has some sweetness to offset the bitterness. These bitter leaves can actually help our digestive process, so they're a great thing to have on the side of a meal as well as being something interesting and delicious to eat.

## Umami/Savouriness

Savouriness or umami, to use the Japanese word, is a recently discovered dimension of flavour. This is a newly recognised taste but is really nothing new. Think grating Parmesan over a plate of pasta or adding ginger, garlic and onions to soups, broths and curries.

A lot of umami flavours are created by ageing or fermentation, such as miso, soy sauce, mustard and kimchi. To me, umami is the hard-to-put-your-finger-on element that rounds off your dinner. Marmite on toast, gyozas dipped in a soy-heavy dipping sauce, the miso next to your plain rice.

## Savoury/umami foods

### Miso
A fermented soybean paste made using a koji, which is a bit like a miso sourdough starter. The type of miso you buy can be denoted by the colour, red or white, or the type of koji that is used, usually soy, barley or rice.

### Mushrooms
Mushrooms are a great way of adding a savoury note. Dried mushrooms can be a particularly good umami hit, as their flavour is more concentrated than that of fresh mushrooms. Soak them in hot water

first to get maximum flavour and use the chopped, dried mushrooms and the water in your cooking.

### Soy sauce/tamari
Soy is made by fermenting soybeans and salt and has a natural savouriness.

### Parmesan cheese
True Parmesan is not vegetarian, so vegetarians should search out a vegetarian Parmesan that is made without using animal rennet. A deep umami flavour comes from the ageing process of the cheese.

### Marmite
Marmite, or yeast extract, is a flavour that splits opinion. It's a great way of adding depth to vegetarian and vegan food. Marmite is a by-product of the beer brewing process, and Vegemite, which is similar (but not as good in my opinion), is a by-product of making brewers' yeast, so as well as eating something delicious you are using up something that would otherwise have been thrown away.

### Seaweed
It was the study of seaweed by Japanese scientists that actually led to the discovery of this umami taste. There is a substance called glutamate which is found in seaweed and lots of other umami-rich foods. It varies depending on which seaweed you're talking about. I like using seaweed to flavour broths and stocks.

### Fermented foods
These are a great way of adding umami – kimchi, sauerkraut and sambal will add flavour to soups and stews but also to dressings, sauces and sandwiches.

## Heat/spice

Heat or spiciness isn't one of our five official tastes. It's the sensation of heat from eating something like chilli. What's actually happening when you bite a chilli, peppercorn or warming spice is that chemicals in the food attach to our sensory receptors, and those receptors get irritated and trick the brain into producing a sensation of heat or pain.

## Foods with heat

### Chillies
When we think about heat, we immediately think of chillies. The heat in a chilli is in the white pith or ribs which hold the seeds. To reduce the heat of a chilli, cut out this white rib and remove the seeds. There is more on chilli on page 174.

### Pepper
There are lots of different types of pepper – from black peppercorns to long pepper and pink, white and green peppercorns. Black tend to be the spiciest. We can use black pepper to create heat in the same way as we might use chilli. Pink peppercorns are best used raw because heat destroys their spiciness. Green peppercorns are often sold pickled, and upgrade curries. Long pepper is a more fragrant pepper and comes in long, tiny pinecone shapes.

### Ginger
Ginger is a favourite way to add heat both to savoury dishes and sweets and cakes – think gingerbread and ginger cake. I love cooking with stem ginger and its sugary syrup.

### Horseradish and wasabi
These are two different plants, but I class the flavour as similar. They give a kind of different heat that goes straight into your nose, which some people love and others find overwhelming. Horseradish is particularly good with yoghurt and dairy in sandwiches. Wasabi I use with rice and noodles but also in dressings where I might use mustard.

## Heat in the kitchen

- Peppercorns are great used in sweet cooking as well as savoury: grinding some pepper over a fruit salad will really enhance the flavour of the fruits.

- Raw onions and alliums like chives are also a great way of adding a slightly more subtle heat to anything you cook. I love adding them to rice and salads to give a subtle, gentle heat.

- Mustard powder and mustard seeds are another great way of adding a more subtle heat.

- The hotter the temperature of the food, generally the fierier the chillies or pepper are going to taste.

- Fried ginger
  A trick I learnt as a young chef was to fry very thin slices of ginger and scatter them over a dish, which gives a hit of texture and heat. The same can be done with garlic.

## Fat

Some form of fat is used in almost everything we cook. It's not part of the accepted five tastes, but considering taste without it feels incomplete. Our food is only as good as the fat it is cooked in. I know that the deliciousness of the tomato sauce I make is entirely dependent on the amount and quality of olive oil I put into it.

Fat carries flavour. While some fats have flavours of their own, all fats coat our tongue and actually allow us to taste food.

## Types of fat

### Olive oil
Olive oil has a distinctive flavour that can range from fiery to buttery. There is as much variety in olive oil as there is in wine. It does not age well, so don't keep a bottle for more

than a year. Olive oil has a lowish smoke point, but most of the food cooked in home kitchens, even when shallow frying, is below that smoke point, so it's safe to use.

### Neutral oils
Oils like sunflower, vegetable, rapeseed or light olive oil (not extra virgin rapeseed or olive oil) are flavourless and good for cooking if you don't want to add the flavour of the oil. I use a light olive oil or rapeseed.

### Ghee
A favourite of mine to cook with, it adds the depth that butter might, but because it's been clarified it doesn't burn or blacken in the same way. Ghee is great for browning, and I always use it for making pancakes and waffles.

### Coconut oil
It comes in two types: one has a coconut flavour that's great in some dishes but overpowers others. Use unflavoured coconut oil if you don't want the coconut flavour. Coconut oil has a really high smoking point, so it's great to use if you are cooking at very high temperatures.

### Yoghurt
I use organic full-fat Greek yoghurt a lot in my kitchen. I use yoghurt both for its gentle acidity and also as a fat to add creaminess. I often use it where you might use mayonnaise, such as in coleslaw, or in place of some or all of the oil in salad dressings to bring a fresher creaminess. Adding cold yoghurt to hot food is also a great way of adding richness as well as being a pleasing temperature contrast.

## Using fats

Using oil to finish a dish is a complete game-changer. Every meal we eat has a drizzle of some sort of oil or yoghurt over it at the end. To me, it just rounds off the flavour and gives a final dimension of richness. I think this is particularly important when it comes to vegetarian cooking.

'There is as much variety in olive oil as there is in wine.'

# Layering texture

When I think about what I'm going to cook, I think about the texture as much as the flavour. Balancing crispy, crunchy, creamy, chewy, soft, wet, crumbly, smooth or sticky is just as important as balancing flavour. Think toasted seeds tossed into a salad; charred, oil-drizzled bread next to a bowl of soup; the crunch of some peppery radishes inside a soft taco; the smooth, spoonable creaminess of Greek yoghurt; the chew of udon noodles.

Texture also hits our tastebuds and tells our brain that this is delicious food and helps us to feel satisfied. An array of different textures builds an interesting eating experience. Have you ever eaten an enormous bowl of porridge that feels texturally monotonous? A bowl with texture from seeds, the crunch of brown sugar and a drizzle of cold cream would send very different messages to your brain, and you would feel full, sated and satisfied in a completely different way.

When we talk about adding texture to food, it's often assumed that we are talking about adding crunch, such as breadcrumbs on top of a bowl of pasta or some crispy sage leaves. While crunch is perhaps the easiest way to think of texture, it is more nuanced than that.

Unlike flavour, though, which for the most part does need to be a balance of all or most of its elements, I don't feel like every dish needs to have a balance of every texture. Some foods, like a roast potato, for instance, will inherently have numerous different textures – the outside will be crisp and crunchy, the deep-golden edges might be a tiny bit chewy, and the inside will be fluffy and soft. So it's important that texture is not always about layering ingredient on top of ingredient. To achieve texture,

One of the most undervalued elements in cooking and eating is texture. Texture is just as key as flavour, particularly in vegetarian cooking. When children respond to food, so much of their response is about the texture rather than flavour; it's a primal part of how we eat. We are all tuned into texture. You might love the spoonable softness of a risotto, the crunch of a pickle or the chew of an udon noodle.

We can appreciate a texture thanks to specialised sensory receptors. The receptors can sense the pressure of something, such as the weight of a liquid like oil or the brittleness of a piece of crunchy food. Other receptors sense temperature and create a painful reaction if something is too hot. Scientists refer to four texture or mouthfeel categories – chewy, crunchy, suckable and creamy.

how you cook and what heat you cook at are key – thinking about what you have, and sometimes keeping things simpler, will amplify the textural sensations.

When we eat food, generally it's nice to have a mixture of at least two textures. Think patatas bravas dipped into alioli or udon noodles in a miso broth. It's having these different textures present on a plate that makes food exciting.

When putting together a plate of food, consider texture. Two opposing textures is a good place to start: crunchy and creamy or chewy and soft. But remember that sometimes one texture can be satisfying or comforting: a heap of mashed potato, a cheesy bowl of polenta, a scoop of ice cream. Here are the ways I think about texture, which I hope will help you consider the various elements of texture in your food too.

## Crunch

Crunch is the easiest and quickest way to make a meal more exciting. When you put crunch next to soft, your tastebuds perk up.

Which crunch you add will depend on the texture you are pairing it with. Soft ricotta gnocchi works perfectly with crispy sage leaves. A bowl of soft, cold yoghurt pairs well with the dry crunch of granola. The juicy crunch of fresh sliced apple might work well next to some very creamy cheese.

- Dry crunch
  Granola, unbuttered toast, breadcrumbs, flaky sea salt, toasted flaked almonds, Demerara sugar, toasted spices.

- Shattering crunch
  Peanut brittle, crispy onions, flaky pastry, toasted coconut, fried sage leaves, fried garlic, crisps.

- Chewy crunch
  The edges of a cheese toastie, an olive oil crouton in a Caesar salad, crumble topping.

- Juicy crunch
  Crisp apples and pears, crunchy vegetables like carrots and celery, samphire.

## Chewy

Chewy is the texture I crave the most, from the sugary pull of a chocolate chip cookie to the puffy chew of a bao bun. I love my food to have chew.

- Brownies, chewy chocolate chip cookies, udon noodles, tapioca pearls, dried fruit, good sourdough, marshmallows, bao buns, tofu, gummy bears.

## Soft

Soft foods are gentle and smooth; a contrast to crunchy and chewy.

- Ripe mango or banana, soft-boiled or scrambled egg, ripe peaches, roast sweet potato, boiled carrots, pillowy whipped cream.

## Creamy

When two liquids that don't usually mix come together to create something that feels and tastes like a perfect mixture of the two. If something is creamy and rich, then it's likely to be an emulsion of liquid and fat.

- Greek yoghurt, ice cream, panna cotta, vinaigrette, mozzarella, tahini, peanut butter, mayonnaise, buttery pasta sauce, fats and oils, coconut milk, hummus.

## One ingredient
### – many textures

One way to add texture without having to add cost or effort is to use the same ingredient two ways. Some corn for a chowder can be kept back and crisped in a pan with chilli to put on top. Raw cauliflower could be shaved on top of some roasted cauliflower soup. Leeks could be cooked slowly in butter and added to colcannon, and some could be kept to sizzle in butter and oil to scatter over the top. One ingredient can give you endless textures.

## Heat and texture

Heat is the element of transformation; it takes food from raw to cooked and from soft to crisp, or vice versa. So far, we've just looked at the different ingredients that can add texture to our food, but how we cook our food also has a dramatic effect on its texture.

Heat and cooking in oil or fat create different types of texture in our food. For instance, if we steam a sweet potato we will get a soft, silky texture on the inside, whereas if we roast a sweet potato we will get a crispy outside and corners and a soft inside.

When you think about heat and texture, consider what you want to end up with and work back from there. It might be a bowl of buttery mashed potatoes, in which case boiling then mashing will give you the creamy effect you are after. But if you want a perfectly crunchy on the outside but melting on the inside cheese toastie, you might need to think more carefully. You may want to butter the outside of your sandwich and toast it in a hot pan until the edges are golden and crisp and the cheese inside is perfectly melted. You will want to eat it warm so that the cheese is still melty.

# Garlic

I buy garlic five heads at a time. I bring it home and peel back the white, papery skin until I get to the stripy lilac cloves. Then it sits there, in the bowl with lemons and limes, pretty and purple. It will be happy there for weeks until I need it. Then a thwack with the side of the knife squashes the clove and loosens the skin. I run my knife through it quickly. I add it to hot butter or oil in the pan and immediately this purple garlic that asked so little of me unleashes its enormous hit of flavour. So much, it's almost not fair on the other ingredients in the kitchen.

# On Garlic

Garlic's transformative power to make food tasty is unparalleled.

I use garlic sparingly, as an accent, not to overwhelm. Often, when I'm making tomato sauce, I will bash the clove with the side of the knife and let it sizzle whole and flavour the oil it's cooking in then lift it out. That hint of garlic is all I need (and is good if you are cooking for gentler palates). Adding a little garlic to your food can sharpen the taste of everything else; adding too much just makes everything taste like garlic.

The amount of garlic flavour you get from a clove will depend on how it is chopped. Kept whole but bashed it will be the gentlest hum of garlic. Finely sliced garlic will add a gentle garlic flavour and will give you pops of garlic flavour. Sliced garlic is also good cooked in oil until golden for a crisp garlic crunch. Minced garlic (or garlic crushed with a garlic press) will give you a more intense garlic flavour throughout what you are cooking. It's good raw too if you like a punchy salad dressing.

Burnt garlic has such a strong flavour it can easily ruin a dish. If you're prone to burning it, you can start your garlic and oil in a cold pan or add the garlic with other ingredients to soften the heat. Garlic really only needs a couple of minutes on a medium heat, less if finely chopped or minced, to cook. If you burn your garlic, start again – you will never get the taste of burnt garlic out of a dish.

I am not a fan of garlic bought peeled or pre-chopped: I think the flavour is acrid. If you find that chopping garlic is too much on a weeknight, chop a head and freeze it under oil in ice cube trays, or peel a head and keep the peeled cloves in a jar in the fridge for up to two weeks.

Hot, Nutty, Mustardy, Sweet

## Types

- **Head of garlic**
  The garlic we know is the picked, semi-dried bulbs of garlic.

- **Young or wet garlic**
  These are the white and purple bulbs picked and sold before they start to dry. It's milder, but you can use it in the same way as normal garlic.

- **Elephant garlic**
  Actually a member of the leek family – with enormous cloves and a milder taste.

- **Wild garlic**
  Is a different species of allium. It has a strong taste when it's raw that mellows when you cook it. It is highly seasonal and grows in woodlands from early spring.

- **Black garlic**
  Heads of raw garlic are fermented until they turn sticky, sweet and black. They go well with eggs and noodle dishes.

- **Confit garlic**
  Cloves of garlic cooked slowly in oil until they are soft, buttery and almost caramel-flavoured. Nothing like raw garlic.

## Goes well with

| | |
|---|---|
| almond | mushroom |
| aubergine | olive |
| basil | onion |
| broccoli | parsley |
| cauliflower | rosemary |
| cheese | shallot |
| chilli | thyme |
| coriander | tomato |
| ginger | walnut |

## Favourite uses

- Ajo blanco (see page 86)
- Smashed cucumber salad
- Fried into golden garlic crisps to top anything
- Confited and jarred for adding flavour to all my cooking
- In equal parts with ginger for a ying/yang feeling
- Fried with a chopped red chilli in oil for an aglio, olio e peperoncino pasta
- Rubbed on toast and topped with fresh tomatoes
- Grated into yoghurt with salt and lemon for serving with flatbreads

## Storage

Store garlic at room temperature in a dry, dark place – this way it will stay fresh for up to six months. Remember, the longer you keep garlic, the stronger the flavour will become. Garlic is fresh and changes flavour as it ages. If it's old or left in a bright spot, a little green shoot will creep out of the top. I think the green sprouts add bitterness, so I always halve the clove, flick the green spouts out with the end of my knife and then use the rest of the clove normally.

Peeled garlic cloves can be stored for up to a week in a container in the fridge.

## What to buy

If you're able, buy UK garlic (the Isle of Wight is a famous producer); cloves bought in the late spring and early summer will be fresher, milder new season garlic. Anything stored through the winter will be stronger. Spain, Italy and France grow good garlic – places like Natoora and good veg suppliers should be able to tell you about the variety and freshness of the garlic they sell.

In recent years, imported Chinese garlic is the main supermarket choice because of price and the fact there is little seasonal variation in flavour.

Easy Wins

# Confit garlic

4 whole heads of garlic
(about 240g)
350ml olive or rapeseed oil
a couple of sprigs of woody
herbs (5g), like bay, rosemary,
savory or thyme

Confit garlic is buttery, sweet and almost caramelly, an entirely different thing from raw or quickly cooked garlic. It can bring big and bold flavour to your cooking. While the word confit sounds like something you'd hear in a restaurant kitchen, it couldn't be simpler to make at home and keeps for months, meaning you have a hit of deep, sweet garlic on hand. Whether smudged over hot grilled toast or used at the start of making a comforting sauce, this is a great thing to have ready all year round, and the oil can be used too, so nothing is wasted.

MAKES 1 × 400G JAR

*Peel the garlic*
Peel 4 whole heads of garlic and add the cloves to a medium saucepan with 350ml olive or rapeseed oil. The garlic cloves should all be covered with oil. If they aren't, simply add a little more oil until they are.

*Confit the garlic*
Cook the garlic over a medium-low heat until the cloves just begin to sizzle gently around their edges, then lower the temperature slightly to maintain that gentle sizzle. Cook for 45 minutes, or until the garlic is completely soft and golden brown.

*Store the confit garlic*
Allow the oil to cool slightly, then add 5g woody herb sprigs to a sterilised jar large enough to hold the garlic confit and oil. Pour the cooked garlic and oil over the woody herbs (be careful, if the oil is too hot it may spit slightly as it hits the herbs) and seal the container. Store the confit garlic in the fridge, covered with the oil, for up to 6 months.

# Garlic and ginger pickle broth

80g fresh ginger, peeled (keep the peelings)
2 tablespoons red miso paste
a bunch of spring onions (about 8), trimmed but kept whole
6 cherry tomatoes
1 whole head of garlic (about 10 cloves), cloves peeled
200g sushi rice, washed until the water runs clear
3 tablespoons groundnut or vegetable oil
1 fresh red chilli, finely sliced
1 teaspoon coriander seeds
2 tablespoons sesame seeds
1 tablespoon maple syrup
1 teaspoon soy sauce or tamari
150g jar pickled ginger, with the pickling liquid

This soup was made one day when Kitty (who helped me test the recipes for this book) and I were sitting around my kitchen table, talking through our day of testing. I was quite pregnant and full of cold, and everything seemed an effort. We settled on the idea of a broth with rice and lots of ginger. It revived me like no other soup I can remember. It was like an IV drip of goodness – plump sushi rice, a gingery garlic miso broth, and then a punchy pickle, half crispy garlic and half pickled and fresh ginger. I made it every day for the next three days. Thanks, Kitty.

SERVES 4

*Make the garlic and ginger broth*
Peel 80g fresh ginger and keep the peelings. Add 1.5 litres water to a saucepan, add 2 tablespoons red miso paste, a bunch of trimmed spring onions, 6 cherry tomatoes, 4 peeled cloves of garlic and the ginger peel. Bring to the boil, then turn down to a low simmer for 20–30 minutes.

*Wash and cook the rice*
Put 200g washed sushi rice and 300ml cold water into a saucepan with a lid. Bring to the boil, cover, then immediately turn the heat down to a very low simmer and cook for 10 minutes. Turn off the heat, wrap the lid of the pan in a tea towel and put it back on the pan, then leave the rice to sit for 10 minutes.

*Slice the pickle ingredients*
Thinly slice 6 cloves of garlic with a knife or very carefully on a mandoline. Chop the peeled ginger into matchsticks as thinly as you can.

*Fry the aromatics*
Put 3 tablespoons groundnut or vegetable oil into a small frying pan or saucepan, followed by the sliced garlic, ginger, 1 finely sliced fresh red chilli, 1 teaspoon coriander seeds and 2 tablespoons sesame seeds. Put the pan over a medium-low heat and allow everything to cook slowly for 5–7 minutes until the garlic and ginger are just golden and crisp. Once crisp, turn off the heat, add 1 tablespoon maple syrup and 1 teaspoon soy sauce and let it bubble. Set aside to cool slightly.

*Finish the pickle*
Empty 150g jarred pickled ginger into a bowl with its liquid (there should ideally be about 75ml of pickling liquid from the jar, but it will vary from jar to jar) then carefully pour in the ginger and garlic mix from the pan with all the liquid.

*Finish the broth*
Spoon the warm rice between four bowls and ladle over the broth. Put the bowl of garlic pickle in the middle of the table and let everyone spoon on as much as they like. Any leftover pickle will keep in a jar in the fridge for up to 2 weeks.

*Add-ons*
I like to eat this broth simply but if you wanted to add more veg, then some quartered pak choi, broccoli, shredded spring greens, or even very thin slices of sweet potato, would work well. Just add them to the broth for the last few minutes of cooking.

# Confit garlic cauliflower cheese

75g butter or vegan butter
75g plain flour
900ml milk or oat milk
2 whole heads (about 20 cloves) of confit garlic (see page 244)
80g Cheddar or vegan Cheddar, grated
50g Gruyère or vegan Cheddar-style cheese, grated
1 large cauliflower, broken into chunky florets, smaller leaves reserved
150g fresh breadcrumbs
zest of 1 unwaxed lemon
a few sprigs of thyme (5g), leaves picked
a few sprigs of sage (5g), leaves picked and chopped

Confit garlic makes everything better, and I feel the same about cauliflower cheese, so together this is a blanket of a dish. Confit garlic, cheesy sauce and burnished cauliflower. Eat this with some lemon-dressed greens or a bitter leaf salad. This is always one of our Christmas Day sides.

SERVES 6

*Make the béchamel*
Preheat the oven to 180°C/160°C fan. Melt 75g butter or vegan butter in a medium saucepan over a medium-low heat, then stir in 75g plain flour until it forms a paste. Cook for a couple of minutes until the paste begins to smell toasty (this will cook the rawness out of the flour). Add 900ml milk or oat milk a little at a time, whisking continuously into a smooth, white sauce.

*Add the confit garlic and cheese to the béchamel*
Take about 20 cloves of confit garlic from their fragrant oil and stir half into the sauce. Add half the grated Cheddar (40g) and half the grated Gruyère (25g), or your vegan alternatives, season well with sea salt and freshly ground black pepper and stir to melt the cheese. It should be quite a loose sauce (it will thicken up as it bakes) so add a little more milk or oat milk if needed.

*Arrange the cauliflower*
Arrange the florets from 1 large cauliflower and some of the smaller cauliflower leaves in a baking dish that will fit everything in nicely, then add the remaining 10 cloves of confit garlic, dotting it into the spaces between the cauliflower.

*Pour over the sauce*
Pour the garlicky cheese sauce evenly over the cauliflower, then top with the other half of the grated Cheddar (40g) and grated Gruyère (25g).

*Make the breadcrumb topping and bake*
Mix 150g breadcrumbs with the zest of 1 unwaxed lemon, 5g thyme leaves and 5g chopped sage leaves, then sprinkle over the cheesy cauliflower. Finally, spoon over some of the oil from the confit garlic and bake for 1 hour, until the cauliflower is soft and golden.

# Roast garlic and white bean soup

200g blanched almonds
1 litre good-quality vegetable
 stock (if using powder
 or cubes use half the
 recommended amount for
 800ml water)
1 large cauliflower (850g), cut
 into florets, leaves kept
a whole head of garlic
1 teaspoon fennel seeds
6 tablespoons olive oil
1 onion, peeled and finely
 chopped
1 stick of celery, finely chopped
200ml white wine or more stock
1 × 400g tin white beans,
 drained (either butter beans
 or cannellini beans)
4 sprigs of thyme, leaves picked

We made this soup one day on the shoot for my last book. It has the comfort of a silky spoonable soup but with a big bold flavour. Mostly on shoot days we eat what we have cooked to take pictures of and most days it's a feast. One of my favourite things about writing a book are these lunches eaten with the friends who help me put my books together.

This day, though, we must have started late or been making sweet things, so we whipped up this soup: buttery roast garlic, almonds, white beans and cauliflower. It was what we had that needed using, but it turned out to be a soup I have repeated a lot since. The tone-on-tone colours in this soup, white on white, had me thinking this is actually a good flavour lesson. Often I'll make something and then realise that every-thing I used was from one colour palette. I think there is some sense in this. Think squash, chilli and orange or peas, broad beans and mint. It's not a hard and fast rule but a way of cooking I sometimes enjoy.

SERVES 4

*Toast the almonds*
Preheat the oven to 200°C/180°C fan. Add 200g blanched almonds to a large shallow baking tray, then place in the oven and toast for 5–10 minutes until lightly golden. Remove from the oven then add three-quarters of them to 1 litre good vegetable stock to soak and leave the other quarter to cool separately.

*Roast the cauliflower and garlic*
Put the florets from 1 large cauliflower into the same tray with a whole head of garlic and add 1 teaspoon fennel seeds, 2 tablespoons olive oil, a generous pinch of flaky sea salt and some freshly ground black

pepper. Toss together so the florets are all evenly coated, then roast in the oven for 30 minutes until golden at the edges. Remove the cauliflower from the tray into a bowl and return the garlic to the oven for a further 15 minutes until it is soft inside.

*Make the soup*
Put 2 tablespoons olive oil, 1 peeled and finely chopped onion and 1 finely chopped stick of celery into a large saucepan. Sauté on a medium heat for 5–10 minutes until soft and sweet but not browned. Add 200ml white wine or more stock and cook until it reduces down to half the amount.

*Add the cauliflower and stock*
Add the roasted cauliflower, 400g tin of white beans, drained, the soaked almonds and vegetable stock to the saucepan with the onion and celery. Bring to the boil, then lower the heat and simmer for 10–15 minutes.

*Squeeze in the garlic*
Cut the top off the roasted head of garlic and squeeze out the soft flesh into the saucepan. Compost the papery skins, then blitz the soup with a hand-held blender until completely smooth, adding hot water if needed to loosen to the consistency of double cream.

*For the topping and serve*
Finely chop the cauliflower leaves and the remaining toasted almonds then add them to a frying pan with 2 tablespoons olive oil, a pinch of sea salt and 4 sprigs of picked thyme leaves. Fry on a high heat for 5–10 minutes until the leaves are crisp and tender and the almonds are more toasted and golden. Ladle the soup into bowls and finish with the crispy cauliflower and almond topping.

# Creamy double garlic and broccoli rigatoni

1 large head of broccoli
  (about 500g)
500g rigatoni
4 tablespoons extra virgin
  olive oil
2 cloves of fresh garlic, very
  finely chopped
10 cloves of confit garlic
  (see page 244 for recipe)
60g Parmesan (I use a vegetarian
  one) or vegan Parmesan-style
  cheese, grated
zest of 2 unwaxed lemons and
  the juice of 1
1 tablespoon black pepper, freshly
  ground (about 10 grinds)

Think cacio e pepe here, but the creaminess comes from confit garlic, not a mountain of Parmesan (though we add some of that too). The confit garlic brings sweet, mellow, creamy garlic flavour which is backed up by a couple of cloves of fresh garlic for heat and spice. The broccoli is cooked almost to the point of collapse, which adds to the soft creaminess of the sauce. All that richness is backed up by a hit of black pepper and just enough umami from some Parmesan. An on-repeat pasta.

If you don't have confit garlic for this recipe (the recipe is on page 244) then you can add a couple of extra cloves of fresh garlic and more Parmesan. It won't be quite as rich or creamy but it will still be a bowl of pasta you will be very happy about.

SERVES 4

*Chop and cook the broccoli*
Cut 500g broccoli into small florets, then roughly chop the stalk into 1cm pieces. Bring a large pot of well-salted water to the boil, add the broccoli florets and stalks and cook for 8–10 minutes until soft. You want it well cooked so it breaks down into a sauce. Drain the broccoli with a slotted spoon and keep the water on.

*Cook the pasta*
Add 500g rigatoni to the same water and boil for a minute less than the packet instructions, which will be about 8–10 minutes.

*Cook the fresh garlic and add the cooked broccoli*
Meanwhile, put 4 tablespoons extra virgin olive oil into a frying pan on a medium-low heat and add 2 very finely chopped cloves of peeled garlic, frying for a minute before adding the cooked broccoli and a few

spoonfuls of the pasta water. Simmer slowly for 5–8 more minutes until it's really soft, mashing some of the broccoli as it cooks with the back of your spoon.

*Make the confit garlic sauce*
In a small bowl, roughly mash 10 cloves of confit garlic with 60g grated Parmesan or vegan Parmesan-style cheese, the zest of 1 unwaxed lemon and 1 tablespoon of black pepper, freshly ground, to make a thick paste. Squeeze in the juice of 1 lemon and add a few spoonfuls of the pasta water until you have a spoonable sauce-like consistency, about the thickness of double cream.

*Finish the pasta*
Drain the pasta, reserving a mugful of the pasta water, then add the pasta to the broccoli pan with the confit garlic sauce. Stir together over a low heat, adding more pasta water until you have a glossy sauce to coat everything, remembering that the sauce will thicken as the pasta sits. Serve immediately, with extra Parmesan, black pepper and lemon zest.

# Confit garlic Caesar salad with herbs

2 slices sourdough bread, torn
 into roughly 2cm pieces
8 cloves of confit garlic, plus
 4 tablespoons of the confit
 garlic oil (see page 244)
zest and juice of ½ an unwaxed
 lemon
100g crème fraîche or oat
 crème fraîche
50g Parmesan or vegan
 Parmesan-style cheese,
 grated, plus extra to serve
2 teaspoons Dijon mustard
1 teaspoon black pepper, freshly
 ground, plus a little extra
2 tablespoons capers, plus
 2 tablespoons caper brine
4 Little Gem lettuces or 2 heads
 of Romaine lettuce
½ a bunch of parsley (15g), leaves
 picked
½ a bunch of chives (10g), finely
 chopped

Like a classic Caesar but fresher. I use confit garlic here to add creaminess to the dressing, with some crème fraîche for bright acidity and lots of herbs to lift it. The confit garlic oil is used to roast the croutons, so there is a mellow double garlic flavour. I eat this as it is on the side, but if you wanted to make it into a meal then a tin of drained white beans, patted dry and cooked until crisp in olive oil in the oven while the croutons cook, would round it out.

SERVES 4

*Preheat the oven and make the croutons*
Preheat the oven to 180°C/160°C fan. Tear 2 slices of sourdough bread into roughly 2cm pieces and place in a large baking tray with 2 tablespoons confit garlic oil, sea salt and freshly ground black pepper. Toss so it's all evenly coated in the oil, then bake in the oven for 10–15 minutes until golden and crisp but still a little soft in the middle. Remove and set aside.

*Make the dressing*
In a bowl, mash 8 confit garlic cloves, then mix with the zest and juice of ½ an unwaxed lemon, 100g crème fraîche or oat crème fraîche, 50g grated Parmesan or vegan Parmesan-style cheese, 2 teaspoons Dijon mustard, 1 teaspoon freshly ground black pepper and 2 tablespoons caper brine from the jar. Mix to a thick dressing, about the same consistency as yoghurt.

*Put the salad together*
Add the leaves from 4 Little Gem lettuces or 2 heads of Romaine lettuce to a serving bowl with the picked leaves from ½ a bunch of parsley (15g), ½ a bunch of finely chopped chives (10g), half the dressing (saving the rest for another day), 2 tablespoons capers and the croutons. Toss everything together, then serve immediately with some more Parmesan grated over the top.

# Crispy garlic egg-fried rice

500g cooked jasmine or
    basmati rice
1 cucumber
150g radishes, leaves trimmed
1 tablespoon crispy chilli oil or
    chilli crisp
3 tablespoons soy sauce or
    tamari
1 teaspoon maple syrup
zest and juice of 1 unwaxed lime
8 cloves of garlic, peeled and
    very thinly sliced (use a
    mandoline if you have one)
3 tablespoons neutral oil (such
    as groundnut)
2 tablespoons sesame seeds
4 free-range eggs
1 bunch of spring onions,
    very finely sliced

Egg-fried rice is made about once every two weeks here. It's a meal we know Dylan will eat and it's what I crave when I'm not feeling like thinking about food, which is surprisingly often. Here, some crispy garlic adds texture and sweet toasty flavour to the rice. Garlic crisped in oil like this will improve just about any meal, so once you have mastered it you can top all your meals with it (and trust me, you just might). The rice comes with an easy little smacked cucumber and radish salad which lifts and adds crunch. I've kept the rice simple, but if you wanted to you could add some shredded greens or blanched frozen peas as well. If you are vegan you could add some crumbled soft tofu instead of the eggs.

SERVES 2 GENEROUSLY, OR 4 AS PART
OF A MEAL

*Cook the rice if needed*
If you don't have leftover rice, cook around 170g rice now, to give 500g cooked rice (see page 194 for a method).

*Make the cucumber and radish salad*
With a rolling pin gently smack 1 cucumber and 150g trimmed radishes so they split but don't break up completely. Chop the cucumber into 2cm pieces and put them into a serving bowl with the radishes. Add 1 tablespoon crispy chilli oil, 2 tablespoons soy sauce, 1 teaspoon maple syrup and the zest and juice of 1 unwaxed lime and mix until everything is coated in the dressing.

*Make the crispy garlic*
Thinly slice 8 peeled cloves of garlic with a knife or very carefully with a mandoline. Put 3 tablespoons of neutral oil into a small frying pan or saucepan and add the sliced garlic and 2 tablespoons sesame seeds. Put

the pan over a medium-low heat and allow everything to cook slowly for 3–5 minutes until the garlic is very lightly golden and crisp. Be careful here to cook until just golden. Taking the garlic too far or too brown will make it bitter, so don't be tempted to cook it on a high heat. Drain the garlic and seeds with a sieve (keeping the oil), then leave to cool on some kitchen paper.

*Beat the eggs and fry the rice*
Beat 4 eggs well with another tablespoon of soy sauce. Put the reserved oil in a large wok or frying pan over a high heat, then, once hot, add 500g cooked jasmine or basmati rice and spread it out in an even layer to heat through for a minute. Now stir until all the rice is coated in a little oil.

*Add the eggs*
Push most of the rice to one side of the pan. Add the beaten egg to the empty side, stir the egg quickly to fry and partly cook it, then stir it into the rice and cook for another minute or two. Take off the heat.

*Serve the rice*
Mix a quarter of the crispy garlic and sesame seeds into the cucumber and radish salad. Divide the rice between four bowls and put some of the salad on the side of each. Finish the rice with the remaining crispy garlic and sesame, and top with 1 bunch of very finely sliced spring onions.

# Lemongrass dal with garlic and curry leaves

1 teaspoon coriander seeds,
   bashed
1 teaspoon cumin seeds
300g red split lentils, rinsed
6 garlic cloves, peeled, 3 left
   whole, 3 finely sliced
2 lemongrass stalks, bashed
1 teaspoon ground turmeric
½ teaspoon Kashmiri chilli
   powder
1 × 400ml tin coconut milk
200g greens, like spinach or
   shredded chard
2 tablespoons coconut oil
1 small red onion, peeled and
   finely sliced
1 teaspoon black mustard seeds
20 fresh curry leaves
1 unwaxed lemon
chapatis or rotis, to serve

The comfort of dal is unmatched, and this gently spiced one comforts as well as lifts, thanks to some lemongrass, greens and lemon. The real star here, though, is the garlic temper, the garlic, red onion, mustard seeds and curry leaves which are spooned over the dal to give tiny pockets of flavour on each spoon. This dal is inspired by one from Cynthia of Rambutan that I've been making a lot.

SERVES 4

*Toast the spices*
In a saucepan big enough to cook your dal, toast 1 teaspoon bashed coriander seeds and 1 teaspoon cumin seeds, then tip into a small bowl.

*Rinse and cook the lentils*
Rinse 300g red split lentils in cold water, then drain, put them in a pan and cover with 1 litre water (about 1cm over the top of the lentils). Add a good pinch of salt and bring to the boil. Once boiling, skim off any scum that has risen to the top, then reduce to a simmer. Add 3 whole cloves of garlic, 2 bashed lemongrass stalks, 1 teaspoon ground turmeric, ½ teaspoon Kashmiri chilli powder, the toasted coriander and cumin seeds and cook for 15 minutes, or until the lentils are velvety soft.

*Add the coconut milk*
Once the lentils are cooked, turn the heat back up to medium, add 400ml coconut milk and 200g spinach and cook for another 10 minutes, until creamy.

*Make the temper*
In a small pan heat 2 tablespoons coconut oil over a high heat, add 1 small red onion, peeled and finely sliced, and cook for 5–6 minutes

until golden brown. Add 3 finely sliced cloves of garlic, 1 teaspoon black mustard seeds and 20 curry leaves and cook for 1–2 minutes more until the curry leaves are crispy and shiny.

*Finish the dal*
Spoon the dal into bowls, top with the garlic and curry leaf temper, add a squeeze of lemon juice to lift everything and eat with roti or chapati.

# Gurd's roasted tomatoes with crispy garlic

125ml olive oil

6 fat cloves of garlic, sliced into thin slivers

1 teaspoon dried chilli flakes

a bunch of parsley (30g), very finely chopped

zest and juice of ½ an unwaxed lemon

4 tablespoons panko breadcrumbs

3 tablespoons dukkah (see recipe below)

1 teaspoon fine sea salt

1kg large ripe tomatoes (I used 4 × 250g tomatoes, halved horizontally)

FOR THE DUKKAH
(MAKES A SMALL JAR)

45g blanched hazelnuts

2 tablespoons sesame seeds

1 tablespoon cumin seeds

1 tablespoon coriander seeds

1 tablespoon fennel seeds

1 teaspoon paprika

1 teaspoon dried oregano

1 teaspoon fine sea salt

2 teaspoons black pepper, coarsely ground

Spending time with Gurdeep feels like time spent in full colour, on fast forward in the most wonderful way. I trust Gurd's opinion on food completely. He is a genius with flavour, and these tomatoes are proof. To Gurdeep, garlic is a unique flavour amplifier whose multiple characters can take a dish into completely different directions depending which is pulled upon. 'Raw garlic imparts sharp spiciness and earthy pungency. Slowly roasted, it's transformed to a fragrant-fudgy butter; and when browned or blackened, it gives an intense tangy-bitterness that shatters with a crunch.' This recipe from Gurd celebrates garlic's diversity – first extracting its allium sweetness into olive oil for roasting with, then crisping it up for some textural peppery bite.

SERVES 4

*Fry the crispy garlic*
Preheat the oven to 195°C/175°C fan. Very gently heat 125ml olive oil in a frying pan, then add 6 fat cloves of garlic, sliced into thin slivers. Fry in the just bubbling oil, low and slow, for 3–4 minutes, watching it closely; you want the garlic to release its flavours into the oil without taking on any colour at all. When the garlic begins to clump together in the oil, add 1 teaspoon dried chilli flakes and sizzle gently for another 1 minute. Pour the oil through a sieve into a jug, keeping the garlic and chilli flakes to one side for now.

*Make the topping*
In a separate bowl, mix together a bunch of very finely chopped parsley and the zest and juice of ½ an unwaxed lemon. Next, stir through 70ml of the garlicky oil, keeping some behind to drizzle over later. Finally, mix through 4 tablespoons panko

breadcrumbs, 3 tablespoons dukkah and a teaspoon of fine sea salt to make a green-zesty crumb crust.

*Prep and top the tomatoes*
Slice 1kg large ripe tomatoes in half horizontally, spread out on a lined baking sheet and sprinkle each one with a pinch of sea salt. Spoon a thick layer of the dukkah-gremolata crust on to each and drizzle liberally with the last of the garlicky oil.

*Bake the tomatoes*
Bake in the oven for 45–50 minutes, until the tomatoes are soft and the tops start to brown. Remove from the oven, baste with the oils from the bottom of the tray, then sprinkle over the fried garlic and chilli flakes. Return to the oven for a further 5–6 minutes until the garlic just turns crispy and the crust is nicely baked. Serve with couscous or warm flatbreads. Enjoy hot or cold.

For the dukkah:
*Preheat the oven and toast the spices*
Preheat the oven to 180°C/160°C fan. Scatter 45g blanched hazelnuts, 2 tablespoons sesame seeds, 1 tablespoon each of cumin, coriander and fennel seeds on to a baking tray. Bake for 6–7 minutes until toasty and just browned. Remove from the oven and cool.

*Grind and mix*
Spoon the cooled nuts and spices into a spice grinder or food processor, along with 1 teaspoon each of paprika, dried oregano and fine sea salt and 2 teaspoons coarsely ground black pepper. Pulse for a couple of seconds to a coarse crumbly rubble. Keep in an airtight jar in a dark place, where it will store well for up to 4 weeks.

# Olia's pampushky

15g fresh yeast or 7g active dry
    yeast
1 teaspoon caster sugar
225ml warm water
400g strong white flour, plus
    extra for dusting
8g fine sea salt
5 cloves (about 20g) wet or
    regular garlic, crushed or
    very finely chopped
3 tablespoons sunflower oil, plus
    extra for oiling
½ a bunch of parsley (15g), finely
    chopped
1 free-range egg, beaten, to glaze

Olia is a dear friend. She writes with great beauty on the food of Ukraine and the surrounding regions. Olia has also provided me and countless others with an unmatched heart-first perspective on the war in Ukraine – standing up and speaking out when it must have been immeasurably hard. Olia has been kind enough to share this recipe with me, and I put it here as a reminder to not forget the war still waged on Ukraine.

Olia tells me that the word 'pampushka' can be used to describe a gorgeous plump woman and is one of her favourite words. Pam-poo-shka! These pampushky are traditionally served with red borshch. In Ukraine, Olia says she would use regular garlic, so if you can't find wet (new) garlic, don't worry – it will still be delicious.

MAKES 8 BREADS

*Make your starter*
First make a 'sponge', which is a type of yeasty starter. Dissolve 15g fresh yeast or 7g active dry yeast and 1 teaspoon caster sugar in 225ml warm water (make sure it's body temperature – hot water would kill the yeast). Add 200g strong white flour and mix roughly. Cover the bowl and leave to prove in the refrigerator overnight or on the counter for 3 hours.

*Make the dough*
The next morning, or 3 hours later, add another 200g strong white flour and 8g fine sea salt to the starter and knead on a well-floured work surface until the dough is smooth and comes away from your hands easily.

*Shape the dough*
Divide the dough into 8 pieces and shape into round buns. Put them side by side in an oiled round ovenproof dish or a 24cm round cake tin, cover and let them prove again, this time in a warm place, until doubled in size. They will join together just like hot cross buns do.

*Make the basting oil*
Meanwhile, preheat the oven to 220°C/200°C fan. To make the basting oil, simply stir 20g crushed wet (new) or regular garlic through 3 tablespoons sunflower oil with a small pinch of sea salt and ½ a bunch of finely chopped parsley, then let it infuse.

*Glaze and bake*
When the pampushky look plump and ready, brush them generously with a beaten egg to glaze and bake for 20–25 minutes or until they form a glistening golden crust. Take them out and baste them with the garlic oil. Serve immediately.

# Onions

Papery skin so thin you can see the light through it. Brown and purple, white and caramel. There is poetry in an onion. Tears when it's peeled, but after a slow cook transformed into a blanket of sweet comfort. Onions cross cultures. The start of so much. The smell of an onion cooking is the smell of promise, of good things to come. A steady assurance of flavour that we can rely on, and we all need something to rely on. Cooked under pastry with cheese and potato, sharp and tempered with acid to lift a tomato salad, charred and blackened but still sweet. All that from one papery allium that lives in the dark.

# On Onions

Every cuisine uses onions. In my kitchen, they are used 100 ways. From slow-cooked and buttery to pickled and punchy. From crispy shards to buttery leeks. Onions and the other alliums (shallots, leeks, spring onions) make my cooking what it is.

To me, an onion needs some cooking: often a long, slow cook until soft and buttery, but I never cook a raw onion for anything less than 10 minutes, until it's softened, broken down and has lost its rawness.

I may be in the minority here, but I am not keen on completely raw onion. If I want the hit of onion freshness, I will quickly pickle it in lime juice and salt or a little vinegar and sugar, depending on what I am eating. The same with a shallot. As well as sweetness and acidity, using onions like this adds their own version of warmth and heat.

My love of nothing but a well-cooked onion has led me to use leeks and spring onions instead of onions when I want to cook quickly. It lends the same allium depth, but you can cook a spring onion in a couple of minutes and a finely sliced leek in five.

Sweet, Hot, Sour, Umami

### Types

- Mild
  Big onions with a soft, mild flavour.

- Yellow
  The most widely used onion in the UK – they have a rich flavour that makes them endlessly versatile.

- White
  More unusual in the UK, white onions are generally cleaner in flavour than yellow, but don't store quite as well as yellow onions do.

- Red
  Slightly sweeter but still punchy when raw. These pickle really nicely.

- Spring onions
  These are very young yellow, red or white onions that are pulled out of the ground before they can turn into onions.

- Leeks
  The milder, milky green cousin of the onion.

- Shallot
  Tapered with a coppery skin – milder and sweeter in flavour than red onions. A staple in French cooking.

### Goes well with

| | |
|---|---|
| beetroot | lemon |
| butter | lime |
| caper | mushroom |
| carrot | pea |
| cheese | potato |
| chilli | red pepper |
| ginger | sage |

### How to cook

- Baking
  Roasting onions turns them into something sweet, rich and earthy – a vegetable all of their own, not a supporting act.

- Soaking
  If you want to use raw onions, but are after a mellower flavour, soak them in a bowl of cold water for a few minutes before using.

- Sautéing
  To sauté an onion, cook over high heat with a little oil until golden brown. If they begin to catch on the bottom of the pan, adding a splash of water (not oil) will unstick them.

- Sweating
  This means cooking over a low heat until the onion becomes soft and transparent, without browning.

- Caramelising
  Caramelisation is a slow, delicate process that combines sweating and sautéing (see following page).

### Storage and tips

Keep onions and shallots in a cool, dark place. Remove them from any plastic bag, as that makes them sweat and go off quicker.

Store a cut onion in the fridge, cut side down, on a plate covered with a bowl or in a jar or glass container so that other foods don't take on the taste of onion.

### What to buy

Try to buy onions grown in the UK when you can.

Look for firm red or yellow onions with taut skin that feel heavy for their size, with no green sprouts.

I buy escallion shallots, also known as banana shallots. The flavour is sweeter, and they are less annoying to peel than the small shallots.

For leeks and spring onions, look for perky ones with no dry or browning bits.

# Crispy shallots

6 banana shallots, peeled,
 halved and finely sliced
1 litre sunflower oil

MAKES A SMALL JARFUL

Peel and halve 6 banana shallots,
then remove their tops and finely
slice. Add to a large bowl and,
using your hands, move through
the shallots separating as many
individual slices as possible.

Put 1 litre sunflower oil into a
large saucepan and heat to roughly
180°C, or until a large breadcrumb
turns golden in 30 seconds in the oil.
Add the shallots to the oil and cook,
stirring continuously, for 10 minutes,
or until the shallots are a light brown.
The shallots will continue to cook and
colour for a minute or so once they
are out of the oil, so remove them just
before they're looking done.

Drain on kitchen paper and allow to
cool. Store in an airtight container in

a cool dark place for up to 2 weeks.
Perfect for topping salads, dressing
fried vegetables or simply stirred
through buttery pasta.

*Here are a few easy ways to use your
crispy onions*
- They're great on top of a curry, a
  dal or a laksa.
- You can scatter them over a stir-fry
  or a noodle dish like a pad thai.
- Pile them into a cheese sandwich
  with some pickle.
- To finish scrambled eggs.
- They make any autumnal or
  winter soup much tastier.
- They'll improve a baked potato or
  sweet potato with crème fraîche
  and a pinch of chopped capers.
- Lastly, they are the perfect finish
  to a rich autumn tomato pasta.

# Slow-cooked onions

1.2kg medium brown onions
 (about 6), peeled, halved and
 finely sliced
1 knob of butter
4 tablespoons olive oil
1 tablespoon apple cider vinegar
2 tablespoons light soft brown
 sugar (optional)

These slow-cooked onions bolster
the base of pies, sauces and one-pot
suppers. Make a large batch and keep
them to hand, frozen in ice-cube
trays. Simply knock out a couple of
cubes straight into the pan as and
when you need them.

MAKES A LARGE JARFUL

Add 1 knob of butter and 4 tablespoons olive oil to a large casserole-
style pot and set over a medium-high
heat. As soon as the butter has melted
and begins to sizzle, add the onions
and a generous pinch of salt. Stir to
evenly coat the onions in the buttery-
oil mixture and turn the heat down
to low. Cook, stirring every now and

then, for 30–45 minutes, until the
onions are translucent, sweet and
soft. Add 1 tablespoon apple cider
vinegar and stir to combine.

If you like, you can enhance the
natural sweetness of the onions
by adding 2 tablespoons light soft
brown sugar at this stage. Add to
the pan, stir to mix evenly and
cook for a couple of minutes until
the sugar has dissolved. Take the
onions off the heat and transfer to
a sterilised container where they
will keep, covered in the fridge,
for a week. To preserve them for
longer, simply divide the cooked
and cooled onion mixture between
ice-cube trays and freeze until
needed.

# Sticky onion Eccles cakes with carrot chutney

1 tablespoon coriander seeds
1 teaspoon caraway seeds
400g carrots, peeled and grated
1 small thumb-sized piece of
    ginger, grated
50g caster sugar
zest and juice of 2 unwaxed
    lemons
1 tablespoon butter or olive oil
4 shallots, peeled and finely
    chopped
75ml white wine vinegar
2 cloves of garlic, peeled and
    finely chopped
6 pitted dates, roughly chopped
150g Lancashire cheese,
    crumbled, or a vegan hard
    mature-style cheese
50g almonds, toasted and
    roughly chopped
2 × 320g ready-rolled puff pastry
    sheets (use non-dairy if
    needed)
1 organic egg, beaten (or
    3 tablespoons of non-dairy
    milk)
4 tablespoons mixed seeds
    (I use a mix of poppy and
    sesame)
2 tablespoons Demerara sugar

Eccles cakes are my favourite. There is a bakery in Anglesey, where John is from. The Eccles cakes are off the chart, the bottom sweet and sticky from the filling running out where the pastry joins. I've wanted to try a savoury version for ages. The filling is based on John's mum's carrot chutney.

This Eccles cake brings together a sticky shallot and carrot filling, which is really like a chutney, and some Lancashire cheese topped with Demerara and seeds which form a crunchy seeded top. These travel well.

MAKES 12 ECCLES CAKES

*Mix the spices and carrot*
Bash 1 tablespoon coriander seeds in a mortar and tip into a saucepan. Add 1 teaspoon caraway seeds, 400g peeled and grated carrots, 1 small thumb of grated ginger, 50g caster sugar and the zest of 2 unwaxed lemons. Cover with a lid and set aside while you cook the onions.

*Cook the shallots*
Melt the butter in a frying pan and fry 4 finely chopped shallots with a pinch of salt over a medium-low heat until soft and beginning to turn golden – about 10 minutes.

*Make the carrot chutney*
Add the carrot and spices to the pan with the shallots and place over a medium heat and measure in the juice of 2 unwaxed lemons and 75ml white wine vinegar. Slowly bring to a boil, then reduce the heat and simmer for 10 minutes, until the carrots are tender.

*Make the filling*
Add 2 finely chopped cloves of garlic, 6 roughly chopped pitted dates and 200ml water to the pan and cook until the dates are completely soft and broken down and almost all the liquid has evaporated. You want a thick chutney consistency. This should take 10–15 minutes, and you will need to keep stirring here so it doesn't stick. Leave aside to cool. Once cool, crumble in 150g Lancashire cheese, or a vegan hard mature-style cheese, add 50g toasted and roughly chopped almonds and stir to combine.

*Roll out the pastry*
Unroll 1 × 320g ready-rolled puff pastry sheet on to a well-floured surface and cut it into 6 equal squares. Pile 2 heaped tablespoons of the filling in the middle of one of the squares. Bring the four corners together over the filling to form a sealed round. Repeat with the other 5 squares. Turn the cakes over and, with the pinched side on the work surface, use a rolling pin to gently flatten, then place on a lined baking tray. Repeat with the other pastry sheet.

*Finish and bake the Eccles cakes*
Mix the 4 tablespoons seeds with 2 tablespoons Demerara sugar. Brush the top of each Eccles cake with beaten egg or non-dairy milk. Dip the eggwashed side into the seed and sugar mixture to completely cover the top of the pastry. Transfer the seeded pastries to a baking sheet as you work. Chill in the fridge for at least 20 minutes. When you are ready to bake, heat the oven to 200°C/180°C fan, remove the cakes from the fridge and use a sharp knife to make a couple of slashes in the top of the pastry. Bake them in the oven for 25–30 minutes until deep golden and flaky.

Onions

# Spring onions with bread sauce

700ml whole milk or oat milk
1 onion, peeled and halved
5 cloves
5 black peppercorns
2 bay leaves
250g stale sourdough, blitzed
    to breadcrumbs
90ml double cream or oat cream
⅛ of a nutmeg, grated
a bunch of dill (or fennel tops),
    leaves picked and finely
    chopped
12 spring onions or calçots,
    trimmed and green tops
    finely sliced
4 tablespoons extra virgin
    olive oil
½ teaspoon Dijon mustard
2 teaspoons apple cider vinegar
a little runny honey or agave
    syrup (optional)
rapeseed or sunflower oil,
    for frying
3 shallots, peeled and finely
    sliced into rounds

This is based on a fine plate of food
I ate at 40 Maltby Street last year.
You know a dish is good when you
crave it so much you have to recreate
it yourself. This has a roast dinner
feeling to it. I use dill a lot in this
recipe. If you are not a dill fan, use
fennel or parsley instead for a more
mellow herb hit. I won't hold it
against you.

The bread sauce can be made up
to two days ahead and kept in the
fridge. Reheat and loosen with a little
milk if it's too thick.

SERVES 4

*Infuse the milk*
Pour 700ml whole milk or oat milk
into a medium saucepan. Spike
1 peeled and halved onion with 5 whole
cloves and lower into the milk. Add
5 black peppercorns and 2 bay leaves
and bring the milk to the boil over
a high heat. Remove from the heat,
cover and allow the flavours to
infuse for half an hour.

*Finish the bread sauce*
Sieve the aromatics from the milk
and put the milk back into the
saucepan. Add 250g stale sourdough
breadcrumbs and bring to a gentle
simmer. Stir in 90ml double cream or
oat cream and grate in ⅛ of a nutmeg,
then season well with sea salt and
pepper. Continue to cook over a low
heat until the sauce has thickened.
Stir in half the finely chopped leaves
from a bunch of dill (or fennel tops),
then remove from the heat. Keep
warm if you are planning to eat it
soon. If not, allow to cool before
transferring to a covered bowl until
you're ready to serve.

*Griddle the spring onions*
Heat a dry pan over the highest
heat until smoking hot. Dry-fry

12 trimmed and finely sliced spring
onions or calçots, not overloading
the pan, for 10 minutes, turning
often, until charred all over but
soft inside. Add 200ml water to
allow the onions to soften, and
cook until it's evaporated.

*Make the onion dressing*
Meanwhile mix 4 tablespoons extra
virgin olive oil with ½ teaspoon
Dijon mustard and 2 teaspoons
apple cider vinegar. Taste and
add a squeeze of honey or agave
if needed. Once you're happy with
the balance, drizzle the dressing
over the charred onions and keep
warm in a low oven.

*Cook the shallots*
Heat 2cm of oil in a shallow frying
pan. Separate 3 shallots cut into
rounds into rings. When the
surface of the oil looks as though
it's shimmering, fry the shallot
rings in batches until crisp and
deep golden. Use a slotted spoon
to lift them out on to a plate lined
with kitchen paper.

*Loosen the bread sauce and serve*
If you have let it cool, reheat the
bread sauce in a saucepan, loosening
with a little milk if it's too thick.
Spoon a couple of generous tablespoons of the sauce on to warm
plates or a platter, top with a heap
of the spring onions or calçots, dill
or fennel tops, and thinly sliced
spring onion tops and some of the
crispy shallots and serve with roast
or boiled, buttered potatoes.

# Potato, cheese and sticky onion pie

50g butter

4 tablespoons olive oil

2 large white onions (400g), peeled and thinly sliced

1 tablespoon apple cider vinegar

850ml whole milk

½ a bunch of thyme (10g) and/or oregano

zest of 1 unwaxed lemon

2 cloves of garlic, peeled and finely sliced

1kg potatoes (waxy), peeled and cut into 2mm-thick slices

300g good strong melting cheese (e.g. Ogleshield, Coolea, Cheddar, Gruyère), grated

1 × 320g ready-rolled puff pastry sheet

This recipe came from Hugo Harrison, a brilliant chef who helped me test the recipes for this book. I ate a version at a dinner he cooked and was blown away. It's a lesson in how simple can be the best. The onions bring sweetness to the double carb pastry and potato. It's a rich pie, think dauphinoise inside a crisp pastry crust, so I want it with lemon-dressed greens or a punchy lemony salad to offset the richness.

SERVES 4–6

*Caramelise the onions*
Add 50g of butter and 4 tablespoons olive oil to a large heavy-based pan and set over a medium-high heat. As soon as the butter has melted and begins to sizzle, add 2 large white onions (400g), peeled and thinly sliced, and a generous pinch of salt. Stir to evenly coat the onions in the buttery-oil mixture and turn the heat down to low. Cook, stirring every now and then, for 30–40 minutes, until the onions are translucent, sweet and soft. Add 1 tablespoon apple cider vinegar and stir to combine. Scoop the onions out of the pan and set aside to cool.

*Cook the potatoes*
While the onions are cooking, put 850ml milk into a medium saucepan with ½ a bunch of thyme (or oregano), the zest of 1 unwaxed lemon, 2 finely sliced cloves of garlic, and a pinch of salt and warm over a low heat. Add 1kg waxy potatoes, peeled and cut into 2mm-thick slices, turn the heat up to medium and cook for 8–10 minutes, or until the potatoes are just cooked and tender when tested with a knife. Drain in a colander set over a bowl to catch all the infused milk. Set aside to cool.

*Assemble the pie*
Preheat the oven to 210°C/190°C fan. Layer the bottom of a 25cm pie dish with an even layer of potatoes, followed by a couple of spoonfuls of the slightly cooled milk mixture. Cover with a third of the onions, followed by 100g strong melting cheese like Ogleshield, grated. Repeat this process, finishing with a layer of potatoes on top, until all the potatoes, onions and the cheese have been used up.

*Cook the pie*
Cover the pie with baking paper, pressing down so that it is directly covering the potatoes, then bake on the middle shelf of the oven for 35–40 minutes, or until a knife easily passes through the potato. Remove from the oven, take the paper off and quickly but carefully top the pie with a 320g ready-rolled puff pastry sheet, trimming the edges with the back of a knife. Poke a hole in the centre to allow steam to escape and liberally brush with any remaining infused-milk mixture. Place back in the oven and continue cooking for another 40 minutes, or until the pastry has risen and is a deep golden brown.

Allow to cook slightly before serving and eat with lots of greens or lemony salad.

# Sticky shallot pappardelle

8 banana shallots (600g), peeled
    and finely sliced
75ml olive oil
a knob of butter (optional)
2 cloves of garlic, peeled and
    finely chopped
1 small carrot, peeled and grated
4 tablespoons tomato purée
1 tablespoon sherry vinegar
a small bunch of woody herbs
    (1 sprig each of thyme,
    rosemary and sage)
400g pappardelle (or tagliatelle)
100g Parmesan cheese, grated,
    to serve
½ a bunch of parsley (15g),
    finely chopped

This pasta came from a craving for a rich pappardelle ragù, but mine obviously has to be made with veg, and I wanted it to cook quickly, as I was making it for a weeknight dinner. Here, shallots cook down to form a super-sweet and rich ragù, backed up by tomato purée, woody herbs and garlic. It's inspired by a Rachel Roddy recipe that my kids love. The sauce tastes like it's taken much more work than it has. If you are cooking for fewer than 4, the ragù will keep in the fridge for up to a week.

SERVES 4

*Prep and cook the shallots*
Peel, trim and finely slice 8 banana shallots. If you have one, a mandoline or a food processor with a slicing attachment can be useful here. Add to a cold pan with 75ml olive oil, a pinch of salt and a knob of butter if you are using it. Cook the shallots slowly over a medium-low heat for 20–25 minutes until they have softened but not browned.

*Finish the ragù*
Add 2 cloves of garlic, peeled and finely chopped, 1 small carrot, peeled and grated, and 4 tablespoons tomato purée, and cook for 5–6 minutes, until the tomato purée is beginning to look sticky and thick. Then add 1 tablespoon sherry vinegar and 200ml water. Add a small bunch of woody herbs and cook for another 10 minutes until you have a soft, caramelly ragù.

*Cook and finish the pasta*
Cook 400g pasta in plenty of boiling, well-salted water for a minute or so less than the packet instructions. You want it just before al dente. Drain it, reserving a mug of pasta water, or use tongs to lift the pasta from the pasta pot into the ragù pan. Remove the woody herbs from the pan and season the ragù with salt and freshly ground black pepper. Add enough pasta cooking water to bring it together into a creamy sauce which coats each noodle. If you drained your pasta in a colander rather than using tongs you will need to add a bit more pasta water. Finish in the pan with 100g grated Parmesan. Top with ½ a bunch of finely chopped parsley.

# Esme salad with grapefruit

2 ripe vine tomatoes, finely
　　chopped
1 red onion, peeled and finely
　　chopped
1 clove of garlic, peeled and
　　finely chopped
2 pink grapefruits, peeled and
　　segmented
2 red peppers, deseeded and
　　finely chopped
½ large cucumber, finely
　　chopped
2 tablespoons capers
zest and juice of ½ an unwaxed
　　lemon
2 tablespoons pomegranate
　　molasses
2 tablespoons olive oil
1 tablespoon harissa paste
½ teaspoon sumac
a pinch of chilli flakes
½ a bunch of parsley (15g),
　　leaves picked and chopped

Esme salad is a staple of Turkish cooking. You'll find a bowl of this bright salad in most Turkish mezzes in the restaurants that line the streets of Hackney. I first tried it in one of those places, alongside falafel, Turkish feta and stewed runner beans. I think the onion is key here. It brings sweetness, a bit of savoury and some acidity to balance out the other punchy flavours which make an esme salad. Here it's best to leave the finished salad to mingle for a couple of hours before eating if you can. Mine is not as finely chopped as the ones in the ocakbaşi near my house, and capers are wildly untraditional but I like them. The grapefruit is inspired by a trip to Bubala in London; they put grapefruit in their version.

SERVES 4 AS A SIDE

*Prep the salad*
Put 2 finely chopped ripe vine tomatoes, 1 peeled and finely chopped red onion, 1 peeled and finely chopped clove of garlic, 2 peeled and segmented pink grapefruits, 2 deseeded and finely chopped red peppers, ½ a finely chopped large cucumber and 2 tablespoons capers in a serving bowl.

*Make the dressing*
In a jar or small bowl, mix or shake the zest and juice of ½ an unwaxed lemon, 2 tablespoons pomegranate molasses, 2 tablespoons olive oil, a pinch of salt and pepper and 1 tablespoon harissa paste together. Pour this over the salad ingredients, toss together, then sprinkle over ½ teaspoon sumac and a pinch of chilli flakes.

*Serve the salad*
The salad is best if left to sit for a couple of hours before serving. If

you leave it to sit, drain off most of the liquid before adding ½ a bunch of chopped parsley and a little more olive oil. I serve it with flatbread and dips like hummus, cacik (a Turkish cucumber and garlic dip) or labneh. Any leftovers can be stored in the fridge for up to 2 days and brought to room temperature before eating.

# Jaya's Utsav paneer

1 large white onion, peeled
2 tablespoons thick strained
    yoghurt
½ teaspoon ground red chilli
    powder (ideally Kashmiri
    chilli powder)
½ teaspoon ground turmeric
½ teaspoon ground black
    pepper
½ teaspoon ground kasoori
    methi (dried fenugreek
    leaves)
2 tablespoons vegetable oil
    or ghee
400g paneer, cut into cubes
1 red or green pepper (or half of
    each), deseeded and cut into
    chunks
1 red onion, peeled and cut into
    eighths, or a handful of small
    red onions, peeled
coriander leaves, to serve
garam masala, to serve
rice or chapatis, to serve

FOR THE CURRY BASE
2 tablespoons vegetable oil
    or ghee
2 green cardamom pods, split
2 bay leaves
5cm piece of cassia bark or
    cinnamon stick
½ teaspoon cumin seeds
1 green chilli, pierced and
    left whole
2cm thumb of ginger, grated
2 cloves of garlic, peeled and
    grated
½ teaspoon ground coriander
½ teaspoon ground fennel seeds
½ teaspoon ground cumin
1 × 400g tin good-quality
    chopped tomatoes
½ teaspoon ground red chilli
    powder, to taste (ideally
    Kashmiri chilli powder)

This recipe was kindly passed on to me by Jaya Chandna and her mum. It is insanely moreish and so perfectly spiced, and for days after making it I couldn't think of much else. Jaya tells me this was a recipe developed by her mum and named after Utsav café in Jaipur, where Jaya would go for lunch with her grandad.

She says, 'This was towards the end. Gone were the days of motorcycle rides to eat pakoras on Delhi streets or painting with him in his studio or hearing my mum shout at him for climbing on the wheelie bins to fix the shed roof (!); replaced by quiet walks pushing his wheelchair round the garden, sitting in the late afternoon sun discussing the antics of the other members of the care home and trips to Utsav café for paneer curry and hot rotis. Where somehow there'd always be a reason to share a pista ice-cream afterwards.'

According to Jaya, it's the onions in this recipe that really bring it to life – the juice of the onion tenderises the paneer, and the grated white onion forms the base of the curry. The small red onions add a lovely sweetness and crunch.

SERVES 4, WITH RICE OR CHAPATIS

*Marinate the paneer*
Grate 1 large white onion, place in a muslin cloth or sieve, and squeeze out all the juice into a bowl. Set the onion aside and mix the juice with 2 tablespoons thick strained yoghurt and ½ teaspoon ground red chilli powder, ½ teaspoon ground turmeric, ½ teaspoon ground black pepper and ½ teaspoon ground kasoori methi. Marinate 400g cubed paneer in this mixture for at least 1 hour.

*Make the curry base*
Heat 2 tablespoons vegetable oil or ghee in a heavy saucepan and add 2 split green cardamom pods, 2 bay leaves, 5cm cassia bark or cinnamon and ½ teaspoon cumin seeds. Watch that they don't burn. Once fragrant, add the grated squeezed onion and 1 green chilli, pierced but left whole, and fry until light brown. Add a 2cm thumb of ginger, grated, and 2 grated cloves of garlic and fry. Add ½ teaspoon ground coriander, ½ teaspoon ground fennel seeds and ½ teaspoon ground cumin and a pinch of sea salt, allow to cook briefly, then add 1 × 400g tin of good-quality chopped tomatoes. Fry well until the oil separates. Add a little more sea salt and ground red chilli powder to taste.

*Char the peppers and onions*
Char 1 red or green pepper, cut into chunks, and 1 red onion, peeled and cut into eighths, in a frying pan and add the curry base sauce. Cook the sauce for a few minutes so the vegetables retain their crunch. Tip the curry with the onions and peppers into a bowl and wipe out your pan to cook the paneer.

*Cook the paneer*
Put the pan back on the heat, add 2 tablespoons ghee or oil, then fry the marinated paneer until speckled brown all over. Add the curry to the pan.

*Finish the curry*
Add half a cup of water to the pan and simmer until the paneer is plump and the sauce has thickened. Sprinkle with coriander leaves and garam masala (if you want to add a kick!) and serve with rice or chapatis.

# Mushroom shawarma with sumac onions

½ teaspoon smoked paprika
½ teaspoon cumin seeds,
    ground
½ teaspoon coriander seeds,
    ground
½ teaspoon whole allspice,
    ground
9 tablespoons extra virgin
    olive oil
5 cloves of garlic, left whole
    and unpeeled
4 white onions, peeled and
    quartered, plus 1 more onion
    peeled, halved and very
    thinly sliced, to serve
450g oyster mushrooms
½ teaspoon ground turmeric
250g thick natural yoghurt
1 teaspoon sumac
½ teaspoon red chilli flakes
zest and juice of 1 unwaxed
    lemon
½ a bunch of parsley (15g),
    roughly chopped
4 flatbreads, to serve

I crave this shawarma – the crunchy edges of roasted mushrooms and onions next to the moreish onion and garlic yoghurt that has an serious amount of flavour. This recipe to me feels like a real celebration of onions. They come roasted with the mushrooms, blitzed into the unreasonably delicious yoghurt and in a lemony onion salad on top.

SERVES 4

*Make the spice rub*
In a small bowl, mix ½ teaspoon smoked paprika, ½ teaspoon cumin seeds, ground, ½ teaspoon coriander seeds, ground, ½ teaspoon whole allspice, ground, and 4 tablespoons extra virgin olive oil with a good pinch of flaky sea salt and freshly ground black pepper to form a loose paste.

*Roast the onions*
Preheat the oven to 200°C/180°C fan. Crush 5 unpeeled cloves of garlic slightly with the back of a knife. Put 4 peeled and quartered white onions, all the garlic and the spiced oil into a large, low-sided baking tray and toss together until the onions and garlic are all evenly coated. Roast in the oven for 30 minutes until a little charred and softened.

*Add the mushrooms*
Tear 450g oyster mushrooms into rough bite-sized pieces. Remove the onions from the oven and put half into a bowl with the garlic cloves, then set aside. Add the mushrooms to the baking tray with the remaining onions and toss together so the mushrooms are coated, adding a little more oil if needed. Return to the oven for another 25 minutes until the mushrooms are crisp and golden and the onions are slightly charred and really soft.

*Prepare the onion yoghurt*
Meanwhile, add the cooled onions to a food processor or blender. Squeeze in the garlic flesh from its papery skins and discard the skins. Add 4 tablespoons extra virgin olive oil, ½ teaspoon ground turmeric, 250g thick natural yoghurt and a pinch of flaky sea salt. Blitz until you have a semi-smooth mixture.

*Make the onion salad topping*
Peel, halve and very finely slice 1 onion and add to a bowl with 1 teaspoon sumac, ½ teaspoon red chilli flakes, the zest and juice of 1 unwaxed lemon, ½ a bunch of roughly chopped parsley, 1 table-spoon extra virgin olive oil and a pinch of sea salt and freshly ground black pepper.

*To serve*
Warm the flatbreads and top with the yoghurt, onions and then the mushrooms and more parsley.

# Miso

Sweet, gentle, caramel-coloured white shiro miso sits next to a red miso and a dark barley miso on the top shelf of my fridge. It sits undisturbed for weeks and months until needed, asking nothing. I would wager it would last years. A teaspoon of miso fills a pot with flavour like nothing else. Miso comes from a culture that is not my own, and I have much to learn about how to cook with it. But it holds a place deep in my heart. I stir it into Cheddar for cheese on toast. Beat it into creamed corn with green chilli. Mash it with toasted walnuts for a soupy udon inspired by Shuko. Bake it into scones and whip it with cream and bananas. Learning as I go.

# On Miso

Miso fills a pot with flavour with very little effort. It's great in soups, stews, broths, dressing and marinades and is even good in sweet things like caramel.

Miso is such a useful ingredient in vegetarian cooking, as it brings a hit of umami that can be hard to get with veg alone. It's sweet, nutty, earthy, umami, savoury and briny. Sometimes even with notes of barley, banana or chestnut. Adding miso to a dish gives a flavour that implies whatever it is in has been cooking for hours.

Whilst there is very little miso made in the UK, what is imported generally arrives by sea. If you buy carefully, you support the artisans who make it. It's also quite easy to make yourself, see page 288. As it's fermented, it's also good for your gut. If you want to keep its beneficial properties, you can add it right at the end of cooking.

Salty, Umami, Sweet, Earthy

### Types

Buying miso can be confusing, as there are so many types out there. I am no expert, but here are the three I buy the most.

- White miso
  Lighter in colour and taste, good for light broths, dressings and in baking or caramel.

- Brown rice miso
  Generally darker in colour and a little saltier, good for more punchy dressings to stand up against chilli and for tossing roast veg in for the last 5 minutes of roasting.

- Red miso
  Often made from barley; it's salty and deep in flavour, good for stews, noodle soups and gravies.

### Goes well with

| | |
|---|---|
| aubergine | ginger |
| avocado | honey |
| banana | kale |
| caramel | kimchi |
| chilli | leek |
| chocolate | mushroom |
| egg | |

### Favourite uses

- In a simple miso soup with spring onions and tofu
- As the base for a ramen
- In dressings
- A tablespoon added to soup for depth
- To round out vegetable stock
- In brownies or cookies
- Stirred through roasted squash or new potatoes for the last 10 minutes
- Smothered over aubergines before roasting

### Storage and tips

Miso keeps well as it's already fermented. Store tightly sealed in the fridge for a year or longer. It can discolour, so a layer of greaseproof paper directly on the surface will slow the oxidisation.

If you are using your miso in a soup or a stew, be sure to add miso towards the end of cooking, as it helps retain all its goodness. I mix all of the miso needed with some cold water until I have a thick but pourable paste and then stir it into a soup or a stew once I have turned the heat off.

### What to buy

All of the misos from Clearspring are consistently good. I also like Hikari Organic Miso Paste and Umasa Red Miso.

# Homemade miso

200g dried pulses – soybeans,
    chickpeas, cannellini beans, etc.
40g dried rice koji
40g fine sea salt
15g white miso paste

Making your own miso is really not as complicated as it sounds and it gave me such an insight into the different kinds and flavours. If you make a white miso then you will only need to ferment it for a couple of months rather than the year or so needed for a darker, richer miso. Either way, once you have jarred it up it's completely hands off. The only special thing you need is dried rice koji. I buy mine from souschef.co.uk, but you could buy it from any Japanese food store.

MAKES 2 LARGE JARFULS

*Cook the pulses*
Soak 200g dried pulses in plenty of cold water, cover and leave overnight (they'll double in size). The next day, drain and rinse them a couple of times in fresh cold water. Put in a large saucepan, cover with water, add a good pinch of salt and bring to the boil. As soon as the water is boiling, reduce the heat to a simmer, skim away any white foam from the top and cook for 1–2 hours, or until the pulses are cooked through and they break when squeezed between your fingers. Drain and allow to cool completely.

*Mix the miso*
Put the cooked pulses, 40g dried rice koji, 40g fine sea salt and 15g white miso paste into a large clean bowl and scrunch it all together with your hands. Keep scrunching until everything is well mixed. Measure out 200ml warm water then add a little water a bit at a time, scrunching as you go, until the mixture has the consistency of a thick hummus.

*Ferment*
Put the miso mixture into a clean sterilised 1-litre jar and push it down with your hand to remove any air pockets. Cover with a circle of baking paper and weigh it down (so the liquid which becomes the by-product, 'soy sauce', covers the miso) with something (I use baking beans), then set aside in a cool dark place for 8–12 weeks, checking and tasting each week or two until it's fermented to your liking. The 12-week mark should produce a slightly sweeter 'white' miso, and you can continue fermenting it for anything up to a year for a dark and rich miso. Once it's fermented to your liking, you can store it in the fridge to stop it fermenting any further. It will be happy there for up to a year, probably longer.

# Miso rarebit with Asian herbs

4 thick slices sourdough bread
200g mature Cheddar, grated,
   or vegan-style Cheddar
   cheese
200g crème fraîche or oat crème
   fraîche
3 unwaxed limes
4 spring onions, trimmed and
   finely sliced
1 red chilli, finely chopped
2 tablespoons red miso paste
½ a cucumber
½ a bunch of mint (15g),
   leaves picked
½ a bunch of coriander (15g),
   leaves picked

This is the rarebit/toasted cheese of my dreams. Creamy and rich, umami from miso and a fresh hit of herbs and cucumber to lift it all. We eat it for lunch, but it's filling and interesting enough to eat for any meal. I use red miso here as I like its richness against the cheese. I've tried it with white or shiro miso too, which give a sweeter, more mellow umami note.

SERVES 4

*Prepare the toast*
Preheat the oven to 240°C/220°C fan. Place 4 thick slices of sourdough bread on to a large, flat tray then put in the oven to toast slightly on both sides, turning halfway. This will take about 5 minutes, depending on your oven. Remove from the oven and set aside.

*Make the cheese mixture*
In a bowl, mix together 200g grated mature Cheddar or vegan-style Cheddar cheese, 200g crème fraîche or oat crème fraîche, the zest of 2 unwaxed limes and juice from 1, 4 finely sliced spring onions, 1 finely chopped red chilli and 2 tablespoons red miso paste. Spread the mix over the 4 pieces of toast and place back in the oven for 8–10 minutes until golden and bubbling.

*For the salad*
Split ½ a cucumber lengthways, scoop out the watery centre using a teaspoon and finely chop. Put the cucumber and the picked leaves from ½ a bunch of mint and ½ a bunch of coriander into a bowl with a pinch of salt, the zest of 1 unwaxed lime and the juice from 2, then toss together. Serve the bubbling rarebit next to the herb and cucumber salad.

# Creamed corn and white bean mash with miso butter

4 corn on the cob
2 onions, peeled and very
    finely sliced
1 tablespoon olive oil
2 × 400g tins butter beans,
    drained
75g unsalted butter or vegan
    butter
2 teaspoons white miso paste
2 green chillies, 1 deseeded
    and very finely chopped,
    1 thinly sliced
2 unwaxed limes
a few sprigs of coriander,
    to serve
Parmesan cheese, grated, to
    serve (I use a vegetarian one),
    optional

This is my comfort food. The butter beans and half the corn come together to make a slightly sweet, velvety mash that's served with the other half of the corn, which is crisped in a pan with some of the onions to create a double-textured spoonable bowl of happiness. White miso brings everything together and adds a roundness. Think the texture of polenta with the comfort of creamed corn and you are in the right place. I serve this with a tomato salad and some flatbreads.

SERVES 4

*Cut the corn from the cobs*
Carefully slice the kernels off 4 corn cobs. I do this by putting the base of each cob in a mixing bowl and carefully cutting down the length of each one to remove the kernels. This stops them flying everywhere.

*Cook the onions*
Put 2 peeled and very finely sliced onions into a medium saucepan with 1 tablespoon olive oil and a pinch of flaky sea salt. Cook over a medium-low heat for 15–20 minutes until really soft and beginning to brown, then scoop out 2 tablespoons and put on one side.

*Add the corn and beans*
Add 2 × 400g tins of butter beans to the pan of onions with half the corn kernels and 50ml water. Simmer over a medium heat for 10 minutes, then blitz in a food processor or with a hand-held blender until you have a creamy mash, seasoning with salt and freshly ground black pepper as you go. Put it back into the pan and keep warm.

*Make the miso corn topping*
Put a frying pan over a medium heat, add 75g unsalted butter or vegan butter, 2 teaspoons white miso paste and the remaining corn and cook for 4–5 minutes so the butter browns slightly and the corn becomes slightly soft and bright yellow. Now stir in the reserved onions.

*Finish*
Add 1 finely chopped green chilli to the brown butter and miso pan, along with the zest and juice of 1 unwaxed lime. Scoop the creamy beans on to a platter or plates and spoon over the buttery corn topping, followed by the thinly sliced green chilli, the zest and juice of 1 unwaxed lime, plus freshly ground black pepper, a few coriander leaves and a grating of Parmesan if you like.

# Shuko's celeriac with clementine and miso

a 5g piece of dried kombu kelp
   (to make the dashi)
1 unwaxed clementine
1 large or 2 small celeriac
50g unsalted butter, at room
   temperature, plus a little
   extra for roasting
50g white miso paste, ideally
   saikyo
10g mustard – Japanese
   powdered mustard mixed
   with water, or English
   mustard
20ml rice vinegar

Shuko's food at her restaurant Koya is some of my favourite in London. I've sat at the bar at Koya many times. Her food has healed colds and broken hearts. To me, this recipe tells the tale of Shuko and Koya's food so perfectly – it sits exactly where comfort and brightness meet.

Shuko tells me that miso soup is what she first learned to cook when she was nine years old, and so it was a starting point in her cooking journey. Shuko tells me, 'Miso, like soy sauce, is made from soya beans by mixing them with koji bacteria and fermenting them, and it is a fundamental element of Japanese cooking and meals. There are countless variations of miso, depending on region, and a wide range of methods for how you can use them. This recipe uses a particularly sweet miso called saikyo miso, which has been matured longer than normal miso, and I think it is a great combination with roasted celeriac and citrus.'

SERVES 2 AS A MAIN, 4 AS A SIDE

*Make the kombu dashi*
You need to start this the night before you want to eat the celeriac. Add 5g dried kombu kelp to 40ml cold water and leave it to soak overnight, then take out the kombu before using the dashi.

*Make the dehydrated clementine*
Preheat the oven to 50°C. Peel the zest from 1 unwaxed clementine with a sharp vegetable peeler and spread it in a single layer on a baking paper-lined baking sheet. Bake until the zest is hard but not darkened, about 30–45 minutes. Once cool, blitz it in a clean coffee grinder or blender until you have a coarse powder. Set aside.

*Roast the celeriac*
Turn the oven up to 160°C/180°C fan. Wash and dry 1 large or 2 small whole celeriac, then use your hands to rub with a knob of unsalted butter. Wrap it in foil and place on a roasting tray. Roast for 2 hours or until it feels soft when you squidge it.

*Make the miso mustard*
In a bowl combine 50g saikyo or white miso with 10g mustard, 20ml rice vinegar, 40ml of the kombu dashi and 50g unsalted butter at room temperature and whisk together well.

*Dress and serve*
Once the celeriac is cooked, peel away the skin with a knife, then cut the flesh into bite-size wedges and mix the pieces with the miso mustard butter, enough to dress them generously. Dust with a generous amount of ground clementine peel.

# Miso maple beetroot with goat's curd

2 tablespoons maple syrup
    or runny honey
3 tablespoons white miso paste
3 teaspoons wholegrain mustard
2 unwaxed limes
4 raw beetroot, peeled and
    quartered
3 tablespoons extra virgin
    olive oil
1 sharp, crunchy apple, halved,
    cored and thinly sliced
3 sticks of celery, finely sliced,
    and some leaves if possible
200–300g goat's cheese or curd
sourdough bread, to serve
    (optional)

We so often think of miso for Japanese dishes, but miso is such a versatile flavour that I have found it works incredibly well in lots of other countries' cuisines, from satay sauces to salad dressings. Here, miso pairs with some classically British ingredients. Roasting beetroot in this maple, miso, lime and mustard dressing creates a crispy, crunchy, caramelised umami-sweet coating to the beetroot which counters the earthy character inside. Paired with a crunchy celery and apple salad and served with crumbled goat's curd or cheese, this plate has got all the textures and flavours in one place.

SERVES 4

*Make the miso maple dressing*
In a small bowl, mix together 2 tablespoons maple syrup or honey, 3 tablespoons white miso paste, 3 teaspoons wholegrain mustard and the zest and juice of 1 unwaxed lime.

*Roast the beetroot*
Preheat the oven to 220°C/200°C fan. Quarter 4 peeled raw beetroot and put them into a shallow baking tray. Pour over 2 tablespoons extra virgin olive oil and roast in the oven for 20 minutes. Remove from the oven and toss in the miso maple dressing, making sure all the beetroot pieces are evenly coated. Return to the oven for a further 20 minutes.

*Make the celery and apple salad*
Halve, core and thinly slice 1 sharp, crunchy apple. Put in a bowl with 3 finely sliced sticks of celery, the zest and juice of 1 unwaxed lime, 1 tablespoon of extra virgin olive oil, a pinch of flaky sea salt and some freshly ground black pepper. Add the celery leaves too, if you have some.

*To serve*
Serve the beetroot with 200–300g soft goat's curd, a pile of the celery and apple salad and, if you like, some toasted sourdough for scooping things up.

# Walnut miso udon

100g walnuts

2 spring onions, trimmed and
    left whole

a thumb-size piece of ginger,
    peeled and grated

4 tablespoons mirin

1 teaspoon runny honey or agave
    syrup, plus 1 tablespoon

2 tablespoons soy sauce

300g dried udon noodles

2 teaspoons red miso paste

2 teaspoons white miso paste

4 handfuls of mushrooms –
    I use a mix of shimeji and
    enoki mushrooms

1 head spring greens or
    sweetheart cabbage,
    destemmed and finely
    shredded

This is my homemade version of the walnut miso udon from Koya in Soho. Their udon noodles are from the gods, just the right side of chewy. But it's the walnut miso paste that comes next to them in a little bowl that really makes it. This is a version that I made at home to quell cravings when I first had my son and it was hard to get to the restaurant. This recipe appeared in another form in my first book but it's my favourite way to eat miso, so I felt it needed a spot in this chapter. Be generous when stirring in the walnut miso; the broth is quite simple so it needs a good hit of the miso.

I sometimes add a poached egg. Most vegetables will work well in this broth – chard, asparagus, sugar snaps, spinach. Don't be tied to what I have suggested here.

SERVES 4

*Toast the walnuts*
Put 100g walnuts into an ovenproof frying pan and toast in the oven at 180°C/200°C fan, or in a pan over a medium heat, for 3–5 minutes, until just toasted and smelling great. If any look too dark, you can rub off their skins and discard those bits. Leave to one side to cool.

*Make the broth*
Now get the broth going. Put 2 whole trimmed spring onions and a thumb of peeled and grated ginger in a pan with 2 litres water and bring to the boil. Reduce the heat and simmer for 10 minutes. Turn off the heat then add 4 tablespoons mirin, 1 teaspoon honey or agave syrup and 2 table-spoons soy sauce. Taste the broth and add some sea salt if needed. Put a lid on and turn down the heat to the lowest setting to keep warm.

*Cook the udon noodles*
Meanwhile, bring another pan of water to the boil. Add 300g dried udon noodles and cook for 6–8 minutes (or follow the instructions on the packet). Drain and rinse under cold water.

*Make the walnut miso*
While the udon are cooking, bash the toasted walnuts in a pestle and mortar until they resemble very coarse breadcrumbs. Add 2 tea-spoons red and 2 teaspoons white miso paste and 1 tablespoon of honey or agave syrup and mix to a paste.

*Add the vegetables to the broth*
Remove the spring onions from the broth, add 4 handfuls of mushrooms and leave to cook for a couple of minutes, then add 1 head of destemmed and finely shredded spring greens or sweetheart cabbage and take off the heat.

*Put everything together*
Divide the noodles between 4 bowls, ladle over the broth and the vegetables and serve with little bowls of the walnut miso to generously stir in.

# Miso, lime and sweet potato bake

1 × 400ml tin coconut milk
100g cherry tomatoes
1 green chilli, roughly chopped
a large thumb-sized piece of
    ginger, peeled and roughly
    chopped (about 60g)
3 cloves of garlic, peeled
2 stalks of lemongrass, roughly
    chopped
2 tablespoons white miso paste
750g sweet potatoes, sliced
    about ½cm thick
2 unwaxed limes
a small bunch of Thai or
    normal basil

This has become a favourite dinner. Everyone in our house loves sweet potatoes, and the mellow miso, ginger and coconut flavours of the gratin are universally loved too. This is a gratin with a bit of attitude. White miso brings sweetness but also umami depth here. We eat this with plain rice and some greens (usually cavolo nero) shredded and cooked in a hot pan until the edges are crisp and finished with a squeeze of lime.

SERVES 4

*Make the miso, ginger and coconut sauce*
Put a 400ml tin of coconut milk into a blender with 100g of cherry tomatoes, 1 roughly chopped green chilli, ⅔ (40g) of a large thumb-sized piece of peeled and roughly chopped ginger, 3 peeled cloves of garlic, 2 roughly chopped stalks of lemongrass and 2 tablespoons white miso paste. Blend on high until you have a smooth, fragrant sauce.

*Prepare the sweet potatoes*
Preheat the oven to 180°C/160°C fan. Slice 750g of sweet potatoes about ½cm thick; you can do this by hand or using a mandoline. Season with sea salt then layer them into a round, shallow cast-iron pan or oiled baking dish about 28cm across if round and about A4-sized if rectangular. I like to layer the sliced sweet potatoes overlapping each other in rows or circles to echo the shape of the dish I am using.

*Add the sauce*
Pour over the coconut miso sauce and add the remaining ⅓ (20g) of chopped ginger. Use a couple of spoons to toss the potatoes in the coconut milk to make sure everything is coated.

*Bake the bake*
Cover the dish with foil and bake for 40 minutes until the top is browned and the potatoes are cooked through. Take off the foil and put back into the oven for 15 minutes.

*Finish the bake*
Grate over the zest of 1 unwaxed lime. Toss a small bunch of Thai basil leaves in a little oil and scatter them over the top, then put the bake back into the oven for another 5 minutes. Serve with 2 limes (including the one that has been zested) cut into wedges for squeezing over.

# Mushroom dumplings with crispy kale seaweed

1 stalk of lemongrass, bashed and roughly chopped

1 clove of garlic, peeled

4 spring onions, trimmed and roughly chopped

a small thumb-sized piece of ginger, peeled and roughly chopped

a bunch of coriander (30g), leaves picked and chopped, stalks separated

4 Szechuan peppercorns, toasted

1 teaspoon Chinese five-spice powder

300g shiitake mushrooms

5 tablespoons neutral oil (I used coconut oil)

3 tablespoons dark miso paste

1 teaspoon runny honey or maple syrup

1 teaspoon Chinese rice wine

50g unsalted peanuts, toasted and roughly chopped

24 × 10cm round Chinese dumpling wrappers, defrosted if frozen

juice of 1 unwaxed lime

½ a shallot, peeled and finely chopped

1 tablespoon red miso paste

1 teaspoon toasted sesame oil

¼ teaspoon dried chilli powder

FOR THE CRISPY KALE

400g curly kale, roughly shredded and tough cores removed

1 tablespoon light soft brown sugar

1 tablespoon sesame seeds

½ teaspoon ground turmeric

The food I crave most often is a dumpling. The almost gummy wrapper, steamed or fried to a crisp, a just-the-right-side-of-salty filling and a dipping sauce both sharp and sweet. When I was pregnant they were all I wanted to eat. Since they are not the kind of thing you can whip up in 20 minutes (they take a little more planning), I make them for friends. These dumplings make the most of mushrooms, with the aromatics of lemongrass, ginger and coriander. I serve them with a great dipping sauce and some kale, cooked like the crispy seaweed served in the Chinese takeaways of my childhood.

The dumplings can also be prepared in advance and kept in the fridge or freezer uncooked. Once steamed, serve immediately. If you steam them from frozen, steam for a total of 15 minutes rather than 12. If you want crispy dumplings you could fry them in a little oil in a non-stick pan on a medium heat for 2–3 minutes on each side until golden brown.

The paste makes more than you need. Freeze it to make this again, or use as a base for a fresh coconut curry.

SERVES 6 (MAKES 24 DUMPLINGS)

*Make the paste*
Put 1 bashed and roughly chopped stalk of lemongrass, 1 peeled clove of garlic, 4 trimmed and roughly chopped spring onions, a small thumb of peeled and roughly chopped ginger, the stalks from a 30g bunch of coriander, 4 toasted Szechuan peppercorns and 1 teaspoon Chinese five-spice powder into a food processor. Add a pinch of salt and pulse five or six times to break everything down, then blitz on a high speed for a couple of minutes, stopping the machine and scraping

down the sides every so often, until you have a deeply fragrant paste. Add 300g shiitake mushrooms and pulse until roughly chopped, being careful not to chop too much – you don't want them to make a paste.

*Make the dumpling filling*
Melt 2 tablespoons neutral oil in a large frying pan over a medium heat. When the oil is hot, add the mushroom paste to the pan with a pinch of salt. Fry, stirring regularly, for 7 minutes until the paste is beginning to brown and everything smells fragrant. Remove from the heat and immediately stir in 1 tablespoon dark miso paste, 1 teaspoon honey or maple syrup and 1 teaspoon Chinese rice wine. Tip into a mixing bowl and mix in 50g toasted and roughly chopped peanuts and the picked and chopped leaves from the 30g bunch of coriander.

*Preheat the oven and prepare the steamer*
Preheat the oven to 200°C/180°C fan. Get a large lidded frying pan ready to cook your dumplings.

*Make the dumplings*
Place a dumpling wrapper on a clean work surface and place a heaped teaspoon of the mushroom filling in the centre. Use your finger to wet the edge of the wrapper and bring one side over the other to make a half-moon shape. Pinch the pastry at the top of the half moon to seal, then pinch and pleat from one edge to the other to seal the top completely. Do this with the rest of the wrappers until you have 24 dumplings.

*Continued over...*

*Cook the dumplings*
Heat your large frying pan over a medium heat, add a tablespoon of coconut oil and once hot, add the dumplings flat side down and cook for 2–3 minutes. Then add 150ml water, put the lid on and cook for 5–7 minutes until all the water has evaporated. Take the lid off and cook for another 3–4 minutes until the bottoms are golden and crispy. You may need to do this in batches.

*Make the crispy kale seaweed*
Meanwhile, spread 400g roughly shredded curly kale, with the tough cores removed, over 2 large roasting trays. Mix 2 tablespoons neutral oil with 1 tablespoon light soft brown sugar, 1 tablespoon sesame seeds, ½ teaspoon ground turmeric and 1 tablespoon dark miso paste and pour over the kale. Scrunch everything together, then spread out again so the kale is in a single layer. Place in the oven for 5–10 minutes, opening the oven door once during this time to release the steam. Remove from the oven and toss well before returning to the oven for another 5 minutes, opening the oven door a couple of times to release the steam and help the kale to crisp up. Remove from the oven and scrape into a large serving bowl.

*Make the dipping sauce and serve*
Mix the juice of 1 unwaxed lime, ½ a finely chopped shallot, 1 tablespoon red miso paste, 1 teaspoon toasted sesame oil and ¼ teaspoon dried chilli powder together to make a dipping sauce. Taste and adjust the seasoning if necessary.

Serve the dumplings immediately alongside the crispy kale seaweed and dipping sauce.

# Miso banana caramel whip

2 medium ripe bananas, peeled
and mashed
75g soft light brown sugar
1 tablespoon white miso paste
200ml organic double cream or
whippable vegan cream
200g thick Greek yoghurt or
oat yoghurt
4 ginger nuts or digestive
biscuits
2 tablespoons white sesame
seeds, toasted
a little dark chocolate, grated,
to serve (optional)

Imagine banoffee pie but ready in 15 minutes and spooned into a glass like a sundae. I'm on the fence about bananas but I love them in this caramel. If you are into bananas, some sliced banana with a little lemon squeezed over could be a nice addition. Here, the miso adds a salty back note that offsets the richness of the banana and brown sugar caramel. I think miso and banana are one of the best sweet combinations.

SERVES 4

*Make the banana caramel*
Put 2 peeled and mashed ripe bananas and 75g soft light brown sugar into a small saucepan over a medium heat and cook for 5–7 minutes until the sugar has dissolved and caramelised, stirring all the time until thick and glossy. Stir in 1 tablespoon white miso paste and take off the heat. Remove from the heat and leave to cool.

*Whip the cream*
Use a hand-held whisk or stand mixer to whip 200ml organic double cream or whippable vegan cream a little shy of soft peaks, so you are beginning to see the trail of the whisk but before it feels 'whipped'. It's best to under-whip it slightly, as the yoghurt will make it thicker. Now gently fold in 200g thick Greek yoghurt or oat yoghurt, taking care not to mix it too much. Put to one side.

*Make the sesame crunch topping*
Crumble 4 ginger nuts or digestive biscuits with your hands into a bowl and add 2 tablespoons toasted white sesame seeds.

*To serve*
Spoon a tablespoon of the banana caramel into the bottom of four glasses, then add a layer of the

pillowy cream. Repeat the layers, ending with the sesame ginger crunch topping, and finish with a little grated chocolate if you like.

# Miso, date and honey scones

180ml whole or oat milk, plus extra for brushing on top
zest and juice of 1 unwaxed lemon
450g plain flour, plus extra for dusting
1 teaspoon baking powder
½ teaspoon bicarbonate of soda
1 teaspoon ground ginger
150g cold unsalted butter or vegan butter, cubed
2 tablespoons miso paste
75g soft light brown sugar
5 Medjool dates, roughly chopped
2 tablespoons Demerara sugar
salted butter, runny honey, crème fraîche and some seasonal fruit, to serve

These scones are light and soft, buttery and sweet and sort of treacly all at once. The flavour comes from the combination of miso, ginger and dates. Adding the miso here gives them an underlying sweet and salty depth, which I am sure is why they are so moreish. Once the dough is made, I use a stacking method to build up layers in the scones, which makes them super-short and buttery.

MAKES 8 SCONES

*Make the buttermilk*
In a jug, mix together 180ml whole or oat milk and the zest and juice of 1 unwaxed lemon and set aside to thicken up.

*Mix the dry ingredients*
In a large mixing bowl, combine 450g plain flour, 1 teaspoon baking powder, ½ teaspoon bicarbonate of soda and 1 teaspoon ground ginger.

*Mix the butter into the flour*
Add 150g cold unsalted butter or vegan butter in cubes to the dry ingredients, along with 2 tablespoons miso, then, with your fingertips, gently rub them into the flour until you have a sandy breadcrumb-y texture, leaving some larger petals of butter as this will make the scones more flaky. Stir in 75g soft light brown sugar.

*Add the dates and the buttermilk*
Add 5 roughly chopped Medjool dates to the scone mix, working quickly so the butter stays cold. Make a well in the centre and pour in the thickened buttermilk, roughly mixing it together with a fork so as not to overwork it.

*Bring the dough together*
Tip the rough mixture on to a lightly floured surface, then, without kneading too much, bring it together to form a dough and shape it into a rectangle, neatening the sides with your hands.

*Stack the dough to create layers*
Cut the dough into three equal pieces, then stack these on top of each other. Press down on the top with a rolling pin or your hands, then roll or press out into a 3cm-thick rectangle about 16cm × 16cm.

*Cut the scones*
Cut the dough into 4cm squares using a knife and put on to a baking tray lined with baking paper. Brush the top of each one with a little extra milk or oat milk and sprinkle with 2 tablespoons Demerara sugar. Chill in the fridge for 30 minutes or the freezer for 15 minutes to firm up. At this point you can keep them in the freezer to bake in smaller batches from frozen.

*Preheat the oven and bake the scones*
Preheat the oven to 200°C/180°C fan. Bake the scones for 20–25 minutes until crispy and golden. Bake for another 5–7 minutes if frozen.

*To serve*
I've served the scones with butter, honey, crème fraîche and some fresh cherries, but you could serve them just with honey and butter, or clotted cream and jam if you wanted to keep it more traditional.

# Peanuts

It started when I was four with peanut butter and jam sandwiches, eaten from a Strawberry Shortcake lunchbox. Always requested then and still eaten now. Rich, buttery, creamy and crunchy. I buy it in huge tubs, but when I make it myself it's the best. I roast the peanuts to the point just before they go too dark, a risk worth taking for the deeply golden butter. Swirled with soy, ginger, chilli sauce and rice vinegar, it makes a sauce we eat with rice and greens so often. It's folded into cookies. Spooned into smoothies. It adds a backbone of deep, creamy flavour to so many meals we eat. And the PB&Js remain.

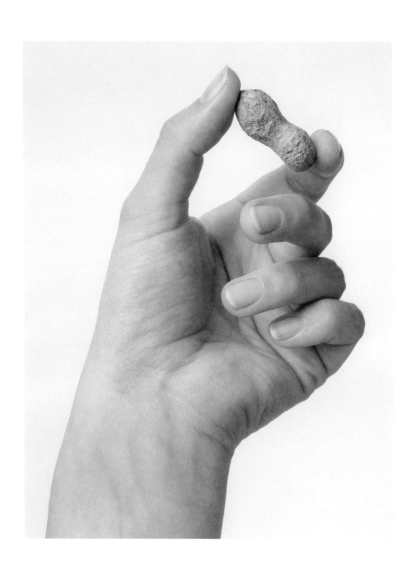

# On Peanuts

Peanut butter is something I crave. It was part of my childhood, eaten on toast or rice cakes for a snack. The hollows of crisp lengths of celery filled with smooth peanut butter and topped with a few raisins – ants on a log. I make the same things now for my own children. The sweet but not sugary flavour of peanut butter is so pleasing to a small person's palate.

Now, though, I use it most in cooking. From a quick cheat's satay sauce to cookies and cakes. Good in soups and stews, it adds a very good creaminess to tomato soup, for example, as well as a richness to a variety of soups and stews. It's especially good whenever I've used a can of coconut milk.

While peanuts are always imported to the UK, most peanut butter comes by sea. There has been a lot of discussion regarding the sustainability of nuts due to the water needed for them to grow, but peanut butter has a relatively low carbon count thanks to how peanuts help to rebuild soil. The shells and peanut plants can be used for energy generation and to feed animals, so if you buy from the right place there is little waste.

To me, making your own peanut butter (see page 314) is worth it. You can control the roast (I like mine deeply roasted), the level of salt and how crunchy or smooth it is.

Nutty, Fatty, Sweet, Salty

## Flavour notes

Peanuts have a nutty, vegetal flavour, to state the obvious. They get a warmer sweetness when they're roasted.

Peanut butter has a nutty, salty and earthy flavour, with a fatty richness.

## Goes well with

| | |
|---|---|
| apple | coriander |
| banana | crunchy veg |
| berries (jam) | cucumber |
| broccoli | lemon |
| carrot | lime |
| celery | potato |
| chilli | soy |
| chocolate | tomato |
| coconut | vanilla |

## Favourite uses

- Stuffed into dates and dipped in chocolate
- Spooned from the jar
- Ants on a log
- Quick cheat's satay – with soy, rice vinegar, chilli sauce, ginger
- Smoothies – date, banana, coffee, vanilla
- In tomato soup
- Added to a coconut-based curry
- Dressing for salad
- In a quick salsa macha
- With banana pancakes
- Spooned next to fruit and yoghurt
- Swirled through brownies
- On top of roast sweet potato with lime and coriander

## Storage

- Peanut butter
  Store out of sunlight and stir before each use to make sure the oil is mixed with the butter. Keeps for months.

- Whole peanuts
  Store in a cool, dark and dry cupboard in a sealed container; buy in small packets as the oil in the nuts can go off. Like all nuts, only keep for a few months.

## Favourite brands and where to buy

Buy the best peanut butter your budget allows; try to steer clear of those containing palm oil, additives and sugars. I buy mine in huge tubs or from refill stores. I buy organic peanut butter from Whole Earth and Clearspring. I am also a fan of ManiLife Deep Roast and Pip & Nut. Koeze from Virginia, USA, is also very good. Asian supermarkets or wholefood stores are a good place to look for whole unsalted peanuts for cooking and to make your own peanut butter with.

Easy Wins

# Easy homemade peanut butter

500g blanched unsalted peanuts
groundnut oil, to loosen

Coating noodles, bolstering a salad or keeping an apple company for an afternoon snack, peanut butter has to be one of my most reached-for ingredients when cooking. It's a perfect example of a couple of things becoming more than the sum of their parts, and this homemade version couldn't be easier. Whether you like it chunky or smooth, you can whip up a batch that's exactly how you like it. This recipe also works with almonds, hazelnuts, macadamia nuts and brazil nuts. You might need to add a little more groundnut oil to loosen, as the amount of oil in the nuts will vary.

MAKES 2 MEDIUM JARS

*Roast the peanuts*
Preheat the oven to 200°C/180°C fan and put 500g blanched unsalted peanuts on to two baking trays so they are in one layer. Roast in the oven for 10 minutes, or until the nuts are golden brown and smelling fragrant. Set aside to cool.

*Blitz and add the oil*
Add the roasted and cooled peanuts to a food processor with a generous pinch of sea salt. Blitz for 3–4 minutes or until all the oil has been released from the nuts and the mixture has turned into a butter. If you're after a chunkier nut butter, then stop blending sooner. In this case, not all the oil from the nuts may have been released, so to get a spreadable consistency add a little groundnut oil and pulse until mixed well.

*Store the peanut butter*
Transfer the peanut butter to 2 sterilised jars and store in a cupboard for up to a month.

# Aubergine, peanut and tamarind curry

2 medium aubergines, cut into
3cm pieces
2 tablespoons coconut oil
or ghee
1 tablespoon black mustard seeds
1 tablespoon cumin seeds
1 tablespoon fennel seeds
1 tablespoon garam masala
1 teaspoon ground turmeric
½ a bunch of coriander (15g),
including stalks
a bunch of spring onions
(about 6)
4 cloves of garlic, peeled
a thumb-sized piece of ginger,
peeled and roughly chopped
1 × 400ml tin coconut milk
4 tablespoons crunchy peanut
butter
2 tablespoons tamarind paste
4 vine tomatoes, roughly
chopped, or 1 × 400g tin
chopped tomatoes
200g paneer or firm tofu,
cut into 2cm pieces
basmati rice, to serve
parathas, roti or chapati,
to serve
pickled onions and raita,
to serve (see introduction)

This curry is unreasonably good.
The peanut butter mixed with coconut
milk and tamarind makes an easy
sauce in the tray which is so so
moreish. As it's all cooked in the oven
it's hands off and pretty quick. I love
how the butteriness of aubergine
stands up well to lots of spice. You
could use squash or sweet potato in
place of the aubergines in winter (you
will just need to cook them for 10–15
minutes longer initially). Vegans can
use firm tofu instead of the paneer; you
can cook it in exactly the same way.

I make some quick pickled red
onions to go on top. Finely slice a red
onion, then scrunch the slices with a
pinch of salt and the juice of ½ an
unwaxed lime (or lemon). They will
keep in a sterilised jar in the fridge for
10 days or so. I also make a quick raita
by mixing roughly chopped cucumber
with yoghurt, lime juice, chopped
coriander and a good pinch of salt.

SERVES 4–6

*Roast the aubergines*
Preheat the oven to 220°C/200°C fan.
Cut 2 medium aubergines into 3cm
pieces and put into a large baking
tray with a couple of tablespoons of
coconut oil or ghee, 1 tablespoon
black mustard seeds and a good pinch
of sea salt. Put into the oven for a few
minutes to melt the coconut oil, then
remove, toss the aubergines until all
the pieces are coated, and roast for
another 20 minutes until golden.

*Toast the spices*
Meanwhile, toast 1 tablespoon cumin
seeds and 1 tablespoon fennel seeds
in a dry pan over a medium heat
until they smell fragrant.

*Make the paste*
Put the toasted spices into a food
processor with 1 tablespoon garam

masala, 1 teaspoon ground turmeric
and the stalks from ½ a bunch of
coriander. Trim the very bottoms
of a bunch of spring onions and
discard, then add them whole to the
processor. Finally, add 4 peeled cloves
of garlic and a peeled and roughly
chopped thumb of ginger and pulse
to a paste. Add 400ml coconut milk
and blitz again before stirring in
4 tablespoons crunchy peanut butter
and 2 tablespoons tamarind paste.
Taste and season with salt if needed.

*Add the tomatoes and paste to the
baking tray*
Once the aubergines have had their
20 minutes' cooking, add 4 roughly
chopped vine tomatoes or a 400g
tin of chopped tomatoes, and 200g
paneer or firm tofu, cut into 2cm
pieces, to the tray and pour over the
peanut and coconut mixture. Toss to
make sure everything is coated in the
sauce, then carefully (it will still be
hot) cover the tray with foil and put
back into the oven for 15 minutes.

*Remove the foil*
After 15 minutes, remove the foil
and put the tray back in the oven
for 15 minutes.

*Prepare the rice, flatbreads and
toppings*
Now is the time to cook your rice and
warm your bread. If you are making
the pickled onions and raita, get on
with those too (see introduction).

*Finish the curry*
Once the curry has had its time,
serve it next to the rice and breads
with the onions and raita and any
chutneys or pickles you like.

# Spring onion pancake with peanut sauce

250g gram flour

2 tablespoons olive oil, plus extra for frying

1 shallot or small red onion, peeled and thinly sliced

zest and juice of 1 unwaxed lime

½ a small red cabbage (300g), finely shredded

1 large carrot, peeled and coarsely grated

a bunch of coriander (30g), chopped

2 tablespoons toasted sesame seeds, plus extra to finish

4 tablespoons soy sauce or tamari

4 tablespoons rice wine vinegar

2 tablespoons maple syrup

2 × 20g pieces of ginger, peeled

125g peanut butter

3 tablespoons sriracha

a bunch of spring onions, trimmed and finely sliced

350g tofu

This has got a California vibe to it, the kind of thing which feels bright and fresh but filling and satisfying all at once. I crave this kind of food and I miss the California cafés it transports me back to. The crossover of cultures here also reminds me of Californian cooking – a little bit Italian farinata and a little bit spring onion pancake with some Indonesian influence from the peanut sauce. It is similar to something I used to order at a now closed but much-loved café in Hackney called Palm Greens. It was always a good place to eat and people watch.

SERVES 4

*Make the pancake batter*
Put 250g gram flour into a bowl with up to 450ml cold water, and mix until you have a thick crêpe batter; gram flour will differ in how much water it will absorb. Whisk in 2 tablespoons olive oil and a generous pinch of sea salt. Leave to sit for at least 30 minutes but ideally for an hour.

*Make the slaw*
Finely slice 1 peeled shallot or small red onion, mix it with the zest and juice of 1 unwaxed lime in a small bowl and leave to sit. Put 300g finely shredded red cabbage into a large mixing bowl with 1 large peeled and coarsely grated carrot, ½ a bunch of chopped coriander and 2 tablespoons toasted sesame seeds.

*Dress the slaw*
Mix 2 tablespoons soy sauce or tamari with 2 tablespoons rice wine vinegar and 2 tablespoons maple syrup, then grate in 20g peeled ginger. Pour over the slaw and leave to sit.

*Make the peanut sauce*
Mix 125g peanut butter with 2 table-spoons soy sauce, 2 tablespoons rice

wine vinegar and 3 tablespoons sriracha, then grate a 20g piece of peeled ginger. Loosen with a little water until the mixture has a drizzling consistency.

*Cook the pancakes*
Once the batter has rested, add a bunch of finely sliced spring onions, reserving a few for serving. There should be enough batter to make 4 large pancakes. Heat a little oil in a frying pan over a medium heat, add a ladleful of the batter and angle the pan so the batter covers the base. Cook for 2–3 minutes until golden brown, then carefully flip on to the other side and cook for another 2–3 minutes until golden. Remove to a plate and keep warm in a low oven while you cook the other 3 pancakes in the same way. You might need to add a little more oil between each one.

*Cook the tofu*
Once all the pancakes are cooked, add a little oil to the same pan, put on a medium-high heat and roughly crumble 350g tofu into the pan in chunks. Cook until golden brown all over, then turn the heat down to low, add 2 tablespoons of the peanut sauce, toss for a minute to coat, then take off the heat.

*Finish the slaw*
Add the limey shallots/onions to the slaw and mix.

*Put everything together*
Serve the pancakes with the slaw and tofu piled on top, with ½ a bunch of coriander, the last of the spring onions and sesame seeds and some of the peanut sauce.

# Peanut and charred tomato broth

400g cherry or small vine
  tomatoes
1 green chilli
2 cloves of garlic, unpeeled
  and bashed
1 tablespoon white miso paste
a thumb-sized piece of ginger,
  peeled and grated
250g soba or egg noodles
1 tablespoon toasted sesame oil
4 tablespoons crunchy peanut
  butter
2 unwaxed limes
½ a bunch of coriander, mint or
  basil (15g), leaves picked, or 5g
  of each
50g roasted peanuts, roughly
  chopped (optional)

We made this one day when I was
feeling less than 100 per cent, and
it brought me back to life. I love it
when food can do that. It can be
everything you need in a bowl. This
hit all the flavours I needed that
day: lots of ginger, garlic, chilli and
lime to liven me up, charred smoky
flavour from the tomatoes which
adds instant depth, and peanut
butter to round it all out with some
creaminess. All those flavours sit on
top of a simple base of soba noodles.

SERVES 4

*Char the tomatoes*
Start by putting 400g cherry tomatoes
and 1 whole green chilli into a large
heavy-based saucepan (that you will
later cook the broth in) on a high
heat. Char the tomatoes and chilli
all over, turning often with tongs for
about 5 minutes. Add 2 cloves of
unpeeled and bashed garlic for the
last minute or so, taking care that
the garlic doesn't burn.

*Make the broth*
Add 1 litre of freshly boiled water to
the tomatoes and chilli along with
1 tablespoon white miso paste and
a thumb-sized piece of ginger, peeled
and grated. Use the back of a spoon
to break up the tomatoes a little,
then bring to a boil and simmer for
30 minutes.

*Cook the noodles*
Meanwhile, boil 250g soba or egg
noodles according to the packet
instructions, then run under cold
water for a minute to remove any
starchiness. Toss in 1 tablespoon
toasted sesame oil and divide
between 4 bowls.

*Finish the broth*
Season the tomato broth with salt
and pepper, then, once you're
happy with the flavour, remove
from the heat and fish out the
garlic cloves and the chilli. Stir in
4 tablespoons crunchy peanut
butter and the zest and juice of 1
unwaxed lime.

*Serve the broth*
Ladle the tomato peanut broth
over the noodles and serve with
more lime zest and juice and the
leaves from ½ a bunch of herbs.
Top with 50g roasted peanuts,
roughly chopped, if you like.

# Sweet lime and peanut slaw

1 large or 2 small red cabbages (850g)
5 tablespoons olive oil
3 unwaxed limes
2 tablespoons runny honey
2 tablespoons soy sauce
a small thumb-sized piece of ginger, grated
1 red chilli, roughly chopped
2 tablespoons smooth peanut butter
1 kohlrabi, leaves trimmed off then peeled and cut into chunky matchsticks
1 pear, cut into chunky matchsticks
100g unsalted roasted peanuts
½ a bunch of coriander (15g), leaves picked and roughly chopped

Cabbage pairs so well with peanuts. The creamy fattiness of peanut butter is a contrast to the fresh, watery crunch of the cabbage. I've added lime, coriander and ginger too, some of peanut's soulmates. In the winter I make this a deeper-flavoured warm salad by charring the cabbage. In the summer I skip the charring part and keep it more crunchy.

SERVES 4–6

*Char the cabbage (optional)*
Remove any wilted outer leaves and chop 1 large or 2 small red cabbages into quarters if small and eighths if large. Season them with some salt and 2 tablespoons of olive oil. Heat a pan or a griddle pan over a high heat, and once it's smoking hot add the cabbage and cook for about 8 minutes on each side until charred and crisp.

*Make the dressing*
Mix the zest of 1 unwaxed lime and the juice of 3 with 2 tablespoons honey or sugar and 2 tablespoons soy sauce. Grate in a small thumb of ginger, roughly chop 1 red chilli and add it too. Pour a quarter of the dressing into a small bowl and set aside, then mix 2 tablespoons smooth peanut butter into the remaining three-quarters of dressing until creamy.

*Chop the fresh vegetables*
Trim the leaves off 1 kohlrabi, if it has them, and peel away the tough outer green or purple skin. Cut this and 1 pear into chunky matchsticks. Roughly chop 100g roasted peanuts and the leaves from ½ a bunch of fresh coriander.

*Dress the cabbage*
Chop the cabbage wedges into smaller pieces. While still warm (if you charred it), pour over the peanut dressing. Pour the remaining soy and honey dressing over the kohlrabi and pear.

*Put everything together*
Put the cabbage on to a big platter and top with the pear and kohlrabi, then the chopped peanuts and coriander.

# Hetty's ginger-peanut warm kale salad

4 heaped tablespoons smooth
    peanut butter
2 tablespoons tahini
2 teaspoons toasted sesame oil
2.5cm piece of ginger, peeled
    and grated
2 cloves of garlic, peeled
    and grated
3 teaspoons tamari or soy sauce
2 tablespoons rice wine vinegar
1 tablespoon runny honey or
    maple syrup
2 bunches of kale (320g), stalks
    removed and leaves roughly
    torn
200g (1 cup) quinoa, rinsed
500ml (2 cups) vegetable stock
    or water
300g extra-firm tofu
extra virgin olive oil
1 red onion, peeled and thinly
    sliced
1 cup unsalted peanuts, roasted
    and roughly chopped
a handful of coriander leaves

Since I discovered this recipe from my friend and cook Hetty McKinnon, it's been one of the meals I have craved most. With this recipe, Hetty manages to tread that elusive line between something tasting so delicious that you can't stop eating it and making you feel so good after eating that you crave it all the time. Hetty says herself, 'This salad comes with a warning: eat at your own risk, as it is very addictive. The combination of kale, tofu and ginger-accented peanut sauce is unexpectedly irresistible.' Hetty wrote this recipe for all the peanut butter obsessives who, like her, are often caught surreptitiously sneaking spoonfuls straight from the jar.

SERVES 4–6

*Make the ginger-peanut sauce*
Place a medium saucepan on a low heat and add 4 heaped tablespoons smooth peanut butter, 2 tablespoons tahini, 2 teaspoons toasted sesame oil, a 2.5cm piece of ginger, peeled and grated, 2 peeled and grated cloves of garlic, 3 teaspoons tamari or soy sauce, 2 tablespoons rice wine vinegar and 1 tablespoon honey or maple syrup, along with 1 cup water. Cook until the peanut butter and tahini have melted, stirring until the sauce is smooth and creamy. If the sauce 'freezes' or is too thick, add more water, a tablespoon at a time, until it's smooth and the consistency of thickened cream. Taste and season with sea salt and black pepper.

*Fold the kale into the sauce*
Fold 320g de-stalked and roughly torn kale leaves into the hot peanut sauce. The heat from the sauce will wilt and cook the kale. Set this aside.

*Cook the quinoa*
Put 200g rinsed quinoa and 500ml vegetable stock or water (if using water, season it with 1 teaspoon of sea salt) into a large pot. Bring to a boil, then reduce the heat, cover and cook for 15–18 minutes, until all the liquid has been absorbed and the quinoa is translucent and you can see the twirly grain. Turn off the heat and set aside, uncovered, while you prepare the rest of the salad.

*Fry the tofu*
Put 300g extra-firm tofu on a chopping board and season well with sea salt and black pepper. Heat a large non-stick frying pan on medium–high, and when it's hot, drizzle with 1–2 tablespoons olive oil. Working in batches, place the tofu in the pan and fry for 2–3 minutes on each side until lightly golden. When all the tofu is cooked, allow it to cool, then slice it into 5mm-thick strips.

*Cook the onion*
Rinse and dry the tofu pan and place it back on a medium heat. Drizzle more olive oil into the frying pan, add 1 peeled and thinly sliced red onion and cook for 12–15 minutes, stirring occasionally, until it is softened and sweet.

*Finish the salad*
Combine the peanut-kale mixture with the quinoa, tofu and onion. Transfer to a large serving plate and top with 1 cup roasted and chopped peanuts and a handful of coriander leaves.

# Peanut butter Rice Krispie bars

110g runny honey
175g smooth or crunchy peanut butter
100g Rice Krispies (I use the brown rice ones)
50g unsalted roasted peanuts, chopped
200g dark chocolate
a pinch of flaky sea salt

These started as a craving for a peanut Tracker bar, if you are in the age range to get that reference. They ended up some way from their original inspiration, as I wanted to keep them full of things which are somewhat good for you. These are a grown-up version of Rice Krispie treats mixed with the flavours of a Snickers.

MAKES 12 BARS

*Prepare your tin*
Depending on how thick you want your bars, line a rectangular or square tin with baking paper (20 × 20cm square, making thick bars, or 20 × 30cm rectangular brownie tin, making medium-thick bars).

*Combine the ingredients*
In a small pan, warm 110g runny honey and 175g peanut butter on a medium heat for a minute until runny, then pour into a large bowl with 100g Rice Krispies and 50g unsalted roasted chopped peanuts. Mix well until everything is evenly coated.

*Pour into the tin*
Pour into your chosen lined tin and press down heavily with the back of a spoon, or even the bottom of a glass, so the mix is evenly compressed into the tin. This will ensure a neat slice once set.

*Melt the chocolate*
Put 200g dark chocolate in a heat-proof bowl set over a pan of barely simmering water, making sure the base of the bowl does not touch the water. Stir occasionally and take off the heat just before it melts – the chocolate will finish melting in the residual heat.

*Add the chocolate*
Pour the chocolate over the Rice Krispies in the tin and spread into an even layer. Place in the fridge to set for 30–60 minutes.

# Peanut butter chocolate-chip cookies

200g plain flour
1 teaspoon bicarbonate of soda
100g rolled oats
250g unsalted butter or vegan
   butter, softened
200g soft light brown sugar
100g caster sugar
125g crunchy peanut butter, well
   mixed
1 teaspoon pure vanilla extract
3 organic or free-range egg yolks
250g dark milk chocolate
   chips or your favourite bar,
   broken up

To me these are the perfect cookies. They have a chewiness from the brown sugar, texture from the oats, melting pools of chocolate, and crunch and saltiness from the peanut butter. Crisp-edged with the perfect chewy bite, these are a mixture of two of my all-time cookies – the Nora Ephron sandwich cookies from *The Dahlia Bakery Cookbook* and Violet Bakery egg-yolk cookies.

MAKES LARGE 18 COOKIES

*Get yourself a baking tray*
Line a baking tray with baking paper. It should be one that will fit into your fridge or freezer.

*Mix the dry ingredients*
In a bowl whisk together 200g plain flour and 1 teaspoon bicarbonate of soda. Stir in 100g rolled oats and ½ teaspoon sea salt and put to one side.

*Mix the butter and sugar*
In the bowl of a stand mixer fitted with the paddle attachment, or with a hand-held mixer, beat 250g softened unsalted butter or vegan butter with 200g soft light brown sugar, 100g caster sugar and 125g crunchy peanut butter until combined but not fluffy and creamy. Too much air will make the cookies cakey, not chewy. Add 1 teaspoon pure vanilla extract and 3 egg yolks and mix in until just combined.

*Finish the cookie dough*
Add the dry mixture to the butter and sugar mixture and mix until it just comes together to form a dough (don't overmix), then stir in 250g dark milk chocolate chips or 250g of your favourite chocolate, broken up.

*Scoop out the cookies*
Use a tablespoon or an ice-cream scoop to scoop out 18 even portions of dough, rolling each one into a rough ball and putting them on the lined tray. Put into your freezer for 2 hours if you have time. If not, it's not a disaster; they will just be a bit flatter.

*Preheat the oven and bake the cookies*
When you are ready to bake, preheat the oven to 180°C/160°C fan. Line a large baking tray or tin with baking paper and put however many cookies you'd like to bake on the tray, leaving enough space between them for them to double in size.

Bake for 7 minutes, then take the tray out and bang it gently on the work surface to remove any pockets of air (this helps make them chewy). Cook for a further 7 minutes until the centre of each cookie is still slightly soft but the edges are crispy and nicely golden. Remove from the oven and allow to cool on the tray for 10 minutes before serving.

*Storing and freezing*
The baked cookies will keep in an airtight container for up to 5 days. The cookie dough balls can stay happily in the freezer for up to 3 months and you can bake them as you need them. To store in the freezer, once the dough balls are frozen remove from the tray and put into a sandwich bag. If you are baking from frozen, allow the cookies 5–10 minutes out of the freezer before placing in the oven.

# Cherry and chocolate peanut butter sundae

400g fresh or frozen cherries
3 tablespoons maple syrup
2 tablespoons smooth peanut
   butter
1 tablespoon cocoa powder
a big pinch of flaky sea salt
8 scoops vanilla ice cream or
   frozen yoghurt, about
    1 × 400ml tub (vegan if
    needed)

There is something about a sundae. They take me back to diners as a kid, waitresses with name badges, fried things on checked paper in red plastic baskets. They feel fun. This is the quickest pudding – the peanut and chocolate sauce is so easy and requires no skill. Peanut butter, chocolate and cherry together is a favourite. Serve the sundaes in tall frosted (pop them in the freezer for 10 minutes) glasses with long sundae spoons for digging right to the bottom of the glass. Any unused chocolate sauce keeps well in the fridge and can be reheated at a moment's notice (or eaten cold by the spoonful).

SERVES 4

*Prepare and cook the cherries*
If you have 400g fresh cherries, congratulate yourself, then stone and halve them and set aside. If you are using frozen cherries, put them into a small saucepan with 1 tablespoon maple syrup and cook on a medium-low heat until they are warm and soft, still with a little liquid. Remember the liquid will thicken as they cool.

*Make the peanut and chocolate sauce*
In a bowl, whisk together 2 table-spoons smooth peanut butter with 2 tablespoons maple syrup (or 3 tablespoons if using fresh cherries), 1 tablespoon cocoa powder and a big pinch of flaky sea salt. You might need to add a little water here if your peanut butter is thick.

*Make the sundaes*
Get yourself 4 glasses or bowls, scoop some cherries into the bottom of each glass, then add a scoop of ice cream, the peanut chocolate sauce, more cherries, another scoop of ice cream and the rest of the cherries and chocolate sauce.

# Dylan's chocolate oat bars

2 tablespoons coconut oil

¼ cup (70ml) maple syrup

1 cup (250g) well-stirred peanut butter (I like crunchy)

2 cups (180g) porridge oats (gluten-free if needed)

½ cup shelled/hulled hemp seeds or sunflower seeds

⅓ cup (60ml) oat or other plant-based milk

150g dark chocolate, broken into pieces

This is a super-simple recipe that gets made once a week in our house. It stops us buying so many after-school snacks but also means we have something sweet on hand during the day. I make batches for people who are feeling ill or need some quick nourishment, like new parents. The peanut butter is the linchpin that these bars are built around; it brings richness to what is a drastically simple recipe. I do feel it's worth saying that while the peanut version is the best, most schools are nut-free, so it's useful to know these also work well with sunflower seed butter. I have kept the measurements in cups as well as grams here, as I find cups an easy way to measure these forgiving bars.

MAKES 24 MEDIUM BARS

*Melt the oil and mix the dry ingredients*
Put 2 tablespoons coconut oil into a small saucepan over a low heat and allow it to melt. Once melted stir in ¼ cup (70ml) maple syrup and 1 cup (250g) peanut butter. Put 2 cups (180g) porridge oats and ½ cup shelled hemp seeds into a mixing bowl.

*Mix and make the oat base*
Pour the peanut butter mixture over the oats and seeds and mix well until everything is coated. You will have a rough sandy texture which will set in the fridge as the coconut oil cools. Line a 23cm square loose-bottomed baking tin with baking paper, press the mixture into the tin and use the back of a spoon to flatten it out.

*Make the chocolate topping*
Put ⅓ cup (60ml) oat milk and 150g dark chocolate into a small saucepan and warm over a very low heat to melt the chocolate. Once the chocolate looks melted, gently stir the milk and chocolate together until you have a thick melted topping. Pour on top of the oats and spread out with the back of a spoon.

*Chill and store*
Put the tin into the fridge to firm up for at least 30 minutes, then cut into pieces. I go for medium bars, but you could do small bite-sized squares if you like. The bars store well in the fridge in a covered container for up to 10 days.

|  | Dill *soft* | Coriander *soft* | Parsley *soft* |
|---|---|---|---|
| Flavour profile | Almost sweet, licorice-like flavour and feathery texture | Gingery Peppery Lemony Floral | Green Fresh Vibrant |
| Info | In German folklore, brides put dill and salt in their shoes for luck. | The classic love it or hate it herb. A staple in Latin American and Asian cuisines. | One of the most versatile fresh herbs. I prefer the flat leaf to the curly one. |
| Goes with | Anything creamy/sour Broad bean Butter Carrot Cucumber Egg Mushroom Pickles Potato | Avocado Chilli Coconut Cumin Garlic Lemon Lime Mint Peanut Peppers Potato Tomato | Caper Carrot Cheese Egg Garlic Lemon Mushroom Potato |
| Favourite uses | I prefer dill raw to cooked. I like to use it bravely in salads, pickles and stews. | There is a huge amount of flavour in the stems, so use them in the base of a curry or soup. | Salsa verde is one my all-time favourites; tabbouleh and gremolata are also classics. |
| Swap with | Feathery fennel fronds. | Not the same but often can be swapped with basil, parsley or mint, depending on the recipe. | Chervil for the same mildness, celery leaves for savouriness or lovage for texture and a close(ish) flavour. |

Herbs

| Mint | Basil | Tarragon | Oregano |
|---|---|---|---|
| *soft* | *soft* | *soft* | *medium* |
| The cleanest flavour of all the herbs | Gently spiced<br>Peppery | Warming licorice | Slightly bitter<br>Aromatic<br>Medicinal |
| There are so many beautiful varieties, but mainly they fall into peppermint and spearmint (garden mint). Peppermint has a much higher menthol content, making it brilliant for teas and desserts. | Known as the king of herbs, there are over 150 varieties of basil – from Thai to lemon, and each has a slightly different flavour and leaf shape. | Used widely, from France to Syria, Iran to Armenia. | All marjorams are oreganos, but not all oreganos are marjorams. |
| Chocolate<br>Coriander<br>Cucumber<br>Feta<br>Garlic<br>Lime<br>Parsley<br>Pea<br>Pineapple<br>Potato<br>Strawberry<br>Tomato<br>Yoghurt | Coconut<br>Egg<br>Garlic<br>Goat's cheese<br>Lemon<br>Lime<br>Mint<br>Mozzarella<br>Nuts<br>Olive Oil<br>Peach<br>Strawberry<br>Tomato | Artichoke<br>Beetroot<br>Capers<br>Cornichons<br>Cream<br>Egg<br>Goat's cheese<br>Mustard<br>Pear<br>Potato<br>Raspberry | Aubergine<br>Courgette<br>Garlic<br>Honey<br>Lemon<br>Mushroom<br>Orange<br>Peppers<br>Potato<br>Tomato |
| Make a peppermint tea with any wilting leaves. | I tear rather than chop basil to stop the edges blackening. | An unusual pairing is with sweet fruits: try raspberries, strawberries, peaches. | Too strong to eat raw, use it in the base of a cooked dish or sauce, or fry in olive oil until crisp to top. |
| Basil is often a good swap in dishes that use fresh mint; thyme can be a good swap for dishes that use it cooked. | Marjoram<br>Mint (good with tomatoes)<br>Oregano | Chervil<br>Tarragon<br>Dill | Thyme<br>Marjoram<br>Basil |

|  | Marjoram<br>*medium* | Rosemary<br>*hardy* | Thyme<br>*hardy* |
| --- | --- | --- | --- |
| Flavour profile | Flowery<br>Sweet<br>Medicinal | Slightly bitter<br>Strong<br>Taste of nutmeg | Earthy<br>Slightly woodsy<br>Flowery<br>Trace of lavender |
| Info | All marjorams are oreganos, but not all oreganos are marjorams. | Traditionally thrown into graves for remembrance. | A bouquet garni is a bundle of herbs that is added to casseroles and soups. Traditionally parsley, a few sprigs of thyme and a bay leaf. |
| Goes with | Chickpea<br>Chilli<br>Egg<br>Garlic<br>Lemon<br>Mozzarella<br>Orange<br>Pasta<br>Tomato (especially sauces) | Chocolate<br>Olive<br>Onion<br>Orange<br>Parsnip<br>Potato<br>Plum<br>Squash<br>Tomato | Carrot<br>Cheese<br>Cinnamon<br>Cream<br>Garlic<br>Leek<br>Mushroom<br>Squash<br>Strawberry<br>Sweet potato<br>Tomato |
| Favourite uses | Always add at the end, as it loses flavour in heat. | Remove whole stems before serving/eating. | Za'atar is the Middle Eastern name for thyme, and also the name given to a seasoning blend containing wild thyme, salt, sumac and sesame. |
| Swap with | Thyme<br>Oregano<br>Basil | Thyme<br>Sage | Rosemary |

Herbs

| Sage | Bay | Lime leaves | Curry leaves |
| --- | --- | --- | --- |
| *hardy* | *hardy* | *hardy* | *hardy* |
| Earthy<br>Eucalyptus<br>Lemon | Balsamic aroma<br>Mellow eucalyptus flavour | Bright, sherbety lemon/lime citrus tang with aromatic almost floral freshness | Hard to place, grounding, earthy, rounded flavour but with an enlivening backnote |
| Good with sweet-savoury foods like squash. | Before vanilla was ubiquitous, bay was used to flavour custards and puddings. | Lime leaves, also known as Makrut lime leaves, are the leaves from a bobbly green citus plant called *Citrus hystrix*. | Curry leaves bear no relation to curry powder. They are the leaves of the curry leaf tree. They are used in ayurveda. |
| Apple<br>Blue cheese<br>Egg<br>Onion<br>Polenta<br>Potato<br>Squash<br>Tomato | Allspice<br>Black bean<br>Cashew<br>Chestnut<br>Chilli<br>Cinnamon<br>Fennel<br>Fig<br>Lemon<br>Lentils<br>Potato<br>Rice<br>Tomato | Chilli<br>Cinnamon<br>Coconut<br>Coriander<br>Cumin<br>Ginger<br>Mango<br>Noodles<br>Peanut<br>Squash | Cauliflower<br>Garlic<br>Mustard seeds<br>Onion<br>Potato<br>Rice<br>Spice |
| Crispy fried sage leaves make most things better, from fried eggs to pasta. | It's best to use fresh leaves. A small bay plant will last forever. | I use whole leaves in curries or broths; very finely shredded fresh leaves can also be used in small amounts as you would a fresh herb like coriander. | They can be added at the beginning of cooking as you would a lime leaf or bay leaf, or cooked in a temper: in hot oil with other spices to be spooned over at the end of cooking. |
| Bay<br>Thyme | Sage | Lemon<br>Lemongrass<br>Lime | Nothing is comparable, just leave them out. |

| | Cardamom<br>*pods and ground* | Cinnamon<br>*sticks and ground* | Coriander<br>*seeds and ground* |
|---|---|---|---|
| **Flavour profile** | Warm<br>Sweet<br>Citrussy | Warm<br>Earthy | Citrussy<br>Lemony<br>Floral<br>Earthy |
| **Info** | Seed pods from various plants in the ginger family. They can be used whole or ground, or just the seeds. There is black, green and white cardamom (bleached green). Green is the most commonly used. | The dried inner bark of the young shoots of the cinnamon tree, an evergreen tree in the laurel family. Dried and rolled into cigar-shaped scrolls. It was so precious to ancient communities that its source was kept a secret. | The fruit from the same plant as the bright, fresh coriander leaves. It's a member of the parsley family, native to the Mediterranean and south-west Europe. |
| **Goes with** | Apricot<br>Banana<br>Cauliflower<br>Chocolate<br>Coconut<br>Coffee<br>Lentils<br>Pear<br>Root vegetables<br>Rose<br>Vanilla | Apple<br>Banana<br>Chocolate<br>Coconut<br>Coffee<br>Cream and dairy<br>Onion<br>Root veg<br>Stone fruit<br>Tomato<br>Squash | Aubergine<br>Blueberry<br>Broccoli<br>Cabbage<br>Cauliflower<br>Celery<br>Citrus<br>Garam masala<br>Goat's cheese<br>Potato<br>Pulses |
| **How to use** | Whole or ground or scrape out the seeds. Toast pods in oil first. Grind the seeds in a pestle and mortar for the best results. | Use as a stick or ground. Ground is less strong/punchy and loses flavour quickly. | Seeds should be toasted and ground, as they are tough/chewy whole, though they are often used whole in pickling and brining. |
| **Swap with** | Hard to match. Leave it out or use more lemon. | Half the amount of nutmeg or allspice. | Caraway seeds, cumin seeds, fennel seeds, or a combination of the three. |

| Cumin | Fennel | Mustard | Nigella |
|---|---|---|---|
| *seeds and ground* | *seeds* | *seeds: yellow and black* | *seeds* |

| Cumin | Fennel | Mustard | Nigella |
|---|---|---|---|
| Warm | Citrussy | Hot | Earthy |
| Earthy | Warm | Warm | Heat |
| Tangy | | Lemony | Smoky |
| Musky | | Earthy | Grassy |
| | | | Verdant |

| Cumin | Fennel | Mustard | Nigella |
|---|---|---|---|
| Dried seeds of the cumin plant, part of the parsley family, used in Latin American, Middle Eastern, North African and Indian cooking. | Native to the Mediterranean, with a stronger flavour than fennel fronds or root. Often chewed instead of chewing gum, it tastes fresh and aniseedy. | Mustard seeds are the tiny seeds from mustard plants, and are grown worldwide. There are three common types: yellow, brown and black. | From the seed casings of the *Nigella sativa* plant, native to the Mediterranean and the Middle East. |

| Cumin | Fennel | Mustard | Nigella |
|---|---|---|---|
| Apricot | Beans | Cinnamon | Breads and savoury bakes |
| Beetroot | Cakes and seeded bread | Coconut | Carrot |
| Citrus | Cheese | Cream | Coconut |
| Chickpeas | Courgette | Cumin | Curry |
| Coriander | Cream | Curry leaves | Date |
| Curry and stew | Cucumber | Pickles | Fennel |
| Squash | Potato | Potato | Lentils |
| Stone fruit | Rye | Preserves | Pickles |
| Yoghurt | Spice blends | Tomato | Pulses |
| | Sweet bakes | | Root veg |
| | Walnut | | Sesame |
| | | | Squash |
| | | | Tomato |

| Cumin | Fennel | Mustard | Nigella |
|---|---|---|---|
| Whole or ground. Whole in a roasting tray with veg, or toasted in oil. A little heat/dry roast is required before grinding the seeds. Add early in the recipe if using seeds. | Toast lightly in a dry pan or fry whole in oil. Always benefits from being ground a little to release its own oils. | Make sure to fry until they pop or they can be bitter. | Use in a spice blend; use to garnish a salad. They don't keep well ground. Grind in a blender, rather than in a pestle and mortar. |

| Cumin | Fennel | Mustard | Nigella |
|---|---|---|---|
| Caraway seeds | Anise | Mustard | Celery seed |
| Coriander seeds | Aniseed | Mustard powder | Cumin seed |
| Garam masala | | | |

Easy Wins

| | Nutmeg<br>*whole* | Peppercorns<br>*whole: white and black* | Pul biber<br>*flakes* |
|---|---|---|---|
| **Flavour profile** | Nutty<br>Earthy<br>Warm | Hot<br>Earthy | Hot<br>Fruity<br>Smoky |
| **Info** | Nutmeg is the inner seed of the nutmeg plant, *Myristica fragrans*, native to Indonesia. It's dried out in the sun. | These are the dried fruits of the pepper plant. Black, white and green peppercorns are all the same seeds of the same plant, just in various stages of development and processed differently. Black pepper is made from picked and dried unripe pepper berries. | Pul Biber is an umbrella term for Turkey's chilli (hot pepper) flakes, which include Aleppo pepper (from the Halaby pepper) and Urfa (cultivated in the Şanlıurfa region, near the Syrian border). |
| **Goes with** | Cheese<br>Cream<br>Kale<br>Lemon<br>Pastry and cake<br>Ricotta<br>Spinach<br>Squash<br>White sauce | Cheese<br>Dairy<br>Egg<br>Parmesan<br>Pasta<br>Potato<br>Tomato<br>Turnip | Avocado<br>Cheese<br>Chickpeas<br>Couscous<br>Dairy<br>Egg<br>Melon<br>Muhummara<br>Stew<br>Walnut |
| **How to use** | It's best when grated fresh, and gives a fresher, cleaner taste. I like to use a microplane. It can be bought ground and is particularly good for baking. It lasts longer as a seed than as a ground spice. | Buy whole peppercorns for the best flavour and scent. Overcooking can make it bitter. | Doesn't need to be heated to remove any rawness, so it's great as a final flourish on soups, salads, eggs. It is traditionally 'bloomed' in hot oil then poured over dishes. |
| **Swap with** | Allspice | White and black pepper can be substituted for each other in small quantities. | A small amount of chilli flakes. |

| Star anise | Smoked paprika | Turmeric | Vanilla |
|---|---|---|---|
| *whole* | *ground* | *ground and fresh* | *pods, paste and extract* |
| Sweet<br>Warm | Smoky<br>Sweet<br>Oaky | Peppery<br>Heat<br>Earthy<br>Floral | Sweet<br>Warm<br>Floral |
| The dried fruit of the Chinese magnolia tree. Star-shaped with eight points, each containing a seed. Both the seeds and the pods are used in cooking and contain the anise flavour. | Chillies smoked in large kilns over fire in the Extremadura region of Spain, then ground to a powder. You can buy picante (hot), dulce (sweet) and agridulce (bittersweet) varieties. | Bright yellow, used in most Indian cooking. You can use it in its fresh form (wear gloves), but most commonly we buy it in powdered form. It's boiled and dried in the sun for a couple of weeks, before being ground. | The second most expensive spice in the world, after saffron. We've been through a vanilla shortage over the last few years, thought to be down to deforestation and the working conditions in Madagascar, where most of the world's vanilla is grown. Vanilla pods are the fruit of certain kinds of orchid. |
| Cabbage and greens<br>Citrus<br>Chocolate<br>Cream<br>Leek<br>Noodles<br>Pear<br>Pho<br>Rice<br>Root veg<br>Soy<br>Squash | Beans<br>Grains<br>Lemon<br>Mayonnaise<br>Parsley<br>Pasta<br>Rice<br>Root vegetables<br>Tomato | Aubergine<br>Cauliflower<br>Coconut milk<br>Dairy<br>Egg<br>Lentils<br>Onion<br>Root vegetables<br>Squash<br>Tomato<br>White chocolate | Apple<br>Banana<br>Blackberries<br>Citrus<br>Melon<br>Pear<br>Rhubarb<br>Stone fruit<br>Tomato |
| Like a bay leaf, it needs to be infused rather than eaten. | A great way to build up smoky flavour. I use a teaspoon in the base of soups and stews and toss root vegetables in a couple of pinches before roasting. It is a good swap for chorizo. | Fresh turmeric keeps for a few weeks in the fridge; dried ground turmeric has a shelf life of at least a year without losing character. | Avoid essence if you can. A good-quality extract is great for baking; look for the plumpest little black vanilla pods you can find. If cooking with the pods, slice lengthways and scrape out the small seeds with a knife. Store in a sealed container, in a dry, dark place. |
| Anise – 5 spice powder. | Other smoked chillies or smoked chilli pastes like chipotle. | Nothing matches it. | Extract for pods in a pinch. 1 tablespoon = 1 pod. |

# Index

# Acknowledgements

A book is written by many people, not just the one named on the cover. This book was written during a bright spring and boiling hot summer heavily pregnant, and when Esca was tiny and was only possible thanks to this tapestry of people.

I feel it is so important to acknowledge the support that allows me to do the work I do. Pretending it all happens with no help feeds the narrative that women must be everything all at once.

First thanks must go to Louise Haines, our fifth book together. For always championing me, being a trusted ear and for never compromising. And for your patience; I feel very lucky to be on your list.

Adriana Caneva, you have approached this book with the care, style and attention to detail I could only have dreamed of. Its beauty is in large part down to you.

Thanks to Mia Colleran for holding the book so completely. Alex Gingell for expertly editing me and Imogen Benson and Victoria Pullen.

Michelle Kane, my heart is full for you, and my thanks are endless. Patrick Hargadon, I feel very lucky to have you on this one. Thanks too to Sarah Bennie for what's to come. Matt Clacher and your team.

To David Roth-Ey and all at 4th Estate, very happy to be part of the 4th collective for five books.

Proofreaders Annie Lee and Laura Nickoll, copy editor Louise Tucker (the safest of hands), and indexer Hilary Bird.

Typesetter Gary Simpson.

To Felicity Blunt, dear friend and excellent person. Thank you for it all. Gracefully supported by Rosie Pierce and Flo Sanderson.

Jess Lea Wilson and Rachael Pilston, I bow down to you both. Jess, ten years and counting and grateful for every one. I am in awe of your endless talents. Rach, your holding and patience this last year have meant so much to me. I strive to be as kind, calm and creative as you. And for your hands – they look excellent.

Hugo Harrison, this book is in large part down to you. Weeks spent testing and retesting recipes, and talking about flavours and food. Your patience, brilliance and grace are endless. Thanks to El Kemp and Chloe Glazier for help testing.

Emily Ezekiel, Aunty Lemony. Five books and everything in between, our friendship has been through it all. No one brings creativity, vision, honesty and Loewe like you.

Rosie Ramsden. Thank you for bringing your painterly ways with food and your steady, uplifting friendship to my life. Golden.

Kitty Coles. 10/10. Always. Thanks for loving egg mayo as much as me and for countless other things.

Christina Mackenzie. Close to twenty years now. Lucky to know and love you. Jodene Jordan, oh babe, the care and love you put into everything, next level. Joe Carey, vibes. Thank you.

Matt Russell, it's been a while since the heady days of the vodka luge. Feel lucky to have called you a friend for so long. You have brought your talent, kind soul and jokes. Thanks to Claudia Gschwend, Aloha Shaw and Gareth Williams. Very lovely to have you.

To the wonderful people who came along on work experience; Hannah Roberts-Owen, Karina Borowiec, Ida Carlins, Freya Pinkerton, Lou Cottle.

Ali Dunwell, a saviour, for my face and my soul.

To the kind people who have allowed me to feature their recipes in the pages of this book, some friends, some just people I greatly admire. All writers and cooks you should know. Jaya Chandna, Maunika Gowardhan, Georgina Hayden, Olia Hercules, Jeremy Lee, Gurdeep Loyal, Hetty McKinnon, Nadya Mousawi, Shuko Oda, Mersedeh Prewer, Sarit and Itamar, Cynthia Shanmugalingam, Kitty Travers, Stanley Tucci and Karla Zazueta.

Thank you to fellow cooks and writers Samin Nosrat (*Salt, Fat, Acid, Heat*), Nik Sharma (*The Flavour Equation*) and Niki Segnit (*The Flavour Thesaurus*) and Mark Diacono (*Herb and Spice*) whose books have informed my writing.

Nadya Mousawi, an actual angel. You came into our lives with Esca, and I know you are here to stay. I am certain without you this book would not exist. Thank you too to Ewa Borowiec who cares for us like family.

Dear friends, many already above, I can feel you cheering me on, always. Special mention to Naomi Annand, Lisa Pfleger and Kate Sessions.

To Mum and Dad, Rog and Gez, you continue to be the life and soul, the friendliest pair and the parents and grandparents who set the bar. I am thankful for you both every day and can't believe my luck.

Laura, having you nearby now is like having half my heart back. I love you. And Jasmin and Jean. Owen, a kind and knowing force in my life. There is so much good to come for you, Hannah and Eli.

Special mention to Liz and Sian Dale for the early days.

John Dale. I am not sure what I did to deserve you. The kindest, steadiest, strongest and funniest. It's been a wild few years. Thanks for holding on to the hope when I couldn't and for making me laugh when I needed it most. For living by example. No words come close.

Dylan, my boy. I am your home, and you are mine. I couldn't be prouder or happier you are my son. I am so excited for a life of great adventures with you.

Esca. I longed for you, and here you are against the odds. With your earnest knowing and ear-to-ear smiles. You fill my heart and our family. Also please sleep a bit more.

To you for buying this book. It will always feel like the greatest thing in the world that you might pick this book up and cook a meal for the people you love. I'll never get over how good that feels.

# Conversion chart

**UK cups**

| | |
|---|---|
| ¼ cup | 62.5ml |
| ½ cup | 125ml |
| 1 cup | 250ml |
| 1½ cups | 375ml |
| 2 cups | 500ml |

**US cups**

| | |
|---|---|
| ¼ cup | 60ml |
| ½ cup | 120ml |
| 1 cup | 240ml |
| 1½ cups | 360ml |
| 2 cups | 480ml |

| Gas | F° | C° | Fan C° |
|---|---|---|---|
| 1 | 275 | 140 | 120 |
| 2 | 300 | 150 | 130 |
| 3 | 325 | 170 | 150 |
| 4 | 350 | 180 | 160 |
| 5 | 375 | 190 | 170 |
| 6 | 400 | 200 | 180 |
| 7 | 425 | 220 | 200 |
| 8 | 450 | 230 | 210 |

4th Estate
An imprint of
HarperCollinsPublishers
1 London Bridge Street
London SE1 9GF
www.4thEstate.co.uk

Macken House,
39/40 Mayor Street Upper,
Dublin 1, D01 C9W8, Ireland

HarperCollinsPublishers

First published in Great Britain
in 2024 by 4th Estate

Design and art direction
Caneva Nishimoto

Typesetting
GS Typesetting

Printed and bound in China
by RR Donnelley APS

This book is produced from
independently certified FSC™
paper to ensure responsible forest
management.

For more information visit:
www.harpercollins.co.uk/green

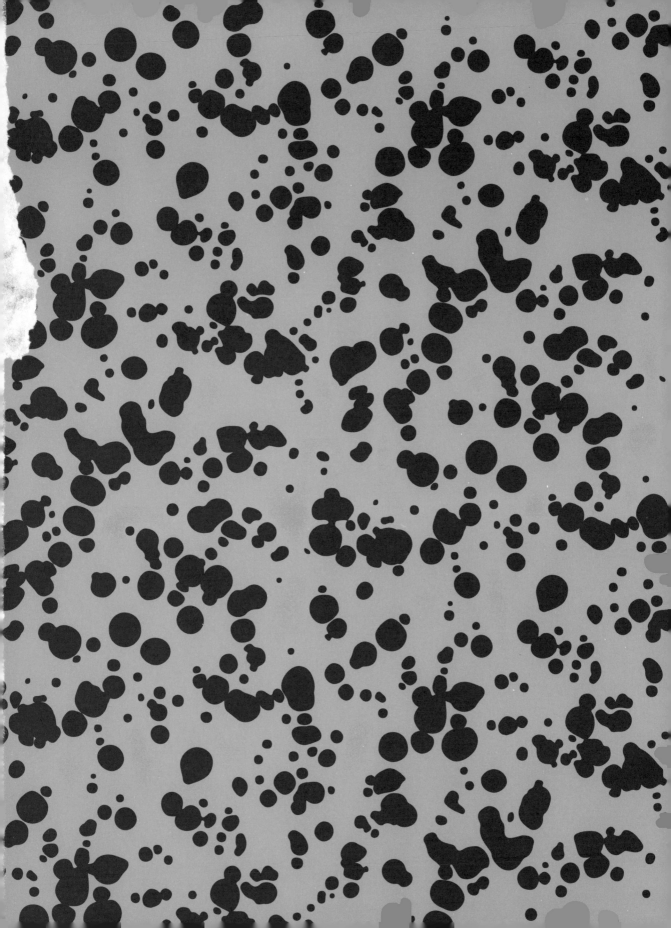

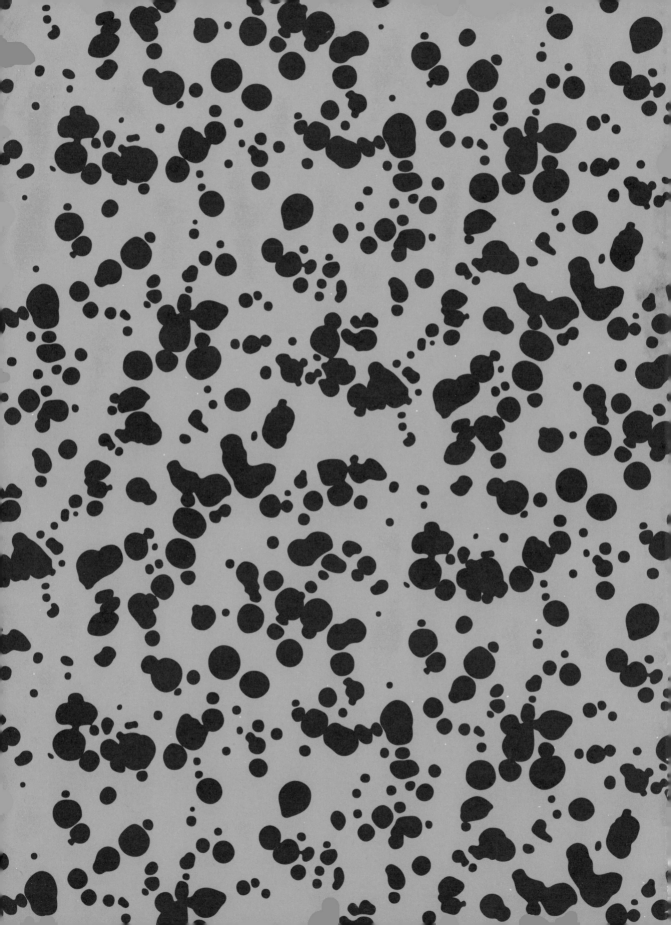